THE
MONEY
TRAIL

Confiscation of Proceeds of Crime,

Money Laundering

and

Cash Transaction Reporting

CANADA AND U.S.A.

The Carswell Company Ltd
Agincourt, Ontario

HONG KONG

Bloomsbury Books Ltd

MALAYSIA

Malayan Law Journal Pte Ltd
Kuala Lumpur

SINGAPORE

Malayan Law Journal Pte Ltd

UNITED KINGDOM

Sweet & Maxwell Ltd
London

U.S.A.

Wm W. Gaunt & Sons, Inc.
Holmes Beach, Florida

THE MONEY TRAIL

Confiscation of Proceeds of Crime, Money Laundering and Cash Transaction Reporting

by

BRENT FISSE
LL.B. (Cantuar), LL.M. (Adel.)
Professor of Law, University of Sydney

DAVID FRASER
LL.B. (Laval), LL.B. (Dal.), LL.M. (Yale)
Senior Lecturer in Law, University of Sydney

and

GRAEME COSS
LL.B., LL.M. (Hons) (Syd.)
Senior Research Assistant, University of Sydney

THE LAW BOOK COMPANY LIMITED
1992

Published in Sydney by

The Law Book Company Limited
  44-50 Waterloo Road, North Ryde, N.S.W.
  490 Bourke Street, Melbourne, Victoria
  40 Queen Street, Brisbane, Queensland
  81 St George's Terrace, Perth, W.A.

National Library of Australia
  Cataloguing-in-Publication entry

The Money trail.

  Bibliography.
  Includes index.
  ISBN 0 455 21064 0.

  1. Money—Law and legislation—Australia—Criminal
  provisions. 2. Money laundering—Australia. I. Fisse, Brent.
  II. Fraser, David, 1953- . III. Coss, Graeme.

345.940268

Designed and edited by Janine Flew.

Typeset in Garamond, 10 on 12 point, by
  Mercier Typesetters Pty Ltd, Granville, N.S.W.
Printed by Star Printery Pty Ltd, Erskineville, N.S.W.

Preface

Few areas of law have developed as rapidly or with such fleeting attention to principle and policy as the money trail legislation we have in Australia. The result today is a complex jumble of provisions. Worse, there are potentially dire implications not only for offenders but also for anyone practising professionally, whether in banking, accounting, engineering, law, medicine, stockbroking, investment-advising, realty, insuring, betting, gun-running, dope-dealing or brothel-keeping.

This book provides a starting point for anyone who wishes to discover what the money trail laws mean. The authors come from widely different backgrounds—legal practice, enforcement administration, prosecution, banking, universities, and consulting in the banking and finance sector. What they have to say represents a cross-section of expertise and opinion. Their contributions also provide a variety of critical and comparative perspectives on crime control strategies against drug trafficking, tax evasion, corporate fraud, environmental despoliage and other major indicia of the relentless modern trend toward uncivilisation. The work is thus partly intended to foster legal and political debate.

We are much indebted to all the authors for their insights and sustained assistance. Much to our regret, none has been named as a recipient of the spoils which governments hope to collect by foraging or ravaging along crime's money trails.

Others have also helped in essential ways. The Institute of Criminology at the University of Sydney hosted a public seminar in June 1990. Risk Management Solutions funded seminars on money laundering and cash transaction reporting in Sydney and Melbourne in August and September 1990, a risk upon which we have capitalised. The Australian Finance Conference has kindly given us the benefit of its experience on a wide range of issues. Printing transactions have been structured throughout by Janine Flew of The Law Book Company, so much so as to transform our deposits into passable currency. Megan Fisse assisted the preparation of the Select Bibliography. On computers, Stephen Fisse of Lexpert Publications has kept the processors in a remarkably steady state of compliance. All suspect data and wire transfers have been reported to the Cash Transaction Reports Agency, or AUSTRAC, to give the agency its newly assumed yet still unverified name.

This project has been self funded except to the extent of various basic forms of support or guidance supplied by the University of Sydney, Risk Management Solutions, Lexpert Publications, the Australian Finance Conference, and The Law Book Company. At a time of pervasive governmental attempts to dictate the course of university research, we profess our lack of allegiance. Support from the Australian Research Council, the Law Foundation of New South Wales, or any other official or semi-official source of funding has been neither sought nor desired.

BRENT FISSE, DAVID FRASER, GRAEME COSS

Sydney
July 1992

Table of Contents

Preface v
Table of Cases ix
Table of Statutes xvii
Table of Other Legislation xxvii
Select Bibliography xxix

Chapter

1. The Money Trail
   Brent Fisse, David Fraser and Graeme Coss 1

2. Confiscating Criminal Assets: The Proceeds of Crime Act
   and Related Legislation
   John Thornton 13

3. Cash Transaction Reporting and Money Laundering
   Legislation: How Will it Come Out in the Wash?
   Graham Pinner 31

4. Lawyers, Guns and Money: Economics and Ideology on the
   Money Trail
   David Fraser 49

5. Confiscation of Proceeds of Crime: Funny Money, Serious
   Legislation
   Brent Fisse 74

6. Forfeiture, Confiscation and Sentencing
   Arie Freiberg and Richard Fox 106

7. Equity and the Proceeds of Crime
   Patricia Loughlan 150

8. The Cash Transaction Reports Act: The Legal Minefield
   John O'Sullivan and Stephen Mitchell 155

9. The Relationship Between the Privacy Act and the Cash
   Transaction Reports Act
   Kevin O'Connor 167

10. Smurfing: Rethinking the Structured Transaction Provisions
    of the Cash Transaction Reports Act
    Brent Fisse and David Fraser 173

11. Smurfs, Money Laundering and the United States Federal Criminal Law: The Crime of Structuring Transactions
Sarah N. Welling 199

12. The Drug Trafficking (Civil Proceedings) Act 1990 (N.S.W.)
Simon Stretton 244

13. Investigating Criminal and Corporate Money Trails
David A. Chaikin 257

14. Finding the Information Trail: Some Experiences in International Tax Enforcement
Lee Burns 294

15. The Confiscation of the Proceeds of Crime in England
G. R. Sullivan 305

16. Cleaning up the Bankers' Act: The United Kingdom Experience
Michael Levi 323

17. Money Laundering Legislation in the United States: A Perspective from the Banking Industry
John J. Byrne 354

18. The Practical Impact of United States' Criminal Money Laundering Laws on Financial Institutions
Whitney Adams 374

19. Minimising Exposure to Liability under the New Legislation: Developing Effective Corporate Compliance Systems
Brent Fisse 407

Index 441

Table of Cases

A.G.I.P. (Africa) Ltd v. Jackson 337
Ahern v. The Queen 191, 192
Alamo Bank v. United States 366
Albernaz v. United States 241
Albertson v. Subversive Activities
    Control Board 229
Allen, Allen & Hemsley v. Deputy
    Commissioner of Taxation 274
Anderson v. Lynch 93, 100, 420
Annandale, The 115
Attorney-General's Reference (No. 1
    of 1988) 308
Attorney-General v. Schmidt 90
Australian Bank Employees' Union,
    Re; Ex parte A.B.N. Australia Ltd   435
A.F.P., Commissioner of v. Butler 20, 22
A.F.P., Commissioner of v. Cornwell
    and Bull 21, 22
A.F.P., Commissioner of v. Cox 89
A.F.P., Commissioner of v. Curran   21, 82
A.F.P., Commissioner of v. Kirk   25
A.F.P., Commissioner of v. Lahood
    (1988) 82
A.F.P., Commissioner of v. Lahood
    (1989) 21
A.F.P., Commissioner of v. Malkoun   24, 26
A.F.P., Commissioner of v. Razzi   20

B.C.C.I. case—see United States v.
    Bank of Credit and Commerce
    International
Babanaft International Co. S.A. v.
    Bassatne 321
Baden Delvaux and Lecuit v. Societe
    General 150
Bailey v. Purser 249
Baker v. Campbell 299, 433
Barclays Bank Plc v. Taylor; Trustee
    Savings Bank of Wales and Border
    Countries v. Taylor 327
Baumgartner v. Baumgartner 153
Beatty v. Guggenheim Exploration
    Co. 150
Beckwith v. The Queen 177
Bert Needham Automotive Co. Pty
    Ltd v. Federal Commissioner of
    Taxation 115
Beresford v. Royal Life Insurance Co.   150
Bond Corporation Holdings Ltd v.
    Australian Broadcasting Tribunal ..   433
Boyce Motor Lines v. United States   230

Brambles Holdings Ltd v. Carey   428
Brauer v. D.P.P.   23
Briggs v. Deputy Federal Commis-
    sioner of Taxation (W.A.); Ex parte
    Briggs   84
Briginshaw v. Briginshaw 182, 248
Browning Arms Co. of Canada Ltd,
    Re   103
Burns Philp Trustee Co. Ltd v. Viney   76
Burton v. Honan 89, 101,
                              106, 115, 116, 140
Calero-Toledo v. Pearson Yacht
    Leasing Co. 81, 101, 395
California Bankers Assoc. v. Schultz   204,
                              227, 228, 374
Callanan v. United States   241
Cameron v. Holt   139
Caminetti v. United States   216
Caplin and Drysdale, Chartered v.
    United States 25, 64, 74,
                              80, 95, 96, 97, 98, 389
Carr v. Atkins   327
Cheatley v. The Queen 87, 101,
                              120, 121
Churchill v. Walton   187
City and Equitable Fire Insurance Co.
    Ltd, Re   414
Cleaver v. Mutual Reserve Fund Life
    Association   150
Clyne v. Deputy Commissioner of
    Taxation   97
Cobiac v. Liddy   112
Cole v. Esanda Ltd   101
Colonnade Catering Corp. v. United
    States   224
Commissioner of Australian Federal
    Police—see A.F.P.
Commonwealth v. Jansenberger   26
Commonwealth v. Kreglinger &
    Furneau Ltd   87
Company Securities (Insider Dealing)
    Act, Re an inquiry under the .. 334, 337
Conally v. General Construction Co.   230
Convery v. Ziino   77
Cooper v. Stuart   87
Corporate Affairs Commission v.
    Yuill   433
Coulter v. The Queen   175
Crime Commission (N.S.W.) v.
    Hawes   255
Crossley Ltd v. North Broken Hill
    Holdings Ltd   270

Cundy v. Le Cocq 139
Customs & Excise Commissioners v.
    Air Canada (1989) 101, 140
Customs & Excise Commissioners v.
    Air Canada (1991) 141
Cutting v. Glover 86

Daire v. Raphael 91
De Courtenay v. The Queen 77
Defendant, Re a 309, 318, 321
Denton v. John Lister Ltd 143
Derby & Co. Ltd v. Weldon
    (No. 1) 321, 322
Derby & Co. Ltd v. Weldon (Nos 3
    and 4) 321
D.P.P. (Cth) v. Jeffery 252
D.P.P. v. Larsson 77
D.P.P. v. Lynch (1989) 23
D.P.P. v. Lynch (1990) 252
D.P.P. v. McCoid 128
D.P.P. v. Nieves 21
D.P.P. v. Saxon 26, 254
D.P.P. v. Walsh 22, 138
D.P.P. v. Ward 25
D.P.P. v. Withers 315
Doe v. United States 298
Drugs Misuse Act 1986, Re an
    Application Pursuant to the 19, 81
Dubai Bank Ltd v. Galadari 326
Ducret v. Colourshot Pty Ltd 136
Dugan v. Mirror Newspapers Ltd 76,
                                                    148

Efstratiadis v. Commonwealth 15

F. v. West Berkshire Health Authority   247
Fa v. Morris 122, 139
Fang Chinn Fa v. Puffett 123
Fazio v. Spitz 120, 123
First Equity Corp. of Florida v.
    Standard and Poor's Corp. 378
Fisheries Inspector v. Turner 110, 118
Forbes v. Traders' Finance Corp.
    Ltd 27, 77, 101
Francis and Francis (a firm) v. Central
    Criminal Court 314
Fraser v. Evans 289
Fraser v. The Queen 136
Frisina v. The Queen 124, 125

Garrett v. United States 234, 236, 238
Gartside v. Outram 289
Gerakiteys v. The Queen 55, 188
Giorgianni v. The Queen 93, 186, 187, 192
Glover v. Zouroudis 118

Goldsmith (J.W.), Jr, Grant Co. v.
    United States 101
Gollan v. Nugent 15
Gordon v. Chief Commander of
    Metropolitan Police 307
Gould v. Mount Oxide Mines Ltd ... 414
Graham v. Allis Chambers 414
Grand Jury Subpoena, Re 435
Grant v. Downs 299, 434, 435
Grayned v. City of Rockford 229
Greathead v. Bromley 248
Griffiths v. The Queen 120
Grosso v. United States 229

H. J. Inc. v. Northwestern Bell
    Telephone Co. 72
Haiti, Republic of v. Duvalier 321, 322
Halabi v. Westpac Banking Corp. 95
Hamilton v. Oades 246
Hampshire, Chief Constable of v.
    A. 309, 311, 316, 322
Hayes v. Weller 116, 117
He Kaw Teh v. The Queen 93,
              139, 174, 175, 176, 177, 420
Helton v. Allen 248
Helvering v. Gregory 218
Holland Furnace Co., Re 427
Hussein v. Chong Fook Kam 288
Hussey v. Palmer 150
Hutton (E.F.) Mail and Wire Fraud
    Case 408
Hwang Ming Heui v. Mellon 123

Illinois v. Vitale 235
Industrial Acceptance Corp. v. R. 133
Initial Services Ltd v. Putterill 289
Internal Revenue, Commissioner of v.
    Newman 218

K. (decd), Re 151
Kain and Shelton Pty Ltd v.
    McDonald 177
Kanbur Pty Ltd v. Adams 17
Kelly v. Kelly 248
Kent, Chief Constable of v. A. 316
Kern Oil & Refining Co. v. Tenneco
    Oil Co. 378
Kirk v. Commissioner of Australian
    Federal Police 77, 96, 99, 132
Kotalla v. Netherlands 312
Kuring-gai Co-operative Building
    Society (No. 12) Ltd, Re 157

Lambert v. California 222, 224, 226
Larmer v. Dome Lighting Products
    Pty Ltd 136
La Trobe University v. Robinson 87
Leader Westernport Printing Pty Ltd
    v. I.P.D. Instant & Duplicating Pty
    Ltd 435
Leary v. United States 229
Leicestershire, Chief Constable of
    v. M. 84, 137, 316
L'Estrange v. Federal Commissioner
    of Taxation 84
Liang v. Mellon 123
Libyan Arab Foreign Bank v. Bankers
    Trust Co. 340
Lim Chin Aik v. The Queen 176
Lucas and Kloss—see R. v. Lucas
Lyons v. Smart 115

M.J.O.'C., Re 352
Macedonia Pty Ltd v. Federal
    Commissioner of Taxation 436
McGovern v. Victoria 101,
                        115, 120, 135, 143
MacKinnon v. Donaldson Lufkin and
    Jenrette Securities Corp. 339, 340
Maher v. Attorney-General (Cth) 96
Malone v. Commissioner of Police of
    the Metropolis (No. 2) 289
Mareva Compania Naviera S.A. v.
    International Bulkcarriers S.A. 321
Margolin v. E. A. Wright Pty Ltd 101
Millar v. Ministry of Transport 176
Morris v. Slappy 97
Murphy v. Farmer 94, 101, 140, 177
Murphy v. Koninklijke-Java-China-
    Paketvaart Lijnen 82
Muschinski v. Dodds 153

National Companies and Securities
    Commission v. Brierley Invest-
    ments Ltd 270
National Employers' Mutual General
    Insurance Association Ltd v. Waind 435
New York Central and Hudson River
    Railroad Co. v. United States 376
Nickmar Pty Ltd v. Preservatrice
    Skandia Insurance Ltd 436
Nn, Dr v. Federal Office of Police
    Matters 274

O'Donovan v. Vereker 98
One Lot Emerald Cut Stones v. United
    States 109
O'Sullivan v. Lunnon 177

Palmyra, The 114
Parramatta, City Council of v. L.
    Shaddock & Associates Pty Ltd 166
Perron Investments Pty Ltd v. Deputy
    Federal Commissioner of Taxation 296
Pinkerton v. United States 241
Powers v. Maher 115
Proudman v. Dayman 139, 174,
    176, 177, 178, 179, 180, 182, 184, 193
Prus-Grzybowski v. Everingham 76
Public Prosecutions, Director of—see
    D.P.P.
Public Trustee v. Evans 151, 153
Public Trustee v. Fraser 151, 153

Queensland Bacon v. Rees 288

R. v. Allen .. 130, 131, 134, 136, 138, 146
R. v. Belcher 136
R. v. Board of Inland Revenue; Ex
    parte Goldberg 326
R. v. Board of Trade; Ex parte St
    Martin Preserving Co. Ltd 247
R. v. Bolger 78, 81, 135
R. v. Bragason 131, 306
R. v. Braham 120, 125
R. v. Brauer 251
R. v. Buddo 125
R. v. Burns 76
R. v. Central Criminal Court; Ex parte
    Adegbesan 327
R. v. Central Criminal Court; Ex parte
    Carr 327
R. v. Central Criminal Court; Ex parte
    Francis and Francis 274, 326
R. v. Chief Metropolitan Stipendiary
    Magistrate; Ex parte Secretary of
    State for the Home Department ... 338
R. v. Chow 191
R. v. Chrastny (No. 2) 310
R. v. Conley 136
R. v. Cotic 136
R. v. Cox and Railton 326
R. v. Crabbe 93, 420
R. v. Crooks 93, 100, 420
R. v. Cuthbertson 76, 124, 145, 148
R. v. D. 94
R. v. Dickens 308, 309, 310, 312, 313
R. v. Enwezor 313
R. v. Everall 77
R. v. Fagher 21, 78, 81, 82,
            83, 84, 85, 87, 88, 128, 129, 253
R. v. Fallon 93, 100, 420
R. v. Freeman 187
R. v. Giorgianni 420
R. v. Good 81, 124
R. v. Grossman 339, 340

R. v. Guildhall Magistrates Court; Ex
parte   Primlaks   Holdings   Co.
(Panama) Inc. 325
R. v. Hadad 19, 77, 412
R. v. Harper 131, 313
R. v. Hedley 313
R. v. Heley 136
R. v. Hoar (F.C.A.) 119, 120, 123, 129
R. v. Hoar (H.C.) 86, 118, 119, 120, 129
R. v. Hopes 310, 311, 313
R. v. Husak 136
R. v. Jansenberger 138
R. v. Johnson 307, 312
R. v. Kakura and Sato 120
R. v. Kingston upon Hull Justices; Ex
parte Hartung 124
R. v. Kneeshaw 319
R. v. Lake 81, 249
R. v. Lewes Crown Court; Ex parte
Hill 327
R. v. Lidster 118, 122
R. v. Loh 86
R. v. Lott-Carter 136
R. v. Lucas 136
R. v. McDermott 130
R. v. McDonald 125
R. v. Manchester Crown Court; Ex
parte Taylor 327, 328
R. v. Mayor of Dover 121
R. v. Menocal 121
R. v. Newman 94
R. v. Nicholson 131
R. v. O'Connor 139
R. v. Ottey 122
R. v. Overell 121
R. v. Parker 93, 420
R. v. Peterson 21
R. v. Po 136
R. v. Pou 86
R. v. Price 77
R. v. Raad 93, 100, 420
R. v. Reynhoudt 175
R. v. Rintel 145
R. v. Robson 306
R. v. Scott 246
R. v. Scully 125
R. v. Seelig 333
R. v. Shields 94
R. v. Small 310, 313
R. v. Smith 310
R. v. Smithers; Ex parte McMillan 21, 88, 89
R. v. Smithson 286
R. v. Southwark Crown Court; Ex
parte   Bank   of   Credit   and
Commerce International 328
R. v. Southwark Crown Court; Ex
parte Customs & Excise 328, 338
R. v. Spagnolo 250
R. v. Spens 333
R. v. Tarzia 125
R. v. Thompson 118, 122, 125

R. v. Vivian 319
R. v. Ward 245, 255
R. v. Ward, Marles and Graham 19,
                                        77, 124, 412
R. v. Warner 140
R. v. Waterhouse 85, 122
R. v. Wattle Gully Gold Mines N.L. 136
R. v. Weller 117
R. v. Woodrow 139
Ralph, Re 121
Rank Film Distributors Ltd v. Video
Information 318
Rasmanis v. Jurewitsch 151, 152, 153, 154
Razzi v. Commissioner of Australian
Federal Police 20
Reading v. Attorney-General 81
Refjek v. McElroy 95
Returned Sailors', Soldiers', and
Airmen's   Imperial   League   of
Australia (Henley and Grange Sub-
branch) Inc. v. Abbott 250
Rewis v. United States 221
Ricci v. Key Bancshares of Maine
(1985) 369
Ricci v. Key Bancshares of Maine Inc.
(1987) 404
Rio   Tinto   Zinc   Corporation   v.
Westinghouse Electric Corp. 338
Rosenfeldt v. Olson (1985) 152, 154
Rosenfeldt v. Olson (1986) 152, 154
Russello v. United States ... 53, 54, 80, 97

Saffron v. D.P.P. 93
Saffron v. D.P.P. (No. 4) 82, 84
St John Shipping Corp. v. Joseph
Rank Ltd 81
Salabiaku v. France 312
Schobelt v. Barber 151
Schultz v. Taylor 160
Scott v. China Navigation Co. Ltd ... 82
Scott v. James Patrick & Co. Pty Ltd 77, 115
Screws v. United States 230
Securities and Exchange Commission
v. Wang and Lee 339
Securities and Investment Board v.
Pantell 316, 322, 341
Sedima, S.P.R.L. v. Imrex 53
Shepard v. Gosnold 142
Sherras v. De Rutzen 139
Sillery v. The Queen 87, 88
Simpson v. United States 236
Smith v. Selwyn 113
Sociedade Nacional de Combustiveis
de Angola v. Lundquist 322
Societe   Internationale   Pour
Participations   Industrielles   et
Commerciales v. Rogers 297
Solem v. Helm 87, 89
Sorby v. Commonwealth 246
South Dakota v. Neville 228

State Drug Crime Commission (N.S.W.), Application of the; Re the Property of Kamal Abi Khalil 253
State Drug Crime Commission (N.S.W.) v. Egan 255
State Drug Crime Commission (N.S.W.) v. Fleming and Heal ... 26, 255
State Drug Crime Commission (N.S.W.) v. Lahoud 247
State Drug Crime Commission (N.S.W.) v. Larsson 255
State Drug Crime Commission (N.S.W.) v. Ujka and Sam 26, 250, 254, 255
State of Norway's Applications (Nos 1 and 2), Re 338
State Superannuation Board v. Trade Practices Commission 158
Stingel v. The Queen 177
Stokes and Difford 187
Stone, Re 151
Stuart v. Guardian Royal Exchange of New Zealand Ltd 434
Surrey, Chief Constable of v. A. 316
Surrey Quarter Sessions; Ex parte Commissioner of Metropolitan Police 121
Sweet v. Parsley 140

Taylor v. Attorney-General 145
Taxation, Commissioner of v. Clyne 89
Taxation, Commissioner of v. Manners and Terrule Pty Ltd 25
Taxation, Deputy Federal Commissioner of v. Allen, Allen & Hemsley 296
Taxation, Federal Commissioner of v. Australian and New Zealand Banking Group Ltd 297
Taxation, Federal Commissioner of v. Barnes 89
Taxation, Federal Commissioner of v. Citibank Ltd 296, 433
Tesco Supermarkets Ltd v. Nattrass 94, 103, 422
Thomas v. The King 175
Tournier v. National Provincial and Union Bank of England 289, 335, 337, 351
Toy Centre Agencies Pty Ltd v. Spencer 116
Trade Practices Commission v. Bata Shoe Co. of Australia Pty Ltd 103
Trade Practices Commission v. B.P. Australia Ltd 427
Trade Practices Commission v. Commodore Business Machines (Australia) Pty Ltd 427
Trade Practices Commission v. Dunlop Australia Ltd 429

Trade Practices Commission v. General Corporation Japan (Australia) Pty Ltd 408, 427, 429
Trade Practices Commission v. Queensland Aggregates Pty Ltd 427
Trade Practices Commission v. Tooth & Co. Ltd 89
Tran v. Commissioner of Australian Federal Police 22
Trautwein v. Federal Commissioner of Taxation 83, 84
Tyler v. Court of Registration 142

United States v. A Fee Simple Parcel of Real Property 397
United States v. Alamo Bank of Texas 376, 403
United States v. All Moneys 395
United States v. Alzate-Restrepo 379
United States v. American Investors of Pittsburgh 379, 380
United States v. Anzalone 200, 206, 207, 208, 214, 217, 237, 380
United States v. Automated Medical Laboratories Inc. 376
United States v. Awan 382, 385, 386, 388, 389, 405
United States v. Badalamenti 96
United States v. Baker 390, 405
United States v. Balint 219, 220, 222
United States v. Banco Cafetero Panama 395
United States v. Banco De Occidente (Panama) 375, 376
United States v. Bank of Credit and Commerce International 364, 375, 393, 394, 395
United States v. Bank of New England 10, 68, 207, 208, 217, 376, 377, 379, 406
United States v. Bassford 405
United States v. Besmajian 378, 380
United States v. Bi-Co Pavers Inc. ... 376
United States v. Blackman 385
United States v. Blankenship 231
United States v. Blockburger 235, 236, 238, 239, 240, 241
United States v. Bosch 378
United States v. Brumlik 384
United States v. Bucey 378
United States v. Busher 81, 87
United States v. Camarena 381
United States v. Carter 377
United States v. Chase Manhattan Bank 339
United States v. Chen 222
United States v. Cincotta 376
United States v. Cogswell 208, 217
United States v. Cook 201, 205, 206, 207
United States v. Culbert 216
United States v. Cure 206

United States v. Davenport 381
United States v. Dela Espriella .. 201, 203,
                              208, 240
United States v. Denemark 207,
                         208, 209, 380
United States v. Dichne 222, 223, 229
United States v. Dickinson 379
United States v. Donahue 380
United States v. Dotterweich 224
United States v. Eisenstein 222
United States v. Feldman 87
United States v. Feola 241
United States v. First Bank of Georgia 375
United States v. Fischbach and Moore,
  Inc. 87
United States v. Freed 219, 220, 222, 223
United States v. Giancola 205,
         207, 208, 210, 212, 217, 240
United States v. Gilliland 241
United States v. Gimbel (1984) 378
United States v. Gimbel (1987) .. 206, 380
United States v. Gold 376
United States v. Granada 222, 239
United States v. Halper 375
United States v. Harriss 229
United States v. Hawley 378
United States v. Hayes 206
United States v. Herron 380
United States v. Heyman 201,
         204, 205, 206, 207, 208, 380
United States v. Hilton Hotels Corp. 376
United States v. Hoyland 243
United States v. International Minerals
  & Chemical Corp. 219,
         220, 221, 222, 224, 226
United States v. Jewell 225,
                226, 376, 377, 379
United States v. Kaatz 227
United States v. Kelly 389
United States v. Kimball 405
United States v. Kington 379, 380
United States v. Konefal 207
United States v. Lafaurie 206
United States v. Lange 215
United States v. Larson 206,
         207, 208, 209, 237, 380
United States v. L.B.S. Bank—New
  York Inc. 377, 378, 381, 382, 384
United States v. Liparota 219,
         220, 221, 222, 226, 242
United States v. Littlefield 87
United States v. Lizza Industries 70, 71
United States v. McKinney 381
United States v. Mainieri 385, 405
United States v. Mangovski 227, 229
United States v. Maroun 381
United States v. Mastronardo 208, 209, 380
United States v. Miller 227, 228
United States v. Mobile Materials Inc. 402
United States v. Monsanto 25, 64, 97, 389
United States v. Morisette 221

United States v. Murphy 378
United States v. Nersesian .. 209, 237, 240
United States v. One Assortment of 89
  Firearms 92
United States v. One Chevrolet Sedan 102
United States v. One Ford Coach 102
United States v. One Ford Coupe 101
United States v. 141st Street
  Corporation 396
United States v. One 1957 Oldsmobile
  Auto 101
United States v. One Single Family
  Residence located at 6960
  Miraflores Avenue, Coral Gables .. 396
United States v. Ortiz 387
United States v. Ospina 386
United States v. Pacific Hide and Fur
  Depot Inc. 377
United States v. Palma 378
United States v. Palzer 208
United States v. Paris 379, 380
United States v. Parramore 388
United States v. Penagaricano-Soler ... 405
United States v. Pilla 380
United States v. Polizzi 231, 387
United States v. Polychron 380
United States v. Ponce Federal Bank
  FSB 69, 375
United States v. Puerto 205,
         206, 209, 215, 234, 240, 380
United States v. Reinis 208
United States v. Restrepo 405
United States v. Richeson 206
United States v. Richter 227, 228, 229
United States v. Rigdon 378, 380
United States v. Russell 405
United States v. St Michael's Credit
  Union 377, 379
United States v. Sanchez Vazquez 207,
                210, 212, 227, 229
United States v. San Juan 228, 229
United States v. Sans 205, 379
United States v. Scanio (1988) ... 380, 381
United States v. Scanio (1990) ... 243, 381
United States v. Schnaiderman ... 222, 223
United States v. Silberman 384, 405
United States v. So 379
United States v. Southside Finance .. 395
United States v. Stowell 395
United States v. Tax Lot 1500 87
United States v. Teemer 231
United States v. Thakkar 381
United States v. Time-D.C. Inc. 377
United States v. Thompson 201,
         203, 205, 206, 207, 208, 209, 217, 380
United States v. Tobon-Builes ... 201, 203,
  205, 206, 207, 208, 209, 214, 217, 237,
                              378, 380
United States v. Tolub 231
United States v. Tota 380
United States v. Turkette 54, 55

United States v. Turley 230
United States v. Twigg 405
United States v. Valdez-Guerro 379
United States v. Valle-Valdex 377
United States v. Varbel 206,
        207, 208, 209, 237, 240, 380
United States v. Vetco Inc. 297
United States v. Warren 222, 223
United States v. Woods 385
United States v. Woodward 215,
                236, 238, 239, 241
United States v. Yermian 237
Universal Telecasters Qld Ltd v.
    Guthrie 427

Van Chen v. Watton 123
Veen v. The Queen 145
Veen v. The Queen (No. 2) 85, 90,
                91, 135, 145, 149
Vickers v. Minister for Business and
    Consumer Affairs 17
Videon   v.   Beneficial   Finance
    Corporation 427

Vogel (L.) & Son Pty Ltd v. Anderson   117
Von Lieven v. Stewart 175, 178

Waterford v. Commonwealth 434, 435
Waugh v. British Railways Board 434, 435
Waugh v. Kippen 177
Weir v. Greening 436
Weld-Blundell v. Stephens (1919) 289
Weld-Blundell v. Stephens (1920) 337
West Mercia Constabulary v. Wagener 316
Wheeler v. Le Marchant 436
Wiedenhofer v. Commonwealth 114
Winters v. New York 229
Wonderheat v. Bishop 113
Woolmington v. D.P.P. 182

X   Ltd   v.   Morgan-Grampian
    (Publishers) Ltd 334
X.A.G. v. a Bank 338

Yick Wo v. Hopkins 405
Young v. United States 404

Table of Statutes

Commonwealth

Bankruptcy Act 1966
  s. 149: 91

Cash Transactions Reports Act 1988: 3, 5,
  6, 10, 11, 31, 36, 38, 43, 155, 156,
  157, 158, 160, 161, 167, 168, 172,
  173, 265, 266, 267, 271, 275, 280,
  281, 285, 298, 407, 419
  s. 3: 32, 156, 157, 158, 173
  s. 3(1): 410, 411
  s. 3(3): 161
  s. 4: 33
  s. 7: 32, 173, 410
  s. 10(2): 5, 159
  s. 10(2)(f): 159, 160
  s. 13: 36
  s. 14: 36
  s. 14A: 36
  s. 15: 32, 160, 161, 174, 286, 411
  s. 15(1): 160, 161
  s. 15(2): 160, 161
  s. 15(3): 160, 161
  s. 15(6): 5, 160, 161
  s. 16: 5, 32, 161, 162, 177, 194, 195,
  281, 410, 431
  s. 16(1): 162, 163, 166, 195
  s. 16(1)(b): 163
  s. 16(1)(b)(i): 163
  s. 16(1)(b)(ii): 163
  s. 16(1)(b)(iii): 163
  s. 16(4): 195, 431, 433
  s. 16(5): 38, 39, 161, 162, 163, 165,
  195, 431
  s. 17: 195, 289
  ss 18-20: 32
  ss 18-23: 410
  s. 18: 411
  s. 23: 32, 430
  s. 24: 265, 411
  s. 27: 33
  s. 28: 412
  s. 29: 5, 161
  s. 31: 6, 32, 47, 173, 174, 175, 176,
  177, 178, 180, 181, 182, 183, 184,
  185, 186, 187, 188, 189, 191, 192,
  193, 194, 195, 196, 197, 198, 271,
  412
  s. 31(1): 173, 174, 176, 178, 180, 181,
  184, 187, 189, 192, 196
  s. 31(1)(a): 181, 182
  s. 31(1)(b)(i): 175, 177, 178, 180

  s. 31(1)(b)(i)(A)-(E): 183
  s. 31(1)(b)(i)(A): 181
  s. 31(1)(b)(i)(B): 181, 185
  s. 31(1)(b)(i)(C): 181
  s. 31(1)(b)(i)(D): 181
  s. 31(1)(b)(i)(E): 181
  s. 31(1)(b)(ii): 175, 177, 178, 180, 181,
  183
  s. 31(1)(b)(iii): 181
  s. 31(1)(b)(iv): 181
  s. 31(2): 174, 189
  s. 31(2)(b)(i): 175
  s. 31(2)(b)(ii): 175
  s. 31(3): 174
  s. 32: 197, 408
  s. 32(1)(b)(i): 178
  s. 32(1)(b)(ii): 178
  s. 33: 285
  s. 34: 159, 192, 193, 194, 197, 198,
  412, 422
  s. 34(3): 193
  s. 34(4): 191, 193
  s. 34(4)(b): 193
  s. 34(5): 193
  s. 35: 33
  s. 38: 165
  Divn 1: 195
  Divn 3: 195
  Pt IV: 171
  Sch. 1: 170
  Sch. 3: 170

Cash Transaction Reports Amendment Act
  1991: 160, 276

Coal Excise Act 1949
  s. 26(1): 113

Commerce (Trade Descriptions) Act 1905
  s. 7(2): 113
  s. 10: 113
  s. 13: 113

Companies Act
  s. 129: 164

Constitution
  s. 51(xx): 157, 165
  s. 51(xxxi): 88, 89

Corporations Law 1989
  s. 232: 413
  s. 232(4): 408, 413, 414
  s. 1324: 413

Crimes Act 1914: 56, 178
  s. 5: 186
  s. 9(1): 113
  s. 10: 296
  s. 30E(3): 113
  s. 30G: 113
  s. 65(3): 113
  s. 69(2): 113
  s. 83(5): 113
  s. 85D: 113
  s. 89A: 113

Crimes (Biological Weapons) Act 1976
  s. 9(1): 113

Crimes (Currency) Act 1981
  s. 29: 113

Crimes Legislation Amendment Act (No. 2)
  1988
  s. 14: 290

Crimes Legislation Amendment Act (No. 2)
  1991: 161
  s. 16(5A): 39

Crimes (Superannuation Benefits) Act
  1989: 129

Crimes (Taxation Offences) Act 1980: 56

Customs Act 1901: 16, 29, 30, 74, 76, 81,
  88, 89, 106, 286, 407
  s. 203: 17, 116
  s. 205: 17
  s. 205(1): 113, 115
  s. 208A: 17
  s. 208D: 17
  ss 228-229: 76
  s. 228: 16, 17, 25, 27, 113, 115
  s. 228A: 113, 115
  s. 228B: 113, 115
  s. 229: 25, 27, 94, 113, 115
  s. 229(1): 115
  s. 229(1)(i): 101, 140
  s. 229(1)(j): 17
  s. 229A: 17, 27, 79, 93, 101, 113, 115,
  421
  s. 229A(8): 27
  s. 230: 113, 115
  s. 233AB: 116
  s. 233AB(1): 116
  s. 233B: 81, 99
  s. 239: 110, 116, 117
  ss 243A-243S: 111
  s. 243A: 20
  s. 243A(3): 132
  s. 243B: 23, 24, 26, 79, 88, 93, 101,
  421
  s. 243B(2): 20
  s. 243B(3): 20
  s. 243B(4): 22
  s. 243C: 20, 22, 77, 79, 88, 93, 101,
  412, 421

  s. 243C(3): 22
  s. 243C(5): 21
  s. 243C(6): 21
  s. 243E: 77
  s. 243E(1): 23
  s. 243E(2): 23
  s. 243E(2)(c): 24
  s. 243E(4)(c): 24, 25, 96
  s. 243E(4A): 25
  s. 243F(1)(a): 24, 25
  s. 243J: 28
  s. 243K: 24
  s. 262: 17
  Pt XIII, Div. 3: 19, 82

Debits Tax Act 1982
  s. 3(1): 156

Defence Act 1903
  s. 82(1): 113
  s. 82(2): 113
  s. 83: 113

Director of Public Prosecutions Act 1983
  s. 6: 127
  s. 6(1)(fa): 15
  s. 6(1)(h): 15
  s. 6(8): 14
  s. 9: 127

Director of Public Prosecutions
  Amendment Act 1985: 14

Excise Act 1901
  s. 93: 116
  s. 96: 113
  s. 116(1): 113, 115

Fisheries Act 1952: 123
  s. 13AA: 120

Freedom of Information Act 1982: 430

Hazardous Waste (Regulation of Exports
  and Imports) Act 1989
  s. 59(2): 194

Income Tax Assessment Act 1936: 42, 296
  s. 221Y(2): 113
  s. 263: 296
  s. 264: 296
  s. 264A: 298
  Pt IVA: 164

Industrial Chemicals (Notification and
  Assessment) Act 1989
  s. 109(2): 194

Law and Justice Legislation Amendment
  Act 1988
  s. 54: 82

Mutual Assistance in Criminal Matters Act
    1987: 290
  s. 3(1): 302
  s. 5: 302
  s. 8: 290
  s. 12: 302
  s. 13: 302
  ss 32ff: 304
  Pt VI: 294

National Crime Authority Act 1984: 41

Navigation Act 1912
  s. 252: 113

Ozone Protection Act 1989: 194
  s. 58: 110
  s. 65: 194, 197
  s. 65(2): 194

Privacy Act 1988: 5, 6, 33, 167, 168, 170,
    172

Proceeds of Crime Act 1987: 2, 13, 14,
    17, 19, 20, 26, 29, 30, 31, 38, 42, 44,
    45, 56, 74, 76, 77, 78, 79, 80, 81, 82,
    83, 85, 89, 90, 91, 92, 95, 97, 98,
    100, 101, 102, 103, 104, 107, 125,
    162, 163, 164, 169, 195, 294, 295,
    304, 407, 410
  s. 3: 29, 79
  s. 3(1): 126
  s. 3(1)(a): 137
  s. 3(1)(b): 135, 137
  s. 4: 99
  s. 4(1): 17, 18, 77, 126, 296
  s. 5: 125
  s. 7: 18, 78, 413
  s. 7(1): 127
  s. 14: 125
  s. 14(1): 126
  s. 18: 85
  s. 18(1): 127, 131
  s. 18(2)(a)-(c): 130
  s. 19: 17, 77, 81, 99, 101, 412, 421
  s. 19(1): 126
  s. 19(2): 126
  s. 19(3): 18, 77, 81, 103, 127, 412
  s. 19(3)(a): 99, 135
  s. 19(3)(4): 82, 85
  s. 19(4): 18, 77, 81, 127, 135, 412
  s. 19(6): 23
  s. 20(1): 18
  s. 20(6): 18
  s. 21: 27, 102, 421
  s. 21(6): 99
  s. 21(6)(b)(ii): 99
  s. 21(7): 421
  s. 21(8): 421
  s. 23: 78, 413
  s. 23A: 78, 413
  s. 26: 77, 412
  s. 26(1): 20, 126

  s. 26(3): 86
  s. 26(4): 82
  s. 26(5): 86, 132
  s. 26(8): 22, 128
  s. 26(9): 128
  s. 27: 20, 77, 128, 137
  s. 27(4)(a): 22
  s. 27(6): 77, 79, 412
  s. 27(7): 21
  s. 27(7)(b): 82
  s. 27(8): 21, 82, 83
  s. 27(10): 21
  s. 28: 22
  s. 30: 18, 28, 77, 78, 88, 102, 127, 412,
    413, 421
  s. 31: 28, 102, 421
  s. 31(6): 252
  s. 36: 29, 433
  s. 43: 23, 78, 413
  s. 43(1): 126, 127
  s. 43(2): 24, 91
  s. 43(3): 96
  s. 43(4): 25, 96
  s. 43d(3)(b): 25
  s. 43(6): 92
  s. 44(1): 23
  s. 44(2): 23
  s. 45: 102, 421
  s. 47: 102, 421
  s. 48: 102, 421
  s. 48(3): 28
  s. 48(4): 18, 251, 252
  s. 48(4)(e): 251
  s. 49(6): 92
  s. 50: 28
  s. 52: 24
  s. 56: 85, 102, 421
  s. 66: 28, 296, 297
  ss 70ff: 297
  s. 71: 29
  ss 73ff: 297
  s. 73: 29
  ss 76-78: 285, 430
  s. 76: 430
  s. 77: 430
  s. 81: 11, 36, 56, 78, 93, 94, 95, 99,
    175, 177, 179, 180, 195, 287, 288,
    408, 413, 419, 420, 422
  s. 82: 11, 36, 78, 94, 177, 195, 287,
    288, 413, 420, 422
  s. 83: 18, 56, 78, 79, 413, 422
  s. 85: 78, 79, 94, 95, 104, 194, 413,
    422
  s. 98(3): 127
  s. 98(5): 128
  s. 99: 22, 128
  s. 100: 128
  Pt III, Div. 1: 78, 413
  Pt III, Div. 2: 78, 91, 413
  Pt IV: 285

Psychotropic Substances Act 1976
    s. 9(2): 113

Spirits Act 1906
    s. 17: 113

Trade Practices Act 1974: 408
    s. 52: 165
    s. 84: 94, 422

New South Wales

Confiscation of Proceeds of Crime Act
    1989: 76, 80, 81, 82, 83, 85, 89, 90,
    91, 92, 95, 98, 101, 102, 104, 107,
    136, 294, 407, 421
    s. 3: 80
    s. 3(b): 135
    s. 4: 126
    s. 4(1): 78, 79, 126
    s. 7: 78
    s. 17(1): 131
    s. 18: 78, 126
    s. 18(1)(b)(ii): 135
    s. 18(2): 85, 86, 132, 135
    s. 24: 126
    s. 24(1): 79
    s. 24(1)(a): 79
    s. 24(2): 86
    s. 25: 79
    s. 25(5): 82, 83
    s. 29: 79
    s. 30(2): 79
    s. 30(4): 82, 83
    ss 43-57: 79
    s. 43: 96
    s. 43(6): 96
    s. 54: 85
    s. 73: 79, 420
    s. 73(3): 100
    s. 73(3)(4): 93
    s. 73(4): 100
    s. 73(5): 196
    s. 76: 79, 94, 104, 422

Crimes (Confiscation of Profits) Act 1985:
    21, 77, 78, 81, 84, 85, 88, 253
    s. 5(1)(b): 249
    s. 5(1)(b)(ii): 249

Crimes Act 1900
    s. 527c: 183
    s. 527c(1): 184
    s. 527c(2): 184

Criminal Appeal Act 1912
    s. 5: 120

Criminal Law Amendment Act 1883: 76

Drug Misuse and Trafficking Act 1985
    ss 23-28: 79. 245

Drug Trafficking (Civil Proceedings) Act
    1990: 7, 79, 107, 111, 244, 256, 286,
    407
    s. 3: 126, 244, 247
    s. 5: 245, 248
    s. 5(1): 132
    s. 6: 245
    s. 6(1): 132
    s. 7: 246, 247
    s. 7(3): 245
    s. 9: 246, 250
    s. 9(5): 245, 250
    s. 9(5)(b)-(f): 250
    s. 9(5)(e): 254
    s. 9(5)(f): 250
    s. 9(9): 250
    s. 10: 245
    s. 10(2): 249
    s. 10(5): 253, 254
    s. 12: 7, 246, 247, 248, 253
    s. 12(e): 245
    s. 12(1)(b): 246, 247
    s. 13: 246, 247
    s. 13(b): 247
    s. 13(c): 247
    s. 14: 253
    s. 16: 255
    s. 16(1): 138
    s. 17: 253
    s. 20: 246
    ss 22-32: 248
    s. 22(4): 249
    s. 22(5): 248
    s. 22(6): 248
    s. 24: 249
    s. 25(3): 250
    s. 26: 252
    s. 27(1): 252
    s. 27(2): 252
    s. 27(7): 252
    s. 28: 252
    s. 28(4): 252
    s. 28(5): 252
    s. 29: 253
    s. 30: 253
    s. 31: 252
    s. 37: 255
    s. 53: 255
    s. 54: 248
    s. 59: 415
    s. 63: 246
    s. 63: 113
    Pt 2: 245
    Pt 3: 248
    Pt 4, Div. 2: 255

Felons (Civil Proceedings) Act 1981: 76

Limitation Act 1969
    s. 14(1): 430

Poisons Act 1966: 245

Secret Commissions Act 1919
  s. 10(1)(b): 84

Supreme Court (Summary Jurisdiction) Act
  1967: 255

Northern Territory

Crimes (Confiscation of Profits) Act 1988:
  294, 407

Crimes (Forfeiture Proceeds) Act 1988: 77,
  107
  s. 3(1): 126
  s. 5(1): 126
  s. 5(1)(b)(ii): 135
  s. 10: 126
  s. 64: 131

Fisheries Act 1965
  s. 48(1): 119
  s. 48(2): 120

Queensland

Crimes (Confiscation of Profits) Act 1989:
  77, 107, 136, 294, 407
  s. 3(1): 126
  s. 6(3): 131
  s. 6(4): 131
  s. 8(1): 126
  s. 8(2)(b): 135
  s. 8(2)(c): 135
  s. 13(1): 126
  s. 71: 129

Drugs Misuse Act 1986: 19, 81
  s. 34: 124

South Australia

Crimes (Confiscation of Profits) Act 1986:
  77, 107, 294, 407
  s. 3a: 128
  s. 4(1): 126

Crimes (Confiscation of Profits) Act
  Amendment Act 1988
  s. 2: 86

Criminal Law Consolidation Act 1935
  s. 329: 76

Criminal Law (Sentencing) Act 1988
  s. 16: 118

Treason and Felony Forfeiture Act 1874:
  76

Tasmania

Poisons Act 1971
  s. 84(2)(g): 124

Victoria

Agricultural Chemicals Act 1958
  s. 18B(5): 113

Crimes Act 1958
  s. 566: 120
  Pt VI: 120

Crimes (Confiscation of Profits) Act 1986:
  77, 107, 146, 147, 294, 407
  s. 1(a): 135
  s. 3(1): 126
  s. 5(3): 130
  s. 5(3)(b): 131
  s. 7: 126
  s. 7(1): 126
  s. 7(2)(b): 135
  s. 12(1): 126
  s. 13: 82
  s. 41Q(3): 196

Crimes (Confiscation of Profits)
  (Amendment) Act 1991
  s. 36: 146

Fisheries Act 1968
  s. 49(3): 113

Forests Act 1958
  s. 79(3): 113

Forfeiture for Treason and Felony
  Abolition Act 1878: 15, 76, 106

Health Act 1958
  s. 293(1): 113

Liquor Control Act 1987
  s. 123(3): 111, 118

Sentencing Act 1991
  s. 5: 146

Stamps Act 1958: 113

Supreme Court Act 1958
  s. 63B: 113

Western Australia

Crimes (Confiscation of Profits) Act 1988:
  77, 107, 286, 294, 407
  s. 3(1): 126
  s. 9(1): 131
  s. 9(2): 130
  s. 10: 126
  s. 10(2)(b): 135
  s. 15: 126

Misuse of Drugs Act 1981
  s. 28(3): 124

Hong Kong

Drug Trafficking (Recovery of Proceeds)
    Ordinance 1989
  s. 25: 257

India

Prevention of Corruption Act 1947
  s. 5(1)(e): 258

New Zealand

Criminal Justice Act 1954
  s. 42: 119
  s. 42(1): 118

Misuse of Drugs Act 1975
  ss 38-42: 83

United Kingdom

Agricultural Holdings Act 1948: 249

Bankers' Books (Evidence) Act 1879: 352

Civil Jurisdiction and Judgments Act 1982
  s. 25: 322

Companies Act 1985
  s. 434(3): 319
  s. 434(5): 319

Companies Act 1989: 352

Companies Securities (Insider Dealing) Act
    1985: 337

Contempt of Court Act 1981
  s. 10: 334

Courts Act 1971
  s. 57: 121

Criminal Court Act 1973
  s. 35: 322

Criminal Justice Act 1986: 317

Criminal Justice Act 1987: 325
  s. 2: 315, 319, 334
  s. 2(8): 319
  s. 2(10): 315, 334

s. 2(13): 334
s. 3: 335
s. 3(4): 335
s. 3(6): 335

Criminal Justice Act 1988: 306, 315, 317,
    330, 343
  s. 71(1): 319
  s. 71(4): 307
  s. 71(5): 308
  s. 71(7): 306, 307
  s. 72(1): 309
  s. 72(3): 307
  s. 72(5): 320
  s. 72(7): 320
  s. 73(1): 309
  s. 73(2): 309
  s. 73(3)(b): 309
  s. 73(5): 307
  s. 74(9): 317
  s. 74(10)(b): 316
  s. 75: 307
  s. 75(1)(c): 316
  s. 76: 316
  s. 77: 316, 352
  s. 77(1): 316
  s. 77(3): 316
  s. 77(5): 316
  s. 77(5)(c): 316
  s. 77(8): 316
  s. 77(10): 316
  s. 78(1): 317
  s. 78(5): 317
  s. 78(7): 317
  s. 80(1): 317
  s. 80(8): 317
  s. 82(4): 305, 308, 317
  s. 89: 318
  s. 96: 305
  s. 98: 314, 330
  s. 99(2): 315
  s. 100: 313
  s. 102(3): 343
  s. 104(1): 319
  s. 105: 320, 322
  Pt IV: 76
  Pt VI: 8, 305, 315, 320
  Pt VII: 305, 306
  Sch. 4: 307

Criminal Justice (International Co-
    operation) Act 1990: 54, 305
  s. 4: 352

Customs and Excise Management Act
    1979: 101
  s. 141: 140
  s. 141(1): 140
  s. 141(3): 140

Drug Trafficking Offences Act 1986: 8,
    38, 76, 81, 107, 305, 306, 307, 311,
    315, 318, 326, 328, 329, 335, 342
    ss 1-5: 79
    s. 1(1): 306, 308
    s. 1(2): 306, 308
    s. 1(5)(c): 312
    s. 2(2): 309
    s. 4(4): 309
    s. 5(7): 317
    s. 11(1): 317
    s. 11(8): 317
    s. 13(4): 305
    s. 24: 257, 281, 314, 328, 330
    s. 24(1): 314, 336
    s. 24(3): 314, 328
    s. 24(4): 329
    s. 26: 305, 311
    ss 27-29: 314
    s. 30: 314
    s. 31: 330
    s. 32(1): 315
    s. 33: 313
    s. 38(1): 308
    s. 38(3): 343

Financial Services Act 1986: 315, 322
    s. 6: 322
    s. 61: 341
    s. 94: 332, 333
    s. 105: 332, 333, 334
    s. 177: 332, 333
    s. 177(3): 319, 333
    s. 177(4): 319
    s. 177(6): 319
    s. 177(8): 333
    s. 178: 333
    s. 178(6): 333

Insolvency Act 1986: 148
    Sch. 13: 332

Forfeiture Act 1870: 15, 76, 106, 148

Navigation Acts 1651, 1660: 16, 76, 114

Police and Criminal Evidence Act 1984:
    325, 326, 330, 352
    s. 8: 325
    s. 8(2): 325
    s. 9: 325, 328
    s. 10(1): 325
    s. 10(2): 326
    s. 14: 325
    s. 27: 328
    s. 27(6): 328
    s. 56(1): 315
    s. 56(2): 315
    s. 56(5): 315
    s. 56(5A): 315
    s. 56(11): 315
    s. 116: 325
    Sch. 1: 325, 328
    Sch. 1, para. 4: 325

Powers of the Criminal Court Act 1972
    s. 38: 322

Powers of Criminal Courts Act 1973: 91
    s. 37(c): 320

Prevention of Oil Pollution Act 1971
    s. 2: 307

Prevention of Terrorism (Temporary
    Provisions) Act 1989: 330, 335, 336,
    342, 343, 351
    s. 9: 314
    s. 11: 331
    s. 11(1): 330
    s. 11(2): 331
    s. 11(3)(b): 330
    s. 11(3)(c): 330
    s. 12(2): 331
    s. 12(2)(b): 331
    s. 18: 330
    Sch. 7: 330

Taxes Management Act 1970
    s. 20(3): 326

United States

Act of 30 April 1790, ch. 9, 1 Stat. 117
    s. 24: 16

Anti-Drug Abuse Act 1988: 200, 355, 356,
    383, 388
    s. 1005: 361
    s. 1359: 374
    s. 4720: 282

Bank Secrecy Act 1970: 3, 9, 32, 35, 47,
    200, 203, 204, 205, 209, 210, 212,
    213, 217, 219, 235, 236, 237, 282,
    283, 354, 355, 356, 358, 359, 361,
    362, 363, 364, 367, 368, 374, 402,
    403, 405, 409, 414, 418, 420, 438

Caribbean Basic Economic Recovery Act
    1983: 301

Cash Transaction Reports Act 1990: 36

Comprehensive Forfeiture Act 1984: 25,
    107

Constitution
    Art. III, s. 3, cl. 2: 16

Continuing Criminal Enterprise Act 1970:
    25, 63, 76, 80, 81, 95, 97, 98, 125,
    294

Continuing Criminal Enterprises Act 1976:
    107

Corrupt Organisation Act 1970: 76

Criminal Money Laundering Control Act
1986: 38, 93, 99, 196, 257, 355, 367,
368, 375, 389, 402, 403, 405, 420
s. 1956: 383
s. 1956(a)(1): 383
s. 1956(a)(2): 383
s. 1956(a)(3): 383

Currency and Foreign Transactions
Reporting Act 1970: 173, 203, 229,
354—see also Bank Secrecy Act 1970

Financial Institutions Reform, Recovery
and Enforcement Act 1989: 375

H.R. 3848
s. 10: 365

Insider Trading Sanctions Act 1984: 340,
341

M.L.C. Act—see Criminal Money
Laundering Control Act 1986

Money Laundering Prosecution
Improvements Act 1988: 213

Omnibus Drug Initiative Act 1988: 358,
361

Organised Crime Control Act 1970: 52,
107

Racketeer Influenced and Corrupt
Organisation Act 1970: 3, 25, 50, 52,
53, 54, 55, 56, 62, 63, 65, 66, 70, 71,
72, 73, 75, 76, 80, 81, 85, 95, 97, 98,
123, 125, 233, 294, 386, 395

Restatement ch. 40 of the Foreign
Relations Law: 339

R.I.C.O.—see Racketeer Influenced and
Corrupt Organisation Act 1970

Right to Financial Privacy Act 1978: 365,
367, 369, 403, 404, 418

Travel Act 1961: 233

Uniform Securities Act 1957: 376

12 U.S.C.
s. 1818(a): 375
s. 1818(c): 375
s. 1818(e): 375
s. 1818(g): 375
s. 1818(h): 375
s. 1818(i)(2)(C): 375
s. 1818(i)(2)(D): 375
s. 1818(s): 375
s. 1829(b): 203
ss 1951-1959 (1982): 203
s. 1953(b): 379

s. 3401ff: 404
s. 3403(c): 404
s. 3412: 403

15 U.S.C.
s. 78o(b)(4): 376
s. 80(b)(3): 376
s. 204(a): 376

18 U.S.C.
s. 2 (1982): 206, 213
s. 2(b): 236
s. 371 (1982): 240, 242
s. 542: 387
s. 549: 387
s. 830: 387
s. 834(f) (1970): 220
s. 857: 387
s. 981: 383, 395
s. 981(a)(2): 396
s. 982: 383, 395
s. 1001: 215, 236, 237, 238, 239, 240,
241, 242, 243
ss 1005-1006: 387
s. 1007: 387
s. 1014: 387
s. 1341: 214
s. 1344 (Supp. III 1985): 214
s. 1590: 387
s. 1951: 214
s. 1952 (1982 and Supp. IV 1986): 233,
390
s. 1952(a)(1982): 214
s. 1952(a)(3): 387
ss 1956-1957 (Supp. IV 1986): 200, 233,
355
s. 1956: 356, 360, 374, 383, 385, 386,
390
s. 1956(a)(i): 384, 385
s. 1956(a)(b): 93, 420
s. 1956(a)(1): 384, 385, 388, 389
s. 1956(a)(2): 384, 387, 388, 389
s. 1956(a)(2)(B): 388
s. 1956(a)(3): 383
s. 1956(c)(1): 386
s. 1956(c)(4): 384
s. 1956(c)(5): 388, 390
s. 1956(c)(7): 386
s. 1956(c)(7)(A) (Supp. IV 1986): 234
s. 1956(f)(1): 384
s. 1956(f)(2): 384
s. 1957 (Supp. IV 1986): 100, 224, 233,
234, 356, 360, 374, 384, 385, 389,
390
s. 1957(b)(1): 389
s. 1957(c): 390
s. 1957 (West Supp. 1989): 234
s. 1956(c)(7)(B): 386
s. 1957(f): 390
s. 1957(f)(2): 390

18 U.S.C.—*Continued*
ss 1961-1968 (1982 and Supp. IV 1986): 233
s. 1961(e): 386
s. 1962 (1982): 233
s. 2319: 387
s. 3623: 389

21 U.S.C.
s. 846: 385
s. 848: 189, 386
s. 881(a): 396
s. 1504: 361

26 U.S.C.
s. 60501 (Supp. IV 1986): 211, 233, 387

29 U.S.C.
s. 1160(a): 376

31 U.S.C.
s. 1052(k)(1976): 215, 238
ss 5311-5314: 203, 224
s. 5311 ff.: 387
s. 5311 (1982): 204
s. 5312: 390
s. 5312(a)(2): 379
s. 5312(a)(2)(H): 390
s. 5313: 199, 236, 378
s. 5313(a) (1982): 199, 203, 209

ss 5316-5322 (1982 and Supp. IV 1986): 203
s. 5316: 222, 232, 233, 238
s. 5318: 374
s. 5321(a)(1) (1982 and Supp. IV 1986): 204
s. 5321(a)(4): 213
s. 5321(a)(4)(C): 213
s. 5321(c) (1982 and Supp. IV 1986): 213
s. 5322 (1982 and Supp. IV 1980): 199, 216
s. 5322(a) (Supp. IV 1986): 204, 213
s. 5322(a): 379
s. 5322(a)-(b) (1982 and Supp. IV 1986): 204
s. 5322(b) (Supp. IV 1986): 233, 242, 379
s. 5324 (Supp. IV 1986): 199, 209, 212, 213, 215, 216, 218, 224, 228, 231, 356, 358, 365, 380
s. 5324 & C: 47
s. 5324(3) (Supp. IV 1986): 216
s. 5325: 209, 213, 359, 379
s. 5326: 209, 213, 359, 360, 380

37 U.S.C.
s. 5324 (Supp. IV 1986): 214

Whistleblower Protection Act 1989: 283

Table of Other Legislation

Bills

Cash Transaction Reports Bill 1987: 31, 35, 36, 38, 42, 163, 172, 266, 271

Confiscation of Profits of Crime Bill 1989: 80

Crime Amendments Bill No. 2 of 1989: 45

Proceeds of Crime Bill 1987: 44, 80, 89, 90, 134

Codes

California Civil Code (U.S.)
 s. 2225: 153
 s. 2225(e)(3): 154

Companies Code (Cth)
 s. 541: 286
 s. 573: 286

Criminal Code (Germany)
 Art. 73 s. 1: 320
 Art. 73: 305
 Art. 74: 305

Criminal Code (W.A.)
 s. 703: 125

Futures Industry Code (Cth): 158

Internal Revenue Code (U.S.)
 s. 982: 298
 s. 7201: 384
 s. 7206: 384
 s. 60501: 233, 269

Model Penal Code (U.S.)
 s. 2.02(a): 221
 s. 2.02(b): 197
 s. 2.04(1)(a): 220

Penal Code (Belgium)
 Art. 42: 305

Penal Code (Denmark)
 Art. 77: 305

Penal Code (France)
 Art. 470: 305

Penal Code (Greece)
 Art. 76: 305

Penal Code (Holland)
 Art. 33: 305

Penal Code (Italy)
 Art. 40: 305

Penal Code (Luxembourg)
 Art. 42: 305

Penal Code (Spain)
 Art. 48: 305

Securities Industry Code (Cth): 158, 164

Securities Industry Code (N.S.W.)
 s. 130(1)(d): 95

Conventions

Convention on Jurisdiction and Enforcement of Judgments: 322
 Art. 24: 322

Council of Europe Convention on Laundering, Seizure and Confiscation of the Proceeds from Crime
 Art. 6: 348
 Art. 6(2)(a): 349
 Art. 6(2)(c): 349
 Art. 12(2): 349
 Art. 13(1): 349
 Art. 18: 349
 Art. 18(7): 349
 Art. 22(2)(a): 349
 Art. 23(2): 350
 Art. 23(3): 350
 Art. 23(5): 350
 Art. 30: 349

European Convention on Human Rights: 311
 First Protocol
  Art. 1: 311
  Art. 3: 312
  Art. 6: 312

Multinational Convention on Mutual Administrative Assistance in Tax Matters: 303

United Nations Convention Against Illicit
  Trade in Narcotic Drugs and
  Psychotropic Substances: 305, 408
  Art. 3(1)(b): 257
  Art. 5: 104

Directives

Draft European Community (E.C.)
  Directive
  Art. 1: 346
  Art. 3: 347
  Art. 3(5): 348
  Art. 3a: 348
  Art. 4: 348

Regulations

Bank Secrecy Regulations (U.S.): 225, 227
  —see also C.F.R. references.

Banking (Foreign Exchange) Regulations
  1946 (Cth): 275

Scheme of Management (Southern Zone
  Rock Lobster Fishery) Regulations
  1984 (S.A.)
  r. 25: 86

12 C.F.R. (U.S.)
  s. 21.11(h)(5): 381
  s. 21.21 (O.C.C.): 391
  s. 208.14: 391
  s. 353.1: 387
  s. 563.17-7: 391
  s. 536.18(d)(iv): 381
  Pt 326: 391

17 C.F.R. (U.S.)
  s. 4.21(a)(13)(i): 376
  s. 4.31(a)(7): 376

26 C.F.R. (U.S.)
  s. 1.60501 (1988): 211

31 C.F.R. (U.S.)
  s. 101.11(g) (1988): 203
  s. 102.1(b) (1970): 199
  s. 103.11(a) (1988): 209
  s. 103.11(g): 209
  s. 103.11(n): 381
  s. 103.11(o) (1988): 216
  s. 103.11(1) (1988): 211
  s. 103.22 (1988): 209, 378
  s. 103.22(a): 378
  s. 103.22(a)(1) (1988): 199, 204, 205,
    210, 211
  s. 103.22(a)(3) (1988): 210
  s. 103.22(a)(4) (1988): 209
  s. 103.22(b)(ii) (1988): 204
  s. 103.26: 380
  s. 103.26(a): 378
  s. 103.26(4) (1988): 204
  s. 103.27 (1988): 212, 378
  s. 103.33(b): 276
  s. 103.33(d): 380
  s. 103.46: 374
  s. 103.47 (1988): 204
  s. 103.47(e) (1988): 213
  s. 103.47(f) (1988): 204
  s. 103.49(d) (1988): 215, 234
  s. 103.53 (1988): 213

Rules

Crown Court (Amendment) Rules 1986
  (Vic.)
  r. 25(B): 326

Supreme Court Rules 1970 (N.S.W.)
  r. 84A: 248
  r. 84B: 246

Supreme Court Rules (S.A.)
  r. 114.06(3): 131

Select Bibliography

Abrams, "The New Ancillary Offences" (1989) 1 *Criminal Law Forum* 1.

Alexander and Caiden, eds, *Politics and Economics of Organised Crime*, Lexington, Mass.: Lexington Books, D.C. Heath and Co., 1985.

Alexander, *Pizza Connection: Lawyers, Money, Drugs, Mafia*, London: Weidenfeld and Nicolson, 1988.

American Bankers Association and American Bar Association Criminal Justice Section, Seminar, *Money Laundering Enforcement: Legal and Practical Developments*, 26-27 October 1989, New York, N.Y.

American Bankers Association and American Bar Association Criminal Justice Section, Seminar, *Money Laundering Enforcement Update: Compliance and Enforcement Issues*, 28-29 October 1991, Los Angeles, Ca.

American Bankers Association and American Bar Association Criminal Justice Section, Seminar, *Money Laundering Enforcement Update: Legislative, Regulatory, Enforcement Developments and Policy Implications*, 24-25 September 1990, Washington, D.C.

American Bankers Association, *Currency Transaction Reporting*, Washington, D.C.: American Bankers Association, 1988.

American Bankers Association, *Money Laundering Deterrence and Bank Secrecy Act Research Report*, Washington, D.C.: American Bankers Association, 1990.

Anon., "The Asset Forfeiture Rap" (rap lyrics).

Australia, Attorney-General's Department, *Cash Transaction Reports, Legislation and Materials*, Canberra: Attorney-General's Department, 1988.

Australia, Attorney-General's Department, *Mutual Assistance in Criminal Matters, Legislation and Materials*, Canberra: Attorney-General's Department, 1987.

Australia, Attorney-General's Department, *Proceeds of Crime, Legislation and Materials*, Canberra: Attorney-General's Department, 1987.

Australia, Director of Public Prosecutions, *Civil Remedies Report 1985-1987*, Canberra: Australian Government Publishing Service, 1987.

Australia, Royal Commission of Inquiry into Drug Trafficking, *Report*, Canberra: Australian Government Publishing Service, 1983.

Blau, "The Right to Financial Privacy and the Criminal Referral Process" (1990) 44 *Consumer Finance Law Quarterly Review* 9.

Block and Barton, "Internal Corporate Investigations: Maintaining the Confidentiality of a Corporate Client's Communications with Investigative Counsel" (1979) 35 *Business Lawyer* 5.

Blum, *Offshore Haven Banks, Trusts and Companies*, New York: Praeger, 1983.

Bostock, "Observations on the Cash Transactions Legislation" (1989) 18 *Australian Tax Review* 147.

Bradley, "Confiscation of Criminal Assets: Recent Developments in New South Wales" (1990) 2(2) *Current Issues in Criminal Justice* 95.

Braithwaite, "Taking Responsibility Seriously: Corporate Compliance Systems", in Fisse and French, eds., *Corrigible Corporations and Unruly Law*, San Antonio: Trinity University Press, 1985.

Brown, "Forfeiture of Property under the Customs Act 1901" (1982) 56 *Australian Law Journal* 447.

California, Department of Justice, *Asset Seizure and Forfeiture Manual*, Sacramento: Bureau of Narcotic Enforcement, 1987.

Cameron, "Making the Offender Squirm—Forfeiture and Confiscation" [1982] N.Z.L.J. 176.

Caplow, "Under Advisement: Attorney Fee Forfeiture and the Supreme Court" (1989) 55 *Brooklyn Law Review* 111.

Carr and Morton, "How to Recognise a Money Launderer" (1989) 7(8) *International Financial Law Review* 10.

Cash Transaction Reports Act 1988 (Cth), Explanatory Memorandum.

Cash Transaction Reports Agency:
    Guideline No. 1, *Suspect Transactions Reporting*.
    Guideline No. 2, *Significant Cash Transaction Reporting*.
    Guideline No. 3, *Account Opening: Verification of Identity Procedures*.
    Guideline No. 4, *Merchant Bankers and Stock Brokers, Suspect Transactions Reporting*.
    I.C. No. 1, *Reporting Suspect Transactions—Principles Involved*.
    I.C. No. 2, *Cash Dealers, Financial Corporation*.
    I.C. No. 3, *Clarification of When a Suspect Transaction Report Must be Given*.
    I.C. No. 4, *Meaning of "Account"*.
    I.C. No. 5, *F.O.I. Access*.
    I.C. No. 6, *Blocking of an Account of an Unverified Signatory*.
    I.C. No. 7, *Insurance Bonds*.

Chaikin, "Money Laundering: An Investigatory Perspective" (1991) 2 *Criminal Law Forum* 467.

Chambost, *Bank Accounts: A World Guide To Confidentiality*, Chichester: John Wiley & Sons, 1983.

Chamness and Cook, *A Guide To The Bank Secrecy Act*, Washington, D.C.: American Bankers Association, 1987.

Clark, "Civil and Criminal Penalties and Forfeitures: A Framework for Constitutional Analysis" (1976) 60 *Minnesota Law Review* 379.

Cloud, "Forfeiting Defence Attorneys' Fees: Applying An Institutional Role Theory To Define Individual Constitutional Rights" [1987] *Wisconsin Law Review* 1.

Coad, "C.T.R.A.: Targeting Money Laundering with Tax Revenue Underpinning" (1990) 2(2) *Current Issues in Criminal Justice* 90.

Coad, "Reporting of Transactions under the Cash Transactions Reports Act 1988", A.I.C., Conference on Organised Crime, 5-7 September 1989.

Committee on Criminal Advocacy, "The Forfeiture of Attorney Fees in Criminal Cases: A Call for Immediate Remedial Action" (1986) 41 *Association of the Bar of the City of New York Record* 469.

Commonwealth Secretariat, *Basic Documents on International Efforts to Combat Money Laundering*, London: Commonwealth Secretariat, 1991.

Commonwealth Secretariat/International Bar Association, *Action Against Transnational Criminality*, Papers from the 1991 Oxford Conference on International and White Collar Crime, London: Commonwealth Secretariat, 1991.

Connelly and Fahner, "Unconventional Strategies in White Collar Criminal Investigations" (1988) 14(2) *Litigation* 17.

Cook and Pollock, "Bank Directors: Understanding Their Role, Responsibility and Liability" (1989) 40 *Mercer Law Review* 588.

Cullen, "Money Laundering Legislation: Perspectives from the Australian Banking Industry", paper presented at R.M.S. Conference, *Cash Transactions Reporting, Money Laundering, and Confiscation of Proceeds of Crime*, Sydney, 21 August 1990.

Dabb, "Cash Transactions Reporting and Proceeds of Crime Legislation: The New Generation of Commonwealth Law Enforcement", paper presented at R.M.S. Conference, *Cash Transactions Reporting, Money Laundering, and Confiscation of Proceeds of Crime*, Sydney, 21 August 1990.

Dodaro, *Asset Forfeiture: An Update*, Hearings Before the House of Representatives Committee on the Judiciary, Subcommittee on Crime, 24 April 1989.

Donald, "A Commentary on the Provisions of C-61: Canada's New Proceeds of Crime Legislation (S.C. 1988, c. 51)" (1990) 47 *The Advocate* 423-424.

Drug Trafficking (Civil Proceedings) Act 1990 (N.S.W.), Explanatory Memorandum.

Efthim, "Dealing with the Money Launderers; Solicitors' Obligations" (1991) 29(11) *Law Society Journal* 40.

Feldman, "Freezing Defendants' Assets before Drugs Trials" (1987) 137 *New Law Journal* 457.

Feldman, *Criminal Confiscation Orders: The New Law*, London: Butterworths, 1988.

Ferris, *Starting Forfeiture Programs: A Prosecutor's Guide*, Washington, D.C.: Police Executive Research Forum, National Institute of Justice, 1989.

Financial Action Task Force on Money Laundering, *Report*, Paris: Financial Action Task Force, 1990.

Finkelstein, "The Goring Ox: Some Historical Perspectives on Deodands, Forfeitures, Wrongful Death and the Western Notion of Sovereignty" (1973) 46 *Temple Law Quarterly* 169.

Fisse, "Confiscation of Proceeds of Crime: Discretionary Forfeiture or Proportionate Punishment?" (1992) 16 *Criminal Law Journal* 138.

Fisse. "Confiscation of Proceeds of Crime: Funny Money, Serious Legislation" (1989) 13 *Criminal Law Journal* 368.

Fisse, "Corporate Compliance Systems: The Trade Practices Act and Beyond" (1989) 17 *Australian Business Law Review* 356.

Fisse, "Fraud and the Liability of Company Directors" in Grabosky, ed., *Complex Fraud*, Canberra: Australian Institute of Criminology, 1991.

Fisse, "Risk Minimisation Through Preventive Law" (1987) 25(7) *Law Society Journal* 54.

Fisse, "The Rise of Money-Laundering Offences and the Fall of Principle" (1989) 13 *Criminal Law Journal* 5.

Fisse, Fraser and Coss, *Money Trail*, Sydney: Lexpert Publications, forthcoming (I.B.M. P.C. hypertext program).

Florez and Boyce, "Laundering Drug Money" (1990) 59(4) *FBI Law Enforcement Bulletin* 22.

Fogel, "Profitability of Customs Forfeiture Program Can Be Enhanced", United States General Accounting Office, Office of the Comptroller General, Washington, D.C., 1989.

Fox and Freiberg, *Sentencing, State and Federal Law in Victoria*, Melbourne: Oxford University Press, 1985.

Fox and Freiberg, "Sentences without Conviction: From Status to Contract in Sentencing" (1989) 13 Crim. L.J. 297.

Fox and O'Hare, "Criminal Bankruptcy" (1978) 4 *Monash University Law Review* 181.

Fraser, "Lawyers, Guns and Money: Towards a Comparative Jurisprudence of Organised Crime" (1990) 2(2) *Current Issues in Criminal Justice* 122.

Freiberg, " 'Civilising' Crime: Parallel Proceedings and the Civil Remedies Function of the Commonwealth Director of Public Prosecutions" (1988) 21 *Australia and New Zealand Journal of Criminology* 129.

Freiberg, "Grandson of Sam in Australia: Confiscating the Proceeds of Criminal Expression and Notoriety", Paper presented at Seventh A.N.Z. Society of Criminology Annual Conference, Melbourne, September 1991.

Freiberg, "Ripples from the Bottom of the Harbour: Some Social Ramifactions of Taxation Fraud" (1988) 12 *Criminal Law Journal* 136.

Freiberg, "Social Security Prosecutions And Overpayment Recovery" (1989) 22 *Australia and New Zealand Journal of Criminology* 213.

Freiberg, "The Monster That Devoured Jurisprudence: Criminal Confiscation, Profit And Liberty", Inaugural Lecture of Foundation Chair of Criminology, Melbourne, 23 April 1991.

Fricker, "Dirty Money" (1989) 75(11) A.B.A. Journal 60.

Fried, "Rationalizing Criminal Forfeiture" (1988) 79 *Journal of Criminal Law and Criminology* 328.

Gallagher, *Management and Disposition of Seized Assets*, Washington, D.C.: Police Executive Research Forum, United States Department of Justice, 1988.

Gaylord, "Chinese Laundry: International Drug Trafficking and Hong Kong's Banking Industry" (1990) 14 *Contemporary Crises* 23.

George, *The Comprehensive Crime Control Act of 1984*, Clifton, N.J.: Prentice Hall, 1988.

Geva, "From Commodity to Currency in Ancient History—On Commerce, Tyranny, and the Modern Law of Money" (1987) 25 *Osgoode Hall Law Journal* 115.

Gold, *Proceeds of Crime: A Manual with Commentary on Bill C-61*, Ontario, Canada: Carswell Company Limited, 1989.

Goode, "Confiscation of Criminal Profits: Tangles in the Net" (1986) 24(6) *Law Society Journal* 36.

Goode, "The Confiscation of Criminal Profits" (1986) 67 *Proceedings of the Institute of Criminology, University of Sydney* 35.

Harmon, "United States Money Laundering Laws: International Implications" (1988) 9 *New York Law School Journal of International And Comparative Law* 1.

Hewett and Kalyk, *Understanding the Cash Transactions Reports Act*, Sydney: C.C.H. Australia, 1990.

Hodgson, *Profits of Crime and Their Recovery*, London: Howard League for Penal Reform, 1984 (Cambridge Studies in Criminology, No. 52).

Hughes, "Policing Money Laundering through Funds Transfers: A Critique of Regulation under the Bank Secrecy Act" (1992) 67 *Indiana Law Journal* 283.

Hughes and O'Connell, "In Personam (Criminal) Forfeiture and Federal Drug Felonies: An Expansion of a Harsh English Tradition into a Modern Dilemma" (1984) 11 *Pepperdine Law Review* 613.

I.B.C. Conference, *Money Laundering: The Legal Regime*, London: I.B.C. 1991.

Intriago, *International Money Laundering: A Eurostudy Special Report*, London: Eurostudy Publishing, 1991.

Irvine, *When You are the Headline: Managing a Major News Story*, Homewood, Ill.: Dow Jones-Irwin, 1987.

Janzen, *Asset Forfeiture: Informants and Undercover Investigations*, Washington, D.C.: Police Executive Research Forum, United States Department of Justice, 1990.

Karlan, "Discrete and Relational Criminal Representation: The Changing Vision of the Right to Counsel" (1992) 105 *Harvard Law Review* 670.

Koenig and Godinez-Taylor, "Criminal Forfeiture: Attacking the Economic Dimension of Organized Narcotics Trafficking" (1982) 32 *American University Law Review* 227.

Koenig and Godinez-Taylor, "The Need for Greater Double Jeopardy and Due-Process Safeguards in R.I.C.O. Criminal and Civil Actions" (1982) 70 *California Law Review* 724.

Kohler, "The Confiscation Of Criminal Assets In The United States And Switzerland" (1990) 13 *Houston Journal of International Law* 1.

Kurisky, "Civil Forfeiture of Assets: A Final Solution To International Drug Trafficking?" (1988) 10 *Houston Journal of International Law* 239.

Levi, "Regulating Money Laundering: The Death of Bank Secrecy in the U.K." (1991) 31 *British Journal of Criminology* 109.

Levi, *Customer Confidentiality, Money Laundering, And Police-Bank Relationships: English Law and Practice In A Global Environment*, London: Police Foundation, 1991.

Levi, *Regulating Fraud: White-Collar Crime and the Criminal Process*, London: Tavistock Publications, 1987.

Linscott, "Asset Forfeiture (Modern Anti-Drug Weapon): Is Bankruptcy a 'Defence'?" (1990) 15 *Tulsa Law Journal* 617-637.

Lynch, "Drug Kingpins and Their Helpers: Accomplice Liability under 21 U.S.C. Section 848" (1991) 58 *University of Chicago Law Review* 391.

Lynch, "R.I.C.O.: The Crime of Being a Criminal, Parts I & II" (1987) 87 *Columbia Law Review* 661.

Maroldy, "Record-keeping and Reporting in an Attempt to Stop the Money Laundering Cycle: Why Blanket Recording and Reporting of Wire and Electronic Funds Transfers is Not the Answer" (1991) 66 *Notre Dame Law Review* 863.

Mass, "Forfeiture of Attorney's Fees: Should Defendants Be Allowed to Retain the 'Rolls Royce of Attorneys' with the 'Fruits of the Crime'?" (1987) 39 *Stanford Law Review* 663.

Mathews, "Internal Corporate Investigations" (1984) 45 *Ohio State Law Journal* 655.

Maxeiner, "Bane of American Forfeiture Law—Banished At Last?" (1977) 62 *Cornell Law Review* 768.

McCay, "Forfeiture of Attorneys' Fees Under R.I.C.O. and C.C.E." (1986) 54 *Fordham Law Review* 1171.

McLean, "Mutual Assistance In Criminal Matters: The Commonwealth Initiative" (1988) 37 *International and Comparative Law Quarterly* 177.

McLean, "Seizing the Proceeds of Crime: The State of the Art" (1989) 38 *International and Comparative Law Quarterly* 334.

Meese, *Attorney General's Guidelines on Seized and Forfeited Property*, Washington, D.C.: United States Department of Justice Office of the Attorney General, 1987.

Money Laundering Alert (monthly periodical).

Morley, *Dirty Money: A Banker's Guide To Self Defence, Bank Manager's Guide*, Arlington, Va.: C.G.M. Group, 1985 (video).

Morvillo, "Voluntary Corporate In-House Investigations—Benefits and Pitfalls" (1981) 36 *Business Lawyer* 1871.

Mutual Assistance in Criminal Matters Act 1988 (Cth), Explanatory Memorandum.

Nadelmann, "Unlaundering Dirty Money Abroad: U.S. Foreign Policy and Financial Secrecy Jurisdictions" (1986) 18 *Inter-American Law Review* 33.

National Crime Authority, *N.C.A. Operation Silo: Report of an Investigation*, Canberra: Australian Government Publishing Service, 1987.

National Crime Authority, *Taken to the Cleaners: Money Laundering in Australia*, Vol. 1, Canberra: Australian Government Publishing Service, 1991.

Nicol, "Committee on the Forfeiture of Assets in Criminal Offences of the Howard League of Penal Reform" (1983) 35(2) *Bulletin on Narcotics* 71.

Nicol, "Confiscation of the Profits of Crime" (1988) 52 *Journal of Criminal Law* 75.

Nilsson, "The Council of Europe Laundering Convention: A Recent Example of a Developing International Criminal Law" (1991) 2 *Criminal Law Forum* 419.

Note, "A Proposal To Reform Criminal Forfeiture Under R.I.C.O. And C.C.E." (1984) 97 *Harvard Law Review* 1929.

Note, "Victim Restitution in the Criminal Process: A Procedural Analysis" (1984) 97 *Harvard Law Review* 931.

O'Neill, "Functions of the R.I.C.O. Enterprise Concept" (1989) 64 *Notre Dame Law Review* 646.

Obermaier and Morvillo, eds., *White Collar Crime: Business and Regulatory Offences*, New York: Seminar Press, 1990.

Okuda, "Criminal Antiprofit Laws: Some Thoughts In Favour of Their Constitutionality" (1988) 76 *California Law Review* 1353.

Pianin, "Criminal Forfeiture: Attacking the Economic Dimension of Organised Narcotics Trafficking" (1982) 32 *American University Law Review* 227.

Pickering, "Does Australia need R.I.C.O.?" (1988) 62 *Law Institute Journal* 939.

Pickering, "Some More Thoughts on R.I.C.O." (1989) 63 *Law Institute Journal* 11.

Pitz, "Letting the Punishment Fit the Crime: Proportional Forfeiture under Criminal R.I.C.O.'s Source of Influence Provision" (1991) 75 *Minnesota Law Review* 1223.

Plombeck, "Confidentiality and Disclosure: The Money Laundering Control Act of 1986 and Banking Secrecy" (1988) 22 *International Lawyer* 69.

Popham and Probus, "Structural Transactions in Money Laundering: Dealing with Tax Evaders, Smurfs, and Other Enemies of the People" (1988) 14 *American Journal of Criminal Law* 83.

Powis, *Bank Secrecy Act Compliance*, Rolling Meadows, Ill: Bank Administration Institute, 3rd ed., 1989.

Powis, *The Money Launderers: Lessons from the Drug Wars: How Billons of Illegal Dollars are Washed through Banks and Businesses*, Chicago, Ill.: Probus, 1992.

Preventive Law Reporter (quarterly periodical).

Proceeds of Crime Act 1987 (Cth), Explanatory Memorandum.

Queensland, *Report of a Commission of Inquiry Into Possible Illegal Activities and Associated Police Misconduct*, Brisbane: The Commission, 1989.

Reuter, MacCoun and Murphy, *Money from Crime: A Study of the Economics of Drug Dealing in Washington, D.C.*, Santa Monica: Rand Corporation, 1990.

Reynolds, "E.C. Briefings" (1990) 9(3) *International Financial Law Review* 43.

Roberts, "Constitutional Law—The Eighth Amendment As Applied To R.I.C.O. Criminal Forfeiture—*United States v. Busher*, 817 F. 2d 1409 (9th Cir. 1987)" (1988) 10 *Western New England Law Review* 393.

Ross, "Bankers, Guns, and Money: Financial Assistance for Terrorism under the Prevention of Terrorism Act 1989" (1991) 14 *Boston College International and Comparative Law Review* 770.

Schwartz, "Liability For Structured Transactions Under The Currency And Foreign Transactions Reporting Act: A Prelude To The Money Laundering Control Act of 1986" (1987) 6 *Annual Review of Banking Law* 315.

Scott, "Some More Thoughts on R.I.C.O." (1989) 63 *Law Institute Journal* 11.

Scott, "The Customs Act/The Proceeds of Crime Act 1987" in *Confiscation of Assets*, Sydney: College of Law, Continuing Legal Education, 1988.

Sherris, "Drug Related Forfeitures Land Title Issues" (1990) 4 *Probate and Property* 33.

Short, Colvard and Lee, "The Liability of Financial Institutions for Money Laundering" (1992) 109 *Banking Law Journal* 46.

Singh, "Nowhere to Hide: Judicial Assistance in Piercing the Veil of Swiss Banking Secrecy" (1991) 71 *Boston University Law Review* 847.

Sigler and Murphy, *Interactive Corporate Compliance*, New York: Quorum Books, 1988.

Skalitzky, "Comments: Aider and Abbettor Liability, The Continuing Criminal Enterprise, and Street Gangs: A New Twist In An Old War On Drugs" (1990) 81 *Journal of Criminal Law and Criminology* 348.

Skorcz, "Comment: R.I.C.O. Forfeiture: Secured Lenders Beware" (1990) 37 *U.C.L.A. Law Review* 1199.

Slater, "Revealed at Last: What the Lawyers told Westpac", *Canberra Times*, 21 February 1991, p. 1.

Smith, *Prosecution and Defence of Forfeiture Cases* [looseleaf service on forfeiture], New York: M. Bender, 1985.

Smith, "Modern Forfeiture Law and Policy: A Proposal For Reform" (1978) 19 *William and Mary Law Review* 661.

Smith, "The Scope of Real Property Forfeiture for Drug-Related Crimes under the Comprehensive Forfeiture Act" (1988) 137 *University of Pennsylvania Law Review* 303.

Spaulding, "Hit Them Where It Hurts: R.I.C.O. Criminal Forfeitures and White Collar Crime" (1989) 80 *Journal of Criminal Law and Criminology* 197.

Spencer, "Bank Liability under the U.N. Drug Trafficking Convention" (1990) 9(3) *International Financial Law Review* 16.

Stolker, *Financial Search Warrants*, Washington, D.C.: Police Executive Research Forum, United States Department of Justice, 1989.

Strafer, "Money Laundering; The Crime of the '90s" (1989) 27 *American Criminal Law Review* 149.

Symposium, "Law and The Continuing Enterprise: Perspectives on R.I.C.O." (1990) 65 *Notre Dame Law Review* 873.

Symposium, "Limitations on the Effectiveness of Criminal Defence Counsel" (1988) 136 *University of Pennsylvania Law Review* 1779.

Symposium, "The 20th Anniversary of the Racketeer Influenced and Corrupt Organisations Act (1970-1990)" (1990) 64 St. John's Law Review 701.

Talbot and Hinton, "Confiscation Orders: A Guide To Their Making And Enforcement" (1991) 55 *Journal of Criminal Law* 504.

Taylor, "Forfeiture under 18 U.S.C. 1963— R.I.C.O.'s Most Powerful Weapon" (1980) 17 *Amercian Criminal Law Review* 379.

Temby, "Taking Assets off Criminals—Attainder in Australia Today?" (1988) *University of Western Australia Law Summer School, Paper 14.*

Temby, "The Proceeds of Crime Act: One Year's Experience" (1989) 13 *Criminal Law Journal* 24.

Temby, "The Pursuit of Insidious Crime" (1987) 61 *Australian Law Journal* 510.

Thornton, "Confiscating Criminal Assets: The New Deterrent" (1990) 2(2) *Current Issues in Criminal Justice* 72.

Touchstone, "Crime, Confiscation and the Conveyance" (1990) 139 *Solicitor's Journal* 537.

United Nations, *Convention Against Illicit Traffic in Narcotic Drugs And Psychotropic Substances*, Vienna: United Nations, 1989.

United States Congress, House Committee on Banking, Finance and Urban Affairs, *Drug Money Laundering*, Hearing Before the Senate Committee on Banking, Housing and Urban Affairs on s. 571, 28 January 1985 (Senate Hearing 99-8).

United States Congress, Senate Committee on the Judiciary, *Money Laundering Legislation*, Hearing Before the Senate Committee on the Judiciary, 29 October 1985 (Judiciary 99-67, Senate Hearing 99-540).

United States, Department of Justice, *Drug Agents' Guide to Forfeiture of Assets*, Washington, D.C.: National Institute of Justice, 1981.

United States, Department of Justice, *Investigation and Prosecution of Illegal Money Laundering—A Guide to the Bank Secrecy Act*, Washington, D.C.: National Institute of Justice, 1983.

United States, Department of Justice, Office of the Attorney General, *Drug Trafficking: A Report to the President of the United States*, Washington, D.C.: United States Department of Justice, Office of the Attorney General, 1989.

United States, General Accounting Office, *Seized Conveyances: Justice and Customs Correction of Previous Conveyance Management Problems*, Washington, D.C.: United States General Accounting Office, 1988.

United States, House Committee on the Judiciary, *Forfeiture Issues*, Hearing Before the House Subcommittee on Crime, 25 November 1985.

United States, House of Representatives, *Asset Forfeiture: An Update*, Hearings Before the House of Representatives Committee on the Judiciary, Subcommittee on Crime, 24 April 1989.

United States, House of Representatives, Subcommittee on Crime of the House Committee on the Judiciary, *Forfeiture Provisions of the Comprehensive Crime Bill and the Anti-Drug Abuse Act of 1986*, Hearing, 100th Cong., 1st Sess., 1987.

United States, House of Representatives, Subcommittee on Crime of the House Committee on the Judiciary, *Forfeiture Issues*, Hearing before the House Subcommittee on Crime, 99th Cong., 1st Sess., 25 November 1985.

United States, President's Commission on Organised Crime, *The Cash Connection: Organised Crime, Financial Institutions and Money Laundering*, Washington, D.C.: Government Printer, 1984.

United States, Senate, Committee on Banking, Housing, and Urban Affairs, *Drug Money Laundering*, Hearing on S 571, 99th Cong., 1st Sess., 1985.

United States, Senate, Committee on Banking, Housing, and Urban Affairs, *The Drug Money Seizure Act and the Bank Secrecy Act Amendments*, Hearing, 99th Cong., 2nd Sess., 1986.

United States, Senate, Committee on Foreign Relations, Report, *Drug Money Laundering, Banks and Foreign Policy*, 101st Cong., 2nd Sess., 1989.

United States, Senate, Committee on Government Affairs, *Banking Secrecy Act*, Hearing before the Permanent Subcommittee on Investigations, 99th Cong., 1st Sess., 1985.

United States, Senate, Committee on the Judiciary, *Attorneys' Fees Forfeiture*, Hearing, 99th Cong., 2nd Sess., 1986.

United States, Senate, Committee on the Judiciary, *Money Laundering Legislation*, Hearing, 99th Cong., 1st Sess., 1985.

United States, Senate, Committee on the Judiciary, Report, *The Money Laundering Crimes Act of 1986*, 99th Cong., 2nd Sess., 1986.

United States, Senate, Permanent Subcommittee on Investigations of the Committee on Governmental Affairs, Report, *Crime and Secrecy: The Use of Offshore Banks and Companies*, 99th Cong., 1st Sess., 1985.

United States, Senate, Subcommittee on Narcotics and Terrorism of the Foreign Relations Committee, *Drug Money Laundering, Banks and Foreign Policy*, 101st Cong., 2nd Sess., 1989.

Victoria, Director of Public Prosecutions, *Issues Paper*, Confiscation of Proceeds of Crime, Drugs Legislation Working Party, November 1990.

Villa, "A Critical View of Bank Secrecy Act Enforcement and the Money Laundering Statutes" (1988) 37 *Catholic University Law Review* 489.

Villa, *Banking Crimes: Fraud, Money Laundering, and Embezzlement*, New York: Clark Boardman Company, Ltd, 1988.

Walter, Ingo, *$ecret Money*, Lexington, Mass.: Lexington Books, D.C. Heath and Company, 1985.

Wardlaw, "Organised Crime and Drug Enforcement" (1986) 67 *Proceedings of the Institute of Criminology, University of Sydney* 17.

Weerasooria, "Money Laundering, Cash Transactions Legislation and the Banker-Customer Relationship" (1991) 2 *Journal of Banking and Finance Law and Practice* 84.

Weinberg, "The Proceeds of Crime Act 1987—New Despotism Or Measured Response?" (1989) 15 *Monash University Law Review* 201.

Weinstein, "Prosecuting Attorneys for Money Laundering: A New and Questionable Weapon in the War on Crime" (1988) 51 *Law and Contemporary Problems* 369.

Weiss, "The Poor Tax Revisited: The Effects of Shifting the Burden of Investigating Drug Crimes to Lenders" (1992) 70 *Texas Law Review* 717.

Welling, "Smurfs, Money Laundering, and the Federal Criminal Law: The Crime of Structuring Transactions" (1989) 41 *Florida Law Review* 288.

Winick, "Forfeiture of Attorney's Fees Under R.I.C.O. and C.C.E. and the Right to Counsel of Choice: The Constitutional Dilemma and How to Avoid It" (1989) 43 *University of Miami Law Review* 765.

Winn, "Seizures of Private Property in the War Against Drugs: What Process is Due?" (1988) 41 *Southwestern Law Journal* 1111.

Winters, "Criminal Forfeitures and The Eighth Amendment: 'Rough' Justice Is Not Enough" (1987) 14 *Hastings Constitutional Law Quarterly* 451.

Wolfteich, "Making Criminal Defence a Crime Under U.S.C. Section 1957" (1988) 41 *Vanderbilt Law Review* 843.

Woltring, "Forfeiture of Criminally Obtained Assets under Australian Federal Law and Associated Laws to Render Forfeiture More Effective at both the National and International Level", paper presented at Fourth International Anti-Corruption Conference, Sydney, 1989.

Young, " 'Son of Sam' and His Legislative Offspring: The Constitutionality of Stripping Criminals of Their Literary Profits" (1988) 4 *Intellectual Property Journal* 25.

Zagaris and Kingma, "Asset Forfeiture International and Foreign Law: An Emerging Regime" (1991) 5 *Emory International Law Review* 445.

Zahra and Arden, *Drug Law in New South Wales*, Sydney: Federation Press, 1991.

1

The Money Trail

BRENT FISSE, DAVID FRASER and GRAEME COSS

A NEW REGIME OF LEGAL CONTROLS

Political moves during the 1980s to attack the money trail in crime have resulted today in a legal edifice that has far-reaching implications for many people in society. Serious yet sweeping offences have been created to combat money laundering. Extensive provision is made for forfeiture of tainted property. Pecuniary penalties can be imposed to recover the gross benefits derived directly or indirectly from crime. Cash dealers are required to report significant cash transactions and suspect transactions. Broad powers of investigation have been enacted. The Cash Transaction Reports Agency has been established and is busily hoisting up leads from its well of data. Existing enforcement agencies have re-oriented their policing or prosecution strategies, as evidenced by the National Crime Authority's reference on money laundering. A dinosaur of our times, the Authority has sensed that engorgement of the proceeds of crime might well be a feeding habit upon which its own survival partly depends.

The new legislative regime has potentially drastic effects not only for hard-bitten drug traffickers and tax evaders but also for banks, finance companies, accountants, solicitors, barristers, land agents, and other persons accustomed to professing innocence. A common misapprehension entertained in such circles is that the legislation relates only to drug and tax offences. Another is that the legislation impinges upon criminals and that companies or professional advisers acting in good faith have nothing to fear. Whatever solace these assumptions may provide for the uninitiated, they do not reflect the position in law. The scope of the legislation is broad, so much so that it is easy for people in commercial or professional walks of life to become entangled, even where they have acted honestly. Remarkably, the legal profession in this country, unlike that in the United States, has been slow to heed the dangers and has done little to oppose even the most extreme and objectionable features of the legislation.

Numerous legal problems arise in this area, partly by reason of novelty, partly because the legislation has not been adequately thought through, and mainly because the basic concepts are inherently problematic. This can be seen from the fundamental yet amorphous notion of "proceeds of crime". "Proceeds of crime" is much wider than the concept of profit

1

and includes interests which have been acquired indirectly from the commission of offences. Moreover, the interests that are vulnerable extend far beyond the property that would be traceable as a matter of equitable remedy. Where exactly the limit is to be drawn is far from clear and depends greatly on the extent to which the courts are prepared to read down the legislation or to use their discretion to relieve hardship. These and other departures from the rule of law have led one American judge to describe confiscation of proceeds of crime legislation as "the monster that ate jurisprudence".[1] Taming this monster is likely to take decades of further legal development, if indeed that challenge can ever be met.

In this collection of essays and papers we have brought together a range of material that sets out the legal dimensions of money laundering, cash transaction reporting, and confiscation of proceeds of crime. Our criterion of selection has been simply that which seems useful at the present formative stage of Australian proceeds of crime laws. Some of the contributions focus on the more technical elements of the law. Others address critical underlying issues of principle and policy. Comparative material from the United States and the United Kingdom has been included. There is also a chapter on corporate compliance and liability control. The thrust of these offerings is summarised below.

A MONEY TRAIL-BLAZER'S GUIDE

The opening contribution to this collection is John Thornton's "Confiscating Criminal Assets: The Proceeds of Crime Act and Related Legislation". This chapter provides an incisive overview of Commonwealth confiscation legislation and the more important issues that arise under it. These issues also arise under State legislation, which follows the same general pattern albeit with much variation in detail. The topics canvassed by Thornton include forfeiture of property connected to an offence or derived from the proceeds of the offence; pecuniary penalties based on benefits derived from the offence; restraint of property pending determination of applications for forfeiture or pecuniary penalties; and investigative powers. The vexed issue of release of funds for legal expenses is reviewed sensitively, as are a number of other difficulties, including the protection of third party interests and the scope of the offence provisions relating to money laundering. Thornton's conclusion is that the Commonwealth confiscation legislation has worked reasonably well but that some of the provisions have the potential to operate oppressively if used indiscriminately, and that the legislation has novel features which are bound to reveal problems and anomalies when they are tested before the courts.

Graham Pinner's "Cash Transaction Reporting and Money Laundering Legislation: How Will it Come Out in the Wash?" provides an account

---

1. Judge David Sentelle of the United States Court of Appeal (D.C.), *Washington Times*, 27 November 1989.

of the operation of the *Cash Transactions Reports Act*. After highlighting
the radically new nature of the enforcement strategy that has now been
implemented under the Australian money trail legislation, Pinner, the
Deputy-Director of the Cash Transactions Reports Agency, explains the
nature of the various reporting obligations under the Act, including the
far-reaching obligation to report suspect transactions. This explanation
leads to a useful reconsideration of the policy behind the legislation.
Pinner supports the legislative objectives in a point by point discussion
of the more significant criticisms that have been made. In his view, the
Australian data collection system avoids the weaknesses that have
emerged under the United States' *Bank Secrecy Act*. Although there are
gaps in the legislation that can be exploited by criminals, he defends the
money trail legislation on the ground that money is a basic medium of
exchange in society and that crime-connected money will be handled by
banks rather than by less reliable underground banking systems. The
scope of the legislation is accentuated by the rather ominous warning
that the legislation is aimed not merely at drug trafficking but also at
white collar and corporate crime. The overall tone of the chapter is
cautious optimism, coupled with professional determination to make the
legislation work.

A much less optimistic view of the new legislative regime is presented
by David Fraser in his challenging critique, "Lawyers, Guns and Money:
Economics and Ideology on the Money Trail". Fraser starts from the
postulation that the object of the legislation is to regulate the market
behaviour of drug traffickers and other offenders. The implications
drawn are not flattering to our lawmakers. The first is that the legislation
should focus on enterprise liability but, unlike the United States' R.I.C.O.
legislation, does so only in a half-hearted and ill-conceived way.
Secondly, it is far from obvious that asset forfeiture and cash transactions
reporting are in fact efficient mechanisms of social control. Fraser
criticises the crude cost-benefit assessments that have been made in this
area previously, as by Lionel Bowen, Gareth Evans and other political
money trail-blazers. Market conditions for drugs conduce to
monopolistic behaviour and, given the demand for the product supplied,
busting such monopolies is much easier said than done. Account must be
taken of the market efficiencies that may result from the licit use of
illicitly-derived capital, especially in times of recession. Enforcement is
costly, both for the state and for the banks and other financial institutions
who have been conscripted as watchdogs. The amounts actually
recovered in practice from asset confiscation are much lower than
political fantasies would have one believe. Entrepreneurial criminals can
and are likely to become more law evasive, as by increasing their capacity
for smurfing and other money laundering practices that are difficult to
control. Moreover, the cost-benefit studies made so far confirm the need
for scepticism, as is evident from the estimate in one recent study that
only $0.0062 out of every illegally earned dollar from narcotics traffic in
the United States is subject to government recovery action. Thirdly, a
market-oriented analysis may shed light on controversial questions of
implementation. Thus, the issue of whether legal expenses should be

excluded from restraining or forfeiture orders would be assessed in hard-nosed economic terms rather than by reference to class-biased notions about the value of being able to employ the lawyer of one's choice. An economic analysis is also revealing when it comes to the question of working out what allowance should be made for expenses and outgoings; if the true costs of crime are to be internalised by drug traffickers and other offenders then there is a case for confiscating the gross profits rather than the net benefits from offences.

The next contribution is "Confiscation of Proceeds of Crime: Funny Money, Serious Legislation" by Brent Fisse. This chapter questions the breadth of the legislation in a number of respects. First, the legislation was introduced partly on the basis of the political representation that the object was to make criminals give up their ill-gotten gains. The truth is that the amount of property that can be confiscated by means of forfeiture orders and pecuniary penalty orders may far exceed the amount of unjust enrichment flowing from offences. Secondly, the maximum amount of the forfeiture or pecuniary penalty that may be ordered is not governed by the traditional sentencing principle that punishment should be proportionate to the offence. Thirdly, the use of forfeiture and pecuniary penalties in order to incapacitate offenders is difficult to reconcile with the utilitarian principle of least drastic means. Less draconian possibilities include official management of an offender's property, along the lines of bankruptcy controls or custody of enemy property during wartime. Fourthly, criminal liability is a precondition of confiscation but traditional principles of criminal liability have been compromised partly in order to facilitate the imposition of forfeiture orders and pecuniary penalties. Fifthly, access to legal assistance in defending charges against a range of serious offences is vulnerable on several fronts, including the risk of forfeiture of fees paid for defending clients. Sixthly, confiscation of the proceeds of crime can have severe and questionable overspill effects on relatives and other persons who were not implicated in the offence that triggered the confiscation. Fisse concludes that the legislation is not only extreme, but represents a deodand-like strategy of social control: targeting the money trail enables the state to defy reality by maintaining an appearance of supremacy and transcendental sanctity.

Arie Freiberg and Richard Fox, in a contribution entitled "Forfeiture, Confiscation and Sentencing", argue that forfeiture and sentencing have become two hopelessly unco-ordinated systems. These two disconnected systems have emerged largely as a result of historical forces, unsound conceptual distinctions and "anti-libertarian and myopic political imperatives". Six different paradigms for the operation of forfeiture and sentencing are identified: (1) automatic on commission of offence; (2) automatic on conviction of offence; (3) mandatory on conviction of offence; (4) discretionary on conviction of offence: criminal court; (5) discretionary on conviction of offence: civil court; and (6) discretionary on civilly proscribed conduct. Current legislative approaches in Australia are compared by reference to these paradigms. The central point of comparison is the extent to which account is taken of forfeiture in imposing sentence or, depending on timing, the extent to which account is taken of the sentence when ordering forfeiture. Chaotic legislative patterns are revealed. The solution commended by Freiberg and Fox is to make forfeiture a conviction-based sentence and to bring its operation under sentencing principles. On this approach, the overall impact of forfeiture and imprisonment or other sanctions would be taken into account and would be subject to the principle that punishment is not to be disproportionate to the offence. Bringing forfeiture and confiscation orders into line as part of a coherent modern system of sanctions is seen as an essential protection against "the mistaken, arbitrary or unjust application of state power". The issue is thus pivotal to the design and operation of our system of criminal justice, but has yet to be addressed seriously by Australian legislators.

Patricia Loughlan's chapter, "Equity and the Proceeds of Crime", explores the ill-defined and previously little-used equitable jurisdiction to deprive criminals of the proceeds of their crimes. The constructive trust can be used to "lasso" the profits of crime and force both the criminals themselves and third persons who take from those criminals to hold such profits on trust. The relevant categories are: (1) constructive trusts imposed on property acquired by reason of an unlawful killing; and (2) constructive trusts imposed to prevent the defendant from being unjustly enriched. It is argued that the first and second categories are intertwined and that the underlying concepts of unconscionability and unjust enrichment hold the key to the development of coherent equitable doctrine in this area.

Two commercial lawyers, John O'Sullivan and Stephen Mitchell, explore a number of practical difficulties in "The Cash Transaction Reports Act: The Legal Minefield". One troubling implication they discern in the definition of "cash dealer" under the *Cash Transaction Reports Act* is that most solicitors, real estate agents and travel agents are likely to be cash dealers. If so, they are subject to the onerous reporting and account opening obligations under the Act. O'Sullivan and Mitchell also discuss what they see as the impracticality of the reporting exemption under s. 10(2), which exempts transactions between financial institutions and high cash flow businesses if the amount of currency involved in the transaction is not in excess of the "amount that is reasonably commensurate with the lawful business activities of the customer". Criticism is also directed at the absence of a requirement of subjective blameworthiness for criminal liability under s. 15(6) where a cash dealer fails to make a required report, and the requirement of knowledge for the offence of providing false or misleading information under s. 29. Attention is also drawn to the difficulties that surround the meaning and scope of the suspect transaction reporting requirement under s. 16. It is maintained that the section presupposes an understanding of fine legal distinctions that tellers and other counter staff are most unlikely to have.

Kevin O'Connor, the Federal Privacy Commissioner, has provided a commentary entitled "The Relationship Between the Privacy Act and the Cash Transaction Reports Act". The privacy rights of individuals are

significantly affected by the Cash Transaction Reports Act (C.T.R. Act).
All customers of financial institutions are affected by the C.T.R. Act's
account identification requirements. There are also far-reaching
reporting obligations, including the obligation to report suspect
transactions. O'Connor questions the need for a suspect transaction
reporting requirement and highlights the possibility of its discriminatory
use against small-deposit customers. Doubt is also expressed as to the
extent of the legislative web of controls that are used in order to catch
the relatively small group who belong to the organised
crime/underground cash economy population. O'Connor's ultimate
concern is the threat to privacy created by modern technology and the
way in which recent government initiatives have led to surveillance of
the day-to-day activities of the ordinary law-abiding population. The
range of agencies given access to information collected under the C.T.R.
Act is wide and yet State agencies are not subject to the controls imposed
under the *Privacy Act* 1988 (Cth).

Brent Fisse and David Fraser, in "Smurfing: Rethinking the Structured
Transaction Provisions of the Cash Transaction Reports Act", provide a
critique of the attempt in s. 31 to deal with structured transactions. The
offence of smurfing is aimed at cases where money launderers try to
defeat the operation of the significant transaction reporting requirements
by depositing funds in amounts which individually fall below the
$10,000 reporting threshold but which in total may far exceed it. The
uninitiated might well be inclined to think that this is a relatively
straightforward problem to cover. As s. 31 reveals, however, the task is
beset with major complications none of which has been resolved by the
section. Difficulties and ambiguities are apparent at many levels: the
mental element of the offence; the "reasonable to conclude" criterion;
the availability of a defence of reasonable mistaken belief; the "sale or
dominant purpose" test; the element of "transaction"; the concept of a
"party" to a transaction; the relevance or otherwise of vicarious liability;
the aggregation question; the application of attempt, complicity and
conspiracy; the absence of a safe harbour provision; the inter-
relationship between civil and criminal liability; the allocation of
individual and corporate liability; and the interaction between s. 31 and
other money laundering and proceeds of crime provisions. These
pervasive failures of definition make the Australian law against smurfing
an ass, a consequence that might be tolerable were it not for the severe
threat of criminal liability to which financial institutions and their
employees are exposed.

The United States experience with anti-smurfing laws is traced in Sarah
Welling's "Smurfs, Money Laundering and the United States Federal
Criminal Law: The Crime of Structuring Transactions". Welling traces
the background to the Federal anti-smurfing legislation and pinpoints the
difficulties which have arisen. As she explains, a central challenge in
curbing manipulation of the bank reporting requirements is drafting a
law that is broad enough to be effective yet limited enough to avoid
abuse. The anti-smurfing legislation reviewed by Welling is much more
tightly drafted than s. 31 of the *Cash Transaction Reports Act* yet a

variety of problems nonetheless remains. One major risk of abuse is that of multiple punishment in situations where liability for smurfing might be added to liability for the mainstream offences behind the smurfing activities which appear at the surface. Welling cautiously supports the approach taken in the United States legislation but the detailed and intricate analysis she provides will come as a shock to those who believe that the legislative task of designing a well-measured prohibition against smurfing is a simple one. Some may also be surprised to find that, contrary to the political pretence, the Commonwealth legislation on smurfing bears little or no resemblance to United States law but is an invention from Canberra.

Simon Stretton's account of the *Drug Trafficking (Civil Proceedings) Act* 1990 (N.S.W.) focuses on a legislative approach which to date other States have been reluctant to adopt. The *Drug Trafficking (Civil Proceedings) Act* establishes a framework whereby civil proceedings may be taken against drug traffickers independently of the criminal process. The Act, which is aimed at wiping out a trafficker's entire accumulation of unlawfully obtained assets, wheresoever located in the world, makes extensive provision for restraining orders, assets forfeiture orders, and proceeds assessment orders. Stretton provides a comprehensive review of this formidable legal artillery. He also addresses a number of important related questions, including the nature and scope of examination procedure under s. 12, and the provision made for reasonable legal expenses. Given the large number of suspects who are being proceeded against under the new civil regime of confiscation, this is a timely report on the Act and its operation to date. The nature of enforcement action against drug traffickers in New South Wales has been radically changed, to the unwelcome surprise of some offenders, and to the consternation of solicitors who are called upon to represent clients of no visibly unfrozen means of support.

David Chaikin's chapter, "Investigating Criminal and Corporate Money Trails", examines the significance of the money trail in providing evidence. Money laundering is the lifeblood of organised crime because it prevents the detection and punishment of those most responsible for directing and financing the criminal organisation. The money trail will often be the only link between the leaders of the criminal organisation and the crime itself. Unfortunately, there are as many techniques for laundering money as there are money launderers. Chaikin canvasses the more popular modes of laundering, including casinos, legitimate business fronts, nominee shareholdings, wire transfers and underground banking systems. He explains why the detection of money laundering is very difficult, one reason being the absence of an identifiable victim, and another the sheer complexity of well-designed money laundering operations. Law enforcement agencies should therefore focus on cash transactions at the beginning of the criminal money laundering cycle because this is the point at which traffickers are most vulnerable to exposure. Chaikin then turns to the question of international enforcement. Money laundering is an international problem which requires the highest degree of co-operation between countries. Australia is a leading advocate of mutual assistance in criminal matters (M.A.C.M.) treaties and arrangements. M.A.C.M. treaties are assisted by Interpol, which provides technical support services through collaboration and communication. A specialist unit, FOPAC, has been set up to help monitor the financial operations of organised crime and drug trafficking. There is also a joint working group consisting of bank security officers from the international banking security association (IBSA) and Interpol. This group is charged with the function of developing methods of preventing, detecting and resolving financial crimes. These initiatives at the international level, however, serve little point unless the problem of money laundering is also combated on the home front. As Chaikin observes, a prime haven for money launderers in this country has been the ineffectual enforcement of our corporations and securities laws.

Lee Burns, in "Finding the Information Trail: Some Experiences in International Tax Enforcement", takes up the problem of collecting information held offshore. Although tax administrators have broad investigative powers, territorial limits often obstruct their use because one state is under no obligation to recognise the taxation laws of another. This prevents administrators from carrying out investigations offshore and from using the judicial process of other states to recover tax due. Local jurisdictional footholds may therefore be critical. One major issue is whether powers of investigation can be used against a director of an Australian company to compel the production of the books and records of a tax haven subsidiary. Burns discusses the authorities which now support a "practical control" test and argues against the more legalistic test that has sometimes been suggested. Even so, many other areas of investigation are limited by territorial sovereignty. The solution adopted by tax administrators is co-operation with other jurisdictions, as through mutual assistance treaties. There is also a growing move toward multilateralism, as signified by the Multinational Convention. Multinational taxpayers have held the upper hand through their ability to structure transactions in ways which effectively prevent national administrators from gaining access to key information about their activities. Burns supports this movement, on the basis that tax administrators need to organise their enforcement activities in the same way that multinationals organise their tax affairs.

Bob Sullivan's review, "The Confiscation of the Proceeds of Crime in England" discusses the *Drug Trafficking Offences Act* 1986 and Part VI of the *Criminal Justice Act* 1988. These provisions, which are far-reaching, raise many questions. One issue is whether the *Criminal Justice Act* provisions comply with the minimum standards mandated by the European Convention on Human Rights. Although the position is not free from doubt, it seems that the legislation will probably withstand constitutional attack. The point nonetheless is that principle has been eroded on dubious grounds. Another controversy is the policy behind the suspect transaction reporting obligation which has been imposed on financial institutions. In England the obligation is restricted to suspicions that particular clients are drug traffickers or terrorists. Should the obligation extend to all serious offences? The views expressed by

Sullivan on this question provide a timely background to the current debate in Australia about suspect transaction reporting at the State level. Sullivan also assesses the role of the Mareva injunction in relation to confiscation of proceeds of crime and in particular the advantage it may still have where the defendant has assets abroad.

Michael Levi's chapter, "Cleaning up the Bankers' Act: The United Kingdom Experience", explores the policing function that financial institutions have been called upon to perform under money trail legislation. Former protections of client privacy have largely been swept aside. Indeed, the banks have been turned into "an unpaid, involuntary High Street Watch scheme of pressed informants." Levi traces the way in which this transformation has occurred and examines the extent to which client information is now accessible by enforcement authorities. He also discusses the impact within banks, including the conflicts that arise between sales and security staff. There is also the sheer difficulty of changing decision-making procedures so as to comply effectively with the new reporting requirements. One particular issue here is the meaning, in operational terms, of a "suspect" transaction. Thus, given the widespread use of nominee companies for criminal purposes, when is it legally safe not to look into the rationale behind their use? Another dimension is the extra territorial invasion of banking privacy, an arena where there has been a shift toward greater openness to foreign courts. In Levi's view, the English courts are likely to take a less protective jurisdictional line in relation to offences of drug trafficking, terrorism, and insider dealing than in relation to anti-trust and other offences that they may deem to be "purely economic". Ultimately, the question is what all the extra policing of banking transactions is likely to achieve. Levi is sceptical about the crime-reducing effects of conviction and confiscation. So much depends on the organisation of the criminal markets and upon the willingness and capacity of new or existing offenders to enter them. Moreover, the aim of policing banking transactions is often forgotten in "the thrill of the chase."

John Byrne, in "Money Laundering Legislation in the United States: A Perspective from the Banking Industry", traces the role of the United States banking system in combating drug trafficking. The *Bank Secrecy Act* 1970 introduced record-keeping and reporting requirements, including the obligation of financial institutions to report all transactions in currency over $10,000 to the Internal Revenue Service. Financial institutions were also required to have compliance procedures. A paper mountain of reports has been created as a result and it is far from clear that effective use has been made of it by the authorities. Apart from the question of overall costs and benefits, numerous particular problems have arisen. One is the lack of an adequate safe harbour for financial institutions which, in assisting enforcement, expose themselves to criminal or civil liability. Another area of difficulty is the reporting of electronic wire transfers. Wire transfers are often used for money laundering but introducing a comprehensive reporting system has been easier said than done given the huge volume of transfers, the large number of United States banks, the lack of compatible computer information systems, and the diversity of wire transfer practices in different countries. These and other facets of the United States experience provide an interesting and informative background to the initiatives that have been taken under the *Cash Transaction Reports Act* to computerise the reporting of significant cash transaction reporting, to provide safe harbours from liability and, more recently, to introduce a computerised system of wire transfer reporting.

Whitney Adams' "The Practical Impact of United States Criminal Money Laundering Laws on Financial Institutions" addresses the legal issues that have arisen. Criminal liability can lead to serious fines and heavy forfeiture and various collateral consequences can flow from indictment or conviction. Banks face potential termination or suspension of F.D.I.C. insurance, revocation of federal or State banking charters, and the imposition of cease and desist orders the violation of which under the new Financial Institutions Reform, Recovery, and Enforcement Act (FIRREA) can expose the bank to additional civil penalties of $1 million per day. Securities and commodity brokers can be barred from the mutual fund business, and broker dealers face suspension or licence revocation. These consequences are all the more significant given the general rule of vicarious corporate criminal liability in the United States, the sufficiency of wilful blindness for money laundering, and the emergence of the problematic concept of collective knowledge in the *Bank of New England* decision. Adams' analysis of the United States legislation and recent case law highlights the dangers than can flow from the ill-developed conceptual underpinnings of corporate criminal liability. Another feature of Adams' chapter is the discussion of the implications for corporate compliance and liability control systems. These implications include the need for a diligent "Know Your Customer" (K.Y.C.) policy, procedures designed to minimise the risk of forfeiture of secured interests, and due diligence checks against contingent liability for money laundering offences or forfeiture where another company is being acquired.

The last paper in the collection is "Minimising Exposure to Liability under the New Legislation: Developing Effective Corporate Compliance Systems", by Brent Fisse. Given the high potential costs of punishment, forfeiture, and directors' liability for failing to exercise due care, it is essential for financial institutions to have a liability control system in place. A framework for such a system is suggested. Twelve elements are discussed in all. These include: review of loan and other contractual documentation in order to optimise the degree of self-protection; control of documentation, including standard contractual terms for protection where secured assets are subject to confiscation, and procedures for avoiding the creation or retention of unnecessarily damaging or incriminating documentation; action plans in the event of discovery of illegality and for resolution of complaints received from employees, clients, members of the public, or enforcement agencies; education and training of personnel; and regular interaction with enforcement agencies. The suggestions made are based on the liability control systems devised by leading United States and Australian companies in other fields of corporate regulation, and try to distil what can usefully be learnt from that experience.

THE MONEY TRAIL: AUSTRALIAN FEDERALISM AND OTHER ISSUES

The contributions which follow provide only a starting point for those who wish to unlock the secrets of the Australian money trail legislation. There is much room for a fuller discussion of many of the issues that have been raised and further questions are constantly emerging.

Key concepts like "cash dealer" and "account" under the *Cash Transaction Reports Act* warrant detailed explication. The meaning of "benefit" and "expenses and outgoings" in the setting of pecuniary penalties is elusive and calls for full analysis. The operation of restraining orders and the scope of related examinations is critical in practice and needs to be examined. The array of wire transfer controls to be introduced in mid 1992 is a large topic in itself. The account opening requirements under the *Cash Transaction Reports Act* are potentially a source of intense fascination. There are issues of constitutional power that need to be resolved by the High Court, one being the validity or otherwise of the money laundering offences under ss. 81 and 82 of the *Proceeds of Crime Act*. The nature and efficacy of the statutory safeguards now in place against evasive tactics (for example, moving assets abroad; structuring one's activities so as to be in a highly geared state of debt) require elaboration. Confiscation of proceeds made from writing about crime adds another problematic dimension to the subject, as does the introduction of measures to take superannuation benefits away from certain types of offenders. The application of confiscation of proceeds legislation and money laundering offences to corporations and corporate officers is a major although as yet little explored domain. International enforcement measures raise many questions which few have the expertise or official contacts to be able to answer.

Perhaps above all, there is an urgent need to address the many deficiencies in the law that stem from Australian federalism. Diverse and complex laws have proliferated, to the great complication of enforcement, and to the jeopardy or cost of individuals and corporations. A national law is needed. This is widely recognised but the experience to date has been disappointing. The challenge of preparing a draft national law on money laundering and confiscation of proceeds was not taken up by the Gibbs Committee on the Reform of Commonwealth Criminal Laws. Nor does much progress appear to have been made by the Standing Committee of Attorneys-General. The National Crime Authority was given a reference on money laundering in 1991 but the fruits of its inquiries remain to be seen. Meanwhile, the follies of Australian federalism proliferate. A recent example is the introduction of a suspect transaction reporting obligation in Victoria in relation to offences under Victorian law. Given the mischievous quirks of the Australian federal system, this kind of State initiative is dangerously inept. Situations may easily arise where a suspect transaction report in accordance with the Victorian requirement is made or disseminated in such a way as to be an actionable defamation or breach of confidence in another State. The statutory immunity under the Victorian legislation hardly provides adequate protection in such cases, a point drawn to the attention of the Victorian government, but to no effect.

Material on these and other topics is listed in the select bibliography contained in this book.

2

Confiscating Criminal Assets

The Proceeds of Crime Act and Related Legislation

JOHN THORNTON[1]

The traditional response of prosecution followed by punishment is seldom of itself an adequate response to large-scale criminal activity which is aimed at accumulating wealth.[2] The motivation for such crime is greed and the aim is profit. To remove the profit is to reduce the motivation. As one commentator has observed:

> The first thing to remember is that the organisation of crime is directed towards the accumulation of money and with it power. The possession of the power that flows with great wealth is to some people an important matter in itself, but this is secondary to the prime aim of accumulating money. Two conclusions flow from this fact. The first is that the most successful method of identifying and ultimately convicting major organised criminals is to follow the money trail. The second is that once you have identified and convicted them you take away their money; that is, the money which is the product of their criminal activities.[3]

In recent times there has been a variety of new legislation, both in Australia and in other common law countries,[4] aimed at confiscating the benefits derived from criminal conduct. I refer to this legislation generically as confiscation legislation. Few, if any, would disagree with the aim of this legislation, the general thrust of which would make true such hallowed maxims as "crime does not pay" and "no-one should profit from an illegal act", but issue has been taken with some of the measures adopted to achieve this aim.[5]

1. Senior Assistant Director, Office of the Commonwealth Director of Public Prosecutions. Paper delivered at a public seminar entitled, "Money Laundering, Cash Transactions Reporting and Confiscation of the Proceeds of Crime", convened by the Institute of Criminology, University of Sydney, 6 June 1990. Published by permission of *Current Issues in Criminal Justice*.
2. Fox and Frieberg, *Sentencing State and Federal Law in Victoria* (1985), p. 210; "Profits of Crime and Their Recovery" (1984) *Cambridge Studies in Criminology* Vol. III, p. 6 (The Hodgson Report).
3. Costigan Q.C., "Organised Fraud and a Free Society" (1984) 17 A.N.Z.J. Crim. 7 at 12.
4. See generally McLean, "Seizing The Proceeds of Crime: The State of the Art" (1989) 38 I.C.L.Q. 334.
5. See e.g. Goode, "The Confiscation of Criminal Assets" (1986) 67 *Proceedings of the Institute of Criminology* 35; Fisse, below, Chapter 5.

Confiscation legislation is premised on the basis of combating organised crime.[6] In the international sphere significant impetus was provided by the 1987 Vienna Conference dealing with organised crime and money laundering, although countries such as the United States of America and the United Kingdom already had legislation in place. In Australia, a series of Royal Commissions called for action against organised crime and the large funds it generated. The Williams and Stewart Royal Commissions explored the ramifications of large scale drug dealing. To this, the Costigan Royal Commission added the significant impact of large scale revenue fraud.

General agreement for confiscation action against those convicted of narcotics offences, was reached at the Special Premiers' Conference on Drugs in 1985. Model uniform legislation was agreed at the Standing Committee of Attorneys-General. As it transpired, uniform legislation did not eventuate, but all States except Tasmania now have confiscation legislation. Having a common origin, many of the principles in the various Acts are consistent as regards the freezing and confiscation of assets.

The legislation is new. Many of the provisions have yet to be tested. Experience has shown that it takes at least two years to complete a large confiscation action under Commonwealth law even where there is a plea of guilty to the associated criminal charge.

The aim of this chapter is to give an overview of Commonwealth confiscation legislation and some of the issues that have arisen under it.

BACKGROUND

The Commonwealth Director of Public Prosecutions' Office has been active in the field of recovering ill-gotten gains associated with criminal activity since 1985. Some of the legislation I will refer to predates this time. The impetus provided in 1985 was the expansion of the D.P.P.'s civil remedies function[7] and the allocation of resources with the specific task of implementing the legislative initiative.

The civil remedies function gives the D.P.P. a role in normal civil recovery action by government agencies in matters connected with, or arising out of, actual or proposed prosecutions, or a course of activity which is being considered for the purpose of deciding whether to institute a prosecution.[8] This function involves no new powers of recovery or forfeiture.

Action taken in response to the revelation of the "bottom-of-the-harbour" tax frauds gave rise to the civil remedies initiative. Royal Commissioner Costigan Q.C. advocated that large scale tax fraud be tackled with task forces that would carry out criminal prosecutions and initiate civil proceedings to recover the tax. The special prosecutors,

6. See e.g. the Second Reading Speech on the Commonwealth Proceeds of Crime Act, *Parliamentary Debates*, H. of Rep., 1987, Vol. 154, p. 2317.
7. *Director of Public Prosecutions Amendment Act* 1985 (Cth).
8. *Director of Public Prosecutions Act* 1983 (Cth), s. 6(8).

appointed in 1982 to handle these tax prosecutions, were the first to have an ancillary function to take or co-ordinate or supervise the taking of civil remedies on behalf of the Commonwealth and its authorities.

The power to take civil remedies is not exclusive of the power of the defrauded agency to recover on behalf of the Commonwealth.[9] To date the function has been exercised mainly by way of supervision and co-ordination with the litigation being conducted through the Australian Government Solicitor. The function applies in relation to the recovery of taxes[10] and other matters or classes of matters specified in writing by the Attorney-General.[11] The Attorney-General has by instrument specified 26 matters. The most important are three class instruments covering respectively, social security fraud, medifraud and nursing home fraud.

The D.P.P.'s involvement in civil remedies comes from it being in a unique position to assemble information from a variety of Commonwealth agencies and to co-ordinate the activities of these agencies against particular individuals or entities with outstanding liabilities to the Commonwealth. The civil remedies function is also a recognition that where criminal means are used to obtain or keep funds from the Commonwealth there is a particular community interest in seeing that the funds are recovered. This may require that resources are applied to difficult recoveries in matters where direct cost benefit analysis, without law enforcement considerations, might not dictate that the resources be so applied.

The recovery of taxes has an important role to play in the effort to remove illegally obtained benefits from criminals. In the case of taxation fraud the benefits are recovered directly. With respect to other types of crimes, few criminals pay tax on their income. The raising and enforcement of default assessment can be an effective way of removing some or all of the proceeds from the offender. Since 1985 recoveries of tax pursuant to the civil remedies function total more than $72 million to 30 June 1990. Non-tax recoveries in the same period total more than $2.7 million.

CONFISCATION LEGISLATION

There is no common law crime-based forfeiture.[12] The ancient concepts of attainder and corruption of blood[13] were abolished in the United Kingdom in 1870[14] and in the Australian colonies shortly after.[15] These old common law rules were also anathema in the American colonies. The

9. *Efstratiadis v. Commonwealth* (1990) 22 F.C.R. 167.
10. *Director of Public Prosecutions Act* 1983, s. 6(1)(fa).
11. *Director of Public Prosecutions Act* 1983, s. 6(1)(h).
12. *Gollan v. Nugent* (1988) 63 A.L.J.R. 11.
13. See generally Chitty, *A Practical Treatise on the Criminal Law*, Vol. II, Ch. XVII; Blackstone, *Commentaries on the Laws of England*, Vol. IV, Ch. XXIX.
14. *Forfeiture Act* 1870 (U.K.).
15. See e.g. *Forfeiture for Treason and Felony Abolition Act* 1878 (Vic.).

framers of the United States Constitution and members of the First Congress rejected them.[16]

Having effectively abolished common law forfeiture, the United States Congress then set about including in rem forfeiture provisions in a variety of statutes. These were originally patterned on the English Navigation Acts and involved the concept of the "guilty chattel". Because it was often difficult to locate the owner of the ship or goods on board, transgressions of the Navigation Acts were dealt with by action against the vessel or goods themselves. Forfeiture could be ordered unless a claimant appeared and proved that the property at issue had not been used in violation of the Acts. Many of these early forfeiture provisions were to be found in customs legislation.

Australian customs legislation has from its early inception also contained forfeiture provisions triggered by the use of ships or other conveyances for the importation of goods in contravention of the legislative provisions. More recently, steps taken to combat the illegal use of narcotics have led to the extension of these provisions to cover money or goods derived from narcotics dealings as well as the notion of a pecuniary penalty order against a person based on the value of benefits derived by the person from her or his connection with narcotics.

The recent confiscation legislation enacted in Australia has a number of common features. Generally the legislation includes the following powers:

- forfeiture of property connected to an offence or derived from the proceeds of the offence;
- pecuniary penalties based on benefits derived from the offence;
- restraint of property at an early stage pending determination of the substantive applications; and
- investigative powers.

FORFEITURE

Customs Act Forfeiture

As discussed above, the forfeiture provisions in the *Customs Act* 1901 (Cth) developed from the need to control the importation of goods. They do, however, have important application in relation to narcotic goods and it is this aspect upon which I will concentrate. The scheme is that ships, aircraft and goods used in contravention of the Act are declared forfeit. These may be seized and it is incumbent upon any claimant to seek to prevent their condemnation and disposal by the Commonwealth. Section 228 provides, inter alia, that ships not exceeding 80 metres in

---

16. United States Constitution, Art. III, s. 3, cl. 2 provides: "no attainder of Treason shall work Corruption of Blood or Forfeiture except during the Life of the Person attainted." The First Congress supplemented the Constitutional proscription with a statutory bar providing that no conviction for any crime would be permitted to work a corruption of the blood or any forfeiture of estate: Act of 30 April 1790, ch. 9, 1 Stat. 117, s. 24.

length and aircraft will become forfeit if used to smuggle goods or knowingly used to convey prohibited imports or exports. Ships over 80 metres in length are not forfeited but the owner is liable to a penalty not exceeding $100,000 and the ship may be detained as security.

Paragraph 229(1)(j) provides that any carriage or animal used in smuggling or in the unlawful importation or conveyance of any goods, is forfeited to the Crown. This provision applies in relation to ships and aircraft notwithstanding the more specific provision in s. 228. Typically these provisions are applied to vessels used to import narcotics and vehicles used to convey illegally imported narcotics.

Section 229A covers moneys or goods that come into the possession or under the control of a person by reason of that person's dealing in narcotic goods. These moneys or goods are deemed to be forfeited upon being seized. The section allows for tracing into moneys or goods exchanged for, purchased or otherwise acquired out of the original moneys or goods. Section 229A does not extend to things that are neither goods or moneys such as a bank account.[17] The section does allow tracing through a bank account to goods in the possession or under the control of a person that were purchased or otherwise acquired out of moneys to which the section applies.[18] The section does not cover real property.

A police officer may seize any forfeited goods or any goods believed on reasonable grounds to be forfeited goods.[19] A seizure notice must be served. Any claimant must then make a claim within 30 days and, if required, follow up with an action to recover the goods within four months. The usual action is a claim in detinue or for conversion. If these time frames are not met the goods are automatically condemned as forfeited to the Crown.[20]

Where the forfeiture of goods is as a result of the commission of an offence, the conviction of any person for the offence shall have effect as a condemnation of the goods.[21] Narcotics-related goods which are condemned as forfeited to the Crown are disposed of in accordance with the directions of the Commissioner or Deputy Commissioner of the Australian Federal Police.[22]

Proceeds of Crime Act (P.O.C. Act) Forfeiture

The *Proceeds of Crime Act* 1987 (Cth) is conviction based. Where a person is convicted of an indictable offence a court may order that "tainted property" be forfeited to the Commonwealth.[23] Tainted property is property used in, or in connection with, the indictable offence or property derived or realised directly or indirectly by any person from the commission of the offence.[24]

17. *Vickers v. Minister for Business and Consumer Affairs* (1982) 43 A.L.R. 389.
18. *Kanbur Pty Ltd v. Adams* (1984) 55 A.L.R. 158.
19. *Customs Act*, s. 203.
20. *Customs Act*, ss 205 and 208A.
21. *Customs Act*, s. 262.
22. *Customs Act*, s. 208D.
23. P.O.C. Act, s. 19.
24. P.O.C. Act, s. 4(1).

The application for a forfeiture order is made by the D.P.P. and the court has a discretion to grant the order. The court may have regard to any hardship that the order may reasonably be expected to cause to any person, the use that is ordinarily made or is intended to be made of the property and the gravity of the offence concerned.[25] Property ordered to be forfeited vests absolutely in the Commonwealth except that registrable property vests in equity until the applicable registration requirements have been complied with.[26] The property cannot be dealt with by the Commonwealth until the end of the appeal periods in relation to the making of the forfeiture order and the person's conviction.[27]

The other forfeiture provisions in the P.O.C. Act are triggered by what are called "serious offences". These are defined to mean:[28]

- a narcotics offence involving more than a traffickable quantity of drugs;

- an organised fraud offence which is created by s. 83 of the P.O.C. Act; or

- a money laundering offence in relation to the proceeds of a serious narcotics offence or an organised fraud offence.

Where a person is convicted of a serious offence any property which has been restrained under the P.O.C. Act, and which remains restrained at the end of a period of six months after the date of conviction, is automatically forfeited to the Commonwealth at the end of that period.[29] This forfeiture occurs simply by elapse of the six-month period following conviction and does not require any assessment or order by the court.

To avoid automatic forfeiture a person must have a court lift the restraining order prior to the end of the six-month period. To do that, the person must satisfy the court that the property was not used in, or in connection with, any unlawful activity and was not derived by any person from any unlawful activity, and that the person's interest in the property was lawfully acquired.[30]

It is not sufficient to satisfy the court that the property was not linked to the offence for which the person was convicted. Unlawful activity means conduct that constitutes an offence against a law of the Commonwealth, a State, a Territory or a foreign country.[31] All these possibilities must also be ruled out.

A person can make an application to have property unrestrained, for the purposes of statutory forfeiture, at any time following the making of a restraining order. It would be wise to make such an application at an early stage. Statutory forfeiture is not prevented by the making of an application but only by its determination by a court in favour of the applicant.

25. P.O.C. Act, ss 19(3) and (4).
26. P.O.C. Act, s. 20(1).
27. P.O.C. Act, s. 20(6).
28. P.O.C. Act, s. 7.
29. P.O.C. Act, s. 30.
30. P.O.C. Act, s. 48(4).
31. P.O.C. Act, s. 4(1).

Different approaches have been taken in relation to the phrase "in connection with" in its application to narcotics offences. The Queensland Court of Criminal Appeal has expressed the view that there must be a substantial connection between the use of the property and the conviction of the offence.[32] It must be such that the offence could not have been committed without the use of the property. A vehicle used to convey drugs to the place of sale is unlikely to satisfy this test, nor is a house used to store drugs prior to sale. On a charge of possessing narcotics, no property may be liable to forfeiture as the place of possession may be thought irrelevant to the commission of the offence.[33]

This approach was rejected by the New South Wales Court of Criminal Appeal.[34] The phrase "in connection with" should be given its ordinary grammatical meaning. The court's wide discretion on the question of forfeiture would enable it to avoid forfeiture in appropriate cases. A car used to convey drugs to the place of sale is tainted, but the court declined to forfeit it because of the hardship it would cause to an innocent third party having an interest in the vehicle.

The approach adopted in interpreting the phrase is of particular importance in respect of serious offences. Forfeiture depends on whether the defendant can satisfy the court that the property was not used in connection with any unlawful activity. The width given to the phrase "in connection with" may be determinative because there is no discretion not to forfeit the property.

PECUNIARY PENALTIES

Forfeiture operates against goods or property which are linked to, or not shown not to be linked to, the conduct which renders them forfeit or liable to forfeiture. Pecuniary penalty provisions operate against persons who have obtained benefits from the commission of certain acts. A penalty equal to these benefits can be ordered against the person and enforcement action taken against any of the person's property regardless of whether it can be linked to the acts from which the benefits were derived.

The *Customs Act* and P.O.C. Act contain similar schemes covering pecuniary penalties.[35] The most notable differences are that the

---

32. *R. v. Ward, Marles and Graham* [1989] 1 Qld R. 194. Carter J., with whom Kneipp J. and Demack J. agreed, found that forfeiture of a vehicle used to convey drugs to the place of sale should have been refused in the exercise of the court's discretion. He reiterated views about the need for a substantial connection between the property and the offence, that he had previously expressed in *Re An Application Pursuant To The Drugs Misuse Act 1986* [1988] 2 Qld R. 506.

33. *Re An Application Pursuant To The Drugs Misuse Act 1986* [1988] 2 Qld R. 506 at 512.

34. *R. v. Hadad* (1989) 16 N.S.W.L.R. 476.

35. Pecuniary penalty provisions were inserted into the *Customs Act* 1901 (Cth) in 1979 under Div. 3 of Pt XIII. The pecuniary penalty provisions of the P.O.C. Act were largely based on those in the *Customs Act* with a number of improvements added. In turn the *Customs Act* provisions were amended drawing on the improvements in the P.O.C. Act, particularly in relation to the restraint of assets and lifting the corporate veil. Many of the operative provisions of the two Acts are therefore the same or very similar.

Customs Act pecuniary penalty provisions apply only to dealings in narcotics and they are not conviction based. The proceedings are civil in nature and the court has to be satisfied that the person engaged in a prescribed narcotics dealing. These are defined to include such things as importing, conspiring to import, possessing and selling narcotic goods in contravention of the *Customs Act*.[36] These dealings largely mirror the narcotics offences in the *Customs Act* except that there is no offence in relation to selling narcotic goods.

A pecuniary penalty can be ordered under the *Customs Act* regardless of whether or not a person has been convicted of an offence or had proceedings instituted against them in respect of any offence.[37] Where the ingredients of the prescribed narcotics dealing are the same as an offence of which the defendant has been convicted "the court is bound by evidence of a conviction and cannot go behind it or permit a collateral attack on some element critical to it".[38]

If the court[39] is satisfied that a person has engaged in prescribed narcotics dealings under the *Customs Act* then it shall assess the value of benefits derived and order that a pecuniary penalty equal to that value be paid to the Commonwealth.[40] The P.O.C. Act provides the court with a discretion. Where the court is satisfied that the person derived benefits from the commission of an offence it may assess the value of benefits so derived and order the person to pay the Commonwealth a pecuniary penalty equal to that value.[41]

In many cases there will be difficulties in quantifying benefits derived by a person from criminal activity. It is unlikely that the documentation and records usually associated with legitimate enterprises will be available. Relationships and dealings will be known only to those involved. They will not be the most credible source of information. Both Acts provide that the penalty shall be assessed by the court having regard to all or any of a number of prescribed factors.

The factors to be considered include the money or value of property coming into the possession or under the control of a person, the value of the defendant's property, before during and after the relevant event and, in the case of the *Customs Act*, the market value of similar narcotics to those sold.[42] A comparable scheme for assessing benefits was described as "a somewhat rough and ready approach" in which the

36. *Customs Act*, s. 243A.
37. *Customs Act*, s. 243B(3). This section has been applied in *Commissioner of Australian Federal Police v. Razzi* (unreported, Fed. Ct, Wilcox J., 24 August 1989). The decision was overturned on appeal. The appeal court agreed that the defendant had engaged in a prescribed narcotics dealing but was not satisfied that she derived a benefit. *Razzi v. Commissioner of Australian Federal Police* (1990) 97 A.L.R. 349.
38. *Commissioner of Australian Federal Police v. Butler* (1989) 91 A.L.R. 293 at 301.
39. Pecuniary penalty applications under the *Customs Act* are brought in the Federal Court while the P.O.C. Act gives the State courts jurisdiction. P.O.C. Act applications are brought by the D.P.P. Until the recent amendments the Commissioner of the Australian Federal Police was the relevant applicant under the *Customs Act*. The recent amendments provide that the D.P.P. can also make an application under the *Customs Act*.
40. *Customs Act*, s. 243B(2).
41. P.O.C. Act, s. 26(1).
42. P.O.C. Act, s. 27; *Customs Act*, s. 243C.

"niceties of accountancy principles or of the classification of legal relationships are not significant".[43]

In assessing the benefit in relation to narcotics the court may have regard to expert evidence from a police or customs officer about the market value of narcotic goods at a particular time or during a particular period.[44] In ascribing a value the court may take into account whether a defendant is likely to have sold on a wholesale or retail basis.[45]

It is the gross and not the net benefit which must be assessed.[46] Expenses or outgoings in connection with deriving the benefit are not to be taken into account.[47] Plainly this may lead to a penalty which far exceeds the actual benefit derived or retained by a person.

The approach in *Commissioner of Australian Federal Police v. Curran*[48] would ameliorate some of the potential harshness which may be thought to arise from these provisions. A distinction was drawn between expenses or outgoings which are not deductible in assessing the penalty, and moneys which pass through the hands of a particular defendant before being disbursed by way of division of the proceeds among several participants. Roden J. in *R. v. Fagher* did not find this approach attractive. To follow it would mean that the "deductability of moneys paid to a co-offender would appear to depend upon whether what was paid was an agreed fee or a percentage of the proceeds".[49] It would be difficult to discern such fine legal relationships in most criminal transactions.

Such a finding was made in *Commissioner of Australian Federal Police v. Lahood.*[50] After the importation of cannabis resin, the defendant paid a bribe of $130,000 previously promised to a police officer to ensure that the drugs passed through customs. In assessing the penalty this payment was disregarded as an expense or outgoing. The court found that the defendant did not receive the money on trust for or subject to any obligation to pay the money to the policeman.

Where receipts are passed between co-offenders it can lead to difficulties in assessing the penalty. Assessing the same benefit in the hands of more than one defendant does not sit easily with the concept in s. 27(7) of the P.O.C. Act of not imposing a pecuniary penalty more than once in respect of the same benefit.

To some extent the size of the benefit may depend on which factors the court relies on in making its assessment. Assessment by reference to money or the value of property coming into a person's possession will

43. *R. v. Fagher* (1989) 16 N.S.W.L.R. 67 at 80. The Act under consideration was the *Crimes (Confiscation of Profits) Act* 1985 (N.S.W.).
44. P.O.C. Act, s. 27(10); *Customs Act*, s. 243c(5).
45. *Commissioner of Australian Federal Police v. Cornwell and Bull* (1989) 43 A. Crim. R. 313.
46. *R. v. Smithers; Ex parte McMillan* (1982) 152 C.L.R. 477.
47. P.O.C. Act, s. 27(8); *Customs Act*, s. 243c(6).
48. (1984) 55 A.L.R. 697. See also *D.P.P. v. Nieves* (unreported, Vic. C.C.A., 25 January 1991) and *R. v. Peterson* (unreported, Vic. C.C.A., 15 March 1991).
49. (1989) 16 N.S.W.L.R. 67 at 74.
50. Unreported, Full Fed. Ct, 9 June 1989.

make no allowance for any outgoings. Asset betterment assessment will mean that any outgoings in connection with the offence will be allowed for as they will not have been used in accumulating the assets.

THE BASIS OF CONFISCATION

Forfeiture and pecuniary penalty provisions in the *Customs Act* are not conviction based. In the case of the forfeiture provisions it is the owner or possessor of the property prior to seizure that must bring the action to claim them back. However, when a claim for conversion or in detinue is made, the onus is on the person who seized the goods to show that they are forfeited goods.[51] In other words the Commissioner of the Australian Federal Police will have to establish, for example, that a motor vehicle was used to carry narcotics. The standard of proof is on the balance of probabilities.

Under the *Customs Act* pecuniary penalty provisions the applicant has to establish that the defendant engaged in prescribed narcotics dealings. The proceedings are civil in nature but the standard of proof is high based on the principles enunciated by Dixon J. in *Briginshaw v. Briginshaw*.[52]

Once a court is satisfied that the defendant engaged in prescribed narcotic dealings the Act provides some assistance, in assessing the benefit derived from that dealing and the property that can be attached to satisfy the debt. For example, there is a rebuttable presumption that the benefit will be not less than any increase in the value of a defendant's property over the period of engaging in prescribed narcotics dealings.[53] The amount of the pecuniary penalty order becomes a debt due to the Commonwealth.[54] The debt may be enforced against property in which the defendant has no legal or equitable interest but which the court finds is under the defendant's effective control.[55]

Conviction of an indictable offence is a prerequisite to obtaining any final orders under the P.O.C. Act. Any question of fact to be determined in respect of an application under the Act is to be decided on the balance of probabilities.[56] With pecuniary penalties, once a conviction is obtained, the position with respect to quantifying the benefit and the property against which the debt can be enforced, is the same as under the *Customs Act*.

In the case of forfeiture orders the court must be satisfied that the property is tainted in respect of the offence. Assistance is given in respect of property in a person's possession at the time of, or immediately after,

---

51. *Tran v. Commissioner of Australian Federal Police* (unreported, N.S.W. Sup. Ct, Studdert J., 5 April 1990).
52. (1938) 60 C.L.R. 336 at 368-369. See *Commissioner of Australian Federal Police v. Butler* (1989) 91 A.L.R. 293 at 295; *Commissioner of Australian Federal Police v. Cornwell and Bull* (1989) 43 A. Crim. R. 313.
53. *Customs Act*, s. 243c(3); P.O.C. Act, s. 27(4)(a).
54. *Customs Act*, s. 243B(4); P.O.C. Act, s. 26(8).
55. *Customs Act*, s. 243c; P.O.C. Act, s. 28. This section has been used to recover against property held by companies and involving a trust; *D.P.P. v. Walsh* [1990] W.A.R. 25. It would have been difficult, if not impossible, to recover against the properties through general insolvency laws.
56. P.O.C. Act, s. 99.

the commission of the offence. In the absence of evidence to the contrary such property is presumed to have been used in, or in connection with, the offence.[57]

Once a person is convicted of a serious offence, property derived from or used in prior criminal activity may be forfeited without the need to prove anything in relation to the prior criminal activity. The onus is on the defendant to establish that the property was not used in connection with or derived from any unlawful activity. In considering the amount of evidence required, the court will take into account any difficulties that may exist in proving a negative and the extent to which a defendant is in a position to know and prove the facts required.[58]

The source of property may be determined on a practical basis rather than applying strict legal concepts.[59] In many cases establishing a legitimate source of income commensurate with ownership of the assets in question may take a defendant a long way towards satisfying the onus.

This reversal of onus in respect of serious offences is the highwater mark under Commonwealth legislation in terms of assistance in establishing the basis for confiscation. Its application is restricted to those convicted of the more grave offences. It might be thought that many who engage in this type of activity are unlikely to have done so on a one-off basis.

RESTRAINING ORDERS

To ensure that the assets of criminals are not dissipated prior to the obtaining of final orders both the *Customs Act* and the P.O.C. Act provide for the restraining of assets at an early stage. Under the *Customs Act* a restraining order may be sought once a proceeding for a pecuniary penalty under s. 243B has been instituted.[60] Usually the two applications are made at the same time. To grant the restraining order the court has to be satisfied that there are reasonable grounds to believe that the defendant engaged in prescribed narcotic dealings and derived a benefit.[61]

Restraining orders may be sought under the P.O.C. Act from the time a person is charged or up to 48 hours prior to a charge being laid.[62] Before it can make a restraining order the court has to be satisfied that there are reasonable grounds for believing that the person committed an indictable offence, and that the property concerned is tainted, or that the person derived a benefit from the commission of the offence.[63] In the case of serious indictable offences it is only necessary to show that there are reasonable grounds for believing that the defendant committed the offence.[64]

57. P.O.C. Act, s. 19(6).
58. *Brauer v. D.P.P.* (1989) 98 F.L.R. 57.
59. *D.P.P. v. Lynch* (unreported, W.A. Sup. Ct, Commissioner Templeman Q.C., 6 October 1989).
60. *Customs Act*, s. 243E(1).
61. *Customs Act*, s. 243E(2).
62. P.O.C. Act, s. 43.
63. P.O.C. Act, s. 44(2).
64. P.O.C. Act, s. 44(1).

The restraining order may direct that the property is not to be disposed of or dealt with by any person. Where the court is satisfied that circumstances so require it may also direct the Official Trustee to take custody and control of the property.[65] This latter order will normally be sought to protect property such as money or other liquid assets that can easily be disposed of or where for some other reason it is necessary to provide an extra safeguard in respect of the restrained property. The other main reason to involve the Official Trustee is where there is a need to manage or maintain the property in question, for example, in one matter the Official Trustee is responsible for the management of a valuable horse stud.

Breach of a restraining order is an offence and any dispositions so made may be set aside.[66] The Commonwealth is required to give an undertaking as to damages and wherever possible restraining orders are sought over assets that are unlikely to depreciate in value or lead to other losses. Real estate generally fits this description. Businesses are avoided.

Restraining orders may involve a serious interference with a person's ability to deal with their property prior to any conviction. The decision to seek a restraining order is not taken lightly. In larger matters approval is normally only given at the highest levels within the D.P.P. Every effort is made to inconvenience people as little as possible in their use of restrained property. Usually a sale of restrained property by a defendant will be agreed to provided the proceeds of the sale, or sufficient of them to cover any likely confiscation order, are themselves restrained.

However, restraining orders are a key element in ensuring the effectiveness of confiscation legislation. Without them, many who are charged with offences would hide, transfer, consume or otherwise ensure that their assets were not available to meet any final orders. To allow this to happen would effectively defeat the objects of the legislation.

PAYMENT OF LEGAL FEES OUT OF RESTRAINED ASSETS

One of the most vexed questions under confiscation legislation is the extent to which a defendant should have access to restrained property to defend criminal charges. Competing interests are involved and there is no simple answer as to where to draw the line. The task involved was aptly described by Ryan J. in the Federal Court:

> In my view, the task of the court in exercising the discretion conferred by s. 243E(4)(c) or s. 243F(1)(a) is to strike a balance between the interest of the defendant in having recourse to his assets to enable his defence in the criminal trial to be prepared and conducted as he thinks appropriate, and the interest of the community in preserving those assets intact to satisfy any pecuniary penalty that the defendant might ultimately be ordered to pay under s. 243B.[67]

65. P.O.C. Act, s. 43(2); *Customs Act*, s. 243E(2)(c).
66. P.O.C. Act, s. 52; *Customs Act*, s. 243K.
67. *Commissioner of Australian Federal Police v. Malkoun* (unreported, Fed. Ct, 1 February 1989, p. 36).

One of the difficulties is who should represent the community interests in striking this balance? It may involve assessing the actions proposed and costs to be expended on the defence. While the D.P.P. has responsibility for recovering proceeds, as the prosecuting authority it is in an awkward position to test these issues.

In striking the balance the first point to note is that Parliament has decided that legal expenses can be paid out of restrained property.[68] It may be thought this is stating the obvious but there are other models. In the United States, the *Racketeer Influenced and Corrupt Organisation Act* 1970, the *Continuing Criminal Enterprise Act* 1970 and the *Comprehensive Forfeiture Act* 1984 do not exempt legal fees from restraint and forfeiture.

The United States Supreme Court has found that the failure to provide such an exemption does not breach the Sixth Amendment right to counsel.[69] Part of the reasoning relied on the "relation-back" principle under which title in the property vests in the United States upon the commission of the act giving rise to forfeiture. Similarly under ss 228 and 229 of the *Customs Act*, ships and other conveyances become forfeited from the time they are involved in the prohibited conduct. They may be subject to a claim in detinue or conversion but in the meantime the Crown holds a defeasible title and a defendant has no access to them for legal fees.

Both under the *Customs Act* and the P.O.C. Act the release of restrained funds is subject to the court being satisfied that the defendant cannot meet the expenses out of unrestrained assets.[70] This is a matter which the D.P.P. can and does test. Relevant information may be available from the financial investigation. There are provisions for ancillary orders to require a person to furnish a verified statement of her or his property and for the examination of a person concerning, inter alia, the nature and location of any property. A relevant consideration may be whether it can be shown that funds have been sent offshore and they cannot be located and brought under any restraining order.[71]

The court has a discretion to release funds for legal expenses. No criteria are laid down to guide the exercise of this discretion. In *D.P.P. v. Ward*,[72] Kennedy J. referred to three factors in exercising his

---

68. P.O.C. Act, s. 43(3)(b). The *Customs Act* makes no specific mention of legal costs. In releasing funds for this purpose reliance has been placed on s. 243E(4)(c), "reasonable living and business expenses" and s. 243F(1)(a), "may make such orders in relation to that property as the court considers just". Pincus J. has been critical of the lack of guidance in the *Customs Act* on the question of legal fees: *Commissioner of Australian Federal Police v. Kirk* (unreported, Fed. Ct, 26 March 1990). He noted that approximately $1.3 million out of restrained assets had been expended on legal costs in the matter before him.

69. *Caplin and Drysdale, Chartered v. United States* 57 U.S.L.W. 4836 (1989); *United States v. Monsanto* 57 U.S.L.W. 4826 (1989).

70. P.O.C. Act, s. 43(4); *Customs Act*, s. 243E(4A).

71. Cf. *Commissioner of Taxation v. Manners and Terrule Pty Ltd* (1985) 81 F.L.R. 131. There was evidence that funds had been sent offshore and out of the reach of a Mareva injunction. The court refused to relase funds for legal fees. The defendants had not discharged their onus of showing that there were no other assets out of which they could pay legal fees.

72. Unreported, W.A. Sup. Ct, 23 December 1988. The release of funds for legal expenses was also refused. Ward had made full admissions and there was nothing before the court to indicate that he was seeking to defended the criminal charges.

discretion to refuse an application for living expenses. The first was that Ward had at all times admitted the offences of defrauding the Commonwealth and there was no suggestion that he would retreat from admissions made. The second was that the funds out of which living expenses were sought were moneys due from the Department which had been defrauded by Ward. The third factor was that in relation to benefits obtained there was likely to be a shortfall of some $120,000 even if all Ward's assets were applied to satisfy his liability for the moneys defrauded.

Commonwealth v. Jansenberger[73] involved a civil claim for amounts allegedly defrauded from the Department of Social Security. A Mareva injunction was obtained over all of the defendant's assets. Southwell J. refused to release funds for legal fees in respect of the associated criminal charges. He referred to the strong prima facie case that the defendant had defrauded the Commonwealth of significantly more than the assets secured and there was no evidence that any of the assets were obtained by lawful means or from lawful sources.

It may be that the courts will draw a distinction between property allegedly derived from an unlawful activity and property lawfully acquired but restrained to meet any pecuniary penalty order. In the case of the former, the courts may be slow to release funds particularly where there is a strong prima facie case including unretracted admissions.

The court is only empowered to release funds to meet "reasonable" expenses. This requirement poses a dilemma for the D.P.P. as well as the court. It is not an unnatural reaction that a person facing serious charges will want to explore every possible avenue of avoiding conviction, regardless of how futile some actions may seem on any objective analysis. Combined with the knowledge that conviction may lead to the loss of all restrained property, the incentive to exhaust this property on even the most hopeless of defences is great. The property will be lost in any event. Why not spend it on legal fees rather than leave it to be recovered? Where the action itself is reasonable there is no incentive to limit the amount spent pursuing it.

To the extent that assets are spent on legal fees they are not available to meet any final orders. Under the P.O.C. Act the D.P.P. is charged with the responsibility of recovering proceeds. As the prosecution authority it is not in a position to comment on the merits of defence action. It is also difficult for a court to decide what is reasonable without some preliminary hearing of the issues, a course which it would be reluctant to embark on, particularly in the presence of the D.P.P.[74]

---

73. Unreported, Vic. Sup. Ct, 3 October 1985. See also *D.P.P. v. Saxon* (unreported, N.S.W. Sup. Ct, 3 August 1990, per Studdart J.) and *State Drug Crime Commission of N.S.W. v. Ujka and Sam* (unreported, N.S.W. Sup. Ct, 20 December 1990, per Badgery-Parker J.).

74. In *Commissioner of Australian Federal Police v. Malkoun* (unreported, Fed. Ct, 1 February 1989), Ryan J. did refuse to allow the defendants unrestricted access to restrained assets "so as to allow a hopeless or extravagant defence to be mounted in the expectation that any funds left will inevitably be subsumed by orders for pecuniary penalties under s. 243B": see above, p. 25, n. 68. He allowed each defendant up to $30,000 with liberty to apply. See also *State Drug Crime Commission v. Fleming and Heal* (unreported, N.S.W. Sup. Ct, 16 May 1991, per Mathews J.).

This issue is not about the release of funds for legal expenses but rather about having some mechanism to allow the community's interest to be given sufficient weight in determining the "reasonableness" of the amount of funds required. One possible mechanism would be to have a body such as a Legal Aid Commission oversight the expenditure of funds, not at the usual legal aid rates, but also not on hopeless causes.

THIRD PARTY RIGHTS

Action taken against property in connection with criminal activity has the capacity to seriously impinge on the rights of innocent third parties who have an interest in the property. The protection given to these third parties varies under the different legislation.

Forfeiture is not limited to property owned by an offender.[75] To so limit forfeiture would mean that the legislation could easily be circumvented by not using one's own property and there would be no incentive for the owner to be concerned about its use. Ownership is not a relevant issue if the conditions enabling forfeiture are satisfied.

Where property is forfeited pursuant to ss 228 or 229 of the *Customs Act* there is no protection at all for an owner who was not involved in its unlawful use. The only way they can retain or recover their property is if a discretion is exercised not to seize the property in the first place or if in disposing of it the Commissioner of the Australian Federal Police, in exercising his wide discretion, gives the property back to the owner. An innocent owner's only remedy lies in an action for damages against the user whose unlawful conduct caused the property to be forfeited.

The position is different in respect of money or goods forfeited under s. 229A of the *Customs Act*. In an action for condemnation or recovery, the court shall return the money or goods to an innocent third party into whose hands the forfeited money or goods have passed, if satisfied that the third party took them without knowledge of or reason to suspect their unlawful origin.[76]

The P.O.C. Act has a far more elaborate scheme protecting the rights of innocent third parties. Mortgagees may have more at risk under the P.O.C. Act which covers both real and personal property. Persons claiming an interest in property may apply before, or with leave after, the forfeiture order is made, for orders to protect their interest.[77] The court can either require the Commonwealth to transfer the interest to them or pay an amount equal to the value of the interest held. The person must satisfy the court that they were not involved in the commission of the connected offence. Where the interest is purchased after the commission of the offence the person must have acquired it for sufficient consideration and without knowledge and in circumstances that would

75. *Forbes v. Traders' Finance Corp. Ltd* (1971) 126 C.L.R. 429. A commercial conveyance is not forfeited merely because a passenger carries narcotics on it. It is only forfeit if the person in control of it is engaged in the illegality. See at 445 per Windeyer J.
76. *Customs Act*, s. 229A(8).
77. P.O.C. Act, s. 21.

not give rise to a suspicion that it was tainted. Financial institutions, for instance, would need to be careful with suddenly rich customers with no apparent legitimate source of income. Similar protection exists for persons with an interest in property statutorily forfeited pursuant to s. 30.[78]

Mortgagees in particular will be concerned to protect their interest at the restraining order stage. In the more serious cases it will not be unusual for offenders to be held in custody. It will take considerable time before final orders are sought and mortgagees can exercise their third party rights in relation to forfeiture. In the meantime they face the prospects of repayments ceasing and equity diminishing. There is power to exclude a person's interest from the restraining order.[79] The tests are similar to those applicable to the forfeiture provisions. The most satisfactory solution for all may be to sell the property, pay any mortgages and restrain the balance. In most instances the D.P.P. would have no objection to this course being taken on the initiative of either a defendant or a mortgagee. There is however a difficulty where the basis of final orders will be that the restrained property was used in or in connection with the offences. To convert the property restrained would eliminate the basis for forfeiture. It cannot be argued that the proceeds of the property are connected to the offence. There is no power to trace in respect of this element of tainted property.

Third parties are protected in relation to pecuniary penalty orders. A charge over the restrained property is created at the restraining order stage under the *Customs Act* and the pecuniary penalty order stage under the P.O.C. Act. In both instances the statutory charge is subject to prior changes.[80]

INVESTIGATIVE POWERS

The P.O.C. Act contains a number of provisions for orders to assist in gathering financial information. These orders can be obtained before a person has been charged provided there are reasonable grounds for suspecting that an indictable offence has been or, in the case of monitoring orders, is about to be committed. Orders available under the Act are production orders, search warrants and monitoring orders.

Production orders[81] are aimed at obtaining property tracking documents. These are documents which are relevant, for example, to identifying, locating or quantifying property of the alleged offender. These orders are obtained from a judge of the Supreme Court and may provide that documents be produced to a police officer or be made available to a police officer for inspection. Bankers books need only be made available for inspection, not produced. Because the recipient is put on notice to produce material, production orders are normally used to obtain information from financial institutions and other parties unlikely to be involved in the alleged offence.

78. P.O.C. Act, s. 31.
79. P.O.C. Act, s. 48(3).
80. P.O.C. Act, s. 50; *Customs Act*, s. 243J.
81. P.O.C. Act, s. 66.

Search warrants[82] are provided as an alternative to production orders. They allow for the seizure of property tracking documents. The main advantage of a search warrant is that the possessor of the document is not put on notice. Search warrants may be obtained in the same circumstances as production orders, with the added requirement that before issuing a search warrant a judge must be satisfied that the use of a production order would not be effective. Search warrants are normally used to obtain documents from suspected offenders or persons associated with them.

Monitoring orders[83] are restricted to situations where serious indictable offences are alleged. They are an innovative and effective investigation technique which can be used at a very early stage. The orders require a financial institution to inform officers of either the Australian Federal Police or the National Crime Authority about transactions conducted through an account held by a person with the institution. The orders are for a specified period not exceeding three months. It is an offence to make an unauthorised disclosure of the existence or operation of a monitoring order. The orders are issued by a judge of the Supreme Court. In the first two years of operation of the P.O.C. Act, 27 production orders, 14 search warrants, and 11 monitoring orders were obtained.

In addition to these information gathering powers the P.O.C. Act also provides for warrants to search land and premises for tainted property.[84] Any property seized must become the subject of a restraining order within 14 days of seizure or be returned. Warrants are issued by a magistrate.

CONCLUSION

The rationale for confiscation legislation has been variously described as including:

- deterrence;

- attacking the economic base of criminal enterprises;

- engendering public confidence in the criminal justice system by demonstrating that crime does not pay.

Qualitatively one would expect confiscation legislation to have these effects. It is of course very difficult to measure the extent to which the legislation is successful in achieving these aims.

The principle objectives set out in the P.O.C. Act are in more concrete terms. They include the recovery of proceeds and benefits derived from, and the forfeiture of property used in connection with, the commission of Commonwealth offences.[85] The P.O.C. Act together with the *Customs Act* provisions provide a very powerful armoury for achieving

82. P.O.C. Act, s. 71.
83. P.O.C. Act, s. 73.
84. P.O.C. Act, s. 36.
85. P.O.C. Act, s. 3. It has been suggested that these objectives are really means rather than ends. Fisse, below, Chapter 5, p. 80.

these objectives in respect of those convicted of Commonwealth offences.[86] They have been effective. Recoveries and forfeited property resulting from the use of both Acts total approximately $9 million to 30 June 1991. In addition, the net value of property restrained to meet future orders is more than $42 million.

Much has been achieved in a relatively short time. The pecuniary penalty provisions of the *Customs Act* have only been pursued with any vigour since June 1985. The P.O.C. Act commenced on 5 June 1987. It provides a complex and far-reaching scheme to assist in combating what was seen as the pressing problem of major crime in relation to drug trafficking and serious fraud on the revenue. The confiscation provisions have been assessed as being far from perfect but "a sensible and sane mechanism for dealing with an urgent and difficult problem".[87] Some of the provisions have the potential to operate oppressively if used indiscriminately. Adjustments will need to be made. Problems and anomalies will come to light as a variety of provisions are fully tested before the courts. It is early days yet. At this stage Commonweath confiscation legislation would appear to be working reasonably well, at least in terms of achieving the principle objectives as set out in the P.O.C. Act.

86. Although the confiscation provisions of the *Customs Act* are not conviction based, in the vast majority of cases there is an associated criminal prosecution.
87. Weinberg Q.C., "The Proceeds of Crime Act" in "New Despotism or Measured Response?" (1989) 15 Mon. L. Rev. 201. The paper is highly critical of the offence provisions in the P.O.C. Act. For criticisms of the offence provisions see also Fisse, "The Proceeds of Crime Act; The Rise of Money Laundering Offences and The Fall of Principle" (1989) 13 Crim. L.J. 5.

3

Cash Transaction Reporting and Money Laundering Legislation
How Will it Come Out in the Wash?

GRAHAM PINNER*

> Money get back
> I'm alright Jack keep your hands off my stack
> Money it's a hit
> Don't give me that do goody good bullshit
> I'm in the high-fidelity first class travelling set
> And I think I need a Lear Jet.
>
> *Pink Floyd*[1]

INTRODUCTION

Money is said to be the source of all evil, but it may be that is not necessarily the case. There are of course many crimes where money may not be an issue, such as rape or assault. But here we are talking about crimes of avarice. The fact is that people are involved in organised crime and tax evasion for the money. The *Cash Transaction Reports Act* 1988 (Cth) (C.T.R. Act) focuses in on the money trail and is part of a legislative package which is aimed at detecting and tracing criminals' moneys so that the criminal money and the assets obtained through those activities can be seized under the *Proceeds of Crime Act* 1987 (Cth) and States' confiscation of assets legislation. Before the passage of these measures, traditional investigative techniques had shown to be ineffective in identifying financiers of major crime because of the ease with which such persons were able to distance themselves from the actual criminal conduct.[2]

CASH TRANSACTION REPORTS ACT

The legislature has addressed the perceived shortcoming in the traditional law enforcement approach. It has addressed this problem by focusing in on the experience both in Australia and overseas that criminal

---

* LL.B. (Tas.); Deputy Director, Cash Transactions Reports Agency.
1. "Money", © 1973 Pink Floyd Music Publishers Ltd. For Australasia: E.M.I. Songs Australia Pty Ltd (A.C.N. 000 063 267), P.O. Box C156, Cremorne Junction N.S.W. 2090.
2. Senator Michael Tate, Second Reading Speech on the Cash Transaction Reports Bill 1987, *Parliamentary Debates*, Senate, 1987, Vol. No. 123, p. 2413.

financiers are more closely associated with the profits of crime than the crime itself and that cash is an important part of financing criminal activity.[3] In the case of the C.T.R. Act it has done so by placing obligations upon people designated as cash dealers and on the general public. Cash dealers are defined as financial institutions (banks, building societies and credit unions) and other what I will term "quasi" financial institutions and gambling institutions such as "TABs, casinos, bookmakers and on course totalisers".[4] The Act then imposes upon the cash dealers an obligation to report all significant cash transactions (cash transactions of $10,000 and above)[5] and suspect transactions (a suspect transaction is a transaction of any kind, of any amount, where the cash dealer suspects on reasonable grounds that the transaction involves tax evasion, some offence against a law of the Commonwealth or may assist in an investigation relating to the *Proceeds of Crime Act*).[6]

The Act also places obligations for reporting on the general public and cash carriers where amounts of $5,000 or more in Australian currency or foreign currency are taken into or out of Australia (international currency transfers).[7]

In addition to the reporting requirements the C.T.R. Act has since 1 July 1988 made it an offence to open or operate an account in a false name.[8] This has already proven to be an effective law enforcement weapon. From 1 February 1991 the C.T.R. Act will require a statutory regime to be followed[9] for the identification of a person opening a new account or for a change of signatory on an existing account. The Act provides for the retention of account opening documentation for a period seven years after the day on which an account is closed for the purpose of providing evidentiary material in relation to criminal investigations.[10]

The C.T.R. Act also states that it is an offence for a person to conduct two or more non-reportable cash transactions where it would be reasonable to conclude that a person is conducting a transaction for the dominant purposes of ensuring or attempting to ensure that no report was made in relation to the other reporting obligations.[11] It should be noted that where a cash dealer recognises what would be termed "structuring" there is an obligation to report that as a suspect transaction under s. 16 of the C.T.R. Act.

ADMINISTRATIVE ARRANGEMENTS IN THE UNITED STATES AND AUSTRALIA COMPARED

For the most part, the reporting provisions of the C.T.R. Act mirror those of the *Bank Secrecy Act* 1970 of the United States which was the former

3. Ibid.
4. *Cash Transaction Reports Act* 1988 (Cth), s. 3.
5. C.T.R. Act, s. 7.
6. C.T.R. Act, s. 16.
7. C.T.R. Act, s. 15.
8. C.T.R. Act, s. 16.
9. C.T.R. Act, ss 18 to 20.
10. C.T.R. Act, s. 23.
11. C.T.R. Act, s. 31.

Attorney-General, the Honourable Lionel Bowen's inspiration for the Australian legislation. Although the substantive provisions of the legislation are very similar, the administrative arrangements between the United States and Australia are quite different. There are a number of reasons for this including the fact that the Australian Agency falls under the control of the federal Attorney-General whereas in the United States the Office of Financial Enforcement falls under the control of the United States Treasury Department. In the United States the various aspects of the reporting are split between a number of arms of the United States Treasury including the Office of Financial Enforcement, the Internal Revenue Service (I.R.S.), and the United States Customs Service. In Australia the entire administration of the legislation falls under the control of the Cash Transaction Reports Agency (C.T.R. Agency) which is itself under the control of a Director[12] appointed by the Attorney-General.[13]

Though it is clear from the objects of the C.T.R. Act that the principle aim of the Act is to facilitate the administration and enforcement of taxation laws, the Agency also has very clear law enforcement objectives[14] and the Agency is clearly a member of the law enforcement community as well as an important new weapon in the Commissioner of Taxation's armoury. It is to be noted that the Commissioner of Taxation is entitled to all of the C.T.R. information whereas the Australian Customs Service, the National Crime Authority and State and federal law enforcement agencies are entitled to information at the Director's discretion.[15] However, the Director has stated publicly that the provision of information to agencies other than the Australian Taxation Office would be liberal subject to adherence to the privacy principles within the federal *Privacy Act*, the secrecy provisions within the C.T.R. Act, the other agencies secrecy constraints and the over-riding proviso that the Director would have the discretion to withhold access in any particular case.

The administrative framework within Australia is much more likely to encourage widespread use of the data for criminal or law enforcement activities than perhaps is the case in the United States, where dissemination of the information to the law enforcement agencies is made through various arms of the United States Treasury. It would seem to the Australian observer that the greatest users of the information for criminal law enforcement purposes are the Criminal Investigation Divisions (C.I.D.) of the I.R.S. and the United States Customs Service, both of which are themselves part of the United States Treasury.

That is not to say that the other United States Agencies such as the F.B.I. and the Drug Enforcement Agency (D.E.A.) have not successfully used bank secrecy information. Indeed, Operation Polar Cap, which was the biggest money laundering operation ever detected in the United States (of which I will speak in some further detail later) was a joint operation of the I.R.S. C.I.D., the F.B.I., the D.E.A. and the United States

12. C.T.R. Act, s. 35.
13. C.T.R. Act, s. 36.
14. C.T.R. Act, s. 4.
15. C.T.R. Act, s. 27.

Customs Service. However, there are a number of features of the United States arrangements which have been avoided in the Australian legislation. In the first place, the significant cash data base in the United States is processed both by the I.R.S. and Customs, that is to say there are duplicated processing sites and the dissemination of material to law enforcement agencies is through both of these federal agencies. The point of dissemination varies in geographic location and the rules under which external agencies may access the federal data bases also vary. In the case of "suspicious transactions" financial institutions report these to the I.R.S. but also send copies to the I.R.S. C.I.D. and the F.B.I. In addition, analysis of databases was until recently carried out independently by the I.R.S. and the United States Customs Service. Following major co-operative efforts like Polar Cap the United States Treasury realised that there was a need for greater co-ordination and in consequence established a joint Treasury operation known as FINCEN to gather money laundering information and intelligence from every known source and to provide a comprehensive analysis of all the source data in support of narcotics money laundering.

Having had the benefit of the United States' experience and considerable advice from its counterparts and various other United States law enforcement agencies, the C.T.R. Agency has been able to avoid the difficulties that this kind of fragmentation causes. In a recent report to the United States Senate Foreign Relations Committee in which these issues were canvassed, the Subcommittee on Narcotics and Terrorism said:

> Other countries have taken the initative on their own to implement anti-money laundering legislation. Australia for instance has a more stringent and more efficient cash transaction reporting system.[16]

One of the other very important differences between the Australian cash transaction reporting arrangements and those prevailing in the United States is that in Australia at least 90 per cent of the data of significant cash transactions will be captured from the cash dealers electronically and that over time that percentage will grow. In the United States the capture of data is, except to a very limited extent, by way of paper reports. Paper processing is not only slow (in the United States it takes an average of 45 days to get a paper report on to the data base), it is very expensive for both the processing agencies and the banks and other cash dealers. The Subcommittee on Narcotics and Terrorism of the United States Senate Foreign Relations Committee said in its report, *Drug Money Laundering, Banks and Foreign Policy*, that the "banking industry by in large recognised the usefulness of the C.T.R. process". One leading American banker had said that the C.T.R. process had "made it very difficult to illicitly get cash into the American banking system", but warned that "the government is literally being drowned in this sea of reports to the point [where] . . . . they might not be making effective use of the data they are getting".[17]

16. United States Senate, Subcommittee on Narcotics and Terrorism, *Drug Money Laundering, Banks and Foreign Policy*, Report to the Foreign Relations Committee (27 September 1989, 4 October 1989 and 1 November 1989), p. 63.
17. Ibid., p. 16.

In reviewing the Cash Transaction Reports Bill, the Senate Standing Committee on Legal and Constitutional Affairs noted that evidence had been presented to them that the C.T.R. Agency would be computer based and that it was anticipated that direct computer links would eventually be set up, for example, between a bank and the Agency.[18]

One of the first actions for the Agency in the setting up phase was to establish a Provider Advisory Group of the Australian Bankers Association (A.B.A.), the Australian Association of Permanent Building Societies (A.A.P.B.S.), and the Australian Federation of Credit Unions (A.F.C.U.L.), as well as consulting with all other cash dealer industry bodies. In the course of early discussions it became evident that financial institutions were not able to provide all of the information specified in the Schedules to the Act electronically or alternatively to amend their systems to capture such information within a time frame that was consistent with the desire of the Parliament to see the legislation in operation.

Following discussions with the finance industry and law enforcement agencies both in Australia and the United States, the Agency formed the view of what information was absolutely necessary to make the C.T.R. system work, and on their parts the financial institutions indicated to the Agency what information could realistically be delivered. The Attorney-General agreed to amend the legislation to enable the Schedules to the Act to be amended by way of regulation and in consequence regulations are now in place that reflect the ability of the cash dealers to report essential information to the Agency electronically. I cannot emphasise too much the level of co-operation that the Agency has received from the cash dealer industry groups and the users of the information. It has placed the Agency in a position where it receives 90 per cent of significant cash transaction data electronically, which we believe is cost-effective and efficient and which the Agency's United States counterparts have said they would like to emulate.

The *Bank Secrecy Act* has been in operation in the United States since 1970, however, there was quite widespread criticism of the legislation and since that time, it would seem, widespread non-compliance. In 1985 the Bank of Boston was fined U.S.$500,000 for failing to report certain transactions and for allowing its exemption from reporting certain business transactions to be used by a criminal organisation. The prosecution was followed by a U.S.$2.25 million civil fine against Crocker National Bank and a U.S.$4.75 million civil fine against the Bank of America.[19] These cases focused attention on the requirement for banks to report cash transactions under the *Bank Secrecy Act* and as a result the Act was substantially amended in 1986. In addition the Federal Bank regulatory agencies directed all banks to establish effective programmes to ensure compliance with the B.S.A. reporting and record keeping requirement. As a result of the Bank of Boston case and these other measures the number of reports doubled between 1985 and

18. Senate Standing Committee on Legal and Constitutional Affairs, *Report on the Cash Transaction Reports Bill 1987* (April 1988), p. 66, n. 34, referring to evidence given by Mr Meaney of the Attorney-General's Department.
19. See Adams, below, Chapter 18.

1986.[20] The C.T.R. Agency does not propose to follow its United States counterparts in this regard.

The focus of the Agency is clearly in providing information that will detect criminals and tax evaders. Whilst the C.T.R. Act contains offences which will be enforced, the Agency does not believe that the management of major Australian institutions would deliberately seek not to comply with the C.T.R. Act. The support to date received from the A.B.A., its member banks and other financial institution bodies indicates that it will not be necessary to do this in the Australian context. Australia has four major banks whereas in the United States they have 14,000 banks and the compliance task is much more difficult. The number of cash dealers in other categories is equally much greater in the United States than in Australia. That does not mean that the C.T.R. Agency will not be seeking to take prosecutions in appropriate cases; it certainly will. The Act gives the Agency a right to conduct audits of cash dealers.[21] The Agency will certainly have a hands-on approach to auditing of cash dealer organisations but cash dealers would not be expected to have our staff looking over their shoulders. The Agency will use comparative statistical data from its computer systems and intelligence from the law enforcement community to determine which cash dealers should be audited. Blatant breaches of the C.T.R. Act will be referred to the Australian Federal Police and the Director of Public Prosecutions.

As was anticipated, the C.T.R. legislation is already of great value in following the money trail for proceeds of all criminal activities including tax evasion and in detecting the financiers of criminal activity such as drug trafficking, as has been the experience in the United States.[22] The theme of this chapter is of course the legislation as a tool in the detection of money laundering and confiscation of the proceeds of crime and I will turn to those issues to describe how the legislation works in practice.

MONEY LAUNDERING

Money laundering is the conversion of profits of illegal activities into financial assets which appear to have legitimate origins.[23] In Australia there are two offences of money laundering under the *Proceeds of Crime Act* 1987 (Cth).[24] The rationale behind focusing upon the money trail rather than traditional law enforcement methods is that "the kingpins put a great deal of distance between themselves and their product but very little distance between themselves and their money".[25] That is appreciated both in Australia and overseas.[26]

20. Hewitt and Kalyk, *Understanding the Cash Transaction Reports Act* (1990), Part 204.
21. C.T.R. Act, ss 13, 14, 14A.
22. Senator Michael Tate, Second Reading Speech on the Cash Transaction Reports Bill 1987, *Parliamentary Debates*, Senate, 1987, Vol. No. 123, p. 2413.
23. United States Senate, Subcommittee on Narcotics and Terrorism, *Drug Money Laundering, Banks and Foreign Policy*, Report to the Foreign Relations Committee, (1989), p. 8.
24. *Proceeds of Crime Act* 1987, ss 81 and 82.
25. Salvatore Martoche, Assistant Secretary for the Financial Enforcement, United States Treasury, to the United States Senate Foreign Relations Committee, October 1989, cited in the Report of the Subcommittee on Narcotics and Terrorism (1989), p. 8.
26. Senator Michael Tate, Second Reading Speech on the Cash Transaction Reports Bill 1987, *Parliamentary Debates*, Senate, 1987, Vol. No. 123, p. 2414.

Although it is recognised that there are many different techniques and methods used to launder money through financial institutions and that the methods used in Australia may be different in some ways from those employed in the United States, it is useful to look at a generic model described in the various stages or "wash cycles" as provided by the United States Senate Committee on Foreign Relations by the United States Customs Service.[27] This model says that money laundering consists of three distinct stages: "placement", "layering" and "integration". "Placement" is the physical disposal of bulk cash, either by combining the cash with the proceeds of a legitimate business, or otherwise converting currency into deposits on the books of a bank or similar financial intermediary. "Layering" is the process of transferring the funds among various accounts through a series of complex transactions designed to disguise the trail of illicit proceeds. The final stage, "integration", is the process of shifting the laundered funds to legitimate organisations with no apparent links to organised crime. Once integrated, the funds can be managed by sophisticated investment managers. Until requested by its criminal owners there is general consensus amongst law enforcement agencies and bankers that the greatest vulnerability of the money launderers is at the placement stage.[28] It is this vulnerability at the placement stage that serves as the basis for operation of both significant cash transaction reports and suspect transaction reports.

In the United States there is a continuing debate as to how useful the C.T.R. process is. On the one hand it is argued that the C.T.R. processes are bearing fruit. Assistant Secretary Martoche in testimony before the Foreign Relations Committee argued that Cash Transaction Reports had been extremely useful in developing new leads; he noted that, in the years 1988 and 1989, over 700 targets had been identified and that many of the cases were ongoing. Assistant Commissioner William Rosenblatt of the Customs Agency claimed that as a result of the artificial intelligence used by the Customs Agency over 60 per cent of the leads resulted in cases.[29] During the year ended 30 June 1991, there were 429,685 significant cash transactions reported by cash dealers. Although our experience in Australia is limited, the early indications are that if the data is properly analysed it will probably be equally as useful as suspect transactions data. Nevertheless, the experience that the Agency is developing in dealing with suspect transactions gives considerable grounds for optimism on the success of the strategy which will be employed by the Agency in Australia.

SUSPECT TRANSACTION REPORTS

Suspect transaction reports reporting obligations commenced on 1 January 1990. Up to 30 June 1991 some 8,135 suspect transaction reports had been received by the Agency.

27. United States Senate, Subcommittee on Narcotics and Terrorism, *Drug Money Laundering, Banks and Foreign Policy*, Report to the Foreign Relations Committee (1989), p. 8.
28. Ibid., p. 12.
29. Ibid., p. 15.

The suspect transaction reporting provisions of the C.T.R. Act are a result of recommendations made to the Senate Committee on Legal and Constitutional Affairs by the Australian Bankers' Association which drew upon the requirements of the *Drug Trafficking Offences Act* 1986 of the United Kingdom.[30] In putting this proposal the A.B.A. was able to secure the statutory protection from civil suit which might arise at common law in relation to their duty of confidentiality to their customers.[31] It is also to be noted that in the United States the *Money Laundering Control Act* 1986 required cash dealers to report "suspicious" transactions but not much attention was given to the sweeping provisions of the Act until 1988.[32] Like the C.T.R. Act the American *Money Laundering Control Act* does not contain a definition of a suspicious transaction. The definition offered to the United States Senate Foreign Relations Committee by Mr Bernard Bailor, Chairman of the American Bar Association Committee on White Collar Crime, was:

> simply put, a suspicious transaction is a transaction that is inconsistent with a customer's legitimate business activities. Thus, the first key to identifying suspicious transactions is knowing enough about the customer's business to recognise that a transaction or series of transactions is unusual for a particular customer.

(He then gave a list of potential danger signals such as a reluctance to furnish reference, reluctance to provide financial statements and so on.) Because the C.T.R. Act likewise does not define what a suspect transaction is, the Agency has taken legal advice on various aspects of suspect transaction reporting and reproduced this advice in the documents in which the principles involved are set out.[33] The C.T.R. Act requires a cash dealer to report a cash transaction where there are reasonable grounds to suspect that information the cash dealer has concerning the transaction may be relevant to:

- investigation of tax evasion;
- investigation or prosecution of an offence against a law of the Commonwealth;
- or may be of assistance in the enforcement of the *Proceeds of Crime Act* (including money laundering).

There are a couple of things I wish to say about suspect transaction reporting. The first is that it has been put that the Agency's position that a transaction can include a negotiation (that is to say, dealings that are not yet completed) but does not include a mere inquiry, has been disputed.[34] The Agency's position on this point is based upon the advice of senior counsel having regard to the pronouncement of the courts cited in the Agency's principles document. The Agency's position is also stated in the *Suspect Transaction Reporting* guideline developed

---

30. Senate Standing Committee on Legal and Constitutional Affairs, *Inquiry into Cash Transaction Reports Bill* (10 March 1988, Transcript of Proceedings), p. 292.
31. C.T.R. Act, s. 16(5).
32. See Adams, below, Chapter 18.
33. *Cash Transaction Reports Act 1988: Reporting Suspect Transactions, Principles Involved* (20 February 1990).
34. Kriewaldt, *Cash Transaction Reports Act 1988* (Paper presented to C.L.E. Seminar, Law Society of Queensland, 27 June 1990), p. 14.

in conjuction with the Provider Advisory Group on the basis of the legal advice from senior counsel and a major law firm.[35]

Another issue on which I wish to comment is that the C.T.R. Agency guideline states that cash dealers should *not* advise the person being reported on that suspect transactions report that they are being reported. A view has been expressed that the cash dealer should advise the customer that he or she is filing such a report.[36] A subsequent amendment to the C.T.R. Act now prohibits such advice being given.[37]

The final issue I wish to discuss is related to a view which has been circulated that a statement in C.T.R. Agency Guideline No. 1 is incorrect, in that subs. 16(5) would not attach unless a cash dealer was aware that "an investigation is being conducted" or "a prosecution is underway". This does not accord with the Agency's legal advice. Clearly the Act refers to where there are reasonable grounds to suspect that information *"may be relevant to investigation"*. It is to be noted that the Act does not contain either the definite or indefinite article before the word "investigation"; the Act talks about "investigation" in a general sense not "an/the investigation". This is an issue which would be tested in the courts in an appropriate case.

The American Bankers Association testified to the United States Senate Foreign Relations Committee that the suspicious transaction law requires a level of judgment in the bank that is not required with the C.T.R. Act.[38] That is certainly also the case in Australia, but it does not mean that bank tellers are being turned into police; the Act simply gives protection in cases where they are suspicious. Nevertheless, I believe the Australian Bank Employees Union is correct in saying that bank employees are proving to be a formidable weapon in Australia's war against crime.[39]

The United States Senate Foreign Relations Committee was told how extremely valuable suspicious transaction reports had proved in Operation Polar Cap.[40] Although Operation Polar Cap was in the United States, it is instructive in terms of understanding the potential use of this kind of information.

POLAR CAP

Operation Polar Cap came to light in January 1988 when a vice-president of the Wells Fargo Bank in San Francisco was examining computer-produced reports on cash surpluses returned to the United States Federal

35. C.T.R. Agency Guideline No. 1, *Suspect Transaction Reporting.*
36. Hewitt and Kalyk, op. cit., p. 82.
37. *Crimes Legislation Amendment Act (No. 2)* 1991, s. 16(5A).
38. United States Senate, Subcommittee on Narcotics and Terrorism, *Drug Money Laundering, Banks and Foreign Policy*, Report to the Foreign Relations Committee (1989), Earl Hadlow of the Barnett Bank.
39. Australian Bank Employees Union, *Bank Staff Turn Crime Fighters* (Media Release, 20 June 1990).
40. United States Senate, Subcommittee on Narcotics and Terrorism, *Drug Money Laundering, Banks and Foreign Policy*, Report to the Foreign Relations Committee (1989), p. 31.

Reserves (the equivalent of the Australian Reserve Bank). On making inquiries with a particular branch in Los Angeles which disclosed a high cash surplus it was revealed that a new account opened by a gold brokerage firm called Andonian Brothers had been depositing millions of dollars a week into the account since it was opened. As the company had deposited $25 million into the account in a three-month period, Jack Kilhefner, Senior Vice-President of the bank, told his chief of compliance, Don Reid, to report the matter to the Criminal Investigation Division of the I.R.S.

At about the same time an armoured car company, Loomis Armoured Transports Company (a subsidiary of the Australian company Mayne Nickless), was checking a nightly shipment of so-called gold "scraps" being sent from a New York jewellery store to a firm called Ropex in Los Angeles. An employee noticed a tear in the box, through which could be seen neatly bundled stacks of banknotes. The employee was suspicious and called the transport company, the explanation was given that the money was being moved from the east coast to Los Angeles to take advantage of better short term interest rates in a local bank. The Loomis employee sent the delivery, but at the same time provided a suspicious report to the F.B.I.

The investigations officer quickly realised that they were dealing with a major money laundering operation of the Medellin cocaine cartel turning "drug tainted cash from the streets of major United States cities into pristine funds which they could draw from secret bank accounts" and transfer to destinations overseas and throughout the United States. It soon became obvious to both agencies that they were dealing with a massive operation which they could not handle and there was a joint meeting of the Drug Enforcement Agency, Customs, F.B.I. and I.R.S. from which a major task force was set up. The arrangement was known by the Colombian bosses as La Mina, the (Gold) Mine. The gold, which was in fact cash, was estimated to amount to U.S.$1.2 billion over a three-year period. The task force ran a major surveillance and undercover operation for some 18 months during which time they identified the members of the syndicate, traced money flows, assets and gathered evidence for subsequent prosecutions.

As part of the operation F.B.I. agents posed as janitors and collected the rubbish from one of the syndicate's suites. A perusal of the rubbish revealed the name of a cheque cashing company in San Jose. That name linked the syndicate to yet another syndicate in the San Jose region which had been under the investigation by the I.R.S. C.I.D. branch as a result of another suspicious report. That report had been lodged because the cheque cashing company (in the United States, commercial companies cash cheques for a commission) which had regularly been obtaining cash from a major United States bank, suddenly ceased drawing cash for change but continued to deposit large amounts of cheques and funds transferred to various foreign countries. Investigation revealed that the Medellin cartel had subverted the cheque cashing company and enlisted it as part of its money laundering operations.

A number of major United States banks co-operated with the joint task force throughout the period of the surveillance operation. When the operation was brought to an end, 127 people were indicted and large amounts of cash seized. As a result of the roles played in the operation, the Wells Fargo Bank and the Bank of America received congressional presentations.[41]

A number of important facets of Operation Polar Cap should serve as lessons for the Australian law enforcement community. First, it was quite by accident that the F.B.I. and I.R.S. C.I.D. got together on Polar Cap and then called in the other Federal agencies. There is clearly a need for suspect transaction reports to go to a central agency so that information can be shared by the various agencies, and this of course has been done in Australia. It is interesting to note that the subcommittee on Narcotics and Terrorism submitted to the United States Senate Foreign Relations Committee that the Internal Revenue Service should explore the possibility of centralising its investigations of suspicious transactions.[42]

Secondly, it is clear that in relation to a major operation, a task force type of approach where the expertise of various agencies can be brought together is a model that should be very closely looked at in Australia. Through its role as a provider of intelligence to both the Federal and State agencies, the C.T.R. Agency is able to facilitate the process of co-ordination of law enforcement agencies of their resources in relation to C.T.R. information. Already a number of task forces have been set up under the *National Crime Authority Act* 1984 (Cth) in relation to suspect transaction reports which indicate involvement of major criminal organisations.

The final thing I would like to say about Polar Cap is that in the course of discussions with the investigators involved and senior officials of the Wells Fargo Bank, I was told that it was not necessary to call bank officers in the course of the subsequent prosecutions. I believe that this is very important because this is consistent with the guidelines that the Agency has issued following discussions that it has had with industry body representatives and bank unions. In the Memoranda of Understanding between the Agency and the law enforcement agencies it is made clear that the information provided under suspect transactions is intelligence and not evidence; law enforcement agencies must take all reasonable steps to ensure that cash dealer staff are not involved in prosecutions arising from suspect transaction reporting.

AUSTRALIAN EXPERIENCE

What then is the experience in Australia with suspect transaction reports to date? Of the 8,135 reports lodged, the majority involve low to

41. Ibid. Evan Lowell Maxwell, "Gold, Drugs and Clean Cash", *Los Angeles Times Magazine*, 18 February 1990. I would also like to thank Jack Kilhefner and Don Reid of the Wells Fargo Bank and Alex Seddio of the North West, Organised Crime Drug Enforcement Task Force I.R.S. C.I.D. San Francisco, California (Alex is a world acknowledged expert on money laundering investigations), for the valuable insight they gave me on Operation Polar Cap, in which they all played key roles.
42. United States Senate, Subcommittee on Narcotics and Terrorism, *Drug Money Laundering, Banks and Foreign Policy*, Report to the Foreign Relations Committee (1989), p. 33.

medium tax cheats of amounts under $50,000, 1,881 cases involving money laundering. There are more than 20 cases which appear to involve high level corporate tax cheating and fraud worth more than $30 million and also 30 to 40 transactions at the organised crime end of the scale indicating major tax evasion and significant drug money laundering. Up to a dozen of these cases involve sums in the millions of dollars. In the larger cases major investigations are underway by either individual law enforcement agencies and in many cases joint task forces.

There have been a number of prosecutions under that Act for false name accounts which have themselves resulted in obtaining quite large amounts of revenue using both the *Income Tax Assessment Act* 1936 (Cth) and the *Proceeds of Crime Act* 1987 (Cth). It is worth noting that the first prosecution under the provisions of the C.T.R. Act resulted in the offender receiving three months' imprisonment and the payment to the Taxation Commissioner of a very substantial part of the tax assessment of $2.8 million raised. In that case when police executed a search warrant on the defendant's premises they found a newspaper article which provided an analysis of the Cash Transaction Reports Bill and set out details of the offences. [43]

THE SIZE OF THE UNDERGROUND ECONOMY

What then is the size of the underground economy which might be able to be detected through cash transaction reporting and which might be the subject of forfeiture under federal and State laws? In other words, what is the potential size of money laundering? It is not very easy to say: the report by the Parliamentary Joint Committee on the National Crime Authority said that the size of the estimated turnover of cannabis, heroin and cocaine in Australia was $A2.617 billion. [44]

In its annual report for the year ending 30 June 1989 the Reserve Bank of Australia reported that there were $A4.781 billion $100 notes in circulation, an increase of 18.77 per cent over the previous year, which is substantially greater than any other denomination. Experience from the United States tells us, in relation to drug moneys, that small denominations ("street" notes) are converted into $100 notes in order to facilitate the money laundering process and that this process is itself an indication of money laundering. [45] One report says that a kilogram of heroin which costs between $A12,000 and $A15,000 in Asia can be sold from between $200,000 and $250,000 in Australia. Seizure of heroin in the luggage of a courier may represent a loss to the importer of $A30,000 plus the cost of an air ticket, which is quite inconsiderable in terms of the profits that can be made. [46]

In its report, the Parliamentary Joint Committee on the National Crime Authority looked at the recommendations of the Williams Royal

43. Director of Public Prosecutions, *Annual Report 1988-1989*.
44. *Drugs, Crime and Society* (1989), p. 52.
45. C.T.R. Agency Guideline No. 1, *Suspect Transaction Reporting*.
46. Dobinson and Poletti, *Buying and Selling Heroin* (New South Wales Bureau of Crime Statistics and Research, Sydney, 1989), and Parliamentary Joint Committee on the National Crime Authority, Report, *Drugs, Crime and Society* (1989), p. 61.

Commission on targeting of major traffickers. They observed that if wholesalers are imprisoned or leave the trade for some reason, there would be a number of lower level dealers ready to take their places; importers may be more difficult to replace depending upon whether the confederates in their organisation remain at large. The Parliamentary Committee concluded that given the profits to be made, even if major traffickers are apprehended others would be prepared to take their place and increasingly they would be drawn from the ranks of professional criminals. They said that the best that law enforcement could probably hope for was to keep drug abuse in society within acceptable limits and that even that prospect seemed to have disappeared in the United States. It would seem that we are dealing with a very large problem and it would seem that there is a great deal of potential for law enforcement agencies to utilise both the C.T.R. Act and forfeiture legislation both to deny criminals of the proceeds of their criminal activities and with some recent initiatives, to fund the operation of law enforcement.

In a paper presented to the Institute of Criminology, University of Sydney, David Fraser questioned the whole economic rationale for both the C.T.R. reporting and for Proceeds of Crime legislation. He said that criminalisation and law enforcement practices often operate as a barrier to entry or to eliminate competition.[47] I don't know whether that is correct or not but I doubt whether anybody in this country knows whether the drugs or any other organised crime groups work within a monopoly, an oligopoly or whether there are numerous large or small criminal organisations.

In the New South Wales Drugs Royal Commission, Mr Justice Woodward held the view that the marijuana traffic in eastern Australia was controlled wholly by an organised group of Calabrian-Italians. On the other hand he was of the view that importation and distribution of heroin was in the hands of a number of small ventures which was not highly organised or monopolistic in structure and not under the control of a single Mr Big.[48] In response to evidence presented that there was "no Mr Big" to the federal Royal Commission of Inquiry Into Drugs, Mr Justice Williams remarked that there were "plenty of Mr Big Enoughs".[49] Looking at the apparently different conclusions of the two Royal Commissions and the question of whether there was organised crime in Australia, Dr Alfred McCoy concluded "it was clear then, that organised crime not only existed in Australia, but it had moved collectively into the drug traffic using its characteristic milieu—style of operations".[50]

The situation in Australia on organised crime, is that nobody appears to know the precise nature of it as to whether it is monopolistic or otherwise; at least that knowledge is not within the public domain and if somebody does know it they are certainly not telling anyone. The C.T.R. Agency and law enforcement agencies are going to have to get to know the nature of the structure of organised crime in this country

47. See below, Chapter 4.
48. New South Wales Royal Commission, *Drug Trafficking* (October 1979), pp. 22-24, 32.
49. *The Bulletin*, 28 August 1979.
50. *Drug Traffic—Narcotics and Organised Crime in Australia* (1980), p. 337.

before money laundering can be tackled in any effective ongoing manner. You cannot deal with money laundering effectively without knowing precisely how it is being carried out. It does not seem to be very useful to make economic assumptions about Australian organised crime and drug trafficking without understanding the market and the organisations that operate within that market. We probably cannot say much more in relation to the drug trade than that the existence of major drug traffickers would probably act as a barrier to entry for small traffickers, and that removal of the major traffickers provides an opportunity for expansion of existing enterprises for new entrants into the market place.

CAN THIS APPROACH WORK?

Ultimately the measure of success of the C.T.R. legislation will be whether the law enforcement agencies can use the information provided by the Agency to deprive criminals of their assets obtained through their criminal activity and at the same time help to keep down revenue outlays. It has been suggested that asset forfeiture legislation itself will depend upon a cost benefit analysis for its practical success and what is required is a theoretically sound and perfectly verified idea about the actual decision making processes of members of organised crime as well as an accurate assessment of the economic value of their activity.[51] With respect, it is naive to expect that the general public or the governments are going to look at the cost of law enforcement in those terms, at least in the immediate future. In any event, "conventional" law enforcement is an expensive business but it is regarded as a social necessity. A rough calculation by the Parliamentary Joint Committee on the National Crime Authority placed the annual cost of drug law enforcement in Australia at $123.2 million.[52]

The purpose of the *Proceeds of Crime Act* 1987 (Cth) was not, as has been suggested, to expand the purse of the Crown or to act as a competition regulator.[53] The purpose of the Proceeds of Crime Bill is set out in the Second Reading Speech to the House of Representatives as being "to strike at the heart of major organised crime by depriving persons involved of the profits and instruments of their crime. By so doing, it will suppress criminal activity by attacking the primary motive—profit—and prevent the reinvestment of profit in further criminal activity."[54] It is clear that the aims of the *Proceeds of Crime Act* go beyond simply removing the profit; it also goes to removing the means of financing of further criminal activities. It is not simply a matter of closing down one business in economic terms, but in closing down the capital base of a business. In my view this provision is simply not one of deterrence but it is also a provision of retribution.

51. See Fraser, below, Chapter 4.
52. *Drugs, Crime and Society* (1989), p. 76.
53. See below, Chapter 4, pp. 56ff.
54. The Honourable Lionel Bowen, Deputy Prime Minister and Attorney-General, Second Reading Speech on the Proceeds of Crime Bill 1987, *Parliamentary Debates*, House of Representatives, 1987.

Well, does the *Proceeds of Crime Act* work? The answer is yes. Even though it is very early days, the federal Director of Public Prosecutions has at this moment in excess of $50 million in assets subject to restraint orders. That may be very small compared with the U.S.$500 million that the F.B.I. seized in the last 12 months but it is not an insignificant amount. The developments that are occurring with the setting up of a trust fund are to be shared by drug rehabilitation centres and law enforcement bodies. At least some part of the expense of law enforcement can be met through this legislation. I think that one of the other things that is often overlooked at this debate is that this legislation is not limited just to criminal activity such as drug trafficking but has great potential in relation to white collar and corporate crime. This is one of the reasons the Australian Securities Commission was made a recipient of C.T.R. information in amendments which were passed late in 1989. [55]

In my view the potential lies there for the forfeiture legislation to be used successfully in money laundering investigations. The next question to be answered is: can the C.T.R. system be used successfully to facilitate that process? I say that the answer is yes. We are already seeing just that in relation to suspect transaction reporting and I feel confident that the different arrangements that we have in place in Australia will put us ahead of our United States counterparts. As I have said elsewhere in this paper, the United States authorities recognise a number of weaknesses in their present system. The Subcommittee on Narcotics and Terrorism of the United States Senate Foreign Relation Committee said that the "money laundering law enforcement may offer the most 'bang for the buck' in the war on drugs" but went on to say what was needed to accomplish the mission was "more people, particularly trained financial investigators to analyse the suspicious activity reports and C.T.Rs pouring in from banks; improved computers, artificial intelligence and on-line telecommunications and reporting and database management are needed to make the most effective and timely use of existing information to put money launderers out of business and behind bars". [56]

Although I cannot say that the C.T.R. Agency is flushed with resources, particularly human resources, I can say that most of the measures that have been recommended by the United States Senate Committee have been addressed in Australia. The Agency is staffed by a very small team of highly skilled professionals with many cumulative years of experience in financial investigation, taxation matters, the banking industry and computer aided investigations. It is the intention of the Director that the Agency will become a centre of excellence in investigative techniques and computer-based financial analysis. But it is clear from operations like Polar Cap that this system cannot operate without the co-operation of the financial institutions on the one hand and between law enforcement bodies on the other.

In my view the reason that there is some criticism of the system in the United States is that the application of the reporting is patchy; in those areas where there is close co-operation between financial institutions and law enforcement agencies the system works well, for example, Polar

55. Crime Amendments Bill No. 2 of 1989.
56. *Drug Money Laundering, Banks and Foreign Policy* (1989), p. 71.

Cap, and in other areas where it is not done it simply does not work. In Australia the Agency has received the very strong support of the financial industry bodies. The Agency recognises that, with very complex commercial dealings which may be involved, it does not have all of the expertise that is necessary to recognise the kind of things which might perhaps indicate that particular transactions of a series of transactions involve tax evasion or criminal activity. Some of that expertise is certainly held by financial institutions. It will be some time before the Agency staff will be able to get on top of all of these issues. The Australian Bankers Association has offered its support to the Agency in gaining an understanding of these intricate financial dealings and the Agency welcomes this assistance.

As I said, on the other hand, for this legislation to work and for money laundering prosecution to be successfully undertaken requires not only expertise on the part of law enforcement agencies but that the law enforcement agencies work together. It is interesting to note that in his report, Commissioner Fitzgerald had a section entitled "Organised Crime" and in the same section another part "Disorganised Law". In that section, Commissioner Fitzgerald said:

> Comprehensive accurate information is essential to combating crime, especially organised crime. Yet our national system of sharing and acting on intelligence about crime is hopelessly inadequate.
>
> A fragmented, inefficient or incomplete gathering network is an enormous reassurance for organised criminals. It means that essential connections will be missed, and only an incomplete and distorted picture will be gained of their activities.
>
> At it stands, Australian law enforcement agencies and government instrumentalities are fragmented and hampered by jealousies, rivalries and lack of co-operation. Information exchange, when it happens at all, is on an ad hoc basis.
>
> Our law enforcement agencies are failing to keep up with organised crime. As a result, criminal organisations are flushed with increasing profits, more adept staff and the latest equipment.[57]

It is clear from the United State experience that it is necessary for Australian law enforcement agencies to delineate their particular areas of responsibility for money laundering matters. For example, in the United States, the role of the F.B.I. is to concentrate on organised crime families, the Drug Enforcement Agency's role is to attack drugs and drug organisations, the C.I.D. of the I.R.S. has money laundering financial experts concerned with following the money, and Customs' role was, until recently, not only the traditional customs role but included some of each of all of the other organisations. That caused a problem, but it seems now to have been addressed, at least in part, by the setting up of FINCEN. There is certainly a role for all of the Australian law enforcement agencies in combating money laundering; it is simply a question of working out what their respective roles might be. For its part, the Agency will provide assistance in money laundering investigative techniques to law enforcement agencies.

57. *Report of a Commission of Inquiry Pursuant to Orders in Counsel* (Queensland, 1989), p. 168.

It has been suggested that this package of legislation, in particular C.T.R. reporting, cannot work since it is based upon a myth and ignores that fact that criminals can avoid the institutions from which C.T.R. reports are filed.[58] I simply do not agree with that. With respect, I believe that this is simply an academic observation with no real knowledge of how criminals deal with their money. It is certainly not backed up by empirical evidence. The C.T.R. reporting system is not perfect, there are certainly gaps in it; there are certainly ways of spending money on cars and real estate that are not covered by the legislation in Australia. There are systems of underground banking such as that known amongst the Chinese as "Chop Shop Banking" and in the Indian subcontinent as "Chiti Banking", "Hindi Banking" or "Hawalla Banking".

In the case of cash purchase of real estate and expensive cars, proceeds of those purchases will in the ordinary case enter the banking system, and are therefore vulnerable. Money being carried in and out of the country is subject to international currency transfer reporting. Such moneys are vulnerable to law enforcement agencies, though perhaps they are more vulnerable to other criminals. Experience in the United States shows that criminals will use physical movement of cash in and out for the country to avoid reporting obligations. Yet our United States counterparts tell us that the vast majority of money enters the banking system. The reason for that is that in the usual case there is simply no trust between criminals.

There is a myth governing the likely success of C.T.R. and it is that there is "honour amongst thieves". That myth is the reason why C.T.R. works. The experience in the United States is that when the Cash Transaction Reporting started, the crooks moved outside of the banking system by, for example, taking their money for drug purchases out in suit cases or containers. Very quickly the crooks started to rob the crooks because a person carrying a suitcase is a much easier target than a bank. The crooks then moved back into the banking system and they used some other devices to avoid reporting. They started to structure their transactions and they started to buy front business to move the money through. The response to that in the United States was to challenge the structuring arrangements under the *Bank Secrecy Act* 1970. Following a number of adverse decisions which said that customers who structure to evade the reporting requirements could not be held responsible under the *Bank Secrecy Act*, Congress passed legislation to overrule these decisions by prohibiting "structuring".[59] This approach is mirrored in the C.T.R. Act in s. 31. The anti-structuring provisions not only increase the cost to the criminals, they make the logistics of the operation very much more complicated and they expose criminals to suspect reporting. The vast majority of suspicious transaction reports in the United States are from blatant structuring, that is, when the person depositing is asked for identity and is told that there is a requirement to report all $10,000 reports to a federal agency, the depositor reduces the amount to deposits below $10,000 or splits the deposit into two or comes back again with

58. Alan Tyree, April 1990, *Journal of Banking and Finance Law* 57.
59. U.S.C. s. 5324 and C; see also Adams, below, Chapter 18.

a lower deposit. That is already the experience in Australia since the significant cash transaction reporting commenced on 1 July 1990.

As to the "Hawalla" banking systems, these types of systems only work in particular groupings, usually ethnic groupings, where for cultural reasons a trust system has developed. Without these trust systems these kinds of underground banking arrangements cannot work, and that is probably the case with most Australian criminal organisations. I cannot profess to know all the answers and to know precisely how successful this legislation will be because I do not think anybody knows enough about the way criminals deal with their money in Australia. That is necessary before action can be taken to deal with money laundering in this country. However I can say those who suggest that this legislation cannot work are not in any position to make any such judgment.

CONCLUSION

If we are able to use the United States as a model, I believe that the legislative package which targets criminals' moneys can and will work and I believe that the short experience of the Agency to date is that that will be the case. The key is getting the support of the financial community and to get law enforcement agencies to work together to deal with organised crime. Support from the financial community is already forthcoming. There is a lot of work that needs to be done to build up and maintain the relationships between the Agency, the institutions and the law enforcement community. In the case of the law enforcement community I believe that there is a need for law enforcement agencies respective roles to be clearly defined; it really calls for a team effort. At the C.T.R. Agency our machine is on, we are seeing lots of suds and I believe that things will come out very bright indeed.

4

Lawyers, Guns and Money
Economics and Ideology on the Money Trail

DAVID FRASER*

> I'm hiding in Honduras
> I'm a desperate man
> Send lawyers, guns and money
> The shit has hit the fan
>
> *Warren Zevon* **

INTRODUCTION

Police and government sources confirm the story. We are "at war"—the enemy—organised crime, their chief weapon—drugs. As President Bush sends the United States Navy off the shores of Colombia, calls are made for the government here to use the Royal Australian Navy in drug interdiction.

As the propaganda reaches a fever pitch, the "law and order" rhetoric intensifies—truth in sentencing, longer terms for convicted drug dealers etc. etc. But the enemy is not so easily defeated. Stronger, more effective measures are required successfully to combat a foe that is "organised"— cunning, strong and resourceful—most of all, resourceful. The rewards associated with drugs are enormous. Not only do drugs eat away at the very moral fibre of our society, but the enemy drug lords, "drug barons" or "narco-terrorists", make huge profits. A successful strategy in the war on drugs will require innovative new weapons and tactics. We must attack the enemy where it lives. Now, instead of bombing Berlin or Tokyo or the Ho Chi Minh trail, we must attack the "money trail"—asset seizures, forfeitures, money laundering offences—these are the saturation bombing of the war on drugs.

Of course, as is always necessary during wartime, certain sacrifices must be made for the greater good. Banking security and privacy must be sacrificed to ensure more accurate cash transaction reporting. Notions of burden of proof must be limited if assets are to be seized effectively. For some, this is an unwarranted assault on civil liberties. For others, the real culprit is organised crime. Police Minister Ted Pickering claimed:

* Faculty of Law, University of Sydney. This is a modified version of a paper first presented at the Institute of Criminology, University of Sydney, 6 June 1990. Published by permission of the author.
** "Excitable Boy" by Warren Zevon (Zevon Music). Reprinted by permission of Rondor Music (Aust.) Pty Ltd.

It's an infringement of my civil liberties to have the drug trade securing the assets they do.[1]

Mr Pickering has, probably unwittingly, given the absurd nature of his statement, stumbled upon a fundamental truth of the so-called "war on drugs". The real issue here is not a struggle for the moral fibre of society against a foreign conspiracy.[2] Nor are the major issues such legal niceties as "burden of proof", "civil liberties" or "the rights of third parties" (see below). The real nature of the war on drugs and of legislation dealing with assets seizure and forfeiture and money laundering is nothing more complex than a battle over control of the market. The struggle is not one of good against evil, but of capitalist against capitalist. In some instances, it is a conflict over the very existence of a market (for example, the "black market" in drugs). In others, it is simply an attempt to regulate activities to ensure that the market functions in a neutral and fair way (for example, use of so-called organised crime statutes against insider trading or fraud; see below, pp. 71-73).

The issues, rhetoric and ideology of the "war on organised crime" are nothing new. The use of asset forfeiture as a weapon to protect the market or the fisc is hardly without precedent. Nor, as history amply demonstrates, is the invocation of the threat of a "foreign devil" a new tool to be employed by a government or a police force which wants new and more extensive powers.

THE LESSONS OF HISTORY

> You see it in the headlines
> You hear it every day
> They say they're gonna stop it
> But it doesn't go away
>
> *Glenn Frey*[**]

The extension of the powers of the state to seize and make forfeit assets connected with the commission of crimes appears, on the surface at least, to be a return to the days of the Star Chamber, attainder and the

---

1. Quoted in Quinn, "Spoils of War: Drugs Lords' Assets to be Caught up in Legal Net", *Sunday Telegraph*, 18 March 1990, p. 139.
2. It is interesting to note the ideological/rhetorical parallels between the "war on drugs" and the "threat of international communism" after World War II. Both involve an "enemy" which is highly organised, structured in secrecy and dominated from abroad. Both are bullshit. See Bradley, "Racketeering and the Federalisation of Crime" (1984) 22 Am. Cr. L. Rev. 213 at 236 and Lynch, "R.I.C.O.: The Crime of Being a Criminal, Parts I & II" (1987) 87 Columbia L. Rev. 661 at 668. Another parallel exists on the flipside of the ideological coin. Just as the enemy must be portrayed as epitomising evil, so must the agents of law and order symbolise virtue. From the pastel-clad post-modern heroes of Miami Vice to the favourable reports of law enforcement success in the war on drugs, the ideological image machinery grinds on. See Stark, "Perry Mason meets Sonny Crockett: The History of Lawyers and the Police as Television Heroes" (1987) 42 Miami L. Rev. 229.
** "Smuggler's Blues". Reproduced by kind permission of Warner Chappell Music Australia Pty Ltd.

deodand.[3] Asset seizure and forfeiture seems contrary to the individualised and personalised utilitarianism which has characterised much of our criminal law since Mill. Moreover, the concept of offending property might well strike us as a reified abstraction which has no place in today's criminological theory or practice.

However, what the history of attainder, deodands and statutory seizure of property shows is a certain continuity in our notions of criminal law and criminal justice. As others have pointed out, asset seizure and forfeiture:

> is one of the oldest sanctions of Anglo-American law, originating with the beginning of public wrongs during the Anglo-Saxon period.[4]

Thus the deodand, the forfeiture of the instrument of crime, although perhaps sui generis, was a well-known concept of criminal law. Similarly, various statutory provisions, particularly those related to customs and navigation,[5] gave extensive rights of forfeiture to the Crown. Similar statutes were adopted, to a greater or lesser extent, in the American colonies and continued as part of the legal system of the newly-formed United States.

As Maxeiner points out, courts were reluctant to allow in personam forfeitures and sought to limit the extent of in rem forfeitures. A national emergency ideologically not dissimilar to today's war on drugs, the Civil War:

> brought about a change in the law of forfeiture. Congress abandoned pre-War constitutional limitations on forfeiture and approved the use of in rem proceedings to impose purely punitive sanctions. Shortly after the War began, it became clear that traditional treason statutes were inadequate to punish the Southern rebels; most rebels were safely behind Confederate lines, protected from treason prosecutions. Nevertheless, many Confederates owned property in the North that was subject to confiscation.[6]

After the War, federal power was invoked against other forms of organised crime. Anti-lottery legislation[7] allowed for seizures as did Prohibition era statutes.[8] Modern anti-organised crime measures can be seen, then, as a simple continuation of this trend.

While in each modern instance of asset forfeiture legislation one can find rhetoric about decaying moral fibre and fundamental values, it is quite easy to see that a fundamental purpose of forfeiture has not changed from the earliest days of attainder and deodand. That purpose is simply the augmentation of the Crown's coffers. In other words, *a*

3. See Bracton, *On the Laws and Customs of England* (Thorne trans., 1968), p. 328; Pollock and Maitland, *The History of English Law* (2nd ed., 1911), p. 474, and Finkelstein, "The Goring Ox: Some Historical Perspectives on Deodands, Forfeitures, Wrongful Death and the Western Notion of Sovereignty" (1973) 46 Temp.L.Q. 169.
4. Maxeiner, "Bane of American Forfeiture Law—Banished At Last?" (1977) 62 Cornell L. Rev. 768 at 770 (footnote omitted).
5. Ibid. at 774ff. See also Bradley, op. cit., and Lynch, op. cit.
6. Maxeiner, op. cit. at 785-786.
7. Bradley, op. cit. at 215ff.
8. Ibid. at 225ff.

fundamental motivation, if not *the* fundamental motivation, behind asset forfeiture as a part of the criminal law has been, and remains, economic. At one level, the economic rationale has been the expansion of the purse of the Crown. At another, and interacting with the first, the function of asset seizure has the happy blending of the public and the private. The assets of the Crown are increased and government regulation (customs, navigation, lotteries, drugs), effectively enforced while at the same time the private interest of the market is protected. Those who buy and sell goods subject, for example, to customs duty, are not undercut by those who would buy and sell the same goods smuggled without the additional cost of customs duties. The market is restored to, and remains at, an equilibrium. Those who would circumvent the level playing field of a properly regulated market are punished by forfeiture and deterred from future illicit economic activity. The cost of doing illegal business is dramatically increased as both capital and income are forfeited and, if the regulation is properly effective, illicit activity is made unprofitable. In a real sense, the purpose of asset forfeiture legislation has always been to ensure that "crime does not pay".

THE UNITED STATES LEGISLATION AND JUDICIAL EXPERIENCE

Others have detailed the legislative and judicial history of United States' efforts to combat organised crime through asset forfeiture legislation[9] and I will not attempt to replicate their efforts here. I wish to focus on two basic points which come from the American legislative and judicial history and which indicate quite clearly the strengths and weaknesses in the current "war on organised crime".

These two points are relatively basic. The first is that the American legislation, unlike its Australian counterparts (see below) is targeted specifically at organised crime. The second basic point is that the American legal system has from the very beginning recognised the primarily economic nature of the "war on crime".

This latter point is crucial. From the very beginning both legislators and judges made it abundantly clear that the aim of their efforts was to root out organised crime from the American economy.[10] They recognised that the most effective way of getting organised crime out of the economy was to use economic measures, that is, forfeiture. In a statement of legislative purpose in relation to the "Racketeer Influenced and Corrupt Organisations" statute (R.I.C.O.),[11] we find that it:

9. See Bradley, op. cit. and Lynch, op. cit. See also Spaulding, "Hit Them Where It Hurts: R.I.C.O. Criminal Forfeitures and White Collar Crime" (1989) 80 J. of Crim. Law & Criminology 197.
10. Indeed, Lynch argues that the original intent of the American legislation was to combat organised crime's infiltration into legitimate enterprise. Attacks on illegitimate enterprises per se (e.g. drugs) was not envisaged at the outset. Op. cit.
11. Passed as part of the *Organised Crime Control Act* 1970, the "Racketeer Influenced and Corrupt Organisations" statute (R.I.C.O.) 18 U.S.C. 1961-1968 (1986) is "one of the most controversial statutes in the federal criminal code". Ibid.

attacks the problem by providing a means of wholesale removal of organised crime from our organisations, prevention of their return and, where possible, forfeiture of their ill-gotten gains.[12]

The Senate Report is even more directly on point:

What is needed here, the committee believes, are new approaches that will deal not only with individuals, but also with the economic base through which those individuals constitute such a serious threat to the economic well-being of the Nation. In short, an attack must be made on their source of economic power itself, and the attack must take place on all available fronts.[13]

Nor did the Supreme Court attempt to shrink from these clear statements of legislative intent and purpose. In a leading case on R.I.C.O., Blackmun J. speaking for the court held:

the R.I.C.O. statute was aimed at organised crime's economic power in all its forms[14]

and he added that:

The legislative history clearly demonstrates that the R.I.C.O. statute was intended to provide new weapons of unprecedented scope for an assault upon organised crime and its economic roots.[15]

The primary rhetorical focus of United States activity against organised crime has been aimed at the heart of crime, that is, the economic gains and power which come with success.

The second element in the American scheme, closely connected to "the money trail", is indicated in the R.I.C.O. title. Its focus is collective, it aims at organisations because it is attempting to deal with organised crime and because it is attempting to deal with the economic power of organised crime which comes through profits derived from enterprises and firms (see below) which act in an "organised" or collective fashion.

This collective approach, epitomised in the title of the statute, is embodied in its substantive provisions. In its key section, R.I.C.O. attacks "a pattern of racketeering activity" which leads to an interest in "any enterprise". While each of these concepts, "pattern"[16] and "enterprise",[17] is, in its own way, complex and problematic, each clearly shifts the focus of the legal inquiry from the traditional individualised idea of crime, criminality and the criminal to a more collectivist notion of an "organisation".

In the leading case, Sedima, S.P.R.L. v. Imrex,[18] the Supreme Court clearly emphasised that the key to R.I.C.O. was this shift away from notions of an isolated act by an individual, to a new approach. Thus:

12. 116 Cong. Rec. 591 (1970).
13. S. Rep. No. 91-617, p. 79 (1969).
14. Russello v. United States 464 U.S. 16 at 25 (1983).
15. Ibid. at 26.
16. See, inter alia, Goldsmith, "R.I.C.O. and 'Pattern': The Search For 'Continuity Plus Relationship' " (1988) 73 Cornell L. Rev. 971.
17. See O'Neill, "Functions of the R.I.C.O. Enterprise Concept" (1989) 64 Notre Dame L. Rev. 646.
18. 473 U.S. 479 (1985).

the compensatable injury necessarily is the harm caused by predicate acts sufficiently related to constitute a pattern, for the essence of the violation is the commission of those acts in connection with the conduct of an enterprise.[19]

The pattern is a "factor of *continuity plus relationship*".[20] The move to an enterprise/pattern concept is not a total abandonment of traditional ideals of criminal liability. The statute aims at "systematic organised crime" but still continues to prosecute "individuals". Liability is based upon the commission of predicate crimes[21] which then are found to fit into a "pattern" involving an "enterprise". Criminality is simply enhanced by its organisational or "organised" nature.

While the pattern and enterprise requirements of R.I.C.O. share in a collectivist origin, they remain conceptually distinct, constituting independent and separate elements of R.I.C.O. offences, each of which must be proved. At the same time, the courts have given an expansive reading to each. While *Sedima* broadened "pattern", other Supreme Court cases have broadened "enterprise". In *United States v. Turkette*,[22] the court held that "enterprise":

includes any union or group of individuals associated in fact. On its face, the definition appears to include both legitimate and illegitimate enterprises within its scope; it no more excludes the criminal enterprises than it does legitimate ones.[23]

This should come as little surprise given the court's clear practice of giving an expansive reading to R.I.C.O. in order to ensure that legislative purpose is attained. In both *Turkette* and *Russello* (above) the court gave a broad reading to the statute because in each case it recognised that the intent of Congress was to attack organised crime and to attack it at its economic roots.

Some, like Professor Lynch,[24] argue that the "transaction-based model of crime", that is, the traditional ideal of an individual committing an illegal act, is essential if the purposes of the criminal sanction are to be well-served. For him, R.I.C.O.'s emphasis on "enterprise" and "pattern", in other words, collective concepts, is inimical to the function of a criminal justice system.

There are several reasons why Lynch's critique should be rejected. First, as I have already mentioned, R.I.C.O.'s focus on a collective approach is nonetheless based on the prosecution establishing the necessary "criminal" predicate act(s) and the defendant's participation therein. At this level, it is indeed based upon a "transaction model" of crime. R.I.C.O. simply expands and extends the criminal sanction to acts

19. Ibid. at 498.
20. Ibid.
21. 18 U.S.C. 1961(1) (1984).
22. 452 U.S. 576 (1981).
23. Ibid. at 580-581.
24. "R.I.C.O.: The Crime of Being A Criminal: Parts III & IV" (1987) 87 Columbia L. Rev. 920 at 932ff.

which might otherwise not be criminal. In this, it is no different from any statute which imposes a "new" criminal liability.

Secondly, as I have pointed out elsewhere,[25] the concept of the individual committing "individual" acts is a highly problematic social construct which masks the complexity of human existence. One could perhaps speculate that R.I.C.O., with its emphasis on a more "social" approach to crime, more closely reflects the complex nature of human society and interaction.

Next, while it may be true that the collectivist approach of R.I.C.O. extends beyond traditional transaction-based models, this does not mean that it is completely and totally isolated from common law principles. To take an obvious example, the common law itself has always been concerned with "criminal combinations". The law of conspiracy is an almost trite example of the law making an act illegal simply because it involves more than one person. Of course it can be objected here that conspiracy remains nonetheless attached to the transaction model and *Gerakiteys v. The Queen*[26] offers ample proof of this.

On the surface, this argument that R.I.C.O. merely extends the common law appears to founder in the conspiracy example. As Lynch points out,[27] the facts in *Turkette* extend criminal liability beyond that of a traditional conspiracy count. Turkette was charged under R.I.C.O. with participating in several arson-for-profit schemes. On the facts, there were at least four different schemes. In two, Turkette hired a third party to burn down properties, collecting a fee from the owners. In the other cases Turkette himself was the insured. Yet the court found that Turkette was involved in a "pattern of racketeering" through which he obtained an "interest in an enterprise", in this case the "enterprise" being "arson-for-profit". While there is, as Lynch points out, a degree of confusion in the court's decision concerning the distinction between the pattern and enterprise requirements, and while this case clearly involves liability greater than a *Gerakiteys* conspiracy, it is no more revolutionary or artificial than most concepts of the criminal law. Given the clear legislative intention behind R.I.C.O., the expansive reading of the court's decision is hardly surprising. Nor is there anything conceptually difficult in its reasoning. Why should not the arson-for-profit schemes be seen to constitute a pattern even though the parties change? Turkette remains the central figure in each "scheme" extracting profit for violence against property. Is this conceptually more difficult than believing that a "corporation" is different from the people who constitute or work for it? For lawyers, each involves only a little imagination and no revolutionary upheaval in the way we see the world. Legislators and judges expand (and contract?) criminal liability all the time. On this level, R.I.C.O. is no big deal.

25. See Fraser, "Still Crazy After All These Years: A Critique of Diminished Reponsibility" in Yeo (ed.), *Partial Excuses to Murder* (1991).
26. (1984) 153 C.L.R. 317.
27. Op. cit. at 704ff.

THE AUSTRALIAN EXPERIENCE

Others[28] have chronicled the still nascent Australian legislative and judicial history of the use of asset seizure and forfeiture to combat organised crime and again I will not duplicate their efforts here. Nor will I offer a detailed exegesis of the Australian or New South Wales legislation. Suffice it to say that while many objections can be raised against these statutes, all debate must take place within the traditional and normal paradigm of criminal law. Unlike the United States where R.I.C.O. is seen by legislators and judges as a tool in the "war against organised crime" and where consequently, it is structured to deal with "collective" crime, one can find little such evidence of a collective approach in Australia.

Rather, Australian legislation deals with these matters as if they were simply part of the traditional common law. For example, the Commonwealth *Proceeds of Crime Act* 1987, creates in s. 81 the offence of money laundering. Yet money laundering is defined in terms of a single transaction. Some apparent attempt at a more refined approach is made in s. 83 which creates a new offence of "organised fraud". Organised fraud means, inter alia, "acts or omissions that constitute three or more public fraud offences" which are defined to include various violations of *Crimes Act* and the *Crimes (Taxation Offences) Act* 1980, but not repeated or patterned violations of the *Proceeds of Crime Act*. Thus while R.I.C.O. focuses on "pattern" with its requirement of continuity and relation, the *Proceeds of Crime Act* focuses solely on "three or more acts", like a simple repeat offender statute. It seems quite clear that while we may be involved in a "war on organised crime", like others before us, we are fighting the new battles with weapons and tactics from the previous war.

AN EXEGESIS ON THE ECONOMICS OF ORGANISED CRIME

> It's the lure of easy money
> It's got a very strong appeal
> Perhaps you'd understand it better
> Standing in my shoes
> It's the ultimate enticement
> It's the smuggler's blues
>
> *Glenn Frey*[**]

Whether the American approach with its collectivist emphasis on "enterprise" and "pattern" will, in the long run, be more succesful than the Australian insistence on traditional transaction-based criminal law

---

28. See Fisse, "The Proceeds of Crime Act: The Rise of Money-Laundering Offences and the Fall of Principle" (1989) 13 Crim. L. J. 5; Fisse, below, Chapter 5; Temby, "The Proceeds of Crime Act: One Year's Experience" (1989) 13 Crim. L. J. 24; Aarons, "The National Crimes Commission: a focus on legislation relating to illegal 'laundering of money' and 'the paper trail' " (1982) 57 Law Inst. J. 1349.

** "Smuggler's Blues". Reproduced by kind permission of Warner Chappell Music Australia Pty Ltd.

models remains to be seen. Indeed, the first thing which must be done is to define our ideal of success. Current trends in N.S.W. Inc. would indicate that rates of incarceration are seen by some as an important bench-mark. Such a standard is, however, problematic because it ignores the reality of criminal enterprise.

Nothing could more succinctly explain the reality of criminal enterprise than the following quote, attributed by Temby to Bruce Richard "Snapper" Cornwell while doing a minimum sentence of 14 years:

I don't give a fuck what they do to me as long as we keep safe all that we have worked for. [29]

Faced with attitudes like this, incarceration is not likely to win the "war on drugs".

The real goal of asset seizure and forfeiture is to hit the crims where it hurts. Criminal forfeiture and money laundering statutes, as I stated above, are economic measures. They are intended to remove valuable assets from criminals (or criminal enterprises) in order to make crime an economically unviable occupation. Success in the war on organised crime, then, must be measured in terms of its effectiveness in achieving this goal. In other words, success here is to be measured in economic terms. Rhetoric and propaganda about moral fibre notwithstanding, the goal of asset forfeiture must be to make criminals operate at a loss, to make marginal cost exceed marginal profit, thereby putting them out of business.

Before beginning a somewhat more detailed analysis of this ideal of economic control of organised crime, it should be noted that different considerations may apply to an economic analysis of various organised crime activities. For example, some types of organised crime, such as drugs, may involve problems of cartel or monopoly, while other types of activity covered by these statutes, such as white collar fraud, may involve simpler forms of market imperfections such as increased transaction costs and information disequilibrium. Thus while the goal of asset forfeiture remains the same, its actual or even potential effectiveness may depend on any number of case-specific factors. Among these are factors as diverse as climatological concerns and consumer preference. For example, the weather for growing opium poppies in the Golden Triangle was so good that the 1989 crop was "the largest produced ever". [30] This should mean, all other factors being equal, that we will see a fall in heroin prices as the end product reaches the market. Effective law enforcement may have resulted in a sharp rise in cocaine prices in the United States and a concomitant drop in consumption of

---

29. Op. cit. at 30. Further evidence of the risk-preferring nature of the drug entrepreneurs can be found from the fact that in Malaysia, for example:

[T]ough anti-drug laws, which include mandatory death penalties, have not deterred drug traffickers from smuggling drugs or using the country as a trans-shipment point, according to the Anti-Drug Deputy Director, Mr Muhammed Said Awong.

Pillai, "Hangman fails to stop drug runners", *Weekend Australian*, 14-15 July 1990.

30. Cameron, "Warning Over New Flood of Heroin", *Sydney Morning Herald*, 11 August 1990, quoting Bill Ruzzamenti of the United States D.E.A.

that drug. At the same time, however, the market in cocaine may have shifted its geographical location to accommodate consumer trends as:

> Western Europe has replaced the United States as the biggest market for cocaine from Columbian drug cartels.[31]

It remains nonetheless a self-evident truth that criminals like all other rational wealth-maximising capitalists are in it for the money. From the paradigmatic junkie stealing a television set, to Ivan Boesky and Michael Milken, people commit crimes for purposes of personal utility—more money, more power, more drugs. This is the reality at which asset forfeiture legislation is aimed, for if the state can reduce or eliminate the profit margin of crime, crime will diminish or cease. At this very basic level, then, asset forfeiture legislation is another form of market regulation by the state.

What "organised crime" has realised, just like General Motors or B.H.P., is that the most important economic actors in the capitalist system are corporate entities or firms. As Hirshleifer puts it:

> Firms are the crucial *productive* agents of society, engaged in the conversion of resources into final goods.[32]

Just as the move to corporate identity allowed capitalism to flourish, the move to organised crime allows crime to flourish. Economies of scale and limited liability operate within a criminal organisation just as they operate for B.H.P. Entrepreneurship is rewarded and profit maximisation is the ultimate goal of both the legal and illegal enterprise. Costs are internalised and the possibility of monopolistic pricing is ever-present.

It is, I think, this prospect of monopolisation which most raises the ire of the state and which is behind the move to asset forfeiture. We are constantly assaulted with dollar figures in the hundreds of millions or even the billions when the spectre of organised crime is raised. However speculative or unscientific those figures may be, it is nonetheless an obvious experiential truth that organised crime, as epitomised by the drug trade, makes lots of money. And the reason that it makes lots of money is that, at a theoretical level at least, it functions like a monopoly or a cartel. The manufacture and distribution of a commodity, for example, cocaine, is controlled by a single entity (a firm, a "family", a "gang"), or a grouping of entities (the infamous Colombian or Medellín cartel) which can, because it is a monopoly, price in a fashion which allows enormous profits. In the case of a cartel, an agreement is entered

---

31. See Isikoff, "Cocaine Price Rise Encourages U.S.", *International Herald Tribune*, 19 July 1990; "Cocaine prices jump in the U.S.", 1 *Money Laundering Alert*, No. 10, July 1990, p. 2; *Sydney Morning Herald*, 28 August 1990.

32. Jack Hirshleifer, *Price Theory and Application* (3d ed., 1984), p. 173. Again, what I am describing here is a paradigm. Empirical research in Australia is lacking and what we *know* about "drug markets" in this country appears to be apocryphal. Some studies from the United States point to monopolisation while others (cf. Reuter et. al., *Money from Crime—A Study of the Economics of Drug Dealing in Washington D.C.* (1990) and Headley, "War in a 'Babylon': Dynamics of the Jamaican Informal Drug Economy" (1988), 15 *Social Justice* 61, point to a more dispersed market, at least at the level of street sales. A recent British study suggests that there is a competitive market in drugs and that there are at least seven types of "firms" engaged in trading activity. See Dorn and South, "Drug Markets and Law Enforcement" (1990) 30 Brit. J. Criminology 171.

into to engage in monopolistic price-fixing. In general economic theory, cartels are less stable than monopolies, because any of the parties may, if the incentive is strong enough, enter into competition by leaving the cartel, thereby dragging down profits to a market, rather than a monopolistic, rate. This scenario is less likely in a criminal cartel situation both because the other members have greater scope in available remedies to deter those who might want to leave (murder, kneecapping, kidnapping) than do cartel members involved in otherwise legal enterprises, and because of the nature of the commodity involved in the cartelisation. Because of the alleged addictive nature of cocaine or heroin, the demand for the product is likely to be highly inelastic in relation to price. In other words, the market for the product will not be adversely affected by monopolistic pricing, therefore, economic incentive to abandon the cartel may be much lower than in ordinary cartel situations.

This monopolistic pricing is highly profitable for the members of the cartel, but for the market, it is a classic example of inefficiency. Because monopoly causes lower output and higher price than a competitive situation, trade in a monopoly situation is coercive and not naturally beneficial. Therefore, the fundamental norms of free market transactions are violated and there is an overall loss of efficiency.[33] At this basic level then, organised crime is extracting exorbitant profit. The only effective means of deterring such conduct, on the rules of the market, is to engage in trust-busting economic sanctions like asset forfeiture. Moreover, it should also be noted that these profits, unless and until they are laundered (see below), are not subject to taxation. All the social costs of the "drug monopoly" are therefore, in the absence of an effective forfeiture mechanism, subsidised by the general tax market. The "externalities" are not internalised by the cartel, they are simply passed along to third parties and the monopolistic profit is further increased as real costs of the transaction are made irrelevant to the profit taker.

It should be noted, however, that not all forms of vertical integration, even to the extent of monopolisation or cartelisation, are completely inefficient in a welfare sense. The savings through integration in terms of management expertise as well as the potential employment benefits are only two examples of such welfare efficiency.[34] Thus, while it may well be argued that organised crime is an evil presence in the economy, especially if it uses monopolistic racketeering practices against legitimate, "efficient" business, or if it uses monopolistic or cartel-based practices

33. While this analysis is focused on the drug trade, the same outlook can be applied to white collar crime. If we look, for example, at insider information, it can be argued that not only does this violate fundamental norms of "the equal playing field" of the market, but it allows someone trading in such information to obtain not only "speculative" profits, but to engage in monopolistic pricing in the sale/use of that information.

34. For a more detailed analysis, see Williamson, *Markets and Hierarchies* (1975). Headley's study (op. cit.) of Jamaican "posses" points out that those organisations engage in vertical integration from importing to street dealing and: " 'This gives them a much higher income because one kilogram of cocaine they buy for $5,000 from the Colombians can earn them $120,000 in street sales', according to an official of the U.S. Bureau of Alcohol, Tobacco and Firearms (B.A.T.F.) in a July 1987 *New York Times* story". Headley, op. cit. at 64.

to prevent further competition once it gains control of legitimate businesses, it should and must be recognised that crime, organised or not, often serves a valuable economic function. At the basic level, it provides goods and services for a demand which exists in the marketplace. There is, whether the government of N.S.W. Inc. or the United States wants to recognise it or not, a market for marijuana and cocaine. Depending on the demand elasticity of different commodities, for asset forfeiture to be successful, it must recognise this fact. Crime-fighting strategy must be so efficient that there is no profit to be made in the supply to meet consumer demand. If the American experience of Prohibition is any example, the likelihood of such efficiency in a state trust-busting process is minimal.

It must also be recognised that organised crime often provides a service at a lower cost than the market or a state monopoly. The example of gambling is the classic one. Even where gambling is legalised, illegal forms of gambling continue to exist and flourish because they offer services or returns to their customers which are not met in the legal, "white" market. "Black market" gambling can offer higher returns in part at least because it is not subject (until the money is laundered) to taxation. Again, to cope with this problem, asset forfeiture can only be successful if enough money or value is seized so that marginal cost exceeds marginal revenue. There is no evidence that this is likely to be the case.

More important, however, is that, outside the problem of monopolisation or cartelisation, organised crime often brings certain attributes and skills to the market which the market values. Criminals are often non-risk averse, that is, they possess entrepreneurial verve and skill and are willing to take chances for the possibility of profit. They possess exactly the same skills and attributes that we appear to honour and cherish in an Alan Bond or a Kerry Packer except that they often put these skills to work in illegal activities. At the same time, these activities, illegal or not, create employment and provide services for which there is a demand. In some instances it might also be possible to suggest that illegal funds might well keep an otherwise inefficient, legitimate business in operation where predatory market forces (L.B.Os (leveraged buy outs) etc.) might force the break-up of the same enterprise with resultant social dislocation through unemployment and unproductive profit taking by the predators.

Similarly, because they are cash-rich, organised crime groups may be able to enter the legitimate market at times when market forces or monetary policy (for example, high interest rates, recession) might prevent other actors from doing so:

> A continuous cash-rich position suggests that members of organised criminal groups may have a competitive advantage in industries where providing capital is a means of competing.[35]

Some might argue that because of the illegal origin of such capital, steps must be taken to keep it out of the legitimate market. Such an argument, however, has little to do with efficiency criteria. The capital, whatever

---

35. Anderson, *The Business of Organised Crime: A Cosa Nostra Family* (1979) p. 115.

its source, may be put to efficient use, even if it has been originally gained through illegitimate means. There is little difference here between illicit organised crime capital or that obtained through tax avoidance schemes or inheritance. The only distinction is the licit or illicit nature of its origin. In other words, the policy makers behind asset forfeiture legislation and practice must recognise that certain decisions may well have both long and short term efficiency or welfare consequences. Again, such decisions can be justified only if their programme reaches the level of marginal profit.

Similarly, once it has entered legitimate business, organised crime may well bring its skills gained in criminal activity to the legitimate market. For example, as Anderson points out,[36] the ability accurately to assess credit risk gained in loan-sharking is a skill clearly transportable to the legitimate world of banking and insurance.

Indeed, her study points clearly to the fact that there is no per se competitive injury in the market when organised crime enters legitimate business:

> None of the major reasons for entry of members of the group into legitimate business—to acquire tax covers, establish fronts, and diversify—in itself leads to damage to competition, consumers, or taxpayers. The group's legitimate business activities are not generally predatory and cannot be characterised as an aggressive effort to achieve profits through illegal means.[37]

If organised crime brings valuable skills to the market and if it does not engage in illegal activity once it is in the market, as Anderson's study suggests, then asset forfeiture practised against interests in such activities must be justified on a broader efficiency basis. Asset forfeiture of legitimate businesses must be shown to affect adversely the marginal profit/cost ratio of the illicit activities. Again, there is no evidence that such is the case.

In order to demonstrate effectively that asset forfeiture can and does work, we need something more concrete than "hitting them where it hurts". What is required is a theoretically sound, empirically verified idea about the actual decision-making processes of members of organised crime as well as an accurate assessment of the economic value of their activity.[38] In addition to the factors of monopolisation and cartelisation mentioned above, such a model/study would also have to consider such elements as entrepreneurial skill and risk-preference which appear to characterise participants in organised crime. Also necessary to the calculus would be the impact (positive/negative) of organised crime on the economy at large—for example, employment creation, risk or venture capital availability, the demand for black market goods and

36. Ibid. at 121ff.
37. Ibid. at 140-141.
38. While the latter is probably impossible, interesting studies and theoretical models of organised crime do exist. See e.g. Anderson, op. cit.; Ehrlich, "Participation In Illegitimate Activities: A Theoretical and Empirical Investigation" in *The Economics of Crime and Law Enforcement* (McPheters and Stronge eds, 1976), p. 141; Schelling, "Economic Analysis and Organised Crime" in *An Ecomonic Analysis of Crime* (Kaplan and Kessler eds, 1976), p. 367.

services, tax and welfare consequences etc. Moreover, the other costs and benefits of organised crime, especially of criminalisation, must be carefully examined.

For example, an almost necessary consequence of criminalisation and the creation of black markets is police and government corruption. Corrupting police and government officials is simply a necessary cost of doing business for the "organised" criminal. Not only do bribes or other emoluments ensure non-enforcement of criminal sanctions (acting therefore as insurance and cost-cutting measures at the same time), but they may also serve further to enhance the monopolist's position. While criminalisation itself serves as a barrier to entry into the (black) market, selective enforcement, insured through corruption, against potential or existing competitors may result in the strengthening or creation of a monopoly. Thus, monopoly practices are enforced by both licit and illicit police practices.

At the same time, corruption of public officials may permit a non-competitive entry into a limited legitimate market (for example, licensing) or into a legal monopoly (for example, municipal contracted refuse services). Such an entrée may not merely harm competition for that particular market or monopoly, but may also harm competition within the broader market if the original contract allows a front for laundering or extortion through racketeering. At the same time, of course, money for bribes enters the economy in one form or another and may create wealth or employment. Again, the fisc may find itself deprived of income in any number of forms. Finally, the cost of policing corruption (see below) will be increased and passed along to the innocent consumer/taxpayer.

Other ideas which might be considered in such a model must take into account the actual choices of organised criminals and the factors which influence such choices.

For example, among such factors I have just mentioned, both the law itself and corruption may operate as a form of insurance for the criminals. The availability of other forms of insurance may also influence their cost/benefit analysis. Three main types of "insurance" are available: (i) real insurance against liability; (ii) the availability of legal representation to "insure" protection against forfeiture and (iii) the "insurance" of asset divestiture to avoid seizure and forfeiture. Each of these these will be examined briefly.

Even though it is likely that criminals are more risk-preferring than the population at large, it should be noted that even for those who are not risk-averse, the availability of insurance may be a relevant consideration. Moreover, American experience clearly demonstrates that R.I.C.O. forfeitures can be employed not only against the paradigmatic "criminal" but against so-called "legitimate" businessmen, for example, white collar criminals, etc. etc. In those cases, the availability of insurance may be relevant.

In the R.I.C.O. scenario, insurance is of course not relevant when considering criminal sanctions. R.I.C.O., however, permits a civil suit by a party damaged by racketeering activity and permits recovery of treble damages. A detailed analysis will not be entered into here.[39] Suffice it to say that the availability of insurance protection of R.I.C.O. treble damages depends on the future judicial characterisation of such damages. If they are compensatory, they are insured; if they are punitive, they are not. Thus, not only is the availability of insurance coverage likely to be a relevant economic consideration for asset forfeiture legislation but if civil R.I.C.O. losses are insurable, this is likely to result in increased costs of insurance for all business (and perhaps for other consumers as well) and increased costs in the use of public resources through litigation as insurers and insured fight out the limits of coverage in court.

The second factor—the availability of legal coverage—is not only likely to be an important factor in any criminal's cost/benefit analysis, but is one of the most controversial in both Australia[40] and the United States.[41] Critics of asset forfeiture often single out the problem of attorneys' fees. Under R.I.C.O. and similar Australian legislation, *all* proceeds of crime, including cash paid to attorneys, may be seized (assuming the nexus broadly defined is established to make such cash "proceeds of crime"). This deprives accused persons of representation of counsel of their choice and therefore of a fundamental right.

Response to such criticism is relatively obvious. First, it does not deprive the accused of representation, simply of "Rolls-Royce" representation. Secondly, if asset forfeiture is to be effective as an economic deterrent, no assets should be immune if they are indeed proceeds of crime. (Unless the value of the right to an attorney of choice is priced more highly in a welfare sense than the value of asset forfeiture as a weapon.)

In other words, at the level of economic analysis, the issues appear to be relatively simple. If the unavailability of "Rolls-Royce" "drug" attorneys will provide a disincentive to criminals to engage in their nefarious activities, seizure of attorneys' fees is a useful weapon. On the other hand there is clearly a social cost in interfering with the availability of qualified criminal defence attorneys. In response to this, however, one might argue that "fundamental", value-based, normative arguments in relation to the forfeitability of lawyers' fees often hide both an inherent class bias and the self-interest of the legal profession. In so far as this latter point is concerned, it is self-evident that it is in the interest of the profession to be immune from seizure and forfeiture of fees, regardless of the "fundamental values" involved. Secondly, it is true that there is little attempt from either the profession or the legislature to deal with the problem of "Rolls-Royce" attorneys in any other context. In all other cases, "you get what you pay for". Only the rich can afford "Rolls-Royce" lawyers, whether they are rich "criminals" or simply "rich". Arguments about "fundamental values" hide the real social costs of the inequalities of the legal system based on an ability-to-pay market scheme.

39. For a cogent and complete exposition of the issues, see Hellerstein and Mullins, "The Likely Insurance Treatment of Treble Damage R.I.C.O. Judgments" (1986) 42 *Business Lawyer* 121.
40. See Fisse, op. cit. (1989) 13 Crim. L. J. 5.
41. See, inter alia, Winick, "Forfeiture of Attorney's Fees Under R.I.C.O. and C.C.E. and the Right To Counsel of Choice: The Constitutional Dilemma and How to Avoid It" (1989) 43 U. Miami L. Rev. 765.

In short, we must determine whether the social and personal cost of forfeiting attorneys' fees is greater than the benefit in providing a further economic disincentive to criminals by forcing them to be even more self-insured. We must consider not only those costs mentioned already, but the cost of lawyers dropping out of criminal practice, in general, and in particular the cost of further enforcing the prosecution's power by diminishing the strength of the defence Bar.[42]

It must also be noted that entrepreneurial types may well be simply more inventive when it comes to developing self-insurance schemes. In a recent Florida case, a lawyer was convicted for taking fees from drug dealers before their drug-running trips. If the smuggling trip was successful, he would keep the $U.S.10,000, if unsuccessful, he would defend them without further charge. Although he was caught, it is not unlikely to assume that similar "legal lottery" schemes would be one possible self-insurance mechanism.[43]

In the end, however, it seems that current policy is moving towards the rationale announced by the Supreme Court of the United States in its latest decisions on the question[44] where White J. said simply:

> There is a strong governmental interest in obtaining full recovery of all forfeitable assets, an interest that overrides any Sixth Amendment interest in permitting criminals to use assets adjudged forfeitable to pay for their defence.

Again, however, it remains to be seen whether this interest analysis will reflect the actual cost/benefit analyses upon which asset forfeiture legislation must depend for practical success.

The third type of insurance which a criminal might employ to avoid forfeiture of valuable assets is a pre-trial disposal of these assets to a third party. Such transactions are not unfamiliar to taxation or bankruptcy practitioners, nor is the idea of tracing such assets in the hands of third parties. The legislative practice, however, has been to simplify the procedure to ensure that the state has assets against which it can act effectively.

Two mechanisms are used to prevent asset dissipation. The first is a pre-trial order freezing assets pending the outcome.[45] While such orders may appear harsh and in violation of the "golden thread" presumption of innocence, certain due-process provisions alleviate many of these difficulties. Given the growth of Mareva injunctions and Anton Piller orders in equity, the criminal law pre-trial freezing of assets is hardly revolutionary or without antecedents.

The second mechanism is the relation-back provision.[46] Under these provisions property is deemed forfeit at the time the criminal act occurred, not at the time of conviction. Thus, assets which have been transferred in the period between the commission of the offence and

42. There is some anecdotal evidence that this may be happening in the United States. See Fricker, "Dirty Money" A.B.A. Journal, November 1989, 60 at 64.
43. Anderson, "Illegal Legal Insurance" A.B.A. Journal, November 1989, 34.
44. *United States v. Monsanto* 109 S. Ct 2657 (1989) and *Caplin and Drysdale v. United States* 109 S. Ct 2646 (1989).
45. For a discussion, see Fisse, op. cit., and Spaulding, op. cit. at 215ff.
46. Ibid.

conviction are traceable because they actually belong to the government during this period. Indeed, recent amendments to R.I.C.O. permit the state to trace and seize other assets in place of forfeit property which has been dissipated, transferred or hidden.[47]

It is clear that such provisions potentially increase the efficiency of asset forfeiture legislation by permitting the government greater scope in the assets it may seize, by establishing a legislative nexus between the assets and the crime, thereby greatly reducing burdens and costs of proof and by removing another form of self-insurance from the criminal. At the same time, in the absence of data, we must ask again whether in practice even this greater scope and cost-reduced enforcement scheme can be effective against monopolistic pricing by organised crime. We are, as they say, "talking big bucks here".

The cost of enforcement practices is, of course, an important factor in determining the effectiveness or efficiency of asset forfeiture legislation. Not only must the government succeed in bridging the gap between the marginal profit and the marginal cost of organised crime, it must do so in a way that the cost to society (or taxpayers) does not exceed the benefit we derive from law enforcement.

One mechanism for reducing the so-called "social" cost of law enforcement is the much touted "privatisation" route. In the United States, R.I.C.O., as I have mentioned, allows a "private" civil action, with treble damages, to parties injured in their business by "organised crime" racketeering activities. Although subject to the criticism of misuse,[48] civil R.I.C.O. does appear to offer several advantages often seen as flowing from "privatisation" and from the public/private distinction in law. Thus, civil R.I.C.O. claimants operate under the less onerous civil burden of proof. Remedial provisions in civil R.I.C.O. permit, in addition to the already mentioned treble damages, divestiture orders, restrictions on activities by racketeers and dissolution or reorganisation of the infiltrated enterprise.

Thus, one can achieve the economic goal of driving out predators and restoring the market to a "level playing field" while reducing the costs of the heavy criminal law burden of proof. At the same time, the availability of treble damages may encourage litigants to act more willingly as private attorneys-general. In addition, under a contingent fee arrangement, impoverished litigants may still sue and lawyers may be more willing to undertake such actions because of the possibility of increased recovery.

The treble damages rule serves not only to compensate the victim for the loss, it also insures that some losses which might not be provable but which nevertheless were incurred, are recovered. It also punishes and deters not only directly, but indirectly as well, by making it more difficult to hide profits or assets because the treble damages rule may get at such assets anyway.

On the other hand, it may well be that again even treble damage awards do not effectively attack the profit margin. Moreover, private

47. 18 U.S.C. s. 1963 (n) (1988).
48. See Abrams, "A New Proposal For Limited Private Civil R.I.C.O." (1989) 37 U.C.L.A. L. Rev. 1.

remedies are not without their public costs. The lower standard of proof may unjustly deprive an innocent of assets. The costs of court time etc. are borne by the public, as are the costs of other trials moved down the docket by the plethora of civil R.I.C.O. cases. As usual, of course, the costs of unsuccessful contingent litigation are borne by the public, as successful litigants subsidise the unsuccessful or lawyers simply refuse to take cases which are difficult, thereby depriving litigants of recovery and allowing potential illegal profits and assets to escape detection and forfeiture.

It is the possibility that assets may escape detection and forfeiture which most concerns law enforcement. One cannot seize what one does not know exists. Thus, measures must be adopted to make hiding assets more difficult and eventually inefficient. Thus do we have Cash Transaction Reporting and anti-money laundering legislation.

Money laundering is quite simply the process through which "dirty" money (proceeds of crime), is washed through "clean" or legitimate sources and enterprises so that the "bad guys" may more safely enjoy their ill-gotten gains.[49] Money laundering is important in the economics of organised crime because it is here that the assets of criminals come close to the surface. Criminals must launder to enjoy the proceeds, the state must stop laundering because once "dirty" money becomes "clean" it is practically beyond their grasp, except as legitimate money, subject to the same rules as everyone else's money.

Again, to determine whether legislative and police efforts are successful, we must determine whether they effect the profit/cost margin to such an extent that "crime does not pay" at a cost that does not burden society. In other words, it must be both internally and externally efficient. And again, the evidence is either not there or what evidence there is indicates that, so far, the state has failed in its saturation bombing of the money trail.

One of the real difficulties with any analysis of money laundering is that we really cannot know what sums are involved. Evidence is either journalistic and anecdotal or partial at best. Thus, recent journalistic reports state that "as much as $600 million in ransom proceeds of organised crime (in Italy) had been laundered in Australia".[50] Another story, in the same newspaper tells us:

> After 15 years, there's still no evidence of Mafia ransom laundering.[51]

Aarons reports that:

> Figures provided by Mr Justice Williams in the Report of the Australian Royal Commission of Inquiry into Drugs indicate that as much as $A16 million leaves Australia each year to buy heroin and when subsequently, the proceeds of such supply leave the country to be "laundered", the amount increases to $A100 million.[52]

49. It should be noted that at this level at least, this is the one area where the fisc benefits from proceeds of crime. As money is "cleaned", it can be reported as income.
50. Mike Seccombe, "Inquiry Ordered into claims of Mafia money link", *Sydney Morning Herald*, 5 April 1990.
51. Evan Whitton, *Sydney Morning Herald*, 9 April 1990.
52. Op. cit. (footnote omitted).

In two cases cited by the President's Commission on Organised Crime, one group laundered \$U.S.25 million in under two years and in a similar period another group laundered \$U.S.94 million.[53]

Although we have no idea of how much money is involved in money laundering, we can say with some certainty that there is a lot of money to be made. And because there is so much money to be made, there is a great incentive to be involved in such activities. The government anti-money laundering scheme must therefore provide a sufficient and efficient disincentive. As has been said, there is little evidence to support a government claim to such effectiveness. Figures from 1981 in the United States indicate that at that time, government efforts were highly ineffective and inefficient. Karchner states:

> one concludes that \$0.0062 out of every illegally earned dollar from narcotics traffic is subject to the initiation of some type of government removal action. This figure loses further significance when one looks at the outcome of various removal actions: less than half the amounts involved in seizure and forfeiture actions were actually surrendered to the government, and no more than two per cent of I.R.S. jeopardy and termination assessments (which totalled \$81.3 million in 1981) ended up being collected. In light of these statistics, the value of asset removal strategies is highly questionable.[54]

Even assuming that, with increased resources, better focus and legislative intervention, the forces of law and order have significantly lifted their game, we must also assume that entrepreneurial criminals have reacted in kind with practices such as smurfing[55] and more sophisticated international banking and business practices.

Also, it should be noted that it is possible that partial government success in this field might simply exacerbate the problem by raising "criminal" profit. As has been argued above, criminalisation and law enforcement practices often operate as a barrier to entry or to eliminate competition so that, in combination, they may well result in monopoly or cartel situations. If money laundering legislation operates against only some criminals, that is, those whose activities are detected, it might simply decrease competition and increase profits, thereby increasing the amount of money being laundered.

Furthermore, as I also argued above, "clean" money enters the fisc and the legitimate economy, often providing economic benefit through growth, employment and increased efficiency. Again Karchner succinctly summarises the situation:

> Overall it could be argued that society stands to suffer relatively less harm from the investment of racketeering proceeds in sectors where

---

53. *The Cash Connection: Organised Crime, Financial Institutions and Money Laundering* (1984), p. viii. The first case involved the infamous "Pizza Connection", the second the Great American Bank.
54. Karchner, "Money Laundering and the Organised Underworld" in *The Politics and Economics of Organised Crime* (Alexander and Caiden eds, 1985), pp. 39-40.
55. Welling, below, Chapter 11; and Popham and Probus, "Structural Transactions in Money Laundering: Dealing with Tax Evaders, Smurfs, and Other Enemies of the People" (1988) 14 Am. J. Crim. L. 83.

financial transactions are expected to conform to certain basic standards that govern the uses which those assets can be put consequently [sic.] criminals whose laundered funds come to reside in banking, real estate, and securities investment must sacrifice a degree of discretion to behave illegally with respect to those investments in order that they might preserve the illusion of propriety, which, after all, is largely responsible for laundering activity in the first place.[56]

In summary, there is no evidence that anti-money laundering legislation is effective in reducing the profit/cost margin of crime. While activities like smurfing might involve additional cost to the criminal, it is not likely that these costs approach the margin. Indeed, there is some evidence to support the argument that some social benefit might arise from the insertion of laundered funds into the economy. Money laundering-related legislation does not appear, in the absence of evidence to the contrary, to be externally efficient.

Is it internally efficient, that is, what are the actual costs of enforcement? Again there is little evidence here. While there are occasional announcements of the government's intention to dedicate funds to eradicate drugs or stop money laundering, there is no comprehensive analysis of all the costs associated with such programmes. Police and civilian staff must be trained in specialised investigative techniques. Expert computer applications must be developed and people trained in their use and application. International co-operation must be obtained and maintained and prosecutions must be successfully launched. Assets must be tracked down and seized. These are all obvious, but so far, undocumented and unanalysed data.

Moreover, the actual offence of money laundering and associated offences related to Cash Transaction Reporting apply primarily to banking and financial institutions. These institutions often have the burden of reporting potential violations of statutory provisions and face severe penalties for non-compliance. However, compliance itself may be costly and complex. Changes in corporate culture and corporate management techniques are often required.[57] The responsibility for spotting suspicious transactions is placed most immediately on often under-paid, under-trained clerks and tellers. Corporate compliance calls for masses of paperwork and/or complex computer operations, all of which are costs imposed on a private party who in all likelihood, will simply pass them on to its customers.

It is little wonder, then, that:

> The American Bankers Association has urged the Treasury Department to assume most of the responsibility for policing large scale money laundering activities, and not to expect banks to uncover suspicious transactions in their international funds transfer operations.

> . . .

56. Op. cit. at 43-44.
57. See e.g. *United States v. Bank of New England* 821 F. 2d 814 (5th Cir. 1987).

The banking trade group expressed concern that compliance with anti-laundering regulations would disrupt service to companies and institutions that require rapid processing of large-dollar payments.[58]

The banking establishment's clear objection to its watchdog role is premised on business (economic) principles and on the public/private distinction. The role of law enforcement and crime detection is, for the bankers, a public one and the costs should not be imposed upon private institutions like banks, nor should such regulation operate in such a way as to infringe on this commercial/customer service relationship.

On the other hand, it appears unlikely that banks will be relieved of responsibility, especially since many cases indicate the banks' willing participation in laundering.[59] Given this reality, it may well be that some banks may actually profit from their role in Cash Transaction Reporting. At the very least, banks will avoid potential losses due to adverse publicity which arises if they are seen to be "soft on drugs". They may also benefit from positive publicity if they are seen to participate, or promote themselves as participating, in "the war on drugs". Moreover, there exists the possibility that certain industry leaders might well market (as is happening in the United States) their expertise in compliance systems and management training to other banks and financial institutions. Thus, while money laundering may not prove to be successful against "organised crime", it may well serve as yet another money-maker for the banks, and, after all, what's good for the banks is good for us all. In the banking industry's objection to bearing the administrative and financial burdens of monitoring money laundering, we can see a complaint which is often raised by critics of asset forfeiture legislation—the imposition of burdens on innocent third parties. While many such objections might appear to be justified given the sometimes extravagant nature of recent legislative language,[60] they founder in both theory and practice. For example, American third party seizures are governed by stringent due-process standards which clearly protect bona fide purchasers.[61] In both theory and practice, then, the innocent third party is protected.

Particular third parties, that is, family members, are singled out as potentially innocent victims.[62] For the objectors, this is particularly nefarious and smacks of ancient and outdated ideas of the loss of rights of inheritance following attainder. But current legislation does not aim at "inheritance" as a legal category. Rather it aims at "proceeds of crime". At this level, it is hardly surprising that government might target assets in the hands of family members since this is an obvious choice for someone who might wish to transfer assets to avoid liability. In addition, it should be pointed out that while defining family members as "innocent" third parties may well be a technically correct legal categorisation, it is a somewhat disingenuous treatment of reality. Bobbie

58. "Bankers Want Smaller Role In Drug Probes", *American Banker*, 4 January 1990, p. 3. See also Intriago, "Money Laundering: New Penalties, Risks, Burdens for Bankers", *The Bankers Magazine*, March/April 1990, p. 50.
59. See e.g. *United States v. Ponce Federal Bank* 883 F. 2d 1 (1st Cir. 1989).
60. See e.g. Fisse, op. cit.
61. See Spaulding, op. cit. at 284.
62. See Fisse, op. cit.

and Susie only go to the private school and drive a Porsche, if Daddy is a racketeer, *because* Daddy is a racketeer. In a very direct and real way, all the material benefits of family life they enjoy are a result of organised crime. To attack the family, in this way, if the family is a valuable asset to the criminal, may have a definite deterrent effect. Finally, it is always the case in the criminal justice system that innocent third parties are affected, especially members of the criminal's family. If the objection is valid in relation to asset forfeiture, it is equally valid for incarceration.

Finally, opponents of asset forfeiture legislation as it now exists argue that forfeiture should somehow be limited to profits, usually net profits, rather than proceeds because to attack proceeds may constitute a form of double jeopardy or disproportionate punishment.[63] While the Australian experience is still in an embryonic form and offers little, if any, guidance on this question, American experience points to the problematic nature of the profits versus proceeds debate.

Congress, in passing R.I.C.O., specifically adopted the term "proceeds" rather than "profits", in part at least, "to alleviate the unreasonable burden on the government of proving net profits".[64] Despite this, the issue of exactly what "costs of doing business", if any, should be taken into account in determining liability for forfeiture remains hotly contested.

In *United States v. Lizza Industries*,[65] the defendant argued that the trial judge erred in calculating seizures under R.I.C.O. on a gross profits basis. The defendant was convicted of participating in a bid-rigging conspiracy for public road building contracts. The trial judge:

> calculated the forfeiture by deducting from the money received on the illegal contracts *only* the direct costs incurred in performing those contracts.[66]

The court points out, correctly I think, that:

> R.I.C.O.'s object is to prevent the practice of racketeering, not to make the punishment so slight that the economic risk of being caught is worth the potential gain. Using net profits as the measure for forfeiture could tip such business decisions in favour of illegal conduct.[67]

The preventive/deterrent nature of forfeiture under R.I.C.O. virtually compels this result if this role as an economic sanction is to make any real impact. Marginal profit is more likely to be attacked under the gross profit approach. In addition, prosecution costs are lessened because net profits are more difficult to prove than gross profits, especially when:

> Often proof of overhead expenses and the like is subject to bookkeeping conjecture and is therefore speculative.[68]

63. Ibid.
64. Spaulding, op. cit. at 260.
65. 757 F. 2d 492 (2nd Cir. 1985) cert. denied, 475 U.S. 1082 (1986).
66. Ibid. at 475. The government did not appeal this direct cost deduction although logically it would appear inconsistent with the financial disincentive function of R.I.C.O. to permit even this deduction.
67. Ibid. at 498-499.
68. Ibid. at 491.

The net profit approach would simply put the amount of seizure within the control of the avoidance-wise "criminal", hardly a deterrent. In addition, as Spaulding points out,[69] there is some confusion in the legal test for forfeiture because of the varying nature of activities caught under R.I.C.O. *Lizza Industries* involved white collar crime where deductible expenses were presumably incurred in the execution of an otherwise legitimate contractual obligation. In drug cases, on the other hand, the serious question remains as to whether expenses like the purchase price of heroin, aeroplane fuel used in smuggling, laboratories etc. should be deductible. Of course, this problem arises only if the direct expenses deduction is the proper approach. One could argue, persuasively I think, that *no* deduction for expenses should be permitted so that, consistent with the disincentive function of R.I.C.O., the defendant must eat her or his loss, thereby, in good market fashion, being forced to calculate the cost/benefit ratio on the basis of fully internalised costs.

TOWARDS A JURISPRUDENCE OF ORGANISED CRIME

> It's a losin' proposition
> But one you can't refuse
> It's the politics of contraband
> It's the smuggler's blues
>
> *Glenn Frey*[**]

A fundamental conceptual and practical difficulty which surrounds any attempt to analyse asset forfeiture legislation is to define, in any meaningful way, the target. While rhetorical invocations about racketeers and organised crime are numerous, little, if any, agreement about what these terms mean can be found. While our popular culture is full of Brandoesque images of "The Family" or the "The Mob" or "La Cosa Nostra", there is little or no evidence[70] to indicate that such organisations play a major role in crime. Nor is there any evidence that Italians or Colombians are more prone to organised criminal activity than W.A.S.Ps. In 1977, the Comptroller-General of the United States claimed:

> There is no agreement on what organised crime is and, consequently, on precisely whom or what the government is fighting.[71]

But the difficulty of defining organised crime and the ubiquitous and offensive stereotypes of popular culture are not merely semantic or symbolic difficulties. They actually affect in a serious way the manner in which R.I.C.O. works in practice. The recent decision of the United

69. Op. cit. at 264.
** "Smuggler's Blues". Reproduced by kind permission of Warner Chappell Music Australia Pty Ltd.
70. For a detailed analysis, see Mack and Kerner, *The Crime Industry* (1975).
71. *Report to the Congress: War On Organised Crime Faltering—Federal Strike Forces Not Getting the Job Done.*

States Supreme Court in *H.J. Inc. v. Northwestern Bell Telephone Co.*[72] epitomises this tension. At issue in this case was the definition of "pattern" and the holding by the appellate court[73] that a pattern must involve multiple schemes. Behind this somewhat technical argument was an attempt by white collar institutions and pressure groups:

> to resurrect previously rejected doctrine limiting R.I.C.O. to traditional organised crime. Various *amici* representing white collar interests have filed briefs arguing that pattern must be interpreted in light of a supposed congressional intent to limit R.I.C.O. to organised crime.[74]

The court rejected these propositions in no uncertain terms.

The ideological basis of such a position is of crucial importance in defining not only organised crime but the function and purpose of asset forfeiture legislation. If white collar crime is excluded from the concept of organised crime, not only will we perpetuate racist notions that only Italians or Colombians participate in organised criminal activity, but our conception of criminal justice will be unduly narrowed.

The idea that white collar crime is not really crime is not a new one. It is however a wrong-headed and dangerous one. White collar crime is enormously burdensome to society as a whole and in many cases more dangerous to our collective well-being and moral fibre than a few pounds of marijuana or an S.P. betting operation. To adopt the "Godfather" definition of organised crime is not only based on biased stereotypes, but it allows the major criminals who engage in activities in concert to escape with their ill-gotten gains.

If R.I.C.O. and similar asset forfeiture and related provisions are to be effective in their primary aim, that is, to get to the economic roots of organised crime, then clearly an expansive idea of the concept is required. It seems quite clear that the greatest amount of anti-competitive, anti-market behaviour comes not from black market activities (which after all, are market activities) but from crimes like organised fraud, insider trading and stock manipulation, which distort and destroy the market. If one values "the market" and its ideals, one must support an expansive effort to eradicate anti-competitive

---

72. 57 U.S.L.W. 4951 (1989). Before I had heard of this case I developed, along with Cary Lederman J.D. and Michael Sobel J.D., a similar theory. According to this theory, the collective versus the individual approach to economic crime can be seen in terms of religion. The collective approach is a Catholic one, the individual, a Protestant one. On the jurisprudential origins of this idea, see Fraser, "Truth and Hierarchy: Will the Circle Be Unbroken?" (1985) 33 Buffalo L. Rev. 727 at 757ff. R.I.C.O.'s collective approach was adopted and implemented because it targeted Catholic groups (Italians, Colombians). It became problematic when it sought to invoke a Catholic approach against traditional Protestant capitalists (W.A.S.P. stock brokers, investment bankers etc.). See Weber, *The Protestant Ethnic and the Spirit of Capitalism* (1958). I call this the "Stella Blue" theory of R.I.C.O., after its place of origin, Stella Pastry in San Francisco and also after the Grateful Dead song of the same name. In its own way, it makes as much sense as any other theory of organised crime.
73. 829 F. 2d 648 (8th Cir. 1987).
74. Goldsmith, op. cit. at 687.

combinations. If this is, as I have suggested, the motivating force behind asset forfeiture legislation, then we must adopt the R.I.C.O. approach that, as Professor Lynch (somewhat disapprovingly) puts it:

Organised crime is as organised crime does.[75]

ON THE SUCCESS OR FAILURE OF ASSET FORFEITURE

The success or failure of asset seizure and forfeiture, on its own terms, depends on very complex efficiency analyses based in a mass of detail about profits, losses, costs, benefits, risk-preference, risk-aversion, insurance etc.

On these terms, it is perhaps impossible to offer a scientific analysis of the current success/failure status of R.I.C.O. and Australian statutes. On the available evidence however, it is quite feasible to speculate that, given the enormous profits to be made and the incentive to entrepreneurial skills and monopolisation or cartelisation within "black" or illegal "white" markets, and given the enormous costs of detection, prosecution and forfeiture, it is most unlikely that *any* asset forfeiture programme will put an end to the profitability of any market.[76]

Indeed, it would appear that the only "success" for which anyone can hope in relation to asset forfeiture is its failure. From this:

a fundamental bureaucratic principle emerges: *failure is success.*[77]

In other words, as the evil of the exorbitant profits made by organised crime emerges (an evil so great that in the opinion of our Police Minister, above, our civil liberties are threatened by its very existence), the need to combat it emerges. As the nature of the evil grows, stronger measures are required. Yet these measures, and the police and enforcement agencies which must implement them, depend for their very existence on the continuing evil. Thus the all too familiar scenario: "we are making headway, here are our statistics to prove it. We could make much more headway with more ————— (money, computers, personnel—you fill in the blank)." Organised crime and the police have a symbiotic relationship not only through the exchange mechanism of corruption, but because at a basic ideological level, they ensure each other's existence.

Those who believe that organised crime is an evil will continue to try to root it out. Those who believe that it is primarily an economic evil will continue to try to root it out through asset forfeiture so that the forces of the free market may continue to rule. Those of us who believe that the "free market" is itself a form of organised crime can only continue to shake our heads in disbelief as mere intra-capitalist struggles are portrayed in terms of a battle for the heart and soul of our moral fibre.

75. Lynch, op. cit. at 687.
76. On these difficulties in the corruption market, see Findlay, "Institutional Reponses to Corruption: Some Critical Reflections on the I.C.A.C." (1988) 12 Crim. L. J. 271 at 280 and sources.
77. Bradley, op. cit. at 215.

5

Confiscation of Proceeds of Crime
Funny Money, Serious Legislation

BRENT FISSE[1]

INTRODUCTION: THE INSIDIOUS PURSUIT OF CRIME?

The *Proceeds of Crime Act* 1987 (Cth) (P.O.C. Act) and similar legislation at the State level provide a new regime for controlling crime.[2] The distinctive method of control under this regime is to attack the money trail by confiscating the proceeds of crime, usually by proceedings in personam. By confiscating the proceeds of serious offences it is hoped that organised crime, especially organised drug-related crime, will be dealt a crippling blow. As one commentator has observed:[3]

> Incarcerating ringleaders of large scale narcotics operations while leaving intact their illegally obtained empires allows illicit enterprises to continue in operation.[4] Criminal forfeiture affords law enforcement officials the opportunity to attack drug traffickers

1. Professor of Law, University of Sydney. Paper presented at 26th Australian Legal Convention, Sydney, August 1989. Thanks are due to Graeme Coss, Matthew Goode, Arie Freiberg, Lee Burns and Grant Wardlaw for assistance with research material. I am also indebted to a number of colleagues for various suggestions. As usual, however, attainder is confined to the author.
2. See generally Scott, "The Customs Act/The Proceeds of Crime Act 1987" in *Confiscation of Assets* (College of Law, Continuing Legal Education, 1988); McClean, "Seizing the Proceeds of Crime: The State of the Art" (1989) 38 Internat. & Comp. L. Q. 334; Goode, "Confiscation of Criminal Profits: Tangles in the Net" (1986) 24(6) Law Soc. J. 36; Goode, "The Confiscation of Criminal Profits" (1986) 67 *Proceedings of the Institute of Criminology, University of Sydney* 35; Temby, "The Proceeds of Crime Act: One Year's Experience" (1989) 13 Crim. L. J. 24; Temby, "Taking Assets off Criminals—Attainder in Australia Today?" (Paper 14, University of Western Australia Law Summer School, 1988); Temby, "The Pursuit of Insidious Crime" (1987) 61 A.L.J. 510; Australia, Director of Public Prosecutions, *Civil Remedies Report 1985-1987*; McKerlie, "The Crimes (Confiscation of Profits) Act 1986" [1989] L. Soc. Bull. (S.A.) (March) 37; Aarons, "The National Crimes Commission: A Focus on Legislation Relating to Illegal 'Laundering of Money' and the 'Paper Trail' " (1983) 57 L. Inst. J. 1349. The main etiological factors have been tax fraud and drug-related crime. See further Freiberg, "Ripples from the Bottom of the Harbour: Some Social Ramifications of Taxation Fraud" (1988) 11 Crim. L. J. 136.
3. Pianin, "Criminal Forfeiture: Attacking the Economic Dimension of Organised Narcotics Trafficking" (1982) 32 Am. U. L. Rev. 227 at 254-255.
4. See also Temby, "Taking Assets off Criminals—Attainder in Australia Today?" (Paper 14, University of Western Australia Law Summer School, 1988), pp. 5-6 (quoting reaction of "Snapper" Cornwell to lengthy jail sentence: "I don't give a fuck what they do to me as long as we keep safe all that we have worked for"); *Caplin and Drysdale, Chartered v. United States* (1989) U.S. Lexis 3124; 57 U.S.L.W. 4836 ("[t]he image of convicted drug dealers returning home from their prison terms to all the comforts their criminal activity can buy is one Congress could not abide").

where they are most vulnerable—in their pocketbooks. Incarcerated individuals can be replaced, but without financial support the well-insulated criminal empire cannot continue as a viable enterprise. In addition, seizure and forfeiture statutes that strike at the economic base of organised crime have the potential to provide funding for further narcotics investigations. Through forfeiture, law enforcement may produce large amounts of revenue . . . The concept of having multi-million dollar drug rings pay for criminal investigations, convictions, and incarcerations through criminal forfeiture is of significant import.

Although the policy of cracking down on the money trail of crime has much appeal, the legislative implementation of that policy in Australian jurisdictions, as elsewhere, is not free from difficulty or controversy.[5] There are a number of major concerns:[6]

- First, the forfeiture orders and pecuniary penalty orders that can be made are not limited to the amount of unjust enrichment flowing from offences.

- Secondly, the maximum amount of the forfeiture or pecuniary penalty that may be ordered is not governed by the traditional principle that punishment should be proportionate to the offence.

- Thirdly, the use of forfeiture and pecuniary penalties in order to incapacitate offenders is difficult to reconcile with the utilitarian principle of least drastic means.

- Fourthly, criminal liability is a precondition of confiscation but traditional principles of criminal liability have been compromised partly in order to facilitate the imposition of forfeiture orders and pecuniary penalties.

- Fifthly, access to legal assistance in defending charges against a range of serious offences is vulnerable on several fronts, including the risk of forfeiture of fees paid for defending clients.

- Finally, confiscation of the proceeds of crime can unduly penalise relatives and other third parties.

The purpose of this chapter is to review these concerns, which relate more to matters of principle and policy than to distinctions flowing from the in personam or in rem nature of proceedings under the legislation.

5. See generally Hodgson, *Profits of Crime and their Recovery* (1984); Levi, *Regulating Fraud* (1987), pp. 334-338; McClean, "Seizing the Proceeds of Crime: The State of the Art" (1989) 38 Internat. & Comp. L. Q. 334; Nicol, "Confiscation of the Profits of Crime" (1988) 52 J. Crim. L. 75; Lynch, "R.I.C.O.: The Crime of Being a Criminal" (1987) 87 Columbia L. Rev. 661, 920; Goode, "The Confiscation of Criminal Profits" (1986) 67 *Proceedings of the Institute of Criminology, University of Sydney* 35.
6. This is hardly an exhaustive list. Consider also: (i) adequacy of procedure at freezing order stage; cf. Note, "Due Process in Preliminary Proceedings under R.I.C.O. and C.C.E." (1983) 83 Columbia L. Rev. 2068; (ii) inversion of burden of proof re issue of benefit obtained from offences; see Nicol, "Confiscation of the Profits of Crime" (1988) 52 J. Crim L. 75; Cameron, "Making the Offender Squirm" [1982] N.Z.L.J. 176; (iii) difficulty of achieving consistency in sentencing given disparate range of orders available; see Hodgson, *Profits of Crime and Their Recovery* (1984) Ch. 14; Freiberg, "Social Security Prosecutions and Overpayment Recovery" (1989) 22 A.N.Z.J. Crim. 213.

Terminology: "D" stands for defendant; "P" for prosecution; and "confiscation" for deprivations of property, whether by way of forfeiture order, pecuniary penalty, or remedial exaction.

THE NEW LEGISLATIVE REGIME OF CONFISCATION

Several forms of crime-based confiscation existed at common law.[7] The prime weapon was attainder,[8] a mechanism whereby a capital felon lost the use of his land for a year and a day and he and his heirs lost their rights of inheritance and title. Attainder and other common law forms of confiscation were eventually abolished by statute,[9] mainly by reason of the stark injustice they could and did occasion defendants and their relatives. Statutory provisions for confiscation of contraband and instruments of crime subsequently proliferated, especially under customs legislation.[10] More recently, statutory confiscation has been deployed as a weapon against drug trafficking and organised crime, the focus being not so much on contraband items or dangerous instruments of crime as on tainted property and proceeds of crime. The modern focus on tainted property and proceeds of crime began with the "R.I.C.O." and "C.C.E."[11] legislation in the United States[12] and has since been reflected in legislation in the United Kingdom and Australia. In Australia, the position is governed by Commonwealth legislation (primarily by the *Proceeds of Crime Act* 1987),[13] and by legislation at the State and Territorial level (for example, the *Confiscation of Proceeds*

7. See generally Blackstone, *Commentaries* Vol. IV, pp. 374-389; Chitty, *A Practical Treatise on the Criminal Law* Vol. 2, Ch. 17; West, *A Discourse Concerning Treasons* (1717); Yorke, *Some Considerations on the Law of Forfeiture for High Treasons* (1745); *R. v. Cuthbertson* [1981] A.C. 470 at 472-476; Note, "Bane of American Forfeiture Law—Banished at Last?" (1977) 62 Cornell L. Rev. 768.
8. See further *Dugan v. Mirror Newspapers Ltd* (1978) 142 C.L.R. 583; Temby, "Taking Assets off Criminals—Attainder in Australia Today?" (Paper 14, University of Western Australia Law Summer School, 1988).
9. *Forfeiture Act* 1870 (U.K.); *Forfeitures for Treason and Felony Abolition Act* 1878 (Vic.); *Criminal Law Amendment Act* 1883 (N.S.W.); *Felons (Civil Proceedings) Act* 1981 (N.S.W.); *Treason and Felony Forfeiture Act* 1874 (S.A.); *Criminal Law Consolidation Act* 1935 (S.A.), s. 329. See further *Dugan v. Mirror Newspapers Ltd* (1978) 142 C.L.R. 583; *Prus-Grzybowski v. Everingham* (1983) 67 F.L.R. 132; *Burns Philp Trustee Co. Ltd v. Viney* [1981] 2 N.S.W.L.R. 216; *R. v. Burns* [1975] V.R. 241 at 248.
10. See e.g. *Customs Act* (Cth), ss 228-229. As to the historical development, see Harper, *The English Navigation Laws* (1939). There is a miscellany of statutory provisions authorising the forfeiture of contraband items or instruments of crime; see further Fox and Freiberg, *Sentencing* (1985), Ch. 6.
11. *Racketeer Influenced and Corrupt Organisation Act* 1970; *Continuing Criminal Enterprise Act* 1970.
12. See further Troland, *Asset Forfeiture: Law, Practice and Policy*; Taylor, "Forfeiture under 18 U.S.C. 1963—R.I.C.O.'s Most Powerful Weapon" (1980) 17 Am. Crim. L. Rev. 379; Tarlow, "R.I.C.O. Revisited" (1983) 17 Georgia L. Rev. 291; Lynch, "R.I.C.O.: The Crime of Being a Criminal" (1987) 87 Columbia L. Rev. 661, 920; Pianin, "Criminal Forfeiture: Attacking the Economic Dimension of Organised Narcotics Trafficking" (1982) 32 Am. U. L. Rev. 227.
13. For a useful review, see especially Scott, "The Customs Act/The Proceeds of Crime Act 1987" in *Confiscation of Assets* (College of Law, Continuing Legal Education, 1988). Cf. *Criminal Justice Act* 1988 (U.K.), Pt IV; *Drug Trafficking Offences Act* 1986 (U.K.).

of Crime Act 1989 (N.S.W.) (C.O.P.C. Act).[14] The elementary features of these intricate Acts are as follows.

Proceeds of Crime Act 1987 (Cth)

The P.O.C. Act provides for discretionary forfeiture and/or pecuniary penalties where D has been convicted of an indictable offence.[15] Provision is also made in some circumstances for automatic forfeiture of property subject to a restraining order.[16]

"Tainted property" is subject to forfeiture where a forfeiture order is made after D has been convicted of a relevant offence. "Tainted property" is defined in s. 4(1) as property used in, or in connection with, the commission of the offence, or proceeds directly or indirectly derived from the offence.[17] "Property" is defined as real or personal property of every description (whether tangible or intangible (thus, bank accounts are covered) and wherever situated), and any interest in relation to such property.[18] A court has discretion as to whether a forfeiture order should be made, and in exercising that discretion may take into account such factors as hardship,[19] the use to which the property is ordinarily put or is intended,[20] and the gravity of the relevant offence.[21]

Pecuniary penalties may be imposed where D has been convicted of an indictable offence.[22] D may be ordered to pay a penalty equal to the value of the benefit to D resulting from the commission of the offence. Penalties are assessed according to s. 27 which details a number of guides for making assessments.[23] In the case of "serious offences" all of D's property at the time the application for a pecuniary penalty order is made, and all property since the earliest relevant offence (or within the previous five years if the earliest offence occurred more than five years previously) is presumed to be proceeds of crime.[24]

14. See also *Crimes (Confiscation of Profits) Act* 1986 (S.A.); *Crimes (Confiscation of Profits) Act* 1986 (Vic.); *Crimes (Confiscation of Profits) Act* 1989 (Qld); *Crimes (Confiscation of Profits) Act* 1988 (W.A.); *Crimes (Forfeiture of Proceeds) Act* 1988 (N.T.).
15. P.O.C. Act, ss 19, 26.
16. P.O.C. Act, s. 30.
17. The nexus between offence and property forfeited is a perennial issue in forfeiture legislation: see e.g. *R. v. Hadad* (1989) 16 N.S.W.L.R. 476; 42 A. Crim. R. 304; *R. v. Price* (unreported, Vic. C.C.A., No. 26/87); *R. v. Everall* (1987) 30 A. Crim. R. 207; *R. v. Ward* (1987) 33 A. Crim. R. 60; *Convery v. Ziino* (1985) 9 F.C.R. 544; *De Courtenay v. The Queen* (1984) 15 A. Crim. R. 263; *Forbes v. Traders' Finance Corp Ltd* (1971) 126 C.L.R. 429; *Scott v. James Patrick & Co. Pty Ltd* (1968) 42 A.L.J.R. 38.
18. Cf. *Kirk v. Commissioner of Australian Federal Police* (1988) 81 A.L.R. 321 (re *Customs Act* 1901 (Cth), s. 243E; there is no beneficial interest in fees paid to a solicitor in advance, but a possessory lien to secure payment to extent of work performed); *D.P.P. v. Larsson* (1989) 18 N.S.W.L.R. 499; 40 A. Crim. R. 313 (re *Crimes (Confiscation of Profits) Act* 1985 (N.S.W.) (C.(C.P.) Act 1985 (N.S.W.))); D, as object of discretionary trust, had no interest in property).
19. P.O.C. Act, s. 19(3).
20. P.O.C. Act, s. 19(3).
21. P.O.C. Act, s. 19(4).
22. P.O.C. Act, s. 26.
23. *Customs Act* 1901 (Cth), s. 243C.
24. P.O.C. Act, s. 27(6).

Where D has been convicted of a "serious offence", and a restraining order remains in force in relation to D's property six months after that conviction, the property is automatically forfeited.[25] "Serious offence" means a "serious narcotics offence" as defined (that is, an offence involving a trafficable quantity of drugs), organised fraud, or money laundering in relation to the proceeds of a serious narcotics offence or organised fraud.[26]

Restraining orders may be made in relation to the property of D where D has been convicted of an indictable offence, or has been or is about to be convicted of such an offence.[27] Detailed provision is made for ancillary orders, variation and revocation.[28]

Several new major offences have also been created, namely money laundering,[29] receiving or possessing money or property reasonably suspected to be the proceeds of crime,[30] and organised fraud.[31] All of these offences carry severe maximum punishments (for example, for money laundering, human offenders face $200,000 and/or 20 years jail). They also impose vicarious liability on individual as well as corporate persons for the conduct of their agents and employees.[32]

The Act covers a wide range of other matters, including mutual assistance in enforcement,[33] and search and seizure.[34]

Confiscation of Proceeds of Crime Act (N.S.W.)

The recent New South Wales Act, in many ways an improvement upon its precursor, the *Crimes (Confiscation of Profits) Act* 1985 (C. (C.P.) Act 1985 (N.S.W.)),[35] has much in common with the P.O.C. Act.

As under the P.O.C. Act, provision is made for discretionary forfeiture orders. A forfeiture order may be made against "tainted property" where D has been convicted of a "serious offence", a term that includes a "drug trafficking offence".[36] "Tainted property" means property used in or in connection with the commission of a "serious offence", or proceeds derived directly or indirectly from the commission of such an offence.[37] "Serious offence" includes an indictable offence or a prescribed offence.[38] "Drug trafficking offence" means an offence

25. P.O.C. Act, s. 30.
26. P.O.C. Act, s. 7.
27. P.O.C. Act, s. 43.
28. P.O.C. Act, Part III, Div. 2.
29. P.O.C. Act, s. 81.
30. P.O.C. Act, s. 82.
31. P.O.C. Act, s. 83.
32. P.O.C. Act, s. 85.
33. P.O.C. Act, ss 23, 23A. See further United Nations, *Conviction against Illicit Traffic in Narcotic Drugs and Psychotropic Substances* (1988), Art. 7; McClean, "Mutual Assistance in Criminal Matters: The Commonwealth Initiative" (1988) 37 Internat. & Comp. L. Q. 177.
34. P.O.C. Act, Part III, Div. 1.
35. As to problems of interpretation under this Act see *R. v. Bolger* (1989) 16 N.S.W.L.R. 115; *R. v. Fagher* (1989) 16 N.S.W.L.R. 67.
36. C.O.P.C. Act, ss 18, 7.
37. C.O.P.C. Act, s. 4(1).
38. C.O.P.C. Act, s. 7.

against ss 23-28 of the *Drug Misuse and Trafficking Act* 1985 (N.S.W.).[39]

Pecuniary penalties may be imposed on D where D has been convicted of a serious offence other than a drug trafficking offence.[40] The measure of the penalty is the value of the benefits derived because of the commission of the offence.[41] Assessment of penalty is governed by rules largely corresponding to those under the P.O.C. Act.[42]

Persons convicted of a drug trafficking offence are subject to drug proceeds orders.[43] The effect of a drugs proceeds order is to impose a pecuniary penalty in relation to the aggregate amount of any payment or reward in connection with drug trafficking. The amount is assessed under s. 30, one feature of which is to create a presumption that all property received by D in the six years preceding the institution of proceedings was received as a payment or reward in connection with drug trafficking.[44]

Unlike the P.O.C. Act, the C.O.P.C. Act 1989 (N.S.W.) does not authorise automatic forfeiture of property subject to a restraining order still in force six months after conviction for a serious offence. Like the *Proceeds of Crime Act* (Cth), however, extensive provision is made for restraining orders.[45]

Money laundering is an offence under the C.O.P.C. Act 1989 (N.S.W.)[46] but there is no offence of organised fraud.[47] Vicarious liability for offences is imposed under s. 76, which corresponds to s. 85 of the P.O.C. Act.

Legislative Aims

The ostensible aims of the P.O.C. Act, and the C.O.P.C. Act are various. The principal objects of the P.O.C. Act, as stated in s. 3, are threefold:

(1) to deprive persons of the proceeds of, and benefits derived from, the commission of offences against the laws of the Commonwealth or the Territories;

(2) to provide for the forfeiture of property used in or in connection with the commission of such offences; and

(3) to enable law enforcement authorities effectively to trace such proceeds, benefits and property.

39. C.O.P.C. Act, s. 4(1).
40. C.O.P.C. Act, s. 24(1).
41. C.O.P.C. Act, s. 24(1)(a).
42. C.O.P.C. Act, s. 25.
43. C.O.P.C. Act, s. 29 (the provisions dealing with drugs proceeds orders have not been proclaimed; reliance is placed on the dragnet provisions of the *Drug Trafficking (Civil Proceedings) Act* 1990 (N.S.W.), discussed below, Chapter 12). Cf. *Customs Act* 1901 (Cth), ss 229A, 243B, 243C; *Drug Trafficking Offences Act* 1986 (U.K.), ss 1-5.
44. C.O.P.C. Act, s. 30(2). Cf. P.O.C. Act (Cth), s. 27(6) (five years).
45. C.O.P.C. Act, ss 43-57.
46. C.O.P.C. Act, s. 73.
47. Cf. P.O.C. Act (Cth), s. 83.

The principal objects of the C.O.P.C. Act are stated in the same terms[48] save for one addition, namely the enforcement of forfeiture and other orders made in respect of offences against the laws of other States.

The legislative objects as stated in the P.O.C. Act and the C.O.P.C. Act specify means rather than ends; to speak of depriving persons of the proceeds or benefits of offences is hardly to reveal the purpose of the exercise and possibly reflects undue preoccupation with the tool in hand. Moreover, no clear idea is conveyed as to the relative importance of the various underlying goals. This opacity bears out Michael Levi's observation that the sanction of asset confiscation means different things to different people: "It may be viewed as a general or individual deterrent, as retribution, and—inasmuch as money may be needed as capital to commit other major crimes (including the establishment of businesses as fronts for crime)—as incapacitation."[49] Another goal, much stressed by the political sponsors of the P.O.C. Act and the C.O.P.C. Act, is deprivation of unjust enrichment.[50] Some have also emphasised the value of confiscated property as a means of bolstering enforcement resources.[51]

Given the sweeping extent of the legislation, it may be argued that the real purpose is to purge society of unwanted criminal *enterprises*.[52] From this perspective, the legislation enables organisations, including business corporations, unincorporated ventures, families and other units, to be stripped of their assets and placed in a position of financial impotence should they or one of their members commit a serious offence. The social and political implications of so ruthless a strategy are daunting, as are the legal problems in implementing it.[53] It is therefore difficult to believe that the legislation is meant to pursue an enterprise-oriented policy of fund-razing. As we shall see, however, extensive provision is made for vicarious liability,[54] and the family does appear to have become a target of punishment.[55]

48. C.O.P.C. Act, s. 3.
49. *Regulating Fraud* (1987) 334. Cf. *Russello v. United States* 465 U.S. 16 at 28 (1983).
50. See *Hansard*, Senate, 30 April 1987, p. 2314 (Lionel Bowen re Proceeds of Crime Bill 1987 (Cth)), echoed in relevant part by John Dowd in his Second Reading speech on the Confiscation of Profits of Crime Bill 1989 (N.S.W.).
51. See *Hansard*, Senate, 30 April 1987, p. 2317 (Lionel Bowen re financial impact of Proceeds of Crime Bill 1987 (Cth)); United Nations, *Convention against Illicit Traffic in Narcotic Drugs and Psychotropic Substances* (1988), art. 5(5); *Caplin and Drysdale, Chartered v. United States* (1989) U.S. Lexis 3124; 57 U.S.L.W. 4836. In the United States about U.S.$171 million in profits were generated in 1986 and 1987: United States, General Accounting Office, *Asset Forfeiture Programs: Corrective Actions Underway but Additional Improvements Needed*, Report (4 March 1988). The same report instances various problems of asset management and auditing.
52. An enterprise-oriented approach is explicit in the *Racketeer Influenced and Corrupt Organisation Act* 1970 (U.S.); *Continuing Criminal Enterprise Act* 1970 (U.S.). The Australian legislation is substantially different in design. I am grateful to my colleague, David Fraser. for highlighting the different angles from which legislation in this area may be seen.
53. For an excellent analysis sympathetic to the need to reflect the organisational dimensions of major crime, see Lynch, "R.I.C.O.: The Crime of Being a Criminal" (1987) 87 Columbia L. Rev. 661, 920.
54. See below, p. 94.
55. See below, pp. 100-104.

UNJUST ENRICHMENT: PROCEEDS OR NET PROFITS?

Few would dispute the principle that offenders are disentitled to profits derived from the commission of offences. Indeed, David McClean has asserted that "[e]very legal system would accept as axiomatic that an offender should not enjoy the profits of his criminal activities".[56] To the extent that the P.O.C. Act and the C.O.P.C. Act reflect the principle of deprivation of unjust enrichment they are hardly controversial. However, the Acts authorise recovery of "tainted property" and "proceeds of crime", concepts which extend much further than the profit made from an offence.[57]

Assume that D, a businessman, imports a quantity of prohibited drugs, say cannabis resin, from Papua New Guinea in an ocean cruiser.[58] The cannabis resin has a street value of $100,000 in Australia. The cruiser is worth $1 million. D's intention was to use the cruiser to bring like quantities of the drug into Australia on his next annual holiday cruise in the South Pacific. D is convicted of unlawfully importing drugs contrary to s. 233B of the *Customs Act* 1901 (Cth), and jailed. Proceedings are then taken under s. 19 of the P.O.C. Act for forfeiture of the cruiser as tainted property. The discretionary factors specified under s. 19(3) (hardship; ordinary or intended use of property),[59] and s. 19(4) (gravity of offence), hardly preclude forfeiture: D is wealthy and unlikely to suffer hardship, he intends to use the vessel for a similar episode of drug running, and the offence is no peccadillo.[60] Forfeiting D's cruiser, however, bears no relation to the profit he intended to make, or would have made, from importing the cannabis resin.

Pecuniary penalties under the P.O.C. Act and the C.O.P.C. Act are also geared to expropriation of property and not merely recovery of unjust enrichment. Pecuniary penalties are related to the value of the "benefit" from an offence. "Benefit" does not mean the net profit flowing from an

56. "Seizing the Proceeds of Crime: The State of the Art" (1989) 38 Internat. & Comp. L. Q. 334 at 334. Cf. *St John Shipping Corp. v. Joseph Rank Ltd* [1957] 1 Q.B. 267 at 292 per Lord Devlin. As to "unjust enrichment", see further *Reading v. Attorney-General* [1951] A.C. 507; Friedmann, "Restitution of Benefits Obtained through the Appropriation of Property or the Commission of a Wrong" (1980) 80 Columbia L. Rev. 504.
57. See editorial (1988) 12 Crim. L. J. 61. For a similar critique of the *Drug Trafficking Offences Act* 1986 (U.K.), see Nicol, "Confiscation of the Profits of Crime" (1988) 52 J. Crim. L. 75 at 79. As regards the United States legislation, see especially Lynch, "R.I.C.O.: The Crime of Being a Criminal" (1987) 87 Columbia L. Rev. 661, 920; Note, "A Proposal to Reform Criminal Forfeiture under R.I.C.O. and C.C.E." (1984) 97 Harvard L. Rev. 1929. But see Smith, "The Scope of Real Property Forfeiture for Drug-Related Crimes under the Comprehensive Forfeiture Act" (1988) 137 U. Pa L. Rev. 303.
58. Cf. *Calero-Toledo v. Pearson Yacht Leasing Co.* (1974) 416 U.S. 663. More recently, a yacht worth U.S.$2.5 million dollars was seized by the United States Coast Guard when a boarding party found less than 0.1 of an ounce on board: (1988) 10 National L. J. 5. The example in the text would create comparable hardship if the vessel were forfeited under the *Customs Act* 1901 (Cth) rather than under the less extreme discretionary forfeiture provisions of the P.O.C. Act.
59. Cf. C.(C.P.) Act 1985 (N.S.W.), as interpreted and applied in *R. v. Bolger* (1989) 16 N.S.W.L.R. 115; 41 A. Crim. R. 222; *R. v. Fagher* (1989) 16 N.S.W.L.R. 67; *R. v. Lake* (1989) 44 A. Crim. R. 63. Cf. also *Re An Application Pursuant to the Drugs Misuse Act 1986* [1988] 2 Qd R. 506; *R. v. Good* (1986) 82 F.L.R. 418.
60. Cf. *United States v. Busher* 817 F. 2d 1409 (1987).

offence but rather the gross proceeds.[61] Thus, it is expressly provided that, in calculating the value of benefit from an offence, account is not to be taken of "any expenses or outgoings".[62] Assume that D traffics in heroin. She pays $1 million to a supplier for a consignment, and $1 million to corrupt police in an attempt to ensure that the consignment reaches her undetected. The consignment reaches her and is then sold for $3 million. Plainly the profit is $1 million, not $2 million, and yet the legislation authorises a pecuniary penalty of $2 million: the cost of bribing the police is "an expense or outgoing" and hence not deductible.[63] If such a penalty is imposed, the result is expropriation of $1 million, not merely exaction of the ill-gotten gain of $1 million.

How far the P.O.C. Act and the C.O.P.C. Act are taken beyond the confiscation of unjust enrichment depends on the exercise of the discretion the courts have under the legislation. Thus, under the P.O.C. Act account may be taken of the factors of hardship and gravity of offence when imposing discretionary forfeiture orders.[64] A court also has a wide discretion when imposing financial penalties.[65] Nonetheless, the point remains that discretionary forfeiture and pecuniary penalties under the P.O.C. Act and the C.O.P.C. Act are not limited to recovery of the net profits from an offence. On the contrary, the courts are expressly authorised to confiscate tainted property and proceeds of crime.

It may be noted that the approach adopted under the P.O.C. Act and the C.O.P.C. Act departs from the position taken by the Hodgson Committee in England when it reported on the subject of recovery of the proceeds of crime in 1984.[66] The Committee stressed that confiscatory orders aimed at stripping D of profit made from an offence should be limited to restoring the status quo. In the opinion of the Committee, it was important not to confuse the difference between removal of unjust enrichment and punishment:[67]

61. Under P.O.C. Act, s. 26(4), provision is made for reducing a penalty where tax has been paid on benefits from an offence.
62. P.O.C. Act, s. 27(8); C.O.P.C. Act (N.S.W.), ss 25(5), 30(4).
63. *Australian Federal Police v. Lahood* (unreported, Fed. Ct, Sweeney J., 23 May 1988). Cf. C.(C.P.) Act 1986 (Vic.), s. 13 (no express exclusion of expenses and outgoings). The cost of supply is deducted when assessing the "benefit" received by D, at least according to a decision on this issue as it arose under C.(C.P.) Act 1985 (N.S.W.): *R. v. Fagher* (1989) 16 N.S.W.L.R. 67, Roden J. dissenting on this point; *R. v. Taylor* (unreported, N.S.W. Dist. Ct, Parker D.C.J., 1989). Where proceeds are received by D and then distributed to co-offenders, the cost of the distribution of the proceeds is also deducted when assessing D's benefit: *Commissioner of Australian Federal Police v. Curran* (1984) 55 A.L.R. 697. In *Saffron v. D.P.P. (No. 4)* (1989) 39 A. Crim. R. 353 it was held that P.O.C. Act, s. 27(7)(b) excluded direct and indirect benefits derived from an offence under "another law of the Commonwealth" in relation to which a penalty order had been imposed (since amended by *Law and Justice Legislation Amendment Act* 1988 (Cth), s. 54, which substitutes the words "Division 3 of Part XIII of the Customs Act").
64. Section 19(3)(4).
65. Cf. *Murphy v. Koninklijke-Java-China-Paketvaart Lijnen* (1975) 49 A.L.J.R. 230; *Scott v. China Navigation Co. Ltd* [1972] A.L.R. 721; Freiberg, "Monetary Penalties under the Trade Practices Act 1974 (Cth)" (1983) 11 A. B. L. Rev. 4.
66. Hodgson, *Profits of Crime and Their Recovery* (1984).
67. Ibid., p. 75.

If drug traffickers have paid their suppliers, confiscation of the gross proceeds would go further than would be necessary to put them in the same position as if they had not offended. Similarly, the owner of a listed building will no doubt have had to incur expense in demolishing it; the court need only confiscate the amount by which the value of the land has been increased less these expenses to ensure that no profit is made from the offence. Of course, some additional penalty may be appropriate, but this ought to be considered separately and openly and not imposed under the guise of confiscation.[68]

Under the P.O.C. Act and the C.O.P.C. Act the "benefit" from say a drug trafficking offence appears to mean D's "take" from selling drugs; the measure is what D has left after paying for the supply.[69] Unlike the position taken by the Hodgson Committee, however, no allowance is made for "any expenses or outgoings" in connection with the commission of the offence.[70]

Relating the approach of the Hodgson Committee to the P.O.C. Act and the C.O.P.C. Act, unjust enrichment would be removed not through pecuniary penalties but by means of a conviction-based confiscation order. A confiscation order would be remedial, not punitive, and would be made upon application by the Director of Public Prosecutions in a civil proceeding. The measure of recovery would be the net profit from an offence rather than the gross proceeds. Alternatively, fines could be adapted specifically for use as a means of depriving D of unjust enrichment, a route adopted in the *Misuse of Drugs Act* 1975 (N.Z.).[71]

Although the principle of recovery of unjust enrichment may be appealing in theory, it may be thought unworkable because of the difficulty in assessing net profits. Drug traffickers and others of like ilk are not noted for maintaining accounting records from which the relevant financial information can be obtained. As Latham C.J. observed in the context of tax evasion:

In the absence of some record in the mind or in the books of the taxpayer, it would often be quite impossible to make a correct assessment. The assessment would necessarily be a guess to some extent, and almost necessarily inexact in fact. There is every reason to suppose that the legislature did not intend to confer upon a potential taxpayer the valuable privilege of disqualifying himself in that capacity by the simple and relatively unskilled method of losing either his memory or his books.[72]

68. As to the punitive and remedial status of pecuniary penalties, see Note, "Statutory Penalties: A Legal Hybrid" (1938) 51 Harvard L. Rev. 1092; Freiberg and McCallum, "The Enforcement of Federal Awards: Civil or Criminal Penalties" (1979) 7 A. B. L. Rev. 246.
69. See *R. v. Fagher* (1989) 16 N.S.W.L.R. 67.
70. P.O.C. Act, s. 27(8); C.O.P.C. Act, ss 25(5), 30(4).
71. Sections 38-42. See further Cameron, "Making the Offender Squirm" [1982] N.Z.L.J. 176.
72. *Trautwein v. Federal Commissioner of Taxation* (1936) 56 C.L.R. 63 at 87.

In *Fagher*,[73] a recent decision of the New South Wales Court of Criminal Appeal, Roden J. drew attention to a similar difficulty in the context of the C. (C.P.) Act 1985 (N.S.W.):

> Calculation or assessment of the value of the benefits derived by a particular offender from any criminal transaction, is likely to be difficult. There will be no audited accounts available, nor can one expect a contract or other documentation evidencing the nature of the dealings among the several participants who may be involved. Additionally, if the participants themselves give evidence of the details of those transactions, their evidence is unlikely to be the most reliable, and to the extent that it may be relied upon is unlikely to disclose clearly defined legal relationships.

There are however a number of reasons for believing that workable assessments of the net profit from offences could be made. First, the Hodgson Committee, after a detailed inquiry into the subject, stood by such an approach. In order to alleviate the task of assessment the Committee recommended that P be required to establish the level of gross profits, with D carrying the persuasive burden of establishing deductions.[74] Secondly, assessing the amount of net profit could be assisted by guidelines as under the present provisions for assessing pecuniary penalties, subject to modifications consistent with the need to measure net rather than gross profit.[75] Thirdly, the problem at hand is one that the Australian Tax Office has to grapple with in assessing the net taxable income of drug traffickers, organised crime leaders, and other offenders.[76] As was accepted by the High Court in *Trautwein v. Federal Commissioner of Taxation*,[77] assessments of the taxable income of tax evaders may come close to guesswork and yet still be lawful.[78]

---

73. (1989) 16 N.S.W.L.R. 67.
74. Hodgson, *Profits of Crime and Their Recovery* (1984), p. 75:

    > The burden would . . . be on the defendant to show that he has been paid less [for drugs supplied] and to show any expenses that reduced the net profit he had made. The expenses ought only to be allowable if actually paid; an uncompleted promise to pay his suppliers may well be unenforceable as illegal contracts. Consideration could also be given to making the deduction of expenses contingent on disclosure of the identity of the payee. If an offender preferred to suffer a heavier penalty than to "grass" on others that is not a matter of concern to us.

75. One issue is whether secondary profits derived from e.g. investment of profit derived immediately from an offence counts as net profit. From the standpoint of deprivation of unjust enrichment, it is difficult to see why secondary profit should be excluded: consider *Saffron v. D.P.P. (No. 4)* (1989) 39 A. Crim. R. 353; but see *Chief Constable of Leicestershire v. M.* [1989] 1 W.L.R. 20; Goode, "The Confiscation of Criminal Profits" (1986) 67 *Proceedings of the Institute of Criminology, University of Sydney* 35 at 42.
76. See generally *Briggs v. Deputy Federal Commissioner of Taxation (W.A.); Ex parte Briggs* (1987) 87 A.T.C. 4,278; *L'Estrange v. Federal Commissioner of Taxation* (1978) 78 A.T.C. 4,744; *Trautwein v. Federal Commissioner of Taxation* (1936) 56 C.L.R. 53; Harmer, "Tax Investigations, Including Betterment Statements" [1985] *Taxation Institute of Australia, 20th Annual Convention* 15.
77. (1936) 56 C.L.R. 63.
78. Cf. *Secret Commissions Act* 1919 (N.S.W.), s. 10(1)(b) (provision, now repealed, making D liable to repay "the amount or value, according to the estimation of the court, of any valuable consideration received or given by him").

DETERRENCE, RETRIBUTION AND PROPORTIONALITY

Deterrent and retributive sentences against offenders are governed by the principle of proportionality, as reaffirmed by the High Court of Australia in *Veen v. The Queen (No. 2)*.[79] Proportionality is a complex and elastic concept,[80] yet nonetheless serves as a major constraint upon the imposition of punishment by the courts. However, this constraint does not apply to the total impact of the sentence imposed for an offence and the confiscatory orders that may be made under the P.O.C. Act and the C.O.P.C. Act.[81]

In *Veen (No. 2)* all members of the High Court endorsed the principle that a sentence should not be disproportionate to the gravity of the offence. They rejected the view that a sentence could be increased beyond the level of proportionality where necessary to protect society against repetition of offence.

The permissible total impact of sentence and confiscatory orders made under the P.O.C. Act and the C.O.P.C. Act is not limited by any ceiling of proportionality.[82] Under s. 18 of the P.O.C. Act a court may defer passing sentence until it has determined an application for a confiscatory order,[83] but this provision falls well short of insistence upon proportionality of total impact. It may also be noted that restraining orders may be revoked where D provides sufficient security for the payment of any pecuniary penalty that may be payable,[84] but again this limitation does not mean that there is any upper limit. This leaves the question whether proportionality is relevant when the courts exercise their discretion to make a forfeiture order or a pecuniary order.

The P.O.C. Act authorises a court to impose discretionary forfeiture of tainted property and, in exercising the discretion, regard may be had to the factors of hardship and gravity of offence.[85] There is no stipulation that hardship and gravity of offence are binding constraints; by plain implication, the impact of forfeiture, or forfeiture and sentence, need not

79. (1988) 164 C.L.R. 465.
80. See further Fox, "The Killings of Bobby Veen: The High Court on Proportion in Sentencing" (1988) 12 Crim. L. J. 339; Levi, *Regulating Fraud* (1987), pp. 315-319; Singer, *Just Deserts: Sentencing Based on Equality and Desert* (1979); Weatherburn, "Sentencing Principles and Sentence Choice" (1987) 11 Crim. L. J. 213. For the view that the theory of just deserts is incoherent and unworkable, see Braithwaite and Pettit, *Not Just Deserts: A Republican Theory of Criminal Justice* (1990).
81. Cf. C.(C.P.) Act 1985 (N.S.W.), as interpreted and applied in *R. v. Bolger* (1989) 16 N.S.W.L.R. 115; A. Crim. R. 222; *R. v. Fagher* (1989) 16 N.S.W.L.R. 67. Cf. also *R. v. Waterhouse* (1984) 14 A. Crim. R. 163 (forfeiture of whole amount of currency ($210,851) taken out of country in violation of foreign exchange regulations). For an earlier critique see Goode, "The Confiscation of Criminal Profits" (1986) 67 *Proceedings of the Institute of Criminology, University of Sydney* 35 at 43-44.
82. This is especially a matter of concern in the context of forfeiture of the assets of a business used partly for legitimate purposes; see Roberts, "Constitutional Law—The Eighth Amendment as Applied to R.I.C.O. Criminal Forfeiture" (1988) 10 West. New England L. Rev. 393 at 415-416.
83. Cf. *Confiscation of Proceeds of Crime Act* (N.S.W.), s. 18(2).
84. P.O.C. Act, s. 56; C.O.P.C. Act, s. 54.
85. P.O.C. Act, s. 19(3)(4).

be proportionate to the offence.[86] The equivalent provisions under the C.O.P.C. Act refer only to hardship as a mitigating factor and, where hardship is considered in relation to a forfeiture order, account is not to be taken of the sentence imposed in respect of the offence.[87]

Similarly, the combined impact of sentence and pecuniary penalties is not bounded by the principle of proportionality. The P.O.C. Act and the C.O.P.C. Act provide that a pecuniary penalty must be reduced by the amount of any property forfeited.[88] The P.O.C. Act also confers a discretion to reduce a penalty by the amount paid by way of fine, restitution, compensation or damages in relation to the offence.[89] However, these provisions do not mean that the overall impact of the sanctions imposed on D must be proportionate to the offence. Assume that D sells a quantity of cocaine for $3 million and makes a net profit of $1 million on the deal. D is convicted on a charge of drug trafficking, jailed for 10 years, and fined $1 million. This sentence, let it be assumed, is proportionate to the offence given the amount of cocaine trafficked, the net profit made, and the degree of blameworthiness. Under the P.O.C. Act and the C.O.P.C. Act a pecuniary penalty equal to the gross proceeds ($3 million) may also be imposed, thereby increasing the overall penalty to a level disproportionate to the offence. Even if the pecuniary penalty were reduced by the amount of the fine imposed, the overall impact would still be disproportionate.

The discussion above may understate the position. The potential reach of the P.O.C. Act beyond the limits of proportionate punishment has been depicted in much more ominous terms, notably by Ian Temby Q.C. in his then capacity as Director of Public Prosecutions for the Commonwealth:[90]

> Putting it shortly, a person who is convicted of one of the major drug offences, or meets the statutory criteria for the conclusion that he or she is involved in organised crime, faces the risk of not just

86. Cf. *Cutting v. Glover* (unreported, S.A. Sup. Ct, Olsson J., No. 3306 of 1986) (re *Scheme of Management (Southern Zone Rock Lobster Fishery) Regulations* 1984 (S.A.), r. 25):
    It is to be remembered that the power is enormously wide and potentially draconian in its effect. In theory an offender is liable not only to specific prescribed penalties and (where applicable) a severe so-called "additional penalty" under s. 66 but he may also have had fish, valuable equipment or even his boat seized. Great care therefore needs to be taken to ensure that there is (in de facto terms) no undue double counting as to penalty and that, in totality, the orders made constitute a reasonable reflection of the total degree of criminality involved in the offending.
87. Section 18(2). Cf. *Crimes (Confiscation of Profits) Act Amendment Act* 1988 (S.A.), s. 2, which provides that: "A court, in determining sentence for a prescribed offence, must not have regard to the question of whether or not the offender's property is, or could be, the subject of an application for forfeiture under this Act." Contrast *R. v. Hoar* (1981) 148 C.L.R. 32 at 39 where the High Court took the view that, had forfeiture been authorised, its impact could have been taken into account in assessing sentence notwithstanding a statutory provision that "forfeiture shall be in addition to and not a part of a penalty". See also Thomas, *Principles of Sentencing* (2nd ed., (1979)), p. 336.
88. P.O.C. Act, s. 26(3); C.O.P.C. Act, s. 24(2).
89. P.O.C. Act, s. 26(5). What if the profit has been taken into account in determining a sentence of imprisonment? Compare *R. v. Pou* (1988) 33 A. Crim. R. 99; *R. v. Loh* (1987) 34 A. Crim. R. 252.
90. (1988) 23(3) Aust. L. N. 10 at 11-12.

imprisonment, or the payment of a fine, or forfeiture of the proceeds of crime, or loss of property involved in the commission of the offence, but the loss of everything of a material nature.

The danger referred to arises in the context of the automatic forfeiture provisions under s. 30 of the P.O.C. Act. As we have seen, where D's property is subject to a discretionary forfeiture order, account can at least be taken of the factor of hardship.[91]

Constitutional limitations may also apply. In particular, account should be taken of the constraints upon cruel and unusual punishment[92] and acquisition of property otherwise than on just terms as required by s. 51(xxxi) of the Constitution.

In determining the amount of discretionary forfeiture or pecuniary penalty under the P.O.C. Act and the C.O.P.C. Act the courts, in heeding the "silent constitutional principle" proscribing cruel and unusual punishment,[93] are likely to seek assistance from interpretations of the Eighth Amendment of the United States Constitution.[94] Recent interpretations of the Eighth Amendment have taken the prohibition against cruel and unusual punishment to mean that the punitive impact[95] must not be grossly disproportionate to the offence. This test was applied in the forfeiture case of *United States v. Busher*,[96] a decision of the United States Court of Appeals, Ninth Circuit in 1987.

In the *Busher* case, D was convicted on fraud charges under R.I.C.O. His entire interest in two companies was forfeited as well as certain real

91. P.O.C. Act, s. 19(3)(4).
92. The prohibition against excessive fines and cruel and unusual punishment in the English Bill of Rights of 1689 is embodied in our law as a "silent constitutional principle": *Sillery v. The Queen* (1981) 55 A.L.J.R. 509 at 513, citing *Commonwealth v. Kreglinger and Furneau Ltd* (1926) 37 C.L.R. 393 at 413; *Cooper v. Stuart* (1889) 14 App. Cas. 286 at 293. See further *La Trobe University v. Robinson* [1972] V.R. 883; Mason, "Future Directions in Australian Law" (1987) 13 Mon. L. Rev. 149; Castles, *An Australian Legal History* (1982), Chs 1, 15. The prohibition is also echoed in the Eighth Amendment to the United States Constitution; see further *Solem v. Helm* 463 U.S. 277 (1983); Granucci, " 'Nor Cruel and Unusual Punishment Inflicted': The Original Meaning" (1969) 57 California L. Rev. 839; Wheeler, "Toward a Theory of Limited Punishment: An Examination of the Eighth Amendment" (1972) 24 Stanford L. Rev. 838; Posner, "Law and Literature: a Relation Reargued" (1986) 72 Virginia L. Rev. 1351.
93. *Sillery v. The Queen* (1981) 55 A.L.J.R. 509 at 513.
94. See especially *Solem v. Helm* 463 U.S. 277 at 284 (1983) (Eighth Amendment prohibits not only barbaric punishments but also sentences that are grossly disproportionate to the crime committed).
95. See *Cheatley v. The Queen* (1972) 127 C.L.R. 291 at 310 per Mason J. (forfeiture characterised as punishment); cf. *R. v. Fagher* (1989) 16 N.S.W.L.R. 67 (pecuniary penalties under C.(C.P.) Act 1985 (N.S.W.) characterised as penalties, not punishment).
96. 817 F.2d 1409 (1987). See also *United States v. Littlefield* 821 F. 2d 1365 (1987); *United States v. Feldman* 853 F.2d 648 (1988). See further Lynch, "R.I.C.O.: The Crime of Being a Criminal" (1987) 87 Columbia L. Rev. 661 at 754-755; Roberts, "Constitutional Law—The Eighth Amendment as Applied to R.I.C.O. Criminal Forfeiture" (1988) 10 West. New England L. Rev. 393; Winters, "Criminal R.I.C.O. Forfeitures and the Eighth Amendment: 'Rough' Justice is Not Enough" (1987) 14 Hastings Constitutional L. Q. 451. Compare *United States v. Fischbach and Moore, Inc.* 750 F.2d 1183 (1984), cert. denied 470 U.S. 1085 (1985) ($1 million fine for antitrust offence not disproportionate); *United States v. Tax Lot 1500* 861 F.2d 232 (1988) (held that Eighth Amendment did not apply to civil as opposed to criminal forfeiture provision).

estate. The loss from D's fraud was $335,000; the value of the property forfeited was much greater—the forfeited interest in one company was worth approximately $2.75 million. The United States Court of Appeals referred the issue of forfeiture back to the District Court for a determination that the forfeiture order was not so grossly disproportionate as to amount to cruel and unusual punishment contrary to the Eighth Amendment. It was held that the Eighth Amendment requires a court when imposing forfeiture to consider the harshness of the penalty (that is, the total punishment imposed for the offence, including not only the forfeiture but incarceration, fines or probation) in light of the gravity of the offence (including the circumstances surrounding D's criminal conduct, harm to victim, and D's culpability). However, forfeiture is not unconstitutional if it merely exceeds the harm to victims or the benefit to the defendant. In the opinion of the Court of Appeals, the Eighth Amendment prohibits only forfeitures that, in all the relevant circumstances, are grossly disproportionate to the offence committed.

The prohibition against cruel and unusual punishment may also prompt a constitutional challenge to the automatic forfeiture provisions of the P.O.C. Act under s. 30. It can be argued that the automatic forfeiture provisions of the P.O.C. Act in some circumstances mandate the infliction of cruel and unusual punishment. Section 30 decrees the forfeiture of property subject to a restraining order still in force six months from the day of conviction for a serious offence. Cases conceivably may arise where the value of the property restrained is very high and where D is unable to have the restraining order varied or revoked before forfeiture is automatically triggered under s. 30. If the value of the property forfeited is grossly disproportionate to the offence, and if the forfeiture is characterised as punishment,[97] the result could amount to cruel and unusual punishment as that term is understood under the Eighth Amendment. It might then be argued that, in mandating cruel and unusual punishment in such a case, the P.O.C. Act goes beyond the Commonwealth's express powers (which warrant legislation "for the peace, order, and good government of the Commonwealth"), and are also outside the scope of the incidental power.[98]

The forfeiture and pecuniary provisions of the P.O.C. Act might also be challenged on the ground of acquisition of property on unjust terms contrary to s. 51(xxxi) of the Constitution.[99] Attempts have been made to challenge the forfeiture and pecuniary penalties provisions under the *Customs Act* 1901 (Cth) on this ground, but to date the High Court has refused to characterise forfeiture or pecuniary penalisation as an

97. See further Clark, "Civil and Criminal Penalties and Forfeitures" (1976) 60 Minnesota L. Rev. 379. Cf. the artificiality of *R. v. Fagher* (1989) 16 N.S.W.L.R. 67 where pecuniary penalties under C. (C.P.) Act 1985 (N.S.W.) were characterised as penalties, not punishment.
98. See *Sillery v. The Queen* (1981) 55 A.L.J.R. 509 at 513.
99. *R. v. Smithers* (1982) 44 A.L.R. 53 it was also argued, unsuccessfully, (i) that s. 243B of the *Customs Act* 1901 (Cth) was supported neither by the trade and commerce power or by the external affairs power, and (ii) that s. 243B, read together with s. 243C, conferred an administrative power on a federal court in which a judicial power of the Commonwealth was reposed.

acquisition of property within the meaning of s. 51(xxxi). [100] However, the High Court may be prepared to re-examine the question. [101]

Assume that the P.O.C. Act made provision for writs of attainder or mandatory pecuniary penalties equal to the entire value of an offender's estate. It is submitted that expropriation of property of that kind would be an acquisition of property within the meaning of s. 51(xxxi). [102] If so, the key question is not whether forfeiture or penalties amount to "acquisition of property" but whether there is acquisition of property on "just terms". In applying this test, the High Court is most unlikely to invalidate legislation merely because of departure from the principle of proportionate punishment, [103] but it might be prepared to employ a standard of gross disproportionality akin to that relevant under the Eighth Amendment prohibition against cruel and unusual punishment. [104]

Constitutional constraints aside, the question remains whether there is any good reason for abandoning the traditional principle of proportionate punishment in the context of the P.O.C. Act and the C.O.P.C. Act. In the parliamentary debates ushering in the legislation [105] there are numerous assertions to the effect that serious drug-related offences are so prevalent and so difficult to enforce that exceptional measures are required. Without denying the prevalence of such offences or the difficulty in enforcing them, it is questionable whether the asserted need for exceptional measures requires that the principle of proportionality be over-ridden.

100. *Burton v. Honan* (1952) 86 C.L.R. 169, especially at 180 where Dixon C.J. expressed the view that:

> it has always been treated as obvious that if the purpose of the forfeiture is to bring a penalty upon the offender it could not come within s. 51(xxxi), it not being an acquisition of property for any purpose in respect of which Parliament has power to make laws within that provision. Alternatively it has been said that even if it was within s. 51(xxxi) there is nothing unjust in a provision forfeiting the property of the offender as part of the punishment for the offence.

See also *R. v. Smithers* (1982) 44 A.L.R. 53; *Trade Practices Commission v. Tooth & Co. Ltd* (1979) 142 C.L.R. 397 at 408 per Gibbs C.J.; *Commissioner of Australian Federal Police v. Cox* (1986) 70 A.L.R. 509. See further Brown, "Forfeiture of Property under the Customs Act 1901" (1982) 56 A.L.J. 447. Similarly re taxation penalties: *Commissioner of Taxation v. Clyne* (1958) 100 C.L.R. 246; *Federal Commissioner of Taxation v. Barnes* (1975) 133 C.L.R. 483 at 494-495.

101. It seems immaterial that the P.O.C. Act may not be characterised as a law with respect to the acquisition of property, or that the acquisition of property is merely incidental: *Trade Practices Commission v. Tooth & Co. Ltd* (1979) 142 C.L.R. 397; commentary by Walker (1980) 54 A.L.J. 37. But see *Commissioner of Australian Federal Police v. Cox* (1986) 70 A.L.R. 509 at 515.

102. Consider *Commissioner of Australian Federal Police v. Cox* (1986) 70 A.L.R. 509 at 514-515; *Trade Practices Commission v. Tooth & Co. Ltd* (1979) 142 C.L.R. 397 at 454-458 per Aicken J.

103. As to the meaning of "just terms" see *Trade Practices Commission v. Tooth & Co. Ltd* (1979) 142 C.L.R. 397 at 416-422 per Stephen J.

104. See *Solem v. Helm*, 463 U.S. 277 (1983).

105. See especially *Hansard*, 30 April 1987, pp. 2314-17 (Lionel Bowen re Proceeds of Crime Bill 1987 (Cth)). Cf. *Burton v. Honan* (1952) 86 C.L.R. 169 at 178-179 per Dixon C.J. (re the stringency of forfeiture provisions under the *Customs Act*).

The need asserted is not so much for increased deterrent punishment[106] as for incapacitating offenders by denying them opportunity to use their economic power to commit or assist the commission of further offences. Once this is seen, it becomes apparent that the central issue is not deterrence versus proportionate punishment. The question is why the P.O.C. Act and the C.O.P.C. Act have employed ostensibly punitive measures (namely forfeiture and pecuniary penalties) to achieve the remedial aim of incapacitation. To that issue we now turn.

INCAPACITATION AND OVERREACH

One major goal of the legislation is to incapacitate offenders, especially those engaged in drug trafficking, by depriving them of the economic power to promote or assist the commission of further offences.[107] Since incapacitation is a remedial goal it may be argued that the constraint of proportionality in punishment is irrelevant when assessing the degree of incapacitation required:[108] the point of incapacitation, like quarantine, is not punishment but prevention by means of civil restraint. However, it hardly follows that incapacitation should be pursued without limit.[109] In particular, there is the utilitarian principle that social control should be achieved by the least drastic means. The P.O.C. Act and the C.O.P.C. Act are difficult to reconcile with this principle.

The modes of incapacitation authorised under the P.O.C. Act and the C.O.P.C. Act are restraining orders prior to trial, and forfeiture and pecuniary penalisation upon conviction. Forfeiture and pecuniary penalisation are extreme methods of achieving the goal of incapacitation. The object of incapacitation is not to beggar defendants but to deprive them of the economic power to commit offences. If so, incapacitation could be achieved by much less drastic means.

In order to deprive someone of workable economic power to engage in drug-trafficking offences it hardly seems necessary to resort to forfeiture of property or exaction of a monetary penalty. Another possible solution, in addition to providing a remedy for recoupment of unjust enrichment,[110] would be to sequester D's property for a

---

106. A controversial issue: see Levi, *Regulating Fraud* (1987), p. 315; Reuter, *Disorganised Crime: The Economics of the Visible Hand* (1983); Wardlaw, "Organised Crime and Drug Enforcement" (1986) 67 *Proceedings of the Institute of Criminology, University of Sydney* 17; Fox and O'Hare, "Criminal Bankruptcy" (1978) 4 Mon. L. R. 181 at 201.

107. See e.g. *Hansard*, Senate, 30 April 1987, p. 2314 (Lionel Bowen re Proceeds of Crime Bill 1987 (Cth)).

108. Compare *Veen v. The Queen (No. 2)* (1988) 164 C.L.R. 465 at 495 per Deane J. The degree of incapacitation ordered is however relevant when assessing the proportionality of the punishment imposed. See further Wood, "Dangerous Offenders and the Morality of Protective Sentencing" [1988] Crim. L. Rev. 424.

109. A point often neglected in wartime provisions for confiscation of the property of enemy aliens: see e.g. *Attorney-General v. Schmidt* (1961) 105 C.L.R. 361.

110. Such a remedy would be aimed at depriving D of the enjoyment of criminally-made profit after release from jail whereas an incapacitation order relates to the prevention of further offences.

substantial period and to require the approval of the Official Trustee in Bankruptcy or the Public Trustee for the disposition of assets or the expenditure of funds during the period of restraint.[111] This approach would require the use of incapacitation orders comparable to the restraining orders now provided for in the P.O.C. Act and the C.O.P.C. Act but adapted to suit the purpose of controlling and monitoring the use of D's property after conviction and sentence.[112] Incapacitation orders of this kind would bear some resemblance to the criminal bankruptcy orders formerly available under the *Powers of Criminal Courts Act* 1973 (U.K.)[113] in so far as administrative control would be exercised over all of D's property (tainted or untainted). Unlike criminal bankruptcy orders, however, the prime purpose of incapacitation orders would not be to distribute D's estate for the benefit of victims. The object would be to shackle D's economic power and thereby prevent him from assisting the commission of further offences with the financial resources that would otherwise be at his disposal.

Without attempting here to present a detailed possible legislative scheme, it may be surmised that incapacitation orders would be available upon conviction for an offence within the range subject to restraining orders under the P.O.C. Act and the C.O.P.C. Act. As in the case of restraining orders, there could well be a broad discretion to make an incapacitation order, and to impose such conditions as are seen fit.[114] The duration of an incapacitation order might be left to the discretion of the court imposing sentence, subject to a limit of five years[115] or the period, if longer, of a sentence of imprisonment. Legislative provision could be made for automatic discharge at the end of the specified period of incapacitation unless the court extended the period of restraint.[116] Extension could be preconditioned upon a showing of probable cause to believe that the resources released will be used by D to assist the commission of further offences.[117]

The thrust of the discussion above is consistent with the view expressed in *Veen (No. 2)*[118] by Deane J. that the need for preventive restraint of dangerous offenders is best met, not by abandoning or

111. In the case of corporations a possible mechanism would be receivership or possibly conditions of probation akin to those of receivership. See further Gruner, "To Let the Punishment Fit the Organisation: Sanctioning Corporate Offenders through Corporate Probation" (1989) 16 Am. J. Crim. L. 1.

112. See P.O.C. Act, Pt III, Div. 2.

113. See further Fox and O'Hare, "Criminal Bankruptcy" (1978) 4 Mon. L. Rev. 181.

114. Cf. P.O.C. Act, s. 43(2).

115. Cf. *Bankruptcy Act* 1966 (Cth), s. 149.

116. Subject perhaps to an upper limit on the period of extension.

117. Cf. the issue of threshold requirements in the context of the use of covert facilitation of the commission of offences where some have advocated that the test be one of reasonable suspicion rather than probable cause: see Whelan, "Lead Us not into (Unwarranted) Temptation: A Proposal to Replace the Entrapment Defence with a Reasonable Suspicion Requirement" (1985) 133 U. Pa L. Rev. 1193 at 1216; Gershman, "Abscam, the Judiciary, and the Ethics of Entrapment" (1982) 91 Yale L. J. 1565 at 1588-1589. But see Braithwaite, Fisse and Geis, "Covert Facilitation and Crime: Restoring Balance to the Entrapment Debate" (1987) 43 *Journal of Social Issues* 5 at 9-10, 30-31, 110-116. Cf. also *Daire v. Raphael* (1983) 35 S.A.S.R. 302.

118. (1988) 164 C.L.R. 465 at 495.

distorting the principle of proportionate punishment, but by introducing an appropriate statutory system of civil preventive restraint.[119] There are however further concerns.

A system of incapacitation orders may be considered impractical given the length of time for which D's property may need to be sequestered. Restraining orders under the P.O.C. Act or the C.O.P.C. Act are relatively limited in duration and hence do not impose the same burden of administration. However, it would be possible to give the Official Trustee in Bankruptcy and the Public Trustee power to streamline the management of D's property, as by converting D's assets into a readily manageable fund for investment.[120] Even a "fire sale" of the property would leave D and his relatives in a better position than if the same property were forfeited, as is now authorised under the P.O.C. Act and the C.O.P.C. Act.

Another understandable concern is the degree of interference with liberty if the property of offenders were subject to sequestration for substantial periods of time. It may be thought that incapacitation orders are too oppressive a means of social control and represent a leap in the direction of a totalitarian state, or perhaps even a regression toward the dark age of attainder. Incapacitation orders conceivably could be hedged around with sufficient safeguards to allay much of this concern (for example, a requirement of probable cause that D will use his financial resources to assist the commission of a similar offence).[121] The limited claim made here is that incapacitation orders, coupled with orders for the recovery of unjust enrichment, would provide a less drastic means of incapacitation than the more absolute solution, as adopted under the P.O.C. Act and the C.O.P.C. Act, of confiscating D's property without any right of return.

PRINCIPLES OF CRIMINAL LIABILITY: COMPROMISES

The P.O.C. Act and the C.O.P.C. Act are conviction based and hence do not allow forfeiture and pecuniary penalties to be used as a means of circumventing the stricter procedural and evidentiary requirements of the criminal process.[122] This approach is commendable, certainly as

119. See Wood, "Dangerous Offenders and the Morality of Protective Sentencing" [1988] Crim. L. Rev. 424.
120. Cf. P.O.C. Act, ss 43(6), 49(6).
121. Alternatively, a more demanding test would be one of high likelihood.
122. The bypass role of forfeiture in the United States is notorious; see *United States v. One Assortment of 89 Firearms* 465 U.S. 354 (1983); Koenig and Godinez-Taylor, "The Need for Greater Double Jeopardy and Due Process Safeguards in R.I.C.O. Criminal and Civil Actions" (1982) 70 California L. Rev. 724; Smith, "Modern Forfeiture Law and Policy: A Proposal for Reform" (1978) 19 Wm & Mary L. Rev. 661; Grilli, "Preventing Billions from Being Washed Offshore: A Growing Approach to Stopping International Drug Trafficking" (1987) 14 Syracuse J. Int. L. & Com. 65; Winn, "Seizures of Private Property in the War against Drugs: What Process is Due?" (1988) 41 So. West. L. Rev. 1111; Kurisky, "Civil Forfeiture of Assets: A Final Solution to International Drug Trafficking?" (1988) 10 *Houston Journal of International Law* 239; Maxeiner, "Bane of American Forfeiture Law—Banished at Last?" (1977) 62 Cornell L. Rev. 768.

compared with the far-reaching provisions for civil forfeiture and penalties under the *Customs Act* 1901 (Cth).[123] However, making criminal liability a precondition of forfeiture and pecuniary penalties under the P.O.C. Act and the C.O.P.C. Act appears to have created some pressure to compromise accepted principles of criminal liability. Compromise is especially apparent under the P.O.C. Act.[124]

The P.O.C. Act creates the serious offence of money laundering.[125] This offence provides an additional basis for the consequential application of forfeiture and pecuniary penalty orders but much of the utility of the offence in this respect has been achieved by relaxing the guilty mind required. Although the offence carries a maximum jail term of 20 years and, in the case of individuals, a maximum fine of $200,000, the mental element is not confined to intention, knowledge or recklessness. Liability extends to an unreasonable failure to know that the money or other property is derived or realised, directly or indirectly, from some form of unlawful activity. This objective test of liability is inconsistent with the emphasis traditionally attached to subjective tests of liability for serious offences.[126] Subjective blameworthy states of mind have been insisted upon in a long line of High Court decisions, from *R. v. Parker*,[127] to *R. v. Crabbe*,[128] to *He Kaw Teh v. The Queen*[129] and *Giorgianni v. The Queen*.[130] It should also be realised that s. 81 does not adhere to the model provided by the money laundering offences in the *Money Laundering Control Act* 1986 (U.S.); knowledge is required under the corresponding United States provisions.[131] Knowledge is also required for the money laundering offence enacted under the C.O.P.C. Act.[132]

123. *Customs Act* 1901 (Cth), ss 229A, 243B, 243C. Cf. Fox and Freiberg, "Sentences Without Conviction: From Status to Contract in Sentencing" (1989) 13 Crim. L. J. 297.
124. See Fisse, "The Rise of Money-Laundering Offences and the Fall of Principle" (1989) 13 Crim. L. J. 5, from which part of this section is adapted. Note also the criticism expressed in *Saffron v. D.P.P.* (unreported, N.S.W. C.C.A., Kirby P., No. 40150 of 1989).
125. P.O.C. Act, s. 81.
126. It is also remarkable that the mental element of money laundering is so radically different from the mental element of receiving, the offence that is the most obvious forbear of the offence of money laundering. The mental element required for receiving is knowledge, or at least belief, that the goods received are stolen: *R. v. Raad* [1983] 3 N.S.W.L.R. 344; *Anderson v. Lynch* (1982) 17 N.T.R. 21; *R. v. Fallon* (1981) 28 S.A.S.R. 394; *R. v. Crooks* [1981] 2 N.Z.L.R. 53; cf. *R. v. Fallon* (1981) 28 S.A.S.R. 394 at 404-409 per Legoe J.; and *Anderson v. Lynch* (1982) 17 N.T.R. 21 at 28-30 per Nader J., where "knowledge" was interpreted to mean knowledge and not merely belief. See further Spencer, "Handling, Theft and the Mala Fide Purchaser" [1985] Crim. L. Rev. 92.
127. (1963) 111 C.L.R. 610.
128. (1985) 156 C.L.R. 464.
129. (1985) 157 C.L.R. 523.
130. (1985) 156 C.L.R. 473.
131. U.S.C. s. 1956(a)(b). See further United States, Senate, Committee on the Judiciary, *The Money Laundering Crimes Act of 1986*, Report (99th Cong., 2d Sess., 1986); Plombeck, "Confidentiality and Disclosure: The Money Laundering Control Act of 1986 and Banking Secrecy" (1988) 22 *International Lawyer* 69; Popham and Probus, "Structured Transactions in Money Laundering: Dealing with Tax Evaders, Smurfs, and other Enemies of the People" (1988) 15 Am. J. of Crim. L. 83.
132. C.O.P.C. Act, s. 73(3)(4).

The rigour of s. 81 might be alleviated to some extent by feats of restrictive interpretation. In the event of genuine ambiguity, doubt is to be resolved in favour of the defendant, a canon of interpretation reaffirmed in *Murphy v. Farmer*.[133] In *Murphy v. Farmer* a majority of the High Court restrictively construed the forfeiture provisions under s. 229 of the *Customs Act*; in the opinion of Deane, Dawson and Gaudron JJ.:[134]

> clear words should be required before there is attributed to the Parliament an intention to take the draconian step of imposing automatic forfeiture as a penalty for "*any*" wrong "entry invoice declaration answer statement or representation" regardless of whether the wrong information was provided as the result of an innocent mistake or excusable ignorance. The effect of the penalty of automatic forfeiture under s. 229(1)(i) can be devastating and quite disproportionate in that it applies regardless of the value of the goods or the importance or effect of the wrong statement which was made.

Similar considerations are relevant in the context of s. 81. It might thus be argued that the words "ought reasonably to know" in s. 81 should be interpreted as requiring a high degree of negligence equivalent to that required for manslaughter by criminal negligence.[135] However, it is questionable whether the framers of the P.O.C. Act meant the section to be read down in such a way.

Another example of the compromise of principle is the extensive provision of vicarious liability under s. 85 of the P.O.C. Act (Cth).[136] The effect of s. 85 is to impose vicarious and hence strict liability on individual and corporate defendants for the offences prescribed by s. 81 (money laundering), s. 82 (receiving or possessing money or property reasonably suspected to be the proceeds of crime), and s. 83 (organised fraud). The general principle at common law is that liability is personal, not vicarious,[137] and although there are numerous statutory exceptions to that principle it is rare to find vicarious liability in the context of offences carrying jail terms.[138] Given the severe jail terms possible under s. 81 and s. 83, the imposition of vicarious liability under s. 85 is extraordinary. Assume, for example, that one partner of a law firm commits an offence against s. 81. By virtue of s. 85 all partners in the firm are vicariously and hence strictly liable for the same offence. Imposing vicarious liability would be understandable in the context of a civil remedy for recovery of unjust enrichment, but that is not the context. Here again, one suspects that the tail of civil forfeiture and pecuniary penalties has wagged the dog of criminal liability.

133. (1988) 165 C.L.R. 19.
134. Ibid. at 28.
135. Cf. *R. v. Newman* [1948] V.L.R. 61 at 67; *R. v. Shields* [1981] V.R. 717; *R. v. D* [1984] 3 N.S.W.L.R. 29.
136. See also C.O.P.C. Act, s. 76.
137. *Tesco Supermarkets Ltd v. Nattrass* [1972] A.C. 153.
138. P.O.C. Act, s. 85 echoes s. 84 of the *Trade Practices Act* (Cth) as amended in 1986 but it should be noticed that, unlike the offences under the P.O.C. Act, the offences and violations under the *Trade Practices Act* do not expose defendants to jail sentences.

These and other examples of the compromise of principles of criminal liability invite statutory revision. Two suggestions may be made. The first is that principle be adhered to, and that s. 81 and s. 85 of the P.O.C. Act and other offending provisions be revised accordingly. The second is that consideration be given to the possible merit of relaxing the conviction-based approach under the P.O.C. Act and the C.O.P.C. Act to the extent of introducing an independent civil remedy for recoupment of the unjust enrichment flowing from offences.

To the extent that pressure exists to allow recovery of unjust enrichment on the basis of principles of civil liability, that pressure might best be relieved by providing a suitable civil remedy upon application by the D.P.P.[139] Such a remedy would not require proof of a criminal guilty mind, and would impose vicarious liability in relation to enrichment derived from the conduct of an agent. It may be noted that the main reason for a conviction based approach is that criminal liability is a trade-off for the high and possibly disproportionate level of expropriation that may be inflicted through forfeiture and pecuniary penalties.[140] The civil remedy suggested is limited to the exaction of unjust enrichment and hence would not create the same need for criminal liability as a threshold requirement.

LEGAL ASSISTANCE AT RISK?

A well-known danger of legislation for confiscating the proceeds of crime is that the controls imposed may unduly impede access to legal assistance.[141] Funds available to defendants for lawyers to act on their

---

139. Cf. *Securities Industry (N.S.W.) Code*, s. 130(1)(d); N.C.S.C., *Insider Trading Legislation for Australia* (1986), pp. 106-110. The quantum of proof required in a civil action in tort founded on facts which also constitute a criminal offence is proof on the balance of probabilities: *Refjek v. McElroy* (1965) 112 C.L.R. 517. As to the inter-relationship between civil and criminal proceedings, see generally Freiberg, " 'Civilising' Crime: Parallel Proceedings and the Civil Remedies Function of the Commonwealth Director of Public Prosecutions" (1988) 21 Aust. & N.Z.J. of Criminology 129. Note also *Halabi v. Westpac Banking Corp.* (1989) 17 N.S.W.L.R. 26; 39 A. Crim. R. 194 (noted 64 A.L.J. 295) (the felony-tort rule has been replaced in New South Wales by a general power to prevent abuse of process).

140. Another reason is the inversion of the burden of proof in relation to the issue of the amount of benefit derived from an offence: Hodgson, *Profits of Crime and their Recovery* (1984), p. 83.

141. As is apparent from the immense volume of literature on the subject, especially in the United States. See especially Freiberg, " 'Civilising' Crime: Parallel Proceedings and the Civil Remedies Function of the Commonwealth Director of Public Prosecutions" (1988) 21 Aust. & N.Z.J. of Criminology 129 at 136-137; Winick, "Forfeiture of Attorneys' Fees under R.I.C.O. and C.C.E. and the right to Counsel of Choice: The Constitutional Dilemma and How to Avoid It" (1989) 43 U. Miami L. Rev. 765; Weinstein, "Prosecuting Attorneys for Money Laundering: A New and Questionable Weapon in the War on Crime" (1988) 51 *Law & Contemporary Problems* 369; Committee on Criminal Advocacy, "The Forfeiture of Attorney Fees in Criminal Cases: A Call for Immediate Remedial Action" (1986) 41 *Association of the Bar of the City of New York Record* 469. In *Caplin and Drysdale, Chartered v. United States* (1989) U.S. Lexis 3124; 57 U.S.L.W. 4836 the majority thought the problem was minor, on the optimistic ground that defendants "may be able to find lawyers willing to represent them, hoping that their fees will be paid in the event of acquittal, or via some other means that a defendant might come by in the future. The burden placed on defendants by the forfeiture law is therefore a limited one."

behalf may be subject to restraining orders. Fees paid to defence counsel may be vulnerable to forfeiture as proceeds of crime. Moreover, the receipt of such fees may constitute the offence of money laundering. These risks should not be exaggerated but do exist.

Restraining orders and other asset freezing measures can leave a defendant with insufficient funds to employ a solicitor or barrister of choice, or to employ a legal representative for the time needed to mount a well-prepared and sustained defence. The potential threat has been described by Mark Weinberg in these terms:[142]

> A judge should be conscious of the dangers of oppression inherent in a situation where the de facto prosecutor can rely on unproven allegations, made ex parte, and thereby prevent a defendant from being able to defend himself against criminal charges by the simple expedient of drying up his funds.[143]

Legal aid may be provided but plainly this is a second best solution. The money available under legal aid schemes is limited and this factor may restrict both the counsel available and the time that can be expended on cases assisted.[144] Rather than forcing defendants to depend on legal aid, the P.O.C. Act and the C.O.P.C. Act provide that a restraining order may allow D "reasonable expenses"[145] in defending a criminal charge. This exemption is expressly qualified under the P.O.C. Act by the proviso that D cannot meet his expenses from property that is not subject to the restraining order.[146] The allowance for reasonable expenses in defending a charge may well be interpreted generously by the courts and in practice perhaps few will be denied unlimited access

142. As quoted in Freiberg, " 'Civilising' Crime: Parallel Proceedings and the Civil Remedies Function of the Commonwealth Director of Public Prosecutions" (1988) 21 Aust. & N.Z.J. of Criminology 129 at 137.

143. The problem has recently been described in more colourful language by a minority of the Supreme Court of the United States in *Caplin and Drysdale, Chartered v. United States* (1989) U.S. Lexis 3124; 57 U.S.L.W. 4836: "it is unseemly and unjust for the government to beggar those it prosecutes in order to disable their defence at trial." The minority also observed, inter alia, that:

> Had it been Congress' express aim to undermine the adversary system as we know it, it could hardly have found a better engine of destruction than attorney's-fee forfeiture. The main effect of forfeitures under the Act, of course, will be to deny the defendant the right to retain counsel, and therefore the right to have his defence designed and presented by an attorney he has chosen and trusts. If the government restrains the defendant's assets before trial, private counsel will be unwilling to continue or to take on the defence. Even if no restraining order is entered, the possibility of forfeiture after conviction will itself substantially diminish the likelihood that private counsel will agree to take the case. The "message [to private counsel] is 'Do not represent this defendant or you will lose your fee.' That being the kind of message lawyers are likely to take seriously, the defendant will find it difficult or impossible to secure representation.' " *United States v. Badalamenti* 614 F. Supp. 194 at 196 (1985).

144. Consider e.g. *Maher v. Attorney-General (Cth)* (1985) 60 A.L.R. 373. Maher's application for legal aid was much resisted by the authorities. Moreover, the political will to provide legal aid under the *Judiciary Act* to persons of conspicuously suspect wealth was tested to the brink, with then Prime Minister Hawke informally threatening to amend the legislation if the application was successful.

145. P.O.C. Act, s. 43(3); C.O.P.C. Act, s. 43(6). Cf. *Customs Act* 1901 (Cth), s. 243E(4)(c); *Kirk v. Commissioner of Australian Federal Police* (1988) 81 A.L.R. 321.

146. Section 43(4). Cf. C.O.P.C. Act, s. 43.

to the lawyer of their choice.[147] It should also be remembered that a defendant against whom a restraining order is made can have the order revoked if he is able to provide adequate security for the payment of a pecuniary penalty that may be imposed in the event of conviction.[148]

There is however a possible risk that the "reasonable expenses" limitation on exclusion of funds from a restraining order will be applied less than generously. Many in the community appear to believe that drug traffickers and other major offenders do not deserve to be defended by "Rolls Royce" counsel.[149] This sentiment is reflected by *Caplin and Drysdale, Chartered v. United States*,[150] a recent decision of the Supreme Court of the United States. A majority rejected the argument that the right to counsel under the Sixth Amendment required that lawyers' fees be exempted from forfeiture under the *Racketeer Influenced and Corrupt Organisation Act* 1970 and the *Continuing Criminal Enterprise Act* 1970.[151] The reasoning, in relevant part, was as follows:[152]

> a major purpose motivating congressional adoption and continued refinement of the R.I.C.O. and C.C.E. forfeiture provisions has been the desire to lessen the economic power of organised crime and drug enterprises.[153] This includes the use of such economic power to retain private counsel. As the Court of Appeals put it: "Congress has already underscored the compelling public interest in stripping criminals such as Reckmeyer of their undeserved economic power, and part of that undeserved power may be the ability to command high-priced legal talent."[154] The notion that the government has a legitimate interest in depriving criminals of economic power, even in so far as that power is used to retain counsel of choice, may be somewhat unsettling.[155] But when a defendant claims that he has suffered some substantial impairment of his Sixth Amendment rights by virtue of the seizure or forfeiture of assets in his possession, such a complaint is no more than the reflection of "the harsh reality that the quality of a criminal defendant's representation frequently may turn on his ability to retain the best counsel money can buy."[156] Again, the Court of Appeals put it aptly: "The modern day Jean

147. See Temby, "Taking Assets off Criminals—Attainder in Australia Today?" (Paper 14, University of Western Australia Law Summer School, 1988), pp. 9-10; "New Head of D.P.P." (1989) 1 Criminology Aust. 16 at 17. Cf. *Clyne v. Deputy Commissioner of Taxation* [1983] 1 N.S.W.L.R. 110.
148. A limited escape route given that the penalty that may be imposed is not limited to unjust enrichment but extends to gross profit from an offence.
149. See Temby, "The Proceeds of Crime Act: One Year's Experience" (1989) 13 Crim. L. J. 24 at 29; Mass, "Forfeiture of Attorneys' Fees: Should Defendants be Allowed to Retain the 'Rolls Royce of Attorneys' with the 'Fruits of Crime'?" (1987) 39 Stanford L. Rev. 663.
150. (1989) U.S. Lexis 3124; 57 U.S.L.W. 4836.
151. See also *United States v. Monsanto* (1989) U.S. Lexis 3132; 57 U.S.L.W. 4826, where the same approach was taken with respect to pre-trial orders and assets not yet judged forfeitable.
152. (1989) U.S. Lexis 3124.
153. *Russello v. United States* 464 U.S. 16 at 27-28 (1983).
154. 837 F.2d 637 at 649 (1988).
155. See e.g. Tr of Oral Arg. 50-52.
156. *Morris v. Slappy* 461 U.S. 1 at 23 (1983) (Brennan J. concurring in result).

Valjean must be satisfied with appointed counsel. Yet the drug merchant claims that his possession of huge sums of money . . . entitles him to something more. We reject this contention, and any notion of a constitutional right to use the proceeds of crime to finance an expensive defence."[157]

With respect, this line of argument begs the question. Criminals are not entitled to enjoy undeserved economic power but until criminality is established it is premature to say that they should be stripped of economic power. Since the confiscation provisions of the P.O.C. Act and the C.O.P.C. Act are conviction based, it is especially difficult to see why D should not be allowed to spend whatever he or she considers necessary to obtain genuine legal assistance in defending herself or himself against charges. The main purpose served by restraining orders is to prevent D from dispersing assets in such a way as to defeat the operation of confiscation orders. Provided that steps are taken to ensure that payment of legal fees is not a subterfuge for dispersion of assets to D's associates, that purpose can still be achieved.[158] It may be added that the value of independent legal representation should not be depreciated by reducing it merely to one factor in the equation of economic power. Lawyers transcend the balance of market power "not because of any professional or moral superiority, but because they play a unique and essential institutional role in our criminal justice system. They serve as the necessary advocates of defendants' rights".[159]

The availability of legal advice may also be prejudiced by the possible chilling effect of the P.O.C. Act and the C.O.P.C. Act upon lawyers asked to act on behalf of persons charged with serious offences, especially drug- or tax-related offences.[160]

157. 837 F.2d 637 at 649, n. 7 (1988).
158. See *Caplin and Drysdale, Chartered v. United States* (1989) U.S. Lexis 3124; 57 U.S.L.W. 4836 where the minority observed that:
> [t]he government's interests are adequately protected so long as the district court supervises transfers to the attorney to make sure they are made in good faith. All that is lost is the government's power to punish the defendant before he is convicted. That power is not one the Act intended to grant.

This is not to deny that solicitors' trust accounts may represent an attractive avenue for money laundering: see Temby, "The Proceeds of Crime Act: One Year's Experience" (1989) 13 Crim. L. J. 24 at 28; Temby, "Taking Assets Off Criminals—Attainder in Australia Today?" (Paper 14, University of Western Australia Law Summer School, 1988), p. 9; Australia, Royal Commission of Inquiry into Drug Trafficking, *Report* (1983), pp. 629-630. Nor is it to deny that the criminal law should be used against lawyers who unjustifiably assist offenders to escape justice: see further *O'Donovan v. Vereker* (1987) 76 A.L.R. 97; Gyles, "Criminal Liability of Professional Advisers" (1989) 23 Taxation in Aust. 480; Redlich, "Criminal Liability of Professional Advisers" (1989) 68 Vic. Bar News 12.
159. Cloud, "Forfeiting Defence Attorneys' Fees: Applying an Institutional Role Theory to Define Individual Constitutional Rights" [1987] Wisconsin L. Rev. 1 at 65.
160. See Tracy, "R.I.C.O. and the Forfeiture of Attorneys' Fees: Removing the Adversary from the Adversarial System" (1987) 62 Washington L. Rev. 201; Cloud, "Forfeiting Defense Attorneys' Fees: Applying an Institutional Role Theory to Define Individual Constitutional Rights" [1987] Wisconsin L. Rev. 1; Mass, "Forfeiture of Attorneys' Fees: Should Defendants be Allowed to Retain the 'Rolls Royce of Attorneys' with the 'Fruits of Crime'?" (1987) 39 Stanford L. Rev. 663; Brickey, "Forfeiture of Attorneys' Fees: The Impact of R.I.C.O. and C.C.E. Forfeitures on the Right to Counsel" (1986) 72 Virginia L. Rev. 493; McKay, "Forfeiture of Attorneys' Fees under R.I.C.O. and C.C.E." (1986) 54 Fordham L. Rev. 1171; Frame, "The 1984 R.I.C.O. Amendments: Will Defendants and their Attorneys be Short-Changed?" (1986) 18 Pacific L. J. 31.

Assume that D, who is widely reputed to be a drug trafficker, is convicted of a drug importation offence under s. 233B of the *Customs Act* 1901 (Cth). B, D's barrister, is paid fees at her usual rate of $2,000 per day. She is paid by D's solicitor and knows that the funds have come from D's bank account. She is aware of D's reputation as a drug trafficker and knows that the offence charged has generated approximately $2 million in proceeds. Assuming that the funds in D's bank account were in fact derived from the commission of an offence against s. 233B, the fees received by B are subject to forfeiture under s. 19 of the P.O.C. Act. B may apply under s. 21(6) to have her interest recognised and validated, but this avenue of protection requires, inter alia, that B received the fees "without knowing, and in circumstances such as not to arouse a reasonable suspicion, that the property was, at the time of the acquisition, tainted property."[161] It is difficult to see how B could satisfy this requirement and yet she has acted in good faith and for sufficient consideration. Perhaps this is a case where a forfeiture order would not be made, on the ground of "hardship" under s. 19(3)(a). Yet is there "hardship" if B knew that her fees were derived from D's offence? If B was reckless? If B suspected? If B did not suspect but had reason to do so? Does it matter that B is a wealthy barrister? That B occasionally undertakes criminal defence work without fee? It is submitted that lawyers acting in good faith on behalf of clients should not be required to work in peril of having the fees confiscated as proceeds of crime, especially under so ill defined a standard as that of "hardship". The danger, it may be noted, cannot be avoided by the tactic of receiving fees in advance.[162]

The offence of money laundering may be even more chilling for lawyers.[163] Take the case of a solicitor or barrister representing an accused charged with a major tax fraud. If the solicitor or barrister accepts a fee from the accused he or she may easily be in jeopardy of committing an offence against s. 81 of the P.O.C. Act. The money handed over may well amount to "proceeds of crime", as widely defined under s. 4, and receiving the money is plainly a prohibited transaction. Whether an offence is committed will depend on whether the solicitor or barrister ought reasonably to have known that the money was of illicit derivation. This objective test may easily catch the lawyer who does not go to considerable lengths to try to ensure that her or his fees come from

---

161. P.O.C. Act, s. 21(6)(b)(ii).
162. See *Kirk v. Commissioner of Australian Federal Police* (1988) 81 A.L.R. 321 (there is no beneficial interest in fees paid in advance but a possessory lien to secure payment to extent of work performed).
163. A similar problem arises under the *Money Laundering Control Act* 1986 (U.S.): Weinstein, "Prosecuting Attorneys for Money Laundering: A New and Questionable Weapon in the War on Crime" (1988) 51 *Law & Contemporary Problems* 369; Irvine and King, "The Money Laundering Control Act of 1986: Tainted Money and the Criminal Defence Lawyer" (1987) 19 Pacific L. J. 171. The problem featured in a recent episode of the television programme *L.A. Law* and has therefore ingrained itself in Australian as well as American social culture. The outreach of the offence of money laundering is hardly confined to lawyers, it may be noted, but extends to wives and other intimates of D: see Nicol, "Confiscation of the Profits of Crime" (1988) 52 J. Crim. L. 75 at 82-83.

a legitimate original source.[164] Compare the requirement for the offence of receiving stolen goods that D must know or believe that the items received were stolen.[165] It is this requirement, together with the defence of claim of right, that spares lawyers from liability for receiving if they accept fees for acting on behalf of reputed gangsters and crooks. It may be noted that the offence of money laundering under the C.O.P.C. Act requires that D knew that the property received represented the proceeds of a serious offence.[166] More circumspect as this definition is, lawyers may still find themselves in a predicament. Assume that S, a solicitor, knows that his fees have come from a serious offence but that he has acquired this knowledge only as a result of information obtained from questions asked of D for the purpose of representing D.[167] S might be forgiven for believing that he is legally entitled to be paid for his services in these circumstances but it is most unlikely that the defence of claim of right applies to the offence of money laundering.[168]

One response to these concerns is that it is fanciful to suppose that the legislation would be invoked in such cases.[169] However, in the emotionally and politically charged atmosphere of drug-related offences and major tax or bribery scandals, this response is unconvincing.[170] A preferable approach, it is submitted, is to delimit the scope of offences as a matter of legal definition. In the context of money laundering this would mean defining the offence not only in terms of a mental element of knowledge, but also in terms of an exemption for legal professional fees received for sufficient consideration and in good faith.[171]

THIRD PARTIES: THE FAMILY AS A TARGET OF PUNISHMENT?

The laws of forfeiture have an inglorious history. For innocent third parties, the evolution of our modern proceeds of crime legislation has

164. Cf. *Sydney Morning Herald*, 10 July 1989, p. 10 (spokesman for the New South Wales Law Society reported as saying that solicitors conveying property are under no obligation to ask the source of the funds).
165. *R. v. Raad* [1983] 3 N.S.W.L.R. 344; *Anderson v. Lynch* (1982) 17 N.T.R. 21; *R. v. Fallon* (1981) 28 S.A.S.R. 394; *R. v. Crooks* [1981] 2 N.Z.L.R. 53.
166. C.O.P.C. Act, s. 73(3). See also s. 73(4).
167. Cf. Wolfteich, "Making Criminal Defence a Crime under U.S.C. Section 1957" (1988) 41 Vanderbilt L. Rev. 843.
168. See Fisse, "The Rise of Money Laundering Offences and the Fall of Principle" (1989) 13 Crim. L. J. 5 at 15-16.
169. See Temby, "The Proceeds of Crime Act: One Year's Experience" (1989) 13 Crim. L. J. 24.
170. Consider e.g. the allegation that some lawyers "disgrace their profession by becoming the handmaidens of crime": Queensland, *Report of a Commission of Inquiry Into Possible Illegal Activities and Associated Police Misconduct* (1989), p. 166.
171. Cf. Wolfteich, "Making Criminal Defence a Crime under U.S.C. Section 1957" (1988) 41 Vanderbilt L. Rev. 843 (proposal exempting knowing receipt of lawyers' fees derived from illicit conduct where knowledge was gained independently of or prior to representing client).

been severe.[172] Ships, yachts, fishing boats, motor vehicles, and aircraft have been seized and forfeited by customs and related authorities with legislatively condoned abandon.[173] Little attention has been paid to the interests of owners, lenders, and other luckless victims whose only connection with the events leading to seizure has been their beneficial interest in the "guilty" item seized.[174] By welcome contrast, the P.O.C. Act and the C.O.P.C. Act provide an extensive array of safeguards for third parties. These safeguards greatly minimise the risk of injustice. Some problems nonetheless remain. As explained below, the automatic forfeiture provisions under the P.O.C. Act may sometimes work harshly and, as we have seen, lawyers' fees may warrant further protection. The main source of concern, however, is not the risk of third parties being deprived of their interest in property. The greater worry is the adverse indirect impact that confiscation orders may have upon the members of an offender's family. The vicarious punishment of members of an offender's family has been seen in some quarters as a useful method of deterring major crime but such a view is highly controversial.

The P.O.C. Act and the C.O.P.C. Act provide important safeguards for protecting the property interests of innocent third parties. Discretionary forfeiture orders require that an offender by convicted of an offence;[175] by contrast, there is no such requirement under the forfeiture provisions of the *Customs Act* 1901 (Cth).[176] Where third parties have an interest in

172. See especially Finkelstein, "The Goring Ox: Some Historical Perspectives on Deodands, Forfeitures, Wrongful Death and the Western Notion of Sovereignty" (1973) 46 Temple L. Q. 169 at 213-227. See also *Cheatley v. The Queen* (1972) 127 C.L.R. 291; *Forbes v. Traders' Finance Corp. Ltd* (1971) 126 C.L.R. 429; *Burton v. Honan* (1952) 86 C.L.R. 169 at 178-179, 180; *McGovern v. Victoria* [1984] V.R. 570; *Margolin v. E.A. Wright Pty Ltd* [1959] V.R. 455; *J.W. Goldsmith, Jr, Grant Co. v. United States* 254 U.S. 505 (1920); *United States v. One Ford Coupe*, 272 U.S. 321 (1926); *United States v. One 1957 Oldsmobile Auto.* (1958) 256 F.2d 931; Fox and Freiberg, *Sentencing* (1985), pp. 222-224; Goode, "The Confiscation of Criminal Profits" (1986) 67 *Proceedings of the Institute of Criminology, University of Sydney* 35; Smith, "Modern Forfeiture Law and Policy: A Proposal for Reform" (1978) 19 Wm & Mary L. Rev. 661; Maxeiner, "Bane of American Forfeiture Law—Banished at Last?" (1977) 62 Cornell L. Rev. 768; Hughes and O'Connell, "In Personam (Criminal) Forfeiture and Federal Drug Felonies: An Expansion of a Harsh English Tradition into a Modern Dilemma" (1984) 11 Pepperdine L. Rev. 613.
173. See *McGovern v. Victoria* [1984] V.R. 570; *Cole v. Esanda Ltd* [1982] Tas. R. 130; *Cheatley v. The Queen* (1972) 127 C.L.R. 291; *Forbes v. Traders' Finance Corp Ltd* (1971) 126 C.L.R. 429; *Margolin v. E.A. Wright Pty Ltd* [1959] V.R. 455; *Calero-Toledo v. Pearson Yacht Leasing Co.* (1974) 416 U.S. 663; *United States v. One 1957 Oldsmobile Auto.* (1958) 256 F.2d 931. Cf. *Customs and Excise Commissioner v. Air Canada* [1989] 2 W.L.R. 589. In this case 331 kg of cannabis resin was found in a container carried on an Air Canada jumbo jet at Heathrow Airport. This discovery led the United Kingdom customs officials to seize the plane and the aircraft was released on payment of £50,000. It was held that although a literal interpretation of the words "been used for the carriage" under s. 141 of the *Customs and Excise Management Act* 1979 (U.K.) meant that the plane could lawfully be forfeited, the section was to be interpreted as requiring knowledge or recklessness as to illicit use. Cf. *Murphy v. Farmer* (1988) 165 C.L.R. 19 at 28 per Deane, Dawson and Gaudron JJ. (view expressed that it may not be permissible to read in a word such as knowingly into a forfeiture provision such as s. 229(1)(i) of the *Customs Act* 1901 (Cth)); see also *Forbes v. Traders' Finance Corp Ltd* (1971) 126 C.L.R. 429 at 432-433.
174. See e.g. *Forbes v. Traders' Finance Corporation Ltd* (1971) 126 C.L.R. 429.
175. As under *Proceeds of Crime Act* (Cth), s. 19.
176. See ss 229A, 243B, 243C.

property subject to a forfeiture order they may apply to a court to have their interest restored;[177] to succeed they must satisfy the court that they were not involved in the commission of an offence in respect of which the forfeiture order was made or, where the interest was acquired at the time of or after the commission of such an offence, that the interest was acquired for sufficient consideration and without knowing or being placed on reasonable suspicion that the property was tainted. The automatic forfeiture provisions are also conviction based, but there must be a conviction for a "serious offence".[178] Forfeiture takes place not by court order but spontaneously where property subject to a restraining order remains in force six months after the conviction. As in the case of discretionary forfeiture, innocent third parties may apply to a court to have their interest restored.[179] Restraining orders are circumscribed by a variety of protections for third parties, including notice of application for an order, notice of an order, and rights of exemption from and revocation of an order.[180]

Although there are many avenues of protection some potential difficulties remain.[181] One potential hazard is the automatic forfeiture process under s. 30 of the P.O.C. Act.[182] Where a third party's property is subject to a restraining order it can be forfeited upon effluxion of six months from the time when another person has been convicted of a relevant serious offence. Although provision is made for innocent parties to protect interests in the property subject to potential forfeiture, the onus is on them to come forward and make application to a court. Passive neglect or casual inaction may thus lead to loss.

A greater danger in practice is the indirect adverse effect that forfeiture orders and pecuniary penalties orders may easily have upon the members of an offender's family. The punitive impact of confiscation under the P.O.C. Act and the C.O.P.C. Act is not bounded by the limit of proportionality,[183] and the amount of loss that can be inflicted is not subject to any fixed amount. Although in law it is the offender who is

177. P.O.C. Act, s. 21.
178. P.O.C. Act, s. 30.
179. P.O.C. Act, s. 31.
180. P.O.C. Act, ss 45, 47, 48, 56.
181. There are a number of possible difficulties beyond the matters discussed below: (1) a reason to suspect test for disqualifying third parties from restoration of their interest in property subject to forfeiture may work harshly; many people in ordinary life interact with others whose source of funds is suspicious but where it would verge on fantastic to expect them to make the inquiry necessary to allay suspicion; there is a difference between having (a) a reason to suspect, and (b) a reason to suspect that one should act on by making diligent and effective inquiry; (2) the issue of notice has attracted concern in the literature; see further Goode, "Confiscation of Criminal Profits: Tangles in the Net" (1986) 24(6) L. Soc. J. 36 (have all the concerns raised been covered in the more recent legislation?); (3) the scope of the property subject to restraint may be too wide, as in cases where X steals Y's car and uses it to commit robbery; cf. *United States v. One Chevrolet Sedan* 12 F. Supp. 793 (1935); *United States v. One Ford Coach* 307 U.S. 219 (1939); (4) wives are in jeopardy of losing their interest in property subject to forfeiture if they were "involved in" a relevant offence; the meaning of "involved in" is not entirely clear (e.g., what if V lends D property used in commission of offence but does so under duress?).
182. There is no equivalent under the C.O.P.C. Act.
183. See above, pp. 85-87.

punished, the offender's family is also likely to be financially devastated. Hardship to others can be taken into account when a court is imposing a discretionary forfeiture order or a restraining order[184] but it remains unclear how far the courts' sense of familial justice will temper the imposition of punishment on drug-running or tax-evading offenders.

Some have seen merit in the capacity of forfeiture to inflict vicarious deterrent punishment. For Blackstone this was one rationale for attainder in treason:[185]

> Such forfeitures moreover, whereby his posterity must suffer as well as himself, will help to restrain a man, not only by the sense of his duty, and dread of personal punishment, but also by his passions and natural affections; and will interest every dependent and relation he has to keep him from offending: according to that beautiful sentiment of Cicero, "nec vero me fugit quam sit acerbum, perentium scelera filiorum poaenis lui: sed hoc praeclare legibus comparatum est, ut caritas liberorum amiciores parentes rei publicae redderet."[186]

Cicero's "beautiful sentiment" may have had some influence upon the thinking behind the P.O.C. Act. Certainly the Act has been viewed as imposing vicarious punishment. Ian Temby Q.C., when speaking of relatives and intimates of offenders subject to confiscatory orders under the Act, issued this unsentimental warning:[187]

> All such people will now be interested, for selfish if not principled reasons, to persuade major crime figures to give up their nefarious activities and find some legitimate pursuit, for otherwise the law may do great harm to malefactors directly, and indirectly to those around them.[188]

The pursuit of vicarious punishment against the members of an offender's family cuts against the grain of the common law. At common law, the general principle is that criminal liability is personal, not vicarious,[189] and that the person sentenced is the offender, not his or her parent or child.[190] The confiscatory sanctions available under the P.O.C. Act, by contrast, operate not only in personam; in practical effect, the impact may be in familiam. This goes to an extreme. The alternatives mooted earlier, namely remedies for recovery of unjust enrichment[191]

---

184. See e.g. P.O.C. Act, s. 19(3).
185. Blackstone, *Commentaries*, Vol. IV, p. 382.
186. "Nor indeed does it escape me that, however harsh it may be, the crimes of the sons are to be atoned by the punishment of the parents, but this is clearly settled by laws, so that the high protection accorded to free men will provide the republic with better parents".
187. (1988) 23(3) Aust. Law News 10.
188. Ibid. at 12.
189. *Tesco Supermarkets Ltd v. Nattrass* [1972] A.C. 153. See further Williams, *Criminal Law: The General Part* (2nd ed.), Ch. 7.
190. See Fox and Freiberg, *Sentencing* (1985), pp. 160-161. A subsidiary company is to be fined in light of its own resources, not those of its parent corporation: *Browning Arms Co. of Canada Ltd* (1974) 18 C.C.C. 2d 298; Hale, "The Twenty-Nine Million Dollar Fine" (1908) 41 Am. L. Rev. 904. Cf. *T.P.C. v. Bata Shoe Co. of Australia Pty Ltd* (1980) 44 F.L.R. 145.
191. See above, p. 90.

and financial incapacitation short of forfeiture,[192] offer less drastic and yet potent means of dealing with the high profit seekers in crime. Moreover, the deterrent impact of vicarious punishment on an offender's family and acquaintances is speculative, especially in a context where, at least according to folklore, godfathers rule the roost. Finally, to the extent that an offender's family and friends are guilty of complicity, they may be prosecuted accordingly.

CONCLUSION: THE RE-INCARNATION OF DEODANDS IN THE NEW INDUSTRIAL STATE?

Legislation for the confiscation of proceeds of crime, as exemplified by the *Proceeds of Crime Act* 1987 (Cth) and the C.O.P.C. Act 1989, has been introduced in an attempt to deal with insidious forms of crime for profit. In pursuing the illicit money trail the legislation has much to commend it. However, the extent of the measures taken is open to criticism.[193] The use made of forfeiture and pecuniary penalties seems drastic and unnecessary. Assuming that the major underlying aims are removal of unjust enrichment, retribution, deterrence, and incapacitation, the provisions for forfeiture and pecuniary penalties legislation are sweeping. Indeed, in stepping beyond the boundaries of unjust enrichment, proportionality, and least drastic means, the legislation authorises a degree of expropriation of property that seems unprincipled. Moreover, there are significant departures from fundamental principles of criminal liability. The principle that criminal liability requires a subjectively blameworthy state of mind has been qualified under the P.O.C. Act by the provisions on money lending offences.[194] The principle that liability is personal, not vicarious, has been abandoned under the P.O.C. Act[195] and the C.O.P.C. Act.[196] And, in effect if not original intention, both statutes pursue the aim of deterrence by vicariously punishing the members of an offender's family.

Instead of using forfeiture and pecuniary penalties to supplement the operation of punitive sentences, an alternative would be to rely on essentially two remedies: one designed to recoup unjust enrichment from offences, and another to incapacitate the economic power of offenders, not by forfeiture but by a form of restraining order.[197] This more circumspect approach would preserve the line between

192. See above, pp. 90-92.
193. Notwithstanding constraints imposed by international law, Australia is a signatory to the recent United Nations *Convention against Illicit Traffic in Narcotic Drugs and Psychotropic Substances* (1988), art. 5 of which requires that a party to the convention make provision for confiscation of the proceeds of crime. However, the definition and implementation of that requirement are left to domestic law (art. 5(9)). The goal of confiscation may therefore be pursued subject to the principles of proportionately limited punishment and least drastic means.
194. See above, pp. 93-94.
195. P.O.C. Act, s. 85.
196. C.O.P.C. Act, s. 76.
197. Pre-trial restraining orders would be necessary to complement the operation of the orders outlined above and, as at present, to help ensure that D does not dispose of property before conviction in such a way as to defeat the legislation.

punishment and remedy, the object being to avoid the obscure middle ground occupied by the present regime of forfeiture and pecuniary penalties.[198] The remedies envisaged would not be geared to deterrence but their combined impact potentially could achieve a high degree of prevention.[199] To make these suggestions, it should be stressed, is hardly to contend that the present legislation be scrapped. On the contrary, the task would be more one of paring back the existing provisions and adapting them for use within a framework of more tightly defined goals and constraints.[200]

These simple thoughts lead to an ultimate perplexity. Given the extremist features of the new legislation, there is reason to question the conventional wisdom that the legislation represents a paradigm shift away from deodands and other ancient forms of punishment in rem. In an illuminating account,[201] Jacob Finkelstein has traced the development of deodands and other forms of forfeiture as a means of upholding the sovereignty of the state where the legal system had yet to provide any workable method of social control. He observed that more modern forms of forfeiture, including confiscation of vehicles used in connection with crime, exemplifed the same "transcendent sanctity of the community" as the deodand. In his conclusion:[202]

[the sovereign may impose forfeiture penalties] whenever it considers its corporate well-being threatened or even vaguely challenged. And these forfeitures may, in the name of a "higher morality", be imposed as "objectively" upon the person as was the condemnation of the goring ox in biblical law, and the confiscation of the "guilty automobile" in our day.

Just as stoning and killing the ox that gored once allowed the state to maintain its transcendent sanctity, it may be that targetting the money trail enables the state to maintain an appearance of supremacy over drug trafficking and tax fraud, the industries that gore. If so, the deodand has been reincarnated.

198. See above, pp. 90-92. See further Clark, "Civil and Criminal Penalties and Forfeitures" (1976) 60 Minnesota L. Rev. 379.
199. In Operation Silo (see Australia, National Crime Authority, *Operation Silo: Report of an Investigation* (1987)) e.g. a remedy for the recovery of unjust enrichment would have enabled recovery of the amount recouped by means of pecuniary penalty. Account must also be taken of other civil remedies, especially those pursuable by the D.P.P.: see Australia, Director of Public Prosecutions, *Civil Remedies Report: 1985-1987*.
200. Cf. the crime control and due process models of criminal justice developed in Packer, *The Limits of the Criminal Sanction* (1968). The challenge ahead, however, is not so much model building as revision of the legislation along more defensible functional and principled lines. A useful starting point, in my view, would be to express the principal objects of the legislation in terms of the central aims rather than by reference to the legislative instrument of depriving offenders of the proceeds of crime. These aims appear to be removal of unjust enrichment, deterrence (specific and general), retribution and incapacitation. It would then be helpful to set out the primary and secondary means by which the aims are to be achieved together with the main constraints upon their pursuit.
201. Finkelstein, "The Goring Ox: Some Historical Perspectives on Deodands, Forfeitures, Wrongful Death and the Western Notion of Sovereignty" (1973) 46 Temple L. Q. 169. Cf. Evans, *The Criminal Prosecution and Capital Punishment of Animals* (1906).
202. Ibid. at 290.

6

Forfeiture, Confiscation and Sentencing

ARIE FREIBERG AND RICHARD FOX*

> a farrago of injustices sanctified by tradition.
>
> *Fried*[1]

PROBLEMS AND PARADIGMS

Sentencing law in Australia has been in a state of turmoil for over a decade, yet the special inquiries and new legislation at State and federal levels have rarely ventured beyond a restructuring of the conventional forms of monetary, custodial and non-custodial sanctions which traditionally count as sentences. In recent years, however, forfeiture as a crime control technique has been revived with a vengeance in Australia. Despite the abolition of common law forfeiture for crime by the *Forfeiture Act* 1870 (U.K.) and its local colonial analogues,[2] the measure survived into the 20th century. It lay, semi-dormant, in quasi-criminal statutory forms, particularly those relating to the enforcement of federal customs and excise matters. Almost 40 years ago former Chief Justice of the High Court, the late Sir Owen Dixon, recognised its potential as "drastic and far-reaching".[3]

In a fragmented Australian criminal justice system, federal legal initiatives are often adopted as models for the States, usually with the active encouragement of the Standing Committee of Attorneys-General. Until recently, the *Customs Act* 1901 (Cth) was the principal vehicle for national attempts to control access to illicit drugs. Powerful forfeiture measures, originally included in that legislation for the protection of federal revenue in customs matters generally, were remodelled into potent weapons against illegal drug importation and the proceeds of such importation. The confiscatory concepts enshrined in that legislation were soon applied to other forms of profitable crime at State as well as

---

* Professor of Criminology, Melbourne University and Professor of Law, Monash University, respectively. A revised version of a paper presented at the Sixth Annual Conference of the Australian and New Zealand Society of Criminology, Sydney, 24-26 September 1990. Our thanks to Judge Hassett of the County Court of Victoria for his comments upon an earlier draft of this paper.
1. Fried, "Rationalising Criminal Forfeiture" (1988) 79 J. of Crim. L. and Criminology 328 at 331 writing of civil forfeiture in the United States.
2. E.g. *Forfeitures for Treason and Felony Abolition Act* 1878 (Vic.).
3. *Burton v. Honan* (1952) 86 C.L.R. 169 at 178 per Dixon C.J.

federal levels. The redeployment of forfeiture in the mid 20th century in this country and elsewhere[4] has been rapid and remarkable. It is a measure advanced with almost messianic zeal by prosecutorial authorities who press for its even wider use. Yet it is replete with difficulties.

First, it comes in many different forms and guises. In the strictest sense the penalty of forfeiture is a sentence only when the legislature directs or permits it to be included in the judgment by which a criminal court disposes of guilty persons.[5] But the sanction of forfeiture can also be triggered simply by the commission of certain offences (whether or not a charge has been laid), or by the fact of conviction alone irrespective of judicial order, or formal sentence. Secondly, confiscatory orders can be made by courts exercising criminal, civil or quasi-criminal jurisdiction before or after a sentence has been imposed. The different sanctions need not be imposed by the same judge or the same tribunal. Thirdly, there is a want of consistency in the legal and criminological theories which support the use of forfeiture type sanctions. Are they to be used punitively or reparatively? Are the limiting principles central to sentencing systems based on desert and proportionality, and which allow for the mitigating effect of hardship, to be applied to them? Though many of the conventional justifications for punishment are also advanced in aid of procedures for the confiscation of assets, there are significant differences in aim and emphasis. Fourthly, its place in the general array of criminal sanctions is ill defined. There is no common legislative or judicial position regarding what account, if any, ought to be taken in sentencing of the actual or potential consequences of forfeiture. Much of modern forfeiture legislation appears deliberately to dissociate the sentencing and confiscatory processes, treating them as though they were competing sanction systems, even to the point of express statutory directions that forfeiture is to be ignored in sentencing. Fifthly, even when legislation does evince an intention to keep the two systems of sanction separate, deprivation of assets is so significant a sanction that courts tend to baulk at treating it as irrelevant to sentence. There is evidence that sentencers are reluctant to create a total punitive effect that is disproportionate to the offending. Finally, the ability of the courts to avoid apparent injustice is often constrained by the degree of discretion left to them by the legislature, and by the order in which the separate confiscatory and sentencing orders are handled.

4. The Australian legislation is: *Crimes (Confiscation of Profits) Act* 1986 (Vic.) (C.(C.P.) Act 1986 (Vic.)); *Crimes (Confiscation of Profits) Act* 1986 (S.A.) (C.(C.P.) Act 1986 (S.A.)); *Proceeds of Crime Act* 1987 (Cth) (P.O.C. Act 1987 (Cth)); *Crimes (Confiscation of Profits) Act* 1988 (W.A.) (C.(C.P.) Act 1988 (W.A.)); *Crimes (Forfeiture of Proceeds) Act* 1988 (N.T.) (C.(F.P.) Act 1988 (N.T.)); *Crimes (Confiscation of Profits) Act* 1989 (Qld) (C.(C.P.) Act 1989 (Qld)); *Confiscation of Proceeds of Crime Act* 1989 (N.S.W.) (C.O.P.C. Act 1989 (N.S.W.)); *Drug Trafficking (Civil Proceedings) Act* (N.S.W.) 1990. See also *Organised Crime Control Act* 1970 (U.S.); *Continuing Criminal Enterprises Act* 1976 (U.S.); *Comprehensive Forfeiture Act* 1984 (U.S.); *Drug Trafficking Offences Act* 1986 (U.K.).
5. There is no all-inclusive common law or statutory definition of what constitutes a sentence. We offer "any dispositive order of a criminal court consequent upon a finding of guilt, whether or not a formal conviction is recorded". Fox and Freiberg, *Sentencing: State and Federal Law in Victoria* (1985), para. 1.101.

Discussion of the place of forfeiture and confiscation in the sentencing of criminals is sparse. This chapter aims to explore the dimensions of the problem. It will demonstrate that the two sanctioning techniques remain intimately connected, but in an unsystematic fashion and will canvass the possibility of better integrating them. Its contention is that the disconnection between forfeiture and sentence is the product of historical forces now spent, of unsound conceptual distinctions and of anti-libertarian and myopic political imperatives.

Attainder, deodand and customs seizures

Much of the confusion which permeates this field is the result of forfeiture being historically rooted in a number of quite separate concepts. Foremost was that of *attainder* under which the civil rights and capacities (including the right to hold, inherit or dispose of property) were deemed to have been automatically extinguished on sentence of death or outlawry of those convicted of treason or felony. No judicial order of forfeiture was required. This form of forfeiture was grounded in the feudal notion that all property or offices were held by the grace of a superior lord and were to be subject to surrender for breach of fealty. The latter would be particularly revealed in acts of treason or felony. Forfeiture was also possible at common law, without the recording of a conviction, if persons fled from justice when confronted by allegations of serious crime. Their guilt was presumed from their absconding.

There was also the parallel concept of *deodand*. It permitted the confiscation to the Crown, on coronial order, but irrespective of any conviction, of the very instruments themselves of crime or damage, at least where a death had been caused. The purpose was more than removal of dangerous things from circulation. There was a mystical and redemptive connection with the wrongdoing. The deodand ("that which is given to God") was applied to pious and charitable uses. Though the benefit could find its way back to the victim's family, compensatory functions were not central to this form of forfeiture.

In addition, there is a background of at least 400 years of customs law which made use of seizure and forfeiture under statute, rather than criminal prosecution and conviction, as its principal mode of enforcing laws designed to raise revenue for the state. The various types of common law forfeiture have disappeared in Australia, having generally been abrogated by statute, but the diverse collection of statutory provisions which have replaced them still show signs of their common law lineage. The influence of the long-standing customs approach to law enforcement continues unabated.

Uncertain terminology

The term "forfeiture" is bound up with that of "confiscation". Both terms are used loosely and interchangeably. Each describes the alienation or withdrawal of certain legal rights. In both, the divestment of proprietary interests is ordinarily for the benefit of the Crown rather than a private complainant or victim.[6] The proprietary interest appropriated need not necessarily be that of the offender. No compensation is payable. As understood at common law, the subject matter of forfeiture is generally specific property immediately connected with the commission of an offence. Confiscation is a more modern term often used, in contradistinction to forfeiture, to denote deprivation of an offender of assets being the proceeds or profits of crime.[7] But the difference between forfeiture and confiscation is now blurred in Australia because the new "proceeds of crime" legislation relies on the concept of "confiscation orders", which themselves embrace both orders for forfeiture and orders for confiscation.

Civil or criminal

Deciding the place of forfeiture within the general scheme of criminal sanctions is handicapped by the problem of characterising forfeiture as civil or criminal.[8] This is particularly true of enforcement procedures under customs and excise Acts which rely on a unique admixture of conventional criminal prosecutions, "civil" procedures, and non-judicial administrative penalties and forfeitures.[9] The last are neither direct punishment for a crime, though a crime has generally been committed when a forfeiture is incurred, nor are they regarded as damages in tort awarded to compensate for a civil injury. They are said to be, in essence, civil measures protective of the revenue. On the other hand, their effect is often excessive and patently punitive.[10]

Statutory paradigms

In considering the relationship between forfeiture and sentencing, too wide a generalisation is dangerous. The various statutory schemes for forfeiture allow different degrees of leeway in their linkage with conventional sentencing. Forfeiture may be invoked in respect of many different types of act or omission. Criminality may only have to be alleged or charged rather than be proven by conviction, or the equivalent of a conviction. The divestment of rights may be mandatory or discretionary. If mandatory, forfeiture may occur wholly automatically by operation of statute, or may require an order from a judge or magistrate who is left no discretion in the matter. If judicial discretion is allowed, it may be exercised by the same court as that responsible for fixing sentence, or by an entirely different court

6. As opposed to orders for compensation or costs.
7. Fox and Freiberg, op. cit., Ch. 6; Hodgson, *Profits of Crime and Their Recovery* (1984) p. 5.
8. Maxeiner, "Constitutionalising Forfeiture Law—The German Example" (1979) 27 Am. J. of Comparative L. 635 at 659; see also Clark, "Civil and Criminal Penalties and Forfeitures: A Framework for Constitutional Analysis" (1976) 60 Minnesota L. Rev. 379.
9. Australian Law Reform Commission, *Customs and Excise: Customs Prosecutions, Jurisdiction and Administrative Penalties*, Discussion Paper 42 (1990); Australian Law Reform Commission, *Customs and Excise: Seizure and Forfeiture*, Discussion Paper 43 (1990).
10. Clark, op. cit. at 411; *One Lot Emerald Cut Stones v. United States* 409 U.S. 232 at 237 (1972).

exercising what appears to be civil jurisdiction. Forfeiture may be ordered before sentence has been imposed or afterwards. The combinations and variations are numerous. Six major paradigms can be identified.[11]

- **Paradigm 1: Automatic on commission of offence.**

  Where forfeiture is a non-discretionary, non-judicial consequence of the *commission* of an offence. No criminal proceedings are required to establish the alleged offence. In these cases the forfeiture is, by statute, wholly automatic. There is no requirement of judicial involvement.[12] A prosecution need never be instigated, nor a sentence imposed, but those possibilities are not excluded.

- **Paradigm 2: Automatic on conviction of offence.**

  Where forfeiture is a non-discretionary, non-judicial consequence of *a conviction* (including a deemed conviction) of an offence.[13] No judicial order is required, nor is any exercise of judicial discretion called for in relation to the forfeiture.[14] It is, by statute, wholly automatic. But it must be supported by a prosecution to conviction. The court retains its discretion regarding sentence, including a discretion to enter the conviction itself.

- **Paradigm 3: Mandatory on conviction of offence.**

  Where the forfeiture is a non-discretionary, judicial consequence of *a conviction* (including a deemed conviction) of an offence. A criminal court must, as part of its judgment on recording a

11. Cf. *Fisheries Inspector v. Turner* [1978] 2 N.Z.L.R. 233 at 238-239 per Richardson J. In that case Somers J. stated at 244-245:

    There are numerous enactments which provide for forfeiture of property . . . as a result or consequence of unlawful conduct. But the manner in which or the event upon which that result or consequence takes or may take effect varies. The principle division is between those statutes in which an order or direction of the court brings about forfeiture . . . and those in which that consequence occurs without any direct order by the court. And within that division there are other differences. . . .

    The range of the different formulae adopted by Parliament . . . indicates that the modes of working a forfeiture and the events upon which it depends are the result of deliberate choice.

12. An example of this is found in s. 239 of the *Customs Act* 1901 (Cth) which provides that: "All penalties imposed under the *Customs Act* 1901 (Cth) are in addition to any forfeiture." There may be no judicial discretion in regard to the forfeiture, but there may be in relation to the subsequent sanction: see further below, pp. 115-118.

13. Or equivalent.

14. The *Ozone Protection Act* 1989 (Cth), s. 58 provides that where a person is convicted of an offence against the Act "all forfeitable goods to which the offence relates are, by force of the conviction, forfeited to the Commonwealth". In *Fisheries Inspector v. Turner* [1978] 2 N.Z.L.R. 233 at 244, Somers J. said of a provision of this type that it was not "properly to be described as the exercise of an executive power. It is a consequence ordained by the legislature itself as following on conviction". In some ways this is the closest analogue to common law forfeiture. At common law, forfeiture for treason or felony was not an express part of the sentence, but an automatic result of the conviction. The very word felony has been said to contain a reference to the forfeiture which follows the crime, i.e., "fee" (a feudal holding) and "lon" (price): Blackstone, *Commentaries on the Laws of England*, Vol. IV, p. 95.

conviction, make a forfeiture order.[15] No discretion as to the making of the forfeiture order is allowed, but discretions regarding recording a conviction or the type of sentence are retained.

• **Paradigm 4: Discretionary on conviction of offence: criminal court.**

Where the forfeiture is a discretionary, judicial consequence of *a conviction* (including a deemed conviction) of an offence. A *criminal* court may, as part of its judgment on recording a conviction, make a forfeiture order. The court has a discretion in respect of conviction, sentence and forfeiture.

• **Paradigm 5: Discretionary on conviction of offence: civil court.**

Where the forfeiture is a discretionary, judicial consequence of *a conviction* (including a deemed conviction) of an offence. A court, in the exercise of *civil* jurisdiction, subsequent to conviction may make a forfeiture or similar order. The court has a discretion in respect of the order, but none in respect of the conviction or sentence.

• **Paradigm 6: Discretionary on civilly proscribed conduct.**

Where the forfeiture is a discretionary judicial consequence of the offender engaging in civilly proscribed conduct. The conduct need not amount to a criminal offence, nor is any actual or deemed conviction required, though that possibility is not excluded. A court in the exercise of *civil* jurisdiction, may make a forfeiture or similar order. The court has a discretion in respect of the order, but none in respect of any conviction or sentence.

The first four paradigms represent the statutory forfeitures generally found in customs and excise legislation and other traditional statutory forfeitures, while the fifth is more akin to the confiscation orders available under state and federal "proceeds of crime" legislation. The sixth represents the pecuniary penalty provisions of the *Customs Act* 1901 (Cth)[16] and the more recent confiscation provisions of the *Drug Trafficking (Civil Proceedings) Act* 1990 (N.S.W.).

In tabular form, these paradigms can be depicted as follows:

Paradigm Number	Offending Behaviour	Judicial Intervention	Type of Court	Discretion
1	Commission of offence	No	—	—
2	Conviction	No	—	—
3	Conviction	Yes	Criminal	No
4	Conviction	Yes	Criminal	Yes
5	Conviction	Yes	Civil	Yes
6	Proscribed Conduct	Yes	Civil	Yes

15. *Fisheries Inspector v. Turner* [1978] 2 N.Z.L.R. 233 at 239 per Richardson J. See e.g. *Liquor Control Act* 1987 (Vic.), s. 123(3): "a court shall in the case of an offence under this section also order all liquor which is found in the possession of the person convicted and the liquor and the vessel containing it to be forfeited".
16. Sections 243A-243S, *Customs Act* 1901 (Cth).

For each of the above paradigms, the inescapable question arises[17]—what account should be taken of the fact of forfeiture in imposing sentence or, depending on timing, what weight should be given to the nature of the sentence when ordering forfeiture?

Mandatory or discretionary

The answer will be partly affected by whether the statutory forfeiture, or prescribed sentence, is mandatory or discretionary in nature. When Parliament prescribes a maximum penalty for a class of crime it is setting a known and legally defined limit on punishment for that misconduct. In theory this is set high enough to accommodate the worst envisaged examples of that class of offending while, at the same time, indicating the relative seriousness with which that type of act or omission is regarded by the state.[18] It assumes that judicial discretion will be exercised in determining where, within the boundary set by the maximum, an appropriate sentence should be fixed in the individual case. The higher the potential penalty, the greater the need for some discretion in fixing it. It is assumed that the courts will have regard to factors which were unable to be comprehensively enumerated in the legislation itself. It is regarded as a serious departure from this well understood division of sentencing responsibilities if Parliament demands mandatory penalties or directs the courts to ignore apparently mitigating factors in order to exclude the adjusting power of the judiciary.[19]

Mandatory sentencing and automatic forfeiture provisions purport to render irrelevant the personal circumstances of the offender, or the value of the property expropriated, or the effect of the disqualification imposed or any other mitigating considerations.[20] Whether the sanction be custodial, financial, or disqualificatory, the rigidity this creates is certain to cause hardship. The answer given is that executive remission of the penalty or forfeiture, in full or in part, is the means of amelioration. While such executive discretion has always had a legitimate role in sentencing, it is unprotected by procedural safeguards and less visible and principled than judicial decision making.

In any event, the problem of the relationship between forfeiture and sentencing will be rarely rendered academic by the restraining influence of mandatory provisions. It would be exceptional for conduct to be punished by both a mandatory sentence and mandatory forfeiture. There will inexorably be some element of discretion; if not in the imposition of the forfeiture or sentence, then as to its quantum. To confine discretion in one class or dimension of penal sanctions only enhances its importance in others. And if the sentencing system of sanctions is wedded to the idea that the totality of punishment must be proportionate

17. The question appears not to arise in the first and sixth paradigms, but will do so if there is a later successful prosecution.
18. Victoria, Sentencing Task Force, *Review of Statutory Maximum Penalties in Victoria* (1989) pp. 22-25.
19. See *Cobiac v. Liddy* (1969) 119 C.L.R. 257.
20. Note that, in relation to forfeiture orders, although no discretion may be allowed regarding whether an order is to be made, a discretion may exist regarding what is to be forfeited.

to the crime, it will be under pressure to adjust its allocations of punishment somewhere along the line to counterbalance the rigidity of a confiscatory system that denies either that it is punitive, or that proportionality has any application to it.

Priority

Part of the problem relates to which sanction is imposed first. At common law criminal prosecutions had priority over civil ones; in particular, a civil action for damages could not be commenced until a charge of felony was disposed of by prosecution.[21] The common law thus excluded from consideration at sentencing the effect on an accused of an award of damages arising out of the same transaction as was being prosecuted as criminal. And no subsequent award of damages could be mitigated by reference to the hardship occasioned by the prior criminal punishment. Statutory forfeiture schemes which benefit the Crown are not subject to any general priority rule, save that those which depend on an actual conviction must necessarily await the conclusion of the criminal prosecution.[22] If sentence and forfeiture are being decided by the same judicial officer, and the legislation is couched in discretionary terms, it is easier for the global effect to be calculated and adjustment made to the sanctions. But if mandatory forfeiture comes after sentence, particularly if ordered by a different tribunal, the leeway for adjustment is negligible. In theory the sentence could be deferred to await the result of forfeiture proceedings, but if these are likely to be protracted, and the offender is being held in custody awaiting sentence, the understandable tendency is to impose sentence immediately.

FORMS OF FORFEITURE

Paradigm 1: Automatic on commission of offence
History

There are many statutory provisions that declare items of property to be forfeited to the Crown simply on the commission of an offence that involves those items.[23] This also extends to other property (such as

---

21. *Smith v. Selwyn* [1914] 3 K.B. 98; *Wonderheat v. Bishop* [1960] V.R. 489; abolished in Victoria, *Supreme Court Act* 1958, s. 63B.
22. Cf. s. 63, *Drug Trafficking (Civil Proceedings) Act* 1990 (N.S.W.): "The fact that criminal proceedings have been instituted or have commenced (whether or not under this Act) is not a ground on which the Supreme Court may stay proceedings under this Act that are not criminal proceedings."
23. Some examples can be found in the *Agricultural Chemicals Act* 1958 (Vic.), s. 18B(5); *Fisheries Act* 1968 (Vic.), s. 49(3); *Forests Act* 1958 (Vic.), s. 79(3); *Health Act* 1958 (Vic.), s. 293(1); *Stamps Act* 1958 (Vic.); *Coal Excise Act* 1949 (Cth), s. 26(1); *Commerce (Trade Descriptions) Act* 1905 (Cth), ss 7(2), 10 and 13; *Crimes Act* 1914 (Cth), ss 9(1), 30E(3), 30G, 65(3), 69(2), 83(5), 85D, 89A; *Crimes (Biological Weapons) Act* 1976 (Cth), s. 9(1); *Customs Act* 1901 (Cth), ss 205(1), 228, 228A, 228B, 229, 229A, 230; *Excise Act* 1901 (Cth), ss 96, 116(1); *Defence Act* 1903 (Cth), ss 82(1) and (2), 83; *Income Tax Assessment Act* 1936 (Cth), s. 221Y(2); *Navigation Act* 1912 (Cth), s. 252; *Psychotropic Substances Act* 1976 (Cth), s. 9(2); *Crimes (Currency) Act* 1981 (Cth), s. 29; *Spirits Act* 1906 (Cth), s. 17.

forms of transport) used in the offending. Divestment of title does not depend upon any judicial process, criminal or civil. No one has to be charged, or convicted, nor any judicial order obtained. Such legislation affects rights in rem, rather than ones in personam. Even the acquittal of the defendant of the offence in respect of which the forfeiture relates will not operate as a bar to this type of forfeiture.[24] These forms of forfeiture offer the least room to manoeuvre in adjusting the effect of the sanction either directly or indirectly. They have a long history which is often invoked to defend their retention as a form of sanction.

Forfeiture based upon unlawful activity, but not upon conviction, originally derives from actions for seizures and forfeitures taken in the revenue side of the exchequer jurisdiction of the courts. The Court of Exchequer was concerned with managing the king's revenue. It developed prerogative processes designed expeditiously to recover money due to the Crown. These were ultimately translated into forms of legislation. Of particular significance was English customs legislation. It made use both of forfeiture and conventional prosecution. The former measure was deliberately chosen for the administrative convenience it offered over standard criminal enforcement:[25]

> [T]he effort was to free the customs staff from the necessity or proving the evil intent and the overt acts usually required to convict of crime, and to reduce the task to one of merely discovering goods unladen or shipped without accompanying documents to prove that they had been duly declared.

This meant that proceedings could be brought either against the smuggler by what was in effect an action in personam, or, in those days, against the offending ship and its illegal cargo by an action in rem. Exchequer had used in rem procedure from the distant past to give the sovereign title to treasure trove, wrecks and the like where there was no obvious owner against whom action could be brought. The latter device was well suited to customs seizures because the authorities apprehended smuggled goods more often than smugglers.[26] The procedure was geared to permit a summary disposal of the seized articles, though the legislation allowed the owner to challenge the forfeiture or otherwise recover the goods on entering a compromise with the customs authorities. Compromises had to be approved by a court. The owner's lack of knowledge or intention in respect of the breach of the revenue law was irrelevant to the forfeiture. The fact of forfeiture, or any later compounding of proceedings, did not bar criminal prosecution of the actual participants for breach of the law involving the same property. Any such prosecutions were not regarded as part of the same proceedings because non-judicial, or in rem forfeitures, did not derive from common law forfeiture in criminal matters.

The latter always required the prerequisite of the conviction of the offender for felony or treason. In *The Palmyra*, Story J. explained:[27]

---

24. *Wiedenhofer v. Commonwealth* (1970) 122 C.L.R. 172 at 175-176.
25. Harper, *The English Navigation Laws: A Seventeenth-Century Experiment in Social Engineering* (1939), p. 87.
26. Ibid., p. 111.
27. 25 U.S. (12 Wheat) 1 at 12; 6 L. Ed 531 at 535 (1827).

It is well known, that at the common law, in many cases of felonies, the party forfeited his goods and chattels to the Crown. The forfeiture did not, strictly speaking, attach in rem; but it was a part, or at least a consequence, of the judgment or conviction. It is plain from this statement that no right to the goods and chattels of the felon could be acquired by the Crown by the mere commission of the offence; but the right attached only by the conviction of the offender. The necessary result was, that in every case where the Crown sought to recover such goods and chattels, it was indispensable to establish its right by producing the record of the judgment of conviction. In the contemplation of the common law, the offender's right was not divested until the conviction. But this doctrine was never applied to seizures and forfeitures, created by statute, in rem, cognizable on the revenue side of the exchequer. The thing is here primarily considered as the offender, or rather the offence is attached primarily to the thing; and this, whether the offence be malum prohibitum, or malum in se. The same principle applies to proceedings in rem, on seizures in the admiralty. Many cases exist where the forfeiture for acts done attaches solely in rem, and there is no accompanying penalty in personam. Many cases exist where there is both a forfeiture in rem and a personal penalty. But in neither class of cases has it ever been decided that the prosecutions were dependent upon each other. But the practice has been . . . that the proceeding in rem stands independent of, and wholly unaffected by any criminal proceeding in personam. This doctrine is deduced from a fair interpretation of the legislative intention apparent upon its enactments. Both in England and America, the jurisdiction over proceedings in rem is usually vested in different courts from those exercising criminal jurisdiction.

Effect on sentence

One of the most commonly used of these automatic forfeiture powers in Australia is to be found in the *Customs Act* 1901 (Cth).[28] The first effect of this legislation is that, immediately upon the occurrence of certain circumstances specified in the legislation, the property in the goods involved is divested from the owner and vested in the Crown.[29] The characteristic common to each situation is a dealing with goods or chattels in contravention of the provisions of the Act.[30] However, the transfer of title does not depend upon any act of seizure on behalf of the Crown, nor any prosecution of the offence in question.[31] Secondly, the goods now forfeited may be seized by those empowered under the Act

28. *Customs Act* 1901 (Cth), ss 205(1) 228, 228A, 228B, 229, 229A, 230; see also A.L.R.C., Discussion Paper No. 42 and A.L.R.C., Discussion Paper No. 43 (1990).
29. *The Annandale* (1877) L.R. 2 P.D. 179 at 185; *Lyons v. Smart* (1908) 6 C.L.R. 143 at 161; *Burton v. Honan* (1952) 86 C.L.R. 169 at 176; *Powers v. Maher* (1959) 103 C.L.R. 478 at 483; *Scott v. James Patrick & Co.* (1968) 117 C.L.R.. 242. See also *Bert Needham Automotive Co. Pty Ltd v. Federal Commissioner of Taxation* (1976) 10 A.L.R. 501 for other consequences of such divestment.
30. E.g. *Customs Act* 1901 (Cth), s. 229(1). See also *Excise Act* 1901 (Cth), s. 116(1).
31. *McGovern v. Victoria* [1984] V.R. 570.

to do so.[32] Thirdly, though no further proceedings are necessary in order to make title, they may be allowed for under the statute either in order to vindicate the title of the Crown to the goods, or to exclude the claim of some person asserting a right to them.[33] Customs and excise legislation usually also provides that the conviction of any person for the offence which caused the forfeiture is to have the effect of condemning the goods in respect of which the offence is committed. The idea of "condemned" goods does not refer to the passing of title, for ownership has already vested in the Crown, it means that the conviction of the offender is decisive of all matters of fact upon which the forfeiture of the goods depends.[34]

Despite the automatic nature of the forfeiture, in most cases a prosecution does follow a seizure where the offender is amenable to the jurisdiction. At that point the question of the relationship between the sentence to be imposed and the prior forfeiture has to be faced. The *Customs Act* 1901 (Cth), s. 239 blankly states that: "all penalties shall be in addition to any forfeiture." Is the sentencer being directed to ignore totally the effects of the prior automatic forfeiture? There is little authority on the operation of s. 239. In *Hayes v. Weller*[35] the defendants were involved in smuggling a car into Australia. The car was forfeited and sold by customs authorities, reaping them some $46,600. On later being prosecuted by the Comptroller-General of Customs the defendants faced liability for substantial fines as well. If, on conviction, fines were imposed in accordance with the formula provided for under the Act,[36] a minimum of $45,984 would be payable in at least one case. It was contended that the defendants should therefore be discharged without being convicted or suffering any further penalty because of the severity of the forfeiture and incidental losses they already had suffered.[37]

The trial judge thought that the statute gave him some leeway:[38]

> Whilst the terms of s. 239 clearly provide that the penalty required by s. 233AB is in addition to the forfeiture, I do not think it follows that the fact of the forfeiture is irrelevant in determining penalty. . . . [T]he likely impact of the penalty on the defendant must be assessed having regard to the state of his depleted assets. The imposition of a penalty of almost $46,000 would virtually strip him of the assets which he has accumulated throughout his working life. Even where the offence involves a serious and deliberate scheme to defraud the revenue, the *ordinary principles of sentencing have application*.

32. *Customs Act* 1901 (Cth), s. 203; *Excise Act* 1901 (Cth), s. 93. A person does not have a right to be heard before the exercise of the power of seizure under this section is exercised: *Toy Centre Agencies Pty Ltd v. Spencer* (1983) 46 A.L.R. 351.
33. *Burton v. Honan* (1952) 86 C.L.R. 169 at 176.
34. Ibid. at 179.
35. (1988) 33 A. Crim. R. 305.
36. The penalty provided by s. 233AB(1) of the *Customs Act* 1901 (Cth) was an amount not exceeding five times the duty evaded and a minimum of not less than two times that amount.
37. The cost of the car and shipping was $32,000.
38. *Hayes v. Weller* (1988) 33 A. Crim. R. 305 at 310-311, emphasis added.

His last phrase refers to his view that later or concurrently imposed sentences should be mitigated if the total punitive and confiscatory effect will be disproportionate to the offence committed. The judge made reference to the combined impact of the loss of money due to the forfeiture and the proposed minimum penalty which would amount to approximately $77,000. He proposed to construct a *penalty package*[39] which "in totality appropriately meets the circumstances of the case"[40] by forbearing to enter a conviction for the offence to which the minimum penalties applied.

The Crown successfully appealed against the leniency of the sentence.[41] It submitted that the judge had failed to give expression to the legislative policy of the Act which was designed to make use of two forms of penalty to meet the difficulties of policing customs offences.[42] The South Australian Supreme Court agreed. In its view, the gravity of the financial impact and the defendants' good character and other mitigating factors were insufficient to offset the weight that had to be given to the legislative policy that penalties were to be supplementary to any forfeiture.[43] However, the case cannot be read as supporting the proposition that express provisions of this sort absolutely deny sentencers the opportunity to treat the prior automatic forfeiture as mitigatory. In any event, the future of s. 239 of the *Customs Act* 1901 (Cth) is uncertain. The Australian Law Reform Commission, has tentatively proposed that s. 239 be repealed, arguing that:[44]

> Forfeiture is a consequence of the same conduct as that constituting the offence and, notwithstanding that it results from a different process, it is intended as a deterrent and shares that characteristic with punishment. Accordingly, it would seem that, upon ordinary sentencing principles, forfeiture should be regarded as relevant. It would be a matter for the sentencing court to determine the weight to be attributed to it.

In similar vein, Hodgson[45] has argued that automatic forfeiture provisions in effect create a strict liability criminal offence for which the sole penalty is the loss of property concerned. It penalises conduct without the substantive or procedural safeguards of the ordinary criminal process. In some cases the loss can exceed by many times the maximum fines which a criminal court could impose. He asserts this type of forfeiture is in effect a fine in specie[46] and, in order to redeem the imbalance of rights, ought to be allowed to be considered as such in determining its relationship to conventional sentences imposed in respect of the same act or omission. This means that any later imposed penalties

39. Ibid. at 312.
40. The total penalty in the most serious case amounted to $10,000 plus the loss of the value of the forfeited car. The effect of the minimum penalty was obviated by the court entering no conviction but entering convictions on two other less serious offences and imposing discretionary fines in respect of each offence.
41. *R. v. Weller* (1988) 37 A. Crim. R. 349.
42. *L. Vogel & Son Pty Ltd v. Anderson* (1968) 120 C.L.R. 157 at 164 per Kitto J.
43. *R. v. Weller* (1988) 37 A. Crim. R. 349 at 355 per Perry J.
44. A.L.R.C. Discussion Paper No. 42, p. 17.
45. Hodgson, op. cit., p. 95.
46. Ibid., p. 99.

should reflect the loss of forfeited goods[47] and should be adjusted if the total effect would be too onerous.[48] This view has found support in the High Court in the case of *R. v. Hoar*[49] where the relevant statute declared, in the case of discretionary forfeiture, that "the forfeiture shall be in addition to and not part of a penalty imposed."[50] The statute was read as intended to distinguish forfeiture from sentence, but not to deny the possibility of recognising the effect of one upon the other.

Paradigms 2 and 3: Automatic or mandatory on conviction

Paradigms 2 and 3 depend on some judicial process in the criminal courts but, in both, the legislative intention is to rule out discretion. Forfeitures which attach automatically to convictions are not part of the judgment of the court and leave sentencers no leeway in relation to the forfeiture of the property.[51] Though it is clear that the amount of any later imposed penalty cannot alter the reach of a prior automatic forfeiture, if the forfeiture is dependent on conviction, it can be forestalled in its entirety by judicial refusal to enter a conviction.[51a] This is legitimate; conditional or unconditional discharge without conviction is a standard sentencing option. No matter whether the forfeiture operates as an immediate statutory consequence of the conviction, or must be ordered by the sentencer under mandatory provisions binding the court,[52] no conviction means no forfeiture.

But the right to discharge an offender without conviction may itself be qualified by statute in order to ensure that minimum penalties are not thus avoided. Is a forfeiture a minimum penalty? In the New Zealand case of *Fisheries Inspector v. Turner*,[53] the respondent had been found fishing illegally and had been charged with an offence under the fisheries regulations. The automatic consequence of a conviction would have been that the fishing vessel, estimated to be worth $65,000, would have been forfeited and the offender would, as well, be subject to any penalty imposed for the offence itself. The magistrate found the fisheries offence proven, but discharged the offender without conviction on payment of costs. He did so to avoid the forfeiture which he regarded to be out of proportion to the nature and gravity of the offence. Section 42(1) of the *Criminal Justice Act* 1954 (N.Z.) upon which he relied permitted the discharge of an offender "unless by any enactment applicable to the offence a minimum penalty is provided for". On appeal by the fisheries to the New Zealand Court of Appeal, it was argued that the forfeiture constituted a "minimum penalty" and thus excluded the power to discharge without conviction.

47. *R. v. Lidster* [1976] Crim. L. R. 80.
48. *R. v. Thompson* (1977) 66 Cr. App. R. 130.
49. (1981) 148 C.L.R. 32.
50. See below, pp. 119-120.
51. *Fisheries Inspector v. Turner* [1978] 2 N.Z.L.R. 233 at 242 per Richardson J.
51a. Cf. *Glover v. Zouroudis* (1990) 54 S.A.S.R. 200 where the Court's discretion as to when to decline to convict was carefully circumscribed by statute: see *Criminal Law (Sentencing) Act* 1988 (S.A.), s. 16.
52. E.g. *Liquor Control Act* 1987 (Vic.), s. 123(3).
53. [1978] 2 N.Z.L.R. 233.

In the Court of Appeal, Woodhouse J. rejected this contention. The word "penalty" referred to a sanction judicially imposed as part of criminal proceedings.[54] Here the forfeiture operated as a "collateral and entirely independent consequence of conviction" and did not constitute an exclusionary "minimum penalty". On the other hand:[55]

> it would be entirely unreal to exclude the statutory consequence of forfeiture as an irrelevant factor for the purpose of deciding whether the discretion to discharge without conviction should be exercised. The consequences of entering a conviction is the very matter with which s. 42 of the *Criminal Justice Act* is concerned.

Richardson J. likewise agreed that the "statutory consequences of a conviction may be taken into account and given weight as considerations relevant to the exercise of the discretion" and if the direct and indirect consequences of a conviction were "out of all proportion to the gravity of the offence", it would be proper for a discharge to be given.[56] His Honour also saw another subtle significance in the distinction between automatic statutory imposed forfeiture and mandatorily awarded judicial forfeiture:[57]

> The [minimum] penalty must be "provided for" in the enactment. It is not enough that it is provided in the enactment. That language is apt to cover an enactment which provides for the imposition of the penalty by the court, but not one where the penalty accrues automatically on conviction and without any further act or step.

Paradigm 4: Discretionary on conviction—criminal process

Is forfeiture part of the sentence?

Forfeiture may be ordered, as a matter of discretion, following conviction at what would normally be regarded as the sentencing stage of a criminal trial. Whether it is an integral part of the sentence properly so called, or is a collateral order, is not always clear. Yet, even when the legislative language strongly intimates that it is not intended to be an integral component of the sentence, the fact that seizure and forfeiture of the defendant's property has occurred is regarded as directly relevant to the nature and quantum of the formal sentence handed down. The latter can then be adjusted to take account of it, or the discretion can be utilised to manipulate either or both the forfeiture and the sentence to achieve a desired total effect.

In the Northern Territory case of *R. v. Hoar*,[58] there were convictions relating to a conspiracy to fish for barramundi during a prohibited period. Forfeiture of plant, freezing equipment, etc. had been ordered by the sentencing judge under the *Fisheries Act* 1965 (N.T.). Such forfeiture was discretionary on conviction under s. 48(1) of the Act,

---

54. Ibid. at 236.
55. Ibid.
56. Ibid. at 241.
57. Ibid.
58. (1981) 34 A.L.R. 357 (F.C.A.); (1981) 148 C.L.R. 32 (H.C.).

but s. 48(2) declared that "the forfeiture shall be *in addition to and not part of* a penalty imposed."[59] The sentencer did in fact take into account the losses that would follow the forfeiture order when deciding to award non-custodial rather than custodial sentences. The Crown appealed against the leniency of the sentences imposed. In the Full Court of the Federal Court, Muirhead J. explained that s. 48(2) was inserted to declare that an order of forfeiture was to be regarded as an exercise of power distinct from the imposition of a penalty, but it was not to be taken as a legislative direction that the loss occasioned by the forfeiture was to be disregarded by a court imposing penalty when the defendant is also the person suffering deprivation or loss by seizure or forfeiture. Indeed losses from the initial seizure would remain relevant to sentence even if the forfeiture order was later quashed. The actual situation of the accused (including losses as the result of a court making ancillary order) must always be relevant: "It would be wrong . . . for a judge deciding an appropriate sentence to put out of his mind that the prisoner had by seizure or a concurrent forfeiture order been deprived of substantial property or means of legitimately earning his living by utilisation of his equipment and plant."[60] On the case reaching the High Court,[61] Gibbs C.J., Mason, Aickin and Brennan JJ. confirmed the correctness of this general line of approach.

When the legislature does not so obviously exclude forfeiture as a sentence, but makes use of more bland wording such as that which declares that offences may be punishable by fine or imprisonment and, "if the court so orders, by the forfeiture of any [property] used in the commission of the offence",[62] criminal courts are more willing to assume they can treat it as part of the sentence for the purposes of imposition or appellate review.[63] They find support for this view in the assimilation of rights of appeal against forfeiture orders with rights of appeal against sentence. For the purposes of a criminal appeal, the order on conviction described as the "sentence" must generally be made with reference either to the person convicted, or any property, or any moneys to be paid by him.[64] While in this context the phrase "with reference to the convicted person" is narrowly construed to encompass only orders imposing physical restraint upon the offender's person,[65] orders relating to property or money to be paid is read to include orders for the payment of money by way of compensation,[66] disqualification or

59. See also *Fazio v. Spitz* (1972) 21 F.L.R. 154.
60. (1981) 34 A.L.R. 357 at 366-367. See also at 362 per Fox and McGregor JJ. to the same effect.
61. *R. v. Hoar* (1981) 148 C.L.R. 32 at 39.
62. Section 13AA, *Fisheries Act* 1952 (Cth). The section was discussed by the High Court in *Cheatley v. The Queen* (1972) 127 C.L.R. 291.
63. *McGovern v. Victoria* [1984] V.R. 570.
64. E.g. Pt VI of the *Crimes Act* 1958 (Vic.), "sentence" is defined, by s. 566 of the *Crimes Act* 1958 (amended in 1989), to include: (a) any order of the court made on or in connection with a conviction with reference to the person convicted or any property or with reference to any money to be paid by the person convicted: cf. *Criminal Appeal Act* 1912 (N.S.W.), s. 5; *R. v. Kakura and Sato* (1990) 51 A. Crim. R. 1.
65. *Griffiths v. The Queen* (1977) 137 C.L.R. 293 at 325 per Jacobs J. (Stephen J. concurring at 312).
66. *R. v. Braham* [1977] V.R. 104 at 107.

cancellation of licences,[67] and orders for restitution of property or forfeiture of goods.[68]

In England, an objection to a ruling that the word "sentence" includes a forfeiture order for the purpose of appeal,[69] was taken on the ground that forfeiture was solely for the public good and not by way of punishment. Lord Salmon castigated this differentiation of purposes as "unsound and contrary to common sense" and went on to say that:[70]

> All prison and other sentences against a convicted person, including money penalties and forfeitures of money in relation to an offence, have two purposes (1) to punish the offender and (2) to support the public good by discouraging the offender and other potential criminals from committing such an offence in the future.

A more significant objection to subsuming forfeiture under sentence relates to the identity of the persons subject to the order. Forfeiture orders can be directed against the property of third parties who have not been charged with any offence and are not before the court. It is said that no such order can be a sentence since a sentence must always be directed against the accused. This line of argument was run in the High Court in *Cheatley v. The Queen*.[71] There the offence was that of fishing in proclaimed waters. It was declared to be "punishable" by discretionary fine, imprisonment, or forfeiture. The master of the fishing boat was fined and the boat was ordered to be forfeited. The latter order affected the overseas owner, rather than the master of the vessel. It was argued that a forfeiture, which was primarily directed against a person other than the accused, could not lawfully be ordered under the Act because it was not punishment of the accused. The High Court held that the legislation clearly envisaged orders being made against property owned by third parties. Despite the forfeiture not relating to the property of the person who committed the offence, it remained, in the High Court's judgment, a form of punishment of the accused under the statute. McTiernan J. held that: "punishment includes a penalty occasioning retributive loss of the possession *or use* of property imposed by a court of justice on a convicted offender."[72]

Menzies J. thought it was not unlike the old law of deodand under which third parties could forfeit right to property used in a killing even though they were not a direct party to the crime itself.[73] Mason J.[74] noted that, historically, forfeiture had been regarded as a "mulct or fine—a punishment for an offence"[75] and that to bring into the penalty third parties might be justified legislatively by circumstances such as the

---

67. *R. v. Overell* [1961] V.R. 95.
68. *Surrey Quarter Session; Ex parte Commissioner of Metropolitan Police* [1963] 1 Q.B. 990; *Re Ralph* [1940] V.R. 99 at 101.
69. The *Courts Act* 1971 (U.K.), s. 57 defines the word "sentence" as including "any order made by a court when dealing with an offender".
70. *R. v. Menocal* [1980] A.C. 598 at 607.
71. (1972) 127 C.L.R. 291.
72. Ibid. at 300, emphasis added.
73. Ibid. at 305.
74. Ibid. at 310.
75. Citing *R. v. Mayor of Dover* (1835) 1 C.M. & R. 726 at 736; 149 E.R. 1273 at 1277.

nature of the goods, the need for a deterrent penalty, or the difficulty of enforcing provisions against foreign owners.

This last justification for accepting that a sentence could include orders affecting third parties was recently reinforced in *Fa v. Morris*,[76] another case involving forfeiture of a fishing vessel for fishing without a licence. The contention that the forfeiture of the vessel made the sentence manifestly excessive was met by observations from the bench on the profitability of the fishing industry and how fining individuals usually did not meet the justice of the case because the person before the court either did not have the wherewithal to pay, or assets only in another country. Moreover, heavy fines could work injustice on those merely following orders. Forfeiture of the vessel put direct pressure on the foreign owner to comply with the policy of the Act.

Adjusting the components

Once forefeiture is discretionary and treated as a component of the final judgment of the sentencing court (whether or not counted as a formal sentence), the judge or magistrate is at liberty to adjust any of the primary sanctions, or the order for forfeiture itself,[77] to achieve a proportionate sentencing result[78] or to maintain parity between co-defendants.[79] The adjustment must be a balanced one. Statutory maxima for fines are common; they set a monetary limit to the exaction that may be imposed, but specific guidelines or fiscal restraints are almost non-existent for forfeitures. Notwithstanding the silence of the legislature regarding a ceiling for forfeitures, it is arguable that the most far-reaching forms of forfeiture must be reserved for the most serious examples of the wrongdoing in question. There should, in theory, be a high degree of congruence between the seriousness ranking of the wrongdoing for the purpose of the primary sanction and the seriousness ranking for the purposes of forfeiture. This accords with conventional sentencing wisdom.

A contrary view is that the requirement of proportionality that comes with sentence would inhibit the use of forfeiture as a form of crime prevention. It is argued that to be restrained by the gravity of the particular crime charged or the totality of any other sentence or sentences imposed at the same time when deciding whether property should be confiscated (or how much should be expropriated) would defeat the preventive and public safety objectives which aim at removing from circulation all of the property specifically adapted to the commission of the offence in question and which has little other legitimate use to the offender, or whose possession by anyone is unlawful. For instance, drugs, counterfeit money, unregistered guns and the like.[80] This may also apply to property thought to be so inherently injurious to the public that summary action to remove without limit as

76. (1987) 27 A. Crim. R. 342 (N.T. Sup. Ct).
77. Thus exercising a discretion both as to whether a forfeiture order is to be made and, where the subject matter of the order is divisable property (e.g. currency), as the amount to be forfeited: *R. v. Waterhouse* (1984) 14 A. Crim. R. 163.
78. *R. v. Thompson* (1977) 66 Cr. App. R. 130.
79. *R. v. Lidster* [1967] Crim. L. R. 80; *R. v. Ottey* (1984) 6 Cr. App. R. (S.) 163.
80. Hodgson, op. cit., p. 98; Clark, op. cit. at 478.

to quantity is called for.[81] Only where the property in question is capable of being used for a wide variety of legitimate purposes and is used only incidentally in connection with the offence should sentencers treat an order for forfeiture as analogous to a conventional monetary sentence.[82]

An example of a court applying conventional sentencing principles to a forfeiture decision is to be found in *Fang Chinn Fa v. Puffett*.[83] There a Northern Territory magistrate imposed a fine of $500 for each of two offences against the *Fisheries Act* 1952 (Cth) for unlawful fishing by foreign ships in proclaimed waters. The maximum fine provided for each separate offence was $1,000. The offences were obviously regarded as mid-range ones. The magistrate then ordered that the fishing boat in question (worth $750,000), together with its nets and lifting gear and its catch (worth $78,000) be forfeited. Gallop J. of the Northern Territory Supreme Court, treated established sentencing considerations as pertinent to the assessment of the appropriateness of the forfeiture order. In his view the confiscation of the nets, catch and boat came too close to maximum possible form of forfeiture allowed for under the legislation and thus violated the principle which called for maximum sentences to be confined to cases that were the worst of their type.[84] This was not an extremely grave breach and there were mitigating factors in relation to the effect of the sanctions on the captain. The order for forfeiture was therefore modified by confining it to the nets, lifting gear and the catch.[85]

Hwang Ming Heui v. Mellon[86] was again an appeal against sentence on the basis that an order for forfeiture of foreign fishing vessels and equipment under *Fisheries Act* 1952 (Cth) in addition to a fine was excessive. Counsel sought to distinguish *Fang Chinn Fa v. Puffett* by submitting that the legislation should be seen as creating a single scale of stepped penalties with the maximum fine of $5,000 representing the first step, then orders for forfeiture of equipment and finally, forfeiture of the entire fishing vessel itself. Proportionality would be located on a single rather than a dual scale. Muirhead J., in the Supreme Court of the Northern Territory, rejected the idea that forfeiture of vessels could not be ordered until the power of imposing monetary fines had been utilised in full.[87] Forfeiture could be needed when fines were thought to be ineffective in providing protection. Though referring to these different considerations in the use of fines and forfeiture, his Honour did not reject the notion that the two were related, or that each had to be

81. Reed and Gill, "R.I.C.O. Forfeitures, Forfeitable 'Interests', and Procedural Due Process" (1983) 62 Nth Carolina L. Rev 58 at 77.
82. *R. v. Hoar* (1981) 34 A.L.R. 357 at 362 per Fox and McGregor JJ., referring to Thomas, *Principles of Sentencing* (2nd ed., 1979), p. 336. As to the problem of categorisation which this entails, see Edwards, "Forfeitures—Civil or Criminal?" (1970) 43 Temple L. Q. 191 at 194.
83. (1978) 22 A.L.R. 149.
84. Ibid. at 154.
85. See also *Fazio v. Spitz* (1972) 21 F.L.R. 154; *Van Chen v. Watton* (1980) 7 N.T.R. 25; *Liang v. Mellon* (1981) 12 N.T.R. 9.
86. (1980) 5 N.T.R. 9.
87. Ibid. at 15.

proportionate to the gravity of the offence for which they were being ordered.

When the wording of the statute treats forfeiture and conventional sanctions as interchangeable, proportionality will feature more prominently as a consideration in respect of both. In the Tasmanian case of *R. v. Good*,[88] once the court had found the accused guilty of the prescribed drug offence, it was free under the *Poisons Act* 1971 (Tas.), s. 84(2)(g) to decide whether or not to order the forfeiture of any vehicle used in its commission and this measure could be used "in addition to or instead of convicting the person and imposing on him a penalty for the offence". In the particular case it was held that for forfeiture to be added as a further element to the sentence would be too draconian. In addition to an assessment of the total effect of the various sanctions, matters relevant to the exercise of the discretion in respect of the forfeiture were the extent of use of the vehicle for commission of drug related offences and whether the vehicle was necessary to the rehabilitation of the offender having regard to the person's general background.[89] In *R. v. Ward Marles and Graham*[90] the point was made that the mere fact that property is used in connection with an offence does not necessarily mean that a forfeiture order should be made in respect of it. There motor vehicles used to transport persons to a location at which cannabis was being sold were ordered by a magistrate to be forfeited under s. 34 of the *Drugs Misuse Act* 1986 (Qld) because they were "used in connection with the commission of" the relevant offences. In setting aside the order for forfeiture the Queensland Court of Criminal Appeal said that, where a court had a discretion regarding forfeiture, it had to treat the option as being one of an additional penal character and subject to the same mitigating considerations.[91] Forfeiture would only be appropriate if the connection between property and offence was a substantial rather than an incidental one:[92]

> If a person, unlawfully possessing cannabis for his own use, has it in his trousers pocket, are his trousers being "used in connection with" the commission of the offence and, if so, liable to forfeiture?

In the particular case, hardship would be encountered by having to suffer forfeiture of the cars which were largely used for legitimate purposes and had only a tenuous connection with the offences charged.

In *Frisina v. The Queen*,[93] forfeiture of a motor vehicle used by an offender to carry cannabis was ordered under the *Misuse of Drugs Act* 1981 (W.A.), s. 28(3). The forfeiture was in addition to the imposition of a fine of $7,500 and six months' imprisonment. It need not have been directly linked with the punishment for the offence since the statute

---

88. (1986) 82 F.L.R. 418.
89. Ibid. at 420. It is impermissible for forfeiture to be ordered solely to provide security for payment of fines or compensation: *R. v. Kingston upon Hull Justices; Ex parte Hartung* (1980) 2 Cr. App. R. (S) 270 (in making forfeiture order, sentencer stated that the forfeited van was to be sold and the proceeds applied to pay a fine and compensation order with the balance repaid to offender).
90. [1989] 1 Qd R. 194.
91. See also *R. v. Cuthbertson* [1980] 2 All E.R. 401 at 406.
92. [1989] 1 Qd. R. 194 at 199 per Carter J.
93. (1988) 32 A. Crim. R. 103.

allowed forfeiture to be ordered irrespective of any one being convicted. The maximum permitted fine was $20,000 but the vehicle alone was worth more than this. The appeal against the forfeiture was allowed because the Western Australian Court of Criminal Appeal considered that the practical effect of the forfeiture was to impose a punishment which was in excess of the statutory power to fine and to create more than fair punishment for the offence. Burt C.J. noted that under s. 703 of the Western Australian *Criminal Code* an order for forfeiture was treated as a sentence for the purpose of appeal. But even if it was not strictly a form of punishment for the particular drug offence charged,[94] this did not mean that the impact of the forfeiture order upon the offender owning the property was irrelevant to the exercise of the discretion which was involved in making the order itself.[95]

Paradigm 5: Discretionary under proceeds of crime legislation—criminal or civil?

Forms of legislation

The main feature of the resurgence of statutory forfeiture in Australia over the last decade, particularly in relation to drug and organised crime offences, is the new State and federal legislation which gives prosecutorial authorities opportunities to obtain judicial orders to seize, restrain and confiscate property and the proceeds of crime.[96] The local legislation drew its inspiration from United States legislation such as the *Racketeer Influenced and Corrupt Organisations Act* 1970 and the *Continuing Criminal Enterprise Act* 1970. It might have been thought that those drafting the new legislation would have taken time to resolve some of the long-standing problems of forfeiture, but the earlier difficulties with terminology, classification, purpose and relationship to sentencing exist here as well. Although the various pieces of State and federal Australian legislation differ from each other in form, they contain significant common elements.

The *Proceeds of Crime Act* 1987 (Cth) is typical of paradigm 5.[97] It was enacted in 1987 as a measure to enable the federal Director of Public Prosecutions to bring proceedings to recover the proceeds of crime arising out of the commission of federal offences.[98] It builds on the criminal process in that the major orders under the Act depend upon the defendant having been convicted (summarily or on indictment) or deemed to be convicted (absconding is counted as conviction[99]) of a

---

94. See also *R. v. Braham* [1977] V.R. 104; *R. v. McDonald* [1979] N.S.W.L.R. 451 which held that orders for compensation and restitution are not part of the sentence for other purposes.
95. See also *R. v. Thompson* (1977) 66 Cr. App. R. 130; *R. v. Buddo* (1982) 4 Cr. App. R. (S.) 268; *R. v. Scully* (1985) 7 Cr. App. R. (S.) 119. *Frisina* was approved on this point by *R. v. Tarzia* (1991) 52 A. Crim. R. 102.
96. See above, p. 107, n. 4.
97. Temby, "The Proceeds of Crime Act: One Year's Experience" (1989) 13 Crim L. J. 24.
98. P.O.C. Act 1987 (Cth), s. 14.
99. P.O.C. Act 1987 (Cth), s. 5. A person is also deemed to have been convicted if they have been found guilty but discharged without conviction; or who have consented to an offence being taken into account when sentence was passed in respect of another crime.

federal offence. But though conviction based, the proceedings are neither a formal part of the criminal prosecution, nor of the sentence. They appear to be civil in nature. .

The principal objects of the legislation are declared to be:[100]

> (a) to deprive persons of the proceeds of, and benefits derived from, the commission of offences against the laws of the Commonwealth or the Territories;[101]

> (b) to provide for the forfeiture of property used in or in connection with the commission of such offences; and

> (c) to enable law enforcement authorities effectively to trace such proceeds, benefits and property.

The vehicle of divestiture of assets is the "confiscation order".[102] This encompasses two subsidiary forms of order. First, the "forfeiture order"[103] made against "tainted" property[104] (that is, property used in, or in connection with the commission of an offence, or property derived or realised directly or indirectly as a result of the commission of an offence) irrespective of the ownership of that property.[105] This is a form of order in rem. Secondly, the "pecuniary penalty order".[106] This is made against the convicted person in respect of benefits (particularly those which cannot be traced to specific property) derived by that person from the commission of the offence.[107] This is in the nature of an order in personam. An application for either form of confiscation order may be made by the Director of Public Prosecutions at the end of a criminal trial after conviction, or in entirely separate proceedings up to six months later. Orders restraining the disposal of property which may be subject to forfeiture can be obtained at a pre-trial stage when charges are only proposed or pending, or once a conviction has been recorded.[108]

The legislation sets up two separate systems of restraining orders. The first deals with ones in respect of indictable offences against federal law,

100. P.O.C. Act 1987 (Cth), s. 3(1).
101. Cf. *Drug Trafficking (Civil Proceedings) Act* 1990 (N.S.W.), s. 3: "The Principal objects of this Act are: (a) to provide for the confiscation, without requiring a conviction, of the property of a person if the Supreme Court finds it to be more probable than not that the person has engaged in drug-related activities."
102. P.O.C. Act 1987 (Cth), s. 4(1); C.(C.P.) Act 1986 (Vic.), s. 3(1); C.O.P.C Act 1989 (N.S.W.), s. 4(1); C.(C.P.) Act 1988 (W.A.), s. 3(1); C.(F.P.) Act 1988 (N.T.), s. 3(1).
103. P.O.C. Act 1987 (Cth), ss 4(1) and 19(1); C.(C.P.) Act 1986 (Vic.), ss 3(1) and 7(1); C.O.P.C. Act 1989 (N.S.W.), ss 4 and 18; C.(C.P.) Act 1989 (Qld), ss 3(1) and 8(1); C.(C.P.) Act 1988 (W.A.), ss 3(1) and 10; C.(F.P.) Act 1988 (N.T.), ss 3(1) and 5(1).
104. P.O.C. Act 1987 (Cth), s. 4(1); C.O.P.C. Act 1989 (N.S.W.), s. 4(1); C.(C.P.) Act 1989 (Qld), s. 3(1); C.(F.P.) Act 1988 (N.T.), s. 3(1); C.(C.P.) Act 1986 (Vic.), s. 7; C.(C.P.) Act 1988 (W.A.), s. 10; C.(C.P.) Act 1986 (S.A.), s. 4(1).
105. The court is required to specify, in the order, the amount it considers to be the value of the property at the time the order is made: P.O.C. Act 1987 (Cth), s. 19(1) and (2).
106. P.O.C. Act 1987 (Cth), ss 4(1) and 26(1); C.O.P.C. Act 1989 (N.S.W.), ss 4(1) and 24; C.(C.P.) Act 1986 (Vic.), ss 3(1) and 12(1); C.(C.P.) Act 1989 (Qld), ss 3(1) and 13(1); C.(C.P.) Act 1988 (W.A.), ss 3(1) and 15; C.(F.P.) Act 1988 (N.T.), ss 3(1) and 10.
107. P.O.C. Act 1987 (Cth), s. 14(1).
108. P.O.C. Act 1987 (Cth), s. 43(1).

that are not "serious offences".[109] Here restraining orders serve to preserve intact property which might be later subject to a judicially imposed forfeiture order (in relation to "tainted property"), or a pecuniary penalty order (in relation to benefits derived from the commission of the offence).[110] The second relates to cases in which a person has been convicted of a serious offence and provides that all property which is the subject of a restraining order is *automatically* forfeited to the Commonwealth six months after the date on which the person was convicted of the relevant serious offence. No further order from the court is required for this statutory forfeiture to occur.[111]

A court is not empowered to make a forfeiture order in respect of property if it normally lacks jurisdiction with respect to the recovery of property of that kind, or level of value.[112] In considering whether it is appropriate to make a forfeiture order, the court may, under the statute, have regard to factors such as hardship, the ordinary use of the property and the gravity of the offence.[113] Where the application is made for a forfeiture order, or a pecuniary penalty order, to a court which is about to pass sentence on the person for the offence, that court is authorised to defer passing sentence until it has determined the merits of application.[114]

Criminal or civil?

The ambiguity regarding the civil or criminal status of the earlier statutory forms of forfeiture still adheres to the confiscatory mechanisms set up under the federal proceeds of crime legislation, and that of the States. Though the legislation is pointedly directed towards the suppression of crime and, on its face, is conviction based, the dominant view is that it creates proceedings that are civil in nature. At an administrative level this is acknowledged in the statutory description of the functions of the federal Director of Public Prosecution who now not only is responsible for the institution of prosecutions on indictment or summarily for offences against Commonwealth law, but also for the pursuit or co-ordination of civil remedies under this and related Acts on behalf of the Commonwealth.[115] To this end offices of the Director now include civil remedies branches as well as branches which continue to handle prosecutions.

There are a number of internal pointers to the civil character of the orders made under the Act.[116] First, the deeming provisions make the

109. As defined by P.O.C. Act 1987 (Cth), s. 7(1) (major narcotic, organised fraud and money laundering offences).
110. P.O.C. Act 1987 (Cth), s. 43(1).
111. P.O.C. Act 1987 (Cth), s. 30.
112. P.O.C. Act 1987 (Cth), s. 98(3).
113. P.O.C. Act 1987 (Cth), s. 19(3) and (4).
114. P.O.C. Act 1987 (Cth), s. 18(1). In considering a confiscation application a court may have regard to the transcript of any proceedings against the person for the offence. This is designed to expedite proceedings by avoiding the need to rehear evidence which was adduced in the criminal proceedings and to assist in providing the evidentiary basis for the order.
115. *Director of Public Prosecutions Act* 1983 (Cth), ss 6 and 9.
116. The following discussion draws heavily from Hassett, *Confiscation and Forfeiture of Assets*, Unpublished Paper (delivered at the Conference of District and County Court Judges, July 1989).

requirement of a conviction a fiction in many cases. Powers which are available to a court under this Act are capable of being applied to persons who have not been tried, convicted or sentenced in any conventional sense. Secondly the standard of proof applicable to the determination of any question of fact under the Act relevant to the making of orders is declared to be the civil standard of the balance of probabilities.[117] Thirdly, a court may not make a pecuniary penalty order of an amount exceeding the limit of its jurisdiction to order the civil recovery of debts[118] and the order itself gives rise only to a civil debt to the Commonwealth, enforceable as a judgment debt.[119] Moreover, the means of calculating pecuniary penalties under the Act are more elaborate than those appropriate to the fixing of fines since their purpose is nullification of the specific benefits gained by the criminal enterprise.[120] Fourthly, matters arising under the Act can be settled, as in civil matters, by a compromise of proceedings between the parties.[121] The Director of Public Prosecution has been known to give undertakings in respect of damages if restraining orders sought were shown to be unwarranted.[122] Fifthly, the fact that there can be multiple parties to the proceedings points to their civil nature. Criminal litigation is only between the Crown and the accused; in civil litigation multiple parties may be joined. Because the proceeds of crime legislation can affect property interests beyond those of the person charged or convicted, various other affected persons may be before the court as applicants or respondents, indeed the applicant for the confiscation order itself may be someone other than prosecuting authority.[123] On the other hand, the appeal provisions allow appeal "as if it were part of sentence",[124] but that right of appeal is conferred on persons other than respondent or applicant for a confiscation order.

Confiscation orders and sentence

What does the apparent civil nature of forfeiture and related orders under the proceeds of crime legislation do to the relationship between such orders and the sentences which follow conviction for the offence in respect of which the order was made? As has been shown in relation to earlier forms of forfeiture legislation, whatever might be thought to be the implicit relationship between a confiscation order and sentence, the legislature, in some jurisdictions, is prepared explicitly to mandate that a sentencing court must totally ignore the results of any application for a confiscation order. Thus, in 1988, the South Australian equivalent of the federal legislation was amended to declare:[125]

117. P.O.C. Act 1987 (Cth), s. 99.
118. P.O.C. Act 1987 (Cth), s. 98(5).
119. P.O.C. Act 1987 (Cth), s. 26(8) and (9).
120. P.O.C. Act 1987 (Cth), s. 27.
121. *R. v. Fagher* (1989) 16 N.S.W.L.R. 67.
122. Hassett, op. cit., p. 75.
123. Ibid.
124. P.O.C. Act 1987 (Cth), s. 100; see also *D.P.P. v. McCoid* (1988) 35 A. Crim. R. 222 at 226.
125. C.(C.P.) Act 1986 (S.A.), s. 3a.

A court, in determining sentence for a prescribed offence, must not have regard to the question of whether or not the offender's property is, or could be, the subject of an application for forfeiture under this Act.

The Queensland statute similarly provides that:[126]

A court, in determining sentence for a serious offence, shall not have regard to the question of whether or not the defendant's property is, or could be, the subject of an application for forfeiture or a pecuniary penalty under this Act.[127]

These provisions were drafted to counteract judicial views that, despite legislative indicators that forfeiture and sentence were independent sanctions, trial judges could justify awarding lesser sentences because of the actual or potential effects of forfeiture.[128] The South Australian Attorney-General wanted the judiciary to disregard any potential action under confiscation legislation in proceeding to sentence. The issue was less to do with the maintenance of a strict criminal/civil distinction, than the perceived differing purposes of the sanctions:[129]

[I]t is quite inequitable for a sentence to be adjusted in accordance with other independent action by the attorney to recover the proceeds of the original crime. No person should be allowed to profit from criminal activity. . . . The legislation should be allowed to take its full and natural course and not be subject to amelioration by those members of judiciary who would wish to view this legislation in a different way to that which Parliament originally intended.

The federal legislation is more open than that in South Austrtalia to links being maintained between forfeiture and like orders and sentence. However, it does so only tentatively and imperfectly, and mainly through procedural means. It suggests that its preferred order of precedence is that the confiscation order should come ahead of the fixing of sentence and, implicitly, that the sentencer should be informed and take account of what has gone before. It does this first, by providing that where a confiscation order is sought from the court before which person was convicted, but that court has not yet passed sentence, it may, if it thinks it necessary to do so, defer imposing the sentence until it has

126. C.(C.P.) Act 1989 (Qld), s. 71.
127. Recent Commonwealth legislation, permitting confiscation of superannuation benefits by means of a "superannuation order" which can be made against Commonwealth employees convicted of certain offences, provides that: "A court shall not, in sentencing a person convicted of an offence punishable by imprisonment for life or a term longer than 12 months, take into account the possibility that a superannuation order may be made in relation to the person": *Crimes (Superannuation Benefits) Act* 1989.
128. *R. v. Hoar* (1981) 34 A.L.R. 357 (F.C.A.); (1981) 148 C.L.R. 32 (H.C.). See also comments by Judge Lowry of the District Criminal Court of South Australia referred to in *Hansard* (S.A.) House of Assembly, 11 February 1988, p. 2692.
129. *Hansard* (S.A.) House of Assembly, 11 February 1988, p. 2692. In *R. v. Fagher* (1989) 16 N.S.W.L.R. 67 at 75-76 the trial judge refused to make a pecuniary penalty order because he thought that the defendant had already been "sufficiently punished". Roden J. commented that "a pecuniary penalty order is not intended as a form of punishment".

determined the application for the confiscation order.[130] The Victorian Supreme Court, in speculating when it might be "necessary" to know what sort of confiscation order is to be made before fixing an appropriate sentence, observed:[131]

> It is commonplace, when sentencing, to take into consideration the value of any goods stolen or destroyed—and not recovered from the offender. Similarly, the courts invariably take into consideration the fact that an offender has returned goods or money stolen or has made some other form of recompense. Often this is seen, of course, as evidence of remorse, but apart altogether from remorse, it is a relevant circumstance when determining the sentence appropriate to the crime. This being so, although an offender may be sentenced before an application for a confiscation order is made, then if at the time of sentencing it is apparent that the profits of the crime are confiscated, it is appropriate to bear that circumstance in mind when sentencing the offender. The weight to be attached for the purposes of sentencing to the fact that a confiscation order is made is of course an entirely different matter.

But deferral is not mandatory and can easily be avoided. It is not part of the legislative package that confiscation orders be made by the sentencing court, nor even by a judge who was the sentencing judge. Applications for orders can be made to any court exercising federal jurisdiction up to six months after the sentence is imposed. Furthermore, there are sound reasons why trial judges might not wish to deal with an application for a confiscation order at same time as sentencing, even when they have the opportunity to do so. There is the anxiety, often expressed in relation to applications at sentencing for compensation or restitution orders, that the proceedings will become too complex. The dual proceedings may place the defendant in a difficult position in her or his plea in mitigation of sentence because of hesitancy to call evidence of relevance to sentence which might also be pertinent to identifying assets subject to confiscation. The tribunal itself will have to apply different standards of proof. The degree of proof in respect of disputed matters of fact relevant to sentence may have to approximate that of the criminal standard, but for confiscation orders it is set at the civil standard. Indeed if the confiscation proceedings are truly characterised as civil, the respondent could be a compellable witness in respect of forfeiture and like matters in a way that is impermissible at trial or at sentencing. The trial judge may also be loath to defer sentence until resolution of the matter of the confiscation order if the convicted person is detained in custody and an appeal against conviction and/or sentence is likely in any event.

130. P.O.C. Act 1987 (Cth), s. 18(2)(a)-(c). See also C.(C.P.) Act 1988 (W.A.), s. 9(2); C.(C.P.) Act 1986 (Vic.), s. 5(3)—if an application is made to a court before which a person was convicted of an offence before that court has passed sentence for the offence, the court may make a confiscation order at the time of passing sentence, and the court may, if it thinks necessary to do so, defer the passing of sentence until it has determined the application for the confiscation order.
131. *R. v. Allen* (1989) 41 A. Crim. R. 51 at 57; approved in *R. v. McDermott* (1990) 49 A. Crim. R. 105.

If an offender pleads to the criminal offence, but wishes to contest the confiscation order, a court may be placed in an invidious position in relation to the appropriate discount for the plea of guilty and in recognition of the defendant's co-operation or lack of it. In *R. v. Nicholson*[132] the English Court of Criminal Appeal ruled that an offender who contested a confiscation order should not be penalised by a reduction of his discount for his guilty plea. Concomitantly,[133] the discount may not be increased on account of the defendant's co-operation in the confiscation proceedings.

The second procedural link between confiscation and sentencing is found in the federal provisions which allow the evidence adduced at the trial to be used in determining confiscation applications:[134]

> Where an application is made to a court for a confiscation order in respect of a person's conviction of an offence, the court may, in determining the application, have regard to the transcript of any proceeding against the person, for the offence.

This is designed to aid in the task of establishing the evidentiary basis for the confiscation order and thus expedite the proceedings. It also indirectly sets up links between confiscation orders and sentence but is not without its problems. The transcript may be of *any* proceeding against the person for the offence and not just of the "convicting" court. It is not at all clear whether this includes depositions and statements in committal proceedings, or the information supplied or admissions made in the plea in mitigation at the sentencing stage of the trial if that has already taken place.

It is to be noted that the wording of the section is not apt to allow evidence given in respect of confiscation proceedings to be used at sentencing, even though the former have been completed first. However, because the rules governing the factual bases of sentencing are so ill defined, evidence or submission regarding the making and likely effect of a confiscation order will readily be received as mitigation if there is no statutory rule against its reception. However, there is the risk that the material adduced in support of confiscation in concurrent "civil" proceedings may contain information, particularly in relation to the scope of other offending, that could serve to aggravate the ultimate sentence.[135] The general principle is that offenders can only be sentenced on the basis of offences of which they stand convicted or to which they have admitted. If the fact of forfeiture and confiscation is treated only as mitigatory, this principle is not violated, but if there is a

132. [1990] Crim. L. R. 530.
133. But contrary to *R. v. Allen* (1989) 41 A. Crim. R. 51.
134. P.O.C. Act 1987 (Cth), s. 18(1); see also C.O.P.C. Act 1989 (N.S.W.), s. 17(1); C.(C.P.) Act 1986 (Vic.), s. 5(3)(b); C.(C.P.) Act 1988 (W.A.), s. 9(1); C.(F.P.) Act 1988 (N.T.), s. 64; C.(C.P.) Act 1989 (Qld), s. 6(3) and (4). In South Australia, *Supreme Court Rules*, r. 114.06(3), states that if all of the parties to the proceedings under the Act are before the court on criminal proceedings, the judge may direct that any evidence given in the proceedings under the Act, but without prejudice to the right of any party to adduce further evidence.
135. *R. v. Harper* [1989] Crim. L.R. 755 and commentary. See also *R. v. Bragason* (1988) 10 Cr. App. R. (S.) 258.

real risk that confiscation information may aggravate the sentence, it may be better for the sentence to be settled before the confiscation application is attended to.

On the other hand, if the confiscation order is made contemporaneously with, or after, sentencing, the federal legislation does allow certain matters relating to the sentence to be taken into account in calculating the level of exaction. For instance the amount payable under a pecuniary penalty order may be reduced by an amount equal to the sum already payable by the person under sentencing orders made in relation to the offence (for example, fines, restitution, compensation, or damages).[136]

Paradigm 6: Discretionary under civil process

This paradigm is the Australian precursor of the previous one. Here there is no doubt that the proceedings are civil in nature. The paradigm is represented by the pecuniary penalty provisions of the *Customs Act* 1901 (Cth), which were originally added to the Act in 1979. Under these, the court may order the payment to the Crown of a pecuniary penalty equal to the value of the benefits the defendant gained from engaging in "prescribed narcotic dealings".[137] The relevant standard of proof is the civil one on the balance of probabilities.[138] No criminal prosecution needs to have been instituted. The order gives rise to a civil debt in favour of the Commonwealth. In like fashion, the confiscation provisions in the new *Drug Trafficking (Civil Proceedings) Act* 1990 (N.S.W.) empower a court, in the exercise of its civil jurisdiction, "to order confiscation or forfeiture of assets gained in drug-related activities".[139] The legislation states unequivocally that: "For the purposes of this Act, proceedings on an application for a restraining order or a confiscation order are not criminal proceedings."[140] This does not prevent charges being laid in respect of those activities, nor a criminal court later taking account of the effects of those orders when imposing sentence in respect of those charges.

OBJECTIVES IN COMMON OR IN COMPETITION?

It can be seen that some Acts allow for links between sentencing, and confiscation orders, while others try to treat the two sanction forms as discrete and separate processes. Complete bifurcation, which the courts are obviously reluctant to accept, brings risk of dangerous disproportion

136. P.O.C. Act 1987 (Cth), s. 26(5); cf. C.O.P.C. Act 1989 (N.S.W.), s. 18(2) (a court may take into consideration any hardship likely to arise following the making of a forfeiture order, but *shall not take into account* the sentence imposed in respect of the offence).
137. *Customs Act* 1901 (Cth), s. 243A(3).
138. *Kirk v. Commissioner of Australian Federal Police* (1988) 81 A.L.R. 321 at 338 per Davies J. where it was held that a proceeding for the recovery of a pecuniary penalty is a civil proceeding not dependent upon a conviction for, or proof of, the commission of a crime.
139. *Drug Trafficking (Civil Proceedings) Act* (N.S.W.) 1990, s. 6(1).
140. *Drug Trafficking (Civil Proceedings) Act* (N.S.W.) 1990, s. 5(1).

in punishment and an unintegrated system of sanctions. A rational connection between the two should be possible, but underlying the inconsistent and unsatisfactory state of the law sketched out above is lack of agreement about the purposes of forfeitures and the differences between these sanctions and conventional forms of judicial punishment.

Since there is no common agreement about the purposes of punishment, or which purpose, if any, should be paramount, it comes as no surprise that there is a similarly diverse and mutually inconsistent set of explanations for the use of forefeiture. The legislative and judicial justifications for forfeiture or confiscation are similar to those brought out to explain conventional sentences: incapacitation; deterrence; retribution; community protection, etc. but there are differences in emphasis which need to be explored.

Incapacitation

The incapacitative purpose of the main forms of sentence is well understood. Incapacitation aims at depriving a person of the physical or financial ability, power, or opportunity to continue to engage in proscribed conduct.[141] It is commonly said that the best way to strike at commercialised crime, particularly the high profit crimes against which proceeds of crime legislation is directed, is through economic sanctions calculated to decrease the profits of the enterprise and strip it of its major capital assets. MacFarlane[142] notes that the acquisition of capital forms the very heart of all business, both legal and illegal. Estimates of revenue generated by illegal activity runs to millions of dollars. Depriving major criminals of assets and income is seen as an essential step in crippling their unlawful entrepreneurial activities. In *Industrial Acceptance Corp. v. R.,* Rand J. noted:[143]

> The forfeiture of property used in violation of revenue laws has for several centuries been one of the characteristic features of their enforcement and the considerations which early led to its adoption as necessary are not far to seek. Smuggling, illegal manufacture of liquor, illegal sale of narcotics and like activities, because of their high profits and the demand, in certain sections of society, for them, take on the character of organised actions against the forces of law; and with the techniques and devices, varying with the times, that have been open to these enemies of social order, the necessity to strike against not only the persons but everything that has enabled them to carry out their purposes has been universally recognised . . . The absolute forfeiture is an inseparable accompaniment of punitive action, and the administration of the law would be seriously impeded were any obstacles to prompt and conclusive action placed in the way of its enforcement.

141. We distinguish this from special and general deterrence. The former may overlap with the incapacitation rationale in that an offender who is deprived of the economic means of committing crime may be both disabled from, *and personally unwilling to*, commit a further crime. However, they are separate and distinct concepts. General deterrence refers to the use of a sanction so as to disincline others to commit an offence.
142. MacFarlane, "Confiscating the Fruits of Crime" (1984) 27 Crim. L. Q. 408.
143. (1953) 107 C.C.C. 1 at 5-6.

This rationale was echoed by the Commonwealth Attorney-General in introducing the Commonwealth legislation: [144]

> The Proceeds of Crime Bill provides some of the most effective weaponry against major crime ever introduced into this Parliament. Its purpose is to strike at the heart of major organised crime by depriving persons involved of the profits and instruments of their crimes. By so doing, it will suppress criminal activity by attacking the primary motive—profit—and prevent the re-investment of that profit in further criminal activity.

The difficulty in squaring the incapacitative rationale for forfeiture with that of conventional sentences is that any effort at crippling a criminal enterprise by stripping it of its assets will itself be crippled if only a proportion of the assets can be seized because the offence proven is not grave enough to warrant expropriation on a large scale.

Deterrence

Deterrence is a well-accepted penal aim both in the sentencing and confiscation contexts. Where forfeiture can occur without conviction, it is said to present a significant deterrent which may be lessened if conviction is a prerequisite.[145] Orders under the confiscation legislation are regarded as deterrent measures and, indeed, "part of the retribution exacted from offenders on behalf of the community".[146]

It is often difficult to separate the incapacitative from the deterrent arguments. The incapacitating effect on the criminal enterprise of lack of income of capital is not the same as using loss of profit as a deterrent. If the primary motive for crime is profit, many offenders will be prepared to run the risk of prosecution and imprisonment as long as their gains will be available on their eventual release. The proceeds of crime legislation seeks to deter from crime by undermining the ultimate profitability of the venture. It seeks to render criminal enterprises profitless, thus creating a disincentive for like-minded persons to engage in similar activity in the future.[147] Again, as with incapacitation, those supporting forfeiture as an independent sanction, would regard its deterrent effect as being diminished if the confiscation of profits was tied to the gravity of the current charges.

Protection and prevention

It is often put that forfeitures are merely preventive actions designed to curb the circulation of prohibited items, particularly ones that are inherently injurious such as narcotics, obscene publications, illicit intoxicants, contaminated food, etc., or items which are adapted for or

144. *Hansard*, H. of Rep., 30 April 1987, p. 2314.
145. A.L.R.C., Discussion Paper No. 43, p. 11.
146. *R. v. Allen* (1989) 41 A. Crim. R. 51 at 56.
147. Temby, "The Pursuit of Insidious Crime" (1987) 61 Aust. L. J. 510 at 519; Commonwealth Director Public Prosecutions, *Annual Report 1987-1988*, 1990.

used in the commission of crime.[148] This justification is closely allied to that of incapacitation, but is usually brought out when discussing forfeiture of the instruments through which crime is committed. This is said to be the basis of in rem procedure in which action is taken against property without reference to those who possess or own it.[149]

The emphasis on the value of forfeiture in revenue protection and crime control, rather than on its oppressive effect on those who have chosen the path of entrepreneurial crime, serves to deflect questions about its proper limits. It is here that the chief obstacle to proportionality is met. Conventional retributive and deterrent sentences are well understood to be subject to the principle of proportionality.[150] It is a major constraint upon imposition of punishment. The supporters of statutory forfeiture as crime prevention openly concede it to be a drastic measure, but claim that it is intended for use only in settings in which conventional criminal detection and enforcement is notoriously difficult.[151]

From their point of view, the full protective benefits to the community will be lost if disproportion in impact on the offender of seizing all her or his illicit goods (for example, the drugs, the fishing catch etc.), or of confiscating property used in the commission of the crime, even if it still has a lawful use (for example, boats, aircraft and vehicles), is accepted as justification for restricting the scope of confiscatory orders. Indeed, on this line of argument, the inclination of modern proceeds of crime legislation, to allow hardship to the offender[152] or gravity of the offence[153] to be taken into account in exercising the discretion to order forfeiture is to be deplored. It is interesting that Fried[154] has pointed out that, in the United States, no court has refused to order an in rem forfeiture on grounds of disproportionality.

This means that, unless the sentence itself is adjusted, the combined impact of both the sentence imposed for the offence and the associated forfeiture order will likely exceed the limits of punishment that would

---

148. Parcels, "An Analysis of Federal Drug-related Civil Forfeiture" (1982) 34 Maine L. R. 435 at 456. The preventive aspect was stressed in *McGovern v. Victoria* [1984] V.R. 570 at 572 where the relevant legislation permitted seizure and forfeiture of boat "for *preventing the commission or repetition or continuation* of any offence." Australian proceeds of crime legislation expresses the preventive objectives in less forthright terms: "to provide for the forfeiture of property used in or in connection with the commission of such offences": P.O.C. Act 1987 (Cth), s. 3(1)(b); C.O.P.C. Act 1989 (N.S.W., s. 3(b); C.(C.P.) Act 1986 (Vic.), s. 1(a).
149. Edwards, op. cit. at 193.
150. *Veen v. The Queen (No. 2)* (1988) 164 C.L.R. 465.
151. A.L.R.C., Discussion Paper No. 43, paras 23-27.
152. P.O.C. Act 1987 (Cth), s. 19(3)(a); C.(C.P.) Act 1989 (Qld), s. 8(2)(b); C.O.P.C. Act 1989 (N.S.W.), s. 18(1)(b)(ii); C.(F.P.) Act 1988 (N.T.), s. 5(1)(b)(ii); C.(C.P.) Act 1986 (Vic.), s. 7(2)(b); C. (C.P.) Act 1988 (W.A.), s. 10(2)(b). However, in New South Wales C.O.P.C. Act 1989, s. 18(2) prohibits the court from taking into account the sentence imposed on the offence in considering "hardship": see *R. v. Bolger* (1989) 16 N.S.W.L.R. 115 at 126 (hardship is not to be assessed by simply asking whether the sentence—or pecuniary penalty order or imprisonment—and the consequences of the making of a forfeiture order amount, in total, to a disproportionately severe punishment for the offence).
153. P.O.C. Act 1987 (Cth), s. 19(4); C.(C.P.) Act 1989 (Qld), s. 8(2)(c).
154. Fried, op. cit. at 380.

have applied had both forms of sanction been components of the same criminal sentencing process. The value of the property forfeited may vastly exceed the proceeds of the criminal venture, or of any fine a court might impose, particularly now that the new legislation allows for the forfeiture of real property. This is an unprecedented extension of forfeiture of the instrumentalities of crime, which had hitherto been confined to personalty, such as equipment, vehicles and ships.

Restoration

Fried argues that while standard forms of punishments are meant to express moral obloquy, and give vent to denunciatory impulses, sanctions like forfeiture are not intended to reprove the transgression.[155] Their primary function is to return the offender to his or her position prior to the offending. The aim of forfeiture and confiscation orders (as well as other ancillary orders such as compensation and restitution) is to eliminate the advantages and benefits which the person has gained through her or his illegality. The orders try to restore the status quo, not to punish.[156] This is not unlike the civil use of orders for restitution in response to unjust enrichment.

Though this is said to be one of the main differences between forfeiture and conventional sanctions, this restorative function is also visible in fines. Under present law, heavy fines (with imprisonment as the default penalty) may be deliberately set to force the disgorging of profit derived from acquisitive crime.[157] Fines and forfeiture could, in theory, be jointly used to restore the status quo.[158] But it may equally be argued that the passing of State and federal proceeds of crime legislation has pre-empted the use of fines for this purpose. If both forms of sanction are to be used for disgorgement purposes, which one takes priority? If confiscation comes first, the capacity of the person to pay any later imposed fine will be diminished. Non-payment of the fine may lead to imprisonment. However if the fine is exacted first, the fact that there are now no assets to forfeit carries no further sanction. In either event the Crown is the beneficiary. The resolution of these conflicts is not aided by having these related sanctions imposed by unrelated tribunals.[159]

---

155. Fried, op. cit. at 333. Cf R. v. Allen (1989) 41 A. Crim. R. 51 at 56: "Orders under the Crimes (Confiscation of Profits) Act . . . are obtained on the application of the Director of Public Prosecutions and are clearly intended to be part of the retribution exacted from offenders on behalf of the community."
156. Hodgson, op. cit., p. 133. see also Phipps (unreported, Demack J., Qld C. A., 14 June 1990) "That order [under the Crimes (Confiscation of Profits) Act 1989 (Qld)] only means that the money that had been stolen is required to be returned. That in itself in not punishment for its theft." (Emphasis added.)
157. Larmer v. Dome Lighting Products Pty Ltd (1978) A.T.P.R. 40-070; R. v. Wattle Gully Gold Mines N.L. [1980] V.R. 622; Ducret v. Colourshot Pty Ltd (1981) 35 A.L.R. 503; R. v. Belcher (1981) 3 A. Crim. R. 124. See also Fraser v. The Queen (1985) 63 A.L.R. 103 at 108. Fines can be used to disgorge profits: R. v. Lott-Carter (1978) 67 Cr. App. R. 404; R. v. Po [1974] Crim. L. R. 557; R. v. Cotic (1984) 12 A. Crim. R. 208.
158. R. v. Heley [1989] Crim. L. R. 842.
159. See cases cited in Rinaldi, Drug Offences in Australia: Volume 1: Sentencing (1986) p. 43. Where money or property has been forfeited this is naturally not available to pay any fine so it is prudent to advise the sentencing judge of any forfeiture: see R. v. Weaver (unreported, N.S.W., 25 June 1981); R. v. Husak (unreported, N.S.W., 30 Oct 1970). Cf. R. v. Lucas (1982) 9 A. Crim. R. 268; R. v. Conley (1982) 30 S.A.S.R. 226; 6 A. Crim. R. 51.

The restorative and disgorging function is far more apparent in the procedures for depriving the offender of the proceeds and benefits of crime than in the steps available for forfeiting the instruments of crime.[160] The latter types of forfeiture are very resistant to proportionality limits, but the former have them built in. In theory, the deprivation should not exceed the benefit gained. The sanction is thus directly proportionate to the seriousness of offence, at least on economic measures. This squares with the view that these forms of forfeiture[161] are merely fines calculated by reference to profits[162] and therefore open to being treated as a conventional sentence.

However the proportionality principle is not wholly satisfied. This is because of the manner in which forfeiture is calculated under proceeds of crime legislation. It is one thing to say that offenders should be disentitled to profits derived from the commission of offences and that this is proportional to their wrongdoing, but it is another to call for them to repay a sum based on the *proceeds* (that is, gross receipt) rather than the *profits* (that is, net receipts) of crime.[163] If no account is taken of expenses and outgoings the result is not recovery of unjust enrichment, but expropriation of property.

Rehabilitation

If forfeiture and confiscation have any rehabilitative or educative attributes, they are very much underplayed. This dimension is rarely mentioned in the literature and never in the cases. After all, deodand and other forms of in rem forfeiture were concerned with objects not people. The sanctions of forfeiture and confiscation are ill-suited to the treatment model of sentencing and are not designed to provide ongoing supervision of the offender's financial affairs, nor any form of social, psychological, of fiscal re-education.

SCOPE FOR INTEGRATION

The intuitive and practical need to forge a relationship between confiscation orders and sentencing has been expressed in a number of contexts. In its influential report on the confiscation of the proceeds of crime, the Hodgson Committee in the United Kingdom[164] envisaged confiscation orders becoming part of sentence and subject to sentencing principles. The Committee envisioned that imposition of all or part of the sentence could be deferred while the court inquired into profits obtained

160. This is the language of P.O.C. Act 1987 (Cth), s. 3(1)(a) and (b), and State legislation.
161. I.e. pecuniary penalty orders.
162. Goode, "The Confiscation of Criminal Profits" (1986) 67 *Proceedings of the Institute of Criminology, University of Sydney* 35 at 45.
163. P.O.C. Act 1987 (Cth), s. 27; Fisse, "The Rise of Money-Laundering Offences and the Fall of Principle" (1989) 13 Crim. L. J. 5 at 7. From the standpoint of unjust enrichment, there is no reason why secondary profits (e.g. interest on investment of profit) would not be counted as net profit: *Chief Constable of Leicestershire v. M.* [1989] 1 W.L.R. 20; see also *R. v. Jansenberger* (unreported, Vic. Sup. Ct, 3 October 1985).
164. Hodgson, op. cit., p. 81.

by the offender from the crime. The sentencer would then be in a position to fix an appropriate mix of confiscation and other penal sanctions. In coming to that decision, the sentencer would be able to take into account other factors such as remorse or co-operation which mitigate sentences and which feature strongly in forfeiture and restitution situations.[165]

The Discussion Papers emerging out of the current Australian Law Reform Commission reference on customs and excise legislation are already exploring the possibility of greater "criminalisation" of forfeiture mechanisms under such legislation with a view to incorporating sanctions of this type into the established scheme of sentencing options. This approach is said not only to provide greater due process rights to those whose property is affected, but also to incorporate a wider range of dispositional options thus allowing the courts to tailor sanctions in a more co-ordinated, responsible and rational fashion.[166]

Appearance and reality

Despite appearances to the contrary, it is obvious that the modern forfeiture and confiscation orders have a closer affinity to the law of sentencing than to the civil law of remedies. It has become increasingly apparent that the traditional, but ill-defined, division between civil and criminal is inadequate to explain why the effect of one set of measures should be ignored in allocating sanctions for the same misconduct, particularly when each of the measures inures for the benefit of public coffers, or the public good. The civil and criminal labels tell only the form of process employed without describing the character of the sanction inflicted. That a suit is labelled civil does not imply that it does not impose punishment.[167]

The line between civil and criminal punishment is unclear as is the line between punitive and remedial. The new fashion for truth in sentencing requires more honesty in bringing within the criminal fold those sanctions that are in effect, if not in intent, unquestionably punitive. The ambiguity of the new confiscatory sanctions was even apparent to politicians who introduced the legislation. In the New South Wales Legislative Council, one speaker labelled the pecuniary penalty order "a sort of fine though not really a fine; for it comes after the major penalty required by the law has been applied".[168] In Queensland, the Attorney-General described the pecuniary penalty order as a type of "super fine".[169] A broader law of sanctions will have to replace the narrow law of sentencing if there is to be an advance on this front.

165. *R. v. Allen* (1989) 41 A. Crim. R. 51; *D.P.P. v. Walsh* [1990] W.A.R. 25. The Hodgson approach was not adopted in the United Kingdom.
166. A.L.R.C. Discussion Paper No. 42 and Discussion Paper No. 43.
167. See Clark, op. cit.
168. *Hansard* (N.S.W.), Legislative Council, 25 Nov 1985, p. 10, 469, Sir Adrian Solomons.
169. *Hansard* (Qld), Legislative Assembly, 4 April 1989, Attorney-General Clausen, p. 4039. Another such indirect indication can be found in s. 16(1) of the *Drug Trafficking (Civil Proceedings) Act* 1990 (N.S.W.) which allows a court to impose a fine for contravention of a restraining order "equivalent to the value of the interest".

Culpability and sanction

The growth of the substantive criminal law has been accompanied by a shift from objective to subjective grounds of culpability. The law of sanctions has revealed a similar dynamic in the shift to individualised and treatment models. Common law and statutory forfeiture is rooted in objective theories of criminal liability: it allows little scope for distinguishing culpability on the basis of subjective states of mind. In customs forfeitures there was often no offender amenable to prosecution, only property to be seized. The doctrine of "guilty res", reinforces the concept of objective liability which underpins much of forfeiture law. The interests at stake were commercial and the sanctions utilised were functional in terms of protection of the revenue, or the maintenance of those minimum standards of health, safety, or quality upon which an orderly commercial world depends. It was not fertile ground for development a jurisprudence of sentencing or sanctions.

The demise of common law forfeiture coincided with the birth of modern doctrines of strict liability and the attendant statutory forfeitures. [170] The emerging industrial revolution and the evolution of the modern state required the protection of the state's new revenue sources, of the health and safety of its workers and of the quality of its products. Statutory forfeiture provisions proliferated together with the regulatory offences to create and support the modern administrative state. As a general rule, the collective interest in conviction took precedence over the concept of personal guilt: [171]

> By the middle of the 19th century, and indeed for a considerable period of time before then, the exaction of forfeitures by the sovereign in such circumstances were clearly anachronistic and . . . were subject to wide public opprobrium. But the right of the sovereign to impose and exact forfeiture and fines, with or without proof of mens rea against the defendant, was never questioned *in principle*, for it was tacitly conceded that some arbitrariness might at times be required under the necessity of maintaining the public revenues, which—while working an occasional hardship on the few—serves the "higher good" of the corporate whole.

The tensions between subjectivism and objectivism in the sphere of civil or regulatory offences have been evident since late last century. [172] Although mediated by such defences as honest and reasonable mistake, [173] a strong judicial current is discernible, in Australia and elsewhere, against objectivism in the substantive criminal law. [174] Similar trends can be detected in respect of statutory forfeitures.

---

170. Finkelstein, "The Goring Ox: Some Historical Perspectives on Deodands, Forfeitures, Wrongful Death and the Western Notion of Sovereignty" (1973) 46 Temple L. Q. 169 at 199. Deodands were abolished in 1846, the same year as the landmark decision in *R. v. Woodrow* (1846) 15 M. & W. 404; 153 E.R. 907.
171. Finkelstein, op. cit. at 204.
172. *Sherras v. De Rutzen* [1895] 1 Q.B. 918; cf. *Cundy v. Le Cocq* (1884) 13 Q.B.D. 207.
173. *Proudman v. Dayman* (1941) 67 C.L.R. 536; see also *Fa v. Morris* (1987) 27 A. Crim. R. 342.
174. *Cameron v. Holt* (1980) 142 C.L.R. 342; *R. v. O'Connor* (1980) 146 C.L.R. 64; *He Kaw Teh v. The Queen* (1985) 157 C.L.R. 523.

In *Murphy v. Farmer*[175] the plaintiff, Farmer, had imported a motor vehicle into Australia but had erroneously, albeit unintentionally, answered a question on a customs form. Under the relevant provision, s. 229(1)(i) of the *Customs Act* 1901 (Cth), where a false answer is given, the goods are forfeited to the Crown. By a majority decision the High Court held that the word "false" in s. 229(1)(i) of the *Customs Act* 1901 (Cth) meant deliberately or intentionally untrue. The prior interpretation of the section, that "false" meant "wrong in fact" was rejected.[176] Underlying the majority's reasoning was a consideration of effect of the automatic forfeiture sanction which attended the commission of the offence. The majority of the High Court, after noting earlier authorities supporting such a result[177] said:[178]

> [I]t seems to us to be more strongly arguable that clear words should be required before there is attributed to the Parliament an intention to take the draconian step of imposing automatic forfeiture as a penalty for *"any"* wrong "entry invoice declaration answer statement or representation" regardless of whether the wrong information was provided as the result of an innocent mistake or excusable ignorance. The effect of a penalty of automatic forfeiture under s. 229(1)(i) can be devastating and quite disproportionate in that it applies regardless of the value of goods or the importance or effect of the wrong statement which was made.

In the United Kingdom a comparable prospect of an egregiously disproportionate sanction compelled a court to import an element of subjectivity into Customs legislation. In *Customs & Excise Commissioners v. Air Canada*[179] an aircraft operated by Air Canada was found to have cannabis, a prohibited import, in one container. The aircraft was later seized by customs as liable to forfeiture under s. 141 of the *Customs and Excise Management Act* 1979 (U.K.).[180] In an action commenced by the customs authorities for the condemnation of the aircraft the plaintiff argued that because s. 141 was absolute in terms and provided a remedy in rem, no mens rea was required. It argued that the overall purpose of the section was to prevent smuggling and to impose severe penalties in order to deter any person from attempting to commit such an offence and that such purposes would be served by strict liability. The defendant argued in response, by analogy with cases such as *R. v. Warner*[181] and *Sweet v. Parsley*[182] that it was unlikely that

175. (1988) 165 C.L.R. 19.
176. Section 229(1)(i) was repealed in 1989 as a result of this decision and replaced by an administrative penalty.
177. *Burton v. Honan* (1952) 86 C.L.R. 169.
178. (1988) 165 C.L.R. 19 at 28.
179. [1989] 2 W.L.R. 589; see also commentary by McFarlane, "Carrying Prohibited Goods: Is the Law Absolute?" (1988) 138 New L. J. 860.
180. Section 141(1) renders a ship, aircraft etc. used for carriage of things liable to forfeiture as also liable to forfeiture. Under s. 141(3) the owner or master is liable on summary conviction to a penalty equal to value of ship, aircraft etc. or £2,000 whichever is less. Schedules to the Act deal with seizure. The Act contains similar provisions to the Australian legislation in respect of seizure, forfeiture and condemnation, however the Australian legislation limits forfeiture to ships of less than 80 metres in length: see A.L.R.C., Discussion Paper No. 43, p. 14.
181. [1969] 2 A.C. 256.
182. [1970] A.C. 132.

Parliament intended that section to have such a draconian effect at least in the absence of mens rea. Tucker J. agreed with the defence stating that:[183]

> there is something wrong about a provision which entitles the commissioners to a right of forfeiture in rem without recourse to the courts . . . It seems to me to be unlikely that Parliament intended that such power should be given to the commissioners without proper supervision by the courts, in such situations as the present . . . I cannot see how the forfeiture of an aircraft belonging to an operator who has no knowledge of, and can have no knowledge of, the contents of a container being carried in its cargo hold can possibly deter the operators of aircraft or any potential smuggler from any illegal act.

In the event, Tucker J. implied knowledge into the relevant provision, despite a strong line of authority to the contrary, ultimately being persuaded by the oppressive and disproportionate result which would flow from a contrary construction.[184]

These judicial reactions to the arbitrary and oppressive effects of the objectification of the offending conduct do not yet amount to a wholesale repudiation of the imposition of sanctions without proof of personal culpability. But they can be seen as initial efforts at bringing the concepts of customs and forfeiture law into the mainstream of penal jurisprudence. These efforts are hampered by the persistence of the idea that forfeiture is an order against objects not people.

In rem/in personam forfeiture

One of the most powerful themes implicitly supporting the view that orders for forfeiture need not concern themselves with the culpability of, or effect on, the individual is the persistence of the idea that there can be forfeitures that have effect in rem which are quite distinct from forfeitures that operate in personam. The in rem forfeitures are said to be the result of judgments which apply to a nominated object and affect its status, while in personam ones are those in which the order is addressed to a specific person. By focusing on control of property through in rem forfeitures, rather than control of persons in the effort to protect revenue and suppress crime, issues of culpability, proportion and mitigation can be largely swept aside.

183. [1989] 2 W.L.R. 589 at 601.
184. The decision in this case was overturned on appeal: see *Commissioners of Customs and Excise v. Air Canada* [1991] 2 W.L.R. 344. The Court of Appeal although expressing sympathy for the judge's views and noting the harshness of the result, concluded that the relevant provisions of the customs legislation were ones that operated in rem and were therefore "wholly independent of the knowledge, motive or attitude of owners or other persons associated with the thing". The authorities relied upon by Tucker J. were criminal offences which operated in personam. The only relief available to the operators of the aircraft was by an application to the Commissioners of the Excise for remission of the forfeiture. Although the result is arguably correct as a matter of law, the decision reinforces the view that major legislative reform is required: see below, pp. 143-148.

This distinction between the two types of forfeiture has more currency in United States jurisprudence than here, where it has been recently rejected as "too formalistic to be relied on as a contemporary justification".[185] In that country the constitutional ramifications of categorising a forfeiture as in rem (and essentially civil in nature) as opposed to in personam (criminal) are profound. By labelling a forfeiture as civil, protections available in criminal proceedings are deemed to be inapplicable. Constitutional attacks on the grounds of unreasonable search and seizure, or of double jeopardy, or failure to provide due process are likely to fail if proceedings are classified as ones in rem.[186] However the increasing number of constitutional challenges to such forfeitures in the United States in response to the injustices wrought by their use, indicates that the theory is beginning to wear thin, "representing only a persistent judicial adherence to the ancient, anthropomorphic deodand".[187]

The notion that property or goods can, of themselves, offend can be traced back, in history, to biblical times[188] and, in law, to deodand under which liability was independent of all notion of fault on the part of the owner. Modern reliance on the idea that liability can attach to an inanimate res has come under severe criticism on the grounds that the concept is conceptually unsound, that it perpetuates legal fictions and that it is subversive of rights. Property cannot enjoy rights, nor owe rights to another. Goods, qua goods, cannot offend.[189] The purpose of the law is to regulate the conduct of human beings and ultimately:[190]

> All proceedings, like all rights, are really against persons. Whether they are proceedings or rights in rem depends upon the number of persons affected.

The expressions "in rem" and "in personam" are ambiguous and misleading. Paton warned how, in the process transferring them from Roman law, they have caused confusion to those who could not resist translating the phrases literally as meaning *a right to a thing* as opposed to *a right against a person*.[191] He agreed that, with rights in rem, the link to the res seemed more prominent, whereas in the case of rights in personam the concentration was upon the particular relationship between definite parties, but he was adamant that, in either case, the rights and liabilities were not vested in objects, but in persons. Austin said that the phrase in rem denoted the compass and not the subject of the right. It referred to a right which availed against people generally, as opposed to a right availing exclusively against a determinate person or

---

185. A.L.R.C., Discussion Paper No. 43, para. 21, n. 20.
186. Parcels, op. cit. at 449.
187. Smith, "Modern Forfeiture Law and Policy: A Proposal for Reform" (1977-78) 19 Wm & Mary L. Rev. 661 at 709.
188. Finkelstein, op. cit.
189. Vaughan C.J. in *Shepard v. Gosnold* (1672) Vaughan 159 at 172; 124 E.R. 1018 at 1024.
190. *Tyler v. Court of Registration* 175 Mass. 71 at 76; 55 N.E. Rep. 812 at 814 per Holmes C.J. (1900).
191. Paton, *A Textbook of Jurisprudence* (3rd ed. by Derham, (1964)), p. 262.

persons.[192] Hohfeld, too, was highly critical of the alleged in rem/in personam distinction.[193]

Such concepts are no longer useful in the classification of forfeitures. Whatever their origins in Roman law, they have become a thin veil for the fiction of the personification of objects. This fiction was born in superstition and ignorance, fostered by administrative convenience and perpetuated by sovereign fiscal greed. From the age of the deodand, through to modern admiralty and customs law, its pretence was that property exists in a vacuum. By mislabelling, in Latin, things as offenders, the state has claimed the right to ignore the effect of its "punishment", that is, its forfeiture, on the humans who are caught up in the transaction as innocent third parties, be they the owners of the property used in the enterprise or others with more indirect interests.[194]

Reconstructing the law of forfeiture

Abolition or restriction of non-judicial forfeitures

The foundation of any reformation of this area of sanction law[195] will have to be the melding of forfeiture powers with general sentencing ones. The minimum prerequisite of expropriation of property as direct or indirect punishment for crime should be a judicial order pursuant to a finding of guilt, or conviction of an offence.[196] Property should not be liable to be permanently confiscated simply upon the "commission" of an offence, or for allegations of crime proven to non-criminal standards of proof. In rem proceedings brought against property alone should be abolished or restricted. Forfeiture should be more clearly defined and accepted as punishment, so that questions of burden of proof, res judicata, double jeopardy and search and seizure would be settled on the same basis as in criminal proceedings. Third parties should be accorded rights of due process appropriate to the acceptance of forfeiture as a criminal sanction.[197] Personal blameworthiness[198] should form the basis both of liability and of sanction.

192. Discussed in Hohfield, "Fundamental Legal Conceptions as Applied in Judicial Reasoning" (1916-1917) 26 Yale L. J. 710 at 720-729; see also Weir, *Criminal Forfeiture Law and its Effect on Third Parties: An Historical and Comparative Analysis*, unpublished LL.B. (Hons) Thesis (Monash University, 1990); p. 10. A modern example of the use of this distinction under a forfeiture statute is found in *McGovern v. Victoria* [1984] V.R. 570 where the court held the effect of a judgment which affect title to or affects property in a thing in possession is a decision that determines the status of the thing and is conclusive in rem. The judgment, however, supports Hoffeld's anlaysis that the proceedings themselves were against a human being, although the effect of them bound others. It was the effect of the judgment, not the status of the proceedings, which made them in rem; cf. *Denton v. John Lister Ltd* [1971] 3 All E.R. 669.
193. Hohfeld, op. cit. at 745.
194. Hodgson, op. cit, p. 95.
195. See also A.L.R.C., Discussion Paper No. 43 (1990).
196. This should, but does not necessarily, entail that mandatory judicial forfeitures should also be abolished.
197. Kramer, "Forfeiture of Property Used in Illegal Act" (1962-63) 38 *Notre Dame Lawyer* 727 at 738.
198. This could also include responsibility for the actions of others through forms of direct or vicarious liability.

Seizure to be separated from forfeiture

The seizure of property as a preventive measure to protect society from a specific danger has always been accepted as a legitimate instrument of the social order.[199] Seizure should continue to be used as a prophylactic measure, to prevent the use or distribution of goods or property of an inherently dangerous character, or which have no purpose other than an illegal one.[200] Seizure may be used to prevent the further commission of offences, to assist in the investigation of the offence, and to secure evidence of the commission of the offence.[201] However, the power to seize should be divorced from the power to forfeit and the lawfulness of seizure should not automatically settle the lawfulness of forfeiture. Seizure is not the same as forfeiture. It should be regarded, as it is in the general criminal law, as a power prior to, but independent of, the ultimate power of disposition of property. As the Australian Law Reform Commission has pointed out:[202]

> A seizure power based on the above principles would differ from the present power to the extent that it would not be based on forfeiture without conviction. It would be independent of any action directed towards the forfeiture of goods which would arise as a penalty. However, it would be substantially the same and at least as effective as the present seizure power in achieving the objective of the customs laws. In fact, it would go further to the extent that it would enable seizure of goods for evidentiary purposes, whether or not those goods were liable to be forfeited.

Judicial forfeitures to be limited by principle of proportionality

The origins of the problem of disproportion in the use of forfeiture as a sanction lie in the nature of the primary sanction in medieval times. The death or outlawry of a person convicted of treason or felony was accompanied by the attainder of the offender, that is the extinction of all the person's civil rights and capacities, including property rights.[203] The loss of these rights could be considered as either proportionate to the gravity of the offence[204] or, more probably, as wholly irrelevant to the offender who was now dead or outlawed.[205]

The early writings on forfeiture are remarkable for the paucity of their coverage of the justifications of forfeiture as a sanction. Blackstone asserted that:[206]

> the true reason and only substantial ground of any forfeiture for crimes consist in this; that all property is derived from society, being one of those civil rights which are conferred upon individuals, in exchange for that degree of natural freedom, which every man must

---

199. Maxeiner, op, cit. at 649.
200. E.g. diseased animals, contaminated food, obscene publications, illicit drugs, explosives, firearms, toxins, dangerous structures or property and the like.
201. A.L.R.C., Discussion Paper No. 43, pp. 9-10.
202. A.L.R.C., Discussion Paper No. 43, p. 10.
203. Fox and Freiberg, op. cit., para. 6.101.
204. Blackstone, op. cit., pp. 373ff.
205. Although of course it was not irrelevant to her or his family.
206. Blackstone, op. cit., p. 299.

sacrifice when he enters into social communities. If therefore a member of any national community violates the fundamental contract of his association, by transgressing the municipal law, he forfeits his right to such privileges as he claims by that contract; and the state may very justly resume that portion of property, or any part of it, which the laws have before assigned him. Hence, in every offence of an atrocious kind, the laws of England have extracted a total confiscation of the moveables of personal estate; and in many cases a perpetual, in others only a temporary, loss of the offender's immovables, or landed property; and have vested them both in the king, who is the person supposed to be offended, being the one visible magistrate in whom the majesty of the public resides.[207]

This Blackstonian view of society, grounded as it is in its 17th century Hobbesian concept of the "social contract", can no longer be a satisfactory basis for the imposition of forfeitures of any kind. First, apart from the inappropriateness of the underlying social theory, official responses to public transgression need no longer be an all-or-nothing affair. The elaborate range of modern sentencing options is ordered in a sufficiently recognisable hierarchy of inflictiveness to enable the selection of degrees of punishment commensurate with culpability. Secondly, it is now acknowledged that official reactions to crime may be excessive. The limiting principle of proportionality is intended to restrain the state's punitive response even in relation to sanctions that are intended to satisfy retributive feelings, or to produce deterrent effects.[208] Because forfeitures have not been fully acknowledged to be an official punitive response to crime, and are often not even a consequence of conviction, the significance of the principle of proportion as a link between offending and sanction has been slow in receiving judicial or legislative recognition.[209] That recognition needs to be more forthcoming, but some major issues will have to be resolved.

First, a clear distinction will need to be made between different forms of confiscation order with different objectives. The principle of

207. See also *Chitty on Prerogatives of Crown* (1820), pp. 213-226 cited in *R. v. Cuthbertson* [1981] A.C. 470 at 471-477. Forfeiture was not intended to deprive an offender of the fruits of a crime but was seen as a "natural" consequence of the offender's violation of obligations to society. The threat of the loss of property was seen as a most effective incentive to loyalty and obedience. Forfeiture applied to both real and personal property because both were seen as product of man's feudal estate.
208. *Veen v. The Queen* (1979) 143 C.L.R. 458; *Veen v. The Queen (No. 2)* (1988) 164 C.L.R. 465; see also Fisse, above, Chapter 5; Maxeiner, op. cit. at 641.
209. The ambivalent attitude of the courts is highlighted in this observation of Debelle J. in *Taylor v. Attorney-General* (1991) 160 L.S.J.S. 210 at 223 on the impact of the confiscation legislation:
    "At the end of the day it is necessary to have regard to whether the order of forfeiture would be severely disproportionate to the circumstances of the offence and the nature and degree of offending. The fact that there is some disproportion is not necessarily a reason for refusing to order forfeiture: that would fail to recognise Parliament's intention to create an additional deterrent. However, if forfeiture were to result in unnecessary hardship, having regard to the circumstances of the offence, a court might be justified in refusing the order."
    See also *R. v. Rintel* (1991) 52 A. Crim. R. 209 and discussion by Fisse, "Confiscation of Proceeds of Crime: Discretionary Forfeiture or Proportionate Punishment", paper delivered at 27th Australian Legal Convention, Adelaide, 1991.

proportionality is not offended by confiscatory steps whose goal is restitution or the prevention of unjust enrichment. Thus, pecuniary penalty orders producing disgorgement of the proceeds of crime should not be regarded as disproportionate, so long as there is a direct and justifiable link between the illegal activity and the sanction. As Goode argues,[210] a "profits fine" can be clearly understood and justified as a special sanction for those who disobey the law for personal gain. The deprivation can be regarded as quasi-retributive in the sense that it restores the legal order by denying the illegitimate receiver the unlawfully obtained enrichment.[211] In any event, as has been argued earlier in this chapter,[212] if the deprivation is linked to and does not exceed the benefit gained[213] the sanction will be directly proportionate to the seriousness of the offence, at least as measured in economic terms.

Secondly, there is the problem of whether the principle of proportionality should limit the confiscation of real or personal property that has had a significant role in the actual execution of the criminal enterprise. Impounding the "instruments of crime" can affect property of such high value as to make the sanction appear to be grossly disproportionate to the gravity of the particular offence charged.[214] Making it an exception to the proportionality principle can be defended, but only on preventive and incapacitative grounds. The types of property which fall into this category are difficult to define. At minimum they will include items which facilitated the crime, but which have no recognised lawful purpose in the hands of the person from whom they are being confiscated. In such cases the value of the property forfeited can be disregarded in assessing whether the proportionality principle has been infringed, but in all other cases, the value of the property can be taken into account in sentencing.

A pioneering attempt to draw these distinctions can be found in the *Crimes (Confiscation of Profits) (Amendment) Act* 1991 (Vic.), s. 36, which amends s. 5 of the *Sentencing Act* 1991 (Vic.). It states:

In sentencing an offender a court—

(a) may have regard to a forfeiture order made under the Crimes (Confiscation of Profits) Act 1986 in respect of property—

(i) that was used in, or in connection with, the commission of the offence;

(ii) that was intended to be used in, or in connection with, the commission of the offence;

(iii) that was derived or realised, directly or indirectly, from property referred to in sub-paragraph (i) or (ii);

210. Goode, op. cit. at 45.
211. Maxeiner, op. cit. at 656: see also comments of the Victorian Court of Criminal Appeal in *R. v. Allen* (1989) 41 A. Crim. R. 51 at 56 when it stated that confiscation orders could be regarded as part of the retribution exacted from offenders on behalf of the community.
212. See above, p. 137.
213. Major problems exist in relation to the difference between net and gross proceeds and profits, but these are not pursued here: see Fisse, above, Chapter 5.
214. This is more likely to be so where real property is concerned.

(b) must not have regard to a forfeiture order made under that Act in respect of any other property;

(c) may have regard to a pecuniary penalty order made under that Act to the extent to which it relates to benefits in excess of profits derived from the commission of the offence;

(d) must not have regard to a pecuniary penalty order made under that Act to the extent to which it relates to profits (as opposed to benefits) derived from the commission of the offence.

(2B) Nothing in sub-section (2A) prevents a court from having regard to a confiscation order made under the *Crimes (Confiscation of Profits) Act* 1986 (Vic.) as an indication of remorse or co-operation with the authorities on behalf of the offender.

Thirdly, the differential impact of confiscation orders on co-offenders will need to be determined. Where a number of offenders are involved, but the property of only one was utilised in the offence, the burden of the penalty will seem to fall disproportionately upon the person whose property is forfeited. This would also appear to violate the principle of parity, namely that, as a general rule, where parties to a crime are of equal culpability, the weight of punishment should fall equally on each. Here the argument can be mounted that those who provide the means for the crime share greater culpability than those who do not. Such persons cannot complain of disparate punishment if the property of theirs which facilitated the crime is taken from them. It can also be argued that the problem of parity does not arise in the same way in respect of pecuniary penalty orders designed to recover the profits of crime. Here the order against one party is intended to have the effect of restoring the pre-offending status quo. The burden will fall according to who profited and, as such, is not disproportionate. It should not then be a factor to be weighed heavily when considering the proportionality of the total sanction package, or when comparing sentences between co-offenders. It may, however, have a mitigative effect if the surrender of the property indicates contrition or co-operation.

Finally, if proportionality is accepted as a limiting principle and the property to be confiscated can be divided in some fashion, orders for partial forfeiture should be made so as to produce the necessary balance. If division of the property is not possible, adjustment of the primary penal sanctions will be needed to produce a proportionate end result. The latter technique can be used to resolve parity problems as well. Where the primary sanction is a fine, greater flexibility in balancing fines and forfeitures could be obtained if the legislation allowed the forfeiture to be treated as a fine in specie. Instead of forfeiture being levied in addition to the fine, the property confiscated could be sold and the proceeds applied in payment of the fine.

Judicial forfeitures limited by principle of least restrictive alternative

The principle of least drastic means, or the least restrictive alternative, holds that if a less drastic measure is available to achieve a desired preventive result, then that should be used in preference to a more severe measure. Complete forfeiture of an offender's assets would only be the ultimate sanction. Thus, property may first be rendered unusable, certain fixtures or marks may be removed, goods may be controlled temporarily or sequestered,[215] illegally obtained drugs could be returned to a pharmacist, cars can be impounded until an unlicensed driver obtains a licence, illegally imported goods could be returned to owners if the owners were willing to pay duties and otherwise comply with regulations. The forfeiture of everyday items should rarely be warranted as a preventive measure.

Judicial forfeitures to be part of "sanction package"

Because the concept of forfeiture conforms easily to the traditional concept of sentence[216] it is contended that orders for imprisonment, or pecuniary penalties, or reparation, or forfeiture should all be seen as forming the elements of a total sanction package, with the sentencing court having regard to the overall impact of the set of orders on the defendant. The nature of the relationship between the different types of order would need to be worked out, and particular attention would have to be given to the sequence in which sanctions were imposed and the importance of them all being awarded by the same tribunal, or if by different ones, of the need for full awareness of what has gone before.

CONCLUSION

Forfeiture and confiscation orders must be brought into a modern system of sanctions, one of both rewards and penalties attended by measures designed to ensure the protection of the individual interests which are affected by the intrusion of the governmental function. The application of these safeguards to criminal confiscation must not depend, as under present forfeiture law, on historical accident. They should be deliberately incorporated to limit the mistaken, arbitrary or unjust application of state power and to preserve the dignity of the individual and the right of that individual to her or his property.[217]

Modern "proceeds of crime legislation" provides supplementary sanctions to buttress the traditional penal methods that are now regarded as inadequate to suppress organised crime, drug trafficking and the like.[218] Yet the legislation hesitates to define forfeiture as criminal *punishment*. It ought now to do so openly. Then at least the criminal

215. One could also draw an analogy here with the notion of forfeiture under *Forfeiture Act* 1870 model: see *R. v. Cuthbertson* [1981] A.C. 470 at 471-477. After 1870, a convicted felon could still be deprived of property while serving a sentence of penal servitude or imprisonment. The felon's property was vested in an administrator who had full power over it during custody but who had to account for it at end of sentence. See also *Dugan v. Mirror Newspapers Ltd* (1978) 142 C.L.R. 583 at 597 per Stephen J. who noted as a matter of historical interest that the provisions of the *Forfeiture Act* 1870 provided a scheme whereby the *Insolvency Act* was used to vest property in an administrator and administered for the benefit of the prisoner's creditors and family.

216. Reed and Gill, op. cit. at 105.

217. Frankel, "Preventive Restraints and Just Compensation: Toward a Sanction Law of the Future" (1968) 78 Yale L. J. 229 at 237.

218. Smith, op. cit. at 310; *Hansard* (Cth) House of Representatives, 30 April 1987, p. 2314, Attorney-General Bowen.

level of proof and procedural standards will, prima facie, apply both to offenders and affected third parties.[219] However, at a substantive level, a major conflict will have to be resolved. Either forfeiture and confiscation sanctions will have to succumb to some of the restraints imposed by general sentencing principles, such as proportionality with its built-in concepts of mitigation, or these general sentencing principles and concepts will have to give way to the utility of special forms of sanction, or the correctional needs of special classes of offender.

Some evidence of the latter occurring can already be found in the willingness of the High Court to incorporate concepts of community protection into the calculus of proportionality so as to deny mental disorder any mitigative effect in sentencing when raised in relation to dangerous offenders.[220] While the argument of this chapter is that forfeiture and confiscation should be subject to the general principles of sentencing, it has been shown a like refinement is open to being made in respect of the weight to be given to forfeiture or confiscation orders at sentencing in estimating whether the total sanction package is proportionate to the crime committed. Sentencers need not take forfeiture into account as mitigation when the prime purpose and effect of the order is disgorgement of profits and the restoration of the status quo, but should do so when the purpose and effect is to strip the offender of assets in an incapacitative, deterrent and punitive fashion. Whether such distinction can be maintained in a meaningful way through the enormous range of situations in which forfeiture is being called for is problematic, but it is unlikely that sentencers will ever accept that prior confiscation or forfeiture of an offender's assets has nothing to do with the manner in which the sentencing discretion is to be exercised.

219. Kramer, op. cit. at 738.
220. *Veen v. The Queen (No. 2)* (1988) 164 C.L.R. 465. Fox, "The Killings of Bobby Veen: The High Court on Proportion in Sentencing" (1988) 12 Crim. L. J. 339 at 358-362.

7
Equity and the Proceeds of Crime

PATRICIA LOUGHLAN*

There is an existing, though ill-defined and distinctly under-utilised, equitable jurisdiction to deprive criminals of the proceeds of their crimes. The thesis of this brief paper is simply that the flexible, conscience-based principles of equity, especially as manifested in the remedial constructive trust, can function to enforce the public policy, curially articulated both at law[1] and in equity,[2] that no criminal shall profit from her or his own crime.

The imposition of a constructive trust has personal and proprietary consequences for the constructive trustee—it is a dramatic and onerous burden. The beneficiary of the trust has an equitable interest in the property subject to the trust and can assert that proprietary interest both against the constructive trustee and against any subsequent holder of the property except for a bona fide purchaser for value without notice. If the property itself cannot be recovered in full or in part because, for example, it is no longer identifiable and cannot be traced, the constructive trustee, like any other trustee, can be made personally liable to pay equitable compensation to the beneficiary for the loss of the property.

But what is the constructive trust and when can it be imposed? The constructive trust is, at least in principle, "the formula through which the conscience of equity finds expression".[3] It is said to be "an instrument created by the law to do justice",[4] a trust imposed by law where justice and good conscience require it, regardless of the express or implied intentions of the parties concerned.[5] Unfortunately, it is also, in practice, a trust imposed only when circumstances of any particular case fall within one or more of a few well-established categories of liability, categories which, in England and Australia at any rate, defy any attempt at a unifying and ordered analysis.

* Faculty of Law, University of Sydney. Published with permission of *Current Issues in Criminal Justice*.

1. *Cleaver v. Mutual Reserve Fund Life Association* [1892] 1 Q.B. 147; *Beresford v. Royal Life Insurance Co.* [1938] A.C. 586.
2. Earnshaw and Pace, in "Let the Hand Receiving It Be Ever So Chaste . . ." (1974) 37 M.L.R. 481 trace this principle of public policy back to the inception of modern equity and describe it as the precursor of the common law rule to the same effect which was later developed in the 19th century.
3. *Beatty v. Guggenheim Exploration Co.* 225 N.Y. 380 at 386 (1919) per Cardozo J.
4. Maudsley, "Constructive Trusts" (1977) 28 N.J.L.Q. 123 at 137.
5. *Hussey v. Palmer* [1972] 1 W.L.R. 1286 at 1289-90; *Baden Delvaux and Lecuit v. Societe General* [1983] B.C.L.C. 325.

In the view of the present writer, however, one or more of these established categories can be developed and used, without violating accepted equitable doctrine, to lasso the profits of crime and force both the criminals themselves and third persons who take from those criminals to hold such profits on trust. The categories are these: (i) constructive trusts imposed on property acquired by reason of an unlawful killing; and (ii) constructive trusts imposed to prevent the defendant from being unjustly enriched. It will be argued here that the reach of the first category of constructive trust liability can be extended to cover other crimes besides wrongful killing and other benefits besides payments under wills and life insurance policies. And it will be further argued that the doctrinal key is to be found in the concepts of unconscionability and unjust enrichment found in the second category.

It is clear law that a constructive trust will be imposed to prevent the perpetrator of a wrongful killing from taking a beneficial interest in any property which accrues to her or him as a direct result of that killing. Where the legal estate becomes vested in the killer,[6] the killer holds it for the benefit of the victim's estate. The slaying of one joint tenant by another entails that, at law, by the jus accrescendi, the slayer becomes entitled to the whole of the property held in joint tenancy. And equity has responded by compelling the criminal to hold the entire legal estate on a constructive trust for herself or himself and for the estate of the victim in equal shares.[7]

A number of difficult problems are contained in and masked by those abstract propositions of law,[8] but the issue for present purposes is how close the connection must be between the act of killing and the acquisition of property before the principle of public policy will engage to attach the property. Since the equitable jurisdiction is not penal and the principle requires deprivation but not punishment, the courts scrupulously avoid any return to the ancient and statutorily abolished regime of escheat and forfeiture:[9]

> The principle of public policy operates only to deny the felon the enjoyment of any benefit which might otherwise flow from his

6. It is often the case that the legal estate never in fact vests in the killer, because the common law, acting under the same principle of public policy, prevents the vesting. Ames, in *Lectures On Legal History* (1897), p. 313, distinguished two legal strategies for depriving the criminal of the profits of the killing. One is to prevent the legal title from ever passing to the killer and the other is to allow the title to pass but compel the killer to hold it on constructive trust. In "Killing The Goose That Lays the Golden Eggs" (1958) 32 A.L.J. 14 at 16, Toohey J. noted that Anglo-Australian courts have generally used the former strategy and American courts the latter.

7. *Rasmanis v. Jurewitsch* (1968) 88 W.N. (N.S.W.) 59; *Re Stone* [1989] 1 Qld R. 351; *Re K. (decd)* [1985] 2 W.L.R. 262; *Schobelt v. Barber* (1966) 60 D.L.R. (2d) 519.

8. Whether e.g. any form of wrongful killing is sufficient to engage the principle of public policy: see *Public Trustee v. Fraser* (1987) 9 N.S.W.L.R. 433 and *Re Stone* [1989] 1 Qld R. 351 (manslaughter with diminished responsibility); and the relevance of a criminal conviction or acquittal to the issue of whether a constructive trust should be imposed: see *Public Trustee v. Evans* (1985) 2 N.S.W.L.R. 188.

9. See Pollock and Maitland, *The History of English Law* (reissued 1968, ed. Milsom) Vol. I, p. 477 for an account of the law in Bracton's day governing the consequences of a declaration of "outlawry". "Of every proprietary, possessory contractual right he is deprived; the king is entitled to lay waste his land and it then escheats to his lord; he forfeits his chattels to the king."

felonious act; it does not cross the line and take from him rights or interests which are not consequential upon his felonious act.[10]

One important restriction on equity's jurisdiction to impose trusts on the proceeds of crime is therefore the need to ensure that only property which can be attributed to the crime itself can be attached.

The causal nexus between the crime and the benefit must, judging from the cases, be close and direct—an inheritance from the will or the intestacy of the victim or a payment under the victim's life insurance policy or pension fund or a survivorship right under a joint tenancy. But Street J., in the passage cited above, speaks in terms of benefits "flowing from" or "consequential upon" the criminal act, terms which, within the limits of avoiding forfeiture of the criminal's own property, do not suggest that there is a particularly stringent causal connection test.

There is one recent rather spectacular instance of a judicial loosening of the causal connection requirement. In the case of *Rosenfeldt v. Olson*,[11] a decision of the British Columbia Supreme Court, a killer was deprived of certain benefits which were found to have accrued to him by reason of crime, in the following unusual circumstances: Olson was a serial killer of children. When he was apprehended, he entered into negotiations with the Royal Canadian Mounted Police which resulted in payment of $100,000 by the R.C.M.P. into a trust fund for the benefit of Olson's family in exchange for information given by Olson as to the locations of the bodies of the children whom he had murdered. The moneys paid were solely for the benefit of Olson's family and not for the benefit of Olson himself. Some of the parents of the murdered children brought an action claiming, inter alia, that the money was impressed with the constructive trust in their favour. The court agreed. Although the judgments proceeded on the basis of the unjust enrichment of the defendant and that Olson was unjustly enriched by the payment, the court had to address the issue of the connection between the act of killing and the receipt of benefit. Trainor J. said this:

> The question is whether that fund came into being or was acquired as a direct result of the killings. Is there the necessary causal connection? . . . I know the fund came into being after the killings had occurred, to be paid out in exchange for information of identity and location of bodies, but I have no problem concluding that the establishment of the fund was as a direct result of those killings.[12]

This is little more than unsubstantial assertion and it may be that the notion of a benefit being a "direct result" of a crime must be an elastic one and dependent upon judicial instinct rather than judicial reasoning. The "direct result" test does seem, in substance, to be a kind of "but for" requirement—the benefit would not have accrued to the criminal but for

10. *Rasmanis v. Jurewitsch* (1968) 88 W.N. (N.S.W.) 59 at 63.
11. [1985] 2 W .W.R. 502; revd [1986] 3 W.W.R. 403 (British Columbia CA); leave to appeal to the Supreme Court of Canada refused.
12. *Rosenfeldt v. Olson* [1985] 2 W.W.R. 502 at 530. The Court of Appeal decision did not disturb Trainor J.'s finding on the causal connection between the crime and the acquisition of property. The reversal of the trial court decision was on the basis that, contrary to Trainor J.'s view, the plaintiffs had not suffered the deprivation necessary to found a constructive trust based on unjust enrichment.

the fact of the crime. If money paid to a killer to acquire information about the crime is a benefit that directly results from that crime, then it seems plausible to suggest that profits accruing to a killer from a book written about the crime are also benefits directly resulting from that crime. And if that is true about profits from a book, then what about the sale of movie rights? This is not, in the view of the present writer, a matter of opening floodgates; it is a matter of opening a window.[13]

That the principle of public policy is indeed a principle and not an inflexible rule of law was recognised by Young J. in *Public Trustee v. Evans*, who found that it is open to a judge to pronounce the limitations of the principle in keeping with the requirements of the particular age.[14] The current widespread social concern, reflected in legislation, over the spectacle of criminals retaining and prospering from the benefits of their crimes may mean that in our age the principle can rightly expand in scope. But persuading the courts of equity to expand the reach of constructive trust hitherto restricted to circumstances such as killers taking benefits under wills may require the exposition of some more established doctrinal basis than a principle of public policy. That doctrinal basis can be found, it is suggested, in the rapidly developing equitable jurisdiction to impose a constructive trust where, in the opinion of the court, it would be unconscionable to allow the person with legal title to property to deny the beneficial interest in that property to the claimant.[15] In *Public Trustee v. Fraser*, Kearney J. expressly recognised that the principle of public policy requiring the attachment of benefits accruing to a criminal from the crime is "itself a rule deriving from the broader concept of unconscionability"[16] and he drew an analogy between that rule and the constructive trust imposed on the basis of "unconscionable assertion or retention of the benefit of property . . . and of unjust enrichment".[17] Kearney J. found that where the constructive trust is expressly imposed on the basis of preventing unconscionable conduct and unjust enrichment, the court's role becomes "not only ascertaining the nature of the crime but also looking to the circumstances in order to evaluate the moral culpability" of the offender.

There is a further problem of the identity of the trust beneficiary. That is, the profits may be held on a constructive trust, but on a constructive trust *for whom*? In *Rasmanis v. Jurewitsch*, Street J. vigorously denounced any principle founding the constructive trust on a

13. The argument here is directed to equity's inherent jurisdiction, through the extension of established doctrine, to impose a constructive trust on the proceeds of crime. It should be noted that in California, a *statute* provides for the mandatory imposition of a constructive trust on profits received by a convicted criminal from the sale of the story of the crime: *California Civil Code*, s. 2225 (West Supp. 1988). For a commentary on the constitutional implications of the statute, see Okuda, "Criminal Antiprofit Laws: Some Thoughts in Favour of their Constitutionality" (1988) 76 California L. Rev. 1353.
14. (1985) 2 N.S.W.L.R. 188 at 192.
15. *Muschinski v. Dodds* (1986) 60 A.L.J.R. 52; *Baumgartner v. Baumgartner* (1987) 76 A.L.R. 75. The domestic context in which the conflict of these two High Court cases arose should not limit the breadth of the principles therein articulated.
16. (1987) 9 N.S.W.L.R. 443.
17. Ibid. at 444.

compensatory basis: "public policy requires deprivation of the felon; it does not require compensation to the victim."[18] In fact, in that case, the benefit was held on a constructive trust for the victim's estate:

> The result is due to equity acting in personam so as to preclude the felon's unconscientious action gaining him this benefit. *A home for the benefit must be found and the estate of his victim is the only available destination.* [emphasis added][19]

The statutory constructive trust in California, referred to above, is imposed in favour of the criminal's victims, for injury or loss resulting from the crime. There is a defined time period within which the victims must file claims and if the time passes without such claims being made, the criminal receives the benefit of the trust.[20] The equitable constructive trust under discussion here, however, is based on the principle that it would be unconscionable to allow a criminal to hold the proceeds of the crime for her or his own benefit. The fact that in any particular case there may be no victims to claim the money should not be a sufficient ground to reverse the operation of the principle.

In *Rosenfeldt v. Olson*, Trainor J. accepted that the parents of the victim were legitimate equitable claimants to the beneficial interest in the fund[21] and found that the money "was a quantification of the loss inflicted by the criminal acts which led to the fund".[22] That finding can be explained by the fact that the constructive trust in the case was expressly based on a principle of unjust enrichment which required both an enrichment of the defendant and a corresponding deprivation of the plaintiff. A deprivation on the part of the parents had to be found to justify the imposition of the trust and, as noted above, the Court of Appeal found that the parents had not suffered the required deprivation:

> The payment to [the trustee] did not deprive the plaintiffs of money which, if it had not been paid to [the trustee], would properly have been payable to the plaintiffs. Thus, the payment to [the trustee] did not result in any corresponding deprivation of the plaintiffs.[23]

But if the constructive trust is founded not on a restitutionary basis but on the basis of unconscionability, then such a deprivation need not be found. And it is suggested that there should be no blanket rule. Where a court decides that a constructive trust should be imposed on the basis that it would be unconscionable for a criminal to retain the beneficial interest in property which accrues as a direct result of the crime, then, in the words of Street J., a home for the benefit must be found and it is up to the court, looking to all the circumstances of the case, to find it. It may be that in most cases the only appropriate beneficiary is the victim or the victim's estate. It may be that in other cases, the property ought to return to the Crown as bona vacantia. The critical point is that the criminal is prevented from retaining the beneficial interest in property where it would be unconscionable for her or him to do so.

18. *Rasmanis v. Jurewitsch* (1968) 88 W.N. (N.S.W.) 59 at 63.
19. Ibid. at 64.
20. *California Civil Code*, s. 2225(e)(3) (West Supp. 1988).
21. *Rosenfeldt v. Olson* [1985] 2 W.W.R. 503 at 533.
22. Ibid. at 526.
23. *Rosenfeldt v. Olson* [1986] 3 W.W.R. 403 at 408.

8

The Cash Transaction Reports Act
The Legal Minefield

JOHN O'SULLIVAN and STEPHEN MITCHELL[1]

SETTING THE SCENE

The *Cash Transaction Reports Act* (1988) (Cth) (C.T.R. Act) is still pretty much "rough justice". Its drafting still needs work. Its concepts still need refining.

This chapter aims to look at some of the problem areas of the C.T.R. Act. If I appear to be critical of the C.T.R. Act or its drafters, I only intend to be constructive. I should also point out at the outset that where one stands on the C.T.R. Act is essentially a matter of political preference. Civil libertarians hate it. Those calling for the death penalty probably love it. I will leave you to form your own political judgments—my aim is simply to comment on some problematic drafting and legal issues.

A QUICK OVERVIEW OF THE C.T.R. ACT

An excellent place to start is the pamphlet published by the Cash Transaction Reports Agency (the "Agency").

That pamphlet starts by pointing out that the C.T.R. Act was initiated for the purpose of assisting the Australian Taxation Office and federal and State law enforcement agencies in the detection of tax evasion and criminal activity, such as money laundering from drug trafficking. To achieve those aims, the C.T.R. Act places certain obligations on cash dealers and on the public.

Obligations on Cash Dealers Arising from the C.T.R. Act

The pamphlet points out that there are three basic obligations on cash dealers:

- cash dealers will need to verify identification of persons opening accounts;
- cash dealers must report to the Agency details of currency transactions (that is, what we think of as "cash") involving $10,000 or more, unless the transactions are exempt;

1. Freehill Hollingdale and Page. Paper delivered at R.M.S. Seminar, "Cash Transaction Reporting, Money Laundering, and Confiscation of Proceeds of Crime", Sydney, 21 August 1990; Melbourne, 24 August 1990.

- cash dealers must report to the Agency "suspect transactions" (whether cash transactions or otherwise).

Obligations on the Public

- Members of the public must produce adequate identification documents when opening accounts with cash dealers;
- It is now unlawful to open or operate a bank account or similar account in a false name;
- Currency transfers to and from Australia of $5,000 or more must be reported to the Agency or to customs.

The Agency

The C.T.R. Act establishes the Agency to receive reports of significant cash transactions, disseminate information from those reports to appropriate bodies, analyse the reports for tax and criminal investigation purposes and generally oversee the C.T.R. Act.

Users of Information Gathered under the C.T.R. Act

- The Australian Taxation Office can automatically access information collected by the Agency.
- The Australian Customs Service, National Crime Authority, Australian Federal Police, State Police, the Australian Securities Commission and other law enforcement agencies can obtain access to the information with the approval of the Director of the Agency (the "Director").

DEFINITIONS

I have no intention of canvassing the definition sections in detail. Let me, however, draw your attention in particular to two troublesome concepts: those of "account" and "cash dealer".

"Account"

An account means any:

facility or arrangement by which a cash dealer does any one or more of the following:

(a) accepts deposits of currency;

(b) allows withdrawals of currency;

(c) pays cheques or payment orders drawn on the cash dealer by, or collects cheques or payment orders on behalf of, a person other than a cash dealer.

This definition of an "account" is much wider than, for example, the definition of "account" found in s. 3(1) of the *Debits Tax Act* 1982 (Cth). The latter refers to "an account kept with a bank or a non-bank financial institution being an account to which payments by the bank or non-bank financial institution in respect of cheques or payment orders drawn on the bank or non-bank financial institution by the account holder or by one or more of the account holders, may be debited".

The opening words in the definition of "account" contained in the C.T.R. Act make it clear that one is to take a "transactional" approach to interpreting what an "account" is, rather than an "accounting" approach. One is to see whether there is a "facility" or "arrangement" of the relevant kind. One does not look to see whether there is a journal or a ledger kept by a relevant body in which entries are made (this being the "accounting" approach).

One can understand why the C.T.R. Act has deliberately taken the transactional approach—it wishes to reach the substance, not the form. However, consider:

- Is the repayment of fixed obligations under the traditional housing loan a "deposit"? I understand the Agency considers it may not be. However, the repayments of a housing mortgage of a "tax effective" kind, for example, the various overdraft products now offered by some banks, would according to the Agency constitute depositing for these purposes;

- When I subscribe for or redeem units in a unit trust (especially a cash management trust with a cheque account facility attached) am I operating a relevant account? There are differing views—depending on the structure, I think probably not.

Who is a Cash Dealer?

Now let me focus for a moment on several of the paragraphs of the definition of "cash dealer":

- Paragraph (b) says that a "body corporate that is, or, if it had been incorporated in Australia, would be, a financial corporation within the meaning of s. 51(xx) of the Constitution" is a "cash dealer".

One needs to be a fairly good constitutional lawyer to understand what kind of organisations will be caught by that paragraph. Mr Justice Deane, then in the Federal Court, considered the phrase in *Re Kuring-gai Co-operative Building Society (No. 12) Ltd*[2] (1978) 22 A.L.R. 621. He said:

the phrase "financial corporation" is a composite one. It does not refer to solvency. An obvious reference point is to the activity of the commercial dealing in finance. Another possible reference point is the provision of management or advisory services in relation to financial matters. I use the words "dealing in finance", for want of a better expression, to refer to transactions in which the subject of the transaction is finance (such as borrowing or lending money) as distinct from transactions (such as the purchase or sale of particular goods for monetary consideration) in which finance, although involved in the payment of the price, cannot properly be seen as constituting the subject of the transaction. A common but not invariable characteristic of the relevant type of transaction is that the obligation on each side is to pay money.

2. (1978) 22 A.L.R. 621.

That description was approved by the High Court in *State Superannuation Board v. Trade Practices Commission.*[3]

It is clear that the expression "financial corporation" is not a precise one. In my view, it is equally clear that there are many organisations which are "financial corporations" who do not realise it. Companies which engage in finance broking or investment advice are, in my view, potentially "financial corporations" and therefore "cash dealers" even though they deal wholly in advice and not cash.

I think that conclusion would surprise (to say the least) a number of investment advisory companies.

• Paragraphs (d) and (e) of the definition of "cash dealer" refer to "securities dealers" and "futures brokers". Those definitions are in turn defined by reference to the definitions found in the *Securities Industry Code* and *Futures Industry Code*. All that is unremarkable. However, it is worth mentioning that one can be a "securities dealer" under the *Securities Industry Code* if one carries on the business of dealing in securities even though not licensed to do so. Similarly one is a "futures broker" under the *Futures Industry Code* if one deals in futures on behalf of others, even though not licensed to do so.

The relevance of this is that when prosecuting authorities are next prosecuting people who should have obtained licences under the *Securities Industry Code* or the *Futures Industry Code*, they may well be able to add charges of failing to comply with the C.T.R. Act. This will attract the significant penalties set out in the C.T.R. Act. The "bucket shop" operators now have another statute to worry about!

• Of greatest personal interest to me is para. (g) which refers to a trustee or manager of a unit trust. "Unit trust" is in turn defined to mean "a trust to which a unit trust scheme relates" and includes cash management trust and property trust. The phrase "unit trust scheme" is defined very widely to mean: "any arrangement made for the purpose, or having the effect, of providing, for a person having funds available for investment, facilities for the participation by the person as a beneficiary under the trust, in any profits or income arising from the acquisition, holding, management or disposal of any property pursuant to the trust."

It is common practice for solicitors, accountants, real estate agents, travel agents and a number of other persons who operate statutorily required trust accounts, to offer arrangements to permit moneys to be swept from those trust accounts to interest bearing accounts of various kinds. Many of them regularly offer investment services (linked to their trust account) of various kinds. In my view, all of those arrangements are likely to fall into the definition of "unit trust scheme".

All of those people are likely to be trustees of a "unit trust scheme".

Accordingly, in my view there is a significant likelihood that most solicitors, real estate agents and travel agents will be "cash dealers".

This, as we will see, has some rather horrifying consequences. In particular it means that I, as a cash dealer, must put in suspect transaction reports. This is discussed below.

3. (1982) 150 C.L.R. 282 at 305.

Without wishing to push the point too far, I should note that the definition of "unit trust scheme" does not contain any limitation by reference to a concept of being available to the public. I think a respectable case can be made out that nearly all trustees, even trustees of private family trusts, are "cash dealers". I doubt I need to develop that thought any further.

- Who "is" the cash dealer?

Where a cash dealer is a corporation it can only act through its servants and agents. Section 34 contains detailed provisions which have the effect that the state of mind of a corporation or conduct of a corporation is to be treated as the state of mind, or conduct, of a "director, servant or agent" acting within the scope of her or his actual or apparent authority.

The explanatory memorandum to the legislation described this section as containing "the standard provisions facilitiating the prosecution of corporations".

It is true that provisions such as those found in s. 34 are now relatively standard in legislation dealing with the conduct of corporations. However, those pieces of legislation usually deal with situations where the relevant conduct or relevant decisions are performed or taken at a relatively high level in the corporation.

What is striking and significantly different about this legislation is that the relevant decisions will be taken at a very low level. In the case of banks, building societies or credit unions, the relevant decisions in relation to whether or not to make a suspect transaction report will frequently need to be taken by tellers. Because those people will be acting in the course of their usual authority, the actions or omissions of the teller will be attributed to the bank or building society (as the case may be).

In effect, this reduces compliance to the lowest common denominator.

SIGNIFICANT CASH TRANSACTION REPORTING

In keeping with my approach of focusing on the difficult areas, let me move straight to s. 10(2) and in particular para. (f) of s. 10(2).

Section 10 sets out the transactions which are eligible for exemption from significant cash transaction reporting.

You will recall that significant cash transactions (that is, cash transactions over $10,000) must be reported unless they are exempt. I will not here go through the exemption process or the keeping of exemption registers but simply say that one of the ways of obtaining exemption is to fall within s. 10(2). Section 10(2) was designed to exempt transactions between financial institutions and so-called high cash flow businesses (for example, certain kinds of retail businesses, entertainment businesses, hospitality businesses and the business of providing vending machines) where the relevant transaction consists of a deposit into or withdrawal from an account maintained for the purposes of that business. The exemption, however, will only be available if the amount of currency involved in the transaction is, in accordance with para. (f) of s. 10(2), not in excess of the "amount that is reasonably commensurate with the lawful business activities of the customer".

Depending on the circumstances, it is quite possible that the decision as to whether the particular amount of currency involved in a deposit or withdrawal does not exceed an amount "reasonably commensurate with the lawful business activities of the customer" will fall to a teller at a bank, building society or credit union.

Most businesses are, at least to some extent, cyclical. Many businesses are subject to quite violent fluctuations depending on the season. Sometimes fluctuations in a business's prospects can depend on something as cyclical as the weather. For instance, businesses which sell umbrellas do very well when it rains whereas businesses selling lawnmowers do very poorly. The owners of the businesses frequently cannot predict their cash flows themselves.

What chance does a teller have?

Whilst by and large the significant cash transaction reporting provisions are relatively easy to observe because they have an objective limit, this is one example where the departure from objective standards makes compliance very difficult.

REPORTING OF TRANSFERS OF CURRENCY

Section 15(1) requires persons transferring Australian currency or foreign currency into or out of Australia with a value of more than $5,000 to make certain reports.[4]

Section 15(2) exempts commercial passenger carriers from making reports in respect of currency in the possession of the carrier's passengers whilst s. 15(3) exempts commercial goods carriers from making reports in respect of currency carried on behalf of another person unless the other person has disclosed to the carrier that the goods include currency.

Two comments are apposite:

- Before dealing with the substantive point that I want to raise in relation to s. 15, first let me make a suggestion. As we all know, the value of a foreign currency is a movable feast. It is not appropriate to attach penal consequences (see s. 15(6)) to a shifting target. I would not have thought it impossible to formulate a valuation provision setting out the means of determining an appropriate exchange rate and time for calculating that exchange rate.

4. The C.T.R. Act has been amended by the *Cash Transaction Reports Amendment Act* 1991 (Cth). This Act addresses the criticism of Duggan J. of the Supreme Court of South Australia in *Schultz v. Taylor* (unreported, 28 June 1991), echoed in this chapter, that s. 15 was "vague" in its wording. The Amendment Act clarifies the last point in time when a person is able to make a report to a customs officer when bringing currency into, or taking it out of, Australia. That Amendment Act also provided for the reporting and analysis of international telegraphic transfer data; changed the name of the Cash Transactions Reports Agency to the Australian Transaction Reports and Analysis Centre and changed the name of the Act to the *Financial Reports Act*.

- The more significant point I wish to raise is the possibility that s. 15 creates a strict liability offence. Where D "transfers" relevant currency into or out of Australia in excess of the relevant value without making a report, D can be guilty of an offence.

It is clear from a reading of s. 15(2) and (3) that the transactions caught by s. 15(1) are very wide ranging. For instance, by inference from s. 15(2) the master of a ship or pilot of a plane will need to make a report in respect of currency in possession of the master or pilot's passengers unless they are a "commercial passenger carrier".

It follows that if I (not being a "commercial passenger carrier") sail my boat from Cape York Peninsula to New Guinea and one of my invited passengers, unbeknown to me, is carrying $5,100 in Australian currency, it would seem that I have to make a report. Ignorance is no defence. The offence appears to be one of strict liability. Contrast s. 29 which says that one will only be guilty of an offence against the provisions set out in s. 29 if one "knowingly" provides false or misleading information. If one provides no information at all, that is, makes no report at all, s. 29 will not apply. Section 15(6) will apply. Section 15(6) contains no requirement of knowledge.

Perhaps even more strange is that it is at least arguable that I have to make a report in the circumstances just referred to even if my guest brings all the cash back from New Guinea on the return trip. This is because there is at least an argument that the concept of "transfer" of currency does not contain any notion of permanence. Rather it focuses on the simple act of "taking or sending" currency out of Australia. If some concept of permanent disposition were intended, it would have been easy enough to say so. However, by focusing on the physical action rather than the consequences or effect of the action, s. 3(3) makes the offence contained in s. 15(6) even easier to commit.

SUSPECT TRANSACTION REPORTING

Here the minefield is at its thickest.[5] Let us see some of the implications.

The position of lawyers and accountants

Because lawyers and accountants usually operate "unit trust schemes" they will usually be "cash dealers".[6]

---

5. Since this chapter was first delivered as a seminar paper on 21 August 1990, the C.T.R. Act has been amended by (inter alia) the *Crimes Legislation Amendment Act (No. 2)* 1991 (Cth) to deal with some of the problems raised by the authors in this chapter. In particular, s. 16(5) of the C.T.R. Act has been amended to ensure that cash dealers or their officers, employees or agents are protected from suit in respect of actions taken by the cash dealer or the person in the mistaken belief that the action complained of was required under s. 16 of the C.T.R. Act. The C.T.R. Act was also amended by the *Crimes Legislation Amendment Act (No. 2)* to confer upon the Director of the Cash Transaction Reports Agency the function of issuing guidelines to cash dealers to assist them in the discharge of their obligations under the Act.
6. See above, pp. 157-158.

Thus, if a lawyer or an accountant:

- is a "party";
- to a "transaction"; and
- has reasonable grounds to suspect that information in possession concerning the transaction may be, inter alia, "relevant to investigation of an evasion, or attempted evasion, of a taxation law", a report must be filed.

It is easy to start conjuring up the possibility that lawyers and accountants may have to report their clients for things their clients seek advice about. That will however only happen if the elements above are satisfied.

At first blush it may seem that the first element will be hard to satisfy. However, assume for a moment that the transaction we are concerned with is the act of receiving the proceeds of sale of an asset on settlement, initially depositing that in a trust account and then transferring it to an interest bearing account. All of those steps are things that lawyers and accountants in private practice frequently do. Clearly, there is a transaction to which the lawyer or accountant is party. Assume further that the lawyer or accountant knows that the client is currently subject to a tax audit. All that has to be done then is to form the view that receipt of the proceeds of sale of the asset "may be relevant" to the tax audit and, likely as not, he or she may be obliged to report the transaction.

What happens in this case to legal professional privilege? Prima facie it would be of no assistance—it would give way to the specific statutory provision.

In any event, the law of privilege is of no assistance to an accountant.

What about bank tellers?

Bank tellers are currently gaily putting in suspect transaction reports. The current approach is "better safe than sorry" and when there is the slightest grounds for suspicion, reports are being put in.

That is done on the basis that s. 16(5) protects cash dealers from any "actions, suits or proceedings" against them "in relation to any action" taken by them "pursuant to" s. 16.

Beware—s. 16(5) is luring many cash dealers into a dangerously unwarranted sense of security.

The protection of s. 16(5) will only apply if the action taken by the cash dealer, or their employee, was taken "pursuant to" s. 16(1). There is a range of preconditions which must be met before an action can be said to be taken "pursuant to" the section. (This all, of course, assumes that an employee ("E") is sufficiently aware of the constitutional meaning of "financial corporation" to understand whether or not E or the employer is a "cash dealer".) These elements include the following:

1. The cash dealer ("D") must be a "party" to the particular transaction which may be relevant to investigation of possible breaches of law or enforcement of the *Proceeds of Crime Act* 1987 (Cth).

2. There must be a "transaction".

3. D must have "reasonable grounds to suspect" that the information possessed falls within s. 16(1)(b).

4. The information that D holds must concern the transaction which falls within s. 16(1)(b)(i), (ii) or (iii).

5. The information must fall within subparas (i), (ii) or (iii) of s. 16(1)(b). This in turn means:

• that, in relation to para. (i) of s. 16(1)(b), it must be relevant to investigation of an "evasion, or an attempted evasion" as opposed to "avoidance";

• it must be relevant to an investigation in relation to a "taxation law" or "an offence against the law of the Commonwealth or of a territory" as opposed to any other kind of federal law and as opposed to any State law;

• the cash dealer must have at least some knowledge of the provisions (and the ingredients of those provisions) of the relevant law.

Turning to these ingredients individually:

1. It is not enough if the cash dealer is told about the transaction. The cash dealer must be a "party" to the transaction. If I tell my bank manager ("B") that I was involved in a bottom-of-the-harbour tax fraud which had nothing to do with B's bank, my bank manager is not required to report the transaction by s. 16(1) and if B does, s. 16(5) will not protect B. I will be entitled to sue B for breach of the banker's duty of confidentiality (not to mention defamation or any other remedy I may have). Section 16(5) is therefore far from being a licence for cash dealers to report bad behaviour.

2. The Agency has suggested in one of its guidelines that a "transaction" can be "constituted by any business dealing between a cash dealer and a customer. It includes negotiations or discussion which may not result in an actual dealing but does not include mere enquiries."

The C.T.R. Act contains no definition of "transaction" (unlike the *Proceeds of Crime Act* which defines "transaction" to include "the receiving or making of a gift"). The word would therefore have its normal English meaning. The *Pocket Oxford Dictionary* defines "transact" as "to perform, carry through" and defines a "transaction" as the "transacting of, any piece of commercial or other dealing". It is a reasonable inference from the *Pocket Oxford Dictionary* that there must be some completed act—otherwise there will be no "performace" or "carrying through".

Even if one accepts the Agency's view that "negotiations or discussion" which do not result in an actual dealing are enough, there is clearly a fine line between "negotiation or discussion" and "mere enquiry".

3. It was pointed out in the Explanatory Memorandum to the Bill that the phrase "reasonable grounds to suspect" was deliberately chosen because it implied a lower standard than "reasonable grounds to believe". This gives the cash dealer therefore at least some measure of protection assuming the other elements referred to above have been satisfied.

4. The information held by the cash dealer must concern the particular transaction which is relevant to investigation of a breach of the tax legislation or other federal law or which may be of assistance in enforcing the *Proceeds of Crime Act*. One cannot report the deposit of a large number of small denomination notes wrapped in a bread wrapper (totalling less than $10,000) because one possesses information that some years ago the depositor attempted unsuccessfully to rob a bakery. The information held is about a past breach of a State's Crimes Act which yielded no proceeds of crime.

5. It is fundamental that the information possessed by the cash dealer concerning the transaction:

- may be relevant to investigation of evasion or attempted evasion of a federal tax law;

- may be relevant to investigation or prosecution of an offence against a federal law or the law of the Australian Capital Territory or the Northern Territory (and other Territories); or

- may be of assistance in the enforcement of the *Proceeds of Crime Act*.

These requirements may not be as well understood as they should be. It is widely thought that one can report transactions relevant to investigations of breaches of almost any law. For instance, one commentator at the Banking Law and Practice Conference in 1989 suggested that a banker with reasonable grounds to suspect a breach of s. 129 of the *Companies Act* or a stockbroker who suspected a breach of the insider trading provisions of the *Securities Industry Code*, would have to make a report. That is incorrect.

With respect to the Agency, I might also mention that I do not believe the guidelines issued by the Agency make this distinction between State and federal law (or a number of other distinctions) sufficiently clearly.[7]

Might I also add to this point (although this is a slight digression) that one of the weaknesses of the suspect transactions reporting legislation is that it must stand or fall in accordance with constitutional limitations imposed on all federal legislation. The constitutional limitation significantly reduces the potential impact of this legislation and it would clearly be preferable for supplementary legislation to be passed in all the States.

In relation to taxation, a report is only required in relation to investigation of an "evasion, or attempted evasion" as opposed to "avoidance". Although the distinction has become blurred over time and has been significantly weakened by Pt IVA of the *Income Tax Assessment Act* (1936) (Cth), the general principle is that "evasion" is illegal whilst "avoidance" (the legitimate ordering of one's affairs so that it attracts a particular kind of tax treatment) is permissible. The distinction between "evasion" and "avoidance" is one of the most difficult in our law. The High Court has wrestled with it on a number of occasions. The drafters of our legislation keep trying to sharpen the concept. It is certainly one which gives me great difficulty—I can imagine what it does for a bank teller.

7. See the discussion below, p. 166.

I would further suggest that one cannot even have "reasonable grounds to suspect" that information concerning a transaction may be relevant to investigation of an evasion of a law or an offence against a law unless one has at least some knowledge of the provisions of the law and of the ingredients of the relevant offices. If one does not have at least some knowledge of the law and its contents, how can one meet even the admittedly low standard of "reasonable grounds to suspect"? To illustrate the point, assume that a bank teller believes there is a federal law which prohibits persons earning more than $5,000 per month and requires them to immediately transfer any excess over $5,000 which they do earn to the federal Treasury. If I deposit into my bank account a cheque for $6,000 together with indisputable evidence that it is my pay cheque for the month of August, the bank teller ("T") is not entitled to report the transaction despite the fact that T has certain knowledge of information which T believes concerns a transaction in breach of federal law. There must in truth be a relevant federal law and, I would submit, it must have the same general characteristics as the cash dealer believes it has.

Earlier, I expressed the view that compliance had been lowered to the "lowest common denominator". Whilst that might be the case, one can now see that the "lowest common denominator" must:

- know enough constitutional law to know what is a "financial corporation" within the meaning of s. 51(xx) of the Constitution (so as to know whether D is a cash dealer);
- know what is a "transaction" and what is a mere enquiry;
- know the legal distinction between "evasion" and "avoidance";
- understand which laws are State and which are federal and what are the contents of each of them.

Unless D gets all of this right, any report submitted will not obtain the benefit of s. 16(5) and D may be successfully sued for defamation and (if a banker) breach of duty of confidentiality. If D takes the easy course and submits no report, D faces a different set of unpalatable sanctions. Life seems very unfair!

The Guidelines

Might I make a few comments in this context about the guidelines issued by the Agency.

First, let me say that s. 38, which deals with the functions of the Director of the Agency, does not appear to authorise with sufficient clarity the preparation and release of these guidelines. Certainly it would have been preferable for the C.T.R. Act to have specifically empowered the Director to issue guidelines (exempting the Director from liability in respect of them—see below).

The *Trade Practices Act* 1974 (Cth) binds the Crown and it is at least arguable that s. 52 applies to the Director. The Director will therefore need to bear in mind s. 52 of the *Trade Practices Act* when preparing the guidelines. If the guidelines in any respect misstate the true legal position, the Director may be in breach of s. 52.

It may also occur that the Director could be liable for negligent misstatement if the guidelines published induce a cash dealer to make a report which is not a report "pursuant to" s. 16(1).[8] A cash dealer might argue that, relying upon incorrect guidelines, he or she made a report which exposed her or him to an action for breach of contract (for example, breach of the implied term in a banker's contract requiring that a customer's affairs be kept confidential) or defamation.[9]

In this context, I do have a number of concerns about the guidelines on suspect transaction reporting. For instance, C.T.R. Agency Guideline No. 1 suggests that cash dealers will be protected against defamation and similar actions in relation to suspect transaction reports made to the agency "provided that the cash dealer suspects, based on reasonable grounds and in good faith, that information it has in respect of a transaction falls within one of the three categories specified in the guideline". It does not, for example, point out that the cash dealer must be a "party" to the transaction. A bank which lodged a report in relation to a transaction of one of its customers to which it was not a party may believe, based on the guideline, that it was entitled to protection from defamation or other law suits. It is not.

There are similar points I could make in relation to the drafting of the prohibition on "structuring" transactions to avoid reporting and about the account verification procedures.

8. See the discussion above, p. 162
9. See *City Council of Parramatta v. L. Shaddock & Associates Pty Ltd* (1981) 36 A.L.R. 385.

9

The Relationship Between the Privacy Act and the Cash Transaction Reports Act

KEVIN O'CONNOR*

INTRODUCTION

Privacy rights of individuals are significantly affected by the *Cash Transaction Reports Act* 1988 (Cth) (C.T.R. Act). All customers of financial institutions will be affected by the C.T.R. Act's account identification requirements from 1 February 1991. Those customers who engage in cash transactions are caught by the reporting requirements placed on cash dealers. The reporting requirements apply to significant and suspect transactions and international currency transfers. The suspect transactions reporting system has been in operation since 1 January 1990. The significant transactions and international currency transfer reporting system commenced on 1 July 1990.

PRIVACY ACT: BACKGROUND

This is not an appropriate place for a detailed discussion of the *Privacy Act* 1988 (Cth). However, to understand better the comments which follow, the following points are relevant.

- The *Privacy Act* came into operation on 1 January 1989.
- It lays down 11 Information Privacy Principles (I.P.Ps) which govern the collection, storage, use and disclosure of personal information.
- The way in which the Cash Transaction Reports Agency (C.T.R. Agency) (as a Commonwealth agency) collects, stores, uses or discloses personal information must comply with the *Privacy Act*.
- Important I.P.Ps from the viewpoint of the C.T.R. Agency are:
  — I.P.P. 1 which allows information to be collected from an individual where it is "lawful", "necessary" and "directly related to the functions of the collector". I.P.P. 3 prevents collection which intrudes "to an unreasonable extent" "upon the personal affairs" of the individual concerned.
  — I.P.P. 11 which prohibits a federal agency from disclosing information unless one of five exceptions applies to the

---

* Federal Privacy Commissioner.

167

disclosure. The two of relevance to the C.T.R. Agency's operation are (d) and (e) which state:

(d) the disclosure is required or authorised by or under law; or

(e) the disclosure is reasonably necessary for the enforcement of the criminal law or a law imposing a pecuniary penalty, or for the protection of the public revenue.

- In regard to the above:
  - The C.T.R. Act deals in detail with the C.T.R. Agency's lawful authority to disclose. Any C.T.R. Agency disclosure made in compliance with I.P.P. 11.1(d) would satisfy the *Privacy Act*;
  - If the C.T.R. Agency breaches an I.P.P. (for example, by misusing information or failing to adhere to adequate security standards) an individual has the right to complain to me and might possibly receive a determination from me which could include an award of damages for any harm suffered.

In this chapter I will address privacy aspects of the three areas of the cash transaction reporting (C.T.R.) scheme: suspect transactions reporting; significant transactions reporting; and account identification. The observations which follow relate to policy aspects of the scheme. I should, I feel, make the point that I believe that the C.T.R. Agency has been conscientiously seeking to observe the requirements of the *Privacy Act* in its administration. But I feel that some aspects of the Act as passed by Parliament raise difficult privacy issues.

SUSPECT TRANSACTIONS

This element of the scheme commenced operation in January 1990. The policy objective for extending the reach of the C.T.R. Act below the usual $10,000 cash transaction is to catch activities which are calculated to avoid the threshold. Identifying a suspect transaction depends on the judgment of, for the most part, frontline public contact staff of cash dealers—who are often junior and inexperienced. They may base their judgment on:

- a principal criterion ("reasonable grounds to suspect") drawn from the language of the criminal law, and which is normally the province of experienced police and magistrates to determine;
- other criteria (for example, personal appearance, behaviour, low-status occupations, confused communication, belonging to pensioned or benefit groups, migrant) which have the potential to allow for stereotyped and prejudiced attitudes to be indulged.

While the public and parliamentary discussion of the C.T.R. proposal concentrated on the value of the C.T.R. system in dealing with "organised crime", large scale tax evasion and the "underground cash economy", my sense of the debate was that the aim was to catch big criminals, not small fry.

The law gives as the situations in relation to which a suspect transaction reported may be lodged:

- the investigation of tax evasion;
- the investigation or prosecution of an offence against Commonwealth laws; or
- assisting the enforcement of the *Proceeds of Crime Act* 1987 (Cth).

These situations alone cover a range of offences from the most trivial to the most serious offences for money laundering or organised fraud.

Recently the Director of the C.T.R. Agency said that in the first six months there had been 3,400 suspect transaction reports. The level of reporting will probably increase over time, as based on United States experience, initial forecasts were that there would be up to 20,000 reports a year.

The suspect transactions element of the scheme means that all personal or business transactions are subject to surveillance by the staff of financial institutions and other "cash dealers". If cash dealers fail to report a "suspect transaction" the individual employee or the employer/cash dealer may be prosecuted.

So, for example, should a bank employee report as "suspicious" the deposit of $1,000 in crisp banknotes by a young woman of Asian appearance who has a small child with her? Is the employee meant to surmise that she is a sole parent, that she may come from a drug-running country and that she probably doesn't work full-time? Obviously examples like this one can be multiplied.

I am aware that the C.T.R. Agency has discussed with relevant unions these issues and that now arrangements exist under which an employee's suspicion will first be examined at senior executive level in the financial institution before being onward reported. Obviously this will burden senior executives with a very difficult role.

Bank clerks have been given a role usually left to police, and one which allows them to apply standards which out of this context may found a complaint of unlawful discrimination. I acknowledge the need for any law which sets a fixed monetary amount as its threshold to have a "safety net" designed to catch transactions which are calculated to avoid that limit. But I feel that the C.T.R. Act's policy aims might largely have been met if a simple money-formula had been used as the basis for identifying artificially constructed below threshold transactions. So, for example, if the Asian mother deposited $1,000 on a very regular or daily basis there would, I acknowledge, be reasonable grounds for suspecting avoidance of the significant C.T.R. threshold.

SIGNIFICANT TRANSACTIONS AND INTERNATIONAL CURRENCY TRANSFERS

This is the main area of operation of the scheme. The C.T.R Agency is anticipating 1.5 million reportable significant transactions and 10,000-20,000 international currency transfers in the year from 1 July 1990.

In comparison with the suspect transactions element of the scheme, at least these transactions are able to be identified clearly by reference to easily applied criteria. The cash dealer is not required to judge the customer and therefore does not have to go beyond the matters listed in Sched. 1 or 3 of the C.T.R. Act to make a report. There is no pressure on the cash dealer to be interested in the private life or activities of the customer. The report need only deal with factual circumstances of the transaction. If the inquiries and collection of information can be limited, I.P.P. 3 is satisfied.

Further, as the reporting scheme becomes more widely known, any person engaging in a cash transaction over $10,000 (or a $5,000 currency transfer) will be aware that a report will be made and of the required contents of a report. They will know that information will be disclosed to the C.T.R. Agency and other particular law enforcement agencies.

As a result, the situation of the large-deposit customer is more in conformity with *Privacy Act* standards than that of the small-deposit customer. The large-depositor will probably be aware of the reporting system; in the case of foreign currency transfers there is an onus on the customer to report the transfer and the report does not intrude into matters of private life or behaviour.

ACCOUNT VERIFICATION

This is the most sweeping aspect of the C.T.R. scheme. It affects all account opening. As from 1 February 1991 it is legally required that the identity of account holders be satisfactorily proven.

It seems that the main way of proving identity is to supply a written reference from a person equivalent in status to those entitled to verify passport applications. This will mean that people choosing that option will have to expose their financial arrangements, to some degree, to the gaze of others. If people do not want to do that then they must run the gauntlet of a complex tiered system for proving identity. The system depends on an individual being able to supply official and other records of their name and other personal particulars. It is not clear where the individual who has insufficient or no such records stands in this system. For example, in the United States members of one community have, because of their religious and cultural traditions, little or no personal documentation. This situation may have parallels among some of Australia's migrant and disadvantaged groups. One must ask the question: why is it necessary to register (over time) the whole of that part of the community which participates in the financial system in order to catch the relatively very small group who belong to the organised crime/underground cash economy population.

A feature of government initiatives of recent times in dealing with serious unlawful conduct has been to employ strategies which sweep into the net of surveillance the day-to-day activities of the ordinary law-abiding population. This development is of course a direct consequence of the facilities given by new information-processing technology.

INVESTIGATION

The use and disclosure of reports for investigation purposes provides the rationale for the creation of the C.T.R. Agency Part IV of the C.T.R. Act provides the Director with the legal basis to disclose C.T.R. information contained in the reports from cash dealers. These disclosure practices are in conformity with I.P.P. 11(1)(d).

The Australian Taxation Office has automatic access to the C.T.R. information while other agencies are permitted access on approved terms by the Director.

For this purpose the Director of the C.T.R. Agency has entered into detailed Memoranda of Understanding with recipient law enforcement agencies. Issues of relevance to privacy addressed to the Memoranda of Understanding include the following:

- the conditions under which on-line access to significant cash transactions reports and suspect transactions reports may be given;

- the nature of the authority by which the Director of the C.T.R. Agency will give access to information on the part of members of other law enforcement agencies;

- providing officers so authorised with individual computer access codes;

- restrictions on reuse and redisclosure of information;[1]

- the extent and nature of reuse or redisclosure of the information for law enforcement purposes. The C.T.R. Act addresses this for C.T.R. information but questions exist for other information obtained by law enforcement agencies in process of investigations;

- restrictions on the location and manipulation of C.T.R. access terminals;

- requiring the recipient law enforcement agency to maintain an effective audit trail in respect of use of the C.T.R. system;

- requirement that officers authorised to receive C.T.R. information acknowledge in writing the existence of the detailed arrangements

---

1. The relevant clause in the agreement with the Western Australian Police Force is as follows:
    The Director is obliged to ensure that the privacy requirements of the Commonwealth are respected. The Agency and the Western Australian Police are required by law to respect the secrecy of C.T.R. information. Thus, Western Australian Police personnel authorised to have access to C.T.R. information are granted such access on the conditions that the officers:
    (a) shall not use the CTR information except for the purposes of performing the officer's function of law enforcement;
    (b) shall not, either directly or indirectly divulge the C.T.R. information to any person except that the information may be communicated to another person as specified herein for the purposes of the enforcement of the laws of the State of Western Australia or the Commonwealth;
    (c) shall ensure that the information is protected by such security safeguards as it is reasonable in the circumstances to take, against loss, against unauthorised access, use, modification or disclosure and against other misuse; and
    (d) shall include in the record containing the information a note of the disclosure of the information to another person pursuant to clause (b), and
    (e) shall abide by the rules and conditions set out herein.

already referred to and that the penalties for unauthorised disclosure of information are $5,000 or imprisonment for two years.

While the C.T.R. Agency itself is subject to the *Privacy Act* those who receive information from the C.T.R. Agency (where they are not Commonwealth agencies) are not subject to the Act. So if there is an improper disclosure or use of information by a non-Commonwealth recipient agency the individual does not have the rights of complaint and to personal remedies provided by the *Privacy Act*. I regard this as a gap in the scheme of the *Privacy Act*, and believe that the Act should at least be amended to give individuals the benefit of Commonwealth laws in regard to any information about them that has emanated from a Commonwealth database.

If it came to my attention (either by way of complaint or through audit) that a non-Commonwealth recipient of personal information had breached the *Privacy Act*, while I might not be able to provide a direct remedy to the individual, I would consider recommending to the Director of the C.T.R. Agency that he consider terminating the agreement or only allowing it to continue to operate on the basis that the wrongdoing agency make amends to the individuals (for example, by payment of ex gratia compensation).

CONCLUSION

The C.T.R. Act and its reporting scheme will have a significant impact on an individual's right to privacy. Aspects of the C.T.R. scheme—suspect transactions and account opening—will affect all people engaging in any form of financial transaction.

In light of the scope of the scheme extra vigilance will be required to protect privacy. This was a major concern highlighted by the Senate Standing Committee on Legal and Constitutional Affairs *Report on the Cash Transaction Reports Bill* (April 1988).

I have questioned in this chapter the reach of the present law in the suspect transactions and account identification areas. The effectiveness of the C.T.R. Act will ultimately be measured by its ability to catch the big criminals and to identify major fraud in the community.

10

Smurfing
Rethinking the Structured Transaction Provisions of the Cash Transaction Reports Act

BRENT FISSE and DAVID FRASER

SMURFING, AUSTRALIAN STYLE

"Smurfing"—the structuring of transactions to avoid reporting requirements—is a major concern in the United States,[1] as Sarah Welling discusses in Chapter 11. Smurfing is also likely to become a prevalent problem under the *Cash Transaction Reports Act* 1988 (Cth) (C.T.R. Act). Successful Smurfing usually requires low cunning and limited personal effort, qualifications hardly likely to discourage locals from entry into the profession.

Section 7 of the C.T.R. Act makes it obligatory to report a "significant cash transaction". Section 3 of the Act defines a "significant cash transaction" as "a cash transaction involving the transfer of currency of not less than $10,000 in value". Section 31(1) makes it illegal to conduct transactions in such a way as to avoid the reporting requirement under s. 7. The evasive techniques against which the section is aimed include the breaking down of what would otherwise be a single deposit of, for example, $20,000 into five deposits each involving the non-reportable amount of $4000.

Section 31 provides as follows:

(1) A person commits an offence against this section if:

    (a) the person is a party to 2 or more non-reportable cash transactions; and

    (b) having regard to:

        (i) the manner and form in which the transactions were conducted, including, without limiting the generality of this, all or any of the following:

            (A) the value of the currency involved in each transaction;

            (B) the aggregated value of the transactions;

---

1. See Welling, "Smurfs, Money Laundering, and the Federal Criminal Law: The Crime of Structuring Transactions" (1989) 41 Florida L. Rev. 288 (reproduced as Chapter 11 of this collection); Popham and Probus, "Structural Transactions in Money Laundering: Dealing with Tax Evaders, Smurfs, and Other Enemies of the People" (1988) 14 Am. J. Crim. L. 83; Schwartz, "Liability For Structured Transactions Under The Currency And Foreign Transactions Reporting Act: A Prelude To The Money Laundering Control Act of 1986" (1987) 6 *Annual Review of Banking Law* 315.

(C) the period of time between any of the transactions;

(D) the locations at which the transactions took place; and

(ii) any explanation made by the person as to the manner or form in which the transactions were conducted;

it would be reasonable to conclude that the person conducted the transactions in that manner or form for the sole or dominant purpose of ensuring, or attempting to ensure, that the currency involved in the transactions was transferred in a manner and form that:

(iii) would not give rise to a significant cash transaction; or

(iv) would give rise to exempt cash transactions.

Subsection (2) creates a similar offence in relation to non-reportable transfers of currency (s. 15). Subsection (3) authorises the imposition of a fine not greater than $10,000 and/or imprisonment of not more than five years for natural persons; corporate offenders are subject to a fine of not more than $50,000.

These provisions raise a number of problems and uncertainties. The discussion following is an attempt to highlight the difficulties which surround the mental element of the offence, the "reasonable to conclude" criterion, the "parties" to a transaction who may be liable, and the position of financial institutions which breach the section but do so in order to assist the enforcement of the statute. Many other issues arise, but we have tried to concentrate on the more significant problems which call for amendments to the section.

THE MENTAL ELEMENT OF THE OFFENCES

Section 31 does not adequately define the mental element required for criminal liability. Little has been learned, it seems, from the spectacle of *He Kaw Teh v. The Queen*[2] and other judicial attempts to divine the mental element of statutory offences from obscurely drafted provisions. The offence under s. 31(1) (or s. 31(2)) is serious but, on a literal interpretation, does not require an intention to evade a reporting requirement.[3] The *Proudman v. Dayman*[4] defence of reasonable mistake of fact may be available as a fall-back position, but even this is unclear. It is therefore necessary to enter that hideous slough of legal despond—the interpretation of the mental element of Australian statutory offences.[5]

The mental element of the offence as defined under s. 31(1) (or s. 31(2)) does not expressly require proof of an intention to evade a reporting requirement of the Act. The wording of the section sets out an

2. (1985) 157 C.L.R. 523.
3. "Intention to evade a reporting requirement" is a shorthand expression used throughout to avoid repeated reference to the cumbersome wording of s. 31 ("an intention to ensure, or an attempt to ensure, that the currency involved in the transaction . . .").
4. (1941) 67 C.L.R. 536.
5. See further Fisse, *Howard's Criminal Law* (5th ed.), pp. 523-539.

objective test, namely that it is reasonable to conclude from the matters stipulated in s. 31(1)(b)(i) and (ii), or s. 31(2)(b)(i) and (ii), that the sole or dominant purpose of the person charged was to evade the reporting requirements. This is hardly the same as requiring that the accused acted with an intention to evade the requirements.

Consider the position where a Smurf innocently makes a deposit on behalf of Pappa Smurf in circumstances where he or she has been duped into acting as a member of the Smurfing enterprise. In such a case the sole or dominant purpose of the transaction, viewed objectively, is to evade a reporting requirement. On a literal interpretation of the section, an accused is subject to liability whether or not he or she acted with an intention (sole, dominant, or incidental) to evade a reporting requirement.

Application of the common law presumption about mens rea

It may be argued that the common law presumption about mens rea as a condition of criminal liability is not rebutted by s. 31 and hence that there is no liability unless the defendant intended to evade a reporting obligation under the Act, or was at least reckless that the other party to the transaction intended to evade such an obligation.

As the law stands, any attempt to ascertain the relevance or otherwise of mens rea from the context of s. 31 is an exercise verging on palmistry:

1. The punishment provided for the offence is serious (the maximum period of jail for individual defendants is five years) but, given the limited weight accorded to the possibility of jail in several previous decisions of the High Court, this factor is far from decisive.[6] It may also be noted that other serious offences relating to money laundering do not require intention or recklessness. In particular, the offence of money laundering under s. 81 of the *Proceeds of Crime Act* 1987 (Cth), which is punishable by a jail term of up to 20 years, is committed where the defendant knows or "ought reasonably to know" that he or she is dealing with tainted property.

2. It seems impossible to measure the stigma associated with the offence in any useful way. The legislation itself is opaque on this question. If the section related expressly to money laundering activities by drug traffickers then perhaps the stigma rating would be high. However, s. 31 has a far more general application which extends to one-off feats of attempted evasion by lone operators who are not drug czars but two-bit tax cheats. The serious level of punishment prescribed does have a stigmatic aura but some judges might nonetheless discount this factor and treat the offence as being not "criminal in the real sense".[7] In any event, there appears to be no survey or other empirical evidence directly in point and, in the absence of prosecutions, public opinion is probably ill formed.

6. The High Court itself has not always upheld the presumption of mens rea where jail has been authorised: see *Coulter v. The Queen* (1988) 164 C.L.R. 350; *R. v. Reynhoudt* (1962) 107 C.L.R. 381; *Thomas v. The King* (1937) 59 C.L.R. 279. See further *He Kaw Teh v. The Queen* (1985) 157 C.L.R. 523 at 535 per Gibbs C.J.

7. Consider e.g. *Von Lieven v. Stewart* (1990) 21 N.S.W.L.R. 52 at 61 per Handley J.A.

3. The factor of feasibility of enforcement is inconclusive.[8] On one hand, it can be argued that a requirement of an intention to evade the reporting obligations would be too difficult to prove. On the other hand, the difficulty or otherwise is highly speculative and, if such a requirement were to prove unworkable in practice, the legislation could of course be amended. Another complication is that no attempt is made in s. 31 to differentiate between the mental element for criminal liability and the mental element for the purpose of civil liability based on a violation of the provisions.[9] The objective test of liability imposed under the section may be defensible for the purpose of civil liability but is much too stringent for serious criminal offences, at least in the context of individual defendants. However, a requirement of intention would detract from the efficacy of the section as a basis of civil liability.

4. The "luckless victims" factor is indecisive. Dispensing with a requirement of an intention to evade the statute would not necessarily lead to draconic injustice if the *Proudman v. Dayman* presumption was upheld. If a defence of reasonable mistaken belief were available to all persons charged with an offence under s. 31 then arguably there would be no significant class of luckless victims.[10]

5. The factor of gravity of social harm or danger is inconclusive. Assuming that Smurfing is a "grave social evil" (whatever so hazy a notion might be taken to mean), is the implication that mens rea is relevant or irrelevant? Some courts appear to have assumed that the more serious the offence the less the relevance of mens rea.[11] From an opposite view, however, the more serious the offence the greater the importance of mens rea. The latter construct is far more tenable but, given the tendency of precedent to perpetuate judicial error, the former could prevail.

If the statutory context fails to resolve the issue whether the common law presumption about mens rea is rebutted, then it may well be argued that, as a matter of statutory construction, the ambiguity is to be resolved in favour of the defendant by requiring proof of mens rea. The force of this argument, however, is difficult to gauge given the absence of guidance from the High Court. In *He Kaw Teh v. The Queen*,[12] the Pythian repository of Australian judicial wisdom on the interpretation of the mental element of statutory offences, the judgments pay little or no attention to the canon of construction that genuine ambiguity in penal statutes is to be resolved in favour of a narrow construction.[13] In

8. It is difficult to understand what exactly this factor is supposed to mean. Compare the uncritical discussion in *He Kaw Teh v. The Queen* (1985) 157 C.L.R. 523 at 529-530 per Gibbs C.J., with that in *Millar v. Ministry of Transport* [1986] 1 N.Z.L.R. 660 at 667.
9. Consider especially the injunctive remedy under s. 32. See further Fisse, "Recent Developments in Corporate Criminal Law" (1990) 13 Uni. N.S.W.L.J. 1 at 28.
10. As discussed below, however, it could be argued that the *Proudman v. Dayman* defence would still leave many luckless victims because few defendants would be sufficiently versed in the section to be able truthfully to say that they entertained a conscious belief going to the relevant matters under s. 31(1).
11. See e.g. *He Kaw Teh v. The Queen* (1985) 157 C.L.R. 523 at 595 per Dawson J.; *Lim Chin Aik v. The Queen* [1963] A.C. 160.
12. (1985) 157 C.L.R. 523.
13. But see (1985) 157 C.L.R. 523 at 594 per Dawson J.

contrast, the later High Court decision in *Murphy v. Farmer*[14] turned on the application of this canon. It is a mystery why the canon of strict construction of penal statutes was applied in the one case and yet not in the other; genuine ambiguity arose in *He Kaw Teh v. The Queen* just as much as it did in *Murphy v. Farmer*.[15] It therefore seems a forensic lottery whether or not the canon would prevail even if the interpretation of s. 31 were to be tested before the High Court.

Application of the common law presumption about the defence of reasonable mistaken belief

If the presumption about mens rea is over-ridden by s. 31, then a further presumption arises, namely that a defendant has available the *Proudman v. Dayman* defence of reasonable mistaken belief. Is this presumption rebutted by the wording and context of s. 31?

The wording of the section makes no reference to a defence of reasonable mistaken belief or any other comparable defence. In contrast, the offence of failing to report a suspect transaction under s. 16 of the C.T.R. Act requires reasonable grounds for suspicion. Sections 81 and 82 of the *Proceeds of Crime Act* 1987 (Cth) may also be compared; s. 81 requires that the defendant know or "ought reasonably to know" that he or she was dealing with tainted property; it is a defence under s. 82 for the defendant to satisfy the court that he or she had no reasonable grounds to suspect that the property was tainted. These provisions are couched in the present tense and refer to the time of the commission of the offence. Section 31, by contrast, imposes an ex post facto objective test, namely whether the nature of the transactions was such that it is "reasonable to conclude" that their sole or dominant purpose was to evade a reporting requirement.[16]

The mere fact that the section makes no reference to the defence of reasonable mistaken belief is no reason for rebutting the common law presumption that the defence is available.[17] It might perhaps be argued, however, that the wording of the section makes the *Proudman v. Dayman* defence superfluous. If the defence relates to all the matters specified in s. 31(1)(b)(i) and (ii) as well as to the question of the sole or dominant purpose of the transaction, then the defence covers the same ground as the "reasonable to conclude" test of liability under the section: it would be splitting hairs to say that there is a difference between a reasonable conclusion and a belief based on reasonable grounds.

A more credible reading of the section is that the "reasonable to conclude" test and the *Proudman v. Dayman* defence serve quite different functions. The "reasonable to conclude" test is for the trier of fact to apply in light of the matters specified in s. 32(1)(b)(i) and (ii). The

14. (1988) 165 C.L.R. 19 at 28. See also *O'Sullivan v. Lunnon* (1987) 163 C.L.R. 545 at 553 per Brennan J.; *Waugh v. Kippen* (1986) 160 C.L.R. 156; *Beckwith v. The Queen* (1976) 135 C.L.R. 569 at 574-575.
15. Compare the principle of equal application of laws, as upheld by the High Court in *Stingel v. The Queen* (1990) 171 C.L.R. 312 at 329.
16. See below, "The 'Reasonable to Conclude' Test", p. 180.
17. See *Kain and Shelton Pty Ltd v. McDonald* (1971) 1 S.A.S.R. 39 at 40-47 per Bray C.J.

test is not that of a reasonable person in the position of the accused, nor is it that of a reasonable person in the position of the other party to the transaction. Rather, the test is whether, at the moment of adjudication, the trier of fact reviewing the factors specified in the section can reasonably draw the inference that the dominant or sole purpose of the accused was to structure the transactions so as to avoid the reporting requirements. In contrast, the *Proudman v. Dayman* defence does not relate to the particular matters specified in s. 32(1)(b)(i) and (ii) but to the central factual issue, which is the purpose of the transaction. On this view, the defence requires the defendant to have believed on reasonable grounds that the sole or dominant purpose of the transaction was not to evade a reporting requirement.

This interpretation is consistent with the wording of s. 31(1). The wording indicates that the matters specified in s. 31(1)(b)(i) and (ii) are to be taken into account by a trier of fact in light of all the evidence in a given case. The same is not true in relation to the *Proudman v. Dayman* defence because a defendant would not necessarily be in a position to consider the significance of all the matters specified in the subsection. Thus, Smurf, a defendant who performs one deposit in a chain of Smurfing deposits organised by Pappa Smurf, would not necessarily be in a position to consider the overall significance of all transactions in the chain. Moreover, the task of assessing the evidentiary significance of any explanation given by the defendant (see s. 31(1)(b)(ii)) seems to be one for the trier of fact rather than for the defendant Smurf.

Although the wording of s. 31 may thus admit the application of the *Proudman v. Dayman* defence, nonetheless it may be argued that the presumed availability of the defence is rebutted by contextual factors. A devil's advocate could easily construct an argument that the *Proudman v. Dayman* defence is rebutted. One predictable line of argument is this:

1. Although the offence is punishable by jail, that has not always been seen by the courts as a sufficient reason for upholding the *Proudman v. Dayman* presumption.[18] Moreover, the courts have a wide discretion in sentencing. Unless the accused is proven to have acted in a significantly blameworthy manner, it is almost inconceivable that a court would impose a custodial sentence. In the unlikely event of a custodial sentence being imposed the safeguard of appeal is available.

2. The section has a wide potential application and is not confined to money laundering activities by drug traffickers. Nor does the offence carry a title which immediately projects a root of evil. Moreover, the legislature has not seen fit to proscribe Smurfing in the *Crimes Act* itself. For these reasons the level of stigma is diluted and the offence is not "criminal in the real sense".[19] In any event, the stigma resulting from conviction depends not so much on the offence in the abstract as on the particular circumstances surrounding its commission. If the defendant did not act in a blameworthy way, then that will be reflected in the sentence; the level and type of sentence imposed will signify a low degree of stigma.

18. See Fisse, *Howard's Criminal Law*, op. cit., p. 534.
19. Compare *Von Lieven v. Stewart* (1990) 21 N.S.W.L.R. 52 at 61 per Handley J.A. See further Fisse, "Recent Developments in Corporate Criminal Law", op. cit. at 26-27.

3. The purpose of the legislation is to target the money trail in crime and to induce persons making or receiving deposits of money to take extreme care to ensure that the transaction is not part of a scheme to evade reporting obligations. Enforcement would be frustrated if defendants were allowed to rely on the defence of reasonable mistaken belief. This is especially apparent in the context of banks and other corporate defendants. There is no reason why a bank should be excused merely because a reasonable mistaken belief happens to be made by one teller. What matters is not the mistake of some individual person within the bank's system of operations but whether, as an organisation, the bank has adequate anti-Smurfing procedures in place.[20] The *Proudman v. Dayman* defence is therefore unsuitable in the context of corporate defendants of the kind most likely to be the subject of Smurfing. If the defence is unavailable to corporate defendants then, applying the principle of juristic personality, the defence is unavailable to individual defendants as well.

4. To exclude the defence from individual or corporate defendants would not create an excessive class of luckless victims. Even if the *Proudman v. Dayman* defence were available to individual defendants they would rarely be able to rely on it successfully. Few will have consciously adverted to the issue whether or not the sole or dominant purpose of the transaction was to evade the reporting requirements under the legislation.[21] Aside from that obstacle, most will be in considerable difficulty pointing to reasonable grounds for their belief because, unlike the trier of fact, they will not have been in a position to assess the significance of all the relevant connected transactions. If honest, they usually would have to say that they lacked enough information to know either way. In any event, luckless pawns are unlikely to be the subject of prosecution. Prosecutors are likely to target the masterminds of Smurfing enterprises and the corporate financial institutions who facilitate their activities. Where financial institutions have taken reasonable anti-Smurfing precautions they are unlikely to be prosecuted. If they are prosecuted and convicted, then they are likely to be put under a bond or required to pay a relatively light fine. Moreover, as indicated in (2) above, the level of stigma attached depends much on the degree of blameworthiness in the particular case.

5. Money laundering, especially in the context of drug trafficking, is a "grave social evil" according to the claims made during the course of parliamentary debate. The more vehement and rabid the expression of political concern, the more likely the legislative intention to over-ride basic principles of criminal responsibility. It may also be argued, from an entirely opposite standpoint, that Smurfing is not a "grave social evil" but a secondary or surrogate offence and that the legislative intention should be seen in light of the mental element prescribed for the much more serious offence of money laundering under s. 81 of the *Proceeds of Crime Act* 1987 (Cth). A reason to know that one is dealing with tainted property is sufficient for the mental element of the offence under

20. See further Fisse, *Howard's Criminal Law*, op. cit., pp. 615-616.
21. Assuming that the defence does require a conscious belief as compared to subconscious assumption or ignorance.

s. 81 of the *Proceeds of Crime Act*. Given that the offence under s. 31 is of a lesser order, and given that a reason to know is comparable to having no reasonable ground to support a *Proudman v. Dayman* defence, there would be no discontinuity between s. 81 and s. 31 if s. 31 were interpreted as excluding the *Proudman v. Dayman* defence.

Whether or not arguments of this kind might ultimately prevail, the scarce time and resources of courts, citizens and corporations should hardly be squandered upon them. If costly test cases are to be avoided then the mental element of the offence of Smurfing needs to be clarified. More fundamentally, the section needs to be revised with due regard to relevant concepts of blameworthiness.

THE "REASONABLE TO CONCLUDE" TEST

Section 31(1) imposes liability in those circumstances where, after determining that the person is a party to two or more transactions and having regard to the factors listed in s. 31(1)(b)(i) and (ii),

> it would be reasonable to conclude that the person conducted the transactions in that manner or form for the sole or dominant purpose of ensuring, or attempting to ensure, that the currency involved in the transactions was transferred in a manner and form that:
>
> (iii) would not give rise to a significant cash transaction; or
>
> (iv) would give rise to an exempt cash transaction.

The scope and application of the "reasonable to conclude" test raise a number of difficulties. As explained below, the test creates more problems than it resolves.

Form and function

The question immediately raised is whether the "reasonable to conclude" test is necessary at all. The main purposes served by the test seem highly questionable.

One conceivable purpose is to displace the common law presumptions about mens rea and the *Proudman v. Dayman* defence of reasonable mistaken belief. If so, the mental element of the offences under s. 31 needs to be redefined in accordance with the principles of blameworthiness discussed in "The Mental Element of the Offence", above. Orthodox legislative models suggest that s. 31 should be amended to provide for liability where an accused, acting without lawful justification or excuse, enters into a transaction with an intention to evade a reporting obligation under the Act, or with awareness of the likelihood that another party to the transaction intended to evade a reporting obligation. It would also be possible to create a less serious offence of engaging in a transaction where:

- there is reason to believe that the defendant intended to evade a reporting requirement;
- the defendant is unable to make out an affirmative defence of lack of intention to evade a reporting obligation and lack of awareness

that any other party to the transaction had an intention to evade a reporting requirement; and

- the defendant is unable to establish any other excuse or justification.

We do not recommend the introduction of such an offence, however, partly because of the potentially oppressive effect of inverting the persuasive burden of proof, and partly because there are other ways of redefining the offences under s. 31 without going to extremes (see "Third Dimension: Parties", below).

Perhaps the most obvious purpose of the "reasonable to conclude" test is to create an offence capable of resisting evasive counter-measures by Brainy Smurfs. The offence is defined in terms which require two or more cash transactions over a period of time but the time-frame is unspecified. The apparent reason for this indeterminacy is to thwart Smurfs who, if presented with more precise rules, might reschedule deposits so as to get around them. The "reasonable to conclude" test limits the scope of liability in a general and relatively Smurf-proof way. Understandable as this rationale is, the result is an objectionably vague offence the indeterminate limits of which are a nightmare for banks and finance companies faced with the task of compliance. As amplified below, it is possible to redefine the offences under s. 31 without relying on the "reasonable to conclude" test and yet in a manner both precise and resistant to Smurfing counter-measures.

Relationship between the "reasonable to conclude" test and the indicia specified

The "reasonable to conclude" test under s. 31(1) requires the trier of fact to take certain statutory indicia into account but does not fully define the relationship between the test and the indicia specified in the section.

The section speaks of "2 or more transactions" and in subsections (a) and (b)(ii), the plural is used, as it is in subsections (b)(i)(B), (C), (D), (E), and (ii) and (iv). Yet subsection (b)(i)(A) speaks of "each transaction" and subsection (iii) of "a significant cash transaction". To what extent must the indicia specified in the section be related by the trier of fact to *each* transaction in the set of transactions allegedly involved in the offence charged?

Take a case of a long standing relationship between a bank and customer where *some* elements of *some* transactions might fit *some* indicia specified under s. 31 but where the relationship was originally an innocent one. Is such a case analogous to the vagaries of the doctrine of continuing trespass in larceny, thereby permitting an innocent relationship to be magically transformed into a criminal one? How far back can or must the trier of fact go in his or her examination of the relationship and the transactions? What, if any, limits are placed on the inquiry by the presence or absence of relevant indicia at different stages in the previous relationship between the parties?

Contrary to the possible semblance of legislative control over what is required for proof of an offence, the "reason to conclude" test under s. 31 has an elusive elasticity. It is pointless to try to pin down the exact nature and limits of its application if, as appears to be the position, the test serves no purpose which cannot be achieved more simply and effectively in other ways.

"Reasonable to conclude" and the persuasive burden of proof

The "reasonable to conclude" test under s. 31 might perhaps be interpreted as pulling out the *Woolmington*[22] Golden Thread of proof beyond a reasonable doubt. Arguably, it is sufficient for the trier of fact to arrive at a reasonable conclusion in the sense of the degree of persuasion required under the *Briginshaw*[23] standard.

There is another interpretation. The requirement that there be some indicia of criminality as specified in s. 31 is consistent with the requirement that the elements of liability be proven beyond reasonable doubt. On this view, s. 31 augments the operation of the *Woolmington* principle by imposing, as a necessary but insufficient requirement of proof, the need for the trier of fact to be satisfied that certain confirmatory indications of Smurfing are present.

To what exactly does the *Woolmington* principle apply? First, proof beyond reasonable doubt is needed in relation to the conduct required for the offence (see s. 31(1)(a)). Secondly, if the common law presumption about mens rea is not rebutted by the section,[24] then the prosecution would also need to establish beyond reasonable doubt that the defendant intended to evade a reporting obligation under the Act, or was at least reckless that the other party to the transaction intended to evade those requirements. Thirdly, if mens rea is irrelevant and the *Proudman v. Dayman* defence of reasonable mistaken belief is available,[25] the defence would succeed if:

- the defendant is able to provide an evidentiary basis for it; and

- the prosecution is unable to prove beyond a reasonable doubt that the defendant did not believe or had no reasonable grounds to believe that the sole or dominant purpose of the transaction was not to evade a reporting requirement.

At the least, the nature and application of the persuasive burden of proof under s. 31 should be clarified if the "reasonable to conclude" test is retained. Our recommendation is that the problem be dissolved by excising the test from the section.

"Reasonable to conclude", retrospectivity, and blameworthiness

Another problematic aspect of s. 31 is the retrospectivity of the "reasonable to conclude" test and the lack of due focus on the blameworthiness or otherwise of the accused.

22. *Woolmington v. D.P.P.* [1935] A.C. 462.
23. (1936) 55 C.L.R. 192.
24. See above, "The Mental Element of the Offences", p. 174.
25. See above, "The Mental Element of the Offences", p. 174.

The "reasonable to conclude" text under s. 31 appears to make the appropriate time for judging the purpose of the transactions not the entry into the transactions but the trial. If so, the test operates retrospectively in light of all relevant evidence that comes to hand. This interpretation is borne out by several features of the wording of s. 31:

1. The factors which are to assist in the determination, as set out in subsection (1)(b)(i)(A)-(E), posit an ex post facto assessment (for example, "the interval of time between any of the transactions" and "the locations at which the transactions took place"). The trier of fact is expected to look back over a series of two or more transactions and then determine whether it is "reasonable to conclude" that the sole or dominant purpose of the transaction impugned was to evade a reporting obligation under the Act.

2. The wording of subsection (1)(b)(ii) requires the trier of fact, when applying the "reasonable to conclude" test, to take into account

"any explanation made by the person as to the manner or form in which the transactions were conducted".

It may be possible to read this provision as relating to an explanation at the time of the transaction, thereby eliminating the ex post facto character of the "reasonable to conclude" test. However, the time-frame of the inquiry contemplated by the subsection seems much wider. The explanation is one "as to the manner or form in which the transactions *were* conducted" (emphasis added). This suggests that the explanation is one given *after* the transactions have occurred and that, as a result, the trier of fact is to relate this factor back in time from the moment of adjudication and to impose a meaning on the transactions from her or his current temporal standpoint.

A defendant thus runs the risk of the trier of fact making a retrospective assessment of the purpose of the transactions in light of information that becomes available only at the trial and which may have been unavailable to the defendant at the time of the relevant transactions. Take the example given earlier where a Smurf innocently makes a deposit on behalf of Pappa Smurf in circumstances where he or she has been duped into acting as a member of the Smurfing enterprise. The sole or dominant purpose of the transaction, viewed objectively in light of all the evidence that later comes to hand about Pappa Smurf and his enterprise, is to evade a reporting requirement but the Smurf is innocent. Examples of this kind indicate that the "reasonable to conclude" test bears no necessary connection with the blameworthiness of the defendant at the time of the alleged structured transaction. The drafting of s. 31 thus departs radically from the standard practice of defining offences in terms which centre on the blameworthy conduct required for liability.

Section 31 compares unfavourably with s. 527C of the *Crimes Act* (N.S.W.), infamous as that last-mentioned section is. Section 527C defines the offence of unlawful possession of property in these terms:

(1) Any person who—

(a) has any thing in his custody;

(b) has any thing in the custody of another person;

(c) has any thing in or on premises, whether belonging to or occupied by himself or not, or whether that thing is there for his own use or the use of another; or

(d) gives custody of any thing to a person who is not lawfully entitled to possession of the thing,

which thing may be reasonably suspected of being stolen or otherwise unlawfully obtained, shall be liable on conviction before a stipendiary magistrate to imprisonment for 6 months, or to a fine of $500.

(2) It is a sufficient defence to a prosecution for an offence under subsection (1) if the defendant satisfies the court that he had no reasonable grounds for suspecting that the thing referred to in the charge was stolen or otherwise unlawfully obtained.

The appropriate time for the "no reasonable grounds to suspect" defence under s. 527C(2) is when the offence was allegedly committed. No such element of concurrent blameworthiness is expressed in s. 31. If concurrent blameworthiness is required under s. 31 then the requirement comes from the common law presumptions about mens rea and the *Proudman v. Dayman* defence of reasonable mistaken belief.[26]

As explained in relation to the mental element of the offence, s. 31(1) can be interpreted as requiring proof of mens rea (in the sense of intention to evade a reporting obligation under the Act, or recklessness that the other party to the transaction intended to evade such an obligation) or as preserving the common law defence of reasonable mistaken belief. If so, then the liability of a defendant depends on whether he or she was at fault at the time of the transactions alleged to have involved a sole or dominant purpose to evade a reporting obligation, or at least at the time of the last transaction in the series of transactions impugned. The application of common law principles may thus avoid the conviction of luckless victims under s. 31. Better still, the issue should be laid to rest by amending s. 31 so as expressly to require mens rea in the sense indicated.

If s. 31 is taken to require mens rea, when exactly must the requisite mens rea be present? At the time of the last transaction in which the defendant participated? At the time of any transaction in which the defendant participated? Perhaps the most commendable reading of s. 31 is that mens rea is required at the time of any one transaction to which the defendant was allegedly a party.[27] This interpretation would help to avoid technical acquittals in so far as it would be immaterial that a guilty mind did not accompany each and every transaction to which the defendant was a party.

The interpretation suggested would leave a gap in the section as far as the anti-Smurfing controls expected of banks are concerned. In normal

26. Other common law presumptions may also be relevant: see Fisse, *Howard's Criminal Law*, op. cit., pp. 524-525.
27. Other time-framing difficulties would arise if the *Proudman v. Dayman* defence of reasonable mistaken belief applies. It is difficult to accept that it should be a defence for an accused to believe that merely one of several transactions did not involve a sole or dominant purpose to evade a reporting requirement.

banking practice, it usually takes some time after a transaction for a bank to check what other deposits or transfers have been made by a client, whether at the same branch or at other branches. Thus, banks typically act in good faith if their conduct is assessed at the time of the last or any other deposit by a client. The more critical question is what if anything has been done to make checks after a deposit has been made. No time period for checking multiple deposits is specified in s. 31 and, given the need for consultation between the banking industry and enforcement agencies on this question, it is hardly the role of the courts to prescribe the period within which checks for Smurfing are to be made. In our view, the legislation should be amended so as to impose a duty on financial institutions to aggregate cash transactions within a time made known to them. To that subject we now turn.

Aggregation

The "reasonable to conclude" test under s. 31 is not related to any given period during which financial institutions are expected to aggregate transactions involving a particular customer. There is no specific obligation under the Act to aggregate deposits or other cash transactions.[28] Instead, "the aggregated value of transactions" is one of the indicia (see s. 31(1)(b)(i)(B)) which the trier of fact is to consider when applying the "reasonable to conclude" test.

The ex post facto nature of the test of liability under s. 31 puts banks and other financial institutions in a precarious or impossible position. The "reasonable to conclude" test implies that financial institutions are under an obligation to aggregate cash transactions yet they are not in a position to know what that obligation requires of them at the time when the transactions take place. Worse, the test is not applied until the matter is determined by the trier of fact. Financial institutions thus remain under an obligation to aggregate until such time as the matter is decided in a prosecution or civil proceeding. So open-ended an obligation to aggregate is not merely vaguely defined but wildly impractical. To comply with it, conceivably a bank would need to aggregate deposits on a perpetually rolling basis, perhaps for years after an initial transaction took place. If the legislation does not require banks to go to such extreme lengths, where is the line to be drawn? Section 31 provides no adequate answer to this question.

It is also unclear whether the required standard of compliance is the same across the wide variety of organisations and bodies subject to s. 31, or whether it varies depending on the technology available to the particular organisation. What exactly are banks and other cash dealers supposed to do to keep track of deposits or other transactions at their various branches? A major interstate or international bank may have a sophisticated computer network which makes the task of aggregation a relatively simple one, whereas a small finance company may lack any corresponding facility. If, for example, a bank has a computer-based

---

28. Contrast U.S. Fed. Reg. Vol. 55, No. 173 (United States Department of the Treasury proposed rules for mandatory aggregation). These rules have not been enacted but have become accepted on an informal basis, according to Mr Peter Djinis, Director, FINCEN.

tracking capability that enables it instantaneously to aggregate all deposits made at any branch within, say, a 24-hour period, then it may well be "reasonable to conclude" on the basis of the information available to that bank that the sole or dominant purpose of the customer was to evade the reporting requirements. On the other hand, if a bank does not have such a computer-based capacity, perhaps it is unreasonable to arrive at the same conclusion. Section 31 fudges the most critical question here, which is whether or not banks are expected to install systems that will enable aggregation of deposits made at all branches, instantaneously or within, say, a daily or other period. Many financial institutions in Australia do not presently have the capacity to aggregate deposits at all branches even on a daily basis. If they are expected to acquire some greater capacity, it seems harsh to make them run the gauntlet of a vaguely defined penal provision. Moreover, installing adequate systems takes time and systems cannot sensibly be installed until it is known what exactly the expected standards of aggregation are.

An aggregation test needs to be worked out in consultation with financial institutions. Can that be done without giving the game away to Pappa Smurfs? Consider the aggregation regulation proposed in 1990 by the United States Treasury.[29] Under that proposal certain categories of financial institution would be required to aggregate client deposits on a business day basis. The danger in such a test is that it will be manipulated by money launderers. A business day aggregation period can be defeated by staging deposits over two days. A weekly aggregation period can be defeated by making deposits over a two-weekly period. This problem could conceivably be resolved by means of a system, developed in conjunction with the banking and finance industry, under which different aggregation periods are used by different financial institutions at different periods arranged on a secret roster basis. Financial institutions would then know exactly where they stand, yet Smurfs and Smurfmasters would not be presented with aggregation rules which could easily be circumvented. Such a system presupposes that banks and other financial institutions have the technical capability to alter the time settings of their aggregation programs periodically at low cost. It also assumes that the roster arrangements could in fact be kept secret from the Smurfing underworld.

Implications for the mental element of complicity, conspiracy and attempt

It is not entirely clear whether or to what extent the "reasonable to conclude" test affects the mental element of ancillary forms of criminal liability, namely complicity, conspiracy and attempt.[30]

Complicity requires knowledge of the essential matters which constitute the principal offence.[31] Is it an essential matter of the

29. U.S. Fed. Reg. Vol. 55, No. 173.
30. Compare Bein, "The 'Completed Offence' and the Attempt: Some Problems in Criminal Law Interpretation" (1969) 4 Israel L. Rev. 216.
31. *Giorgianni v. The Queen* (1985) 156 C.L.R. 473; *Crimes Act* (Cth), s. 5.

principal offence under s. 31(1) that the sole or dominant purpose of the transactions be to evade a reporting requirement? It may be argued that the subject matter covered by the "reasonable to conclude" test is not an essential matter constituting the principal offence but an evidentiary requirement imposed on the trier of fact. Alternatively, the essential matters conceivably could be taken to be the factual basis upon which the trier of fact arrives at a reasonable conclusion that the sole or dominant purpose was to evade a reporting requirement. Although these obscurities result partly from the foggy concept of "essential matters" precipitated by the High Court in *Giorgianni v. The Queen*, they are also inherent in the murk created by the "reasonable to conclude" test itself.

One possible way of avoiding arid disputes as to the "essential" and "non-essential" components of the "reasonable to conclude" test would be to interpret s. 31 as upholding the common law presumption about mens rea. On this interpretation, as discussed earlier, the principal offence would require an intention to evade a reporting requirement, or at least recklessness that the other party to the transaction intended to evade a reporting requirement. This mental element would be an essential matter constituting the principal offence.[32] Complicity would thus require not only knowledge of the actus reus on the part of the principal offender but also knowledge that the principal offender was acting either with an intention to evade a reporting requirement or with recklessness that the other party to the transaction intended to evade a reporting requirement. Logical as this approach might be, sympathy goes out to any judge or jury called upon to apply its convolutions.

A more straightforward basis of liability for complicity is needed. This seems entirely possible. A starting point is to unravel the implications of the present requirement that the defendant be a "party" to two or more cash transactions. As argued in a later section, the "party" concept is unsatisfactory from a number of standpoints, including the failure to differentiate sufficiently between different modes of participation in Smurfing. If liability under s. 31 were recast in the manner suggested below, then the prime forms of complicity in Smurfing activities could be defined in relatively simple terms.

The "reasonable to conclude" test also tends to muddy the mental element of conspiracy. What is the unlawful object which must be mutually intended by the parties to a conspiratorial agreement? Is it sufficient that the object of the alleged conspirators was merely to become a party to, or to bring about, two or more cash transactions in circumstances where it is reasonable for the trier of fact to conclude that the sole or dominant purpose of those transactions was to evade a reporting requirement? Is it necessary that the alleged conspirators intended to evade a reporting requirement? Does the "reasonable to conclude" test apply to the offence of conspiracy at all?

The starting point is the common law presumption that conspiracy requires mens rea even where mens rea is unnecessary for the offence which is the alleged unlawful object.[33] Is this presumption rebutted by

32. *Stokes and Difford* (1990) 51 A. Crim. R. 25.
33. *R. v. Freeman* (1985) 3 N.S.W.L.R. 303; *Churchill v. Walton* [1967] 2 A.C. 224.

the wording or context of s. 31? It is submitted that the presumption is not rebutted, for two alternative reasons:

1. As explained below in "Third Dimension: Parties", liability for conspiracy appears to be excluded where the defendant is a party to the transactions which are the subject of prosecution. On that interpretation, the need to determine the mental element of conspiracy arises only in relation to agreements which are anterior to any actual transactions. The "reasonable to conclude" test under s. 31 applies ex post facto and, on one possible view, presupposes two or more cash transactions which have already occurred. If this is the position, then the test does not apply to the offence of conspiracy and hence cannot rebut the presumption that conspiracy requires mens rea.

2. The complete offences under s. 31 may themselves require mens rea.[34] On this interpretation, the "reasonable to conclude test" operates as a necessary but insufficient condition of the mental element required for liability. If so, the test has the same operation in the context of conspiracy and does not rebut the presumption of mens rea.

On this analysis, conspiracy to commit an offence against s. 31 requires an intention to structure two or more cash transactions with intent thereby to evade a reporting requirement. The intention must be mutually shared by all the conspirators, as required by the decision of the High Court in *Gerakiteys v. The Queen*.[35]

The "reasonable to conclude" test under s. 31 raises similar difficulties in relation to the mental element of attempt. Does the test impose a necessary or sufficient condition? Does it have any application?

As in the context of conspiracy, the starting point is the common law presumption that mens rea is required. It seems that the presumption is not rebutted, on these alternative grounds:

1. The "reasonable to conclude" test under s. 31, it may be argued, does not apply to the offence of attempt. The test applies ex post facto and appears to presuppose two or more cash transactions which have already occurred. If so, the test is irrelevant and cannot rebut the presumption that attempt requires mens rea.

2. The "reasonable to conclude" test does apply to attempt but its role is not to displace the requirement of attempt. Rather, it can be seen as strengthening the requirement of proximity. The fact that the defendant proposes to enter into two or more cash transactions with an intention thereby to evade the reporting requirements does not in itself mean that the danger is sufficient to warrant criminal liability. From this perspective, the "reasonable to conclude" test helps to confine liability to cases where the accused represents a serious threat to the efficacy of the cash transaction reporting requirements.

If the presumption of mens rea is upheld then the mental element of attempt in the context of s. 31 would be an intention to be a party to two or more cash transactions with intent thereby to evade a reporting requirement.

34. See above, "The Mental Element of the Offences", p. 174.
35. (1984) 153 C.L.R. 317.

None of these problems of interpretation would arise if, as we recommend, the "reasonable to conclude" test were abolished. The mental element of ancillary offences might also be usefully clarified by enacting offences that deal specifically with the main forms of participation in Smurfing activities, an approach discussed in the section immediately following.

THIRD DIMENSION: PARTIES

A third major dimension of the Smurfing offences under s. 31 is the nature of the liability of the various parties who may be implicated in or connected with the transactions which are the subject of prosecution.[36] The requirement under s. 31(1) (and s. 31(2)) that the defendant must be a party to two or more cash transactions raises a number of problems which again seem best avoided by redrafting.

Party to two or more transactions

It is difficult to understand why liability is conditioned on the defendant being a party to two or more cash transactions.

The ostensible social danger of Smurfing is not confined to cases where one person makes multiple deposits but also arises where multiple deposits are made by a number of Smurfs each of whom is a party to only one transaction. Similarly, situations can readily arise where multiple deposits are made in a number of banks each of which is a party to only one deposit. What is the point under s. 31 of insisting that Smurfs or banks be parties to two or more transactions rather than one?

The underlying policy may be that there is not enough social harm or danger to warrant criminal liability where someone makes only the first of a number of possible deposits which, if they are all made, will in total exceed the reporting threshold. The making of one deposit at one branch is not proximate to the making of a second deposit at another branch. Nor is the making of one deposit at one branch necessarily proximate to the making of a second deposit at the same branch later the same day. Opportunity should be given for a change of heart. Under the two-transaction rule, at least a second deposit or a later act of withdrawal must be made, and this later conduct confirms that the Smurf is not merely a putative offender who happens to have engaged in wishful foreplay. If this is the rationale, however, it does not account for cases where a single deposit is made by a Smurf with intent to evade or assist in the evasion of a reporting requirement and where, to his or her awareness, further deposits are being made in such a way as to circumvent the reporting threshold. In that context the Smurf is not merely preparing to commit an offence, but is facilitating a scheme of evasion which is already in place. Moreover, the Smurf who knowingly

---

36. See generally Lynch, "Drug Kingpins and Their Helpers: Accomplice Liability under 21 U.S.C. Section 848" (1991) 58 Uni. Chicago L. Rev. 391; Skalitzky, "Aider and Abettor Liability, The Continuing Criminal Enterprise, and Street Gangs: A New Twist In An Old War On Drugs" (1990) 81 J. of Crim. L. and Criminology 348.

makes the last deposit which takes the total over the non-reportable threshold is not merely a facilitator. He or she is a terminator.

Another conceivable rationale is that the two-transaction rule is an attempt to restrict liability to those who organise Smurfing operations and to Smurfs who go beyond one-off participation in a Smurfing enterprise. In other words, the aim is to concentrate liability on Pappa Smurf and the more active members of his family. Again, however, this seems unconvincing. A two-transaction rule is an oblique and inept way of gearing liability to the prime players, whether they be ringleaders or the most Handy or Brainy offspring of Pappa Smurf. Smurfing godfathers orchestrate deposits by the hundreds. Moreover, one does not need to be a Pappa Smurf to realise that Smurfs can be gainfully employed in a series of operations involving only one Smurf per transaction.

The two-transaction rule thus seems more a charter for Smurfhood than an attempt to circumscribe the scope of liability on a well-founded basis. A better approach, it may be suggested, is to restructure liability by creating the following three basic offences:

1. an offence of carrying out two or more cash transactions in such a way as to exceed the non-reportable limit and with intent to evade a reporting requirement;

2. an offence of participation in the management of a scheme or enterprise devised or adapted for the evasion of a reporting requirement by means of cash transactions carried out or to be carried out by another person or persons; and

3. an offence of carrying out a cash transaction with intent to assist or facilitate a scheme or enterprise devised or adapted for the evasion of a reporting requirement.

The point of this suggested recasting of the offences under s. 31 is to target the more likely different categories of offender and to define the scope of liability accordingly. Thus, the lone Smurfer would not be liable merely by making one deposit but, for the complete offence under 1 above, would need to engage in two or more cash transactions exceeding the non-reportable threshold; prior to that point there could be liability for attempt but only if the conduct is sufficiently proximate to the complete offence. Ringleaders and Pappa Smurfs are targeted under 2 above. The offence proposed focuses on the managerial or leadership nature of the defendant's role in schemes for structuring transactions through the use of Smurfs.[37] There is no need for the scheme to be implemented; it is sufficient that the defendant has played a leading role in organising a team of Smurfers. The offence under 3 above relates to Smurfs who enter into a cash transaction as part of a Smurfing operation. Entry into two or more transactions is not required under this proposal, nor is it necessary that the non-reportable limit be exceeded. Smurfs in operations involving one Smurf per transaction would be covered. If such an offence is thought to go too far, the scope could be limited by

37. This approach is consistent with the view that money trail and proceeds of crime legislation should focus more on the enterprise and organisational realities of the money laundering schemes which represent the greatest conceivable anti-social danger. See Fraser, above, Chapter 4, pp. 52-56.

giving Smurfs (but not managers) a statutory defence if they provide full details of their involvement in the scheme and the identity and activities of other persons with whom they have been associated.[38]

Conspirators and accomplices

The "party" element of the offences under s. 31 raises the question whether persons who are parties to a cash transaction can be liable for conspiracy or complicity by reason of their participation in that transaction.

When the definition of the substantive offence includes an "agreement", the parties to an agreement of the kind contemplated by that definition are not liable for conspiracy. In *R. v. Chow*,[39] a decision of the N.S.W. Court of Criminal Appeal, the relevant substantive offence was supplying a prohibited drug. It was held that persons who had entered into an agreement for the supply of drugs could not be held liable for conspiracy to supply drugs because the statutory definition of "supply" included an agreement to supply. The central reason given was that[40]

> a conspiracy requires an agreement between A and B which is anterior in time to the doing of the unlawful act which is the object of the conspiracy, and that unlawful act stands independently of the agreement to do it.

The implications of the *Chow* doctrine under s. 31 are not entirely clear. In order to be a "party" to a cash transaction under s. 31 it would seem that an agreement between the parties to the transaction is necessary. If so, then *Chow* suggests that the parties to the agreement are not liable for conspiracy; the agreement embodied in the cash transaction is covered by the offence under s. 31. However, an agreement among Smurfs and their Pappa Smurf to engage in the structuring of transactions is an agreement anterior to the agreement inherent in a cash transaction with another party and presumably such an anterior agreement can found liability for conspiracy.

But what if Pappa Smurf is charged with conspiracy to structure the very cash transactions which have been carried out? Pappa Smurf may be a party to those cash transactions by reason of the vicarious liability provisions under s. 34(4). If so, is he liable for conspiracy? The position is different from that in *Chow* in so far as vicarious liability under s. 31 does not necessarily presuppose an agreement on the part of the employer. Nonetheless, it may be argued that the legislative intention behind the vicarious liability provisions was to exclude liability for conspiracy where a "party" to the impugned transactions is vicariously liable. This interpretation is consistent with the view that part of the function of the "reasonable to conclude" test is to serve as a proxy for the *Ahern v. The Queen*[41] "reasonable evidence" exception to the

---

38. On withdrawal in complicity see further Fisse, *Howard's Criminal Law*, op. cit., pp. 350-351.
39. (1987) 30 A. Crim. R. 103.
40. (1987) 30 A. Crim. R. 103 at 113.
41. (1988) 165 C.L.R. 87.

hearsay rule.[42] The *Ahern* rule makes the statements and conduct of co-conspirators admissible against each other if there is reasonable evidence of their participation in the alleged conspiratorial agreement. The "reasonable to conclude" test under s. 31 makes the statements and conduct of Smurfmasters and their bankers admissible against each other to the extent that such evidence is relevant to show that the sole or dominant purpose of two or more transactions in which they were involved was to evade a reporting requirement. If so, then it is possible to draw the implication that the legislature saw no need to preserve liability for conspiracy in any case where the defendant is liable, whether personally or vicariously, as a "party" to two or more cash transactions.

The concept of a "party" to a cash transaction also tends to confuse the scope of liability for complicity. Is the term "party" used in the sense that anyone who is an accomplice is to be treated as a principal offender? Or does "party" mean someone who has actually carried out the cash transaction, together with employers or principals who are parties by reason of the vicarious liability provisions under s. 34? The meaning and scope of the concept of "party" may be critical in some cases. Take for example the position of a bank supervisor who innocently assists a transaction carried out by a teller in circumstances where the "reasonable to conclude" test under s. 31(1) is satisfied. If the supervisor is treated as a "party", and if the offence under s. 31(1) does not require mens rea (in the sense of intention or recklessness), then the supervisor is liable as a principal offender. However, if the supervisor is not a "party" and hence not a principal offender under s. 31(1), then liability will turn on the mental element required for complicity. In that event, the central issue is whether the supervisor had knowledge of the essential matters constituting the principal offence. On one view of the law, the supervisor is not liable because he or she lacked knowledge of the evasive purpose served by the particular transaction.[43]

The difficulties outlined above could be resolved partly by redefining the offences under s. 31 in terms which abandon the use of the term "party" and which more adequately differentiate between lone Smurfs, Pappa Smurfs, and members of teams of Smurfs.[44] Clarification of the relevance or otherwise of the offence of conspiracy would also seem desirable in the context where a Pappa Smurf is liable on the basis of vicarious liability under s. 34. The position of banks and other financial institutions seems best dealt with by means of an offence of carrying out a cash transaction with intent to assist or facilitate a scheme or enterprise devised or adapted for the evasion of a reporting requirement, as recommended earlier.

Vicarious and corporate liability

Section 34 provides for vicarious liability on the part of corporate and individual employers. At least two major problems arise. The first is that some Smurfing operations may be structured so as to circumvent or

42. See further Burchett, "The Co-Conspirator Evidence Rule" (1988) 4 Aust. Bar Rev. 115.
43. See *Giorgianni v. The Queen* (1985) 156 C.L.R. 473, and the critique of the concept of "essential matters" in Fisse, *Howard's Criminal Law*, op. cit., pp. 333-335.
44. See pp. 189-190.

obstruct the operation of s. 34. Secondly, the strictness of vicarious liability is objectionable in the context of offences as serious as those prescribed under s. 31.

The first problem emerges from the way in which Smurfing operations are often practised. A drug-lord or king-pin typically gives money to an underling to be laundered, and that underling then approaches other actors who then subdivide the cash among a team of Smurfs. The effect is to insulate or distance the king-pin from the transactions involving a cash dealer. Under such a scheme, the prime "party" is hidden from detection and lacks knowledge of the particular transactions which are carried out. The king-pin is not a "party" to the cash transactions unless vicarious liability is open under s. 34. Individual employers are vicariously liable under s. 34, the relevant provisions of which are as follows:

> (3) Where it is necessary, for the purposes of this Act, to establish the state of mind of a person in relation to conduct deemed by subsection (4) to have been engaged in by the person, it is sufficient to show that a servant or agent of the person, being a servant or agent by whom the conduct was engaged in within the scope of his or her actual or apparent authority, had that state of mind.

> (4) Conduct engaged in on behalf of a person other than a body corporate:

>> (a) by a servant or agent of the person within the scope of his or her actual or apparent authority; or

>> (b) by any other person at the direction or with the consent or agreement (whether express or implied) of a servant or agent of the firstmentioned person, where the giving of the direction, consent or agreement is within the scope of the actual or apparent authority of the servant or agent;

> shall be deemed, for the purposes of this Act, to have been engaged in by the first-mentioned person.

Subsection (4)(b) is perhaps sufficiently broad to make a king-pin vicariously liable as a "party" to cash transactions performed by Smurfs who are employed by an employee or agent of the king-pin. However, if the offence requires mens rea (in the sense of intention or recklessness), or carries a *Proudman v. Dayman* defence of reasonable mistaken belief,[45] subs. (3) applies. This subsection does not impose vicarious liability unless the relevant state of mind[46] was present on the part of a servant or agent "by whom the conduct was engaged in" within the scope of his or her actual or apparent authority. Depending on the skill and cunning of those arranging the Smurfing operation, the Smurfs who engage in the relevant conduct (carrying out two or more cash transactions) may be entirely innocent.

It is therefore conceivable that the vicarious liability provisions under s. 34 will bite banks and middle- or low-level employees within criminal enterprises but will not effectively reach the leaders of highly organised

---

45. See above, "The Mental Element of the Offences", p. 174.
46. As broadly defined in s. 34(5).

money laundering ventures. The vicarious liability provisions under s. 34 thus seem rather mindless. There needs to be more focus on the type of Smurfing operations likely to arise in practice, and liability redefined accordingly. King-pins and Pappa Smurfs could be dealt with by means of an offence aimed specifically at persons of that ilk. As discussed earlier,[47] there seems a need for an offence of participation knowingly in the management of a scheme or enterprise devised or adapted for the evasion of a reporting requirement by means of cash transactions carried out or to be carried out by another person or persons.

A more fundamental problem is the radical departure of s. 34 from the principle that criminal liability requires blameworthiness. Vicarious liability is a species of strict liability and hence is controversial, particularly in relation to offences which, like those under s. 31, carry the possibility of jail.

Section 34, like s. 85 of the *Proceeds of Crime Act*, is wrong in principle.[48] It is significant that, under more recent Commonwealth provisions corresponding to ss 34 and 85, a defence of reasonable precautions is provided.[49] It is difficult to fathom why the principle of blameworthiness should be reflected in, for example, s. 65 of the *Ozone Protection Act* 1989 (Cth) and yet not in s. 34 of the C.T.R. Act. There is no evidence to suggest that the problems of compliance or non-compliance on the part of banks under s. 31 are materially different from those facing manufacturing or other large companies in settings such as the *Ozone Protection Act*. The strategies and tactics of king-pins and drug-lords require special consideration, but this is hardly an argument for scattergun rules of vicarious liability. Nor can any credence be given to the argument that statutes such as the *Ozone Protection Act* deal with a lesser "social evil" so as to make recognition of the principle of blameworthiness less risky.

Piecemeal legislative development thus seems to explain the present form of s. 34. The provisions should now be amended in line with the more principled statutory models adopted by the Commonwealth in recent years.

ASSISTING LAW ENFORCEMENT: DIRE STRAITS OR SAFE HARBOURS?

Section 31 does not contain a safe harbour provision for financial institutions or their employees in cases where cash transactions are entered into in order to discover the identity of Smurfs or the Pappa Smurf. This is surprising and unsatisfactory, especially when one compares the position in the context of suspect transaction reporting under s. 16 of the C.T.R. Act.

47. See pp. 189-190.
48. See Fisse, above, Chapter 5, pp. 94-95.
49. See e.g. *Ozone Protection Act* 1989 (Cth), s. 65(2); *Industrial Chemicals (Notification and Assessment) Act* 1989 (Cth), s. 109(2); *Hazardous Waste (Regulation of Exports and Imports) Act* 1989 (Cth), s. 59(2). See further Fisse, "Corporate Criminal Responsibility" (1991) 15 Crim. L.J. 166; "The Attribution of Criminal Liability to Corporations: A Statutory Model" (1991) 13 Sydney L. Rev. 277.

Section 16 of the C.T.R. Act provides for the reporting of certain suspect transactions:

(1) Where:

    (a) a cash dealer is a party to a transaction; and

    (b) the cash dealer has reasonable grounds to suspect that information that the cash dealer has concerning the transaction:

        (i) may be relevant to investigation of an evasion, or attempted evasion, of a taxation law;

        (ii) may be relevant to investigation of, or prosecution of a person for, an offence against a law of the Commonwealth or of a Territory; or

        (iii) may be of assistance in the enforcement of the *Proceeds of Crime Act* 1987 or the regulations made under that Act;

the cash dealer, whether or not required to report the transaction under Division 1 or 3, shall, as soon as practicable after forming that suspicion:

    (c) prepare a report of the transaction; and

    (d) communicate the information contained in the report to the Director.

Under s. 16(5) cash dealers and their personnel are exempted from civil and criminal liability in relation to any action taken pursuant to the section or in the mistaken belief that it was required by the section. Another safe harbour is created by s. 17, which provides that information communicated under s. 16 is not attributable to cash dealers or their employers for the purpose of the money laundering offences under ss 81 and 82 of the *Proceeds of Crime Act* 1987.

There are no safe harbour provisions under s. 31. Moreover, making a suspect transaction report under s. 16 in relation to a transaction does not immunise a cash dealer or its employees against liability under s. 31. Action taken pursuant to the section (making a suspect transaction report or giving further information required under s. 16(4)) is immunised under s. 16(5) but being a party to structured transactions is hardly action taken pursuant to s. 16. Moreover, the protection afforded by s. 17 is confined to money laundering offences under the *Proceeds of Crime Act*. A cash dealer and its employees are thus placed in an invidious no-win position: to make a suspect transaction report is to run the risk of liability under s. 31, whereas not to make a suspect transaction report is to run foul of s. 16 and, in all possibility, the money laundering offences under s. 81 or s. 82 of the *Proceeds of Crime Act*.

It might be argued that, where a bank strings along a suspected Smurf in order to discover more about the Smurfing operation, there is no liability under s. 31 because the dominant purpose of the bank was not to evade the reporting provisions but to assist the authorities. That argument would be irrelevant, however, if complicity is the basis of liability:[50] complicity in an offence against s. 31 does not require a sole or dominant purpose on the part of the defendant. In any event, it would be difficult for the bank to maintain that its dominant purpose was not to attempt to ensure that the transaction would not give rise to a significant cash transaction: its dominant purpose was to ensure that a significant transaction did not arise because only in that way could the trap be expected to work.

The standard response of enforcement and prosecution agencies to the lack of safe harbour provisions is that banks and other financial institutions have nothing to fear because they will never be prosecuted if they act in good faith. Placatory as this response may sometimes be, it hardly confers a legally effective immunity. One danger is that the situations in the minds of the authorities when offering their assurances may be too idealised and a far cry from the expectations of financial institutions. Another is the highly charged atmosphere of money laundering. Enforcement agencies are under increasing political pressure to justify their existence. Moreover, drug traffickers and those who assist them are a prime target of blood-lust in the community, or at least in the media.

The hazardous position of banks and their personnel is illustrated by the recent money laundering prosecutions against officials of the Stone Oaks neighbourhood bank in San Antonio, Texas.[51] Two key executives, Pounds and Vanderzee, were later indicted for money laundering. The officials reported their suspicions about a customer to the United States Department of the Treasury and filed currency transaction reports as required under United States legislation. They were assured by Treasury that the bank had done all it needed to do. Notwithstanding this assurance, they were later indicted by the United States Justice Department on charges of money laundering. The trial judge directed that the defendants be acquitted, observing that they had done "what any prudent, responsible banker and banking operation would have done". As one might expect, the prosecution undermined the bank's business. The banking industry, understandably enough, has responded by demanding a safe harbour provision under the *Money Laundering Control Act* 1986 (U.S.). From the standpoint of Treasury, the prosecution reputedly has compromised and prejudiced its policy of encouraging banks to report suspect transactions.

Section 31 requires amendment in light of these considerations. Financial institutions and their employees should be given a safe harbour where action is taken in good faith for the purpose of assisting law enforcement and where the C.T.R. Agency is notified within a specified period of the action taken.[52]

50. It can be argued that a defendant who is a "party" to a transaction under s. 31(1) is liable only as a principal offender and not as an accomplice: see above, p. 192.
51. *A.B.A. Bankers Weekly*, April 14, 1992, p. 1.
52. Compare *Crimes (Confiscation of Profits) Act* 1986 (Vic.), s. 41Q(3); *Confiscation of Proceeds of Crime Act* 1989 (N.S.W.), s. 73(5).

CONCLUSION: POLITICAL CARTOONS OR RESPONSIVE LEGISLATION?

The offences of evasively structuring cash transactions under s. 31 seem ill drafted and insensitive to a number of major concerns. In our view, the section needs substantial restructuring and redefinition.

We have suggested that s. 31 be amended so as to provide three basic offences:

1. an offence of carrying out two or more cash transactions in such a way as to exceed the non-reportable limit and with intent to evade a reporting requirement;

2. an offence of participation in the management of a scheme or enterprise devised or adapted for the evasion of a reporting requirement by means of cash transactions carried out or to be carried out by another person or persons; and

3. an offence of carrying out a cash transaction with intent to assist or facilitate a scheme or enterprise devised or adapted for the evasion of a reporting requirement.

If special rules relating to the aggregation of cash transactions by financial institutions are introduced, an offence of non-compliance with such rules would also be required.[53]

The mental element of the offences should be expressly defined. For the first offence proposed, an intention to evade a reporting requirement would be required, together with intention, knowledge or recklessness (awareness of likelihood) in relation to all parts of the actus reus. In order to avoid sterile debates, "intention" should be defined to mean either conscious purpose or awareness of practical certainty.[54] The second offence would require knowledge or recklessness (awareness of likelihood) in relation to all parts of the actus reus. For the third offence, it would be necessary for the defendant to have acted with an intent to assist or facilitate a scheme or enterprise known or known to be likely to be one devised or adapted for the evasion of a reporting requirement. An affirmative defence of reasonable corporate precautions would be provided for corporations charged with offence 1, 2 or 3,[55] and likewise in the context of the supplementary offence of non-compliance with aggregation rules.

The "reasonable to conclude" test would be abolished under the restructured and redefined offences proposed above. Abolition of the test would overcome a variety of problems which now arise, namely:

---

53. The basis of liability for civil injunctions under s. 32 might also be reconsidered, on the ground that the mental element that is appropriate for criminal liability may be too restrictive for the purpose of civil liability. Thus, perhaps it should be sufficient for injunctive liability that the defendant has engaged in, or proposes to engage in, a transaction with a third party where, from the standpoint of the trier of fact looking at all the circumstances of the case, there are reasonable grounds to suspect that the transaction was intended by some person to evade or to help another to evade a reporting requirement under the Act.

54. See further American Law Institute, *Model Penal Code*, s. 2.02(b); Fisse, *Howard's Criminal Law*, op. cit., pp. 481-483.

55. By qualifying vicarious liability under s. 34 along the lines of the *Ozone Protection Act 1989* (Cth), s. 65.

- the inexactly defined relationship between the test and the indicia specified in the section;
- the uncertainty as to whether the "reasonable to conclude" test displaces the *Woolmington* principle;
- the confusion that the "reasonable to conclude" test introduces by focusing retrospectively on the sole or dominant purpose behind transactions rather than on the blameworthiness of defendants at the time they entered into the relevant transactions;
- the absence of any clear rules indicating what financial institutions are expected to do by way of aggregation of multiple deposits; and
- the uncertain implications which the "reasonable to conclude" test holds for the mental element of complicity, conspiracy and attempt.

The concept of a "party" to a transaction would also be eliminated under the new set of offences which we have recommended. The following problems could then be resolved or at least addressed:

- the inefficacy of an offence framed in terms of being a party to two or more transactions rather than in terms of the main forms of participation in Smurfing which need to be covered (namely lone Smurfing, organising Smurfing operations, and assisting or facilitating a Smurfing operation);
- the complexity surrounding the relevance or otherwise of conspiracy and complicity to the offences defined under s. 31; and
- the under-reach and over-reach of the concept of being a "party" on the basis of vicarious liability under s. 34.

Financial institutions and their employees should be exempted from liability under s. 31 where:

- they participate in Smurfing in good faith and with intent thereby to assist law enforcement; and
- the C.T.R. Agency is notified within a specified period of the particular nature of the action taken.

These suggestions are advanced in a constructive spirit. At the same time, they confirm that the money trail in crime is highly resistant to quick political fixes and raises a thicket of legal issues. This seems especially so in the context of structured transactions under s. 31 of the C.T.R. Act. Ask Pappa Smurf.

11

Smurfs, Money Laundering, and the United States Federal Criminal Law

The Crime of Structuring Transactions

SARAH N. WELLING*

INTRODUCTION

In 1970, Congress adopted a statute requiring financial institutions to report cash transactions over $10,000 to the government.[1] Failure to report was a crime.[2] In 1987, Congress made it a crime to structure financial transactions to evade this reporting law. Thus, for example, if Joe arranges his banking so the cash transactions are below $10,000 in order to avoid reporting, Joe commits a federal crime. What brought Congress to this point? Should we be alarmed at the extent of governmental intrusion into the arrangement of our financial affairs, or is the intrusion warranted? This chapter answers these questions and tells a good story as well.

The story begins with money laundering. The following section, "The Setting: Creating an Environment Conducive to Smurfs" (pp. 201-213), provides background on money laundering and describes the government's opening salvo against laundering, a statute requiring financial institutions to report cash transactions over $10,000 to the government.[3] To skirt this law, launderers began to conduct multiple cash transactions just below the $10,000 reporting threshold. The army of persons who scurried from bank to bank to accomplish these transactions became known as "smurfs" because, like their little blue cartoon namesakes, they were pandemic. Smurfs thrived when the 1970 reporting law encountered trouble in the courts. The government's response to this new species was to adopt a new criminal provision, the 1987 anti-smurfing statute.[4]

* Professor of Law, University of Kentucky. This article was previously published in 41 (No. 2) *Florida Law Review* (Spring 1989). The author is indebted to Professors Norman Abrams, Ronald J. Allen, Eugene R. Gaetke, Michael Goldsmith, Christopher Slobogin, John Rogers and George C. Thomas III for their thoughtful comments on prior drafts.

1. Pub. L. No. 91-508, ss 221-223, 84 Stat. 1122 (1970) (codified as amended at 31 U.S.C. s. 5313(a) (1982); 31 C.F.R. s. 102.1(b) (1970)).
2. Pub. L. No. 91-508, ss 205(b), 209-210, 84 Stat. 1120-21 (1970) (codified at 31 U.S.C. s. 5322 (1982 and Supp. IV 1980)).
3. 31 U.S.C. s. 5313 (1982); 31 C.F.R. s. 103.22(a)(1) (1988).
4. 31 U.S.C. s. 5324 (Supp. IV 1986).

Congress adopted the anti-smurfing statute quickly and without careful analysis. The legislative history includes examples of problems with the reporting law[5] and descriptions of cases the government lost.[6] Yet, the history contains little analysis of the elements of this new crime,[7] and no analysis of its basic theory, constitutionality, interaction with other reporting laws, or its relationship to federal criminal law as a whole. The lack of analysis results from several factors. Congress was in a hurry to plug the loopholes in the reporting statute to halt the drain of laundered money.[8] Congress resented the insolence of money launderers, particularly the smurfs who flooded the banks with multiple transactions for $9,900, thereby avoiding the reporting requirement.[9] Finally, the anti-smurfing statute was upstaged, but not obviated, by legislation making money laundering per se a crime.[10]

5. See *The Drug Money Seizure Act and the Bank Secrecy Act Amendments: Hearing Before Senate Committee on Banking, Housing, and Urban Affairs*, 99th Cong., 2d Sess. 22, 41, 82-83, 89 (1986) (hereinafter *Hearing Before the Senate Committee on Banking, Housing, and Urban Affairs*); *Tax Evasion, Drug Trafficking and Money Laundering as They Involve Financial Institutions: Hearings Before the Subcommittee on Financial Institutions Supervision, Regulation and Insurance of the House Committee on Banking, Finance, and Urban Affairs*, 99th Cong., 2d Sess. 179-182 (1986) (hereinafter *Hearings Before the House Committee on Banking, Finance and Urban Affairs*); *Money Laundering Legislation: Hearing Before the Senate Judiciary Committee*, 99th Cong., 1st Sess. 224 (1985) (hereinafter *Hearing Before the Senate Judiciary Committee*).
6. See *Hearing Before Senate Committee on Banking, Housing and Urban Affairs* op. cit. at 53-55, 97, 128-135; *Hearings Before the House Committee on Banking, Finance and Urban Affairs* op. cit. at 179-182, 846-847, 850; *Hearing Before the Senate Judiciary Committee* op. cit. at 224.
7. See *Hearing Before the Senate Committee on Banking, Housing and Urban Affairs* op. cit. at 49-50, 61-62, 66-68, 115, 136-137; cf. *Hearings Before the House Committee on Banking, Finance and Urban Affairs* op. cit. (extensive analysis of elements of 18 U.S.C. ss 1956-57 (Supp. IV 1986)).
8. Congress acted quickly in defining this new crime. As late as 1985, the reporting law appeared to present no significant problems. No improvements to the law were suggested in The President's Commission on Organised Crime, Interim Report to the President and the Attorney-General, *The Cash Connection: Organised Crime, Financial Institutions, and Money Laundering* (1984) pp. vii-viii (hereinafter *The Cash Connection*). The Department of Justice seemed confident of the bank reporting law in 1983. See Narcotic and Dangerous Drug Section, Criminal Division, Department of Justice, *Investigation and Prosecution of Illegal Money Laundering—A Guide to the Bank Secrecy Act*, pp. 11-16, 99-129 (1983). Also, the cases generally upheld prosecutions until *United States v. Anzalone* 766 F.2d 676 (1st Cir. 1985). But see Comptroller General, *Bank Secrecy Act Reporting Requirements Have Not Yet Met Expectations, Suggesting Need for Amendment* (cited in *Anzalone* at 681-682) (identifying aggregation loophole and recommending amendment). Congress passed the anti-smurfing statute on October 27 1986; it became effective three months later. Section 1364(a) of Pub. L. 99-570 provided that: "The amendment made by section 1354 shall apply with respect to transactions for the payment, receipt, or transfer of United States coins or currency or other monetary instruments completed after the end of the 3-month period beginning on the date of the enactment of this Act [October 27 1986]". *Anti-Drug Abuse Act* Pub. L. No. 99-570, s. 1364(a), 100 Stat. 3207 (1986). A gestation period of two years from the time a problem arises until Congress has it solved is short.
9. See *Hearing Before the Senate Committee on Banking, Housing and Urban Affairs* op. cit. at 41, 87, 89, 96; *Hearings Before the House Committee on Banking, Finance and Urban Affairs* op. cit. at 654, 661; *Hearing Before the Senate Judiciary Committee* op. cit. at 221-222.
10. See generally *Hearing Before the House Committee on Banking, Finance and Urban Affairs* op. cit. (analysis of 18 U.S.C. ss 1956-57 (Supp. IV 1986)).

This chapter takes a thorough look at the anti-smurfing statute. The following part presents the setting that facilitated the emergence of smurfs. The third part, "The Anti-Smurfing Statute" (pp. 213-232), examines the statute itself, including its basic theory, elements, constitutionality, unit of prosecution, and practical operation. The fourth part, "The Relationship of the Anti-Smurfing Statute to other Federal Crimes" (pp. 232-242), examines how this new crime fits into federal criminal law as a whole. The chapter concludes that on balance, the reduction in privacy that the anti-smurfing statute effects is warranted by the harm money laundering and the drug trade cause.

THE SETTING: CREATING AN ENVIRONMENT CONDUCIVE TO SMURFS

Some Background on Money Laundering

Money laundering begins with dirty money. Money can get dirty in two ways. One way is through tax evasion; people make money legally, but they make more than they report to the government.[11] Money also gets dirty through illegal generation.[12] Common techniques include drug sales,[13] gambling,[14] and bribery.[15] Once money is dirty, it must be converted into an apparently legitimate form, or "laundered" before it can be invested or spent.[16] " 'Money laundering' is the process by which one conceals the existence, illegal source, or illegal application of income, and then disguises that income to make it appear legitimate".[17]

11. See e.g. *United States v. Heyman* 794 F.2d 788 (2d Cir. 1986), cert. denied, 479 U.S. 989 (1986); *United States v. Cook* 745 F.2d 1311 (10th Cir. 1984), cert. denied, 469 U.S. 1220 (1985); see also *United States v. Tobon-Builes* 706 F.2d 1092 (11th Cir. 1983) (defendant claimed his $185,200 in cash was "poker winnings"; conceivably he generated it legally, e.g. in Las Vegas).
12. Illegally generated money is probably dirty in both ways because after illegal generation it presumably goes unreported.
13. See e.g. *United States v. Dela Espriella* 781 F.2d 1432 (9th Cir. 1986).
14. See H.R. Rep. No. 975, 91st Cong., 2d Sess. 11, reprinted in 1970 Code Cong. & Admin. News 4394 at 4396. ("The money in many of these transactions may represent . . . the proceeds of a lottery racket.")
15. Ibid. ("The money in many of these transactions may represent . . . the bribery of public officials.")
16. Laundering is only required for large amounts of money because small amounts can be absorbed inconspicuously. E.g. a person legally generating and reporting an income of $100,000 could probably dispose of half of it in unlaundered cash on items like clothing, cars, restaurants, and travel without arousing suspicion. But when vast amounts of money are involved, it cannot simply be absorbed and spent as cash. Often drug trafficking is the crime generating the amounts of money that require laundering. See e.g. *United States v. Dela Espriella* 781 F.2d at 1432 (9th Cir. 1986) (money derived from cocaine trafficking); *United States v. Thompson* 603 F.2d 1200 (5th Cir. 1979) (money to be used to purchase cocaine); see below, p. 203, text accompanying n. 24 ($355 million worth of cocaine seized); see also *United States v. Tobon-Builes* 706 F.2d 1092 (11th Cir. 1983) (defendant claimed his $185,200 in cash was "poker winnings", but the court noted that the defendant had trouble speaking English and that his girlfriend possessed the return portion of a round-trip airline ticket from Medellin, Columbia to Miami, Florida).
17. *The Cash Connection*, op. cit. at 7.

Laundering has several goals. One is to hide or sanitise the property so the tax collector does not get it. This aspect of the laundering process has been chronicled in detail.[18] Another goal is to convert the cash into a physically manageable and inconspicuous form. That form often is a postal money order or cashier's cheque,[19] but it also could be gold, stamps, or any form of property. The importance of converting cash into a manageable physical form is illustrated by the case of Anthony Castelbuono. Castelbuono somewhat conspicuously brought $1,180,450 in small bills to a casino. The cash had an estimated volume of 5.75 cubic feet and weighed 280 pounds.[20]

Whatever its goal, money laundering is harmful. Underground money absorbs no portion of the tax burden. More importantly, laundering is harmful because it allows the underlying criminal activity to thrive. Drug sales, gambling, or other crimes that generate cash are pointless if the cash cannot be invested or spent. Without laundering, the risk-reward ratio for the underlying crime is unattractive. Thus, success of the criminal venture depends on laundering.[21] Efficient laundering renders the underlying crime lucrative, and therefore perpetuates it.

Money laundering has become a major concern recently because of the thriving drug trade.[22] Laundering is required only if large amounts of cash are involved, because smaller amounts of dirty cash can be absorbed

18. Ibid. at 13-15, 29-49.
19. Postal money orders and cashier's cheques are the launderers' instruments of choice. Unlike property such as cash, gold, and real estate, money orders and cashier's cheques are physically convenient and extremely mobile. They are better than two-party cheques because they are guaranteed and require no underlying bank account. They are better than certified cheques because no payor need be identified. Although banks and the Post Office keep some records of cashier's cheques and money orders, the documentation is minimal. Postal money orders and cashier's cheques are thus the most flexible and anonymous form of property. In fact, postal money orders became so popular that in August 1987, the Postal Service imposed a temporary ceiling on sales of money orders to $10,000 per person per day. See *Restriction on Purchase of Postal Money Orders* 52 Fed. Reg. 27,992 (1987).
20. See *Hearing Before the Senate Judiciary Committee* op. cit. at 104; see also *Hearings Before the House Committee on Banking, Finance and Urban Affairs* op. cit. at 656 (drug trade worth $110 billion per year in "huge bulky quantities of cash in denominations no larger than $100").
21. "Money laundering . . . provides a function necessary for the effective operation of a number of types of criminal activities conducted on a large scale." *Hearings Before the Senate Committee on Banking, Housing and Urban Affairs* op. cit. at 148 (response to questions by James Knapp and Brian Sun); see also *The Cash Connection*, op. cit. at 3: "Without the means to launder money, thereby making cash generated by a criminal enterprise appear to come from a legitimate source, organised crime could not flourish as it now does."
22. See *Restriction on Purchase of Postal Money Orders* 52 Fed. Reg. 27,992 (1987). See generally Abramovsky, "Money-Laundering and Narcotics Prosecution" (1986) 54 Fordham L. Rev. 471 (foreclosing the opportunity to launder drug dollars can substantially decrease the quantity of drugs imported and sold); Wisotsky, "Exposing the War on Cocaine: The Futility and Destructiveness of Prohibition" (1983) Wisconsin L. Rev. 1305 at 1333 ("Importers and [drug] dealers . . . must confront the problem of processing a volume of cash so enormous that it must be weighed instead of counted, or counted with the aid of high-speed machines. In fact, one informant claims that getting rid of the money has become the hardest part of the dope business.") (footnote omitted).

inconspicuously into a criminal's lifestyle. Huge amounts of cash require attention to disposal, and the drug trade currently generates such huge amounts.[23] For example, in August 1988, 5,000 pounds of cocaine were seized in New York; the estimated street value was $355 million.[24] Had this cocaine reached the streets, that $355 million would exist originally as cash. To put that cash to its best use, it would have to be laundered.

Aside from combating these measurable harms, putting a halt to money laundering also is emotionally appealing. The existence of laundering schemes indicates that some people get rich unfairly because they pay no taxes. Furthermore, the people who need laundering schemes often get rich because they sell drugs in the United States. Drug money laundering is especially unsavoury on an intuitive level, considering the source of the cash that drives it.

The Original Reporting Statute

The government's first attack on money laundering was indirect. In 1970, Congress passed the *Currency and Foreign Transactions Reporting Act*[25] ("the Act") as Title II of the *Bank Secrecy Act*.[26] The Act imposes reporting requirements for certain financial transactions.[27] One statute provides that when a domestic financial institution[28] is involved in a currency transaction under circumstances prescribed by regulation, the bank must file a report with the government.[29] The regulations require that banks report each transaction in currency

23. See e.g. *United States v. Dela Espriella* 781 F.2d 1432 (9th Cir. 1986) (money derived from cocaine trafficking); *United States v. Tobon-Builes* 706 F.2d 1092 (11th Cir. 1983) (circumstances led court to conclude cash was raised in drug transactions); *United States v. Thompson* 603 F.2d 1200 (5th Cir. 1979) (money to be used to purchase cocaine); see also *Hearing Before the Senate Committee on Banking, Housing and Urban Affairs* op. cit. at 125 (estimates of drug trade from $50 to $110 billion); *Hearing Before the Senate Judiciary Committee* op. cit. at 220 (74 pounds of cocaine worth $30 million); *Lexington Herald-Leader*, 25 March 1989, p. A3, col. 6 (Detroit cocaine ring generated as much as $3 million per day from 1982 to 1988).
24. See *Lexington Herald-Leader*, 22 August 1988, p. A3, col. 1.
25. 31 U.S.C. ss 5311-5314, 5316-5322 (1982 and Supp. IV 1986).
26. *Bank Secrecy Act*, Pub. L. No. 91-508, 84 Stat. 1114 (1970) (codified at 12 U.S.C. ss 1829b, 1951-1959 (1982)); 31 U.S.C. ss 5311-5314, 5316-5322 (1982 and Supp. IV 1986).
27. 31 U.S.C. ss 5311-5314, 5316-5322 (1982 and Supp. IV 1986). See generally Note, "The Currency Reporting Laws and the War on Organised Crime" (1986) 20 Suffolk L. Rev. 1061 (discussing a financial institution's liability for its agents' reporting violations and the need for greater deterrence of reporting violations).
28. The reporting law applies to "domestic financial institutions", which include banks, securities dealers, currency exchanges, funds transmitters, telegraph companies, casinos, and anyone subject to state or federal banking authority. See 31 C.F.R. s. 103.11(g) (1988). In this chapter the term "bank" is used for convenience, but the law is not so limited.
29. 31 U.S.C. s. 5313(a) (1982) provides in part: "When a domestic financial institution is involved in a transaction . . . of . . . currency . . . under circumstances the Secretary prescribes by regulation, the institution and any other participant in the transaction the Secretary may prescribe shall file a report . . . in the way the Secretary prescribes."

exceeding $10,000.[30] Failure to report can result in civil[31] and criminal[32] penalties.

The stated purpose of the Act is to generate reports with a "high degree of usefulness in criminal, tax, or regulatory investigations".[33] Congress recognised that criminals deal in cash. Thus, large cash transactions are suspect; they are often a clue to underlying criminal activity.[34] As Congressman McKinney said: "What legitimate business in the United States of America today transfers money in cash?"[35] Cash is the only practical medium in some businesses, and those are recognised in statutory exceptions.[36] Usually, though, large cash transactions are indeed suspect. Moreover, cash is riskier than other types of paper due to the possibility of loss or theft. The willingness to accept the higher risk makes large cash transactions even more suspect. Thus, Congress concluded that reports of large currency transactions would be valuable in ferreting out crime.[37]

30. 31 C.F.R. s. 103.22(a)(1) (1988). The regulation provides in relevant part: "Each financial institution . . . shall file a report of each deposit, withdrawal, exchange of currency or other payment or transfer, by, through, or to such financial institution which involves a transaction in currency of more than $10,000." Ibid. Portions of this regulation reflect an amendment effective April 1987. *Bank Secrecy Act*, 52 Fed. Reg. 11,442 (1987) (codified at 31 C.F.R. s. 103.22(a)(1) (1988)). The amended regulation is discussed below, nn. 74-98 and accompanying text, pp. 209-212.

    The form designed for the report is Treasury Form 4789 (Currency Transaction Report). See *California Bankers Assoc. v. Shultz* 416 U.S. 21 at 39 n. 15 (1974). The form is to be filed with the Commissioner of Internal Revenue, 31 C.F.R. s. 103.26(4) (1988).

31. 31 U.S.C. s. 5321(a)(1) (1982 and Supp. IV 1986); see also 31 C.F.R. s. 103.47 (1988). The Secretary and Congress have amended both these provisions several times since adopting them in 1970. Both 31 U.S.C. s. 5321 (Supp. IV 1986) and 31 C.F.R. s. 103.47 (1988) reflect the progression of amendments in their legislative history sections. The original civil penalty was limited to not more than $1,000; today the same civil penalty for wilful violation is limited to "not more than the greater of the amount (not to exceed $100,000) involved in the transaction or $25,000": 31 C.F.R. s. 103.47(f) (1988).

32. 31 U.S.C. s. 5322(a)-(b) (1982 and Supp. IV 1986). Like the civil penalty statute (see above n. 31), this criminal penalty statute has been amended twice since its adoption to increase the sanctions. Pub. L. No. 99-570, s. 1356(c)(1), 100 Stat. 3207-3224, 3207-3226 (1986); Pub. L. No. 98-473, s. 901(b), 98 Stat. 2135 (1984). The original penalty was limited to a fine of $1,000 or one year in prison or both: 31 U.S.C. s. 5322(a) (1982). Today the penalty is limited to a fine of $250,000 or five years in prison or both: 31 U.S.C. s. 5322(a) (Supp. IV 1986).

33. 31 U.S.C. s. 5311 (1982).

34. H.R. Rep. No. 975, 91st Cong., 2d Sess., reprinted in 1971 U.S. Code Cong. & Admin. News 4396: "Criminals deal in money—cash or its equivalent. The deposit and withdrawal of large amounts of currency or its equivalent (monetary instruments) under unusual circumstances may betray a criminal activity."

35. *Briefing on the 1970 Currency and Foreign Transactions Reporting Act: Hearing Before the Subcommittee on Financial Institutions Supervision, Regulation and Insurance of the House Committee on Banking, Finance and Urban Affairs*, 99th Cong., 1st Sess. 51-52 (1985).

36. 31 C.F.R. s. 103.22(b)(2)(ii) (1988) provides exemptions from the reporting requirement for, inter alia, sports arenas, race tracks, amusement parks, bars, restaurants, hotels and vending machine companies.

37. *California Bankers Assoc. v. Shultz* 416 U.S. 21 at 39 (1974) ("Congress recognised the importance of reports of large and unusual currency transactions in ferreting out criminal activity and desired to strengthen the statutory basis for requiring such reports".); see also *United States v. Heyman* 794 F.2d 788 at 789 n. 1 (2d Cir. 1986)

The reporting statute and regulations take an indirect approach in that they only require information. Large cash transactions are not illegal, but they must be reported. Failure to report such transactions, however, is criminal. Once the bank files the report, people are free to deal in cash without constraints.

The bank reporting law attacks laundering by alerting the government to the process at its earliest point, the initial cash transactions. As the laundering process continues, the transactions become byzantine and more difficult to trace. The initial cash transactions are a vulnerable point because large amounts of cash are difficult to obscure. From the government's perspective, the cash transactions are an attractive target because they occur early in the laundering process and are conspicuous.

Problems with the Statute and the Judicial Response

The Act and regulations became effective in 1971.[38] In the early years banks largely ignored the reporting law.[39] United States attorneys apparently ignored the law as well, because few criminal cases were reported before the late 1970s.[40] At that time, appellate case law began to develop, and the early cases upheld the prosecutions.[41] Beginning in 1985, however, the cases revealed two distinct problems with the law.

One problem was that the regulations imposed the duty to report cash transactions over $10,000 only on banks.[42] The question arose whether bank customers also had a duty to report these cash transactions.[43] Some courts found that customers did have such a duty, and could

37. *continued*
   (large cash transactions are often part of the money laundering process), cert. denied, 479 U.S. 989 (1986); *United States v. Giancola* 783 F.2d 1549 at 1553 (11th Cir. 1986) per Hill J., dissenting: "Currency is the life blood of organised crime"), cert. denied, 479 U.S. 1018 (1986); H.R. Rep. No. 975, 91st Cong., 2d Sess., reprinted in 1971 U.S. Code Cong. & Admin. News 4396-97 ("These reports may be of considerable value to law enforcement agencies in criminal investigations and prosecutions.").
38. Pub. L. No. 91-508, s. 401(a), 84 Stat. 1114 (1970).
39. Few reports were filed in the early years. In 1975, 3,418 reports were filed. In 1979, 121,000 reports were filed. By the next year, the number almost doubled; 241,850 reports were filed in 1980. In 1986, an estimated 3.2 million reports were filed. See *Hearing Before the Senate Committee on Banking, Housing and Urban Affairs* op. cit. at 33 (statement of Brian Bruh, Director, I.R.S. Office of Criminal Investigations). The number of reports filed is also documented in *The Cash Connection*, op. cit. at 9. See generally *United States v. Sans* 731 F.2d 1521 (5th Cir. 1984) (referring to testimony that banks universally ignored the currency reporting requirements); *Hearing Before the Senate Judiciary Committee* op. cit. at 100 (testimony of James D. Harmon, Jr.) (referring to "the banks' . . . now documented abysmal record of ignoring the reporting requirements of the *Bank Secrecy Act*, a law on the books for some 14 years").
40. See *The Cash Connection* op. cit. at 9 ("For most of the first decade after passage of the [Bank Secrecy] Act, the Federal Government did not vigorously enforce its provisions". (footnote omitted).
41. See e.g. *United States v. Cook* 745 F.2d 1311 (10th Cir. 1984), cert. denied, 469 U.S. 1220 (1986); *United States v. Tobon-Builes* 706 F.2d 1092 (11th Cir. 1983); *United States v. Thompson* 603 F.2d 1200 (5th Cir. 1979).
42. See 31 C.F.R. s. 103.22(a)(1) (1988) (quoted above, n. 30).
43. See e.g. *United States v. Puerto* 730 F.2d 627 at 631 (11th Cir.), cert. denied, 469 U.S. 847 (1984).

therefore be held criminally liable for failure to file a report.[44] These courts reasoned that customers were accomplices of the banks.[45] Other courts refused to hold customers liable for failure to file a report[46] on the basis that the regulations did not explicitly impose such a duty. Criminal liability therefore would be unconstitutional because the laws were too vague to provide fair notice.[47] These courts often reasoned that while the enabling legislation granted the Secretary of the Treasury authority to require "any . . . participant" to file reports, the Secretary's regulations required only that "financial institutions" do so.[48] Thus, the courts concluded, although he had the power, the Secretary specifically had chosen not to require reports from individuals.

Another problem with the reporting law was that the regulations imposed a duty to report only if the cash transaction exceeded $10,000.[49] Assume that Joe, a smurf, is in charge of converting cash drug profits into cashier's cheques. To do his job well, he does some research and finds that he can avoid the reporting requirement by manipulating cash transactions so none exceeds $10,000. The cases began to reveal such schemes.[50] The number of variables involved in

44. See e.g. *United States v. Lafaurie* 833 F.2d 1468 (11th Cir. 1987); *United States v. Richeson* 825 F.2d 17 (4th Cir. 1987); *United States v. Cure* 804 F.2d 625 (11th Cir. 1986); *United States v. Puerto* 730 F.2d 627 at 633 (11th Cir. 1984); *United States v. Tobon-Builes* 706 F.2d 1092 (11th Cir. 1983); see also *United States v. Hayes* 827 F.2d 469 (9th Cir. 1987) (person not associated with financial institution could not be punished as aider and abetter for conspiring to avoid currency transaction reporting requirements); cf. *United States v. Heyman* 794 F.2d 788 (2d Cir. 1986) (defendant was not a customer but rather an employee of the financial institution; conviction sustained), cert. denied, 479 U.S. 989 (1986); *United States v. Cook* 745 F.2d 1311 (10th Cir. 1984) (customer liable under the bank reporting law for giving false information on report rather than for failure to file a report), cert. denied, 469 U.S. 1220 (1986); *United States v. Thompson* 603 F.2d 1200 (5th Cir. 1979) (same).

Courts addressing the liability of customers as accomplices of banks did not distinguish among the three statutes (the bank reporting law, s. 1001, and conspiracy) used to prosecute. See e.g. *United States v. Varbel* 780 F.2d 758 (9th Cir. 1986) (customer not liable under s. 1001 and s. 371); *United States v. Anzalone* 766 F.2d 676 (1st Cir. 1985) (customer not liable under s. 5313 and s. 1001); *United States v. Puerto* 730 F.2d 627 (11th Cir. 1984) (customer liable under s. 5313, s. 1001 and s. 371), cert. denied, 469 U.S. 847 (1984); cf. *United States v. Heyman* 794 F.2d 788 (2d Cir. 1986) (account executive liable under s. 5313 and s. 371), cert. denied, 479 U.S. 989 (1986).

45. The courts relied on 18 U.S.C. s. 2 (1982). See *United States v. Puerto* 730 F.2d 627 at 633 (11th Cir. 1984), cert. denied, 469 U.S. 847 (1984); *United States v. Tobon-Builes* 706 F.2d 1092 at 1099-1101 (11th Cir. 1983).

46. See e.g., *United States v. Gimbel* 830 F.2d 621 (7th Cir. 1987); *United States v. Larson* 796 F.2d 744 (8th Cir. 1986); *United States v. Dela Espriella* 781 F.2d 1432 (9th Cir. 1986); *United States v. Varbel* 780 F.2d 758 (9th Cir. 1986); *United States v. Anzalone* 766 F.2d 676 (1st Cir. 1985).

47. See e.g. *United States v. Larson* 796 F.2d 244 at 247 (8th Cir. 1986); *United States v. Varbel* 780 F.2d 758 (9th Cir. 1986); *United States v. Anzalone* 766 F.2d 676 at 678 (1st Cir. 1985).

48. See e.g. *United States v. Larson* 796 F.2d 244 (8th Cir. 1986); *United States v. Varbel* 780 F.2d 758 at 762 (9th Cir. 1986); *United States v. Anzalone* 766 F.2d 676 (1st Cir. 1985). The statute and regulation are quoted above, pp. 203-204, nn. 29-30.

49. 31 C.F.R. s. 103.22(a)(1) (1988) (quoted above, p. 204, n. 30).

50. See e.g. *United States v. Heyman* 794 F.2d 788 (2d Cir. 1986), cert. denied, 479 U.S. 989 (1986). The defendant was an account executive with Merrill Lynch: at 789. On 26 July 1982, he received a briefcase from a client containing $70,000 in cash, and he deposited $7,000 in ten related accounts. On the next day he transferred all the money

financial transactions allowed smurfs like Joe endless opportunities for manipulation. The variables included the number of banks,[51] the number of branch offices of a particular bank,[52] the number of teller stations at one branch office,[53] the number of instruments purchased,[54] the number of accounts at a particular bank,[55] the time period during which the transactions were conducted,[56] and the number of persons doing the transactions.[57] Manipulating these variables to keep each transaction under $10,000 required manpower. The armies of lower level operatives who appeared in banks became known as smurfs. As they scurried from bank to bank executing transactions just under the $10,000 reporting limit, they seemed to be everywhere, much like the little blue cartoon characters.[58]

These schemes exploited the lack of any aggregation requirement in the statutes or regulations that defined a $10,000 transaction. The instructions on the back of the reporting form provided for

50. *continued*

into one joint account. See also *United States v. Cook* 745 F.2d 1311 (10th Cir. 1984) (defendant attempted to avoid the $10,000 reporting requirement by withdrawing money from one bank and re-depositing it in another bank, using a false identity), cert. denied, 469 U.S. 1220 (1986); *United States v. Tobon-Builes* 706 F.2d 1092 (11th Cir. 1983) (defendant and companion simultaneously deposited $9,000 each in ten banks during a six hour period).

51. See e.g. *United States v. Varbel* 780 F.2d 758 at 759 (9th Cir. 1986); *United States v. Denemark* 779 F.2d 1559 at 1560-1561 (11th Cir. 1986).

52. See e.g. *United States v. Giancola* 783 F.2d 1549 at 1551 (11th Cir. 1986), cert. denied, 479 U.S. 1018 (1986); *United States v. Sanchez Vazquez* 585 F. Supp. 990 at 993 (N.D. Ga. 1984).

53. See e.g. *United States v. Larson* 796 F.2d 244 at 246 (8th Cir. 1986).

54. See e.g. *United States v. Bank of New England* 821 F.2d 844 at 847 (1st Cir. 1987) (cheques), cert. denied, 108 S. Ct. 328 (1987); *United States v. Thompson* 603 F.2d 1200 at 1202 (5th Cir. 1979) (nn.).

55. See e.g. *United States v. Heyman* 794 F.2d 788 (2d Cir.), cert. denied, 479 U.S. 989 (1986).

56. Compare *Heyman* 794 F.2d 788 at 789 (transactions occurring simultaneously) and *Bank of New England* 821 F.2d at 844-847 (same) with *United States v. Anzalone* 766 F.2d 676 at 679 (1st Cir. 1985) (transactions occurring over a two week period) and *United States v. Konefal* 566 F. Supp. 698 at 700 (N.D.N.Y. 1983) (transactions over a two month period).

57. See e.g. *United States v. Tobon-Builes* 706 F.2d 1092 at 1094 (11th Cir. 1983) (two people go to each bank; each person buys a $9,000 cashier's cheque).

58. See *Hearings Before the House Committee on Banking, Finance and Urban Affairs* op. cit. at 179 (smurfs scurry from bank to bank with increments of less than $10,000), at 665 (term "smurfs" originated because like the cartoon characters, there are many of them running around everywhere), at 792 (the problem of smurfing), at 818 (smurfs would be good both as defendants and as witnesses); *Hearing Before the Senate Committee on Banking, Housing and Urban Affairs* op. cit. at 21 (the "well known practice of smurfing"), at 41 (smurfs travelled to banks all over the United States), at 61 (structuring is "commonly known as smurfing"), at 79 (structured cash conversion schemes often dubbed "smurfing"), at 87 (long lines at banks discourage smurfs who go to other metropolitan areas to smurf cash), at 89 (law is ineffective, so launderers just "smurf away"), at 124 (referring to an "anti-smurfing" regulatory measure), at 150 (smurfs are relatively low on the organised crime totem pole), at 191 (smurfs convert illegally obtained cash into cashier's cheques), at 226 (smurfs are escaping liability); see also *Restriction on Purchase of Postal Money Orders* 52 Fed. Reg. 27,992 (1987) (temporary restriction on amount of money orders a customer can buy in one day adopted to prevent smurfs from using money orders to launder drug money).

aggregation,[59] but whether these instructions could serve as the basis for criminal prosecution was uncertain at best.[60] Some courts specifically found the instructions to be non-binding.[61]

The judicial response to the smurfs' use of multiple transactions to avoid filing a report was mixed. In some limited circumstances, courts were willing to collapse the transactions and aggregate the amounts to reach $10,000, thus rendering the defendant liable for failure to file.[62] Generally, though, courts refused to aggregate transactions[63] and declared the defendants' conduct non-criminal.[64] These courts reasoned that no language in the statute or regulations imposed a duty to aggregate transactions. A criminal conviction therefore would be unconstitutional because nothing clearly warned the defendant that the conduct was criminal.[65] The courts that refused to find defendants liable often stated that it was for Congress or the Executive to declare conduct criminal, not the courts.[66] Noting further that a Comptroller General's report had identified this aggregation loophole, the courts relied on the Secretary's subsequent inaction to conclude that the Secretary knew of the problem but apparently had chosen not to cure it.[67]

59. See *United States v. Anzalone* 766 F.2d 676 at 679, n. 6 (1st Cir. 1985). The form provided: "Multiple transactions by or for any person which in any one day total more than $10,000 should be treated as a single transaction, if the financial institution is aware of them".

60. See e.g. ibid. at 684 (Aldrich J., concurring); *United States v. Palzer* 745 F.2d 1350 at 1357 (11th Cir. 1984) (no specific ruling but suggests that instructions are binding); *Tobon-Builes* 706 F.2d at 1097-98 (court mentions instructions but extent of reliance thereon is unclear).

61. See *United States v. Reinis* 794 F.2d 506 at 508 (9th Cir. 1986) (bank reporting form not effective as regulation because not in compliance with *Administrative Procedure Act*); *Anzalone* 766 F.2d 676 at 679, n. 6; *United States v. Cogswell* 637 F. Supp. 295 at 298 (N.D. Cal. 1985).

62. See *United States v. Bank of New England* 821 F.2d 844 (1st Cir. 1987) (simultaneous transfer, same teller window, multiple instruments), cert. denied, 108 S. Ct. 328 (1987); *United States v. Heyman* 794 F.2d 788 at 789 (2d Cir. 1986) (simultaneous transfer, same representative, multiple instruments), cert. denied, 479 U.S. 989 (1986); *United States v. Giancola* 783 F.2d 1549 at 1551-1552 (11th Cir. 1986) (same day, same bank but different branches, multiple instruments) (distinguishing *United States v. Denemark* 779 F.2d 1559 (11th Cir. 1986) on the basis that *Denemark* involved different banks), cert. denied, 479 U.S. 1018 (1986); *United States v. Thompson* 603 F.2d 1200 at 1202 (5th Cir. 1979) (simultaneous transfer, same teller, multiple instruments); cf. *United States v. Tobon-Builes* 706 F.2d 1092 (11th Cir. 1983) (defendant and girlfriend went to same branch office of same bank, each completed $9,000 transaction at different tellers; court treated this as one transfer of $18,000).

63. See *United States v. Larson* 796 F.2d 244 (8th Cir. 1986); *United States v. Dela Espriella* 781 F.2d 1432 (9th Cir. 1986); *United States v. Varbel* 780 F.2d 758 (9th Cir. 1986); *United States v. Denemark* 779 F.2d 1559 (11th Cir. 1986); *United States v. Anzalone* 766 F.2d 676 (1st Cir. 1985); *United States v. Cogswell* 637 F. Supp. 295 (N.D. Cal. 1985).

64. See e.g. *United States v. Varbel* 780 F.2d 758 at 761-762 (9th Cir. 1986).

65. See *United States v. Mastronardo* 849 F.2d 799 at 805 (3d Cir. 1988); *Varbel* 780 F.2d 758 at 760-61; *United States v. Anzalone* 766 F.2d 676 at 678 (1st Cir. 1985).

66. See *United States v. Giancola* 783 F.2d 1549 at 1553-1554 (11th Cir. 1986) (Hill J., dissenting), cert. denied, 479 U.S. 1018 (1986); *United States v. Cogswell* 637 F. Supp. 295 (N.D. Cal. 1985).

67. See *Anzalone* 766 F.2d 676 at 681-682; *Cogswell* 637 F. Supp. 295 at 297-298.

Disagreement on the issues of customer liability and aggregation of transactions caused a split in the circuits.[68] The two issues raised distinct questions. Sometimes a case would present just one of these issues,[69] but frequently they were intertwined.[70] When that happened, courts generally failed to distinguish the issues.[71] The law grew into confused disarray.

Governmental Response to Misadventure in the Courts

The government responded to these problems. The Secretary of the Treasury amended the regulations,[72] and Congress passed a new criminal statute.[73]

Revised regulations to address aggregation

The Secretary amended the regulations of the bank reporting law to deal with the aggregation question.[74] First, a new regulation clarified the status of branch banks.[75] The old regulations did not specifically address this issue, but the definitions of "bank" and "financial institution" suggested that each branch was a separate entity.[76] Thus, transactions conducted at multiple branches of one institution would not be aggregated. Despite the language in these definitions, the courts concluded that transactions occurring at different branches of one

68. See above, pp. 205-208, text accompanying nn. 42-67; see also *United States v. Mastronardo* 849 F.2d 799 at 804 (3d Cir. 1988) (noting "severe split among the circuits" on issue of customer liability); *United States v. Nersesian* 824 F.2d 1294 at 1310 (2d Cir. 1987) (noting split of authority on issue of customer liability), cert. denied, 108 S. Ct. 357 (1987); Abrams, *Federal Criminal Law and its Enforcement* (Supp. 1986), p. 19.
69. See e.g. *United States v. Denemark* 779 F.2d 1559 at 1561 (11th Cir. 1986) (aggregation only); *United States v. Puerto* 730 F.2d 627 (11th Cir. 1984) (customer liability only), cert. denied, 469 U.S. 847 (1984).
70. See e.g. *United States v. Larson* 796 F.2d 244 at 246 (8th Cir. 1986).
71. See e.g. *United States v. Varbel* 780 F.2d 758 (9th Cir. 1986); *United States v. Anzalone* 766 F.2d 676 (1st Cir. 1985); *United States v. Tobon-Builes* 706 F.2d 1092 (11th Cir. 1983); *United States v. Thompson* 603 F.2d 1200 (5th Cir. 1979).
72. *Amendments to Implementing Regulations Under the Bank Secrecy Act* 52 Fed. Reg. 11,442 (1987) (codified at 31 C.F.R. s. 103.22 (1988)).
   In addition to these direct responses to loopholes in the reporting law, Congress recently adopted two new statutes which authorise new reporting requirements. See 31 U.S.C. ss 5325, 5326, discussed below, n. 104.
73. 31 U.S.C. s. 5324 (Supp. IV 1986).
74. The Secretary did not amend the regulations to deal with the customer liability issue. Individuals were under no duty to report. The authorising statute would have authorised such a duty, see 31 U.S.C. s. 5313(a) (1982) (quoted above, note 29), but no duty was imposed due to enforcability concerns. Telephone interview with John Landreth, Office of Financial Enforcement, Office of the Assistant Secretary (Enforcement), Department of the Treasury (August 10 1987).
75. See 31 C.F.R. s. 103.22(a)(4) (1988).
76. See 31 C.F.R. s. 103.11(a) (1988) (defining "bank" as "[e]ach agent, agency, *branch*, or office within the United States") (emphasis added); ibid., s. 103.11(g) (defining "financial institution" as "[e]ach agent, agency, *branch*, or office with the United States") (emphasis added).

institution should be combined.[77] The new regulation modified the definition of financial institution[78] to reflect the courts' conclusion.[79] This modification codified the cases and left the law essentially unchanged.[80]

The Secretary also adopted a regulation that codified the aggregation instructions on the back of the reporting form.[81] As noted above, the reporting form included aggregation instructions,[82] but the force of these instructions was unclear and the courts were reluctant to rely on them on the basis of a criminal prosecution.[83] This uncertainty has been cured now that the instructions are embodied in a regulation. The new regulation provides: "Multiple currency transactions shall be treated as a single transaction if the financial institution has knowledge that they are by or on behalf of any person and result in either cash in or cash out totalling more than $10,000 during any one business day."[84]

This regulation requires that three conditions exist before multiple transactions are treated as one. The transactions must be "by or on behalf of any person", the transactions must amount to over $10,000 cash in or cash out in a single day, and the bank must have knowledge of both these conditions.[85] If any one of these conditions fails, then multiple transactions are not treated as a single transaction. Assuming that each individual transaction is for less than $10,000, the bank has no duty to report.

This regulation raises several questions, some of which are resolved in the comments accompanying the amendments. For example, the comments indicate that only total cash in or cash out must be

77. See *United States v. Giancola* 783 F.2d 1549 at 1552 (11th Cir. 1986) ("Exchanges made by a single person or his partners or associates in a single day, in different branches of the same bank, do require the bank to file a [report]"), cert. denied, 479 U.S. 1018 (1986): accord *United States v. Sanchez Vazquez* 585 F. Supp. 990 (N.D. Ga. 1984).
78. See 31 C.F.R. s. 103.22(a)(3) (1988) ("A financial institution includes all of its domestic branch offices for the purpose of this paragraph's reporting requirements").
79. The comments accompanying the new regulations state that the revision modifies the definition of financial institution "to comport with recent case law". *Bank Secrecy Act*, 52 Fed. Reg. 11,436 (3) (1987).
80. But cf. *Giancola* 783 F.2d 1549 at 1554, n. 1 per Hill J., dissenting: "I recognise that there has been a recent amendment to 31 C.F.R. s. 103.22(a) which in the future may or may not be sufficient to pull transactions such as those in this case within the purview of the C.T.R. reporting requirement."
81. See *Bank Secrecy Act* 52 Fed. Reg. 11,442 (1987) (codified at 31 C.F.R. s. 103.22(a)(1) (1988)).
82. See above, p. 208, n. 59 and accompanying text.
83. See above, p. 208, nn. 60-61 and accompanying text.
84. 31 C.F.R. s. 103.22(a)(1) (1988). This change necessitated a regulation to define "business day." See s. 103.11(q) (1988) ("Business day . . . means that day, as normally communicated to its depository customers, on which a bank routinely posts a particular transaction to its customer's account").
85. Section 103.22(a)(1). The comments accompanying the new regulation describe the phrase "has knowledge". The comments state: "Treasury has changed the term 'is aware' to 'has knowledge.' This term means knowledge on the part of a partner, director, officer or employee of a financial institution, or on the part of any existing system at the institution that permits it to aggregate transactions." See *Bank Secrecy Act* 52 Fed. Reg. 11,437 (1987).

aggregated.[86] If $8,000 and then $4,000 are deposited in one account, the transactions must be aggregated, but if $8,000 is deposited and then $4,000 is withdrawn, aggregation is not required. Another question the regulation does not explicitly address is whether deposits one person makes to multiple accounts, or deposits multiple people make to a single account, must be combined into a single transaction. The comments indicate that in these situations, the presence of a single person or single account means that transactions involving that person or account must be combined and treated as a single transaction.[87]

Other questions the regulation raises are not addressed in the comments.[88] One such question is the meaning of the requirement that the transaction be "by or on behalf of any person."[89] The regulations define "person" as broadly as possible.[90] This language is literally meaningless because one cannot possibly conjure up a transaction that is not "by or on behalf of any person." The drafters probably meant to refer to transactions by or on behalf of *a* person or any *single* person, but were wary of limiting the regulation in this way. To have any meaning, the regulation should be interpreted to mean by or on behalf of *a* person.[91]

Another question is whether multiple transactions must be treated as one if all three conditions are met,[92] but the cash in or cash out is

86. *Bank Secrecy Act* 52 Fed. Reg. 11,438 (1987). The relevant comment provides:
    Treasury also wishes to reiterate that "cash in or cash out totalling more than $10,000" means the total of all deposits *or* the total of all withdrawals. Deposits and withdrawals are not to be aggregated together for purposes of the Bank Secrecy Act. However, the total of all deposits or the total of all withdrawals during a particular business day should be aggregated in order to determine if a reportable deposit or withdrawal limit has been reached.
87. *Bank Secrecy Act* 52 Fed. Reg. 11,438 (1987). "Examples of reportable transactions would be two people depositing more than $10,000 in one account, though neither deposited a reportable amount, or one person making a deposit of more than $10,000, but depositing the money in more than one account."
88. One question the regulations raise is how to resolve a conflict between the new regulations on branch banks and aggregation. If transactions are accomplished at multiple banks, the banks have no duty to aggregate the transactions and report, even if the bank has knowledge of the multiple transactions. Yet if the transactions are done at multiple branches of the same bank, the regulations treat them as occurring at one bank, and the bank must combine and report them. But what if the bank does not know of the transactions at multiple branches? Which regulation controls, the one requiring transactions to be combined among branches or the one requiring aggregation only if the bank has knowledge? Treasury comments reveal that the intent was for the knowledge requirement to control. Thus, if branch banks have no knowledge of multiple transactions on behalf of one person, the bank need not combine and report the transactions. See *Bank Secrecy Act* 52 Fed. Reg. 11,437 (quoted above, p. 210, n. 85).
89. 31 C.F.R. s. 103.22(a)(1) (1988).
90. 31 C.F.R. s. 103.11(1) (1988) (" 'Person'. An individual, a corporation, a partnership, a trust or estate, a joint stock company, an association, a syndicate, joint venture, or other unincorporated organization or group, and all entities cognizable as legal personalities.").
91. Compare 26 C.F.R. s. 1.6050I (1988). This regulation provides that for a similar reporting law, 26 U.S.C. s. 6050I (Supp. IV 1986), the aggregation requirement operates when the transaction is on behalf of "a person." See below, p. 233, n. 214 and accompanying text.
92. See above, p. 210, text accompanying n. 85.

transferred at different banks. The government's position is that a bank is under no duty to aggregate transactions conducted at different banks, even if the bank has knowledge of the other transactions.[93] The regulation as originally proposed would have captured this situation and required aggregation,[94] but the Secretary rejected that regulation, at least temporarily, in favour of the one adopted.[95]

The amended regulations leave some options open to the ambitious launderer. For example, Joe can manipulate time by limiting his cash transactions to $10,000 or less each day. This is an unattractive option, however, because the laundering process will be too slow for the volume of cash that many drug organisations generate. Another option, assuming Joe uses only a single bank, is to use multiple accounts and multiple agents to limit the bank's knowledge of the relationship between multiple transactions. If the bank lacks such knowledge, it has no duty to treat multiple transactions as single.[96] Finally, Joe can use multiple banks during a single day because the regulations do not require aggregation of transactions conducted at different banks.[97] So long as the transaction at each bank does not exceed $10,000, the bank has no reporting obligation.[98]

Recognising a new crime

Because launderers still could avoid the aggregation regulations in these ways, the regulations were an incomplete solution to the holes in the reporting law. Thus Congress enacted a new statute, which provides that no person shall for the purpose of evading the reporting requirements: (i) cause a financial institution to fail to file a required report; (ii) cause a financial institution to file a required report with an omission or misstatement; or (iii) structure any transaction with one or more financial institutions.[99] Sanctions for violating this statute include

93. Telephone interview with John Landreth, Office of Financial Enforcement, Office of the Assistant Secretary (Enforcement), Department of the Treasury (10 August 1987).

94. 51 Fed. Reg. 30,233, at 30,234 as proposed (25 August 1986); see also *Hearing Before the Senate Committee on Banking, Housing and Urban Affairs* op. cit. at 56 (prepared statement of Richard C. Wassenaar, Assistant Commissioner (Criminal Investigation), Internal Revenue Service).

95. The comments accompanying the new regulations mention that the regulations encompass all but three of the original proposals. Of the three not implemented: "two proposals, dealing with the purchase of more than $3,000 in monetary instruments, are still under consideration by Treasury and will be the subject of a separate notice to be issued within the next few months." *Bank Secrecy Act* 52 Fed. Reg. 11,436 (1987).

96. The revised regulations include stricter provisions on customer identification that will make it more difficult for smurfs to hide their identity from the banks. See 31 C.F.R. s. 103.27 (1988).

97. See above, text accompanying nn. 93-95.

98. Ibid.; see also *United States v. Giancola* 783 F.2d 1549 (11th Cir. 1986) (bank required to report aggregate transactions over $10,000 at different branches), cert. denied, 479 U.S. 1018 (1986); *United States v. Sanchez Vazquez* 585 F. Supp. 990 (N.D. Ga. 1984) (same).

99. 31 U.S.C. s. 5324 (Supp. IV 1986) provides:
    No person shall for the purpose of evading the reporting requirements of section 5313(a) with respect to such transaction—(1) cause or attempt to cause a domestic financial institution to fail to file a report required under section 5313(a); (2) cause or attempt to cause a domestic financial institution to file a report required under section 5313(a) that contains a material omission or misstatement of fact; or

forfeiture,[100] civil penalties,[101] and criminal sanctions of up to $250,000 in fines, five years in prison, or both.[102] The statute is officially titled: "Structuring transactions to evade reporting requirement prohibited".[103] Unofficially, the statute should be called the "anti-smurfing statute", in honour of the smurfs who prompted it.[104]

THE ANTI-SMURFING STATUTE

Elements and Theory of the Offence

Clause (1)

Clause (1)[105] takes conduct previously defined as criminal, failure of a bank to file a report, and extends liability to any person who causes that failure. This amounts to an accomplice liability provision tailored to the specific crime of failing to file a report. Federal law includes a general accomplice liability statute,[106] but the courts have disagreed on its

99. *continued*
    (3) structure or assist in structuring, or attempt to structure or assist in structuring, any transaction with one or more domestic financial institutions.
        The Secretary adopted a regulation mimicking the statute. See 31 C.F.R. s. 103.53 (1988). The comments accompanying this regulation state that the "amendment merely incorporates into the regulations the new statutory violation of structuring": *Bank Secrecy Act*, 52 Fed. Reg. 11,440 (1987).
100. There is some confusion over forfeiture. See 31 U.S.C.A. ss 5321(a)(4)(C), 5321(c) (1982 and Supp. IV 1986), both of which refer to structured transaction forfeiture provision s. 5317(d). But no s. 5317(d) appears.
101. See ibid., s. 5321(a)(4); 31 C.F.R. s. 103.47(e) (1988).
102. See 31 U.S.C. s. 5322(a) (1982 and Supp. IV 1986).
103. 31 U.S.C. s. 5324 (Supp. IV 1986).
104. In addition to the amended regulations and the anti-smurfing statute which took effect in 1987, the government response to smurfing was bolstered again in November 1988 when Congress added two new statutes with expanded reporting requirements. See *Money Laundering Prosecution Improvements Act* 1988, Pub. L. No. 100-690, November 18 1988, codified at 31 U.S.C. ss 5325, 5326. One statute, s. 5325, basically requires banks to check and verify identification for persons purchasing with cash any instrument over $3,000. This statute authorises the Secretary of the Treasury to adopt regulations defining the type of identification required and the records that banks must keep on the identification. (The Secretary has begun the process of prescribing regulations, see *Advance Notice of Proposed Rulemaking* 53 Fed. Reg. No. 247, pp. 51846-47 (December 23 1988).) All records must be provided to the Secretary upon request: 31 U.S.C. s. 5325. The other statute basically authorises the Secretary to target a particular bank or geographic group of banks and order them to keep such records and provide such information on currency transactions as the Secretary may require: 31 U.S.C. s. 5326.
        These new reporting requirements will make smurfing more difficult. For example, cash purchases of cashier's cheques will have to be below the $3,000 threshold or the identification provisions will increase the likelihood of bank knowledge that separate transactions are all by or on behalf of one person. See above, p. 212, text accompanying n. 96. Or the Secretary might target a particular bank to report all cash transactions over $1,000. Aside from making smurfing more difficult, these new reporting requirements have no impact on the operation of the anti-smurfing statute because the statute is based exclusively on the reporting requirements of s. 5313.
105. 31 U.S.C. s. 5324 (Supp. IV 1986). "No person shall for the purpose of evading the reporting requirements of s. 5313(a) with respect to such transaction—(1) cause or attempt to cause a domestic financial institution to fail to file a report required under s. 5313(a)."
106. 18 U.S.C. s. 2 (1982).

applicability to non-reporting.[107] Congress responded to this disagreement by adopting this particularised accomplice liability provision.[108]

This provision of cl. (1) is obsolete today. Assume Joe goes to Bank A at 10 o'clock, 1 o'clock, and 3 o'clock. Each time he buys a $4,000 cashier's cheque with cash. To find Joe in violation of cl. (1), Bank A must have a duty to file a report, and must fail to do so. Under the regulations, Bank A has a duty to file only if it knows that multiple transactions for one person total cash in or cash out over $10,000 in one day. If Bank A meets these criteria, that is, it knows of Joe's three transactions, how could Joe "cause" its failure to file?

The explanation for this anomaly is historical. Congress drafted and adopted cl. (1) of the anti-smurfing statute before the Secretary of the Treasury revised the regulations to impose the aggregation requirement. Because cl. (1) was designed to impose liability on customers, the bank's knowledge was irrelevant. Under the revised regulation, however, if the bank is ignorant of one person's multiple transactions on one day, it has no duty to combine the transactions and therefore no duty to file a report. Joe's three trips, of course, caused the bank's ignorance and its consequent lack of duty to file. Even so, Joe cannot be held liable for causing failure to perform an act that the bank had no duty to perform.

Clause (1) also contains an attempt provision. Federal law includes no general attempt statute, but instead incorporates attempt language in individual statutes.[109] When Congress defines a new crime, it routinely includes attempt language. The attempt language of clause (1) still is vital under the regulations because it encompasses situations in which a customer attempts to mislead a bank, but the bank discovers the attempt and files a report. For example, assume Joe goes to Bank B at 2 o'clock and pays $9,000 cash for a cashier's cheque, then returns at 4 o'clock and does the same. To avoid a report, Joe uses false identification on the 4 o'clock trip. Bank B discovers that Joe accomplished both transactions and files a report. Under clause (1), the government can charge Joe with attempting to cause Bank B to fail to file.

Clause (2)

Clause (2)[110] makes it a crime to cause a bank to file a report containing a material omission or misstatement. In this situation, the bank is aware of the cash transaction over $10,000. The bank reporting

---

107. Cf. *United States v. Tobon-Builes* 706 F.2d 1092 at 1099 (11th Cir. 1983) (s. 2 is applicable) with *United States v. Anzalone* 766 F.2d 676 at 682 (1st Cir. 1985) (s. 2 is not applicable). See above, pp. 205-206, text accompanying nn. 42-48.

108. At the same time, Congress declined to enact a general criminal facilitation statute. See *Hearings Before the House Committee on Banking, Finance and Urban Affairs* op. cit. at 834 (prepared statement of Assistant Attorney-General Stephen S. Trott); Joost, "Simplifying Federal Criminal Laws" (1986) 14 Pepperdine L. Rev. 1, 15-16.

109. See e.g. 18 U.S.C. ss 1341, 1951, 1952(a) (1982); s. 1344 (Supp. III 1985).

110. 37 U.S.C. s. 5324 (Supp. IV 1986). "No person shall for the purpose of evading the reporting requirements of section 5313(a) with respect to such transaction— . . . (2) cause or attempt to cause a domestic financial institution to file a report required under s. 5313(a) that contains a material omission or misstatement of fact."

law already defines making any misstatement in a report as a crime.[111] Clause (2) of the anti-smurfing statute extends liability to those who *cause* misstatements. Clause (2) also imposes criminal liability for causing a material omission in a report, conduct the bank reporting law does not reach.

Another criminal statute, 18 U.S.C. s. 1001, affects the same conduct.[112] Causing the filing of a bank report with an omission may be criminal under s. 1001,[113] and causing the filing of a false report is always criminal under s. 1001.[114] Therefore, clause (2) of the anti-smurfing statute defines new criminal conduct in some omission fact patterns. In most cases, however, its impact is to impose another layer of liability to conduct already deemed criminal under other laws.[115]

In addition, like cl. (1), cl. (2) prohibits attempts to cause incomplete or false filings. This attempt language defines new criminal conduct.

Clause (3)

Clause (3)[116] defines an entirely new crime. Clause (3) makes it illegal to structure any transaction with one or more banks for the purpose of evading the reporting requirement. This clause addresses both problems the original bank reporting statute raised: customer liability and manipulation of transactions. Clause (3) establishes customer liability by imposing liability on anyone who assists or attempts to assist in structuring a transaction. Yet the crux of cl. (3) relates to manipulation; it closes the loopholes remaining under the revised regulations.

---

111. See 31 C.F.R. s. 103.49(d) (1988) "Any person who knowingly makes any false, fictitious or fraudulent statement or representation in any report required by this part may, upon conviction thereof, be fined not more than $10,000 or be imprisoned not more than five years, or both".
112. See 18 U.S.C. s. 1001 (1982) (discussed below, pp. 236-240, text accompanying notes 236-264).
113. Section 1001 prohibits concealment of material facts, but only by "trick, scheme or device"; *United States v. Woodward* 469 U.S. 105 (1985). Thus, if a report contains an omission, but the omission is not attributable to a trick, scheme, or device, the concealment would not fall under s. 1001. In this circumstance, cl. (2) of the anti-smurfing statute makes otherwise legal conduct criminal.
114. See *United States v. Puerto* 730 F.2d 627 at 633 (11th Cir.), cert. denied, 469 U.S. 847 (1984).
    The elements of s. 1001 in the false statement context have been summarised: "Proof of five elements is essential . . . under the false statement proscription of s. 1001: (1) a statement, (2) falsity, (3) materiality, (4) specific intent, and (5) agency jurisdiction." *United States v. Lange* 528 F.2d 1280 at 1287 (5th Cir. 1976). A false statement on a currency transaction report would satisfy all five elements. Congress intended this result and wrote a statute to insure it. See 31 U.S.C. s. 1052(k) (1976) (repealed 1982): "For the purposes of s. 1001 . . . the contents of reports required under any provision of this title are statements and representations in matters within the jurisdiction of an agency of the United States." This statute was later eliminated as unnecessary. See *United States v. Woodward* 406 U.S. 105 at 107, n. 6.
115. See below, pp. 236-240, text accompanying nn. 236-264.
116. 31 U.S.C. s. 5324 (Supp. IV 1986). "No person shall for the purpose of evading the reporting requirements of section 5313(a) with respect to such transaction— . . . (3) structure or assist in structuring, or attempt to structure or assist in structuring, any transaction with one or more domestic financial institutions." Aside from the basic crime of structuring, this clause also includes complicity and inchoate provisions.

As noted above, launderers have three methods available under the revised regulations to avoid aggregation and the duty to report.[117] Clause (3) covers each of these. First, the crime of structuring is not limited to transactions accomplished in a particular time period. Thus, transactions that would avoid aggregation under the regulations because $10,000 or less was transferred during one day would still qualify as structured transactions under cl. (3). Secondly, because the crime of structuring does not depend on the bank's knowledge, using multiple agents and multiple accounts to keep the bank in the dark on the total transactions would not defeat liability under cl. (3). Thirdly, the crime of structuring includes transactions accomplished at "one or more domestic financial institutions",[118] so conducting the transactions at multiple banks will not avoid liability. This clause is independent of the aggregation regulation, thus it prohibits all structuring regardless of whether the bank has a duty to file a report.

The mens rea required for the crime of structuring is two-tiered. Conviction of any crime under the reporting laws requires wilfulness.[119] In addition, the anti-smurfing statute requires that the defendant act for the purpose of evading the bank reporting law.[120] The combination of these two mens reas, each of which is rigorous alone, makes the mens rea element even more difficult to prove.[121]

The conduct element is defined less precisely. It is illegal to "structure" a "transaction". The regulations define the term "transaction in currency" as a physical transfer of currency.[122] The definition of "structure" is more complicated. The statute contains no explicit definition, and the popular definition is not helpful,[123] so legislative intent is relevant.[124] The legislative history reveals no explicit

117. See above, p. 212, text accompanying nn. 96-98.
118. 31 U.S.C. s. 5324(3) (Supp. IV 1986).
119. See 31 U.S.C. s. 5322 (1982 and Supp. IV 1986).
120. The statute begins: "No person shall *for the purpose of evading the reporting requirements of section 5313(a)*" 31 U.S.C. s. 5324 (emphasis added); see also *Hearings Before the House Committee on Banking, Finance and Urban Affairs* op. cit. at 846 (prepared statement of Assistant Attorney-General Stephen S. Trott) ("structuring" is present when transactions are broken up "in order not to trigger the report filing requirements").
121. The mens rea will be even more difficult to establish if the courts impose a requirement of knowledge of the law. See below, pp. 218-227, text accompanying nn. 135-81.
122. See 31 C.F.R. s. 103.11(o) (1988). " 'Transaction in currency'. A transaction involving the physical transfer of currency from one person to another."
123. See *Caminetti v. United States* 242 U.S. 470 (1917) (reliance on common meaning of statutory term). *Webster's New Collegiate Dictionary* (1981) p. 1146 defines the verb "to structure" as to form into "something arranged in a definite pattern of organisation." Another definition which might apply is provided for the noun "structure": "The aggregate of elements of an entity in their relationships to each other." Ibid. Neither definition is enlightening in this criminal context.
124. See *United States v. Culbert* 435 U.S. 371 (1978) (reliance on legislative intent in construing federal criminal statute); Justice Department Handbook on the Anti-Drug Abuse Act of 1986 (March 1987): "[Subs. (3)] is the only one . . . that presents any significant problems of interpretation because the statute does not define 'structuring.' This definitional problem is hardly insurmountable if care is taken in bringing cases that Congress clearly intended to be covered by this section."

congressional statement of intent concerning the meaning of the term "structure." But the legislative history does include an example of structuring,[125] and the testimony of the government drafters reveals what they intended by the term.[126] In the drafters' view, "structuring" is "breaking up a single currency transaction of more than $10,000 into separate smaller transactions in order not to trigger the [report] filing requirements".[127] This definition is bolstered by the courts' use of the term in this way in cases decided prior to the anti-smurfing statute.[128] These definitions render the conduct element precisely congruous with the mens rea requirement.

Defining a criminal offence based on the structure of one's finances suggests an analogy to tax law. If Joe can legitimately structure his finances to avoid paying taxes, is it not correspondingly legitimate to structure finances to avoid reporting cash transactions? The answer is no. The courts recognised that this analogy was faulty but failed to identify the reason.[129] The analogy fails because the two acts, structuring finances to avoid paying taxes and structuring finances to avoid filing reports, have different purposes. When he structures to avoid taxes, Joe saves money but still provides information to the government. In contrast, when Joe structures to avoid the bank reporting law, he denies the government information. The statutory use of the term "evade"

125. See S. Rep. No. 433, 99th Cong., 2d Sess., 22 (1986). The legislative history provides, in pertinent part:
   [A] person who converts $18,000 in currency to cashier's cheques by purchasing two $9,000 cashier's cheques at two different banks or on two different days with the specific intent that the participating bank or banks not be required to file [reports] for those transactions, would be subject to potential civil and criminal liability. A person conducting the same transactions for any other reasons or a person splitting up an amount of currency that would not be reportable if the full amount were involved in a single transaction (for example, splitting $2,000 in currency into four transactions of $500 each), would not be subject to liability under [clause] (3).
126. See *Hearing Before the Senate Committee on Banking, Housing and Urban Affairs* op. cit. at 66: "structured" currency transactions are "currency transactions which are intentionally broken down into a series of small transactions, each under $10,000, for the purpose of evading the reporting requirements of the *Bank Secrecy Act*". (prepared statement of Deputy Assistant Attorney-General James Knapp); *Hearings Before the House Committee on Banking, Finance and Urban Affairs* op. cit. at 846 (prepared statement of Assistant Attorney-General Stephen S. Trott): " 'Structuring' as used by the government in criminal prosecutions under Title 31 of the United States Code, consists of breaking up a single currency transaction of more than $10,000 into separate smaller transactions in order not to trigger the [report] filing requirements."
127. *Hearings Before the House Committee on Banking, Finance and Urban Affairs* op. cit. at 846 (prepared statement of Assistant Attorney-General Stephen S. Trott).
128. The verb "structuring" was first used in *United States v. Thompson* 603 F.2d 1200 at 1202 (5th Cir. 1979). Other courts also adopted the term. See *United States v. Giancola* 783 F.2d 1549 (11th Cir. 1986), cert. denied, 479 U.S. 1018 (1986); *United States v. Anzalone* 766 F.2d 676 (1st Cir. 1985); *United States v. Bank of New England* 640 F. Supp. 36 at 37 (D. Mass. 1986), affd, 821 F.2d 844 (1st Cir. 1987), cert. denied, 108 S. Ct. 328 (1987); *United States v. Cogswell* 637 F. Supp. 295 at 297 (N.D. Cal. 1985).
   The Senate Report acknowledges the common law definition by stating that the anti-smurfing statute is intended to "codify *Tobon-Builes* and like cases." S. Rep. No. 433, 99th Cong., 2d Sess., 22 (1986).
129. See e.g. *United States v. Thompson* 603 F.2d 1200 at 1203-1204.

rather than "avoid"[130] expresses the congressional conclusion that any reason to resist reporting is illegitimate and therefore an evasion. While one might legitimately avoid taxes,[131] there exists no concept of legitimate avoidance of the reporting requirement.[132]

The anti-smurfing statute is based implicitly on the judgment that resistance to reporting cash transactions is even more suspect than the large cash transactions themselves. This judgment is reasonable because no legitimate reason exists to resist reporting large cash transactions. The time it takes Joe to provide the bank with the information for the report is negligible,[133] and it will not cost him any money when the bank files a report.

Joe might object to the bank filing a report on the basis that the report invades his privacy, and that it is a scary situation indeed when the government is entitled to collect information (unrelated to taxes) on financial arrangements. Perhaps Joe is averse to the government knowing about his transactions. When balanced against the threat to society that the drug trade and money laundering pose, however, the threat to Joe's privacy is not compelling. The reduction in privacy is minimal. The United States has a tradition of protecting individual privacy from governmental interference, but in view of the documented dangers of drugs and laundering, laws that protect individual privacy at all costs have become a luxury. The anti-smurfing statute results in less than perfect individual privacy, but the harms of drugs and laundering warrant the minimal reduction. Congress in effect made this judgment when it defined structuring to evade the reporting law as a crime.

Beyond inconvenience and privacy, Joe may have another reason for resisting the reporting requirement. Joe may need to hide other criminal activity. This reason is patently illegitimate and is one the law should neither recognise nor endorse.[134]

Knowledge of illegality

The anti-smurfing statute applies only when the defendant acts for the purpose of evading the bank reporting requirement.[135] Assume Joe goes to the bank five days in a row and each day pays $9,000 in cash for a cashier's cheque. If Joe is unaware of the bank reporting law, he is not smurfing because he does not have the required motive to evade the bank reporting law. Joe is smurfing, however, if he is aware of the bank

---

130. The anti-smurfing statute begins, "No person shall for the purposes of *evading* the reporting requirements of section 5313(a)": 31 U.S.C. s. 5324 (Supp. IV 1986) (emphasis added).

131. On the concept of legitimate tax avoidance, see *Commissioner of Internal Revenue v. Newman* 159 F.2d 848 at 850-51 (2d Cir. 1947), cert. denied, 331 U.S. 859 (1947); *Helvering v. Gregory* 69 F.2d 809 at 810 (2d Cir. 1934), affd, 293 U.S. 465 (1935). See generally Rice, "Judicial Techniques in Combating Tax Avoidance" (1953) 51 Mich. L. Rev. 1021.

132. But cf. Villa, *Banking Crimes* (1988), s. 6.05[4][a].

133. The relevant form is Form 4789 (Currency Transaction Report).

134. For a discussion of the implications of the privilege against self-incrimination, see below, pp. 228-229, text accompanying nn. 190-99.

135. See 31 U.S.C. s. 5324 (Supp. IV 1986) (quoted above, n. 99).

reporting law and structures his transactions to avoid a report. A smurfing conviction is impossible unless the defendant knows of the bank reporting law.

A separate question is whether a smurfing conviction is possible without knowledge of the anti-smurfing law as well. What happens if Joe knows of the bank reporting law and structures his transactions to avoid reporting, but is unaware that such structuring is itself a crime? In other words, is knowledge of illegality an element of smurfing, thus making ignorance of the anti-smurfing law a defence?[136] Some defendants have recently asserted that ignorance of the law is in fact a defence.[137]

The express terms of the anti-smurfing statute do not require knowledge of the law,[138] so the question of whether knowledge of illegality is an element will be left to the courts.[139] In *United States v. Balint*[140] and *United States v. Freed*,[141] the statutes prohibited selling narcotics[142] and possessing unregistered hand grenades,[143] respectively. Because the materials regulated were physically dangerous,[144] the

136. Asking whether knowledge of illegality is an element of the crime is an alternative way of asking whether ignorance of the law is a defence. If knowledge of illegality is an element, then ignorance of the law is necessarily a defence; if knowledge is not an element, ignorance is not a defence. Either formulation raises the same issue, and this chapter uses the two formulations interchangeably.

137. See *Proposed Amendment to Bank Secrecy Act Regulations Providing for Notice to Customers of Anti-Structuring Provision by Financial Institutions* 53 Fed. Reg. 7948 (1988) (to be codified at 31 C.F.R. Pt. 103) (proposed 11 March 1988) (hereinafter *Proposed Amendment to Bank Secrecy Act Regulations*).

138. The conclusion that the express terms of the statute do not require knowledge of illegality assumes that the anti-smurfing statute's requirement of a purpose to evade the reporting requirement of s. 5313 does not include knowledge of illegality.

139. If a statute is silent or ambiguous, a court tries to discern congressional intent from other sources, like the legislative history. See *United States v. Balint* 258 U.S. 250 at 252 (1922) (mens rea of empty statute is "a question of legislative intent to be construed by the court"); see e.g. *United States v. Liparota* 471 U.S. 419 (1985) (looking to legislative history); *United States v. International Minerals & Chemical Corp.* 402 U.S. 558 (1971) (same). The legislative history of the anti-smurfing statute does not indicate whether Congress intended knowledge of the law to be an element. If the legislative history is unhelpful because it is silent (see e.g. *United States v. Freed* 401 U.S. 601 (1971); *Balint* 258 U.S. 250) or ambiguous (see e.g. *International Minerals & Chemical Corp.* 402 U.S. 558) a court falls back on common law principles to interpret the statute. See e.g. *Liparota* 471 U.S. 419 at 423-28.

140. 258 U.S. 250 (1922).

141. 401 U.S. 601 (1971).

142. *Balint* 258 U.S. 250 at 251.

143. *Freed* 401 U.S. 601 at 602-604.

144. In both cases, the court primarily based its refusal to require knowledge of illegality on the dangerous character of the regulated items. In *Balint*, the court stated: "Congress weighed the possible injustice of subjecting an innocent seller to a penalty against the evil of exposing innocent purchasers to danger from the drug, and concluded that the latter was the result preferably to be avoided"; *Balint* 258 U.S. 250 at 254. In *Freed*, the court stated: "[Hand grenades] are highly dangerous offensive weapons, no less dangerous than the narcotics involved in [*Balint*]"; *Freed* 401 U.S. 601 at 609. However, the court also mentioned other factors indicating that knowledge of illegality should not be an element. In *Balint*, the Court referred (at 254) to the likelihood of the defendant's knowledge and the difficulty of proof. In *Freed*, the court referred to the likelihood of the defendant's knowledge. See *Freed* 401 U.S. 601 at 609 (the statute "may well be premised on the theory that one would hardly be surprised to learn that possession of hand grenades is not an innocent act") (footnote omitted).

Supreme Court declined to infer knowledge of illegality as an element
and thus concluded that ignorance of the law was no defence.[145]
Likewise, in *United States v. International Minerals & Chemical
Corp.*,[146] the court concluded that knowledge of the statute prohibiting
shipping acid without proper documentation was not an element of the
crime.[147] The *International Minerals* court reasoned that the maxim
that ignorance of the law is no excuse was so ensconced in our criminal
law that it trumps ambiguous congressional statements.[148] Moreover,
because acid is inherently dangerous, the probability of regulation was
so great that knowledge of the law could be presumed.[149] The court's
mention of the second basis undermines the first, and indicates the
court's ambivalence toward the maxim that ignorance of the law is no
excuse.

The ambivalence culminated in *United States v. Liparota*,[150] in which
the court held that ignorance of the law was a defence to the crime of
unauthorised acquisition of food stamps.[151] The anti-smurfing statute is
more analogous to the statute construed in *Liparota* than those in *Balint*
and *Freed* because the items the statutes regulate in the former,
structured cash transactions and unauthorised food stamps, pose no
physical danger. Many of the bases for the *Liparota* decision also apply
to the anti-smurfing statute. The *Liparota* court did not rely on
congressional intent in construing the food stamp statute because it
characterised the statutory language as ambiguous and the legislative
history as silent.[152] Likewise, the language and legislative history of the

---

145. *United States v. Balint* 258 U.S. 250 at 251. The language of *Balint* is ambiguous as
to whether the issue was ignorance of law or fact. The indictment charged the
defendants with unlawfully selling opium and coca leaves not on the written order
form required by statute. The court stated: "The defendants demurred to the
indictment on the ground that it failed to charge that they had sold the inhibited drugs
knowing them to be such." Did the defendants not know that the substances were
drugs, or did they not know that the substances were inhibited? At 254, the court
stated that the purpose of the statute was to penalise those who sold the inhibited
drug "in ignorance of its character." Does this mean in ignorance of its character as
opium, or in ignorance of its character as illegal? *Balint* does not adequately resolve
this confusion, but in a later case, the court clarified the matter by characterising the
issue in *Balint* as a question of ignorance of law. See *Freed* 401 U.S. 601 at 609.
146. 402 U.S. 558 (1971).
147. 402 U.S. 558 at 563-64. The statute provided that whoever "knowingly violates any
such regulation" would be fined or imprisoned. 402 U.S. 558 at 559 (quoting 18
U.S.C. s. 834(f) (1970)).
148. 402 U.S. 558 at 563 ("We conclude that the meagre legislative history of the 1960
amendments makes unwarranted the conclusion that Congress abandoned the
general rule and required knowledge of both the facts and the pertinent law before
a criminal conviction could be sustained"). But cf. 402 U.S. 558 at 565-569 (Stewart J.,
dissenting) (describing the "explicit legislative history").
149. 402 U.S. 558 at 565.
150. 471 U.S. 419 (1985).
151. 471 U.S. 419 at 433-34.
152. 471 U.S. 419 at 424-426, 430, n. 13.
     The *Liparota* court also stated that a background assumption of our criminal law
is that criminal offences require a mens rea and Congress's silence or ambiguous
statements in the food stamp statute are insufficient to signal a departure from this
tenet. 471 U.S. 419 at 426. This rationale is disingenuous. Surely our criminal law
assumes that a mens rea is required, but that mens rea has traditionally extended only
to knowledge of facts, not law. Cf. *Model Penal Code* s. 2.04(1)(a) and commentary

anti-smurfing statute both are silent on knowledge of illegality. The *Liparota* court applied the rule of lenity[153] and concluded that because the ambit of the statute was unclear, the defendant should get the benefit.[154] Because the coverage of the anti-smurfing statute is unclear in the same way as the statute at issue in *Liparota*, the rule of lenity would have the same impact on the anti-smurfing statute. Thus *Liparota* would likely control the courts' interpretation of the anti-smurfing statute.

Yet one of the rationales of *Liparota* has questionable impact on the anti-smurfing statute. The *Liparota* court held that requiring knowledge of illegality was appropriate in order to avoid criminalising a broad range of innocent conduct.[155] Applying this reasoning to the anti-smurfing statute, can structuring cash transactions to avoid a reporting law be characterised as innocent conduct?

Structuring cash transactions to avoid reporting might be construed as innocent. One reason is that people may feel that their experience with tax law informs them that structuring cash transactions is acceptable conduct. Although the tax law analogy is defective for reasons discussed above,[156] courts should not expect this level of analysis from the typical bank customer. Another reason that structuring cash transactions might be innocent conduct is that the United States historically has protected individual privacy from governmental intrusion. Arranging cash transactions to avoid a report to the government would strike many people as acceptable conduct, or at least non-criminal. At any rate, structuring cash transactions seems as likely to be deemed "innocent" as the conduct in *Liparota*, in which the defendant furtively bought food stamps that were stamped "non-transferable" at a substantial discount.[157]

On the other hand, structuring cash transactions to avoid reporting to the government arguably is not innocent. To treat smurfing as innocent requires a narrow definition of innocence, one related only to the

152. *continued*
    at 269-271 (1985) (ignorance of fact or law is a defence if it negates the mens rea required for the crime) with *Model Penal Code* s. 2.02(9) and commentary at 248 (mens rea as to illegality of conduct is generally not required). See also Note, "Ignorance of the Law as an Excuse" (1986) 86 Columbia L. Rev. 1392 at 1399-1400 (discussing whether *Liparota* creates a defence of mistake of criminal law). The *Liparota* court cited *United States v. Morisette* 342 U.S. 246 (1952), for the principle that a mens rea is required. *Liparota* 471 U.S. 419 at 425-426. But the mens rea required in *Morisette* extended to knowledge of facts (whether the bomb casings were owned or abandoned), not to knowledge of law (whether stealing was a crime). See *Morisette* 342 U.S. 246 at 276. Thus *Morisette* is no precedent for *Liparota*. Finally, it is ironic that *Liparota* characterised the mens rea of knowledge of illegality as a "background assumption of our criminal law", *Liparota* 471 U.S. at 426, when just 14 years earlier the court emphasised "the general rule that ignorance of the law is no excuse"; *United States v. International Minerals & Chemical Corp.* 402 U.S. 558 at 563 (1971).
153. *Liparota* 471 U.S. 419 at 427.
154. Ibid. (quoting *Rewis v. United States* 401 U.S. 808 at 812 (1971)).
155. *Liparota* 471 U.S. 419 at 425-426.
156. See above, pp. 217-218, text accompanying nn. 129-31 (tax analogy).
157. *Liparota* 471 U.S. 419 at 434 n. 17; see Note, "Ignorance of the Law as an Excuse", op. cit. at 1415, n. 122.

defendant's ignorance of this particular statute. Smurfs know of the bank
reporting law and purposely evade it. As noted above, the only reason
to avoid the reporting law is to hide other crime. Smurfing cannot be
isolated from the laundering process, nor can it be isolated from the
underlying crime that generates the cash. To define smurfing as innocent
conduct demands both that we ignore the impetus for smurfing and adopt
a compartmentalised definition of innocence. The law need not be limited
to a fictional, counterintuitive definition of innocence. Smurfs are not
necessarily innocent, even if they are unaware of the anti-smurfing statute.

The implications of *Liparota* for the anti-smurfing statute are
mixed. [158] Other factors are relevant in analysing whether ignorance of

158. One other case is helpful in understanding the court's approach to ignorance of the
law as a defence. In *Lambert v. California* 355 U.S. 225 (1957), a municipal ordinance
required all convicted felons living in Los Angeles to register with the city: 355 U.S.
225 at 226. The ordinance was silent on knowledge of illegality and the Court
mentioned no legislative history: 355 U.S. 225 at 227-230. The court (at 227) held that
ignorance of the law was a defence and that due process requires notice that conduct
is criminal. Because this ordinance criminalised mere unregistered presence in a city,
due process precluded conviction unless the prosecution showed knowledge of
illegality or the probability of knowledge: 355 U.S. 225 at 229-230.
  Lambert differs from *Balint, Freed, International Minerals & Chemical Corp.*, and
Liparota in two ways. First, the court based its decision on the due process clause
of the Constitution rather than on canons of statutory construction. Of course,
because the case involved a Los Angeles ordinance rather than a federal statute, the
court had to base its decision on the Constitution in order to take jurisdiction; at 266.
Even so, the decision reveals the court's willingness to find that knowledge of
illegality is constitutionally mandated; the decision is important for that reason.
  Lambert also differs from the four cases discussed above because the ordinance in
Lambert criminalised pure omission to act while the other statutes depended on some
element of positive conduct. In *Balint*, the conduct was selling opium and coca leaves
without an I.R.S. form; *United States v. Balint* 258 U.S. 250 at 251 (1922). In *Freed*,
the conduct was receiving unregistered hand grenades; *United States v. Freed* 401
U.S. 601 at 603 (1971). In *International Minerals & Chemical Corp.*, the conduct was
shipping acid without reflecting it on shipping papers; *United States v. International
Minerals & Chemical Corp.* 402 U.S. 558 (1971). In *Liparota*, the conduct was
purchasing food stamps at less than face value; *Liparota* 471 U.S. at 421-422.
  Yet *Balint, Freed* and *I.M.C.* arguably can be characterised as omission cases as
well. In *Balint*, defendants omitted to use the prescribed I.R.S. form; in *Freed*, the
defendant omitted to receive registration papers with the grenades; and in *I.M.C.* the
defendant omitted to list the acid on the shipping papers. These three cases can thus
be characterised as omission cases due to the lack of forms in each case. Even under
this view, they still differ from the *Lambert* ordinance. The *Lambert* ordinance
proscribed unregistered existence in Los Angeles and therefore included no element
of positive conduct at all. As the Supreme Court stated: "Registration laws are
common and their range is wide. But the [*Lambert*] ordinance is entirely different.
Violation of its provisions is unaccompanied by any activity whatever, mere presence
in the city being the test"; *Lambert* 355 U.S. at 229.
  One other line of cases holding ignorance of law to be a defence deserves mention.
Under 31 U.S.C. s. 5316 (1982 and Supp. IV 1986), persons importing or exporting
$10,000 in monetary instruments must file a report with the government. All courts
confronting the issue have concluded that knowledge of the import/export reporting
law is required before the defendant can be convicted of violating it. See e.g. *United
States v. Eisenstein* 731 F.2d 1540 at 1543 (11th Cir. 1984); *United States v. Warren*
612 F.2d 887 at 889 (5th Cir. 1980); *United States v. Dichne* 612 F.2d 632 at 636
(2d Cir. 1979); *United States v. Chen* 605 F.2d 433 at 435-36 (9th Cir. 1979); *United
States v. Schnaiderman* 568 F.2d 1208 at 1210-12 (5th Cir. 1978); *United States v.
Granada* 565 F.2d 922 at 925-27 (5th Cir. 1978). Some courts reached this conclusion

the law should be a defence to the anti-smurfing statute. Inferring knowledge of illegality can be helpful to limit arbitrary enforcement.[159] If a statute is written broadly so that many violate it, the police freely may pursue the most blameworthy violators. Yet wide application allows police so much discretion that they may decide whom to arrest based on factors besides the violation of a statute.[160] If a statute encourages arbitrary enforcement, then ignorance should be a defence. It would ensure that the law apply only to blameworthy people, and would limit police discretion by narrowing the wide net that such a law creates.[161]

The anti-smurfing statute, however, does not encourage arbitrary enforcement. The statutory language defining the conduct of smurfing (to structure a transaction) is broad, but the mens rea requires a purposeful evasion of the bank reporting law.[162] This mens rea limits the number of persons who violate the anti-smurfing statute and limits police discretion as well.

Another relevant question in determining whether ignorance should be a defence is the likelihood that the defendant had notice that the conduct was illegal.[163] If nothing in the situation a statute addresses would alert a person to possible illegality, then ignorance should be a

158. *continued*

based on the statutory language. See e.g. *Schnaiderman* 568 F.2d 1208 at 1211. But the statutory language is unclear; even more so than statutory language the Supreme Court has found ambiguous in the past. See above, p. 220, nn. 146-149 and accompanying text (statute which requires "knowing violation" is ambiguous). Thus the courts relying on the language fail to explain their decisions adequately. The better opinions recognise that knowledge of illegality should be inferred as an element because the statute criminalises omission to report otherwise innocent conduct. See e.g. *Warren* 612 F.2d 887 at 891; *Dichne* 612 F.2d 632 at 636.

These cases construing the import/export reporting law have some predictive value for the courts' response to the anti-smurfing statute. The cases holding that knowledge of illegality is an element based on the statutory language are disingenuous and should be discounted. But if courts applied the language rationale to the anti-' smurfing statute, they would probably conclude that its language requires knowledge of illegality. That conviction requires both a wilful violation and that the defendant act for the purpose of evading the reporting law would support this conclusion. In this way, these import/export cases indicate that knowledge of illegality will be an element of the anti-smurfing statute.

The rationale mentioned in some import/export cases, namely that knowledge of illegality is required because the statute criminalises omission to report otherwise innocent conduct, does not apply to the anti-smurfing statute. Smurfing is not based on an omission to report something, but rather on the positive conduct of structuring a cash transaction. Thus, the omission concept is irrelevant. Moreover, as discussed above, smurfing is not really such innocent conduct that defendants would have no notice that the conduct is criminal. Smurfing is not analogous to the import/export reporting law, and the cases finding knowledge of illegality required for the latter would have little value for predicting whether courts will require such knowledge for smurfing.

159. See Note, "Ignorance of the Law as an Excuse", op. cit. at 1402-1403.
160. Ibid. at 1398.
161. Ibid. at 1408; see also ibid. at 1398 (drawbacks of unbridled police discretion).
162. Of course, this conclusion depends somewhat on what is required to show purpose to evade the reporting law.
163. See *United States v. Freed* 401 U.S. 601 at 609 (1971) (quoted above, n. 144); see also Note, "Ignorance of the Law as an Excuse", op. cit. at 1413 (courts should consider, among other factors, the likelihood that defendant had notice of the law).

defence.[164] Several factors illuminate the likelihood of notice. If the proscribed conduct is malum in se because it involves possible physical harm[165] or has moral overtones,[166] then the likelihood of notice is high.[167] Smurfing involves no phyiscal harm. As for moral overtones, smurfing is not as obviously immoral as fraud or statutory rape, but an effort to avoid the bank reporting law is not morally pure either. Smurfing arises only in the wake of an effort to evade another law. Although smurfing is morally ambiguous, Joe's intuition about criminal law should cause him at least to question its legality.

Other circumstances are relevant to the likelihood of the defendant's notice. One factor is how pervasively the field is regulated.[168] Defendants generally have knowledge of the law if they deal with a highly regulated substance like alcohol.[169] Regulation of cash transactions is not as pervasive. No State laws regulate cash transactions, and the only relevent federal laws are the ones this chapter describes.[170] Nonetheless, a smurf by definition knows of the bank reporting law, although he may be ignorant of the anti-smurfing laws. Because smurfs are aware of at least one law regulating cash transactions, the relatively limited extent of regulation does not indicate that smurfs' knowledge of the anti-smurfing law is less likely.

The specialised nature of smurfing also bears on the likelihood of the defendant's knowledge.[171] A person dealing in an unusual substance like dangerous chemicals or toxic waste is more likely familiar with the law than a person dealing in pencils, dental floss, or paperclips.[172] Cash transactions are not specialised activities, although extremely large transactions subdivided into smaller increments are more unusual. Even so, the basic commodity of the anti-smurfing law is cash transactions, which are difficult to put in the specialised category with acid and toxic waste.[173]

Some factors affecting the likelihood of notice are unique to the anti-smurfing statute. Assume Joe sets out to convert $500,000 in cash into

164. Note, "Ignorance of the Law as an Excuse", op. cit. at 1413-1414. See generally Lambert v. California 355 U.S. 225 (1957) (ignorance of ordinance requiring all convicted felons to register with the city was a valid defence because due process requires notice that the conduct is criminal); above, n. 158 (discussion of Lambert v. California).
165. One example might be possession of hand grenades. See Freed 401 U.S. 601 at 603.
166. An example might be distribution of misbranded and adulterated drugs. See United States v. Dotterweich 320 U.S. 277 (1943).
167. Note, "Ignorance of the Law as an Excuse", op. cit. at 1414.
168. Ibid.
169. Compare Colonnade Catering Corp. v. United States 397 U.S. 72 at 76-77 (1970) (defendants in effect consent to government inspection by engaging in pervasively regulated industry).
170. Those laws include three reporting statutes (the bank reporting law, 31 U.S.C. ss 5311-5314 (1982 and Supp. IV 1986), and the two described below, p. 233, text accompanying nn. 213-214); the anti-smurfing statute, 31 U.S.C. s. 5324 (Supp. IV 1986); and 18 U.S.C. s. 1957 (Supp. IV 1986) (described below, p. 234, text accompanying nn. 221-222).
171. Note, "Ignorance of the Law as an Excuse", op. cit. at 1414.
172. See United States v. International Minerals & Chemical Corp. 402 U.S. 558 at 564-565 (1971).
173. See ibid.

cashier's cheques. Joe learns that the law requires banks to report cash transactions over $10,000 to the government, and he learns that reports can be avoided by simply keeping each transaction under $10,000. As a practical matter, Joe should question whether such easy evasion is too good to be true. The obviousness of the loophole should cause Joe to question its legitimacy, and alert him that he is acting in an area of questionable legality. Moreover, the Treasury Department is considering specific measures to provide notice of the law to bank customers.[174] If any of these proposals is implemented, the likelihood that Joe will have knowledge of the law will be high.

The final issue in analysing whether ignorance of the law should be a defence is whether ignorance of the law is itself blameworthy.[175] If a reasonable person would be on notice of the possibility of criminal liability, then that person should investigate; continuing ignorance of the law is blameworthy in that situation.[176] With regard to the anti-smurfing statute, the blameworthiness of ignorance is fairly clear. Smurfing is morally ambiguous enough that a defendant might not be certain the conduct is criminal. Yet the factors discussed above relating to the likelihood of knowledge indicate that smurfs should be alerted at least to the potential of liability. Once on notice of potential liability, smurfs reasonably may be expected to investigate the law. Smurfs know they are evading the reporting law. They obviously have researched the scope of the law, and know how to avoid it. Because smurfs are sophisticated enough to investigate the bank reporting law, it is reasonable to impose on them a duty to investigate related laws. If smurfs remain ignorant of the anti-smurfing statute, their ignorance is blameworthy and should not be a defence.

In summary, various factors indicate that ignorance of the law should not be a defence to the anti-smurfing statute. Admittedly, dealing in cash transactions is not a specialised activity. Structuring finances to avoid reporting to the government may seem acceptable in view of the tax avoidance analogy and the American tradition of privacy. Nevertheless, an ignorance defence is unnecessary to limit arbitrary enforcement. The likelihood is high that smurfs have notice that their conduct is questionable. Smurfs know of the bank reporting law, so they are aware that laws exist regulating cash transactions. Their effort to evade the bank reporting law also has moral overtones; it only can be deemed innocent by adopting an extremely narrow definition of innocence. Practically, evasion of the bank reporting law is so easy, a smurf should wonder whether it is too good to be true. Once on notice that smurfing may be questionable, continuing ignorance of the law is blameworthy because smurfs have a duty to research the law as they did when they investigated the bank reporting law.

174. See Proposed Amendment to Bank Secrecy Act Regulations, above, n. 137.
175. See Note, "Ignorance of the Law as an Excuse", op. cit. at 1413. This issue is related to the second, namely whether the defendant would have had notice of illegality. See ibid. at 1413-1414.
176. Ibid. This criterion echoes the "wilful blindness" doctrine courts developed to deal with knowledge as a mens rea. See e.g. *United States v. Jewell* 532 F.2d 697 (9th Cir. 1976) (en banc), cert. denied, 426 U.S. 951 (1976).

On balance, ignorance of the anti-smurfing law should not be a defence to smurfing. Nonetheless, excessively cautious courts may establish it as a defence.[177] The innocence and immorality of smurfing are ambiguous, and *Liparota*, although a bad decision, indicates that the Supreme Court is receptive to the defence. At a minimum, courts may fall back on the rule of lenity to establish ignorance as a defence. If the courts infer knowledge of illegality as an element of the offence, they should not require actual knowledge. Rather, the government should be able to establish mens rea by showing that the defendant should have known the law. This latter option, really a mens rea of negligence, is preferable to actual knowledge.[178] The Court has suggested that this alternative is constitutionally acceptable.[179] More importantly, requiring proof of actual knowledge would exceed the legitimate boundaries of ignorance as a defence. As discussed above, Joe has good reason to be on notice that smurfing is questionable, thus he should have a duty to investigate the law. In this context, Joe's lack of actual knowledge is due only to his negligence.[180] Joe should not be allowed to assert his own negligence as a defence. And, as a practical matter, requiring the government to prove

177. If the courts decide to allow ignorance of the law as a defence to smurfing, they would likely do so based on principles of statutory construction rather than constitutional grounds. *Lambert* revealed the Supreme Court's willingness to rely on the due process clause to establish ignorance of the law as a defence. See above, n. 158; see also *United States v. International Minerals & Chemical Corp.* 402 U.S. 558 at 564-565 (1971) ("Pencils, dental floss, paperclips may also be regulated. But they may be the type of products which might raise substantial due process questions if Congress did not require . . . 'mens rea' as to each ingredient of the offence."). Nonetheless, the court is unlikely to choose that approach for the anti-smurfing statute for several reasons. First, the ordinance in *Lambert* is distinguishable from the anti-smurfing statute because the former criminalised an omission to act while the latter criminalises only the positive conduct of structuring cash transactions. Because of this difference, the anti-smurfing statute does not entail the same danger of lack of notice the court found critical in *Lambert*.

Another indication that the court would rely on statutory construction to establish ignorance of the law as a defence is the court's use of that approach in *Liparota*. *Liparota* was explicitly decided on statutory rather than constitutional grounds. See *United States v. Liparota* 471 U.S. at 419 at 431-432 (1985). As described above, the *Liparota* statute is most analogous to the anti-smurfing statute. See above, pp. 220-221, nn. 150-154 and accompanying text. Finally, the court will likely rely on statutory construction because it avoids constitutional questions whenever possible. Using statutory construction, the court has alternative grounds to reach the same result. Although commentators have criticised the use of statutory construction to establish ignorance of the law as a defence (see Note, "Ignorance of the Law as an Excuse", op. cit. at 1401-1403) it is the approach the court likely will take.

178. See ibid. at 1414-1416.

179. In *Lambert v. California* 355 U.S. 225 (1957), the court implied that a showing that knowledge of illegality is probable satisfies the Constitution. "Where a person did not know of the duty to register and where there was no proof of the probability of such knowledge, he may not be convicted consistently with due process"; ibid. at 229-230. Whether the Constitution would likewise be satisfied by a showing that the defendant should have known the law is a slightly different question. If the Constitution allows punishment of a person who "probably knew", it should as well allow punishment of a person who "should have known".

180. Compare *United States v. Jewell* 532 F.2d 697 (9th Cir. 1976) (en banc) (wilful blindness), cert. denied, 426 U.S. 951 (1976). See generally Note, "Ignorance of the Law as an Excuse", op. cit. at 1415-1416 (discussing why a purely subjective standard is undesirable).

actual knowledge of the law would make prosecution for smurfing impossible in most cases.[181]

The mens rea of negligence is a compromise between the alternatives that knowledge of illegality is irrelevant and that knowledge of illegality must be actual. Once the Treasury Department implements measures ensuring that bank customers are informed of the anti-smurfing law, the combination of these measures with the "should have known" standard for knowledge of illegality will eliminate the defence of ignorance of the law.

Constitutionality

The Fourth Amendment

In *California Bankers Association v. Shultz*,[182] plaintiff banks and depositors challenged the constitutionality of the bank reporting law under the Fourth Amendment.[183] The Supreme Court held that the statute did not violate the bank's Fourth Amendment rights, but the court did not decide the issue as to depositors because it concluded that the depositors lacked standing to challenge the statute.[184] In a concurring opinion, Powell J. expressed the view that the reporting law was constitutional, but stated that "[a] significant extension of the regulations' reporting requirements . . . would pose substantial and difficult constitutional questions . . . At some point, governmental intrusion upon these areas would implicate legitimate expectations of privacy."[185] Is the anti-smurfing statute the "significant extension" to which Justice Powell referred?

Under current law, the anti-smurfing statute does not violate the Fourth Amendment. In *United States v. Miller*,[186] the Supreme Court held that a bank customer suffers no search or seizure when bank records are turned over to the government. The statute breaches no legitimate expectations of privacy because the customer voluntarily conveys the information to the bank and assumes the risk that the bank will turn the information over to the government. Relying heavily on *Miller*, lower courts all have concluded that the bank reporting law does not violate bank customers' Fourth Amendment rights.[187] Although the Court's

---

181. See Proposed Amendment to Bank Secrecy Regulations, above, n. 137, at 7948 ("[The] problem of establishing knowledge is presenting difficulties for investigators and prosecutors and is threatening to undermine Treasury's ability to assure compliance with [the anti-smurfing statute]."). See generally Note, "Ignorance of the Law as an Excuse", op. cit. at 1415-1416 (describing reasons mens rea should not be limited to actual knowledge).
182. 416 U.S. 21 (1974).
183. 416 U.S. 21 at 59.
184. 416 U.S. 21 at 67-69.
185. 416 U.S. 21 at 78-79, per Powell J. concurring.
186. 425 U.S. 435 (1976).
187. See *United States v. Kaatz* 705 F.2d 1237 at 1242 (10th Cir. 1983); *United States v. Richter* 610 F. Supp. 480 at 492-93 (N.D. Ill. 1985), affd sub nom. *United States v. Mangovski* 785 F.2d 312 (7th Cir. 1986), cert. denied, 479 U.S. 855 (1988); *United States v. Sanchez Vazquez* 585 F. Supp. 990 at 995 (N.D. Ga. 1984).

rationale in *Miller* is disingenuous and deserves reconsideration,[188] this chapter is not the place. Given the current state of Fourth Amendment jurisprudence, the anti-smurfing statute does not extend the reporting law so dramatically as to conflict with the Fourth Amendment.[189]

The privilege against self-incrimination

Assume that Joe has $450,000 in $20 bills he wants to send secretly and safely to an offshore tax haven. Prior to adoption of the anti-smurfing statute, Joe had two options. He could get one cashier's cheque and let the bank report the transaction or he could get fifty $9,000 cashier's cheques at different banks and avoid a report. The anti-smurfing statute eliminates the latter option by defining it as a crime.[190] Arguably, the anti-smurfing statute creates a dilemma and subtly coerces Joe into choosing the option the government prefers—self-reporting his suspicious activities. The Supreme Court has acknowledged that an odious choice may constitute compulsion for purposes of the privilege against self-incrimination.[191]

Even assuming a compelling effect, however, the anti-smurfing statute does not violate the privilege against self-incrimination because the courts have concluded that reports filed under the bank reporting law are not incriminating. The Supreme Court has yet to rule on this issue,[192] but the lower courts have found no incrimination because the reporting

188. See generally LaFave and Israel, *Criminal Procedure* (1985), p. 107 (*Miller* is "highly questionable" since customer expects bank documents will remain private); Whitebread and Slobogin, *Criminal Procedure: An Analysis of Cases and Concepts* (2nd ed., 1986), pp. 113-114 (the "assumption of risk" rationale of *Miller* is "particularly questionable" in light of necessity of using banking systems).

189. Smurfing rarely will occur in conjunction with a search or seizure. If a customer successfully structures transactions so that no report is filed, no search is made because no expectation of privacy (reasonable or otherwise) was invaded; the government and the customer made no contact. See *Richter* 610 F. Supp. 480 at 492: "If we assume the truth of the facts in the indictment, we find that the defendants managed to deposit their money without triggering the Act's reporting requirements. Thus, no search or seizure actually happened in this case. The defendants successfully *avoided* a search and are being prosecuted for doing so." If, on the other hand, the customer does not structure transactions and the bank files a report, government contact is present and arguably an expectation of privacy is breached, but there is no crime because the customer did not structure transactions. Thus, while arguably there was a search, there will be no prosecution. In that situation, the existence of a search is wholly without criminal consequences. The final fact pattern involves a defendant who tries to structure transactions to evade the reporting law but fails, so the bank files a report. In this situation, the defendant has committed the crime of attempted structuring. The bank files a report, so arguably there is a search. This last pattern is the only one likely to include both a crime and a search, so in only limited circumstances would the question even arise.

190. See 31 U.S.C. s. 5324 (Supp. IV 1986); cf. *United States v. San Juan* 405 F. Supp. 686 at 694 (D. Vt. 1975) (one factor lessening the danger of self-incrimination in the import/export law is the option of avoiding reporting requirements by arranging to carry less than $5,000 at each border crossing).

191. See *South Dakota v. Neville* 459 U.S. 553 at 563-565 (1983).

192. In *California Bankers' Assoc. v. Schultz* 416 U.S. 21 at 75 (1974), the court declined to rule because the plaintiff depositors' claims were premature.

requirement is not targeted at an inherently suspect group,[193] and because no direct nexus exists between the disclosure and potential criminal activity.[194] This definition of incrimination is extremely narrow. It contradicts Congress's express statement[195] and implicit assumptions[196] about large cash transactions. Filing a report brings Joe to the government's attention as a target for criminal investigation, and necessarily exposes him to an increased risk of prosecution.[197] A critique of the courts' definition of incrimination is beyond the scope of this chapter and is available elsewhere.[198] Given the current law, however, the anti-smurfing statute does not violate the privilege against self-incrimination regardless of its compelling effect because the information in the reports has been deemed not incriminating.[199]

Due process

Clause (3) defines a new crime of structuring transactions to evade the reporting requirement. One might challenge cl. (3) as void for vagueness[200] based on the verb describing the actual criminal act, "structure". Such a challenge seems initially strong because the term is not statutorily defined, no popular definition of the term exists, and Congress provided no explicit statement of its intent regarding the term.[201] Nonetheless, the Senate Report includes an example of

193. *United States v. Sanchez Vazquez* 585 F. Supp. 990 at 996 (N.D. Ga. 1984); cf. *United States v. Dichne* 612 F.2d 632 at 639-640 (2d Cir. 1979) (import/export reporting law does not target inherently suspect group); *San Juan* 405 F. Supp. 686 at 692 (same). In these cases, the courts explained that the import/export law applied to all foreign travellers rather than a particular suspect group. In contrast, laws which have been determined to target suspect groups include laws applying to Communists, marijuana dealers, and gamblers. See *Leary v. United States* 395 U.S. 6 (1969); *Grosso v. United States* 390 U.S. 62 (1968); *Albertson v. Subversive Activities Control Board* 382 U.S. 70 (1965).

194. *United States v. Sanchez Vazquez* 585 F. Supp. 990 at 996; cf. *United States v. Dichne* 612 F.2d 632 at 640 (import/export reporting law has no direct link to related criminal activity); *United States v. Richter* 610 F. Supp. 480 at 491-492 (N.D. Ill. 1985) (no standing to assert violation of privilege against self-incrimination), affd sub nom. *United States v. Mangovski* 785 F.2d 312 (7th Cir. 1986), cert. denied, 479 U.S. 855 (1988); *San Juan* 405 F. Supp. 686 at 693 (same).

195. See above, p. 204, nn. 33-34 and accompanying text.

196. See *Briefing on the 1970 Currency and Foreign Transactions Reporting Act: Hearing Before the House Committee on Banking, Finance and Urban Affairs* 99th Cong., 1st Sess. 51-52 (1985) (comments of Congressman McKinney: "What legitimate business in the United States of America today transfers money in cash?")

197. See *United States v. San Juan* 405 F. Supp. 686 at 693 (D. Vt. 1975). *San Juan* dealt with the import/export reporting law, but the impact of filing a report with the government is the same for the import/export law and the bank reporting law.

198. See Comment, " 'Hollow Ritual[s]': The Fifth Amendment and Self Reporting Schemes" (1986) 34 U.C.L.A. L. Rev. 467. See generally Whitebread and Slobogin, op. cit. at 340-343.

199. This conclusion assumes that it is not just the information in the reports that is arguably incriminating, but also the identification as one to whom the law applies. Thus, the self-incrimination claim should not depend on its assertion on the report form itself. See Comment, " 'Hollow Ritual[s]': The Fifth Amendment and Self Reporting Schemes", op. cit. at 479 n. 54. See generally ibid. at 478-480 (comparing cases involving registration forms for Communist Party membership and for income tax on income gained illegally).

200. See *Grayned v. City of Rockford* 408 U.S. 104 at 108 (1972); *United States v. Harriss* 347 U.S. 612 at 617 (1954); *Winters v. New York* 333 U.S. 507 at 518 (1948).

201. See above, pp. 216-217, text accompanying nn. 124-25.

structuring, and the drafters' congressional testimony reveals what they meant by the term.[202] Thus the legislative history provides some meaning to the word "structure". Even more fatal to a vagueness challenge is the fact that "structure" developed a common law meaning before the anti-smurfing statute was born.[203] When a federal statute employs a common law term without defining it, the term retains its common law meaning.[204] Thus one may rely on all the cases concerning "structuring" decided under the basic reporting law when interpreting the anti-smurfing statute. These cases clearly indicate what conduct is criminal.[205] Considered together, these sources provide a sufficiently clear definition of "structure" to satisfy due process.[206]

In summary, the anti-smurfing statute should pass constitutional muster. This result may be attributable in part to dubious definitions of "search" and "incrimination". Assuming no change in these definitions, the anti-smurfing statute plainly is constitutional.

The Unit of Prosecution

Until now the analysis has focused on the point at which Joe's behaviour triggers the anti-smurfing statute. A different question concerns the point at which Joe goes from violating the statute once to twice or more. What is the unit of prosecution for the anti-smurfing statute? Under clauses (1) and (2), which prohibit causing or attempting to cause a bank to fail to file or to file a faulty report, the unit of prosecution is clear. Each time the bank files a bad report or fails to file a required report constitutes one unit of prosecution.[207] Likewise, each time a customer attempts to cause such a result is one unit of prosecution.[208]

202. See above, p. 217, nn. 125-26 (quoting legislative history and congressional testimony regarding the meaning of "structuring").
203. See above, n. 128.
204. *United States v. Turley* 352 U.S. 407 at 411 (1957).
205. See generally *Connally v. General Construction Co.* 269 U.S. 385 at 391-92 (1926) (statute is sufficiently certain if it "employs words or phrases having . . . a well-settled common law meaning").
206. The mens rea element bolsters, in two ways, the conclusion that the anti-smurfing statute is not void for vagueness. First, the anti-smurfing statute requires that the defendant act "for the purpose of evading the reporting requirement." The specificity of this mens rea helps offset an arguably obscure actus reus. See *Screws v. United States* 325 U.S. 91 at 101-102 (1945). Second, knowledge of illegality may be inferred as an element of smurfing. See above, text accompanying nn. 135-81, pp. 218-227. This additional mens rea element will similarly contribute to dispel any vagueness. See *Boyce Motor Lines v. United States* 342 U.S. 337 at 339 (1952) (regulation requiring drivers of vehicles transporting explosives or flammable liquids to avoid, "so far as practicable, and, where feasible" driving through congested thoroughfares, tunnels, etc. was not invalid on the ground of vagueness where statute punished only those who knowingly violated the regulation).
207. The point at which a bank files an incomplete or false report is obvious. As for defining when a bank has failed to file a report that is due, the regulations establish when transactions must be aggregated and reports must be filed. See above, pp. 209-212, text accompanying nn. 74-98.
208. Defining the conduct constituting an attempt is the subject of a voluminous common law that can be used here to define when one or more attempts have occurred.

Under cl. (3), which deals with structuring a transaction, the unit of prosecution is more complex. Assume that each week Joe receives about $90,000 in small bills to launder. Over the course of the week, he goes to ten banks and buys a $9,000 cashier's cheque at each. This might be defined as one unit of smurfing because Joe structured one $90,000 transaction. At the other extreme, Joe's conduct might constitute ten units of smurfing, because each time he entered a bank, Joe structured a transaction. Or this might be defined as five units of smurfing, because assuming that for each unit of prosecution the aggregate amount of cash must exceed $10,000, the transactions can be collapsed into five units of $18,000 as Joe goes from bank to bank.

Joe's conduct is best defined as five units of smurfing. Defining Joe's conduct as ten units of smurfing is unwise because each unit of prosecution requires over $10,000 in order for the government to prove that Joe intended to evade the reporting requirement.[209] Defining Joe's conduct as one unit of smurfing is equally unwise because it relies arbitrarily on a one-week period. Using a time period is problematic because the usual situation will involve converting a continuing cash flow; thus any time period selected will be arbitrary. More importantly, the number of units of prosecution should relate to the amount of money smurfed rather than an arbitrarily selected time period. Focusing on the amount of money smurfed ensures that liability is commensurate with harm and culpability. Focusing on the amount of money smurfed also renders liability consistent from case to case.

Courts interpreting other federal crimes have tended to find multiple units of prosecution.[210] Using $10,000 to define the unit of prosecution furnishes a reasonably bright line. The $10,000 line is certain and therefore predictable; it avoids extensive litigation over the definition of the unit of prosecution.

209. The anti-smurfing statute does not by its terms require the presence of $10,000 for each unit of prosecution. See 31 U.S.C. s. 5324 (Supp. IV 1986). As a practical matter, however, if less than $10,000 is involved, no report is due, and the government will not have the chance to prove that the defendants acted for the purpose of evading reports. See above, n. 125 (splitting up $2,000 is not smurfing). In the example with Joe, assuming the transactions were at different banks, neither bank is under a duty to aggregate, so no reports were due. Joe might still be liable for structuring, but interpreting the ten transactions individually as ten separate crimes of structuring is inconsistent with the purpose of evasion. Only if the transactions are reconstructed and examined as a whole can the government establish that the defendants acted with the purpose of evading reports. The government often will find this impossible.

210. See e.g. *United States v. Blankenship* 746 F.2d 233 at 236 (5th Cir. 1984) (interpreting mail fraud statute unit of prosecution to be each use of mails although only one fraudulent scheme was involved); *United States v. Tolub* 309 F.2d 286 at 289 (2d Cir. 1962) (interpreting Hobbs Act unit of prosecution to be each payment in an extortion scheme even if payments occur during continuance of the same underlying conditions); *United States v. Teemer* 214 F. Supp. 952 at 958 (D.W. Va. 1963) (interpreting Travel Act unit of prosecution to be each use of an interstate facility and each act of interstate travel although only one underlying scheme) (cited with approval in *United States v. Polizzi* 500 F.2d 856 at 898 (9th Cir. 1974)). See generally Thomas, "A Unified Theory of Multiple Punishment" (1985) 47 U. Pitt. L. Rev. 1 (1985) 12-25.

Anti-Smurfing Applied

Investigation of smurfing will be difficult. If a smurf structures transactions so that no reports are filed, the government will have to discover the conduct in some other way. Most discoveries will not result from an investigation targeting smurfing. Accidental discoveries of smurfing surely will occur, but probably not routinely.

Prosecution of smurfing also appears difficult because the government must prove that the defendant structured transactions for the purpose of evading the reporting requirement. Forcing the government to prove motive is onerous.[211] As a practical matter, however, this burden may not be that difficult. Once the government introduces evidence that the defendant engaged in a series of cash transactions, each of which was at or below $10,000, the jury will likely conclude that the defendant intended to avoid reporting. The defendant then must offer some other explanation for his transactions, and a convincing explanation for multiple cash transactions may be difficult to compose.

Regardless of its practical operation, the anti-smurfing statute has a symbolic aspect as well. Societal concern over structuring may be assuaged by this congressional response. Moreover, this particular type of response is significant in that Congress created an entirely new crime rather than amending existing statutes and regulations. The new crime signals a legislative commitment to eradicate money laundering. From this perspective, the statute is important symbolically, its efficacy notwithstanding.

THE RELATIONSHIP OF THE ANTI-SMURFING STATUTE TO OTHER FEDERAL CRIMES

The federal criminal law lacks an organising principle. It is not a code, but rather an assortment of unrelated crimes accumulated over the years. One result of this approach is that the interaction between crimes is often unanticipated and complex. This section explores relationships between the anti-smurfing statute and other federal crimes.

A Comprehensive Reporting Scheme

The bank reporting statute that the anti-smurfing statute aids and abets is part of a comprehensive scheme of reporting laws that captures all large cash transactions. The bank reporting statute is only one of three reporting statutes.[212] The others are 31 U.S.C. s. 5316, which requires each person to report the import or export of more than $10,000 in

211. The anti-smurfing statute is unusual in requiring the government to prove the defendant's motive. Motive is rarely an element of crimes; generally the government must prove that defendants intended to do the prohibited act but not why they did it.
212. In addition, two new statutes authorize the Secretary to adopt expanded reporting requirements. See above, n. 104.

monetary instruments at one time,[213] and 26 U.S.C. s. 6050I, which requires any person who receives more than $10,000 in cash in the course of trade or business in one transaction or in related transactions to file a return.[214] Collectively, these statutes cover all large cash transactions and require that the government be informed of them.[215] Thus, the government receives a report if Joe takes more than $10,000 cash and conducts any financial transaction, sends the cash out of the country, or invests it in diamonds.[216] These laws were the government's first sortie against money laundering.[217]

The Ripple Effect

Although federal criminal laws largely are unrelated, some crimes and sanctions depend on a combination of predicate offences. Therefore, the birth of a new federal crime has a ripple effect. The anti-smurfing statute has made ripples by providing for enhanced sanctions when it is violated in combination with any other law of the United States.[218] Thus, a person convicted of structuring and any other federal crime is subject to more severe sanctions than a person convicted only of structuring. Congress also has included the anti-smurfing statute as a predicate offence for two other crimes, R.I.C.O.[219] and the *Travel Act*.[220] A person chargeable under the anti-smurfing statute also is more likely liable for R.I.C.O. and *Travel Act* violations.

In contrast, one criminal provision declines to rely on the anti-smurfing statute as a predicate offence. Under 18 U.S.C. s. 1957,

213. 31 U.S.C. s. 5316 (1982 and Supp. IV 1986) provides:
>   [A] person . . . shall file a report . . . when the person . . . knowingly . . . (1) transports [or] is about to transport . . . monetary instruments of more than $10,000 at one time . . . from a place in the United States to or through a place outside the United States; or . . . to a place in the United States from or through a place outside the United States; or (2) receives monetary instruments of more than $10,000 at one time transported into the United States from or through a place outside the United States.

214. 26 U.S.C. s. 6050I (Supp. IV 1986) provides: "Any person . . . who is engaged in a trade or business, and . . . who, in the course of such trade or business, receives more than $10,000 in cash in one transaction (or [two] or more related transactions), shall make [a] return . . . with respect to such transaction."

215. The three statutes operate today as a comprehensive scheme but Congress did not enact them as one. The bank reporting law and the import/export report law were enacted in 1970 and s. 6050I was added to the *Internal Revenue Code* in 1984. See Pub. L. No. 98-369, s. 146(a), 98 stat. 685 (1984) (enacting s. 6050I); Pub. L. No. 91-508, ss 221-223, 231, 84 Stat. 1114 (1970) (codified as amended at 31 U.S.C. s. 5316 (1982 and Supp. IV 1986)).

216. Reinvesting the cash in a criminal enterprise may violate R.I.C.O. See 18 U.S.C. s. 1962 (1982).

217. Today this indirect approach is joined by a direct approach in the form of statutes defining money laundering per se as a crime. See 18 U.S.C. ss 1956-57 (Supp. IV 1986).

218. See 31 U.S.C. s. 5322(b) (Supp. IV 1986), which states, in pertinent part:
>   A person wilfully violating this subchapter or a regulation prescribed under this subchapter . . . while violating another law of the United States or as part of a pattern of any illegal activity involving more than $100,000 in a 12-month period, shall be fined not more than $500,000, imprisoned for not more than ten years, or both.

219. 18 U.S.C. ss 1961-68 (1982 and Supp. IV 1986).
220. 18 U.S.C. s. 1952 (1982 and Supp. IV 1986).

conducting a monetary transaction in property derived from specified unlawful activity is defined as criminal.[221] Violations of the anti-smurfing statute and the bank reporting law do not constitute "specified unlawful activity",[222] so the anti-smurfing statute does not contribute to a violation of s. 1957.

Double Jeopardy and the Anti-Smurfing Statute

In some situations, the double jeopardy clause prohibits imposition of multiple punishment in a single trial. The relationship between the anti-smurfing statute and its predecessors must be defined to assure a coherent approach when the double jeopardy issues reach the courts.

The bank reporting statute

The bank reporting law overlaps with the anti-smurfing statute so that often, both statutes define the same conduct as criminal. Clause (1) of the anti-smurfing statute prohibits causing a bank to fail to file a report. As noted above, some circuits hold customers liable for failure to file under the bank reporting law as accomplices of the banks, while others hold that customers are not liable as accomplices.[223] Clause (2) of the anti-smurfing statute prohibits causing a bank to file a report with an omission or misstatement of fact. The bank reporting statute covers the same conduct in that it prohibits any false, fictitious, or fraudulent statement in a report.[224] Unlike the failure to file situation, courts have never hesitated to apply this part of the reporting law to customers.[225] Clause (3) of the anti-smurfing statute prohibits structuring transactions. Some circuits interpret the bank reporting law, coupled with the general accomplice liability statute, to reach some types of structuring on the theory that the customer caused the bank to fail to file.[226] Jurisdictions that have adopted this theory of the bank reporting law only apply it to transactions structured within certain limits.[227] Moreover, the bank reporting statute never directly prohibits structuring transactions. Rather, it only prohibits a particular result—failure to file. Some overlap exists between cl. (3) and the bank reporting law, but it is minimal.

In the circuits in which customers are liable as accomplices under the bank reporting law, are they now also liable under the anti-smurfing statute? If the same conduct violates two statutes, then double jeopardy bars multiple punishment unless Congress has authorised multiple punishment.[228] The existence of statutory authorisation depends on congressional intent. If Congress intended that there be only one offence, then the double jeopardy clause bars multiple punishment. But

---

221. 18 U.S.C.A. s. 1957 (West Supp. 1989).
222. See 18 U.S.C. s. 1956(c)(7)(A) (Supp. IV 1986).
223. See above, pp. 205-206, text accompanying notes 42-48.
224. See 31 C.F.R. s. 103.49(d) (1988) (quoted above, n. 111).
225. See e.g. *United States v. Puerto* 730 F.2d 627 at 629 & n. 2 (11th Cir. 1984) (false information in reports would violate reporting law) and 631 (conspiracy to submit false reports), cert. denied, 469 U.S. 847 (1984).
226. See above, p. 206, nn. 44-45 and accompanying text.
227. See above, p. 208, nn. 62-64 and accompanying text.
228. See *Garrett v. United States* 471 U.S. 773 at 778 (1985).

if Congress intended to create multiple offences, then statutory authorisation exists and multiple punishment is allowed.[229]

The relevant inquiry is whether Congress intended for customers to be liable under both the bank reporting law and the anti-smurfing statute. With regard to the crimes of causing failure to file and structuring transactions under cll. (1) and (3) of the anti-smurfing statute, Congress did not explicity state its intent. However, the legislative history of the anti-smurfing statute indicates that the purpose of the statute was not to impose multiple punishment on customers, but rather to change the law in some circuits to ensure that customers were liable.[230] The anti-smurfing statute ensures customer liability and makes the law consistent nationwide. Nothing indicates that Congress intended to establish two separate offences to increase punishment.

Clause (2) of the anti-smurfing statute is slightly different. The legislative history reveals that the main problems with the reporting law were customers causing failure to file and structuring transactions.[231] Congress addressed these two problems when it drafted cll. (1) and (3) of

229. Ibid.; cf. Thomas, "The Prohibition of Successive Prosecutions for the Same Offence: In Search of a Definition" (1986) 71 Iowa L. Rev. 323 at 340-342 (concluding that a broader double jeopardy protection exists against successive trials than against multiple punishments in a single trial). According to Professor Thomas, legislative authorisation of multiple punishments does not answer whether the double jeopardy clause permits successive trials. See ibid. at 370-75. The successive trial test that Professor Thomas develops is predicated on the underlying conduct rather than the *Blockburger* analysis of the statutory elements. See ibid. at 382-88 (relying principally on *Illinois v. Vitale* 447 U.S. 410 (1980)). If this position is correct, my conclusion that multiple punishment is permissible should be limited to the context of a single trial.

230. See *Hearing Before the Senate Committee on Banking, Housing and Urban Affairs* op. cit. at 22, 30 (anti-smurfing law meant to cure inadequacies in current law in three federal circuits); ibid. at 48-49 (proposed anti-smurfing law corrects the problems revealed in case law); ibid. at 67 (anti-smurfing statute should close money laundering "loophole"; anti-smurfing statute "needed as prosecutions . . . continue to suffer from adverse case law"; anti-smurfing statute "should help clarify the state of the law and permit continued vigorous prosecution"); ibid. at 92 (anti-smurfing statute will cure confusion caused by case law and preclude unjustified dismissals); ibid. at 95 (anti-smurfing statute is designed to cure shortcomings in *Bank Secrecy Act*); ibid. at 134-136 (case law has created two major gaps in reporting law that anti-smurfing law should overcome); ibid. at 226 (anti-smurfing law is designed to overcome several recent court decisions); *Hearings Before the House Committee on Banking, Finance and Urban Affairs* op. cit. at 792 (anti-smurfing statute is aimed at overcoming problems of structured transactions caused by recent cases); ibid. at 846 (describing recent case law as a severe blow to government efforts to use reporting requirements).

231. See *Hearing Before the Senate Committee on Banking, Housing and Urban Affairs* op. cit. at 22, 30 (testimony of Francis A. Keating II, Assistant Secretary for Enforcement, Department of the Treasury): "The [anti-smurfing law] would make a person who structures transactions to avoid the currency reporting requirements, or who causes a financial institution not to file a required report, subject to the criminal and civil sanctions of the *Bank Secrecy Act*." Note that false statements are not mentioned, only failure to file and structuring. See also ibid. at 48-49 (description of anti-smurfing statute as it applies to structuring); ibid. at 55 (description of anti-smurfing law as it applies to causing failure to file); ibid. at 67: "The [anti-smurfing statute] is needed as prosecutions based upon 'structured' transactions and the 'causing' of financial institutions to fail to file currency transaction reports continue to suffer from adverse case law." (prepared statement of Deputy Assistant Attorney-General James Knapp). Again, false statements are not mentioned, only failure to file and structuring.

the anti-smurfing statute. The legislative history mentions liability for incomplete or false statements under cl. (2) only once; a government witness explained that cl. (2) of the anti-smurfing statute is a "restatement" of liability for false statements under the bank reporting statute and 18 U.S.C. s. 1001.[232] The word "restatement" is ambiguous, but it does not necessarily imply additional liability. Regardless of the meaning of "restatement", references throughout the legislative history indicate that the purpose of the anti-smurfing statute was to cure problems with the reporting law by closing its loopholes.[233]

All evidence indicates Congress intended the anti-smurfing statute to tighten the reporting law rather than to define additional crimes to increase punishment. This consistent evidence of congressional intent makes it unnecessary to resort to the *Blockburger*[234] test of statutory construction.[235] Because Congress did not intend to impose multiple punishment, statutory authorisation for multiple punishment is missing; punishment under both laws would therefore violate the double jeopardy clause.

Section 1001

Section 1001 deems it criminal when, within the jurisdiction of any government agency, a person intentionally conceals a material fact by trick, scheme, or device; makes any false, fictitious, or fraudulent statement; or makes or uses any false writing or document knowing it has a false, fictitious, or fraudulent statement.[236] This statute overlaps with the anti-smurfing statute in several ways.

232. "This new language is, in part, a restatement of the law of causation found in 18 U.S.C. s. 2(b) and 31 U.S.C. s. 5313, and the law pertaining to the intentional making of false statements . . . codified at 18 U.S.C. s. 1001." *Hearing Before the Senate Committee on Banking, Housing and Urban Affairs* op. cit. at 67 (prepared statement of Deputy Assistant Attorney-General James Knapp).
233. See above, n. 230; see also *Hearing Before the Senate Committee on Banking, Housing and Urban Affairs* op. cit. at 62 (anti-smurfing statute as "closing the loopholes" created by case law); ibid. at 95 (anti-smurfing statute designed to "cure" shortcomings in *Bank Secrecy Act*).
234. *United States v. Blockburger* 284 U.S. 299 (1932). For a discussion of the *Blockburger* text, see below, pp. 238-239 text accompanying nn. 250-58.
235. See *Garrett v. United States* 471 U.S. 773 at 780-81 (1985); *Albernaz v. United States* 450 U.S. 333 at 343-344 (1981); *Simpson v. United States* 435 U.S. 6 at 11-16 (1977). At any rate, the reporting law and cl. (2) of the anti-smurfing statute would likely fail the *Blockburger* test and would therefore be deemed the "same" offence. As *Woodward* makes clear, the *Blockburger* test is not applied to the facts of the case but to the words of the statute. See *United States v. Woodward* 469 U.S. 105-106, 108 (1985). Thus a more accurate phrasing of the *Blockburger* test might be that each crime *may be established* by proof of a fact the other does not require. Applied to the reporting law and cl. (2) of the anti-smurfing statute, the anti-smurfing statute does not necessarily prove a reporting violation because one can violate the anti-smurfing statute by merely attempting to file a false statement. Conversely, though, it is difficult to imagine how one could prove a "false, fictitious or fraudulent statement . . . in [a] report" under the reporting law without necessarily proving a false report under cl. (2) of the anti-smurfing statute. Because violation of the reporting law could never be proved without establishing a violation of cl. (2), the reporting law does not require proof of a fact the anti-smurfing law does not. Thus, these two offences may be deemed the same offence under *Blockburger*.
236. See 18 U.S.C. s. 1001 (1982).

Clause (1) of the anti-smurfing statute prohibits causing a bank to fail to file a currency transaction report. The circuits are split on whether s. 1001, coupled with the general accomplice liability statute, reaches this conduct.[237] In the circuits that hold s. 1001 applicable, one who causes a bank to fail to report is liable both under s. 1001 and cl. (1) of the anti-smurfing statute.[238]

Clause (2) of the anti-smurfing statute makes it a crime to cause a bank to file a report with a material omission or misstatement. Unlike the failure to file situation in which some courts held that s. 1001 did not apply, the applicability of s. 1001 to incomplete or false filings always was clear.[239] Causing a false filing necessarily would violate s. 1001,[240] and causing an incomplete filing would violate s. 1001 if the defendant used a trick, scheme, or device.[241]

Clause (3) of the anti-smurfing statute prohibits structuring transactions. Clause (3) and s. 1001 overlap only slightly. Some courts hold that s. 1001 reaches conduct also covered under cl. (3), but only when the customer causes the bank to fail to report.[242] In any other situation, s. 1001 does not reach the conduct and does not overlap the anti-smurfing statute.

In circuits holding s. 1001 applicable, would a person be liable both under s. 1001 and the anti-smurfing statute? As noted above, the double jeopardy clause prohibits multiple punishment in a single trial unless Congress intended such a result.[243] As for causing failure to file, some evidence supports the conclusion that Congress did not intend the anti-smurfing statute and s. 1001 to impose multiple punishment. Section 1001 was in place when congress enacted the anti-smurfing statute,[244] and courts were split over the former's applicability to failure to file situations. The legislative history of the anti-smurfing statute indicates that the purpose of the statute was not to add another layer of liability, but to ensure customer liability in the circuits holding other laws, including s. 1001, inapplicable.[245]

---

237. Compare *United States v. Nersesian* 824 F.2d 1294 at 1312 (2d Cir. 1987) (defendant could have been held liable under s. 1001 had he been charged), cert. denied, 108 S. Ct. 357 (1987) and *United States v. Tobon-Builes* 706 F.2d 1092 (11th Cir. 1983) (defendant liable under s. 1001) with *United States v. Larson* 796 F.2d 244 (8th Cir. 1986) (defendant not liable under s. 1001); *United States v. Varbel* 780 F.2d 758 (9th Cir. 1986) (same) and *United States v. Anzalone* 766 F.2d 676 (1st Cir. 1985) (same).
238. See *Nersesian* 824 F.2d 1294 at 1311-12; *Tobon-Builes* 706 F.2d 1092 at 1096-1101.
239. See above, n. 114.
240. Ibid.
241. See above, n. 113.
242. See above, n. 238.
243. See above, pp. 234-235, nn. 228-229 and accompanying text.
244. Congress adopted the predecessor to 18 U.S.C. s. 1001 in 1918. Act of 23 October 1918, ch. 194, 40 Stat. 1015. See generally *United States v. Yermian* 468 U.S. 63 at 70-74 (1984) (the 1918 Act was first federal criminal statute prohibiting making a false statement).
245. See above, n. 230; see also *Hearing Before the Senate Committee on Banking, Housing and Urban Affairs* op. cit. at 67 ("This restatement of the applicability of [s. 1001] to the Bank Secrecy Act was believed necessary following the decision of the First Circuit in *Anzalone*") (prepared statement of Deputy Assistant Attorney-General James Knapp).

But one also can argue that Congress did intend to impose multiple punishment under the anti-smurfing statute and s. 1001. When Congress passed the original reporting laws in 1970, it also passed a statute describing one aspect of the relationship between s. 1001 and bank reports.[246] This statute indicated that Congress contemplated that s. 1001 would apply to bank filings and failures to file.[247] Although Congress later repealed this statute, the repeal only strengthens this argument, because Congress explained that the statute was unnecessary due to the obvious applicability of s. 1001.[248] Therefore, Congress recognised this impact of s. 1001 and intended it to apply to filing or failing to file reports. Congress surely knew that clause (1) of the anti-smurfing statute would impose multiple punishment in the circuits holding s. 1001 applicable.[249]

Because of the conflicting evidence of the congressional intent in the legislative history, the *Blockburger* test[250] defines congressional intent.[251] This statutory construction test provides that Congress intended to define separate crimes if each crime requires proof of a fact that the other does not.[252] The Supreme Court has applied this test to a situation analogous to the anti-smurfing law and s. 1001. In *United States v. Woodward*,[253] the defendant made a false statement in a report required under the import/export reporting statute.[254] He was convicted of violating that statute and s. 1001. The Supreme Court applied the *Blockburger* test and concluded that the statutes defined separate crimes because each required proof of a fact the other did not.[255] The court reasoned that proof of a reporting violation does not necessarily include proof of a s. 1001 violation, because s. 1001 requires proof of a fact the reporting statute does not, a "trick, scheme, or device".[256] Conversely, s. 1001 does not necessarily include proof of an

---

246. See 31 U.S.C. s. 1052(k) (1976) (repealed 1982).
247. The statute provided: "For the purposes of section 1001 of Title 18 . . . the contents of reports required under any provision of this chapter are statements and representations in matters within the jurisdiction of an agency of the United States." Although the statute does not mention failure to file, it presumably covered those situations as well.
248. The statute was repealed as "[u]nnecessary" because "Section 1001 applies unless otherwise provided". H.R. Rep. No. 651, 97th Cong., 2d Sess. 301, reprinted in 1982 U.S. Code Cong. & Admin. News 1895 at 2195; see *United States v. Woodward* 469 U.S. 105 at 110 n. 6 (1985).
249. The Supreme Court relied on a similar congressional intent argument in *Woodward* 469 U.S. at 105. The *Woodward* court cited, at 109, the fact that in passing the import/export law, Congress's attention was called to s. 1001. Ibid. Therefore, the court stated, one cannot assume that Congress was unaware that there were two offences. Ibid. Here, in passing the anti-smurfing statute, Congress's attention was similarly drawn to s. 1001. See above, nn. 246-247. Again, one cannot assume Congress was unaware of the existence of two offences.
250. See *United States v. Blockburger* 284 U.S. 299 (1932).
251. *Garrett v. United States* 471 U.S. 773 at 779-780 (1985).
252. *Blockburger* 284 U.S. 299 at 304.
253. 469 U.S. 105 (1985).
254. Ibid. at 106; see 31 U.S.C. s. 5316 (1982 and Supp. IV 1986) (described above, p. 233, text accompanying n. 213).
255. *Woodward* 469 U.S. 105 at 108.
256. Ibid.

import/export reporting violation.[257] Therefore, Congress intended to define separate crimes and to authorise cumulative punishment.[258]

The *Woodward* analysis requires the same result when the *Blockburger* test is applied to the anti-smurfing statute and s. 1001. Proof of an anti-smurfing cl. (1) violation does not necessarily include proof of a s. 1001 violation because s. 1001 requires proof of either a false statement or concealment via trick, scheme, or device. In contrast, cl. (1) requires only that the person cause the bank to fail to file; presumably this could be accomplished without a trick, scheme, or device. Even assuming that a trick, scheme, or device would be required to successfully cause a bank to fail to file,[259] cl. (1) also prohibits attempts to cause a bank to fail to file. Clearly a person could attempt to cause a bank to fail to file without necessarily violating s. 1001. For example, Joe could conduct three transactions of $4,000 each in one day at a single bank, and just stand silently rather than volunteer information indicating a report is due. Without some affirmative trick, scheme, or device like false identities, the bank would probably discover the situation and file a report. Nonetheless, Joe would have violated cl. (1) by attempting to cause a failure to file. However, because he used no trick, scheme, or device, he would not have violated s. 1001. The Supreme Court relied on an analogous rationale in *Woodward* to hold it possible to violate the import/export reporting law without violating s. 1001.[260] Accordingly, cl. (1) and s. 1001 pass the *Blockburger* test as separate crimes and multiple punishment is authorised.[261]

A slightly different question is whether Congress intended the anti-smurfing statute and s. 1001 to define multiple crimes for incomplete and false filings. The legislative history of the anti-smurfing statute does not explicitly address this point.[262] The argument made above in support of multiple punishment for failure to file under cl. (1) of the anti-smurfing statute and s. 1001 likewise would apply to incomplete and false filings. The statute passed in 1970 and repealed in 1982 indicates that Congress

257. Ibid. at 107, n. 3.
258. Ibid. at 108-110.
259. This might be required as a practical matter, but the Supreme Court is capable of ignoring practical matters. In *Woodward*, it relied on the possibility that persons going through customs might not be asked whether they were carrying enough currency to require a report. See below, n. 260. This is theoretically possible but extremely unlikely, because everyone passing through customs is presented with forms that ask whether the traveller is carrying over $10,000. See e.g. *United States v. Granda* 565 F.2d 922 (5th Cir. 1978) (describing customs declaration cards). See generally Abrams, *Federal Criminal Law and its Enforcement* (1986), p. 574, n. 3.
260. The *Woodward* court stated:
    A person could, without employing a "trick, scheme, or device", simply and wilfully fail to file a currency disclosure report. A traveller who enters the country and passes through Customs prepared to answer questions, truthfully, but is never asked whether he is carrying over [$10,000] in currency, might nonetheless be subject to conviction under [the import/export report law] for wilfully transporting money without filing the required currency report. However, because he did not conceal a material fact by means of a "trick, scheme, or device", (and did not make any false statement) his conduct would not fall within . . . s. 1001.
261. See above, n. 229 for an argument limiting successive trials even when multiple punishment is authorised.
262. See above, pp. 235-236, nn. 231-233 and accompanying text.

intended s. 1001 to apply to bank reports.[263] Courts never doubted the
applicability of s. 1001 to incomplete and false filings.[264] Thus, when
Congress adopted the anti-smurfing statute in 1986, it must have known
that the impact of cl. (2) would be to impose another layer of liability in
addition to s. 1001. One can infer that Congress intended this result.

This evidence of congressional intent on causing the filing of an
incomplete or false report under cl. (2) indicates that Congress intended
to establish multiple liability. Unlike the situation described above for
failure to file, the evidence of congressional intent on false and
incomplete filings is unambiguous. Thus resort to the *Blockburger* test
is unnecessary. Yet if the *Blockburger* test were applied to cl. (2) and
s. 1001, the conclusion that the statutes define separate crimes would be
the same. The analysis would be the same as that used for failure to file.
Clause (2) and s. 1001 pass the *Blockburger* test because each requires
proof of a fact the other does not. Clause (2) includes attempts and
s. 1001 includes a trick, scheme, or device. Either way, the conclusion
is that multiple punishment does not violate the double jeopardy clause
because Congress authorised it.

Conspiracy

The interaction between the anti-smurfing statute and the conspiracy
statute[265] is less complex. As with the laws above, the circuits are split.
Some circuits allow prosecution of bank customers for conspiracy to
violate the reporting law,[266] while others do not.[267] In circuits in which
customers are liable for conspiracy to violate the reporting law, are they
also liable under the anti-smurfing statute? The answer again depends on
whether Congress intended to impose multiple liability.

The legislative history contains no direct evidence of congressional
intent with regard to conspiracy liability, but one can infer the intent to
allow multiple punishment from several factors. Conspiracy is an old and
notorious crime[268] of which Congress surely was aware when it

263. See above, p. 238, nn. 246-247 and accompanying text.
264. See above, p. 215, n. 114.
265. See 18 U.S.C. s. 371 (1982), which provides:
    If two or more persons conspire either to commit any offence against the United
    States, or to defraud the United States, or any agency thereof in any manner or for
    any purpose, and one or more of such persons do any act to effect the object of
    the conspiracy, each shall be fined not more than $10,000 or imprisoned not more
    than five years, or both.
266. See e.g. *United States v. Nersesian* 824 F.2d 1294 at 1309-1313 (2d Cir. 1987), cert.
    denied, 108 S. Ct. 357 (1987); *United States v. Giancola* 783 F.2d 1549 (11th Cir.
    1986), cert. denied, 479 U.S. 1018 (1986); *United States v. Puerto* 730 F.2d 627 (11th
    Cir. 1984), cert. denied, 469 U.S. 847 (1984). See generally Mann, "The Bank Secrecy
    Act: Conspiratorial Liability for Structured Transactions" (July-August 1987) White
    Collar Crime Rep. 2, 9.
267. See e.g. *United States v. Dela Espriella* 781 F.2d 1432 (9th Cir. 1986); *United States
    v. Varbel* 780 F.2d 758 (9th Cir. 1986).
268. Congress enacted the conspiracy statute in 1909 and revised it in 1948. See Act of
    4 March 1909, ch. 321, s. 37, 37 Stat. 1096 (enacting statute); Act of 25 July 1948, ch.
    645, 62 Stat. 701 (condified at 18 U.S.C. s. 371 (1982) (amended version)). Since that
    time it has been used and debated frequently. See generally Marcus, "Conspiracy: The
    Criminal Agreement in Theory and in Practice" (1977) 65 Geo. L. J. 925 (judges,
    practising attorneys, and scholars have had a "love-hate" relationship with
    conspiracy throughout this century).

adopted the anti-smurfing statute. That Congress said nothing about conspiracy suggests approval of its application in addition to the new anti-smurfing offence.[269] This conclusion is strengthened further by the evidence of how Congress treated s. 1001. First, Congress adopted a statute indicating that s. 1001 applied to currency transaction reports, then it repealed the statute and explained that s. 1001 applies unless otherwise provided.[270] Surely Congress intended that the conspiracy statute similarly would apply unless otherwise provided, and Congress made no other provision. Finally, conspiracy does not merge with a completed substantive offence under federal law,[271] on the theory that the crime of conspiracy targets harms distinct from the substantive offence.[272] Congress knew of this established rule and chose by its silence to endorse multiple liability, the usual interaction between a substantive crime and conspiracy.

These factors indicate that Congress intended the anti-smurfing statute and the conspiracy statute to define separate offences; this is sufficient evidence of congressional intent to render the *Blockburger* test inapplicable. At any rate, that test only corroborates the conclusion that Congress intended to authorise multiple crimes.[273]

In summary, the anti-smurfing statute authorises multiple punishment with s. 1001 and with the conspiracy statute but not with the bank reporting law. This conclusion effects rather than offends congressional intent. Congress meant for the anti-smurfing statute to reinforce the underlying reporting law by closing its loopholes, not by imposing additional punishment. Section 1001 and conspiracy are separate crimes directed at distinct evils, unrelated to the anti-smurfing statute.[274] If the

269. The Court relied on a similar rationale in *Woodward*. In that case, the Court stated that in passing the import/export reporting law, Congress's attention had been drawn to s. 1001, and its subsequent silence could not be interpreted to mean that Congress was unaware that it created two offences and authorised multiple punishment; *United States v. Woodward* 469 U.S. 105 at 109 (1985). In passing the anti-smurfing statute, Congress's attention was not specifically drawn to conspiracy, but we must assume that Congress was aware of the statute. Thus silence accompanying the anti-smurfing statute with regard to conspiracy can only indicate that Congress intended two separate offences.
270. See above, p. 238, nn. 246-247 and accompanying text.
271. See *Pinkerton v. United States* 328 U.S. 640 (1946).
272. The primary justification is that collective action presents a greater risk to society than individual action and so warrants punishment in addition to that imposed for the substantive crime. See *United States v. Feola* 420 U.S. 671 at 693 (1975); *Callanan v. United States* 364 U.S. 587 at 593 (1961).
273. Conspiracy and the anti-smurfing statute pass the *Blockburger* test because each requires proof of a fact the other does not. Conspiracy requires proof of plurality, and the anti-smurfing statute requires proof that the defendant acted for the purpose of evading the cash transaction reporting law.
274. See *United States v. Woodward* 469 U.S. 105 at 109 (1985) (congressional intent to allow separate punishment is shown by fact that statutes are directed at separate evils) (quoting *Albernaz v. United States* 450 U.S. 333 at 343 (1981)). Clearly the anti-smurfing law, s. 1001, and conspiracy target separate evils. The anti-smurfing statute was designed to cure the problems with the reporting law, thus enabling it to operate effectively against money laundering. See above, n. 230. Section 1001 was designed "to protect the authorised functions of governmental departments and agencies from the perversion which might result from the deceptive practices described." See *United States v. Gilliland* 312 U.S. 86 at 93 (1941) (quoted in *Woodward* at 109). The conspiracy statute is designed to deter collective action. See above, n. 272.

elements of those crimes happen to be met when the anti-smurfing statute is violated, then multiple evils are present and multiple punishment is appropriate. This is not the case, however, between the anti-smurfing statute and the bank reporting law. Those laws are closely related and are aimed at the same harms. They should not be used to pyramid liability.[275]

CONCLUSION

The anti-smurfing statute resulted from two determined forces converging: the incredibly lucrative drug trade in the United States, and the relentless effort of Congress to halt money laundering and contain the underlying drug trade.

The reporting law scheme was the government's first attack on money laundering. A central part of this scheme is the bank reporting law. When the bankers, prosecutors, and Joes of the world began to notice it, this legislation had an unpredicted consequence—the birth of smurfs. The bank reporting law experienced considerable difficulty in the courts. Soon the case law blossomed into gaudy disarray, and smurfs only occasionally were threatened. Congress quickly adopted the anti-smurfing statute.

The implicit message of the anti-smurfing statute is that no legitimate reason exists to keep large cash transactions secret. The very existence of the transactions is suspect; the bank reporting law acknowledges this. The anti-smurfing statute establishes that avoidance of the reporting law is unjustified. Reporting involves little time and negligible costs. The reports impose slightly on privacy, but weighed against the magnitude of damage that drugs and money laundering cause in our country, the reduction in privacy that the anti-smurfing statute causes is warranted. The only other reason to resist these reports is to hide other crime, either in generating the cash or in tax fraud. This objection to reporting is entitled to no weight and is accorded none.

One of the difficulties of curbing manipulation of the bank reporting law is drafting a law that is broad enough to be effective yet limited enough to avoid abuse. The anti-smurfing statute includes several guarantees against abuse. The mens rea requirement directs the government to prove the defendant acted with the motive of evading the bank reporting law. Smurfing is not totally innocent conduct, so criminal liability should not catch our friend Joe by surprise. Even so, under *Liparota*, the courts may infer knowledge of illegality as an element and thereby protect even further against abuse. Besides the integral rule of mens rea, the anti-smurfing statute should be interpreted to incorporate other controls on abuse. First, the unit of prosecution should be defined

275. At any rate, the government has plenty of weapons in its arsenal. 31 U.S.C. s. 5322(b), discussed above, p. 233, text accompanying n. 218, provides for enhanced sanctions when the anti-smurfing statute is violated with any other federal law. Therefore the availability of ss 1001 and 371 for prosecution with the anti-smurfing law increases the government's power beyond merely the sanctions allowed by multiple counts.

to avoid undue proliferation of counts. Second, courts should define the relationship between the anti-smurfing statute and other federal crimes to allow multiple punishment with s. 1001 and conspiracy, but not with the bank reporting law. Adopting these positions minimises the danger of abuse.

The efficacy of the anti-smurfing statute in stemming the tide of laundered dollars is hard to predict. Investigation will be difficult because smurfs easily can obscure structured transactions. Prosecution also will be difficult, primarily because the government must prove the defendant's motive to evade the reporting law, although as a practical matter, this burden may shift to the defendant. Regardless of its efficacy, the adoption of a new crime also has symbolic importance in that it formally expresses society's condemnation of that conduct. Nonetheless, the symbolic importance of a crime is not a sufficient justification for its existence. The law must confront reality; it cannot lapse into an intricate but irrelevant set of rules to be treated contemptuously and avoided as if in a cartoon. The anti-smurfing statute is a positive step to avoid that result.

Author's Note
In the two years since this article was first published, the most active topic in the smurfing world has been the knowledge of illegality element discussed at pages 218-227. First, the Treasury Department withdrew proposed regulations (cited in nn. 137 and 181) that would have required banks to give notice of the anti-structuring law to customers. Banks today have no obligation to provide notice. Second, the courts have mostly agreed with the article's conclusion that knowledge of illegality is not an element of structuring, so ignorance of the law is not a defence. Although there is some contrary lower court authority, two of the most respected appeals courts have held that the government does not have to prove knowledge of the anti-structuring law. See *United States v. Hoyland* 903 F.2d 1288 (9th Cir. 1990); *United States v. Scanio* 900 F.2d 485 (2d Cir. 1990).

12

The Drug Trafficking (Civil Proceedings) Act 1990 (N.S.W.)

SIMON STRETTON*

The *Drug Trafficking (Civil Proceedings) Act* ("the Act") is New South Wales legislation that was proclaimed on 3 August 1990. It represents a new approach to the scheme of criminal deterrence in that it establishes a framework whereby various types of civil proceedings may be taken against drug traffickers, quite separate from the criminal process. Conviction, acquittal or the existence of pending criminal proceedings are neither trigger nor bar to action pursuant to the Act. Similarly, neither conviction nor criminal penalty flow from a finding of liability pursuant to the Act.

The Act springs from a perception[1] that modern drug crime is often committed by highly organised groups with sophisticated methods, and is in many ways a business. The purpose of the business is long term profit and the assembling of assets. The criminal can continue until detected, be penalised for that one transaction, and retain the fruits of all the previous trafficking. The accumulated wealth of the group can also be used for the restructuring and continuation of the group notwithstanding the apprehension of some of its members, for bribery attempts, and for all the other methods whereby the facilitation of organised crime is achieved. There is a co-related perception that society must choose between allowing the trafficking groups to continue, or augment society's traditional reactive conviction-based criminal deterrence strategies. To this end, the Act seeks to recover all the trafficker's unlawfully obtained assets. At its second reading, the Minister for Police and Emergency Services stated:

> This legislation is aimed squarely at those involved in major drug crime. Its purpose is to deprive those involved in the drug trade of their illicit profits—profits earned at the expense of their victims and of the community generally. Importantly, it is not only the profits of a discrete transaction, but also the proceeds of a life of crime that will be confiscated.

Actions pursuant to the Act are conducted in the Supreme Court and may only be commenced by the New South Wales Crime Commission ("the Commission").

The principal objects of the Act are expressed[2] as the provision for the confiscation, without requiring a conviction, of the property of a

---

* Barrister-at-Law and Counsel assisting the N.S.W. Crime Commission.
1. *Hansard* (N.S.W.) Legislative Council, 23 May 1990, pp. 4627ff.
2. Section 3.

person if the Supreme Court finds it to be more probable than not that the person has engaged in drug-related activities; to enable the proceeds of drug-related activities to be recovered as a debt due to the Crown; and to enable law enforcement authorities effectively to identify and recover property. The Act provides that the onus of proof in all matters except offences against provisions of the Act, is proof on the civil onus of balance of probabilities; and further[3] that civil rules of construction and evidence apply to actions pursuant to the Act. Accordingly, evidential rules applicable only in criminal proceedings such as the challenging of evidence on a voir dire to enquire into its legality, will not ordinarily be available to either party. The Act further provides[4] that property under the "effective control" of a trafficker is subject to forfeiture, as is "drug-derived" property unless it is in the hands of a bona fide purchaser for sufficient consideration without knowledge or suspicion that it is drug-derived or illegally acquired.[5]

This "defence" to an action available to a purchaser involves objective as well as subjective elements.[6]

The two substantive actions available to the State under the Act are for assets forfeiture orders and proceeds assessment orders. These will normally be preceded by restraining orders pursuant to Pt 2 of the Act.

RESTRAINING ORDERS

Where a police officer, member of the Commission, or a person authorised in writing by the Commission suspects a person has engaged in "drug-related activity", or that property of a person is "drug-derived", the Commission may apply ex parte to the Supreme Court for a restraining order.[7] This application must be supported by that person's affidavit containing their grounds for that suspicion. If the court considers that the grounds are reasonable it must make an order restraining the assets applied to be restrained whether they be specific interests, a class of interests or all the interests in property of a particular person.[8] The court may, if it considers the circumstances so require, order the Public Trustee to take control of all or some of the property. No property may be physically seized under the Act unless there is an order of the court either for the Public Trustee to take control, or an ancillary order pursuant to s. 12(e) for seizure.

"Drug-related activity" is defined widely to include offences against ss 23 to 28 of the *Drug Misuse and Trafficking Act* 1985, similar offences against its predecessor the *Poisons Act* 1966, offences under Commonwealth, Territory or other State laws of a similar nature, or indictable offences of certain types committed "in connection" with any of the aforementioned.[9]

3. Section 5.
4. Section 7(3).
5. Section 9(5).
6. See *R. v. Ward* (1989) 42 A. Crim. R. 56.
7. Section 10.
8. Section 10.
9. Section 6.

"Interest" is also widely defined[10] and includes a legal or equitable estate or interest in the property or a right, power or privilege in connection with the property, whether present or future and whether vested or contingent. "Interest" also includes any property of this nature under the effective control of the trafficker, which is in itself widely defined.

"Drug-derived property" is defined such that it may be traced through any number of transactions whereby its nominal form is varied.[11]

When a restraining order is made, it remains in force for only 48 hours unless an assets forfeiture application is made, a proceeds assessment application is made, or there exists an unsatisfied proceeds assessment order or other order under s. 20.[12] If such application or order is made, the restraining order continues.

At the time of the restraining order being made or at any later time the court may make ancillary orders pursuant to s. 12. The court has a discretion to make any order it considers appropriate, including an order for the examination on oath of persons as to the affairs of the owner of an interest in property that is subject to the restraining order.

EXAMINATION

Where the court has ordered the examination of a person pursuant to s. 12(1)(b) of the Act, Rules of Court[13] prescribe that this may take place before a Master or a Registrar of the Supreme Court. The examination must be on oath. Section 13 of the Act abrogates the common law entitling the claiming of privilege against incrimination but at the same time renders any answers given and any evidence obtained as a consequence of the evidence inadmissable in any criminal or civil proceedings subject to certain exceptions. The court has no discretion in the face of a specific statutory abrogation of privilege.[14] The fact that criminal charges are pending is irrelevant.[15] This is recognised in the Act in that s. 63 provides that the existence of criminal proceedings is not a ground for the staying of proceedings under the Act, although it should be noted that the Act provides for the court to prohibit publication of any matter arising under the Act if criminal proceedings are current. No doubt such an order would be made when there exists a real risk that matters arising at any stage in proceedings under the Act may be published and potentially prejudice a future jury. The abrogation of privilege is effective notwithstanding the subject matter of the questioning may be matters occurring prior to the statute's enactment.[16]

10. Section 7.
11. Section 9.
12. Where upon refusal to make a confiscation order the court has a discretion to continue the restraining order, presumably to maintain status pending appeal and for like purposes.
13. Rule 84B.
14. See *R. v. Scott* (1856) D. & B. 47; 169 E.R. 909; *Sorby v. Commonwealth* (1983) 152 C.L.R. 281.
15. *Hamilton v. Oades* (1989) 166 C.L.R. 486.
16. See *Sorby v. Commonwealth* (1983) 152 C.L.R. 281.

This abrogation is understandable, as the "affairs" to which the examination relates necessarily must focus upon distinguishing between legitimate and illegitimate activities to determine the various issues that a court must determine under the Act. To determine the proceeds of trafficking, questions must be asked about trafficking, just as to determine whether an item is drug-derived the derivation from drug-related activity must be asked about. The meaning of "affairs" has always been held to flow from its context, and when used in a statutory context from the Act and the purpose of the Act.[17]

The scope of "affairs" within s. 12 was considered by Master Greenwood in *State Drug Crime Commission v. Lahoud*.[18] At p. 8 the Court said:

> The plaintiff is . . . entitled to seek information from the witness concerning any interest in property which comes within s. 7. The plaintiff is also entitled to establish the source of funds (if any) used to acquire that interest. The term "affairs of the owner" given its normal meaning is expansive. Affair is defined in the Macquarie Dictionary as (1) "anything done or to be done, that which requires action or effort, business concern; (2) (plural). Matters of interest or concern, particular doings or interests." The word affair as used in s. 12(i)(b) includes the nature and location of any property. The definition is therefore wider than the nature and location of the property. It is not restricted to business affairs. The legislature intended the word to be used in its wide sense. In my view without restricting its meaning but by way of guidance "affairs" will refer to any dealing arrangement or activity which would be of interest to the Commission in pursuing the objects of the Act as enunciated in s. 3. In my view the definition should not be read down.

Master Greenwood went on to say that the section could not be used to obtain evidence for a prosecution, and that its ambit could be generally limited to the subject matter of the restraining order. The court also said that the examinee must answer questions about his tax returns notwithstanding that the answering of such questions may give rise to prosecution for a Commonwealth offence. The court noted that s. 79 of the Judiciary Act would in practice extend the s. 13 evidentiary protections to any such prosecution commenced in New South Wales. The extent to which counsel for the examinee may also question this witness was briefly considered, and the Master expressed the "tentative" view that:

> counsel for the witness is entitled to ask questions limited only to dealing with ambiguities or to explaining answers for the sake of clarity. Counsel is not entitled to embark on any other form of evidentiary exercise.

The evidence taken at the examination is then admissible in the confiscation and ancillary proceedings.[19]

17. See *R. v. Board of Trade; Ex parte St Martin Preserving Co. Ltd* [1964] 2 All E.R. 461; *F. v. West Berkshire Health Authority* [1989] 2 All E.R. 545.
18. Unreported, N.S.W. Sup. Ct, 8 March 1991.
19. Sections 13(b) and 13(c).

ASSETS FORFEITURE ORDERS

Part 3 of the Act[20] provides for assets forfeiture orders, proceeds assessment orders, and the establishment of a Confiscated Drug Proceeds Account for the resulting funds.

An application for an assets forfeiture order may only be made if a restraining order is in place, and will seek the forfeiture to the Crown of any or all of the interests in property that are subject to that restraining order. The court must determine on the civil onus whether the person to whom the restraining order relates has engaged in "drug-related activity" in the six years[21] preceding the making of the application. Whilst an indictable quantity of drugs is not required for a restraining order, it is required for a forfeiture order. This reflects the practical reality that many restraining orders will be sought at or about the time of arrest, at which time it will not usually be possible to have an exact analysed weight of drug to aver.

The rules of construction and evidence applicable in civil proceedings apply and the raising of "a doubt" only is insufficient to avoid an order being made.[22] There has been no judicial consideration to date concerning the applicability of the principle concerning civil proof enunciated in cases like *Briginshaw v. Briginshaw*[23] and *Helton v. Allen*.[24] The "reasonable satisfaction" described by Dixon J. in *Briginshaw v. Briginshaw* as necessary for proof on the balance of probabilities was said to be affected in part by the seriousness of the allegation and the gravity of the consequences. If the principle is applied, then the seriousness of the drug trafficking alleged and the amount or proportion of the defendant's assets sought will effect the ease with which a court will be "reasonably satisfied" that trafficking has occurred.

Section 54 renders a Certificate of Conviction admissible as evidence of the commission of the offence to which it relates.

No specific trial procedure is provided for by the Act and accordingly the court may regulate its procedure by s. 12 in accordance with the *Supreme Court Rules*. The court has assigned all proceedings under the Act to its Criminal Division.[25] As s. 5 provides that the proceedings are civil, the various pre-trial procedures provided by the Supreme Court Rules will be generally available except to the extent that the Act excludes them by necessary implication. Section 12 gives the court a wide discretion to make any interlocutory order that the court "considers appropriate". The court can therefore make orders under the Rules, orders under s. 12 in the nature of orders under the Rules, or develop new orders appropriate to the novel actions created by the Act.

20. Sections 22 to 32 inclusive.
21. Section 22(5) provides that this period may operate to cover a period prior to the commencement of the Act.
22. Sections 5 and 22(6).
23. (1938) 60 C.L.R. 336.
24. (1940) 63 C.L.R. 691.
25. Rule 84A. In the absence of procedural specifics, the court has traditionally regulated itself "by analogy to the proceedings at Common Law": *Greathead v. Bromley* (1798) 7 Term Rep. 455; 101 E.R. 1073 as more recently approved in New South Wales in *Kelly v. Kelly* (1950) 50 S.R. (N.S.W.) 261 at 267.

To date, the court has required the filing of affidavits in support and provided time for affidavits in opposition and reply to be filed, as the precursor to the setting of any trial date.

If the court finds that the person subject to the restraining order did engage in drug-related activity within six years of the application, it must make an order forfeiting all the restrained property vesting it in the Public Trustee on behalf of the Crown. Whilst the restraining order may be in general terms and apply to all of a person's assets or a class of their assets, any forfeiture order must specify the exact property to which it applies. [26]

The defendant may give or call evidence in opposition to the application, although there are no provisions relating to privilege as in the case of an examination. The reality of most cases will be that the defendant in opposing the application will be asserting non-engagement in drug-related activity, and so the issue of privilege against incrimination will not arise.

The Act provides relief [27] against hardship for dependants of a person liable to forfeit assets by virtue of an order under the Act. Dependant is defined to mean a spouse, de facto partner, child, or member of the household dependant for support on the person. If the court is satisfied that a person in this category has (in the case of a person over 18) no knowledge of the drug-related activity, and would suffer hardship by the order, then it may order money to be paid from the proceeds of the sale of the forfeited asset to prevent hardship, and provide for the application of such funds if the person is under the age of 18. There are no decisions of the court as to the scope of "hardship" in the Act, however, the Court of Criminal Appeal has considered the word in the context of s. 5(1)(b) of the *Crimes (Confiscation of Profits) Act* 1985 (N.S.W.). In *R. v. Lake* [28] Kirby P. stated:

> In considering hardship, it is necessary to bear in mind that, of necessity, in achieving its objects, the Act will cause a measure of hardship in the deprivation of property. Indeed that is its intention. It is not that kind of hardship, therefore, that can give rise to the relief under s. 5(1)(b)(ii). The provision for relief on that ground must not be so interpreted as to frustrate the achieving of the purpose of Parliament in enacting the exceptional provisions of the Act. Something more than ordinary hardship in the operation of the Act is therefore meant.

Accordingly it is probable that something more than a simple loss or reduction in drug-funded lifestyle will be required to attract the operation of the section. Historically, the scope of "hardship" has been held to be entirely dependent on its statutory context; whilst in the context of the United Kingdom *Agricultural Holdings Act* 1948 [29] it was held to be a concept "wholly unrestricted as a matter of language" the more common view is that "hardship" involves adverse consequences

26. Contrast s. 10(2) concerning restraining orders with s. 22(4).
27. Section 24.
28. (1989) 44 A. Crim. R. 63 at 66.
29. *Bailey v. Purser* [1967] 1 All E.R. 188 at 191 per Lord Parker C.J.

of a serious kind. [30] One of the aims of the legislation is to deprive traffickers of the enjoyment of the fruits of their labours, and undoubtedly the provision of extra benefits to dependants is a part of that. What the avoidance of serious adverse consequences to those dependants will involve will be a question of fact in each case. In seeking an order, an applicant will bear an onus to show that there will be sufficient hardship, that all assets have been disclosed such that the court may be satisfied that the restrained assets must be used, and that there is no reasonable alternative method of avoiding the hardship. A similar approach was taken to the issue of payment out of restrained property for legal expenses by Badgery-Parker J. in *State Drug Crime Commission of New South Wales v. Ujka and Sam* [31] as later discussed.

EXCLUSION ORDERS

As can be seen, there is no nexus required between the drug-related activity and the assets to be forfeited by way of assets forfeiture order. The Act provides for the retention of legally obtained property by way of exclusion order. An "exclusion order" is an order excluding the interest from the operation of the assets forfeiture order or any relevant restraining order. This application may be made by the owner of the property either before a forfeiture order is made or under certain circumstances after it. A person with notice of the forfeiture proceedings may apply with leave to the court within six months of a forfeiture order, and a person who had no notice may apply within six months as of right, and beyond six months with leave. [32] The applicant for the exclusion order must prove on the civil onus that the property is not illegally acquired, to obtain an exclusion order. "Illegally acquired" property is widely defined [33] to include the proceeds of any illegal activity and to retain its "illegally acquired" character notwithstanding any number of transactions and changes of form. It ceases to be illegally acquired in the hands of a bona fide purchaser for value without notice, although it must be noted that the test involves both subjective and objective criteria. [34] There are some further exceptions. [35] The Act is unusual in giving actual examples of its operation in the body of the Act. Section 9(9) provides examples of how property can become and cease to be drug-derived property:

> 9(9) . . .
>
> (a) if money that is the proceeds of a drug-related activity is used to buy land, the land becomes drug-derived property and the money used (which is now in the hands of some other person) continues to be drug-derived property;

---

30. *Returned Sailors', Soldiers' and Airmen's Imperial League of Australia (Henley and Grange Subbranch) Inc. v. Abbott* [1946] S.A.S.R. 270 at 273-274; *R. v. Spagnolo* (1990) 156 L.S.J.S. 262.
31. Unreported, N.S.W. Sup. Ct, Badgery-Parker J., 20 December 1990.
32. Section 25(3).
33. Section 9.
34. Section 9(5).
35. Section 9(5)(b) to (f). There are currently no "prescribed circumstances" pursuant to 9(5)(f).

(b) if the land is then sold it continues to be drug-derived property and the money paid for it becomes drug-derived property;

(c) if the money paid for the land is then used to buy a car, the car becomes drug-derived property and the money used to buy it (now in the hands of the car's former owner) continues to be drug-derived property unless the purchase was for sufficient consideration from an innocent person.

In this way the Act also penalises (and deters) persons who knowingly acquire drug-derived property thereby facilitating the traffickers profit realisation or money laundering activities.

The burden of proof is placed on the person seeking the exclusion order, and there is no evidential onus on the Crown. In *R. v. Brauer*[36] the suggestion that there should be an initial threshold evidential onus before the owner be required to shoulder the legal and persuasive onus was rejected by the Queensland Full Court in relation to similar (but not identical) proceedings to exclude restrained property pursuant to s. 48(4) of the *Proceeds of Crime Act* 1987 (Cth). At the same time, the court recognised the difficulties that persons may have in proving the legality of matters many years after the event and noted that this must be borne in mind in matters of this nature. The s. 48(4) test about which the court was concerned, however, includes the somewhat more onerous requirement that the person must not only prove the property is not unlawfully derived, but must also prove that the property has never been used in or in connection with any unlawful activity. This latter matter does not have to be established for an exclusion order to be obtained under the New South Wales Act.

The degree of proof that an applicant for an exclusion order may bring can widely vary, from the simple verbal assertion of legal acquisition, to detained financial and documentary evidence from independent sources establishing that legal acquisition. What degree of documentation, if any, the court will regard as necessary in addition to the applicant's verbal evidence to satisfy the persuasive onus will depend on many factors including the age of the transaction, the availability of records from the institutions such as banks, registries, and elsewhere to support the legality of the acquisition, and the type of transaction itself. In the context of the aforementioned Commonwealth Act, Thomas J. held in *Brauer*[37] that it should not be assumed that the Crown is in a better position to prove or disprove the legality of the acquisition or use of property. On the one hand the Crown has easier access to public and investigative records, yet on the other hand it is the owner who would ordinarily have been at the centre of the process of acquisition of the property and ought therefore be expected to have reasonable access to evidence concerning the circumstances of that acquisition.

Some judicial consideration has been given to the way courts should approach the fact-finding process in this reverse onus scenario, in the context of the *Proceeds of Crime Act* 1987 (Cth). Section 48(4)(e) of that

36. (1989) 45 A. Crim. R. 109.
37. Ibid. at 113.

Act provides for the release of restrained property if the property in general terms was lawfully acquired. In *D.P.P. (Cth) v. Jeffery*,[38] Hunt C.J. at C.L. observed:

> the legal onus remains at all times upon an applicant for relief pursuant to s. 48(4) of the *Proceeds of Crime Act*. If his sworn denial . . . is accepted as honest and accurate, that onus has been discharged. As a matter of practical reality, what such an applicant must do in most cases in order to establish the negative facts . . . is not only to deny on oath in general terms that the property was so used in or derived from any unlawful activities, but also to establish what activities it was in fact used in and derived from.

Section 31(6) of that Act provides for the recovery of forfeited property under certain circumstances if a similar negative onus is discharged. In *D.P.P. v. Lynch*[39] the Western Australia Supreme Court noted:

> the practical consequence is that an applicant will not succeed unless he can identify some lawful source or activity which produced or generated the monies used to purchase the property.

This approach is certain to be adopted by the court when considering exclusion applications under the Act. The applicant for an exclusion order will need to identify in general terms the lawful source of the property in question and provide such corroboration as might reasonably be expected to be available in all the circumstances.

Where is it proved that part of a forfeited asset is not attributable to illegal activity, then the Act provides for payment of that proportion of the proceeds of sale to be paid to the owner.[40]

PROCEEDS ASSESSMENT ORDERS

A proceeds assessment order is an order by the Supreme Court requiring the payment to the Treasurer of an assessed amount being the value of proceeds derived from drug-related activities since the point in time six years prior to the making of the application for the order.[41] This order may be made in addition to a forfeiture order.

The Supreme Court must make a proceeds assessment order if it is proven on the civil onus that the person against whom the order is sought engaged in any drug-related activity in that six year period.[42] The amount assessed by the court becomes a debt due to the Crown[43] and all the property of the person concerned is charged in favour of the Crown until payment is made or certain other events occur.[44] Proceeds assessment criteria are specified[45] and include proceeds in any form.

38. Unreported, N.S.W. Sup. Ct, Hunt C.J. at C.L., 15 January 1992.
39. Unreported, W.A. Sup. Ct, Commissioner Templeman Q.C., 2 February 1990.
40. Section 26.
41. Section 27(1).
42. Section 27(2).
43. Section 27(7).
44. Section 31.
45. Section 28.

The court may take into account assets betterment considerations in determining the proceeds. Property and proceeds coming into the person's possession or control outside the State are included, and opinion evidence as to the value of drugs by qualified witnesses is rendered admissible and relevant to the assessment.[46]

In calculating the quantum of "proceeds" the Act provides[47] that "expenses and outgoings" are not to be deducted. In *Application of the State Drug Crime Commission of New South Wales; Re The Property of Kamal Abi Khalil*[48] the court distinguished the concept of "proceeds" from "benefit" or "profit", holding that a drug trafficker's expenditure in purchasing the drugs themselves should not be deducted when calculating "proceeds" pursuant to the Act.[49] The court said that whilst "benefit" imported the concept of advantage, "proceeds" did not. Accordingly, the actual gross moneys received by the trafficker will be recoverable, without reference to any cost or expense that may have been incurred in obtaining those moneys.

If an order is sought to satisfy a proceeds assessment order against property on the grounds that whilst it is not legally the property of the trafficker, it is under her or his effective control, the legal owner must be given notice and the opportunity to be heard.[50] In this way the legal owner has the opportunity of resisting the forfeiture by calling evidence to demonstrate that the property is not under the effective control of the trafficker.

There are provisions for the sale of restrained property to satisfy a proceeds order and restrained property may also be sold when it is subject to waste, loss of value, or the cost of controlling it would exceed its value.[51] An order of the court is required.

The money obtained by the sale of property subsequent to a proceeds assessment order is applied firstly to the Public Trustee's fees and expenses, then to the debt created by the order, and then any remainder is returned to the owner unless the property was also subject to an assets forfeiture order. If it was subject to an assets forfeiture order any excess of moneys upon sale over and above the proceeds order is also forfeited.

LEGAL EXPENSES

The Act provides[52] that a restraining order may provide for payment of the reasonable legal expenses of a person in actions under the Act or in criminal proceedings, out of restrained property. On application by the Commission or the Public Trustee, these costs must be taxed. The Act provides no further details concerning the criteria or procedure for the making of such order. In *State Drug Crime Commission of New South*

46. Sections 28(4) and (5).
47. Section 28(4).
48. Unreported, N.S.W. Sup. Ct, Grove J., 26 April 1991.
49. Contrast the interpretation of the *Crimes (Confiscation of Profits) Act* 1985 pecuniary penalty provisions taken in *R. v. Fagher* (1989) 16 N.S.W.L.R. 67.
50. Section 29.
51. Sections 14 and 30.
52. Sections 10(5), 12 and 17.

Wales v. Ujka and Sam,[53] Badgery-Parker J. identified a number of matters the court would consider on an application for the payment of legal expenses out of restrained property. First, the applicant bears an onus on the balance of probabilities to establish that legal expenses will be incurred in connection with the application for the restraining order or confiscation order and that he or she is not able to meet reasonable legal expenses without resort to property the subject of the restraining order. To this issue the court stated at p. 16 of the judgment:

> it is not sufficient for the applicant merely to be able to point to the fact that the restraining order in its terms applies to all of his property; it appears to me that the applicant comes under an obligation to disclose to the court all of his interests in property, and that an order should not be made unless the court is satisfied that it is fully apprised of what property exists.

Secondly, Badgery-Parker J. held that s. 10(5) of the Act did not invite any enquiry as to the reasonableness of the defendants' conduct in defending the charge, and that the importance of committal proceedings must be taken into account when the court considers whether to make an order to fund them.

Thirdly, the court considered the issue of which restrained property ought to be applied to the payment of costs:

> The court has a discretion whether to make any order at all, and has a discretion as to how its order be framed, so as to require the applicant to resort for his legal costs to a particular asset should that appear appropriate.

The court held that the applicant did not have to establish the lawful acquisition of property, to enable it to be paid out in legal expenses, but approved Studdert J. in *D.P.P. v. Saxon*[54] in holding that in a particular case evidence may be so compelling that a particular item of property was acquired unlawfully that it would be inappropriate to allow it to be applied in legal costs, such money thereby becoming unrecoverable pursuant to the provisions of the Act.[55] The court recognised the difficulty that may occur in that payment may be made from property that is eventually found to be illegally acquired and thus that asset is lost to the State when it should be forfeited to it, yet other property legally obtained be returned unaffected as a result of a successful exclusion application. To address this issue, the court held that there be an order of payment out of legal expenses against a certain asset, but that the applicant execute a deed binding himself to pay to the Crown a sum of money equivalent to any amount paid in respect of reasonable legal expenses which were paid out of illegally acquired property as defined in the Act, and charging all of his property with payment to the Crown of those amounts.

In a series of decisions the court has held that costs incurred "defending a criminal charge" will include those incurred in applying for

53. Unreported, N.S.W. Sup. Ct, Badgery-Parker J., 20 December 1990.
54. Unreported, N.S.W. Sup. Ct, Studdert J., 3 August 1990.
55. Section 9(5)(e).

bail,[56] defending a Crown application for revocation of bail,[57] contesting a committal hearing,[58] and in appealing against conviction or sentence.[59]

The parties may request the court to determine in advance at what rate costs are to be paid out of restrained property. The Court of Appeal has given some guidance as to the applicable principles.[60]

OFFENCES

The Act contains various offences. A person contravening a restraining order or any ancillary order made by the court by disposing or otherwise dealing with restrained property commits an offence against s. 16 of the Act and is liable to prosecution before the Supreme Court in its summary jurisdiction,[61] and is liable on a conviction to a fine equivalent to the value of the interest dealt with or by imprisonment for two years or both, unless it is proved that the person had no notice of the existence of the restraining order and no reason to expect that it was in existence. This statutory defence will be one with both a subjective and objective requirement. In *R. v. Ward*,[62] Campbell and Allen JJ. described "no reason to suspect" as an objective test involving whether a reasonable person would have regarded the known fact or facts as giving reason to suspect. The phrase "unless it is proved" casts the onus on the accused to establish the defence, which will accordingly require proof on the balance of probabilities that he or she had no notice of the restraining order and that in the light of all that was known to them there was objectively no reason to suspect the existence of a restraining order.

The Act contains provision for the making of production orders by the Supreme Court on the application of an authorised officer for the production or inspection of documents relating to the assets of a person. Failure to comply with such an order without reasonable excuse is an offence punishable summarily before a magistrate.[63] Whilst the defendant may lawfully resist a production order on the grounds of legal professional privilege,[64] the Act abrogates it as far as third parties are concerned, and provides that the privilege against incrimination is not

56. *State Drug Crime Commission v. Heal and Fleming* (unreported, N.S.W. Sup. Ct, Matthews J., May 1991 at p. 14 and on appeal per Kirby P., 14 August 1991 at p. 26).
57. Ibid.
58. *State Drug Crime Commission of New South Wales v. Ujka and Sam* (unreported, N.S.W. Sup. Ct, Badgery-Parker J., 20 December 1990 at p. 16); *State Drug Crime Commission of New South Wales v. Egan* (unreported, N.S.W. Sup. Ct, Bruce A.J., 17 July 1991 at p. 12).
59. *New South Wales Crime Commission v. Hawes* (unreported, N.S.W. Sup. Ct, Studdert J., 20 December 1991).
60. *State Drug Crime Commission v. Heal and Fleming* (unreported, N.S.W. Sup. Ct, Matthews J., May 1991 at p. 14 and on appeal per Kirby P., 14 August 1991 at p. 26).
61. Section 53. In the absence of any statutory provision requiring an indictment any such prosecution will be by way of summons before a single judge sitting without jury pursuant to the *Supreme Court (Summary Jurisdiction) Act* 1967.
62. (1989) 42 A. Crim. R. 56 at 71.
63. Sections 37 and 53.
64. *State Drug Crime Commission v. Larsson* (1991) 53 A. Crim. R. 131 at 135.

available to prevent the production of any document. However if objection is taken to the order, the document is not admissible in criminal proceedings against the provider of it. Search warrants are obtainable under Pt 4 Div. 2 and the hindering or obstruction of the execution of such warrants are offences punishable summarily. Further, the Act provides for the monitoring of financial transactions by order of the Supreme Court, and for offences of breaching or not properly complying with such order or unlawfully disclosing such order. These offences may only be prosecuted before the Supreme Court in its summary jurisdiction.

CONCLUSION

The *Drug Trafficking (Civil Proceedings) Act* provides a non-criminal, non-conviction-based set of civil proceedings designed to cast the onus on a proven drug trafficker to prove that the assets he or she has are lawfully acquired, or lose them to the State, to enable the State through the Confiscated Drug Proceeds Account to assist law enforcement, drug rehabilitation, drug education and related matters. It provides investigators with powers of search, seizure and monitoring directed towards the financial nature of the issues that are likely to be involved, rather than rely on the limited investigatory powers traditionally available to investigators in civil matters.

13

Investigating Criminal and Corporate Money Trails

DAVID A. CHAIKIN*

INTRODUCTION

What is the money or paper trail?

In the business world most transactions, whether they be legitimate or illegitimate, bring documents into existence. In a non-commercial setting, a large amount of information about individuals and businesses is also generated. Such documents and information may be useful in constructing a picture of assets, income and changes in wealth.[1]

The money or paper trail is the documentation which links an individual and/or organisation to specified criminal activity or to unexplained income/assets. It is the method used by investigators, for example, to show the links between a crime and its financiers or beneficiaries. It is thus said that following the money trail represents the most effective way of combating organised crime and serious white collar crime.

What is money laundering?

There is no universal or comprehensive definition of money laundering. Prosecutors and criminal intelligence agencies, business people and companies, developed and third world countries, each has its own definition based on different priorities and perspectives. Legal definitions for the purposes of prosecution[2] are narrower than definitions for intelligence purposes.

Money laundering has two related processes. Firstly, anyone who hides the existence of money from the authorities is engaged in money laundering. For example, the drug trafficker who salts illicit income in a Swiss bank, or the tax evader who hides earnings in a real estate

---

* Barrister-at-Law, N.S.W. B.Com.LL.B. (N.S.W.), LL.M. (Yale), Ph.D. (Cantab.).
1. For a discussion of investigatory techniques, see generally Chaikin, *Regulation of Commercial Crime* (1983), Chs 2-4, 7; Meagher, *Organised Crime*, paper presented to the 53rd ANZAAS congress (Perth, Western Australia, 16-20 May 1983), pp. 79-145; Comer, *Corporate Fraud* (1985).
2. See United Nations *Convention against Illicit Traffic in Narcotic Drugs and Psychotropic Substances*, 1988, art. 3(1)(b); *Money Laundering Control Act* 1986 (U.S.A.); *Drug Trafficking Offences Act* 1986 (U.K.), s. 24; *Drug Trafficking (Recovery of Proceeds) Ordinance* 1989 (H.K.), s. 25.

investment. Secondly, the money is "cleaned" or sanitised where its true nature, source or use is concealed. Legitimisation provides the avenue for enjoying money without fear of revealing its original source.

Creating a justification for controlling or possessing funds and assets is the essence of laundering. Thus the drug trafficker needs to explain to the police why he or she is living in a Hollywood-style mansion and driving luxurious cars. The tax evader will need to justify to the tax authorities the purchase of a luxurious yacht and investments in shares. The corrupt bureaucrat will have to explain to the anti-corruption commission why her or his lifestyle is not commensurate with income. The accountability of the drug trafficker, tax evader and corrupt bureaucrat will vary from one country to another,[3] and this in turn will influence the type and extent of money laundering.

In this chapter I will use a very wide definition of money laundering:

> The process by which one conceals or disguises the true nature, source, disposition, movement or ownership of money for whatever reason.

Money laundering is used to break the paper trail by, for example, using cash or transferring funds overseas to a tax or bank secrecy haven. Laundering creates obstacles to government investigators, tax prosecutors and private detectives. If money cannot be traced, then a prosecution may be stymied, confiscation of assets may be avoided, and/or debts may not be recovered.

Origin of the terms money laundering and money trail

United States law enforcement agencies first used the term money laundering to refer to Mafia ownership of laundromats. During the 1920s and 1930s the Mafia bought legitimate businesses with illicit profits from bootlegging, gambling and prostitution. Mafia investments in laundromats were popular because many were already owned by small-time Italian families. Dirty money was mixed with cash takings from laundry businesses and it was claimed that illicit cash was legitimate money. The Mafia bosses used the laundromat as a financial and tax alibi for illicit income.

A laundromat changes dirty clothes into clean clothes. A washing machine removes grime and dirt, making the clothes look clean and new. Similarly, a money laundry turns dirty money into clean money by removing the stain associated with dirty money.[4]

---

3. E.g., until recently corruption was virtually an unprosecutable offence in Australia because of the difficulty of proving the offence and the absence of institutional agencies devoted to combating corruption. In contrast, the burden of proof of corruption is placed on the defence in many developing countries where it is a criminal offence for a public servant to be in control of assets that are disproportionate to known sources of income. See e.g. *Prevention of Corruption Act* 1947 (India), s. 5(1)(e).

4. The idea of tainted money is not new. See Matthew, Ch. 27 (reference to blood money and Judas). See also Wiseman, *The Money Motive: A Study of An Obsession* (1974), Ch. 3 (for the concept of good and bad money); Galbraith, *Money; Whence It Came, Where It Went* (1975) (describing the debasement of coinage).

The paper chase or money trail was pioneered by American law enforcement agencies, especially the Internal Revenue Service (I.R.S.), in the 1920s to investigate the syndicate or mob. The most famous target was the gangster Al Capone,[5] who from 1925 to 1931 ran a multi-million dollar illicit business in Chicago. Capone did not pay any taxes and claimed that he earned less than U.S.$5,000 a year. Capone never had a bank account and never bought property in his own name. He paid for everything in cash out of a strongbox hidden under his bed. An I.R.S. special intelligence team targeted Capone for tax evasion. The unit compiled a list of Capone's personal spending, estimating the cost of his custom-made clothes, laundry items, telephone calls, home furnishings, parties and hotel accommodation, and calculated his net worth (assets less debts). With this information and with the assistance of Capone's gambling employees, the I.R.S. was able successfully to prosecute Capone on 22 counts of evading tax of over U.S.$1 million. Capone was fined U.S.$50,000 and sentenced to 11 years in prison, where he died.

The purpose

The wide definition of money laundering which we are using shows that money laundering can be for illegitimate or legitimate purposes. The prime illegitimate purpose is to avoid detection by taxation investigators or criminal law enforcement agencies. Laundering is also often an element of the following illegal activities: narcotics trafficking, organised crime, terrorism, tax evasion and white collar crime.

Narcotics traffickers accumulate huge amounts of cash which must be hidden and laundered—otherwise possession of illicit money will be evidence of drug activity.[6] Similarly, terrorist groups[7] require laundering facilities to fund illegal and violent operations. Money laundering is also an essential prerequisite for tax evasion[8] since any unaccountable income or wealth will attract the attention of tax officials. In the case of investment frauds,[9] criminals will find it difficult to keep their illicit benefits unless they engage in laundering.

Money laundering techniques are used by multinational companies to disguise bribes and sensitive payments to foreign government officials

5. Short, *Crime Inc.; The Story of Organised Crime* (1984), pp. 100-107; Balsamo and Carpozi, *Crime Inc.—The Inside Story Of the Mafia's First 100 Years* (1988), pp. 227-228, 237-241.
6. See generally, United States Senate Governmental Affairs Committee (Permanent Subcommittee on Investigations), *Illegal Narcotics Profits Hearings*, December 1979.
7. See generally, Adams, *The Financing Of Terror* (1986); Clare, *Racketeering In Northern Ireland: A New Version Of The Patriot Game* (1989). The world's richest terrorist group is the P.L.O. which through its various associated groups has an annual income of over U.S.$1.25 million. See "Inside The P.L.O. Finances" (September 1989), *Euromoney*.
8. For the description of various tax schemes, see Redlich, *Annual Report Of The Special Prosecutor: 1983-84* (1984). For a British discussion of tax evasion techniques, see Tuft, *The History Of Tax Avoidance* (1989); Gillard, *In The Name of Charity: The Rossminister Affair* (1987).
9. E.g., the tracing of profits from an insider dealing scam may lead to the discovery of the insider. Similarly determining who has financially gained from a share pushing racket, warehousing scam, or false prospectus will provide intelligence leads and evidence for prosecution. See Chaikin, op. cit., above Chs 2-4.

and "agents", in order to obtain lucrative contracts. Secret funding of political parties is necessary where there are legal restrictions on payment by companies, for example, in Japan and the United States, and to avoid embarrassment.[10]

In the corporate context, laundering is also used to conceal the sources of funds in a takeover bid, or generally to hide the beneficial ownership of shares in a company.[11] Laundering methods can disguise the fact that loans from banks are being used for unauthorised purposes, or to conceal the fact that corporate funds have been improperly removed from personal gain.

Laundered funds are hidden from parties such as spouses, creditors, business partners, competitors and the general public. Money laundering takes place in both the private and public sectors. It is found in the capitalist and socialist political systems.

What is the size of the problem?

It is virtually impossible to estimate accurately the size of money laundering. If criminologists cannot accurately estimate the amount of drug trafficking, organised crime or white collar crime, then it is difficult to see how they can calculate the amount of money produced by those crimes and consequently the extent of money laundering.

The International Monetary Fund (I.M.F.) and the Bank for International Settlements (B.I.S.) have found that it is impractical to make a direct estimate of worldwide drug money flows from international banking statistics and balance of payments accounts. Discrepancies in accounts between various countries can be analysed,[12] but there is no way of distinguishing drug money from illegal arms funds, or from other significant financial crimes. It is likely that drug money flows are only a small percentage of the total international money flows.

The Group of Seven Financial Task Force[13] has used three indirect methods of calculating laundered drug proceeds, namely estimated world drug production, actual seizures of illicit drugs and the estimated

10. See the myriad ways that corporate bribes were paid in the Lockeed arms scandal. The unsavoury world of political funding has been a subject of recent political controversy in France: see Giustini, *Le Racket Politique* (1990). The funding of political intelligence operations and illegal arms deals require laundering services. See e.g. the Iran-Contra arms scandal, as discussed in Cockburn, *Out Of Control* (1988); and *Report Of the Congressional Committees Investigating The Iran-Contra Affair* (1988).

11. E.g., in the takeover of the House of Fraser, it was found that the successful bidders, the Al Fayed family, had lied about their background and wealth. The government inspectors criticised the Fayeds' merchant bank and legal advisers because they had appeared to vouch for the character and financial standing of the Fayeds without making due diligence inquiries. See Brooke Q.C. and Aldous, *The House Of Fraser Holdings Plc*, Department of Trade and Industry, *Report* (1988), Chs 22, 23 and 25.

12. See Walter, *Secret Money: The World Of International Financial Secrecy* (1985), pp. 11-17. The main sources of information on aggregate banking activity in the individual offshore centres are the I.M.F.'s international financial statistics, the Bank for International Settlements, or the centres themselves. Unfortunately, the financial centres do not publish sufficient information so as to determine the size of bank liabilities.

13. *Report Of The Financial Action Task Force On Money Laundering* (7 February 1990), pp. 1-3.

consumption needs of drug users. The task force relied on the uncertain statistics that gross drug trafficking proceeds worldwide were U.S.$300 billion in 1987. Using a combination of these methods, the task force postulated that in the United States and Europe the retail proceeds of dealing in the three main drugs—heroin, cocaine and cannabis— amounted to U.S.$122 billion per year, of which 50 per cent to 70 per cent or as much as U.S.$85 billion was profits. The drug profits were laundered and/or used to finance other drug trafficking and criminal activities, purchase luxury goods, make investments in real estate and undermine legitimate businesses.

In Australia estimates of money likely to be laundered annually include $A2.6 billion from drugs, $A3 billion from tax evasion, and $A2.8 billion from illegal gambling. These figures are only rough estimates. They do not include illicit money sent by overseas criminals to Australia for laundering.

United States cases of drug money laundering indicate that the dimensions of money laundering are staggering. It is not unusual for laundering schemes to involve many millions of dollars. In one case that the author investigated while working for the London-based Common- wealth Commercial Crime Unit,[14] an offshore bank in the Caribbean was asked by a shady group of financiers to accept a deposit of U.S.$300 million at a commission for the bank of 3 per cent. The bank was being offered a fee of U.S.$9 million for merely agreeing to accept money on deposit. This indicates the price that the launderers were prepared to pay to clean the money. The bank officials were very tempted by the easy money, but the government got a whiff of the scheme and suspended the bank's licence.

What is wrong with money laundering?

A significant proportion of money laundering for illegal purposes is carried out at the instigation of organised criminal groups.[15] Money laundering is the lifeblood of organised crime. It prevents the detection and punishment of those most responsible for directing and financing the criminal organisation. Those at the top of the organisation are insulated from the physical acts of the crime. The criminal leaders are extremely difficult to investigate, let alone prosecute. It is the money trail which will often represent the only link between the leaders of the criminal organisation and the crime itself. Here lies the Achilles' heel of the financiers of crime.

Money laundering allows organised crime to maintain illegal profits intact and to enjoy the fruits of their criminal activities. The penetration of legitimate business by organised crime groups, and the consequent corruption of business, is well known and documented in the United

14. See Rider, *Combating International Commercial Crime — A Commonwealth Perspective* (1983) (description of the background and operations of the commercial crime unit).
15. See President's Commission on Organised Crime, *The Impact of Organised Crime Today*, Report to the President and the Attorney-General (April 1986).

States.[16] It has occurred in Australia in the poker machine and club industries,[17] gaming machine concerns,[18] unions[19] and the waterfront.[20] Indeed, concern about organised crime's involvement in Australia's business world was a major consideration in the establishment of the National Crime Authority.

The threat to business and industry is not only of direct penetration, but also grossly unfair competition. Criminals who have made their money from drug trafficking, illegal gambling or fraud are not going to be concerned about complying with tax or other laws that apply to law-abiding business people. They enjoy access to interest-free money created outside the legitimate banking world. They deploy their funds without regard to the general credit and fiscal restraints operating in the economy.[21]

The growth of the underground economy and money laundering saps the strength of the legitimate financial community.[22] The huge amount of money available for laundering has insidious corrupting influence. Business morality declines. Both managers and employees of financial institutions are subject to overwhelming temptations. Public servants and politicians are corrupted. Judicial authorities are compromised. Tax evasion becomes the norm. Indeed, an inevitable by-product of money laundering schemes is the violation of tax laws.

In the worst possible scenario, laundering perverts the economic and political system to such an extent that a country is hijacked for the enrichment of criminals. This has already occurred in some countries,

16. See e.g., Cook, "The Invisible Enterprise: Part 2: Money makes the mob go round", *Forbes*, 13 October 1980, pp. 120-128; Kwitny, *Vicious Circles: The Mafia In The Marketplace* (1979); Pennsylvania Crime Commission, *Racketeering In the Commercial Loan Brokerage Industry* (January 1980). While Reuter has emphasised the economic limitations of organised crime groups, Arlarcchi has argued that they have competitive advantages over non-mafia firms. See Reuter, *Disorganised Crime; The Economics Of The Visible Hand* (1983); Arlarcchi, *Mafia Business; The Mafia Ethic And The Spirit Of Capitalism* (1986).
17. See Mr Justice Moffit, *Report Of Inquiry In Respect Of Certain Matters Relating To Allegations Of Organized Crime In Clubs* (1974); Wilcox, *Report Of Board Of Inquiry Into Poker Machines* (November 1983); Mr Justice Connor, *Report Of Board Of Inquiry Into Casinos* (April 1982).
18. Note the recent allegations concerning criminal associations of gaming machine manufacturers, licensees and repairers. See Queensland Criminal Justice Commission, *Report On Gaming Machine Concerns And Regulations* (May 1990).
19. See Costigan, *Report On The Activities Of The Federated Ship Painters And Dockers Union*, Final Report (1984), Vol. 3, and Interim Report No. 4 (1982), Vol. 1 (1982); Winneke, *Report Of Inquiry Into The Activities Of The Australian Building Construction Employees And Builders Labourers Federation* (1982); Sharpe, *First and Second Reports Nos 87 & 89 Of the Custodian Appointed Pursuant To The BLF (De-recognition Act) 1985* (1988).
20. See Joint Commonwealth and New South Wales Task Force, *Report On Security Of Wharves And Containers* (1985), pp. 225-240; Sweeney, *Final Report Of The Royal Commission Into Alleged Payments To Maritime Unions* (1976).
21. See Rider, *The Promotion And Development Of International Co-operation To Combat Commercial and Economic Crime*, Memoranda of Commonwealth Law Ministers Meeting, Barbados (26 April-2 May 1980).
22. For the view that the underground economy has had substantial beneficial effects in overcoming Peru's complex legal machinery and corrupt bureaucracy, see De Soto, *The Other Path: The Invisible Revolution In The Third World* (1989).

and been attempted in certain Caribbean countries and in some of the small jurisdictions in the Asia/Pacific rim.[23]

The vulnerability of small states to financial manipulation and money laundering should never be underestimated.[24] There are many states where government revenue is considerably less than the profits made by international narcotics organisations. The risk is that such countries may become the washrooms and laundries of vast amounts of money of dubious origins.

Many of these small jurisdictions are presently trying to establish themselves as offshore financial centres, even though they do not have the necessary legal and financial infrastructure.[25] The danger of money laundering is all too obvious. As the United States government has closed the laundering opportunities in the Caribbean region, it is likely that North and South American criminals will look increasingly to the Asia/Pacific region as a venue for money laundering.

LAUNDERING SCHEMES

Structure of laundering

Whereas organised criminals have easy access to the most sophisticated laundering techniques, governments and the public are often ignorant of the latest money laundering schemes.

There are as many techniques for laundering money as there are methods of smuggling contraband or schemes for avoiding tax or exchange control. The potentially infinite variety of laundering schemes is only limited by the creative imagination and expertise of the entrepreneurs who devise such schemes.

The suitability of a laundering technique is influenced by the aims of the criminal and the circumstances concerning the crime. For example, a corrupt police officer in Australia who receives relatively small bribes

23. See report of United States Senate Committee for Foreign Relations, Subcommittee on Terrorism, Narcotics and International Operations, *Drugs, Law Enforcement And Foreign Policy* (December 1988) which discusses the growth of drug-related corruption in the Bahamas, Columbia, Cuba, Nicaragua, Haiti, Honduras and Panama. See also Gould and Amaro-Reyes, *The Effects Of Corruption On Administration Performance: Illustrations From Developing Countries*, World Bank Staff Working Paper No. 5680 (1984) which focuses on bureaucratic corruption in Asia, Africa and Latin America. A recent United States Senate Report accused Vanuatu, Nauru and Anguilla of being centres for drug money laundering. See (May 1990) *Islands Business* (Fiji) 11.
24. See comments of Law Ministers and Attorneys-General of the Commonwealth at the 1977, 1980 and 1983 Law Ministers Meetings. Winnipeg, Barbados and Sri Lanka, *Minutes Of Meetings And Memoranda*. See also the communiques at these meetings, and the communique at the Second Meeting Of Law Officers Of Commonwealth Jurisdiction in Port Villa, Vanuatu, July 1985. See generally, Commonwealth Consultative Group, *Vulnerability: Small States In A Global Society Report* (1985).
25. The lack of local expertise is so serious that the Bank of England has regularly supplied its employees on secondment to many Pacific Commonwealth countries. There is also a shortage of accountants, lawyers and financiers, and insufficient funds properly to vet applicants for bank licences and/or to investigate commercial fraud.

on an ad hoc basis, may merely use false names to invest the illicit money in banks and property. In contrast, a dictator[26] who is looting the nation's treasury on a vast scale will use more sophisticated money laundering techniques. Such techniques include the use of international banking facilities, the processing of funds through layers of fictitious entities and the creation of false documentation.

The success of a laundering scheme will ultimately depend on whether it provides a credible and apparently truthful explanation for the derivation of money. Laundering schemes geared to the specific needs of an individual will usually be more successful than off-the-peg general schemes.

Laundering money within jurisdiction

Using financial institutions

In 1984 the American President's Commission on Organised Crime warned that:

> every financial institution, including banks, savings and loan institutions, currency exchanges, and casinos, should assume that it is a potential target for use by organised crime in money laundering schemes.[27]

Nearly every type of service offered by banks and financial institutions can be used as part of a money laundering scam.[28] The functions of banks in laundering include the following:

- refining illicit money;
- exchanging illicit money for a bank deposit in a false name;
- using a safe deposit box to hide illicit products and money;
- providing transfer facilities so that illicit money can be moved to a convenient destination;
- using electronic funds transfers to pay for an illegal product, such as drugs, or to deposit and distribute the proceeds of an illegal transaction; and/or
- failing to report currency transactions or evading currency laws by smurfing.

The simplest and most common technique is refining of money. Refining is the process of converting small denomination bills ($1, $5, $10) into larger denomination bills ($50, $100).

26. For a description of former Philippines dictator Ferdinand Marcos' and his wife Imelda's theft of billions of dollars, laundering scams and co-operation with organised crime, see Seagrave, *The Marcos Dynasty* (1988), Chs 4, 9, 15-17 and Bonner, *Waltzing With A Dictator* (1987), Chs 11 and 12. The recovery by a new democratic government of money stolen by deposed dictators raises difficult questions of international law, including the constitutionality of anti-corruption bodies, sovereign immunity and personal immunity of a former head of state, the political offence exception to extradition and mutual assistance requests, the enforcement of foreign judgments, and the requirements of a fair trial and due process.
27. President's Commission On Organised Crime, *The Cash Connection: Organised Crime, Financial Institutions, and Money Laundering*, Interim Report (1984), p. 51.
28. See generally, Chaikin, *Money Laundering Techniques And Banking Secrecy*, Fourth International Symposium on Commercial Crime, Jesus College, Cambridge (1986); Mr Justice Stewart, *Report of Royal Commission Of Inquiry Into Drug Trafficking* (1983), pp. 202-327; Pinilla, *The Subversion Of Banking By Organised Crime*, Unpublished Paper (Wolfson College, University Of Cambridge, 1985).

Refining is most likely to occur where large volumes of "street money" (small denomination bills) are produced, for example, at the retail end of drug trafficking. It has been observed that drug addicts do not pay for drugs by credit: they do not use American Express or Mastercard. They use small bills which may be physically tainted by the drug.

There are two motives for refining money. First, refining eliminates the physical taint associated with cash used or produced in an illegal transaction. For example, the cash exchanged in a drug deal is physically tainted with the residue or scent of the drug.[29] Secondly, refining reduces the volume and weight of cash so as to make it easier to carry. For example, the United States government estimates that U.S.$1 million in $100 bills weighs 20 pounds and fills one suitcase, whereas U.S.$1 million in $10 bills weighs 200 pounds and requires 10 suitcases to carry. There is thus a considerable difference in the weight and volume of money when using $10 or $100 bills. Refining of cash is caught by the *Cash Transaction Reports Act* 1988 (Cth) (C.T.R. Act), either because it is a suspicious transaction or significant transaction.

Another method of laundering is opening and operating a bank account in a false name. Section 24 of the C.T.R. Act makes such conduct a criminal offence, punishable in the case of an individual by a fine of up to $5,000 and/or up to two years imprisonment.

Under the C.T.R. Act banks and other cash dealers are required to verify the identity of persons opening or becoming signatories to accounts. Pursuant to the Act, cash dealers have introduced new procedures to prevent future misuse of their facilities. But some doubt has been raised whether cash dealers in Australia have weeded out a significant proportion of existing accounts in false names.[30] There is also the problem that false identification documents are widely available in criminal circles, and that cash dealers do not have the expertise to check identity documents.[31]

29. The spread of drug-tainted dollars in the United States economy is making it more difficult to link drug traffickers and drug-tainted cash. The London-based *Economist* reported in April 1989 that in a random sample of 135 bills in denominations from U.S.$1 to U.S.$100 taken from banks in 12 American cities, it was found that 131 bills were tainted with traces of cocaine, ranging in quantity from one billionth of a gram to one four thousandth of a gram. Defendants in United States drug cases are now claiming that they have innocently picked up traces of cocaine (the "innocent happenstances" defence).
30. See comments by Fitzgerald on the difficulty of obtaining the names of false accounts in Queensland banks; *Report Of A Commission Of Inquiry Into Possible Illegal Activities and Associated Police Misconduct* (1989), pp. 165-166.
31. The abuse of Australian passports by drug dealers was documented in the report by Mr Justice Stewart, *Royal Commission Of Inquiry Into Drug Trafficking, Interim Report No. 2: Passports* (1980) and the widespread problem of false bank accounts was revealed by Costigan, op. cit. The introduction of a new system for obtaining Australian passports and stricter state requirements for obtaining drivers' licences has not deterred organised criminals, who can buy a legitimate passport from certain countries (e.g. Bolivia, Bangladesh, Costa Rica, Gambia, Philippines, Sri Lanka, Tonga). See Glain, "Hong Kong Elite's Ticket To The World: Dollars For Passports", *International Herald Tribune*, 23 August 1990, p. 2; Harriman, "Passports For Sale", *The New Statesman*, 17 March 1989, p. 10. The lack of a national identity card system and the ease with which fraudulent travel and identity documents can be purchased impose serious limitations on the effectiveness of the C.T.R. Act identification requirements.

In the author's experience, since the enactment of the C.T.R. Act, there has been a shift in the opinion of senior management in Australia's banks and major financial institutions. Senior management are well aware of the banks' new legal responsibilities to report suspicious and significant cash transactions. They are determined to keep their institutions clean and prevent any association with or use by criminals. They are encouraging their line managers to take more vigorous action to prevent both fraud and money laundering. It will, however, take some time before every branch manager, teller and employee is sufficiently sensitive to the requirements of the legislation.

Casinos and gambling transactions

Casinos are honey-pots for criminals who go there to cheat, gamble and launder money. Wealthy criminals who are outcasts in polite society are welcome as "high-rollers" in casinos. In such an atmosphere it is easy for a criminal to gamble illicit earnings in relative anonymity.[32]

Although casinos in Australia are generally subject to strict regulations,[33] this does not stop money laundering taking place, either with or without the co-operation of the casino management. Casinos attract money launderers[34] because they are a high cash flow business and provide financial services similar to those supplied by banks.

Some casinos handle more currency than the average bank branch and maintain a huge inventory of cash. Typically, customers of casinos deposit small denomination bills and are paid out in $100 bills or casino cheques. In turn casinos are required to make deposits of small bills at their banks and to withdraw $100 bills. The pattern of bank/casino transactions—small bills in, large bills out—provides an ideal cover for anyone desiring to refine a large volume of street money through casinos. Thus a government programme to analyse the general cash flows through the bank accounts of casinos will be unable to determine whether refining has taken place.

It is not widely known that casinos accept deposits, cash cheques, provide safe deposit facilities and transfer funds offshore.[35] These services are supposed to be used in order to facilitate gambling, but they can be perverted for laundering purposes.

32. For an empirical study of Las Vegas casinos, see Skolnick, *The House of Cards: The Legalisation And Control Of Casino Gambling* (1978).
33. See McMillen, "Gambling For High Stakes: Australian Casino Developments" (September 1987) Cur. Affairs Bull. 20; and by the same author, "The Other Revolution; The Legalisation Of Commercial Gambling In Australia" (1986) 2 Nev. Pub. Affairs Rev. 65 (the main regulatory defects are the preliminary control procedures and the difficulty of cancelling casinos' licences once granted). See also *Submission To The Senate Standing Committee On Legal And Constitutional Affairs By Conrad International Hotels Corporation On The C.T.R. Bill* (1987) and the report by Sir Desmond Sullivan, *The Committee Of Enquiry Into The Establishment Of Casinos In New Zealand* (January 1989).
34. See United States House of Representatives, Committee of Judiciary (Sub-Committee on Crime), *Use Of Casinos To Launder Proceeds Of Drug Trafficking And Organised Crime, Hearings*, 10 February and 21 June 1984 (1985); Mangan, "Casinos And Drug Money: A Laundering Loophole", *Drug Enforcement*, Summer 1984, p. 21.
35. See e.g. how Brian Molony, an assistant manager of the Canadian Imperial Bank of Commerce stole more than $CAN17 million from his employer and used Caesars Palace's Toronto bank account to transfer stolen money from Canada to the United States: Ross, *Sting* (1987).

Casino money laundering is usually detected as a result of "tip-offs" by casino employees or managers or by surveillance of a suspected launderer. Prevention of laundering has been facilitated by new controls introduced by casinos to comply with the obligations under the C.T.R. Act.

In Australia, criminals and corrupt police have claimed[36] that their wealth is derived from successfully gambling on horse-racing, dogs, etc. The Woodward Royal Commission into Drug Trafficking summarised one laundering scheme as follows:

> money can be laundered at a race meeting and race meetings are of considerable value to persons seeking such facility. By way of illustration, a person possessing $A1,000 cash which has been obtained illegally may launder it by producing evidence of an acceptable nature which shows that he has won it at a race meeting. The only certain way of doing this is by producing a betting ticket on the horse that won or by a cheque from the bookmaker . . . with the co-operation of a bookmaker, a winning ticket may be obtained in several ways. One way is to approach the bookmaker after the race is run and place with him a purported bet on the winning horse. In such event, the bookmaker may write a ticket in proper sequence and enter it in the betting slip either as a cash or credit bet. In either way, it will appear as the last bet on the horse in the race.[37]

Another method is to purchase for cash a winning bet from a lucky punter just after a race has been decided but before collection of the bet.[38] The launderer will claim the winning bet as her or his own and this is supported by the betting ledgers. The scheme relies on finding winning ticket holders in a timely fashion, offering that punter a premium for the ticket, and in ensuring that the identity of that punter is kept secret. Moreover, the latter punter must be willing to take the risk of possessing a large amount of cash which has an illicit origin.

In the author's view, a laundering scheme involving only small amounts of illicit cash will probably escape detection. It is difficult to prove that gambling wins have been laundered because gambling is relatively anonymous, betting records are easily reconstructed or manipulated, and bookmakers are often willing to co-operate with launderers.

Where a person is under suspicion, investigators should use forensic techniques to examine documents, and interview betting agents, bookmakers and other witnesses. A thorough investigation may reveal discrepancies in documents and show a pattern of laundering. Reliance on reporting by bookmakers, who are subject to the C.T.R Act, will be very important. The challenge to the C.T.R Agency and government is

---

36. E.g., the notorious drug trafficker Robert Trimbole claimed that he had net winnings of $A1.5 million from betting transactions over a 17-month period immediately following his discharge from bankruptcy. Trimbole manufactured records of his so-called wins but this was easily exposed by government investigators. See Mr Justice Woodward, *Report Of Royal Commission Into Drug Trafficking* (October 1979), pp. 898-979.
37. Ibid., p. 949.
38. Ibid., pp. 943-979.

to change the ethical culture of bookmakers, ensure that suspicious credit bets are reported, and monitor laundering via illegal gambling.[39]

The domestic laundromat

Buying a high cash flow business and putting illicit cash through the till is another favoured laundering method. The illicit funds are disguised as part of business turnover and may even be declared as taxable income so as to ensure complete legitimisation. This method has the secondary effect of increasing the value of the company's shares by artificially increasing its profitability, thereby creating a potentially large capital gain.

A financial adviser to the mob understands the advantages of investing in the legitimate sector. Increases in illicit income or asset wealth can be justified by the legal business. There is the tax alibi to explain extravagant spending and increases in net worth. Businesses offer criminals legitimate sources of employment which help them to cultivate an image of respectability and provide a springboard to political power. The legal operations of businesses also provide a cover for illegal activities.[40]

American organised crime penetrates legitimate businesses for profiteering and/or laundering. Front companies have been used to invest in cash businesses such as bars, restaurants, hotels, car dealerships, vending companies and debt collection agencies.

A variation on this scheme is the direct investment in an unsuccessful business such as a failed property company, travel firm or insurance business.[41] The criminal investor buys a legitimate business which is losing money, and then manipulates the records to show that the business is profitable. Funds requiring laundering are thus channelled through the business as if they are legal profits. Soaking up losses is a very costly laundering strategy and usually only makes sense in the short term.

In all cases the books must be manipulated by using one of the following techniques:[42]

- overstating the amount of revenue generated by the business by inflating sales volume or average prices;

39. For the role of illegal casinos and illegal gambling in financing drug deals and organised crime, see Hickie, *The Prince And The Premier* (1985). For the use of illegal lottery dealers in Puerto Rico to launder drug money, see United States Senate Committee On Governmental Affairs (Permanent Subcommittee on Investigations), *Money Laundering In Puerto Rico Hearings*, 25 July 1985 (1985).
40. For an account of a Mafia family's legitimate business interests in the United States, see Anderson, *The Business Of Organised Crime: A Cosa Nostra Family* (1979), Chs 5-7.
41. E.g., the Oakland chapter of the Hell's Angels laundered their profits from illegal amphetamine trafficking by purchasing failing businesses through "front men". Those businesses which resisted the Angel's buy-out approach were subject to intimidation. The Angels' "buy-out, burn-out, bomb-out" programme of laundering money was completely ineffective because it aroused intense law enforcement interest.
42. The techniques used by so-called respectable companies to cook the books are also used by organised crime to launder money through companies. See Griffiths, *Creative Accounting* (1986); and Murphy, *Use Of Legitimate Business Activity As A Cover For Money Laundering*, Unpublished (Police Executive Research Forum, Washington, 1989).

- overstating reported expenses by paying suppliers for non-existent goods, paying wages for "ghost employees", or invoicing non-existent consultants; and

- creating assets or inflating asset values through fake loans, sales of non-existent property, or purchase of assets at an undervalued price.

The United States, unlike Australia, has a specific law to detect laundering through legitimate businesses. Section 60501 of the American *Internal Revenue Code* provides that any person engaged in a trade or business who receives in the course of that business, cash in excess of U.S.$10,000 in one transaction (or two or more related transactions) must report to the I.R.S. This provision is wide enough to catch accountants, attorneys, [43] real estate agents, and retailers of luxury items, who sell their services, goods and items to drug traffickers and other criminals in return for cash.

There are also specialised investigative methods for detecting laundering in both the income statements and balance sheets of legitimate firms. Reported revenues and expenses can be compared with some independent indicator of revenue and expenses. For example, in France the tax authorities have found that laundry bills (for the number of tablecloths cleaned) and bakery bills (for the number of loaves of bread consumed) of restaurant owners are useful information for making an independent estimate of revenue.

Fabrication of transactions or creation of ghost employees are easier to detect and thus are more risky from the money launderer's viewpoint. For example, completely fictitious sales of motor cars are established by checking actual sales against car registrations. Bogus or ghost employees are also easily established because it is nearly impossible to create a truly convincing false person. There are many indications of the existence of a genuine person, and when these are all examined, the falsity of the identity will be uncovered.

Secret purchases of assets and shares

There are many well-known perfectly legal ways in which an interest in, or control or ownership of, a company may be obscured, if not completely hidden. Organised crime uses Wall Street attorneys and London's bowler hat brigade secretly to acquire companies and even industries. In most cases the lawyers and bankers do not know who their clients are.

Investment bankers in takeover battles are highly imaginative in hiding interests in shares. They use nominees, proxies, options, voting trusts

---

43. About 15,000 American lawyers have reported to the I.R.S. that they had received cash payments for more than $U.S.10,000, but refused to disclose the identity of their clients because they considered that this would violate attorney-client privilege. See Glaberson, "I.R.S. pursuit of lawyers' cash client faces test", *New York Times*, 9 March 1990, p. A1. Lawyers are also contesting prosecutorial practices such as subpoenaing attorneys to testify about their fees, summonses by the I.R.S. and attempts to gain forfeiture of attorneys' fees. See generally, Viles, "Attorney's Fees Forfeitures and Subpoenaing Defendant's Attorneys" [1986] *Ann. Survey Of Amer. Law* 335; United States Senate, Committee On The Judiciary, *White Collar Crime (Money Laundering) Hearings*, 18 & 25 March 1986, pp. 91-102.

and concert parties. Criminals can also use these devices in penetrating legitimate businesses.[44]

The use of a nominee to buy shares in a company breaks the link between a criminal and the cash he or she has made illegally and now wishes to invest. The nominee's name appears on the company's records as the registered holder of the shares, but the nominee is only the agent/trustee for the real owner.

The real owner of the shares may not even be known to the nominee, so that questioning the nominee may not be fruitful. Where shares are purchased in the name of a nominee by a third party acting for the investor, the nominee will not know—and may not want to know—the identity of the investor.

Another way of hiding share ownership is to create a chain of nominees by using companies as shareholders.[45] For example, company A holds the majority of shares in company B, company B owns all shares in company C, and company C owns all shares in company D. Thus company A ultimately owns company D. To break open the corporate chain, an investigator has to unravel the ownership of companies D, C, B and A. In more complex company chains—which may have up to 15 nominee companies spread through several countries—investigators face a near impossible task.

Bearer shares[46] conceal ownership because they are transferred between owners merely by delivery. Just like cash, where bearer shares are issued there is no registration of the holders of such shares and so beneficial ownership cannot be easily determined.

In the United States, Britain and Australia, all substantial real (beneficial) owners of shares in public companies must be disclosed to the government, but this is easily evaded by the use of foreign nominees. Moreover, there is no obligation to disclose the real ownership of private companies—these provide rich pickings for organised crime.

Other domestic devices

Other devices for laundering money within a country include misuse of lawyers' trust accounts,[47] creation of bogus mortgages and investment in real estate. During the boom period in the 1980s when asset prices rose steeply, launderers also invested in shares, futures and

---

44. See New Zealand Securities Commission, *Nominee Shareholdings In Public Companies* (1982) for a useful summary of the various methods of concealing a nominee's interest in a company. See also Chaikin, "Cracking the Nominee in New Zealand" (1982) 3 Commonwealth Law Bull. 814; Ashe, *Nominee Shareholdings*, paper submitted to Commonwealth Law Ministers Meeting, Sri Lanka, Minutes and Memoranda (1983).

45. For the use of multiple nominees to conceal strategic interests in companies, see *Crossley Ltd v. North Broken Hill Holdings Ltd* (1986) 4 A.C.L.C. 131 (Vic. Sup. Ct); *N.C.S.C. v. Brierley Investments Ltd* (1988) 14 N.S.W.L.R. 273 (N.S.W. Sup. Ct).

46. Bearer shares are not available in Australia but are used in Anguilla, Barbados, Cook Islands, Costa Rica, Gibraltar, Liberia, Nauru, Netherlands, Panama, Seychelles, Turks and Caicos and Vanuatu.

47. See Note, "Solicitors' nominee companies laundering profits of criminal activity" (January 1984) Commonwealth Law Bull. 331; Stewart, op. cit., pp. 221-229.

options, as well as in precious metals[48] and collectables. Laundering investments of this nature requires specialised knowledge of the market, so investigators should seek professional assistance when examining financial transactions involving these matters.

There are two other devices which are likely to be increasingly used by money launderers in order to avoid the C.T.R. Act. The first method is called smurfing, whereby a person deposits cash with a cash dealer in amounts less than the reportable amount. If the American experience is any guide, we will witness the rise in Australia of smurfing organisations and a variety of smurfing practices.

The most common smurfing practices[49] are:

- opening multiple bank accounts at one or more banks in the names of offshore companies. Money couriers then make deposits in each account in amounts under $A10,000;

- using different persons as money couriers for depositing illicit cash of amounts less then $A10,000 at the same bank;

- using different branches of the same bank to make several under $A10,000 illicit cash deposits on a daily basis;

- travelling from bank to bank, branch to branch buying bank cheques for cash in amounts under $A10,000.

Some smurfing practices pretend to comply with the reporting rule in such a manner as not to arouse suspicion of money laundering by:

- using a money courier a limited number of times to buy large bank cheques (for example, $A50,000 or $A100,000); or

- using a courier to make occasional large cash deposits to different bank accounts making sure that there is no pattern of deposits to attract attention.

Secondly, criminals will try to arrange their transactions so as to fall within one of the exemptions from the reporting requirement under the C.T.R. Act. Criminals will target financial institutions and attempt to corrupt branch managers and other employees in order to obtain the valuable exempt status.

Section 31 of the C.T.R. Act covers both avoidance schemes by making it a criminal offence to conduct cash transactions so as to avoid the reporting requirements under the Act. However, merely relying on a law will not be a sufficient way of coping with the new threat of laundering. Banks should be aware of the vulnerability of certain types of employees and should train their managers to be aware of the new risks arising from regulation and increased criminal activity.

48. The use of diamonds, gold and precious metals to avoid tax, move money offshore and to clean dirty money is widespread. The C.T.R. Act which applies to bullion dealers is likely to be avoided by small-time miners who will deal in parcels of less than the reportable amounts. See Industries Assistance Commission Report, *Precious Metals, Gems And Jewellery*, No. 412, 3 May 1988, para. 2.1. See also *Submission By The Central Queensland Bullion Traders To The Senate Standing Committee On Legal And Constitutional Affairs Regarding The C.T.R. Bill* (1988).
49. See Morley, *Dirty Money: A Banker's Guide To Self Defence*, Bank Manager's Guide (1985); Chamness and Cook, *A Guide To The Bank Secrecy Act Teacher's And Students Editions* (1987).

Laundering money offshore

In the past twenty years there has been a significant internationalisation of currency, capital and corporate securities markets.[50] Given the ease of international travel and developments in communications, information and technology, a very high proportion of financial crime will be transnational, in conception, execution or realisation. Money laundering schemes for transnational crimes and for significant single jurisdiction crimes will inevitably involve offshore countries.[51]

An offshore laundering scheme involving illicit money, no matter how simple or complex, has three basic steps. First, money will be smuggled offshore either directly or through a financial institution. Secondly, money will be agitated through one or more laundering cycles offshore. Thirdly, a legitimate source will be formed in a foreign country through which the now clean money may be safely repatriated onshore or maintained offshore for investment or other purposes.[52]

Smuggling of funds offshore

There are many ways of smuggling funds offshore, but the most efficient method is to use a bank or financial institution which has access to international money transfer facilities.[53] Money transfer facilities are a vital component of international trade in goods and services. They are used by governments, businesses and tourists. They are also used by drug traffickers, terrorists and white collar criminals.

In terms of the amount of money exported, the single most important element is a bank or financial institution. It is a bank which ordinarily accepts money for export and transmits it abroad. The laundering method may be the issuing of a bank cheque or money order or simply crediting electronically an account. The use of the banking system seldom attracts attention and is not easily identified as part of an unlawful scheme. However, if the government detects the unlawful conduct and follows the transaction to the bank, there should be bank records providing evidence of the currency transfer.

Another method of smuggling funds offshore is actually physically to transport cash or negotiable monetary instruments. Cash is transported in airlines, ships, rail or road. It may be carried by body couriers, as luggage, in carrier or false compartments, as unaccompanied baggage, or as freight.

50. For an analysis of extraterritorial problems, see Chaikin, "Fraud, Securities Laws and Extraterritoriality In The United States", Ch. 11 in *The Regulation Of The British Securities Industry*, ed. Rider (1979); Rider, Chaikin and Abrams, *Guide To The Financial Services Act 1986* (1987), Ch. 13; Levy, "Internationalisation Of The Securities Markets: Jurisdictional And Enforcement Issues" (May 1988) 6 (No. 2) C.S.L.J. 75.

51. The extraterritorial reach of American money laundering legislation has been a subject of some controversy. See Harmon, "United States Money Laundering Laws: International Implications" (1988) 9 (No. 1) N.Y. Jnl Int. & Comp. L. 1.

52. Chaikin, *Money Laundering: Policy And Enforcement Aspects*, Unreported Paper (given at seminar conducted by Queensland Law Society and Bond University Law School, Brisbane, 25 October 1989); Fahlman, "Drug Money Flow" (October 1985) 391 I.N.C.P.R. 147.

53. For a description of the various systems of international payments, see Crawford, *International Money Transfers*, Unpublished Paper (given at Singapore Conference On International Banking And Corporate Financial Operations, 18-20 August 1988).

The physical transportation method is simple and popular with money launderers because it generally leaves no paper trail within jurisdiction.[54] The main disadvantage of smugglers is the substantial risk of loss through accident and theft by employees or rival criminal groups.

The risks of detection of cash smuggling are small, particularly since the introduction of container cargoes and the replacement of body searches with electronic scanning devices at airports. Most money couriers are caught by accident or because of a tip-off. In recent years United States Customs has increased its surveillance by relying on money courier profiles, the system of private aircraft reporting, and targeting mail shipments to haven countries.

Other vehicles for smuggling funds offshore include the use of false or fraudulent customs documentation, the manipulation of securities, commodities and foreign exchange transactions, and the abuse of the international airlines payment system.[55] These smuggling vehicles have been used in evading exchange control, and have been and are being adapted by professional launderers to assist narcotics traffickers and other organised criminals.

Agitation of funds

The first stage of the laundering cycle is completed when the illicit funds reach an offshore jurisdiction, such as a tax haven. Additional secrecy protection[56] is obtained by agitating the funds through one or more laundering cycles. The funds can travel across many countries and pass through many hands, bank accounts and legitimate businesses.

For example, an Australian-based drug trafficker hires a bagman who takes the illicit cash to a tax haven, such as the Cook Islands. The funds are initially processed in the Cook Islands—for example, they are deposited in a local bank account in the name of a trust company—and later are transmitted through bank wire transfer to Hong Kong. The maze of financial transactions will mean that the Hong Kong authorities will not know whether the money entering their country is derived from an illegal source; nor will the receiving bank in Hong Kong necessarily have any grounds for believing that the funds are suspicious.

Offshore laundering cycles rely on traditional secrecy vehicles[57] such as companies, nominees and trusts. Accounting firms assist the laundering process by providing their employees as directors and shareholders of shelf

---

54. There will be some paper records where cash is smuggled as unaccompanied baggage on airlines and ships—e.g. airway bills and shipping manifests. But unlike when the international payments system is used, investigators of the physical transport method will not be able to determine the precise contents of the baggage.
55. For the widespread problem of fraudulent trade documentation, see Ellen and Campbell, *International Maritime Fraud* (1981); International Chamber Of Commerce, *Guide To The Prevention Of International Trade Fraud* (1985). For the use of shares, share options and futures contracts to move money offshore, see Stewart, op. cit., pp. 100, 204-218, 644-647.
56. See report of United States Senate Committee on Governmental Affairs (Permanent Subcommittee on Investigations), *Crime And Secrecy: The Use of Offshore Banks and Companies* (1985); Blum, *Offshore Haven Banks, Trusts And Companies: The Business Of Crime In the Euromarket* (1984).
57. See Chaikin, *Money Laundering Techniques and Banking Secrecy*, op. cit. above; Chambost, *Bank Accounts: A World Guide To Confidentiality* (1983).

companies, while lawyers facilitate the recycling process by opening up bank accounts for their clients in offshore havens. The widespread availability of legal professional privileges is especially important in providing supra-secrecy protection for criminals.[58]

In most instances the professional accountant and lawyer will not be aware that he or she is part of a laundering scheme. But there are also many jurisdictions where the professions are corrupt and have no ethical limitations on their conduct.[59]

The more secrecy vehicles that are inserted in a laundering scheme, the greater will be the difficulty in unravelling the scheme. There are, however, two practical limitations on the recycling process. Secrecy vehicles cost money and will diminish the amount of funds available to the owner. The increasing maze of secrecy also entails greater risks of loss and theft.

Repatriation of funds

After the illicit funds have passed through the laundering cycle, the owner of those funds has the choice of either leaving them in a haven country or arranging to repatriate them. If the laundering scheme is to be successful, the funds must be repatriated in such a way that it appears that they were legitimately acquired from abroad.

The most common scheme for repatriating laundered money is a loan arrangement. Back-to-back loans[60] are a common feature of international commerce, but they are equally valuable to tax evaders and money launderers.

For example, an Australian drug trafficker ("D") has $A500,000 in illicit profits hidden in a Luxembourg bank account. In order to repatriate the money D decides to invest it in a chain of Chinese restaurants costing $A1 million. A down-payment of $A50,000 is made in "clean money" properly declared to the government. D then borrows $A450,000 from a local bank and borrows the remaining $A500,000 from the Luxembourg bank. The latter $A500,000 is a legitimate loan and is secured against D's bank deposit in Luxembourg. Interest on both loans is tax deductible, which thereby reduces the cost of the laundering scam.

58. It is common for lawyers in Switzerland and Liechtenstein to open up bank accounts on behalf of their clients, thereby imposing two layers of secrecy—bank secrecy and legal professional privilege. See Hughes, "Super Secrecy Arrives In Swiss Banking", *Financial Times*, 4 October 1989. But the Swiss Federal Supreme Court has held that an attorney's investment activities on behalf of a client are not covered by the attorney-client privilege. See *Dr Nn v. Federal Office Of Police Matters*, Federal Court, 29 December 1986, Praxis des Bundesgerichts 79 N.R. 188 (September 1987). Similar decisions have been reached in Australia (see *Allen, Allen & Hemsley v. Deputy Commissioner of Taxation* (1989) 20 A.T.R. 321, F.F.C.) and the United Kingdom (see *R. v. Central Criminal Court; Ex parte Francis & Francis* [1988] 3 W.L.R. 989.

59. See allegations of lawyers' involvement in Bahamian offshore drug money schemes in the *Report Of The Commission Of Enquiry* (President Sir J. A. Smith, Nassau, 1984), Ch. xiv; McGee and Hiaasen, "Some Lawyers Accused Of Passing Bribes And Fixing Cases", *Miami Herald Special Reprint* (1984).

60. Back-to-back loans are an efficient method of obtaining a specified currency and provide a method of avoiding the risks which would otherwise apply where the loan is between countries which are parties to the I.M.F. treaty. See Chambost, op. cit., pp. 23-24.

Investigators on loan back arrangements should check the credit record of the borrower, the circumstance of the making of the loan, and the history of payments. They should examine documents in the hands of the borrower which may indicate that there is a back-to-back arrangement.

There are numerous alternative methods of repatriating funds.[61] A criminal uses a foreign shelf company as a front to make a direct investment in a local unit trust, partnership or company. A criminal claims that the illicit proceeds are profits from a successful foreign business, gambling, stock or property transaction. A criminal arranges with a third party to receive funds from a fake insurance settlement or phoney inheritance.

In all cases where large sums of money are involved it is likely that accountants and law firms will have been consulted because there are issues of tax planning, foreign investment law and/or company law. If investigators can interview the accountants and lawyers and examine their documents then the laundering scam can be uncovered.

The main vehicle for detecting international money laundering is the currency import and export reporting requirement of the C.T.R. Act. Under that Act any person who transfers foreign currency out of Australia, or Australian currency or foreign currency into Australia, of a value of not less than $A5,000, must provide a report in respect of that transfer. Any person in Australia who receives Australian or foreign currency from a place outside Australia will be required to report the receipt of those funds if the value of the currency involved exceeds $A5,000. These provisions complement the *Banking (Foreign Exchange) Regulations* 1946 which presently contain a prohibition on the export of Australian currency in excess of $A5,000.

Wire transfers—a money laundering loophole

In the modern world electronic transfers of money constitute the bulk of, and the highest value transactions in, national and international payments. In the United States more than U.S.$1 trillion and over 400,000 transactions pass through the nation's clearing houses every day. Billions of dollars are wire transferred into and out of the United States, with little government monitoring.

Since wire transfers are the fastest and most efficient way to move funds from one bank to another, they have a high potential for abuse. For example, United States bank investigators estimate that over U.S.$100 billion of cocaine money is exported out of the United States by wire transfer each year.

The American Bankers Association[62] stated in 1989 that "wire transfers which are essentially unregulated, have emerged as the primary method by which high volume launderers ply their trade". Senator John Kerry has called for "wire transfer accountability".

---

61. See Chaikin, *Money Laundering Techniques and Banking Secrecy*, op. cit. (for an outline of the other methods of repatriating funds).
62. 135 Cong. Rec. 99555 (18 May 1989).

The United States treasury[63] has proposed that financial institutions keep more detailed records of international payments including wire transfers, which will assist in the detection and investigation of offshore money laundering. Banks are also being requested to develop suspicious wire transfer profiles and to report suspicious payments to the United States treasury. A suspicious transfer[64] would be, for example, the presence of large currency deposits prior to an outgoing transfer, or the existence of an incoming transfer followed by issuance of a bank cheque.

The Australian government plans to introduce a new surveillance system to monitor international electronic money transfers.[65] The precise scope of any new reporting obligation has not yet been established. The usefulness of the reports to law enforcement should be balanced against the effect of any ensuing requirement on the cost and efficiency of the payments system.

The Bank for International Settlements (B.I.S.) is considering whether to pool surveillance knowledge into an expert system to monitor unusual wholesale banking transactions. The idea is for member banks in B.I.S. to pool unusual transactions on a day-to-day basis and feed them into a data base. The information would be useful in preventing fraud, targeting customers and detecting laundering.

Whither exchange controls?

The 1980s witnessed the dismantling of exchange control laws in nearly every country in western Europe, starting with the United Kingdom in 1979 and with more recent changes in France, Italy, Ireland and Denmark. The relaxation of exchange controls is a necessary condition for Europe's single market in 1992. The dismantling of the exchange control laws, coupled with the growing presence of Japanese banks in Europe, have been significant factors in the doubling of business between banks in Europe from U.S.$39 billion in 1988 to U.S.$81 billion in the first three quarters of 1989.

The trend towards lifting exchange controls and freeing capital movements, which has also occurred in the Asia/Pacific region, inevitably undermines efforts to control offshore money laundering scams. There are also increased risks of tax evasion and corporate abuse.

63. Financial institutions are already required to keep some records relating to international transfers of more than U.S.$10,000 to or from any person or account outside the United States (31 C.F.R. 103.33(b)). The main defect is that "financial institutions are not required to obtain or record information from or about the identity of an originator or beneficiary of a payment, about the parties on whose behalf the originator or beneficiary may be acting, or other information beyond what is in their records or necessary to make the wire transfer."

64. See Dudine, *Identification Of Suspicious Wire Transfers Can Be Integrated Into The Bank's Credit Review Systems*, Unpublished Paper (given at conference on money laundering enforcement: legal and practical developments, American Bankers Association/American Bar Association, New York, 26-27 October 1989).

65. The *Cash Transaction Reports Amendment Act* 1991 (Cth) requires the reporting to the C.T.R. Agency by cash dealers in Australia of all international funds transfer instructions (including telex) into and out of Australia sent or received by them which effect a payment of funds either in Australia or a foreign country unless exempted by regulations.

One solution to the problem of tax evasion is to dismantle exchange controls but to require disclosure of cross-border movements of money above a certain level. For example, since 1 January 1990, French residents have been allowed to open bank accounts abroad on condition that transactions involving Ffrs 50,000 (U.S.$8,200) or more are declared to the French tax authorities. At the same time French residents can open foreign bank accounts at their domestic banks. Further, the government has beefed up its tax surveillance apparatus by requiring domestic banks to provide to the tax authorities detailed information about their customers' financial activities.

The experience of countries which have or have had sophisticated exchange control regimes is directly relevant to the so-called battle against money laundering. Most developing countries have currency controls[66] which require extensive reporting of virtually every type of financial transaction with a foreign resident. There is a wide array of prohibitions applying to certain transactions and controls applying to financial institutions, securities and gifts which affect foreign exchange. Typically, the enforcement body of exchange controls is a central bank which has a hugh discretion in giving or denying permission to specific financial transactions.

There are many ways of avoiding and evading exchange control laws.[67] The enforcement record of exchange control countries is generally poor. The system depends on a high degree of voluntary compliance. Exchange controls are often a desperate solution to bad economic policy. There is also the risk that "too effective enforcement" (sometimes called a heavy-handed approach) may result in a bigger economic problem than the one that justified the introduction of exchange controls.[68]

Experience shows that attempts to control capital flight quickly expand to systems regulating all outflows of foreign exchange.[69] Direct controls of capital are evaded through the vehicle of unregulated foreign payments. To deal with misinvoicing of trade, the authorities need therefore to supervise closely import and export payments. Efforts directed at establishing the bona fides of trade transactions involve inevitable delays in payments for goods and services and tend to disrupt the normal commercial life of a country.

Even the most comprehensive enforcement exchange control country has the greatest difficulties in achieving its aims of protecting the local

66. For a description of exchange control laws and policies, see I.M.F., *Annual Report On Exchange Arrangements And Exchange Restrictions* (1989).
67. For a description of exchange control violations, see Mr Justice Stewart's *Report Of The Royal Commission Of Inquiry Into The Activities Of The Nugan Hand Group* (1985), Vol. 2, pp. 939-989; Stewart, op. cit., pp. 643-647; Walter, "The Mechanisms Of Capital Flight", Ch. 5 in Lessard and Williamson (eds) *Capital Flight And Third World Debt* (1987).
68. For the argument that exchange controls are self-defeating, see Brown, *Money Hard And Soft On The International Currency Markets* (1978); and Quirk, "The Case For Open Foreign Exchange Systems", *Finance & Development* (World Bank/IMF, Washington, June 1989). See also Brown, *The Flight Of International Capital: A Contemporary History* (1987); Aliber, *The International Money Game* (1979).
69. Verbit, *International Monetary Reform And Developing Countries: The Rule Of Law Problem* (1975).

currency and the domestic economy. Businesses waste effort in trying to evade the currency controls and intermediaries bribe public servants and the police to avoid compliance with the law.

Just as exchange controls do not work in practice in the long term, similarly a strategy that tries to tackle every type of laundering can lead to totalitarian restrictions which infringe on the liberty of the citizen. The risk is that as governments discover new laundering practices, they will require an increasing level of disclosure from business, financial institutions, the professions and ordinary persons. The incremental increase in regulation will impose major costs on innocent parties and at some point will undermine legitimate business activity.

Where are the money laundering havens?

The naming of money havens is a highly political act, depends on the perspective of the law enforcement agency, and is influenced by matters such as the definitions of money laundering and havens. There are similar problems in describing tax havens, terrorist states and offshore crime financial centres.

The Australian C.T.R. Agency has described the following countries as narcotic source or transit countries: Afghanistan, Bolivia, Burma, Colombia, Honduras, Hong Kong, India, Laos, Lebanon, Malaysia, Pakistan, Peru, Philippines, Thailand, Turkey and Venezuela.

The C.T.R. Agency has also named the following countries as tax havens "known to facilitate money laundering and/or under tax evasion, due to strict bank secrecy laws": Bahamas, Bermuda, British Channel Islands, British Virgin Islands, Cayman Islands, Cook Islands, Gibraltar, Grenada, Hong Kong, The Isle of Man, Liberia, Liechenstein, Luxembourg, Nauru, Netherlands Antilles, Panama, Switzerland, Tonga and Vanuatu.

Presumably the C.T.R. Agency expects that cash dealers should more carefully scrutinise transactions involving the above countries with a view to establishing whether a suspicious transactions report should be filed.

In theory, any state can be a drug money laundering haven or a fiscal paradise. Recently United States authorities have described Canada[70] as a major drug laundering centre and a British parliamentary committee admitted that London[71] is a banking centre for drugs cash.

It is naive to rely on country lists except as a very crude guide to possible problem states, because such lists rely on past experiences that can easily date. Moreover, there are dozens of states which are not mentioned in the C.T.R. tax haven list which have as extensive bank and commercial secrecy laws as Switzerland. Indeed, many of these states will not effectively co-operate in investigations of white collar crime, including money laundering.

---

70. United States D.E.A. and Canadian R.C.M.P., *Money Laundering And The Illicit Drug Trade*, unpublished (D.E.A., Washington 1989).
71. Home Affairs Committee, *Drug Trafficking And Related Serious Crime*, Report and Proceedings of the Committee, House of Commons (1989), Vol. 1, paras 19-20.

New offshore financial centres with bank secrecy laws are emerging. As far back as 1983 the I.M.F. described how the African states of Ivory Coast and Kenya had enacted special laws to attract offshore investment. In the Caribbean states such as St Vincent and Turks and Caicos, in Europe countries such as Cyprus and Monaco, and in the Pacific states such as Western Samoa and Nauru, are for the same reason candidates as money laundering centres.

Underground banking systems

Prior to the development of the modern commercial banking system there were numerous methods of exchange and moving money. These methods depended on personal, especially family and ethnic, contacts, and involved among other features barter trading. Many of these methods have survived among certain ethnic communities, despite the growth of the international commercial banking system. New methods have also developed.

A significant example of the informal method of moving money is the Chinese underground banking system.[72] The Chinese, who normally conduct business within their community without written contracts, are predisposed to transferring money and entering into major commercial/trade deals on the basis of mutual trust and dependence. Faced with political unrest and anti-Chinese sentiments in a number of states in South-East Asia, the sizeable overseas Chinese community has spread its investments throughout the world, placed tremendous faith in the economic value and security of gold and relied on alternative methods of moving money vis-à-vis the commercial banking system.

The Chinese underground banking system operates through gold shops, trading companies, commodity houses, travel agencies and money changers, many of which are run in various countries by members of the same Chinese family. The method of moving money is the chop, which is in effect a negotiable instrument acceptable as valuable money and which can be cashed in Chinese gold shops or trading houses in another country. The value and identity of the holder of the chop is a secret between the parties. The form of chop may vary from transaction to transaction and may be difficult to identify. The chop system allows money to be transferred from country to country instantaneously and anonymously.

For example, funds for a drug deal may be deposited in a gold shop in Sydney's Chinatown in return for a receipt which is in the form of a chop. The chop is couriered to Hong Kong and cashed. The chop owner then makes a claim against the original issuer, who is fronting for an illegal drug syndicate.

72. For a description of the Chinese underground banking system, see Mangan, "The South East Asian Banking System" (Winter 1984) *D.E.A. Quarterly* 7; Posner, *Warlords Of Crime: Chinese Secret Societies* (1988), Ch. 14; McCoy, *Drug Traffic: Narcotics And Organised Crime In Australia* (1980), p. 354; Mills, *The Underground Empire* (1987), pp. 759-761.

The United States Drug Enforcement Agency[73] has claimed that the Chinese underground banking system is responsible for moving the bulk of heroin money throughout South-East Asia. It has also been used for the illegal movement of currency out of Burma, Indonesia and Thailand. The advantages of this system for the money launderer is that it provides complete anonymity, does not involve the keeping of records, and will not leave a paper trail.

There are many other examples of underground banking systems. For example, in India, the "hawala" system[74] has been used for centuries to transfer commodities such as diamonds, gold, precious jewels, as well as currency. Indian criminal networks have extensively used the hawala system to evade exchange controls, finance drug deals and launder illicit profits.

The significance of the underground banking system is that they are not susceptible to traditional law enforcement measures. The underground banking networks are extremely difficult to detect, investigate and prosecute. Legislation such as the C.T.R. Act is an impotent weapon in tracking underground money flows. The National Crime Authority's specialised Chinese Criminal Unit which gathers intelligence on Chinese criminal syndicates is a more promising initiative.

DETECTION OF MONEY LAUNDERING[75]

The detection of money laundering is the most difficult task facing law enforcement. In most criminal money laundering operations there is no identifiable victim, and therefore no complaint to the police and no investigation. A complex laundering scam can confuse unwitting participants, such as bankers, lawyers and accountants, and prevent detection of the underlying purpose of the financial transactions. There are few witnesses to such transactions and they are usually subject to duties of confidentiality. We can further conclude that effective money laundering schemes do not take place on the streets; they are executed in the offices of banks, companies, businesses and the professions.

Law enforcement agencies should focus on cash transactions at the beginning of the criminal money laundering cycle because this is the weakest link. Drug money launderers are most likely to be exposed when they bring substantial amounts of cash into a bank and attempt to

---

73. *Operation Cashflow: The Movement And Impact Of International Drug Money*, Unpublished (D.E.A., Washington May 1983).
74. There are underground banking systems operating in India itself and by ethnic Indians living in the United Kingdom, Middle East and Asia. See Blackhurst, "Underworld Hijacks Underhand Banking" (June 1986) *Business* 86. Informal banking systems are also operated by ethnic Pakistanis in Bangkok, French Arabs in Paris, Russian Jews in New York, and Colombians in London.
75. This section is concentrating on drug money laundering. Some of the views expressed may not be applicable to corporate money laundering scams. For example, in contrast to drug money scams where there is no direct victim, the laundering of kidnapping ransom, stolen money, or bank and/or corporate fraud proceeds do cause loss to an individual or business association. Also a scheme to launder a corporate bribe is most likely to be detected at the end of the laundering cycle.

exchange it for high denomination bills or monetary instruments. The risks of exposure arise because the money is in a suspicious form and the money exchange may be observed by third parties.

Once illicit money is deposited into the banking system, it becomes anonymous and its character obscured by the millions of banking transactions that occur daily. Banks do not generally question wire transfers of millions of dollars by established customers. Traditionally they have considered that it is none of their business to examine the use of their customers' funds, apart from the case where it is patently fraudulent.

Reporting suspicious transactions

The United Kingdom,[76] Australia and the United States have laws requiring the reporting of suspicious transactions.

Section 16 of the Australian C.T.R. Act requires cash dealers to report suspect transactions, that is, where there are reasonable grounds to suspect that the information about the transaction would assist law enforcement in respect of evasion of tax, tracing/confiscation of moneys from criminal activities, and other federal offences.

The suspect transaction does not have to be in the form of cash and applies to any amount of money. The purpose of this provision is to prevent all forms of illegal money laundering through cash dealers. It is wider than the equivalent British provisions which require reporting of suspected drug-money laundering and terrorist laundering.

The C.T.R. Agency Guidelines[77] state that:

> where a transaction causes a cash dealer to have a feeling of apprehension or mistrust about the transaction considering:
>
> — its unusual nature or circumstances or,
>
> — the person or group of persons with whom they are dealing.
>
> And based on the bringing together of all relevant factors including knowledge of the person or person's background, behaviour and personal appearance, it should be reported as a suspicious transaction.

In the first twelve months of the Australian law becoming operational, 6,250 suspicious financial transaction reports were filed. The reports related to drug trafficking, money laundering, false bank accounts, tax evasion, social security fraud and other criminal offences. There were few reports relating to wholesale corporate business transactions.[78]

---

76. In Great Britain there is no specific legal obligation on banks to report suspicious transactions, but banks who disclose their suspicions concerning drug money will avoid prosecution for the offence of assisting a person to retain the benefits of drug trafficking, and can claim immunity from civil action for such disclosures. See *Drug Trafficking Offences Act*, s. 24.
77. C.T.R.A. Guideline No. 1. See Hewitt and Kalyk, *Understanding The Cash Transaction Reports Act* (1990), Ch. 6.
78. *The Cash Transactions Reports Act during 1990 and early 1991*, C.T.R. Agency, Sydney, 1991; Harbutt, "Cash Transactions Referred To N.C.A.", *Weekend Australian* 13-14 January 1990, p. 5; Morgan, "Taxman's Spy; He's In Your Bank", *Sydney Morning Herald*, 31 March 1990, p. 11. The C.T.R. Agency expects that up to 20,000 annual suspect transactions will be reported: see Coad, *The Reporting Of Cash And Banking Transactions—A Means Of Limiting Corruption*, Unpublished Paper (given at the Fourth International Anti-Corruption Conference, Sydney, 12-17 November 1989).

Given that the Australian suspicion-based system also includes tax evasion and social security fraud, the number of reports are not as great as might be expected. The major limitations are inadequate staff training to detect laundering schemes and the lack of comprehensive procedures for detecting non-cash money laundering. Nor are there supervisory procedures for detecting money laundering at the later stages in the laundering cycle. Contra arrangements, credit facilities and barter trading are unlikely to be caught in practice.

Mandatory cash transaction reporting requirements

While the United States, Italy and Australia have mandatory requirements for the reporting of significant cash transactions, Britain and many other jurisdictions have rejected this option.

In Australia all cash transactions over $A10,000 with a cash dealer and all cash movements over $A5,000 into and out of Australia must be reported. The underlying assumption is that major movements of cash raise a suspicion of criminal activity unless adequately explained.

While the American provisions under the *Bank Secrecy Act*[79] have resulted in numerous prosecutions, the Australian law is relatively untested—the significant cash transactions provisions came into force in July 1990.

There are penalties of up to $A5,000 for an individual failing to report a significant or suspicious transaction ($A25,000 for corporations) and $A10,000 or five years for giving false information.

Although these penalties are high, it would be simplistic to believe that a criminal with a long history of breaking the law, would be deterred by yet another law. The true test of whether this new law (which imposes major costs on the banks and ultimately the customers) is effective is the extent to which it imposes high costs on the criminal community. This will only occur if there is a high chance of being caught for violating the C.T.R. Act and other anti-money laundering laws.

INFORMANTS AND UNDERCOVER OPERATIONS

Investigations of money laundering operations depend on the development of sources of information, informants and undercover operations.

Establishing who are the associates of the principal defendant ("D"), what have been D's travel movements (for example, overseas to open a bank account), how D is paying for living expenses and professional advisers, is very useful in a financial investigation.

79. See also s. 4720 of the *Anti-Drug Abuse Act* 1988 which directs the secretary of the United States Treasury to negotiate with countries that do business in United States currency to require their financial institutions to keep records of large dollar currency transactions similar to the domestic requirements under the *Bank Secrecy Act* and to share those records with United States law enforcement upon request. Financial institutions in those countries which fail to negotiate in good faith towards achieving adequate records face significant penalties.

The cultivation of informants[80] is important in following the money trail. Informants may include airport employees who become aware of unusual movements of cash into and out of a country. For example, a major money laundering operator acting for the Medellin drug cartel was identified as a result of an informant in Panama who revealed that millions of dollars in cash were being unloaded at the national airport.

In the United States there is greater ability for law enforcement agencies to pay informants. The I.R.S. in tax matters, the Securities and Exchange Commission in insider trading investigations and the Comptroller of Currency in currency reporting cases use paid informants to develop their cases. Foreign informants can be paid a reward up to U.S.$150,000 for information on *Bank Secrecy Act* violations which lead to criminal fines, civil penalties or forfeiture.

Whether we in Australia should rely on paid informants is a vexed question. In the author's opinion, the first priority should be to create a system where the community has sufficient confidence in the administration of the law that information is volunteered on a regular basis to law enforcement agencies. There are too many cases where members of the public who wished to give information on suspected corporate misconduct have been fobbed off by bureaucrats. In one case the informant, who happened to be a director of the suspect company, was told by a corporate regulator that he would be investigated if he complained any further.

Whistleblowing laws,[81] whereby public servants are given legal protection from dismissal and official harassment if they report on malpractices in their departments, is another option. Unfortunately, martyrs have a bad history. Whistleblowing laws can never give adequate relief, for a public servant who whistleblows on colleagues will find it unbearable to work in the same environment. The ultimate solution is to give monetary rewards so that it is no longer necessary for the party to continue employment in the public service.

Undercover operations[82] have been the most successful method in the United States for penetrating organised criminal groups and money laundering organisations. Undercover agents can pose as criminals in search of laundering services, or launderers willing to exchange illicit money for criminals. Government agents are thus becoming skilled at laundering operations, so much so that in some cases they are actually creating laundering opportunities.

80. See Hirsch, "Confidential Informants: When Crime Pays", (1985) 39 *University Of Miami Law Review* 131.
81. In a United States study of a group of 233 whistleblowers, 90 per cent lost their jobs or were demoted. Study by Soekin, quoted in *The Age*, 8 August 1989, p. 11. For the argument that laws such as the United States *Whistleblower Protection Act* 1989 are worthwhile, see McMillan, *Principled Organisational Dissent: Whistleblowing In Response To Corruption*, Unpublished Paper (given at the Fourth International Anti-Corruption Conference Sydney, 12-17 November 1989).
82. See generally, United States Senate, *Select Committee To Study Undercover Activities Of Components Of The Department Of Justice, Final Report*, 15 December 1982 (1983); United States House Of Representatives Committee Of The Judiciary (Sub-committee on Civil and Constitutional Rights, *Report on F.B.I. Undercover Operations*, April 1984; Levinger, "Covert Facilitation Of Crime" (1987) 43 (No. 3) *Journal Of Social Issues*.

Undercover operations must be carefully designed and controlled, or otherwise they may undermine public confidence in the police and government institutions. There is also a danger that they may damage innocent and uninvolved parties and cause unfair injury to targeted individuals.

Outside the area of drug trafficking and other "hard-core" criminal activities, there is no extensive use of undercover operations in Australia. Such operations are time-consuming and very expensive.

In the United States undercover operations are increasingly relied on to detect and investigate white collar crimes. For example, in "Operation Mish-Mash" F.B.I. agents penetrated the inner workings of the Chicago futures markets by posing as traders, buying seats on the commodity exchanges and secretly recording conversations of both traders and brokers. The operation led to the discovery of a gigantic fraud on the exchange itself and the indictment of over 40 members of Chicago's futures exchanges.

The scope of the futures frauds on the exchanges would never have been discovered in the absence of an undercover operation. Without the fear that undercover operatives could be working in their midst, brokers and traders in the futures markets may feel safe in carrying out illegal and abusive trading practices. [83]

FINANCIAL INVESTIGATIONS AND FINANCIAL ANALYSIS

A financial investigation [84] is an investigation into the financial aspects of a suspected crime, or an individual and/or organisation. It has two aims. The first is to trace the money which has been used in or is derived from criminal activity. This involves identifying criminal activity and the money, and showing the link between the money and crime. Sometimes money must be traced through several layers of insulation to its destination and/or origin. The second is to assess the net worth of the individual and/or organisation being investigated and to identify the sources and applications of her or his wealth. This involves showing the existence of any unexplained income or wealth.

A financial investigator should be fully familiar with all sources of financial information. [85] There is a wide variety in the type and amount of financial information which is available in different countries. There are also different laws and practices for the disclosure of information to private individuals and to law enforcement agencies.

Australian investigators, both in government and in the private sector, do not usually have the knowledge, skills or contact base to ferret out much of the information that is available in foreign countries.

---

83. See Chaikin, "Futures Frauds In The Asia Pacific Region", in Lye and Lazar (eds), *The Regulation of Financial and Capital Markets* (1991), pp. 251-271.
84. See Nossen, *The Detection, Investigation And Prosecution Of Financial Crimes* (May 1982); Costigan, op. cit., Vol. 2; Stewart, above op. cit., pp. 624-629.
85. See e.g. Carrol, *Confidential Informations Sources: Public And Private* (1975).

Financial analysis techniques[86] can be adapted to organised crime and money laundering investigations. An individual's or group's source of cash/income flow may show illegal profits from criminal activities. Following the source of cash/funds to its application may indicate whether illicit profits have been channelled into legitimate enterprises.

There are two methods of estimating income derived from illicit sources. First, income may be established by the direct method which relies upon specific transactions (for example, sales, expenses) to determine income. Secondly, the indirect approach relies upon circumstantial proof of income by the use of such methods as net worth analysis and source and application of funds statements.

Computer software has been developed to make cash and financial reconstructions a manageable task. But there is a tendency for these techniques to be applied in a vacuum. It is vital that information from all sources—discovered court material, seized documents, publicly available material and investigatory material—be compiled, indexed and analysed. Where gaps are found in the material or analysis, these should be the subject of further investigation.

TRACING ASSETS

Money laundering investigations rely largely on the construction of paper trails. Most businesses generate large volumes of documents which will assist investigators. For example, companies have legal obligations to keep certain records, while individuals are required to keep documents relating to their tax returns. In addition, ss 76-78 of the *Proceeds of Crime Act* 1987 (Cth) require financial institutions to retain certain records, including documents necessary to reconstruct transactions for seven years. This is complemented by the C.T.R. Act which provides a mechanism to trace significant cash movements.

There are a range of powers under the *Proceeds of Crime Act* that will assist in a criminal money laundering investigation. The information-gathering powers in Pt IV of that Act are production orders, search powers in relation to property-tracking documents and monitoring orders. These powers can be used at an early stage of a laundering investigation. There is also the unique power of a monitoring order which enables movement of funds through particular accounts to be monitored by law enforcement agencies virtually as the transaction occurs.

There are significant powers under the C.T.R. Act which may assist the detection and investigation of cash smuggling. Under s. 33 of the C.T.R. Act, an Australian customs or police officer has powers of questioning and search of persons entering and leaving Australia. An officer also has

<hr/>

86. See Arenberg and Tanaka, *Link Network Diagraming,* Unpublished Paper (California Department Of Justice Advanced Traning Centre, 1984); Nossen, "One-on-One Uncorroborated Testimony: The Dilemma Of Prosecutors, Defence Attorneys, And The Courts In Fraud, Waste And Abuse Cases" (1983) 58 *Notre Dame Law Review* 1019.

a power to seize currency found during the course of an examination or search provided that he or she has reasonable grounds to believe that it may afford evidence of an offence under s. 15 of the Act.

There are also powers under the *Companies Code* which may be used for the purpose of investigating the nature and extent of the property of individuals. But whereas a provisional liquidator is empowered under s. 541 of the *Companies Code* to apply for and obtain a court order that a person attend before the court to be examined on oath on matters relating to the corporation concerned, there is no similar power in the case of a receiver under s. 573 of the Code.[87]

Although there is much political and law enforcement rhetoric about the importance of going after the money trail, in practice there is inadequate commitment and few resources applied by either the police or the Australian Securities Commission to this task. Only drug money laundering gets priority in investigations.

Investors in companies which have lost large sums of money are increasingly turning to the private sector to recover assets. The traditional accounting firms do not provide an "investigatory service" and tend to be satisfied with earning large fees from receivership rather than assisting investors to claw back some of their defrauded moneys. There are, however, a number of specialised private agencies which are now offering investors the chance to recover their assets.

FREEZING, SEIZING AND CONFISCATING ASSETS

The Commonwealth and most States have legislated to freeze, seize and confiscate the proceeds of crime.[88] The success of these measures is yet to be proved. Apart from provisions relating to drug crimes in the *Customs Act* 1901 (Cth) and the *Drug Trafficking (Civil Proceedings) Act* 1990 (N.S.W.), all other State and Commonwealth laws require a criminal conviction before the making of a confiscation order. In the United States the main success in confiscating criminal proceeds has been through civil procedures.

The powers under criminal confiscation legislation are not generally used to seize money which has disappeared from corporations. However, the task force which has been set up, in the wake of the McCusker Report on Rothwells,[89] has been specifically mandated to seek to freeze and confiscate criminal profits by all available means, including the *Crimes (Confiscation of Profits) Act* 1988 (W.A.).

There are also powers under the civil law which can assist in the freezing and seizing of assets (for example, Mareva injunctions, Banker's

---

87. See *R. v. Smithson* (unreported, Waddell J., 20 December 1984, No. 4314 of 1984).
88. See Bradley, *Confiscation Of Criminal Assets: Recent Developments In New South Wales* (1990) 2 (No. 2) *Current Issues in Criminal Justice* 95 and Thornton, above, Chapter 2.
89. See McCusker, *Report Of Inspector On A Special Investigation Into Rothwells Ltd*, Part 1 (Perth 1990).

Trust and Shapira orders and Anton Piller orders). These powers can sometimes be used to assist criminal investigations.[90]

Money laundering has become a greater necessity as freezing and confiscation laws have come into force. Money laundering scams will become more complex and sophisticated as criminals seek to avoid detection by the police and tax authorities.

PROSECUTION OF MONEY LAUNDERING

Under the *Proceeds of Crime Act* two separate money laundering offences are created. Section 81 makes it an offence to engage in certain conduct "with knowledge or reason to know" that the money or property is derived or realised from some form of unlawful activity. Section 82 is the less serious money laundering offence of being in possession of the proceeds of crime.

The actus reus of both offences is extremely broad and is capable of encompassing normal financial transactions carried out by banks, professional advisers and commercial entities. The acceptance of a deposit, the making of a loan, and the receipt of money in a property or business transaction are examples of conduct which may constitute the actus reus of money laundering.

Under s. 81 (but not under s. 82) the prosecution must also prove that the money or property involved in the transaction in fact represents the proceeds of crime. Proceeds of crime is defined as proceeds of an offence against the law of the Commonwealth or Territory, or conduct occurring in another country which would constitute a narcotics-related offence, if it had occurred in Australia.

Presumably the courts will permit the prosecution to trace property at law and at equity so as to establish this element of the offence. But it will be extremely difficult to prove this element in complex money laundering schemes, especially where the money trail is broken.

The mens rea of the new laundering offences is of special interest to financial institutions. To be held liable under s. 81, one must have "knowledge or reason to know" that the property is derived or realised from some form of unlawful activity. Unlawful activity is defined as conduct that constitutes an offence against a law in force in the Commonwealth, a State, a Territory or a foreign country. This means that a person may be guilty of laundering under s. 81 even if mistakenly thinking that the property is derived from a different offence than it actually is.

For example, a bank teller who has every reason to know that a series of cash deposits, each slightly less than $A10,000, are the proceeds of an illegal gambling operation, but deliberately ignores this situation, may

90. For the advantages of civil remedies especially in international investigations, see Chaikin, *Regulation of Commercial Crime*, op. cit. and Chs 2 and 11; Fleming, *Protecting And Recovering Corporate Assets Overseas*, paper presented at Eighth Symposium On Economic Crime (Jesus College, Cambridge, 29 July-3 August 1990).

create criminal liability for herself or himself and the bank, even if the cash turns out to be drug money.

Section 82 imposes a lower mens rea standard than s. 81. Under s. 82 the mens rea is established if it may "reasonably be suspected" that the property is the proceeds of crime, unless the person charged with the offence can prove that he or she had "no reasonable grounds for suspecting the property was derived or realised from some form of unlawful activity."

In every case under s. 82 the burden of proving innocence[91] is shifted to the accused once it is shown that there are objective indicia of unlawful activity in relation to the property. The accused will be required to prove that there are no reasonable grounds for suspecting; not that he or she did not suspect but the more difficult task that he or she had no reasonable grounds to.

What is a suspicious transaction? In *Queensland Bacon v. Rees*[92] Kitto J. said that:

> a suspicion that something exists is more than a mere idle wondering whether it exists or not; it is a positive feeling of actual apprehension or mistrust, amounting to "a slight opinion but without sufficient evidence" . . .

> Consequently a reason to suspect that a fact exists is more than a reason to consider or look into the possibility of its existence.

How is this dictum applied to money laundering? In the simplest case where a person brings into a bank large amounts of cash in unconventional containers (for example duffel bags), bank tellers should be suspicious. But are banks required to question substantial non-cash transactions which have no clear business purpose? Must banks ferret out additional information about their customers, and if so, will this not effect their competitiveness and impose undue costs on their business?

A difficult case is where banks are acting in an execution-only role. Banks regularly transfer enormous sums of money as part of a chain that might well disappear into an offshore country such as the Cook Islands or Hong Kong. Some banks may argue that such transactions are not inherently suspicious, and that if they report them they can be sued by their customers for breach of their duty of confidence.

For example, a branch of a bank receives a multi-million dollar payment from a foreign-based bank, which was 100 times the average amount received by the bank. Does mere size indicate suspicion?[93] Does the fact that the source of the funds is a tax haven raise suspicion?

91. The justification for reversing the onus of proof under s. 82 is that that "[t]he circumstances in which the person acquires or deals with the property, and the extent of his or her awareness of its tainted nature, are matters peculiarly within the knowledge of the accused who ought, in the light of the significantly reduced penalty for this offence, to lead evidence of these facts." (Letter from Attorney-General to the Chair of the Senate Scrutiny of Bills Committee, Canberra, 13 May 1987).
92. (1965) 115 C.L.R. 266 at 303 (Kitto J.). See also *Hussein v. Chong Fook Kam* [1970] A.C. 942 at 948 ("suspicion in its ordinary meaning is a state of conjecture or surmise when proof is lacking: 'I suspect but cannot prove.' ").
93. In a civil matter in the New South Wales Supreme Court S.B.C. (Australia) Ltd is suing to recover U.S.$20 million payment which was fraudulently obtained, and is arguing inter alia that the State Bank of N.S.W. should have been suspicious because of the size of the transaction. See *Financial Review*, 23 October 1990.

Answers to these questions are also tied to the scope of the immunity clause. Fears that the immunity under s. 17 of the C.T.R. Act will not apply, thereby raising the possibility of civil suit by a customer against a bank for disclosure, are exaggerated. As a matter of practice, it is unlikely that the customer will find out that he or she has been the subject of a suspicious report—for there are very tight secrecy provisions imposed on the C.T.R. Agency. Moreover, there are considerable judicial dicta[94] indicating that banks have taken a too conservative view as to their right to expose their customers' suspected misdeeds.

INTERNATIONAL CO-OPERATION

Money laundering should be seen as an international problem which requires the highest degree of co-operation between countries. The O.E.C.D. Bank of International Settlements, European Community and United Nations consider that drug money laundering is a threat to the world's financial system, and should be tackled by national, bilateral and multilateral initiatives.[95]

Mutual assistance treaties and arrangements

Australia is a leading advocate of mutual assistance in criminal matters (M.A.C.M.) treaties and arrangements. M.A.C.M. treaties expand the areas in which foreign countries can co-operate with Australia in investigating and prosecuting crime. They are wide enough to cover criminal offences such as fraud, insider trading and money laundering.[96]

The assistance available under M.A.C.M. treaties includes the following areas:

- locating and identifying persons;
- examining witnesses;
- obtaining bank and corporate documents;
- search and seizure;
- serving and authenticating documents;
- arranging persons to give evidence or assist investigations; and
- locating, freezing and confiscating proceeds of crime.

94. *Gartside v. Outram* (1856) 26 L.J. Ch. 113 at 114; *Weld-Blundell v. Stephens* [1919] 1 K.B. 520 at 526, 534, 547-8; *Initial Services Ltd v. Putterill* [1967] 3 All E.R. 145 at 148, 151; *Fraser v. Evans* [1969] 1 All E.R. 8 at 11; *Malone v. Commissioner Of Police Of The Metropolis (No. 2)* [1979] 2 All E.R. 620 at 634. See also the classic case of *Tournier v. National Provincial And Union Bank Of England* [1923] All E.R. 550 at 554. Froomkin, *Confidentiality And Banking*, paper given at the Eighth International Symposium On Economic Crime, Jesus College, Cambridge, 29 July-3 August 1990 (for the argument that banks have a common law duty to disclose evidence of crime).
95. See Zagaris, "Dollar Diplomacy: International Enforcement Of Money Movement And Related Matters—A United States Perspective" (1980) Geo. Wash. Jnl. Int. L. 466 (discussion of international initiatives).
96. See generally, *Proceedings Of The Harvard Law School Conference On International Co-operation in Criminal Matters* (Winter 1990), Vol. 31, no. 1, pp. 1-126; Nadelaman, "Negotiations In Criminal Assistance Treaties" (1985) 33 Am. Jnl. Comp. L. 467.

Australia has legislated in this field[97] and has negotiated treaties with over 20 countries, including Switzerland, Luxembourg, Italy and Great Britain. Australia is also a party to the Commonwealth of Nations scheme of mutual assistance which was agreed to by law ministers from 60 countries in Harare, Zimbabwe in August 1986.[98]

Freezing bank accounts and searching documents on behalf of foreign countries are intrusive measures affecting the rights of individuals and businesses in Australia. The justification for taking such action is the efficacy of international law enforcement.[99]

Before the Australian federal Attorney-General's Department (which is the central authority for processing of requests) will act on a foreign request for assistance, it must be satisfied that there is or has been a genuine foreign investigation into a criminal matter.

The *Mutual Assistance in Criminal Matters Act* 1987 (Cth) (M.A.C.M. Act) contains wide-ranging executive safeguards.[100] The federal Attorney-General is under a legal obligation to refuse assistance if the granting of the foreign request would prejudice the sovereignty, security, national interest or essential interests of a state. Assistance must also be refused if the request relates to a political offence or purely military offence.

The scope and value of mutual assistance is still being worked out. One limitation is that countries such as Switzerland refuse to give assistance in tax evasion cases. Also many countries will not give assistance involving compulsory measures (for example, access to bank information) unless the conduct underlying the investigation is criminal in both the requesting and requested country. For example, Hong Kong, Vanuatu and the Cayman Islands will not compel banks to disclose confidential information about their clients in cases of insider trading and warehousing of shares because such conduct is not criminal in their jurisdictions. On the other hand, Switzerland has recently enacted a money laundering law, thereby facilitating greater co-operation in investigating laundering scams involving Swiss banks.

Another difficulty is that there can be considerable delays in obtaining information and evidence in international investigations.[101] Delays can be shortened by sending investigators overseas, reducing the number of

97. See the *Mutual Assistance in Criminal Matters Act* 1987 (Cth).
98. See Chaikin, *Mutual Assistance In Criminal Matters: A Commonwealth Perspective*, Commonwealth Law Ministers Meeting Report, 1mm(83)29 (1983) (for a discussion of existing mutual assistance measures in Commonwealth countries and the need for a Commonwealth scheme); Maclean, "Mutual Assistance In Criminal Matters; The Commonwealth Perspective" (1988) 37 I.C.L.Q. 177 (for a description of the elements of the Commonwealth scheme).
99. See Chaikin, *Mutual Assistance Aspects Of The Proceeds of Crime Act*, Unpublished Paper (presented to the Tenth Australasian Corporate Crime Investigators Course, N.S.W. C.A.C./Mitchell College, Bathurst, 1987).
100. *Mutual Assistance in Criminal Matters Act* 1987, s. 8 and amendment to Political Offences Exception in *Crimes Legislation Amendment Act (No. 2)* 1988, s. 14.
101. See Mann, *Current Issues In International Securities Law Enforcement*, Unpublished Paper (presented to American Bar Association International Litigation and Arbitration Conference, New York, 2-8 April 1986) (1987).

hands through which mutual assistance requests pass, and ensuring that investigators understand the foreign law, procedure and customs.

A problem for corporate regulators has been that the N.C.S.C. and now the A.S.C. are not empowered to use their compulsory powers (for example, subpoena witnesses and produce documents) actively to assist foreign regulators. It is desirable that the A.S.C. gets such powers so that it will be able to obtain similar assistance from foreign agencies. The American Securities and Exchange Commission (S.E.C.), the New Zealand Securities Commission and the British Department of Trade have such powers.

The federal Attorney-General has announced that the government will introduce legislation to give regulators, such as the A.S.C., new powers to co-operate with their overseas counterparts. The legislation will expand the scope of existing mutual assistance treaties for criminal investigations to cover corporate malpractices.

Interpol

The International Criminal Police Organisation (Interpol), which is based in Lyons, France, is a police communications network devoted to furthering mutual assistance between law enforcement agencies. Interpol's role is to provide technical services through collaboration and communication. In contrast to popular opinion, Interpol is not a supra-national body of men and women who rove the world armed with police powers.

In every case where police investigations are required, the co-operation of the local police is a necessity. If there is corruption among the police or prosecutors, or in the highest circles of government, then international co-operation will be seriously undermined. If a particular country is slow in acceding to a foreign police request, then there is little that the General Secretariat of Interpol can do.

Interpol does, however, have important functions in encouraging a political and international police climate attuned to combating the financial aspects of crime.[102]

In 1984 the General Secretariat of I.C.P.O.-Interpol established a specialist unit with the mandate to develop programmes relating to the financial aspects of organised crime and drug trafficking. The unit which is staffed by police officers and customs and tax agents is known as F.O.P.A.C.[103]

The main task of F.O.P.A.C. has been the compilation of a financial assets encyclopaedia, which consists of a summary of existing financial laws and procedures in nearly 60 countries. Other functions of F.O.P.A.C. are the development and propagandisation of an Interpol model law on tracing, seizing and confiscating illicit assets, the provision

102. See Chaikin, *Regulation of Commercial Crime*, op. cit., Ch. 9 (for a discussion of fraud initiatives of Interpol, including the work of the Economic and Financial Crimes Unit).
103. I.C.P.O.-Interpol Circular No. 18/02/F.O.P.A.C., 26 April 1984; I.C.P.O.-Interpol Resolution at 57th General Assembly meeting in Bangkok, 17-23 November 1988.

of training facilities in financial investigative techniques, the arrangement of working meetings on ongoing cases, and the development of liaison contracts with other international organisations.

More recent initiatives of F.O.P.A.C. include the compilation of a list of the ten top money couriers from every country and a study on the underground banking systems. Because Interpol depends on information and contributions by member states to carry out these studies, the initiatives have progressed very slowly. One difficulty is that member police forces are unwilling to share intelligence with the Interpol bureaucracy. Another problem is that some of this work would be better suited to an academic research body, rather than serving police officers.

Perhaps the most significant initiative has been the creation of a joint working group consisting of bank security officers from the International Banking Security Association (I.B.S.A.)[104] and Interpol. The working group is mandated to develop new approaches to prevent, detect and resolve financial crimes. The working group is examining ways to improve co-operation between the banks and the police, to develop guidelines for the exchange of information, and to identify and analyse the modus operandi of financial crimes.

CONCLUSIONS

1. There is no foolproof method of laundering money, just as there is no perfect tax avoidance scheme. There is no such thing as absolute secrecy, at least in the long term.

2. The principal method of detecting money laundering in Australia is the C.T.R. Act which provides for both significant cash reporting and reporting of suspicious transactions by cash dealers. The success of this legislation will depend on the attitude of cash dealers, the prosecution record, the effectiveness of the new C.T.R. Agency, and the usefulness of C.T.R. reports including follow-up action by law enforcement agencies.

3. A major weakness in Australian law enforcement is the lack of adequate information systems. The N.C.S.C. and the State Corporate Affairs Commissions have devoted too few resources to the development and delivery of intelligence systems. It is hoped that the new Australian Securities Commission will play a more prominent role in attacking corporate money laundering.

4. Investigators should concentrate on the most vulnerable points of laundering schemes. In drug transactions, it is the initial cash transactions which are most susceptible to detection. Investigators should also familiarise themselves with the documents likely to be generated by cash dealers, businesses and individuals.

---

104. I.B.S.A., which has observer status at Interpol, has grown into a very practical umbrella organisation for over 40 major international banks. Security officers in member banks are linked to each other by an electronic telecommunications network, and can attend Interpol General Assembly meetings and fraud conferences.

5. An unstated assumption of the anti-organised crime laws of the Commonwealth is that banks should have a larger role in combating money laundering. Given this political imperative, and the danger of organised crime corrupting bank personnel, it is vital that banks equip themselves with defence mechanisms including:

- consolidating good banking practice, such as knowing the customer, and knowing the customer's business. It is not worth the risk for banks to act for customers in transactions which have no commercial sense and may be suspicious;
- instituting training programmes for bank tellers and other employees who deal with cash;
- developing money laundering profiles and suspicious transactions tests/audits;
- instituting comprehensive internal controls so as to detect money laundering; and
- making line management aware of the latest scam, and ensuring that they properly supervise their staff.

6. In the light of the large number of corporate collapses in Australia there is an urgent need not only to prosecute company officials and professional advisers who have assisted in the execution of frauds or corporate money scams, but also to take more effective steps to recover moneys "lost" by investors.

7. The lack of respect for the administration of the law (especially in the corporate and securities fields) in Australia has bred contempt for the law itself. Unless the Australian government takes significant measures to improve the enforcement of corporate securities laws, then the laws are not worth the paper they are written on. They are merely an empty shell—which imposes costs on the law abiding business citizen—but has little, if any, effect on corporate malefactors.

14

Finding The Information Trail
Some Experiences in International Tax Enforcement

LEE BURNS[1]

INTRODUCTION

A recent trend in Australia's fight against organised crime has been to attack the "money trail" by confiscating the proceeds of crime.[2] With the increased use of tax havens to launder the proceeds of criminal activities, the effectiveness of this policy will depend on the ability of enforcement agencies to obtain information concerning the proceeds of crime. The new measures provide for broad information collection powers, including in particular, the possibility of bilateral co-operation between law enforcement agencies pursuant to treaties on mutual assistance in criminal matters (M.A.C.M.).[3] However, the treaties negotiated to date generally have not included assistance in relation to the recovery of the proceeds of crime.

If the experience in the tax area is anything to go by, enforcement agencies will face great difficulties in collecting information which is held offshore. Indeed, there is increasing acceptance among tax administrators that the only way of stemming the growing tide of international tax evasion and avoidance is through effective co-operation.[4] At this stage, most co-operation is bilaterally based, however there is a move, albeit slowly, towards greater multilateralism in international tax enforcement.

---

1. Faculty of Law, University of Sydney. This chapter draws on previous research performed jointly with Associate Professor Robin Woellner, University of Technology, Sydney, and was previously published in (1990) 2 *Current Issues in Criminal Justice* 111.
2. *Proceeds of Crime Act* 1987 (Cth); *Confiscation of Proceeds of Crime Act* 1989 (N.S.W.); *Crimes (Confiscation of Profits) Act* 1986 (S.A.); *Crimes (Confiscation of Profits) Act* 1986 (Vic.); *Crimes (Confiscation of Profits) Act* 1989 (Qld); *Crimes (Confiscation of Profits) Act* 1988 (W.A.); and *Crimes (Confiscation of Profits) Act* 1988 (N.T.). A similar approach was adopted in the United States some years ago: see also *Racketeer Influenced and Corrupt Organisations Act* 1970 (U.S.) and *Continuing Criminal Enterprises Act* 1970 (U.S.).
3. Part VI of *Mutual Assistance in Criminal Matters Act* 1987 (Cth).
4. In the case of the Australian Taxation Office, see D'Ascenzo, "Developments in Transfer Pricing Enforcement and Complex Audit Strategy" (1988) 5 *Australian Tax Forum* 471 at 480.

It is not the purpose of this chapter to consider the policy underlying the Proceeds of Crime legislation.[5] Rather, the chapter will detail some of the experiences of tax administrators, particularly in dealing with the multinational taxpayer, so as to highlight the need for co-operation between law enforcement agencies if this legislation is to be effective.

BACKGROUND

It was observed by Professor Brian J. Arnold that the Revenue's "battle" with the multinational taxpayer is like a local under six soccer side taking on the national team.[6] Professor Arnold's observation related to the ease in which a multinational enterprise can shift profits between discrete entities within the enterprise, and in particular, to the use of tax havens as a means of avoiding tax. The more "organised" are a taxpayer's offshore activities, the greater are the difficulties confronting administrators in collecting the information necessary to enforce national tax laws.

While tax administrators generally have broad investigations powers, territorial limits render them inadequate to deal with international transactions. The principle of sovereignty means that a state is under no obligation at international law to recognise the taxation laws of another state. This prevents administrators from carrying out investigations offshore and from using the judicial process of other states to recover tax due. Indeed, John A. Calderwood, Director-General of the International Audits Division, Revenue Canada has noted that:

> Tax planners are very much aware that if the information is located offshore, not necessarily in the true tax haven, it is much more difficult for a "revenue" to gather evidence to support income tax assessments.[7]

Of course, if tax havens are used the enforcement problem is greater. An important characteristic of tax havens is secrecy laws which invariably forbid the disclosure of banking and commercial information and which prescribe heavy penalties for breaches of such laws.[8] Consequently, for example, it is simply not possible for a national revenue to investigate fully on its own the "simple" flow of funds in payment of goods which is diverted through several interposed companies or "blind" trusts located in tax havens.

Effective tax enforcement at the international level can only be achieved through co-operation between tax administrators. In the past, the barriers of national sovereignty, secrecy laws, concerns about

5. For critiques of the new legislation, see Fisse, above, Chapter 5, and Fraser, above, Chapter 4.
6. The observation was made in the course of delivering a paper entitled "Future Directions in International Tax Reform", at the University of New South Wales Taxation, Business, and Investment Research Centre International Tax Workshop, held at Terrigal on 26-28 August 1988.
7. Calderwood, "Tax Havens: Concept, Magnitude of Problem and Methods Used" (1988) 28 *European Taxation* 330.
8. See generally, Irish, "Tax Havens" (1982) 15 Vanderbilt J. of Transnat. L. 449.

reciprocity, and competition for "tax dollars", have meant that there has been little effective co-operation between tax administrators.[9]

There is now an increasing use of bilateralism in international tax enforcement. However, this has its limits when dealing with the multinational taxpayer. Tax administrators need to "organise" their enforcement activities in the same way that multinationals organise their tax affairs.

UNILATERAL INFORMATION COLLECTION

Investigation powers

The Commissioner of Taxation (the "Commissioner") has broad investigation powers under the *Income Tax Assessment Act* 1936 (Cth) (the Tax Act). In particular, the Commissioner has a right to full and free access to all buildings, places, books, documents and other papers for the purposes of the Tax Act.[10] The Commissioner also has the power to require any person to:

• furnish information;

• attend and give evidence; and

• produce all books, documents and other papers in the person's custody or under their control.[11]

Further, the Commissioner may obtain a search warrant under s. 10 of the *Crimes Act* 1914 (Cth).

It is noted that police officers have similar powers under the *Proceeds of Crime Act* 1987 (Cth) (P.O.C. Act). Where a person has been convicted of an indictable offence and a police officer has reasonable grounds for suspecting that a person has "possession or control" of a "property tracking document(s)"[12] in relation to the offence, the officer may apply to a judge of the relevant Supreme Court for an order requiring the person to produce such documents.[13] A person is not excused from complying with such an order even though compliance may tend to incriminate the person, or expose the person to a penalty, or be a breach of a non-disclosure obligation.

9. For further discussion on these barriers, see Woellner and Burns, "International Information Flows—The Tax Implications" (1989) 6 *Australian Tax Forum* 143 at 145-146. In the area of criminal matters, the traditional position has also been one of co-operation (see McClean, "Mutual Assistance in Criminal Matters: The Commonwealth Initiative" (1988) 37 Internat. & Comp. L. Q. 177 at 178).

10. Section 263 of the Tax Act. For recent cases which discuss the scope of this power, see *Federal Commissioner of Taxation v. Citibank Ltd* (1989) 89 A.T.C. 4268; and *Deputy Federal Commissioner of Taxation v. Allen, Allen & Hemsley* (1989) 89 A.T.C. 4294.

11. Section 264 of Tax Act: see *Perron Investments Pty Ltd v. Deputy Federal Commissioner of Taxation* (1989) A.T.C. 5038.

12. A "property-tracking document" is basically any document relevant to identifying, locating or quantifying the property of a person who has committed the offence or the proceeds of the crime: P.O.C. Act, s. 4(1).

13. P.O.C. Act, s. 66. Note that an order may also be sought where an officer has reasonable grounds to suspect that such an offence has been committed.

There are also provisions for the obtaining of a search warrant in relation to a property-tracking document;[14] and special provisions for monitoring bank accounts.[15]

Application of the taxation investigations powers in the international context

While there are obvious limits on the use of formal investigations powers to obtain information and documents stored offshore, they may be of some assistance. It is usually the case that there is someone, either in-house or a third party adviser, who at least will have some knowledge of the contents of the documents. Consequently, the Revenue should be able to use its investigations powers to compel such persons to provide the information.

In-house personnel

It may be asked whether the investigations powers could be used against a director of an Australian company to compel the production of the books and records of its tax haven subsidiary.

This issue has not really been tested in the Australian courts. It would depend on whether the person had "control" over the books and records.[16] Certainly, the person would argue that the separate legal nature of the two companies would mean that the parent company could do no more than request that the books and records be handed over and that this would not be sufficient to amount to control. On the other hand, what authority there is supports an argument that we should look at "practical" control rather than legal rights to documents.[17]

In the United States, it has long been accepted that a domestic corporation has "control" over the books and records of its foreign subsidiaries.[18] The issue which generally arises is whether the domestic corporation will be compelled to produce the books and records in circumstances where their production will infringe the secrecy laws of a foreign jurisdiction.

It has been held by the United States courts that the mere existence of such laws does not of itself prevent disclosure.[19] The courts have approached the issue as basically one of balancing competing national interests, namely, the interest of the foreign jurisdiction as a sovereign state in enforcing its secrecy laws against the interest of the United States in enforcing its tax laws. Not surprisingly, the courts have generally found that the United States' interest in enforcing its tax laws is the

---

14. P.O.C. Act, ss 70ff.
15. P.O.C. Act, ss 73ff.
16. Note that "control" is also used in s. 66 of P.O.C. Act.
17. *Federal Commissioner of Taxation v. Australian and New Zealand Banking Group Ltd* (1979) 79 A.T.C. 4039.
18. *Societe Internationale Pour Participations Industrielles et Commerciales v. Rogers* 357 U.S. 197 (1958).
19. *United States v. Vetco Inc.* 691 F. 2d 1281 (9th Cir. 1981), cert. denied 454 U.S. 1098 (1981).

greater interest, particularly where the foreign jurisdiction is a tax haven.[20]

Another problem faced by administrators has been that, while taxpayers have been unable to produce documents held offshore at the investigation stage, they have later been able to produce the documents to support an objection to an assessment of liability. To overcome this problem, the United States *Internal Revenue Code* s. 982 establishes a formal document request procedure. If the taxpayer fails substantially to comply with the request, then the taxpayer is precluded from subsequently producing the documents to support its case against an assessment.

A similar procedure has been introduced in Australia.[21] Where a taxpayer refuses or fails to comply with an "offshore information notice", the information or documents sought by the Commissioner are only admissible in proceedings disputing the taxpayer's assessment with the consent of the Commissioner. In exercising his discretion, the Commissioner is to ignore the possible application of foreign secrecy laws.

Third parties

There will often be persons outside the corporate group who either have access to, or knowledge of, documents located offshore.[22] These persons include lawyers, accountants and bankers. The United States experience in this regard is that the courts have been less willing to compel disclosure where a third party is involved, particularly where the third party may be exposed to a penalty under the foreign law.[23]

Foreign secrecy laws are rarely absolute. For example, bank secrecy laws may be waived by the customer. The United States Internal Revenue Service (I.R.S.) has attempted to take advantage of this by obtaining court orders compelling taxpayers to sign a consent form waiving all rights to the protection of the bank secrecy laws of the foreign jurisdiction. This "compelled consent" has been held by the United States Supreme Court not to be a violation of the Fifth Amendment privilege against self-incrimination.[24] However, it is not entirely clear what practical effect a compelled consent will have as the foreign jurisdiction is unlikely to view it as a "real" consent.

In the case of banks, it has been noted that many offshore financial institutions do not have substantial computer installations. This means that major data processing and storage has often been performed onshore at head office installations.[25] Consequently, the fact that the hard copy may be in the Turks and Caicos Islands, for example, should

20. See generally, Crinion, "Information Gathering on Tax Evasion in Tax Haven Countries" (1986) 20 *The International Lawyer* 1209 at 1217-1225.
21. See s. 264A of Tax Act (1988).
22. Indeed, this is the theory of the *Cash Transactions Reports Act* 1987 (Cth).
23. Crinion, op. cit. at 1217-1225.
24. *Doe v. United States* 88-2 U.S.T.C. 9545 (1988).
25. Kelman, "The Computer as Accomplice and Police Informer" (1988) 5 *Offshore Investment* 19.

not be a barrier to compelling the head office to produce the information.

Where the third party is a lawyer there is the additional barrier of legal professional privilege. Privilege attaches to documents created for the sole purpose of obtaining legal advice or for use in legal proceedings.[26] In *Baker v. Campbell*,[27] Gibbs J. observed that privilege was granted:

> to ensure that the client can consult his lawyer with freedom and candour, it being thought that if the privilege did not exist "a man would not venture to consult any skilful person, or would only dare to tell half his case."[28]

Two observations may be made concerning privilege. First, it is noted that the absence of privilege does not appear to have prevented taxpayers from "venturing" to consult an accountant for tax advice. Secondly, there has been a recent example of a law firm using privilege as a marketing tool in an attempt to lure clients away from accounting firms.[29] In these circumstances, it would seem appropriate to re-examine the role of legal professional privilege in the context of tax matters.

Innovative investigative techniques

The I.R.S. has proved itself to be innovative when it comes to obtaining information which is held offshore. For example, in the early 1970s it carried out an investigation referred to as the "Swiss Mail Watch".[30] The aim of this was to identify United States taxpayers with undisclosed Swiss bank accounts. It involved the I.R.S. microfilming the exterior of all envelopes passing through New York mail exchange which were believed to have originated from Swiss banks. The programme identified some 40,000 taxpayers with Swiss bank accounts.

Other investigation activities of the I.R.S. read like something out of a John Le Carré novel. For example, in 1972 the I.R.S. undertook "Project Haven" which investigated the dealings of a narcotics trafficker with a Bahamian bank and trustee company.[31] The I.R.S. used an informant who had developed a close relationship with the vice president of the bank. The banker made regular visits to Miami. On one occasion, the informant arranged a date for the banker with a former policewoman. The banker left his briefcase at the woman's apartment while they dined out. The informant used a key to the woman's apartment to get access to the banker's briefcase which contained a list of the bank's clients. The document was delivered to an I.R.S. agent who copied it. The information obtained disclosed 63 cases of evasion. It also led to the criminal indictment of members of a Chicago law firm who aided and abetted tax evasion activities through the bank.

26. *Grant v. Downs* (1976) 135 C.L.R. 674.
27. (1983) 83 A.T.C. 4606.
28. Ibid. at 4612.
29. See *The Australian Financial Review*, 2 August 1989, p. 1.
30. Crinion, op. cit. at 1228.
31. The description of Project Haven has been summarised from Crinion, ibid. at 1225-1228.

CO-OPERATION BETWEEN ADMINISTRATORS

As stated at the outset, there is increasing acceptance among administrators that the only way of stemming the growing tide of international tax evasion and avoidance is through effective co-operation. At this stage, most co-operation is bilaterally based, however there is a move, albeit slowly, towards greater multilateralism in international tax enforcement.

Bilateral exchange of information

Double Tax Treaties[32]

Australia has entered into comprehensive double tax treaties with 31 nations. Each treaty provides for the exchange of information between the two tax administrations. The information exchange is not unlimited in operation. Each treaty defines the boundaries of the exchange. While the precise boundary varies from treaty to treaty, all but one of Australia's treaties provide for an "extended" exchange. Under an extended exchange, information may be exchanged not only for the purpose of carrying out the treaty, but also for the purpose of enforcing domestic laws which are the subject of the treaty. A "restricted" exchange only permits the exchange of information for the purpose of carrying out the treaty. The only Australian treaty which provides for a restricted exchange is the Swiss Treaty.

The definition of the boundaries of the exchange is important for two reasons: first, the obligation to exchange is mandatory; and secondly, if information is exchanged which is outside the scope of the exchange, then the administration may be in breach of secrecy laws.

Even with the boundaries of the exchange, certain classes of information may be excluded. Under most treaties, there is no obligation to exchange information which would disclose any trade, business, industrial, commercial or professional secret or trade process. Further, there is no obligation to exchange where disclosure would be contrary to public policy. While there is no obligation to exchange such information, most treaties give administrators a discretion to do so.

Generally, there is no obligation to exchange information which the requesting administrator could not obtain under its domestic laws. This is designed to prevent administrators exploiting the broader investigations powers of their treaty partners. Again, while there is no obligation to exchange such information, treaties usually give administrators a discretion to do so.

In most cases, the exchange is not limited to information already in the possession of the administration. The requested authority may be obliged to collect the information and this is the case regardless of whether or not the requested authority has any interest in the information.

Treaties leave the actual design of the exchange to be determined by agreement between the two administrations. In most cases, there is an

---

32. See generally, Burns and Woellner, "Bilateral and Multilateral Exchanges of Information" (1989) 23 *Taxation in Australia* 656.

informal agreement that information will be exchanged automatically, upon request or spontaneously. Some administrations, most notably the United States, prefer to formalise the structure of the exchange by way of an agreement with the other administration.[33]

An automatic exchange involves the regular exchange of agreed classes of information. Such an exchange is generally limited to information which is routinely reported by taxpayers or third parties to the respective administrations. One of the main problems with the automatic exchange is that information is often received in an unusable form, for example, there is inadequate taxpayer identification, or the information may not be in English. This problem is being addressed through the introduction of a standard multi-lingual form. Another problem is that an automatic exchange may in fact generate too much information in that the receiving administration may not have the resources to use all the information received. It is common now for administrators to set tolerance levels (that is, minimum dollar amounts) or to alternate the classes of information exchanged from year to year.

Information may also be exchanged upon request. The quality of the information is very much a function of the terms of the request. One way to ensure the quality of the information exchanged is to have the the requesting authority involved in its collection. For example, the I.R.S. has exchanged representatives with the Canadian and German Revenues to facilitate, inter alia, the exchange of information.

Information may also be exchanged spontaneously. This usually occurs where information is discovered during an investigation which suggests non-compliance with the tax law of a treaty partner.

Treaties limit the use to which the information received may be put. Further, the confidentiality of the information is preserved by a requirement that the receiving authority treat the information as secret in the same way as it would treat domestically obtained information. However, problems may arise where the receiving authority is subject to secrecy laws which are not as strict as those to which the transmitting authority is subject.

Caribbean Basin Initiative

Bilateralism is of limited assistance when tax havens are involved. Not surprisingly, there are very few bilateral treaties with tax havens. Even where there are, they rarely overrides the tax haven's bank and commercial secrecy laws.

The United States has attempted to use economic incentives to encourage Caribbean tax havens to enter into information exchange arrangements. In 1983, the United States Congress passed the *Caribbean Basin Economic Recovery Act* (commonly known as the Caribbean Basin Initiative, hereafter referred to as C.B.I.).[34] The aim of the C.B.I. was to

33. See e.g. the "Working Arrangement Between the United States Inland Revenue Service and the Australian Taxation Office for the Conduct of Simultaneous Examinations Under the Terms of the Exchange of Information Provisions of the Convention for the Avoidance of Double Taxation and the Prevention of Fiscal Evasion With Respect to Taxes on Income", entered into on 2 November 1989.
34. See generally, Sharp and Steel, "The Caribbean Basin Exchange of Information Draft Agreement—A Technical Analysis" (1985) 19 *The International Lawyer* 949.

encourage the Caribbean tax havens to enter into information exchange agreements with the United States which over-rode the Caribbean country's bank and commercial secrecy laws. The "carrot" offered for signing was that under the United States tax law the Caribbean country would be given "North American Area status". This would mean that United States residents would be entitled to deductions for the costs of holding and attending conferences in the Caribbean country.

Of the 28 countries targeted, five such agreements have come into effect and a further five agreements have been signed. One of the first countries to sign such an agreement was Bermuda. It was reported recently that Bermuda was becoming a "legitimate offshore financial centre" rather than simply being an "offshore tax haven".[35] It was also reported that the agreement led to 5 per cent of businesses leaving the island. The interesting statistic though, would be the dollar value which these businesses represented.

Besides being repugnant to the concept of sovereignty of nations, it must be questioned whether the C.B.I. derives any real benefits for the United States. Presumably, those United States taxpayers holding conferences in the Caribbean will do so in a country which has North American Area status, while those United States taxpayers wanting to use a tax haven will simply shift operations to a Caribbean country which has not signed an agreement. From a revenue point of view this seems the worst possible position.

Given the financial benefits of being a tax haven, there will always be countries willing to make themselves available in this capacity. As more countries sign information agreements with the United States, there is a greater incentive for other countries to remain as tax havens (competing with 17 tax havens for international business must be better than competing with 28).

Mutual Assistance in Criminal Matters[36]

In 1987, the Commonwealth Parliament passed the *Mutual Assistance in Criminal Matters Act* 1987 (Cth) (M.A.C.M. Act). The object of the M.A.C.M. Act is to facilitate the provision and obtaining of international assistance in criminal matters, including the obtaining of evidence, documents and other articles (s. 5).

The M.A.C.M. Act applies to foreign countries with which Australia has entered into a Treaty on Mutual Assistance in Criminal Matters. To date, Australia has signed Treaties with the United States, Japan, Vanuatu and Canada. Nothing in the M.A.C.M. Act is to affect the obtaining of assistance in other ways, for example, under a tax treaty.

Under the Act, assistance may be provided in relation to, inter alia, the production of documents for the purposes of proceeding in relation to a criminal matter (ss 12 and 13). In this context, criminal matter includes a taxation offence (s. 3(1)). At this stage, there does not appear to have been much use of these treaties in relation to tax offences.

---

35. "International Tax News—Bermuda" (1989) 44 *Tax Notes* 1243.
36. See generally, McClean, op. cit.

Multilateral exchange of information

While the information exchange articles in Australia's treaties provide the Commissioner with an important source of information concerning international transactions, their bilateral nature limits their effectiveness when dealing with the multinational taxpayer. A multilateral audit can only be carried out if there is an information exchange article in force between all countries involved. Further, the scope of each exchange must be the same for the audit to be carried out effectively.

Effective enforcement at the international level requires multilateral co-operation between tax administrators. A multilateral approach would allow administrators to organise their enforcement activities in the same way as multinationals organise their tax affairs. The latest attempt at achieving multilateralism in international tax enforcement is the *Multinational Convention on Mutual Administrative Assistance in Tax Matters* (the Multinational Convention) which is a joint initiative of the O.E.C.D. and the Council of Europe. At the time of writing, three countries, Sweden, Norway and the United States, have indicated that they will sign. The Multinational Convention requires five signatories before it will come into force. Australia, Luxembourg, Switzerland, the United Kingdom and Germany have indicated that they will not be signing the Multinational Convention. The main reason given in each case is the belief that the Multinational Convention is unnecessary having regard to the existing network of bilateral treaties.

In Australia's case, the decision not to sign was made at the time when the government was attempting to have the tax file number and related privacy legislation passed through Parliament. It may have been that the decision not to sign was taken to "smooth the way" for the passing of that legislation. It is also interesting to note the reaction of the Australian business and professional community to the Multinational Convention. Basically, it was seen as the end of civilisation as we now know it. The reality was that it would merely allow what can be done now on a bilateral basis to be done on a multilateral basis.

In one sense it is not surprising that a number of countries have chosen not to sign the Multinational Convention. This is because this global attempt at international enforcement came at a time when many administrators (the Australian Taxation Office included) were only beginning effectively to use bilateralism. Once networks of bilateral co-operation become more sophisticated, it would seem inevitable that multilateral co-operation on a global basis will be formalised.

CONCLUSION

The experience in the tax arena has been that administrators are severely limited in their attempts to obtain information concerning international transactions. Multinational taxpayers have held the upper hand through their ability to structure transactions in ways which effectively prevent national administrators from gaining access to key information about their activities. It would seem to be generally accepted now that there must be greater co-operation between tax administrators if there is to be effective enforcement at the international level.[37]

While the M.A.C.M. Act provides for assistance between law enforcement agencies in relation to the recovery of the proceeds of crime (ss 32ff), to date only Australia's treaty with Canada provides for such co-operation. Given the tax experience, it is submitted that such co-operation will be essential to the success of the Proceeds of Crime legislation.

---

37. Since this chapter was written, the federal Attorney-General, Mr Duffy, announced that legislation would be passed enabling Australia's business regulators (in particular, the Australian Securities Commission and the Trade Practices Commission) to co-operate with overseas regulators in investigating corporate malpractice. The proposed legislation involves expanding the scope of Australia's treaties on Mutual Administrative Assistance in Criminal Matters so as to cover corporate matters. This continues the trend towards greater co-operation in enforcement activities.

15

The Confiscation of the Proceeds of Crime in England

In a time of "penological pessimism" attention has increasingly focused on using the penal law as a mechanism for compensating the victims of crime[1] and confiscating the proceeds of crime; aims, within their appropriate limits, of self-evident utility. Two recent measures, the *Drug Trafficking Offences Act* 1986 (D.T.O. Act) and Pt VI of the *Criminal Justice Act* 1988, repose in Crown, and to a lesser extent magistrates courts, wide powers to confiscate criminally-based profits. This brings Great Britain into line with other European Economic Community countries whose codes make provision for confiscation.[2] As well as the primary powers of confiscation both Acts contain detailed ancillary powers of pre-trial restraint on a defendant's realisable property and of post-trial enforcement.[3] The exercise of these powers may involve intrusion into third party interests in property, the over-riding of gifts funded from criminal profits with significant implications for banks and financial intermediaries, but subject to the principle that the financial interests of non-implicated third parties other than donees of the defendant should be protected.[4] Both Acts contain provision for the making of arrangements by treaty for the enforcement of foreign confiscation orders in England,[5] pursuant to a government policy of seeking mutual enforcement of confiscation orders.[6] Ultimately, this may result in an internationalised confiscation regime embracing much of Western Europe, the United States of America and the

---

* Senior Lecturer, University of Durham. This chapter is an expanded version of a paper read at the inaugural meeting of the English section of the International Association of Penal Law at the London School of Economics, April 1989. The chapter was prepared for publication in October 1990, and some additions to the footnotes were made before going to press.
1. *Criminal Justice Act* 1988, Pt VII.
2. Belgian *Penal Code*, Art. 42; Danish *Penal Code*, Art. 77; French *Penal Code*, Art. 470; German *Penal Code*, Arts 73 and 74; Greek *Penal Code*, Art. 76; Dutch *Penal Code*, Art. 33; Italian *Penal Code*, Art. 40; Luxembourg *Penal Code*, Art. 42; Spanish *Penal Code*, Art. 48.
3. *Criminal Justice Act* 1988, ss 77-81. Many of the confiscation provisions of the *Criminal Justice Act* 1988 replicate the confiscation provisions in the *Drug Trafficking Offences Act* 1986 (D.T.O. Act). References relating to the latter Act will normally only be given when some point of difference from the former Act is under discussion.
4. *Criminal Justice Act* 1988, s. 82(4); D.T.O. Act 1986, s. 13(4).
5. D.T.O. Act, s. 26; *Criminal Justice Act* 1988, s. 96.
6. The *Criminal Justice (International Co-operation) Act* 1990 empowers the United Kingdom to co-operate with other countries in criminal proceedings, including confiscation, and to implement the *Vienna Convention against Illicit Trade in Narcotic Drugs and Psychotropic Substances*.

Commonwealth.[7] Such arrangements in relation to drug trafficking have already been made with the United States, Canada, Australia, the Bahamas and Switzerland. This chapter will predominantly focus on the confiscation provisions of the *Criminal Justice Act* 1988 which cover most indictable and some summary offences. Consideration will also be given to certain draconian provisions of the D.T.O. Act which have been applied with effect in a growing number of cases. Due to the pariah status of drug offenders, these provisions enjoyed an unopposed passage through Parliament and met with little critical comment.[8] Their influence can be detected in subsequent legislation relating to terrorists.[9] Should Parliament be persuaded that other categories of offenders require similar rigour, the precedent is at hand. Additionally to outlining the confiscation regime itself, the chapter will consider the extent to which the confiscation provisions can forward the complementary policy, enhanced by recent legislation,[10] of affording compensation to victims of crime through the criminal courts.

The effectiveness of the confiscation legislation will, of course, depend upon resources and priorities. In drug trafficking cases the confiscation process is mandatory,[11] thus earmarking resources irrespective of overall budgets and personnel. In other cases there is a monetary filter[12] and prosecutorial discretion. Reservations have been expressed concerning the availability of the resources and trained personnel necessary for the effective implementation of the complex confiscation powers.[13] To some extent successful civil actions by the victims of crime to recover financial and proprietary losses may coincidentally advance the policy of confiscation. Indeed, recent developments in the burgeoning jurisdiction relating to Mareva injunctions establish that in cases with a multijurisdictional dimension, the civil law may reach assets currently beyond the criminal confiscation process. Consequently, this chapter will treat briefly of some recent developments relating to the grant of extraterritorial Mareva injunctions.

THE SCOPE OF CONFISCATION ORDERS

The *Criminal Justice Act* 1988 (the Act) provisions apply to all indictable offences (save drug trafficking offences) and certain non-indictable offences relating to sex shops, unlicensed videos and unlicensed

---

7. For a survey of Commonwealth developments, see McLean, "Seizing the Proceeds of Crime: The State of the Art" (1989) 38 I.C.L.Q. 334.
8. But see Nicol, "Confiscation of the Profits of Crime" (1987) 52 J.C.L. 75; Feldman, "Individual Rights and Legal Values in Proceeds of Crime Legislation: A Comparative Analysis" (1989) 18 Anglo Am. L. Rev. 91.
9. *Prevention of Terrorism (Temporary Provisions) Act* 1989, s. 9.
10. *Criminal Justice Act* 1988, Pt VII.
11. D.T.O. Act, s. 1(1), (2). The court is required to go through the motions of a hearing even where it is obvious from the start that the defendant has no realisable assets: *R. v. Bragason* [1988] Crim. L.R. 778. Where a difficult issue of civil law arises in confiscation proceedings the cost of those proceedings may well exceed the amount realised: *R. v. Robson* [1991] Crim. L. R. 222.
12. *Criminal Justice Act* 1988, s. 71(7)—currently £10,000.
13. Feldman, *Criminal Confiscation Orders* (1988), pp. 6-7.

performances.[14] The jurisdiction is discretionary and can only be invoked if it is established that the defendant ("D") has benefited to a minimum amount—currently £10,000[15]—from offences for which D has been convicted or which D has asked to be taken into account in the same proceedings. Confiscation is not conceived of as a penal measure: though a confiscation order can be taken into account when imposing a fine, forfeiture order or determining compensation, it must be left out of account when fixing the term of imprisonment.[16] In so far as a confiscation order strips an offender of assets to which there is no entitlement at civil law there can be no objection to this approach. But such orders will frequently impinge on property to which the offender has an indefeasible title.[17] In such cases, the impact of the order on the offender is indistinguishable from a fine and may include up to ten years' additional imprisonment for default.[18] In principle, in such a case, the order should be considered as tantamount to a fine when determining the length of a custodial sentence. However, the legislation clearly provides otherwise.[19]

In terms of the Act, a person has benefited from an offence if he or she has obtained property (which includes money) as a "result of or in connection with the commission of an offence".[20] Obviously all forms of "predatory" crimes involving financial or proprietary victims will be covered. So too will be the profits from intrinsically illegal commerce in fields such as sexual services or gaming. Less obviously covered will be lawful activity involving incidental illegality as when a business enhances its profits by avoiding expenditure required to bring its operations in conformity with regulatory laws.

We may use by way of an example of the latter situation a company consistently committing an offence by causing oil pollution to an estuary because it will not make the outlay required for additional storage tanks for its factory, calculating an economic benefit in merely paying any fines that may arise. As the offence charged is indictable,[21] the question arises: has the company obtained a benefit to the minimum extent required? Even if profits are boosted by a sum in excess of £10,000 by the failure to make the expenditure, the profits are obtained by way of trade, the failure to make the expenditure involving merely the retention of profit. However, the Act provides that: "[W]here a person *derives* a

---

14. *Criminal Justice Act* 1988, s. 72(3), Sched. 4.
15. *Criminal Justice Act* 1988, s. 71(7).
16. *Criminal Justice Act* 1988, s. 73(5).
17. Which will be the case where profits arise from illegal commerce in drugs, sex, gaming etc. involving willing buyer, willing seller: *Gordon v. Chief Commander of Metropolitan Police* [1910] 2 K.B. 1080.
18. *Criminal Justice Act* 1988, s. 75. In *R. v. Johnson, The Times*, 4 May 1990, the Court of Appeal ruled that a confiscation order under the D.T.O. Act was to be regarded as part of the sentence for the purposes of an appeal against sentence, a conclusion which should follow for the *Criminal Justice Act* 1988.
19. *Criminal Justice Act* 1988, s. 71(7). Moreover any delay in sentencing caused by confiscation inquiries aggravates the injustice of the refusal to include time in custody on remand as part of the minimum period of six months which must be served before release on licence is possible.
20. *Criminal Justice Act* 1988, s. 71(4).
21. *Prevention of Oil Pollution Act* 1971, s. 2.

pecuniary advantage as a result of or in connection with the commission of an offence he is to be treated . . . as if he had obtained as a result of or in connection with the commission of the offence a sum of money equal to the value of the pecuniary advantage" [emphasis added].[22]

"Pecuniary advantage" is at large and presumably the provision caters, inter alia, for situations where a financial advantage is derived without direct receipts arising from the commission of the offence. The use of the term "derives" rather than "obtains" suggests that the pecuniary advantage need not be achieved by way of direct acquisition as is arguably required to prove an "obtaining".[23] It might be argued that the offence in question—discharging oil into United Kingdom waters—does not of itself give rise to any pecuniary advantage and that the failure to incur compliance expenditure is not of itself an offence. But such failure is so intimately connected with the offence itself that the advantage gained can surely be regarded as derived from a connection with the offence. Such a conclusion will enhance the enforcement potential of much regulatory legislation, where fines in terms of formal limits or sentencing practice can be inadequate. Moreover, if in the future provision is made, as contemplated in the Act, for the enforcement of external confiscation orders,[24] some recourse against multinational companies is in prospect. Much will depend on how prosecutors and judges administer what is a discretionary jurisdiction.

By contrast, the jurisdiction under the D.T.O. Act is mandatory.[25] It is triggered by a conviction for a drug trafficking offence. Drug trafficking offences cover production of controlled drugs, supply, possession for the purpose of supply, importation, exportation, being concerned in arrangements allowing others to retain benefits of drug trafficking and attempts, incitements and conspiracies directed to these ends.[26] The question then becomes one of determining that the defendant has benefited from "drug trafficking".[27] Drug trafficking is a narrower band of conduct than covered by drug trafficking offences and is confined to producing or supplying, transporting or storing or importing or exporting controlled drugs.[28] The defendant need not have a conviction relating to such conduct, nor need an offence relating to such conduct have been taken into account.[29] Moreover, the conduct involved may have taken place anywhere in the world, provided that it constituted an offence in the jurisdiction of commission.[30] It appears that any determination in drug confiscation proceedings must be established on the basis of proof beyond reasonable doubt[31] save where statutory assumptions (to be discussed below) as to

22. *Criminal Justice Act* 1988, s. 71(5).
23. *Attorney-General's Reference (No. 1 of 1988)* [1989] 1 All E.R. 321 construes "obtaining" as covering the passive receipt of information but in circumstances involving direct acquisition.
24. *Criminal Justice Act* 1988, s. 82(4).
25. D.T.O. Act, s. 1(1).
26. D.T.O. Act, s. 38(1).
27. D.T.O. Act, s. 1(2).
28. D.T.O. Act, s. 38(1).
29. D.T.O. Act, s. 1(2).
30. D.T.O. Act, s. 38(1).
31. *R. v. Dickens* [1990] 2 All E.R. 626.

benefit and its extent are applicable. Once the court has determined that the defendant has been involved in drug trafficking, the inference that D has also benefited from such activity is almost overwhelming.[32]

ESTABLISHING THOSE ASSETS SUBJECT TO CONFISCATION

The initiative lies with the prosecution (in non-drug trafficking cases) to establish that the defendant has benefited to the minimum amount.[33] A spur for co-operation is imposed on the defendant in that the prosecution can tender statements to the court in the matter of the defendant's assets which will be treated as conclusive to the extent that the statement or any part of it is not challenged by the defence.[34] If the defence wishes to challenge it must indicate those matters it will seek to rely on in rebuttal of the prosecution's allegations.[35] This procedure does not extend to bare assertions that the defendant has benefited from an offence.[36] Despite this derogation from the defendant's normal right not to have any adverse inference drawn from silence, the ultimate burden of proof as to the amount of benefit lies with the prosecution, which may give rise to difficulty where illicit activity is intermingled with legitimate commerce.[37]

The position under the *Drug Trafficking Offences Act* 1986 (D.T.O. Act) can be far more favourable for the prosecution. The D.T.O. Act allows for assumptions to be made for the purpose of determining whether the defendant has benefited from drug trafficking and for assessing the proceeds derived from such trafficking.[38] The assumptions are that any property held at any time since conviction and any property transferred to D within the six years[39] preceding the institution of proceedings were received as payment or reward for drug trafficking. Additionally all expenditure in the six year period prior to the proceedings is assumed to have been funded from drug trafficking. Once invoked these assumptions will be sustained unless the defendant can, on a balance of probabilities, prove them to be incorrect.[40]

32. *Re a Defendant, The Times*, 7 April 1987.
33. *Criminal Justice Act* 1988, s. 72(1).
34. *Criminal Justice Act* 1988, s. 73(1).
35. *Criminal Justice Act* 1988, s. 73(2).
36. *Criminal Justice Act* 1988, s. 73(3)(b).
37. As occurred in *Chief Constable for Hampshire v. A.* [1985] Q.B. 132. The *Hampshire* case concerned a common law restraint order where the burden of proof was on a balance of probabilities. In the *Criminal Justice Act* 1988 the burden is unspecified. Under the D.T.O. Act the prosecution burden is proof beyond a reasonable doubt, a position established by judicial interpretation (see *R. v. Dickens* [1990] 2 All E.R. 626). Because of salient differences in the confiscation regimes in the two Acts, the position under the *Criminal Justice Act* 1988 is still at large.
38. D.T.O. Act, s. 2(2).
39. Proving that a particular asset acquired within the six year period is untainted, e.g. a house acquired five years prior to the proceedings may, of course, involve proof of matters occurring well before the six year period.
40. The standard of proof is unspecified in the Act. In *R. v. Dickens* [1990] 2 All E.R. 626 the Court of Appeal ruled (at 629) that the standard of persuasion was proof on a balance of probabilities.

The amount subject to confiscation is the defendant's *proceeds* of drug trafficking, a term interpreted as the gross as opposed to the net returns from trafficking.[41] Thus, unless a defendant can displace these assumptions, the quantum of the order could be an aggregation of current capital, the value of all assets held within the previous six years and the gross income and expenditure for that period. The order will be limited to the amount the court is satisfied can be realised.[42] A recent appellate description of these provisions as "intentionally draconian" seems restrained.[43]

These assumptions can be triggered by a "preliminary assessment" of the likelihood of benefits based on the evidence from the trial or the recital of facts on a plea.[44] Frequently a conviction for a drug trafficking offence, particularly if it falls within the narrower category of drug trafficking, will suffice of itself. But not invariably. We may take a case of a person convicted of producing a controlled drug—a drug trafficking offence and a designated example of drug trafficking—on the basis of the home-growing of cannabis. Unless a "commercial" quantity has been grown, such facts should not raise a prima facie case of benefit and, it is submitted, to invoke the assumptions in such a case would constitute an error of law.[45] But if the quantity is suggestive of growing for sale the assumptions may be lawfully applied.

The assumptions are permissive not mandatory and one cannot assume the courts will strive to "clean out" all drug-trafficking offenders. Nonetheless a growing number of cases demonstrate the formidable nature of the confiscation power. In *R. v. Small*,[46] a defendant convicted of possessing cannabis with intent to supply, possessed some of the artefacts associated with contemporary affluence[47] and was reputed to have spent considerable sums of money in pubs, clubs etc. His sole explanation for his economic condition was that he was "a traveller in the black economy".[48] The trial judge estimated the proceeds of his trafficking to be £10,000, a figure which he conceded was "a pure guess".[49] The Court of Appeal, confirming the order, ruled that a determination premised on intuition did not contravene a right to fair hearing in the light of the defendant's unco-operativeness, general unreliability and the lack of financial documentation.

But a defendant who wishes to co-operate in the process may yet be in great difficulty in establishing that any particular assets are "clean". In *R. v. Hopes*[50] an Australian national was convicted of a drug-trafficking offence in England. In addition to drug trafficking, the defendant had

41. *R. v. Smith* [1989] 2 All E.R. 948.
42. D.T.O. Act, s. 4(4). The confiscation order may be realised against legitimately acquired property: *R. v. Chrastny (No. 2)* [1991] 1 W.L.R. 1385.
43. Per Lord Lane L.C.J. in *R. v. Dickens* [1990] 2 All E.R. 626 at 628.
44. Ibid.
45. On such facts a jurisdictional basis for the invocation of the assumptions would be lacking as there would be no evidence on which the judge could base a "preliminary assessment" of benefit.
46. (1989) 88 Cr. App. R. 184.
47. Particular note was made of his car phone.
48. *R. v. Small* (1989) 88 Cr. App. R. 184 at 186.
49. Ibid.
50. (1989) 11 Cr. App. R. (S) 38.

income from a bar he owned in Bangkok and his Sydney car business. An assumption was made that his chief asset within the jurisdiction, a house in Wales, was acquired from the proceeds of drug trafficking. At the hearing the defendant did not try to prove that the house was legitimately acquired but argued that there was no evidence on which to base the order. His appeal was dismissed on the ground that if there was a likelihood that some benefit had been taken from trafficking, the D.T.O. Act entitled the court to make the assumption that any particular asset was so acquired unless the defendant could prove otherwise.

What if the defendant in *Hopes* had attempted to prove the legitimacy of his acquisitions? Let us suppose, for the sake of analysis, that the court had invoked the assumptions against all his known assets wherever they were situated (as it would have been entitled to do, subject to enforcement treaty arrangements).[51] Presumably if he could have established that the assets putatively to be confiscated were his only assets a total clean-out would have been impermissible in the light of evidence of legitimate sources of income of more than de minimis quantity. Such an order could not be characterised as a determination of benefit and should be struck down as a deliberate over-reach, constituting surrogate additional punishment and not bona fide confiscation. But if the court came down on half of his assets, or two thirds or a third, what then? Given the scope the assumptions allow to judicial intuition, prospects for successfully contesting the quantum of the order seem bleak. Even a fully co-operative defendant may experience great difficulty in establishing to the satisfaction of the court the proportion that legitimate income bears to illegitimate income.[52]

A relevant question, particularly if the provisions under discussion prove a tempting precedent for a wider range of offences, is their compatibility with minimum standards mandated by the European Convention of Human Rights. As well as providing a very limited remedy of last resort for those subject to United Kingdom jurisdiction[53] any incompatibility between provisions of the D.T.O. Act and the Convention will be an important issue in those European countries[54] who are parties to the Convention and have made treaty arrangements with the United Kingdom for the mutual enforcement of confiscation orders.

Article 1 of the First Protocol to the Convention guarantees the peaceful enjoyment of possessions. The protection yields to the "public interest", a condition clearly satisfied if the forfeited possessions *are* the

51. D.T.O. Act, s. 26.
52. The situation would be akin to the prosecution's failure in *Chief Constable of Hampshire v. A.* [1985] Q.B. 132 to establish in the context of a common law restraint order what proportion of moneys were the proceeds of crime in relation to an account sourced by licit and illicit funds. There too the burden of persuasion was on a balance of probabilities.
53. The Convention, of course, is not directly applicable in United Kingdom law and any ex gratia payment made by the United Kingdom government in the light of an adverse finding or judgment will, after all relevant hurdles have been cleared, be some few years after the confiscation order.
54. Where, in many cases, Convention provisions will be directly applicable and controlling.

product of drug trafficking. Thus the focus must be on how that issue is determined, invoking Art. 6 of the Convention, which guarantees, inter alia, a fair hearing in the determination of one's civil rights or of any criminal charge against one and which makes explicit reference to the presumption of innocence.

The determination of the precipitating condition, a conviction of an offence of drug trafficking by trial on indictment obviously satisfies the requirements of Art. 6. Any argument contending a breach of Art. 6 must posit that the confiscation proceedings constitute a determination of civil rights[55] or determination of a criminal charge[56] above and beyond the resolution of the charge relating to the drug trafficking offence and any consequent punishment arising therefrom. Such a characterisation gains force from the fact that a confiscation order involves a determination of facts additional to the fact-finding required for the conviction, and the insistence in the D.T.O. Act that a confiscation order is *not* to be taken into account when determining the length of a term of imprisonment.[57] The European Court of Human Rights in *Salabiaku v. France*[58] has indicated that the use of presumption in favour of the prosecution will contravene the guarantee of fair hearing if, in terms of practicability, the burden of rebuttal is too onerous. But if the confiscation process is seen as an integral part of punishment for the drug trafficking offence[59] and not a process separate from the conviction for such an offence the focus shifts to Art. 3 which proscribes inhuman or degrading treatment or punishment. The relevant jurisprudence holds little prospect of establishing that the confiscation process may involve a breach of this article.[60]

The possibility of incompatibility between the statutory assumptions under discussion and the European Convention is arguably diminished by a recent analysis offered by the Court of Appeal in *R. v. Dickens*.[61] Lord Lane L.C.J., giving the judgment of the court, emphasised that the penal context of the Act and the impact of a confiscation order entailed that the burden on the prosecution when establishing the fact and extent

55. The right to hold property consequent on a finding that it represents the proceeds of drug trafficking, a determination additional to the conviction for the drug-trafficking offence.
56. The procedure requires a finding of benefit from drug trafficking, a determination from which additional sanctions flow. As property to which the defendant has an indefeasible title may be confiscated with the prospect of additional punishment for default, the process could be characterised as penal, as seems indicated by the attitude of the Court of Appeal in *R. v. Dickens* [1990] 2 All E.R. 626.
57. D.T.O. Act, s. 1(5)(c).
58. E. Ct H. Rs A 141 A (1988).
59. In *R. v. Johnson, The Times*, 4 May 1990, the Court of Appeal ruled that a confiscation order was part of the sentence for a drug-trafficking offence for the purposes of a sentencing appeal. The obvious concern was to allow appeals against quantum in addition to the more limited recourse in respect of error of law. The decision should not preclude a finding that a conviction for a drug-trafficking offence and the subsequent confiscation hearing involve two distinct procedures and that the procedural adequacy of the former does not immunise the latter from Convention scrutiny.
60. E.g. *Kotalla v. Netherlands* (1978) 14 D.R. 238, holding that a life sentence involving no prospect of release did not contravene Art. 3.
61. [1990] 2 All E.R. 626.

of benefit was proof beyond a reasonable doubt.[62] This burden was "greatly lightened"[63] by the statutory assumptions in as much as if any assumptions survived the defendant's attempt to disprove them, "they will, together with any evidence that the judge may accept, assist the judge to decide whether he is satisfied as to feel sure that the prosecution have made out their case".[64]

Apparently then, the failure of the defence to rebut an assumption does not clinch the prosecution case, it merely assists the yet to be discharged task of establishing beyond reasonable doubt that the assets in question are the proceeds of drug trafficking. Seemingly then there must always be some *real* evidence besides the unrebutted assumption. In order for an assumption to afford assistance it must be capable of re-inforcing evidence which would otherwise be insufficient to discharge the burden of proof. But as the assumptions, by their very nature, are not factually based, it is irrational to maintain that they can make good deficiencies of true evidence—a confusion of two different modes of discourse. However, unless they are to be allowed an evidential impact their only role would be to allow the defence an opportunity to prove on a balance of probabilities that assets are licit, safe in the knowledge that a failure leaves undiminished the prosecution task of proving beyond reasonable doubt their drug-tainted provenance.

Be that as it may, previous appellate cases operate on the basis that the failure to rebut an assumption entails proof of the prosecution case.[65] Indeed such was the basis of the fact finding in *Dickens* itself. The defendant's explanation as to how he obtained an expensive motor vehicle was rejected by the judge: "[C]onsequently the appellant failed to show that the assumption made by the judge was incorrect. Thus the sum paid for the vehicle by the appellant was part of his proceeds from drug trafficking."[66] Lord Lane's vindication of the trial judge cuts across his own analysis, thus demonstrating the potency of the assumptions and the continuing relevance of compatibility with the Convention.

IDENTIFICATION OF PROCEEDS

The effectiveness of these powers will depend on accurate identification of the defendant's assets. Both Acts provide for searches in the Land Register if there are reasonable grounds for thinking that such a search will be of substantial value in relation to a specified person.[67] The drug

62. Ibid. at 629.
63. Ibid.
64. Ibid. at 629-630.
65. *R. v. Small* (1989) 88 Cr. App. R. 184; *R. v. Hopes* (1989) 11 Cr. App. R. (S) 38; *R. v. Harper* (1989) 11 Cr. App. R. (S) 240; *R. v. Hedley* (1989) 11 Cr. App. R. (S) 298.
66. *R. v. Dickens* [1990] 2 All E.R. 626 at 631. There was evidence aside from the assumptions that D was the owner of property but no additional evidence aside from the assumption that it represented the proceeds of drug trafficking. Where the statutory injunctions are not invoked, *Dickens* clearly establishes that proof beyond reasonable doubt is required to establish that assets are the proceeds of drug trafficking: *R. v. Enwezor* (1991) 12 Cr. App. R. (S) 661.
67. D.T.O. Act, s. 33; *Criminal Justice Act* 1988, s. 100.

trafficking provisions go further in allowing a constable to apply to a circuit judge for an order for the production of particular material or for material of a particular description against a person thought to be in possession of same if there are reasonable grounds for believing that a specified person has carried on drug trafficking or has benefited from it and that the material is likely to be of substantial value in any investigation.[68] These powers have been successfully invoked against a firm of solicitors in relation to conveyancing papers for a property to be purchased with drug funds, although the firm was unaware of the illicit nature of the finance.[69] Further powers are provided under the D.T.O. Act 1986 to provide for the disclosure of information held by government departments,[70] of particular value to the police in extracting information from customs officials.

To date, the most productive source of information relating to the proceeds of drug trafficking has been s. 24 of the D.T.O. Act 1986 which makes it an offence to assist another to retain the benefit of drug trafficking, an offence which will inculpate any bank or other financial intermediary with knowledge or suspicion that a client is or was a drug trafficker. Knowledge or suspicion that the funds or property in question represent the proceeds of drug trafficking is not required.[71] The section provides a defence to any person who discloses to a constable relevant knowledge or suspicion and further provides that any disclosure shall not be treated as a breach of any restriction upon the disclosure of information imposed by contract.[72] The prospect of heavy penalties has seemingly precipitated a steady stream of disclosures by banks, though not without complaint at what has been described as a "serious inroad into customer confidentiality".[73] A similar goad to disclosure has recently been extended by adaptation to funds of terrorists[74] but for other offences a bank would commit no offence per se by processing what it knows or suspects to be the funds of an active criminal. However, should a bank or other body or person choose to reveal any knowledge or suspicion relating to a client's funds to the police, the *Criminal Justice Act* 1988 provides that such disclosure shall not be treated as a breach of any restriction upon the disclosure of any information imposed by contract.[75]

On the face of it, it is difficult to discern any obvious reason why banks and other institutions should be, in effective terms, obliged to disclose suspicions that particular clients are drug traffickers or terrorists but not obliged to spill the beans on other serious offenders. Clearly the matter rests on some unarticulated index of heinousness which may reflect a consensus on terrorists but which is likely to dissolve on discussion of the respective positions on a moral scale of, say, cannabis dealers and

68. D.T.O. Act, ss 27-29.
69. *Francis and Francis (a firm) v. Central Criminal Court* [1988] 3 All E.R. 775.
70. D.T.O. Act, s. 30.
71. D.T.O. Act, s. 24(1).
72. D.T.O. Act, s. 24(3).
73. A remark attributed to Professor Robert Jack, chair of a government committee enquiring into the appropriate limits of banking confidentiality: *The Guardian*, 24 February 1989.
74. *Prevention of Terrorism (Temporary Provisions) Act* 1989, s. 9.
75. *Criminal Justice Act* 1988, s. 98.

defrauders of widows and orphans. The matter is all the more anomalous in that the Serious Fraud Office can require information or an explanation of documents from any person[76] but may only put questions to a bank official in relation to a client of the bank if the matter is first cleared by the Director of the Serious Fraud Office or a person designated by the Director for such purpose.[77] It is submitted that banks and cognate institutions should be under a general obligation to report suspicions that particular funds may be the proceeds of serious crime.[78] In relation to the clearing banks and also authorised or exempted persons under the *Financial Services Act* 1986, an argument that these institutions operate in a purely private capacity is difficult to sustain.[79] The obligation should ideally not be imposed on a crime-by-crime basis with consequent anomalies but by reference to a general concept of serious crime.[80]

Along with powers of investigation, the confiscation provisions of both the *Criminal Justice Act* 1988 and the D.T.O. Act 1986 increase police powers to keep arrested persons incommunicado. The *Police and Criminal Evidence Act* 1984 provides that a suspect under arrest can have a named person informed of the arrest[81] and access to a solicitor, save for some exceptions in relation to serious arrestable offences.[82] These rights can now be over-ridden for 36 hours if a police officer not below the rank of superintendent is reasonably of the view that the exercise of these rights will hinder the recovery of the proceeds of crime. This applies to drug-trafficking offences and to all cases where a person is detained for an offence to which Pt VI of the *Criminal Justice Act* 1988 applies.[83] The latter extends to indictable offences whether or not they are serious arrestable offences. The police only need reasonable grounds for believing that the detainee has benefited from the offence. They need not suspect that he or she has benefited to the amount required (£10,000) for a court to make a confiscation order.

RESTRAINT AND CHARGING ORDERS

Obviously, the confiscation jurisdiction would be seriously undermined if suspects, on catching wind that criminal proceedings are imminent, could not be prevented from taking steps to conceal or dispose of their

76. *Criminal Justice Act* 1987, s. 2.
77. *Criminal Justice Act* 1987, s. 2(10).
78. Arguably, there should be knowledge or suspicion that the funds directly or indirectly represent the proceeds of crime rather than merely suspicion that the client is a criminal.
79. Whether bank officials were cognate with public officials or merely private employees was left open in *D.P.P. v. Withers* [1975] A.C. 842.
80. For discussion of a principled approach as to what constitutes degrees of seriousness in relation to offending, see Von Hirsch, *Past and Future Crime* (1985), Ch. 6; Von Hirsch and Jareborg, "Gauging Criminal Harm: A Living Standard Analysis" (1991) 11 Ox. J.L.S. 1.
81. *Police and Criminal Evidence Act* 1984, s. 56(1).
82. *Police and Criminal Evidence Act* 1984, s. 56(2), (5), (11).
83. *Police and Criminal Evidence Act* 1984, s. 56(5A), interpolated by D.T.O. Act, s. 32(1) as amended by *Criminal Justice Act* 1988, s. 99(2).

assets. Prior to the Acts, a restricted common law jurisdiction was created which empowered the prosecutor to obtain an order for the detention of money standing to the credit of a bank account to the extent that it could be shown to have been obtained from another in breach of criminal law.[84] This jurisdiction has not been abolished, but it seems clear that with the advent of a statutory jurisdiction it will no longer be developed.[85] Although it is possible to envisage situations where a common law freezing order may be available on grounds not afforded by statute,[86] the major defect of common law orders is that the moneys to be frozen must be identifiable as the direct proceeds of crime at the time the order is granted.[87]

By contrast, statutory restraint orders may be made against all "realisable property" in which the defendant holds an interest[88] and additionally in respect of any gifts made, directly or indirectly.[89] Of course, ultimate enforcement of a confiscation order will be made against those assets and gifts which can be shown to have been funded from crime or, in the case of drug trafficking when statutory assumptions are invoked, cannot be proved by the defendant not to be funded from the proceeds of drug trafficking. But at the outset of proceedings, all the defendant's realisable assets are potentially subject to restraint.

A restraint order is obtainable ex parte from the High Court by the prosecutor.[90] It may apply to all realisable property held by a specified person, whether the property is described in the order or not and to any realisable property held by a specified person after the order is made.[91] The order prohibits any person from dealing with any realisable property subject to such conditions and exceptions as may be specified in the order.[92] This prohibition affects anyone with notice of the order,[93] a matter of obvious significance for bankers, solicitors, stockbrokers etc. Where the High Court has made a restraint order, a constable may seize any property to prevent its removal from Great Britain.[94] The court may appoint a receiver to take possession of and manage the property.[95] An order may be applied for to operate from when a person is to be charged with a relevant offence and may remain in force until any confiscation order is satisfied.[96] A restraint order is available if there are reasonable grounds for thinking a confiscation order will be made.[97]

---

84. *West Mercia Constabulary v. Wagener* [1981] 3 All E.R. 378; *Chief Constable of Kent v. A.* [1983] Q.B. 34.
85. *Chief Constable of Leicestershire v. M.* [1988] 3 All E.R. 1015; *Chief Constable of Surrey v. A.*, *The Times*, 27 October 1988. But contrast *S.I.B. v. Pantell* [1989] N.L.J.R. 754, discussed below.
86. For example, to freeze an account for the purposes of compensation in circumstances where the police are aware that the defendant's proceeds of crime are less than £10,000.
87. *Chief Constable of Hampshire v. A.* [1985] Q.B. 132.
88. *Criminal Justice Act* 1988, s. 77.
89. *Criminal Justice Act* 1988, s. 74(10)(b).
90. *Criminal Justice Act* 1988, s. 77(5).
91. *Criminal Justice Act* 1988, s. 77(3).
92. *Criminal Justice Act* 1988, s. 77(1).
93. *Criminal Justice Act* 1988, s. 77(5)(c).
94. *Criminal Justice Act* 1988, s. 77(10).
95. *Criminal Justice Act* 1988, s. 77(8).
96. *Criminal Justice Act* 1988, s. 76.
97. *Criminal Justice Act* 1988, s. 75(1)(c).

Alternatively, the prosecution may apply for a charging order over interests in specified realisable property[98] which may include any beneficial interest of the defendant or D's donee in land, government stock, shares and units of any unit trust.[99] Such an order will be particularly appropriate if there are multiple interests in particular assets. The charge operates as a security for the payment of money to the Crown[100] and may subsist until such time as the amount payable under a confiscation order is paid into court.[101]

CONFISCATION AND THIRD PARTIES

The restraint, charging and the realisation of assets may, of course, be disruptive of third party interests in the affected property. It is provided that orders should be exercised with a view to allowing persons other than the defendant or donees "to retain or recover the value of any property".[102] But inevitably sales and other forms of disruption of jointly-held property will, in many readily conceivable circumstances, have an adverse economic impact on the interests of innocent third parties. More fundamentally, these powers may effectively destroy the right to reside in a specific property enjoyed by the offender's spouse and children. Rights to retain possession of matrimonial property do not feature as protected interests under the Acts.[103] Though a spouse or any significant other would obtain value proportionate to the interest held, there is no mechanism based on entitlement to postpone realisation in circumstances of hardship. Persons holding an interest in property must be given a reasonable opportunity to make representations to the court[104] and hopefully the courts will temper the exercise of the powers under the Acts with some humanity.[105]

The right of a third party to make representations falls short of being made a party to the proceedings with legal representation. In *R. v. Robson*[106] the defendant's mother was the legal owner of a house but had received financial support from the defendant. A complicated issue of civil law arose as to whether these arrangements gave the defendant an equitable interest in the property based on a constructive or resulting trust. The prosecution's argument that such was the effect of the financial support succeeded at trial with an order ensuing for sale of the property. This conclusion was reserved on the facts by the Court of Appeal. In the course of his judgment Rose J. remarked: "[I]t was a striking and extraordinary consequence of the 1986 Act[107] that, in a case such as the present, the court's powers were so draconian that it seemed able to

98. *Criminal Justice Act* 1988, s. 78(1).
99. *Criminal Justice Act* 1988, s. 78(5).
100. *Criminal Justice Act* 1988, s. 78(1).
101. *Criminal Justice Act* 1988, s. 78(7).
102. *Criminal Justice Act* 1988, s. 82(4).
103. *Criminal Justice Act* 1988, s. 74(9); D.T.O. Act, s. 5(7).
104. *Criminal Justice Act* 1988, s. 80(8); D.T.O. Act, s. 11(8).
105. In both Acts the final exercise of the power of realisation is expressed in permissive rather than mandatory terms: *Criminal Justice Act* 1988, s. 80(1); D.T.O. Act, s. 11(1).
106. [1991] Crim. L.R. 222.
107. The position under the *Criminal Justice Act* 1988 is the same.

deprive the legal owner of property of some or all of his or her beneficial interests in it without the owner having any opportunity to present the arguments against such a conclusion."[108] The force of these remarks is obvious in a context where the legal position may be complex and where there may be disputation as to the facts not only between the prosecution and the defendant but between the defendant and a third party.[109]

If the substantive proceedings culminate in an acquittal, the quashing of the conviction or a pardon, a person adversely affected by an order may be awarded such compensation as the court considers appropriate but only if there has been *serious* default on the part of the investigators or prosecutors and if *substantial* loss has arisen in consequence.[110] Thus there would be no statutory compensation if the defendant had been, say, the victim of a malicious informer unless it had been manifestly unreasonable for the relevant authority to act on the information. Moreover, it has been recently decided that this limited statutory right is incompatible with the existence of any common law right of compensation against the prosecuting authority.[111]

DISCLOSURE OF ASSETS

Neither Act includes any coercive mechanisms to enforce disclosure of assets. In drugs cases a practice has apparently emerged of officers interviewing suspects after charge in an effort to ascertain what assets might be caught by the D.T.O. Act. Although suspects are assured that answers will only be used in confiscation proceedings after conviction and not to obtain a conviction, unsurprisingly solicitors advise clients not to answer these questions.[112] However, if a restraint order is successfully obtained from the High Court, the prosecutor will then have access to the inherent jurisdiction of the High Court. Under this jurisdiction, discovery may be applied for against a recalcitrant defendant. Such a course was taken in *Re a Defendant*,[113] where the defendant was obliged to give the prosecutor details of his assets or else be found in contempt. Understandably, the defendant complained that this process infringed his right not to incriminate himself. Webster J. considered that this right would be preserved if the prosecutor gave an undertaking to the court to confine his use of the information obtained to confiscation proceedings and not to adduce any of it as evidence at the trial.[114]

108. *The Times*, 7 August 1990.
109. There may, of course, be an incentive for the defendant to exaggerate her or his own interest in jointly held property so that the order may, at least in part, be levied at someone else's expense.
110. *Criminal Justice Act* 1988, s. 89.
111. *Re R.*, *The Times*, 15 July 1989.
112. Feldman, *Criminal Confiscations Orders* (1988), pp. 14-15.
113. *The Times*, 7 April 1987.
114. On the theory that such an undertaking would, unlike a civil plaintiff, bind the prosecutor, thus distinguishing the failure to resolve the self-incrimination problem in *Rank Film Distributors Ltd v. Video Information* [1982] A.C. 380.

At the risk of digression, one may remark that the case affords another example of how the adversarial model of the criminal process has to make increasing accommodation to inquisitorial features. If one uses by example the position pre-trial of persons suspected of some species of fraud, a varying pattern is revealed. As we have just examined, such an offender may be forced to reveal assets under the formal protection of non-admissibility of answers at trial. If the case is under investigation by the Serious Fraud Office D is obliged to answer questions and/or give an explanation of documents[115] but again, save for limited exceptions, the answers are not admissible evidence.[116] If however the defendant is called before inspectors investigating the affairs of a limited company[117] or into alleged insider trading[118] D is obliged to answer questions and the answers can be put in as evidence in any subsequent criminal proceedings. It is difficult to discern any sustainable rationale underpinning this varying pattern.

CONFISCATION AND COMPENSATION

For many offences there will, of course, be identifiable victims. The *Criminal Justice Act* 1988 gives added emphasis to the previous legislation on compensation by criminal courts by providing that a criminal court must give reasons why it has not made a compensation order to a victim occasioned loss by a crime.[119] But the compensation jurisdiction remains discretionary. The most salient judge-made limitation on the award of orders has been the insistence that the procedure is only suitable for "clear and simple" cases. Thus, to take two examples where the factual issues did not appear too intractable, an award was not entertained in a case where the convicted burglar denied that he had stolen certain of the items on a list supplied by the householder[120] and also in a case where the convicted motorist disputed the pre-crash condition of the car he had damaged.[121]

This insistence on expedition in the matter of compensation can be contrasted with the detailed statutory procedure provided to determine confiscation issues. Coupled with the accompanying investigatory powers, restraint orders and enforcement procedures (including the appointment of receivers) we have a potentially serious[122] commitment of court time and enforcement resource. The question arises as to whether in those cases which meet the monetary threshold, the confiscation machinery can be put at the disposal of compensation. In the Federal Republic of Germany, a forthcoming reform will give victims of crime first priority on funds recovered through the confiscation

---

115. *Criminal Justice Act* 1987, s. 2.
116. *Criminal Justice Act* 1987, s. 2(8).
117. *Companies Act* 1985, s. 434(3), (5).
118. *Financial Services Act* 1986, s. 177(3), (4), (6).
119. *Criminal Justice Act* 1988, s. 104(1).
120. *R. v. Kneeshaw* (1974) 58 Cr. App. R. 439.
121. *R. v. Vivian* [1979] 1 All E.R. 48.
122. The confiscation jurisdiction in non-drug cases is discretionary: *Criminal Justice Act* 1988, s. 71(1).

process.[123] It will be contended that such a priority can be achieved in the United Kingdom, de facto, through prosecutorial and judicial discretion operating within the current legislation.

Legislative concern for just compensation to victims in the context of confiscation orders may be discerned in the requirement to take into account any civil proceedings before determining a confiscation order.[124] Doubtless this is to safeguard against double payment by the defendant in respect of the same gain but it will also avoid depleting funds by way of confiscation orders that will be required to satisfy civil judgment. The primacy of compensation is explicitly recognised in a provision dealing with the situation where a confiscation and a compensation order are made in the same proceedings but where the defendant lacks sufficient means to satisfy both orders: in such cases the court "shall direct that so much of the compensation order as cannot be paid shall be paid out of sums recovered under the confiscation order".[125]

Against such a background it is to be hoped, particularly in large scale frauds with multiple victims, that prosecutors will apply for confiscation orders with a view to using the statutory confiscation process in the interests of compensation. Allied to that must be a judicial willingness to allow court time for establishing the particular losses to individual victims. Given that conjunction, the confiscation provisions can considerably enhance the effectiveness of criminal courts as vehicles for compensation without in any way detracting from the purposes of the confiscation provisions.

MAREVA INJUNCTIONS

Because the confiscation process under the D.T.O. Act 1986 is mandatory, prosecuting and investigatory authorities will have to accommodate to it, whatever the given level of resources. But as the jurisdiction under Part VI of the *Criminal Justice Act* 1988 is discretionary, the incidence of confiscation orders will reflect priorities and resources. In cases involving victims, the policy of confiscation might be coincidentally furthered by private action for civil law redress. Moreover, as will be discussed, a successful civil action may recover assets which are situated outside the jurisdiction and beyond the current scope of a statutory confiscation order.

123. Art. 73, s. 1 of the German *Criminal Code* provides for the confiscation of economic gains from offences. The section is displaced by any civil action brought by the defendant. The Article is under review by the Federal Ministry of Justice with a view to granting to victims first priority on any assets recovered in confiscation proceedings. I am grateful to Professor H. H. Jescheck for this information.
124. *Criminal Justice Act* 1988, s. 72(5).
125. *Criminal Justice Act* 1988, s. 72(7). Somewhat paradoxically s. 37(c) of the *Powers of the Criminal Court Act* 1973 (as substituted by s. 105 of the *Criminal Justice Act* 1988) provides that a magistrates court charged with the enforcement of a compensation order can discharge or reduce the order if the defendant lacks the means to satisfy the order and a confiscation order made against her or him in the same proceedings.

If a civil action is to be brought, preliminary action will frequently be required in an effort to identify and preserve assets for the satisfaction of judgment. To this end the still developing Mareva injunction,[126] with its ancillary power providing for disclosure of assets, has proved invaluable. As is well known, a Mareva injunction is a court order, available in ex parte proceedings, restraining the defendant from placing assets beyond the enforcement reach of the court. If necessary, severe restrictions can be placed on the defendant and third parties on dealing in the assets. An order can be made pre or post judgment and is served on the defendant and on any third party (in particular banks) known or believed to have assets within the control of the defendant. If the plaintiff lacks particulars about the defendant's assets, it may suffice simply to provide the court with the names of the defendant's bankers or other financial intermediaries.

The statutory restraint orders are to a large extent modelled on the Mareva injunction. At present statutory restraint orders will in the main be limited in their effect to assets located within the jurisdiction. Although they may place a defendant under compulsion[127] to disclose assets within her or his control located overseas, such orders will lack the vital dimension of collateral enforceability against overseas third parties such as banks located abroad. In the absence of a mutual enforcement treaty, any attempt to have an order recognised by a foreign court will in all likelihood be met by a refusal to apply foreign penal law. An argument can be made the statutory restraint orders should not be regarded as penal law as they emanate from civil courts and are ancillary to a process which, if characterised as purely restitutionary, is non-punitive. It is contended that such a characterisation is implausible given that confiscation orders are imposed by criminal courts as a consequence of a criminal conviction and involve an impost payable to the Crown. In the light of burgeoning international fraud, the abolition of exchange control and the proliferation of offshore havens for cash and securities, this impediment to international enforceability is a significant limitation.

Mareva injunctions are indisputably adjuncts to civil proceedings. A series of recent decisions by the Court of Appeal,[128] resolving uncertainty, have established that these orders can, in certain circumstances, be issued in relation to overseas assets of a defendant subject to the personal jurisdiction of the court. Although a greater readiness to make such an order in relation to the enforcement of a judgment is indicated, orders for pre-trial restraint over overseas assets have been issued.[129] It is stressed that such an order will be exceptional, even "very rare"[130] and yet the guiding criteria for granting such an

---

126. *Mareva Compania Naviera S.A. v. International Bulkcarriers S.A.* [1975] 2 Lloyd's Rep. 509.
127. Not in their own terms but by invoking the inherent jurisdiction of the High Court: see *Re a Defendant, The Times,* 7 April 1987, discussed above, p. 318.
128. *Babanaft International Co. S.A. v. Bassatne* [1989] 2 W.L.R. 232; *Republic of Haiti v. Duvalier* [1989] 2 W.L.R. 261; *Derby & Co. Ltd v. Weldon (No. 1)* [1989] 2 W.L.R. 276; *Derby & Co. Ltd v. Weldon (Nos 3 and 4)* [1989] 2 W.L.R. 412. On these cases, see Collins, "The Territorial Reach of Mareva Injunctions" (1989) 105 L.Q.R. 262; Capper, "Worldwide Mareva Injunctions" (1991) 54 M.L.R. 329.
129. In each of the cases cited directly above, fn 128.
130. *Republic of Haiti v. Duvalier* [1989] 2 W.L.R. 261 at 272.

order—insufficiency of assets within Great Britain to meet judgment; determination to keep assets beyond reach of court; significant quantity of money involved[131]—are likely to feature in many large scale fraud cases. Incidentally to the injunction, the court may also make a disclosure order relating to assets abroad which may facilitate the bringing of attachment proceedings in foreign courts.[132] Any question of an overreaching assumption of extraterritorial jurisdiction is met by an insistence that any enforcement of the order must be processed through the local court. If the local court is situated in a country party to the *Convention on Jurisdiction and Enforcement of Judgments*,[133] there is entitlement as of right to have a preliminary order relating to specific assets enforced by the local court if the order is ancillary to civil or commercial proceedings, provided the defendant was given an opportunity to contest the order.[134]

It would seem that the Mareva injunction, with its extraterritorial dimension, is not available to prosecutors wishing to preserve assets for the purposes of a compensation order imposed by a criminal court. Quite apart from the question of the enforcement of foreign penal law (if such be the case),[135] the Court of Appeal has confirmed the refusal to issue the equivalent of a Mareva injunction in the context of a forthcoming criminal trial.[136] This contrasts with the decision in *Securities & Investment Board v. Pantell*,[137] where a Mareva injunction with extraterritorial effect was granted to the Board in support of the Board's statutory power to bring civil action on behalf of investors caused loss by contraventions of the *Financial Services Act* 1986. The difference is anomalous; despite the penal setting, the role of the prosecutor in seeking compensation is in the like case to the role of the Board. Indeed, the respective empowering provisions employ similar language.[138] For some time to come, the civil law may offer a more effective response to the phenomenon of international fraud than the criminal law.[139]

---

131. Ibid. at 273.
132. An injunction (with ancillary disclosure order) will not normally be made unless the plaintiff gives an undertaking that no attachment proceedings will be taken abroad without first obtaining the consent of the English court: *Derby & Co. Ltd v. Weldon (No. 1)* [1989] 2 W.L.R. 276 at 285.
133. Cmnd. 7395. The E.E.C. and the E.F.T.A. countries.
134. *Convention on Jurisdiction and Enforcement of Judgments*, Art. 24; *Civil Jurisdiction and Judgments Act* 1982, s. 25.
135. Arguably, the fact that the payment is made to the victim and excludes or diminishes the effect of any civil liability of the defendant in respect of the victim (*Powers of the Criminal Court Act* 1972, s. 38 as substituted by s. 105 of the *Criminal Justice Act* 1988) sufficiently distinguishes a compensation order from a confiscation order, to allow recognition of the former in foreign courts.
136. *Chief Constable of Hampshire v. A.* [1985] Q.B. 132. The Court of Appeal ruled that a prosecuting authority seeking to preserve a defendant's assets to satisfy any compensation order lacked locus standi in the sense of any cause of action required for an injunction relating to assets of the defendant unless they could be shown to be directly sourced from criminal offences.
137. [1989] N.L.J.R. 754.
138. The powers of the *Criminal Court Act* 1973, s. 35 provide that a criminal court may award compensation, "on application or otherwise"; the *Financial Services Act* 1986, s. 6 provides that the High Court may pay out compensation to investors damnified by unauthorised investment business "on application" by the Board. In *Pantell*, s. 6 was said to repose a cause of action in the Board; thus an injunction could be obtained.
139. Although the privilege against self-incrimination may impair the effectiveness of an order in some instances: *Sociedade Nacional de Combustiveis de Angola v. Lundquist* [1990] 3 All E.R. 283.

16

Cleaning up The Bankers' Act
The United Kingdom Experience

MICHAEL LEVI*

INTRODUCTION

Willie Sutton, the great American bank robber, was reputed to have replied to a journalist who asked him why he robbed banks, " 'Cos that's where the money is".[1] Alas, that was in a bygone era. Willie's modern counterpart would have had to worry, not just about how he was going to rob the bank (and avoid being identified for the police and jury's benefit by the on-line cameras) but also about what he could do with the money when he got it. The essence of the plethora of legislation which had developed in the United Kingdom has been to make it increasingly difficult for any "non-respectable" embarked upon "the queer ladder of social mobility"[2] to deposit cash or cheques at all without being subjected to a Banking Inquisition, or at best to do so without being passed on to the authorities as a suspected money launderer. So unless he or she hides the money under the bed—which, with inflation running at around 6 per cent, is bad business—or spends it—which is poor entrepreneurship if terrific fun—what is a poor modern robber to do? Before reviewing the contemporary scene, let us go back to the halcyon (for criminals) regulatory days of 1983, when the only legal powers the police had were to inspect bankers' books following the institution of legal proceedings against the person whose books were to be examined, and of 1985—not so long ago—when no United Kingdom money laundering legislation existed.

In the aftermath of the United Kingdom £26 million Brinks-Mat robbery of 1983, a previously obscure firm suddenly generated a large number of transactions and withdrew huge sums in cash. Between September 1984 and January 1985, a company called Scadlynn—which previously had been trading in tens of thousands of pounds monthly— deposited over £10 million, allegedly as the result of dealers buying scrap gold. Once- or twice-weekly cash withdrawals escalated from £20,000 to £300,000 over the four-month period; new cashiers were recruited at the small three-till branch to deal with the account; special arrangements were made with Barclays' Bullion Centre at Bristol to supply £50 notes;

* Professor of Criminology, University of Wales College of Cardiff.
1. Willie Sutton later claimed, plausibly, that the quote had been invented by a journalist. See Sutton, *Where the Money Was* (1981).
2. Bell, "Crime as an American way of life", in Bell (ed.), *The End of Ideology* (1961).

and the firm warned the bank they would soon require £1 million per day, which information was communicated to the Bank of England. It took some time before the upsurge in cash transactions was reported up the line to Barclays' inspection department and, even then, it was not reported to the police: there was no *legal* obligation for the bank to report it.

Scadlynn's managing director had not long before been given a suspended prison sentence for conspiracy to defraud, and had several convictions for fraud, though neither the bank manager nor the bank inspection department knew that: this knowledge might have made a difference in practice to the way they treated the account, though at that time, even had the bank known, it would not have affected the bank's legal duty in relation to its contract with him. In September 1984, the Brinks-Mat ringleader Kenneth Noye approached a branch of the Bank of Ireland in Croydon, flashily dressed, and—probably unknown to the bank—using a false name. He inquired about offshore bank facilities, and opened an offshore Dublin account in his false and his wife's maiden name, stating that he did not want statements sent to him. He also left no means by which the bank could contact him. He allegedly told the bank that he was in the property development business, but had made a killing on the stock market. From September 4 1984, he made five monthly deposits of £200,000 in cash, in new £50 notes. No criminal liability then attached to the bankers involved: now, they could all be facing a maximum 14 years' imprisonment.

The movement in the direction of encouraging—and in an increasing range of cases, requiring—"active citizenship" on the part of banks has as its objectives to prevent criminals from benefiting financially (i) from the offences for which they have been convicted; and (ii) to the extent that monetary gain is the *criminals'* primary goal or is a crucial means to their other (for example, political) goals, to deter or prevent them and others from committing crimes for gain in the future. These objectives are being pursued not only in Britain but also in the international arena, as other articles in this book discuss. The effect of these changes has been to transform (i) the police—and some other regulatory bodies—from financial information supplicants to information demanders; and (ii) the banks into an unpaid, involuntary High Street Watch scheme of pressed informants. How and in what ways has this remarkable transformation been achieved?

Before we embark upon this exposition, we should note that it would be a mistake to view all these developments as unwelcome to the banks, for one universal aspect of such *reactive* court-ordered demands is that they release the banks from any legal liability to clients for breach of confidentiality. These developments in powers remain haphazard, because it is alien to the government in Britain (or elsewhere) to be consistent across the board in setting out the powers of different departments (or, for that matter, in rationalising their policies). Powers have sometimes been rationalised at an intra-agency level, but inter-agency co-ordination—which remains variable in extent—received low legislative priority before criticisms by the Keith and Roskill Commmittees prompted respectively some harmonisation of tax powers and the establishment of the Serious Fraud Office under the *Criminal Justice Act* 1987.[3]

THE POLICE AND CRIMINAL EVIDENCE ACT 1984

Section 8 of the *Police and Criminal Evidence Act* 1984 (referred to hereafter as P.A.C.E. 1984) deals with search warrants issued by magistrates in relation to serious arrestable offences. However, more germane for the purpose of this review are s. 9 and Sched. 1 of P.A.C.E 1984, under which a circuit judge may issue the police with a warrant to search for evidence in relation to "special procedure material"—such as information held in confidence by banks (s. 14)—if he or she is satisfied that there are reasonable grounds for believing, inter alia, that (i) a serious arrestable offence has been committed, this being defined in s. 116, inter alia, as an offence which has led, or is intended or likely to lead, to substantial financial gain or loss to any person;[4] (ii) there is material likely to be of substantial value (whether by itself or together with other material) to the investigation; (iii) the material is likely to be relevant evidence; (iv) there is no prospect of the material being obtained without a Production Order (for example, if bankers' obligations of confidentiality prevent them from disclosing information); and (v) access to the information is overall in the public interest: a term of the utmost flexibility! Applications for orders under Sched. 1, para. 4 must be made inter partes, though under s. 8 of P.A.C.E. 1984, search warrants are available ex parte where bankers themselves are clear suspects and/or service of notice might seriously prejudice an investigation.

Section 8(2) of P.A.C.E. 1984 defines three categories of extraordinary material for which the police might wish to search: "items subject to legal privilege", which cannot be subject to a search warrant from anyone at all; and "excluded material" and "special procedure material", for which warrants may be issued only by a circuit or a deputy circuit judge under s. 9. No warrant may ever be issued to search for evidence which is legally privileged. Such material is defined in s. 10(1) as covering communications between a professional legal adviser and a client or the client's represenative made in connection with the giving of legal advice; communications made between the adviser and the client and any other person that have been made in connection with, or in contemplation of, legal proceedings; and items enclosed with or referred to in such communications and made in connection with the giving of legal advice. Legal advisers include barristers, solicitors, and their clerks, and "any other person" referred to might include an accountant or banker asked to prepare a report "in connection with" legal proceedings. So all documents and other records in the possession of a solicitor *in relation to the affairs of their clients* are either legally privileged or special procedure material.[5]

---

3. See generally, Levi, *Regulating Fraud: White Collar Crime and the Criminal Process* (1987).
4. "Substantial" is defined loosely so that it can represent the subjective perception of the victim or of the police!
5. *R. v. Guildhall Magistrates Court; Ex parte Primlaks Holdings Co. (Panama) Inc.* [1989] 2 W.L.R. 841.

Section 10(2) states that "items held with the intention of furthering a criminal purpose are not items subject to legal privilege". But whose intention is included here? The House of Lords—by a three to two majority decision—has eased the investigative path by upholding the view that legal privilege does not apply, not only where the criminal purpose is that of the client—as was the common law view in *R v. Cox and Railton*[6]—but also where the documents are said to further the criminal intentions of a third party. This was a case where the police believed that a drug trafficker provided substantial sums to members of his family to repay through a floral business a £330,000 mortgage, though the case was pursued on the basis that the family did not know that it was drug money.[7]

It is a matter for speculation whether the same view would have been taken had the suspect been suspected of laundering the proceeds of fraud rather than drug trafficking, or where it was absolutely clear that the solicitor's client was truly unaware of any criminal intention on the part of the third party. In *R. v. Board of Inland Revenue; Ex parte Goldberg*,[8] the Divisional Court held that in a case under s. 20(3) of the *Taxes Management Act* 1970, copies of documents brought into existence for the sole purpose of obtaining legal advice were privileged, even if the originals were not. Thus, though the originals had disappeared, a barrister could not be required to hand over copy documents related to the case of a client whose tax affairs were under investigation—though not at that stage criminal investigation—by the Inland Revenue. However, in the later case of *Dubai Bank Ltd v. Galadari*,[9] the Court of Appeal declined to follow *Goldberg* and held that a copy of an affidavit was not protected by legal professional privilege, as the original was not privileged. *R. v. Central Criminal Court; Ex parte Francis & Francis*[10] applies to all serious arrestable offences pursued under P.A.C.E 1984 and the *Drug Trafficking Offences Act* 1986 (D.T.O. Act): to fraud as well as to drug-trafficking investigations. It applies also where "laundering" offences cannot be laid specifically, since as Lord Goff observed:[11] "The purpose of a bank robber is not just to rob a bank: it is to obtain the money for his own benefit." In ex parte cases where the solicitor is not under suspicion, the order is normally made to take effect within seven days, during which time the solicitor can apply to the judge to discharge the order.[12]

The interpretation of these issues has to be decided on a case-by-case basis, but though commercial fraud (and, a fortiori, drug trafficking and money laundering) have been highlighted as major crimes since 1986, the police and prosecutors cannot confidently expect the courts knowingly to allow these provisions to be used for evidentiary fishing expeditions. The greater independence from the police of judges compared with magistrates, as well as the complexity of some requests

6. (1884) 14 Q.B.D. 153.
7. See *R. v. Central Criminal Court; Ex parte Francis and Francis* [1988] 3 W.L.R. 989.
8. [1988] 3 All E.R. 248.
9. Unreported, 7 August 1989.
10. [1988] 3 W.L.R. 989.
11. Ibid. at 1015.
12. See r. 25(B) of the *Crown Court (Amendment) Rules* 1986 (S.I. 1986, No. 2151).

for access, are the principal (non-political) reasons why magistrates were not given the right to make such production orders. The general inference arising out of the case law is that statutory safeguards are essentially intended for the protection of the person or body against whom production orders are sought, rather than for the protection of the suspect. Thus, the Court of Appeal has ruled that banks are under no contractual duty to their customers either to resist the making of production orders or to inform their customers that production orders have been applied for inter partes. [13] Any protection for suspects lies (i) in the *internal* criteria applied within policing organisations before seeking information from banks (which, in practice, varies both within and between policing agencies); and (ii) in how critical circuit judges are when reviewing, before making a production order, whether or not the access conditions under various statutes have been satisfied. This is subject to potential shifts in judicial attitude towards what they see as "abuse of power".

One problem that sometimes arises relates to the particularisation of documents. The names of account holders regarding whom information is sought can be communicated orally rather than written on the documentation. This is important where it is suspected that there may be leaks inside the bank to the account holders. [14] In *R v. Central Criminal Court; Ex parte Adegbesan* [15]—which concerned allegations of corruption in relation to the administration of funds by a trustee of the Youth Association on the riot-hit Broadwater Farm Estate in London— the Divisional Court quashed the "special procedure" order made by the Common Sergeant, stating that it was the duty of the police to set out a description of all the material that was to be produced. Failure to do so could result in the recipient of the notice unwittingly destroying the material, since it was impossible for him to know whether or not it was covered by the order. When the police did provide further particulars, the defendants appealed once more, on the grounds that the particulars were still inadequate. [16] In argument before the Divisional Court regarding the appeal over the second set of production orders, counsel for the Metropolitan Police accepted that in relation to two of the Production Orders, the evidence before the circuit judge was inadequate to satisfy the access conditions under s. 9, though the judge had in fact

13. *Barclays Bank Plc v. Taylor; Trustee Savings Bank of Wales and Border Countries v. Taylor* [1989] 1 W.L.R. 1066. See Taylor, *The Poisoned Tree* (1990) for a detailed account of a claimed police/political conspiracy which underlay this investigation. The police were heavily criticised subsequently by the judge at Taylor's trial for the spurious grounds on which they allegedly had obtained their search powers. Perhaps influenced by their perception of the risk of abuse in the light of the Taylor case, as well as by the facts of the *Hill* application (below) in which the police had not informed the judge that they already had (unsuccessfully) sought to obtain the information they wanted via a magistrates' order under s. 7 of the *Bankers' Books Evidence Act* 1879, the Divisional Court has subsequently warned that before granting Production Orders, judges must be satisfied that all access conditions are present, such as that other practicable methods of obtaining discovery had been substantially exhausted without success (*R. v. Lewes Crown Court; Ex parte Hill, The Times*, 12 November 1990).
14. See *R. v. Manchester Crown Court; Ex parte Taylor* [1988] 1 W.L.R. 705.
15. [1986] 3 All E.R. 113.
16. *Carr v. Atkins* [1987] 3 All E.R. 684; *R. v. Central Criminal Court; Ex parte Carr* (1987) Lexis, 27 February 1987; *The Independent*, 5 March 1987.

granted those orders. Those orders were quashed, but the others upheld. Leave was then granted to appeal to the House of Lords over whether notices under s. 9 must specify *all* the facts and matters upon which the applicant for the order intends to rely, and whether it is allowable that orders be granted against parties severally, where the applicant does not know which party has which documents.

These inroads into legal privilege—or clarification of its meaning!— make little difference to most banking situations, except where moneys are held in solicitors' clients' accounts. More generally, banking and police sources state that there is very seldom any objection to Production Orders under Sched. 1 of P.A.C.E. 1984 in inter partes hearings (though this may partly reflect pre-application agreement between the parties). It is contempt of court to breach a Production Order, with a potential sanction of imprisonment: to date, such sanctions have not been applied.

DRUG TRAFFICKING OFFENCES ACT 1986

The second major legislative development of the 1980s affecting the policing of banking transactions was more dramatic. The *Drug Trafficking Offences Act* 1986 (D.T.O. Act) required banks to be *proactive* in passing on information about suspected drug traffickers to the police, on pain of imprisonment should they fail to be good citizens. Section 24 of the Act creates an offence of assisting drug trafficking. It also provides immunity from being sued for breach of contract where (subs. 3):

> a person discloses to a Constable a suspicion or belief that any funds or investments are derived from, or used in connection with, drug trafficking or any matter on which such a suspicion or belief is based.

By contrast with P.A.C.E. 1984 Production Orders—which are inter partes—s. 27 Production Orders from a circuit judge are ex parte, though s. 27(6) does allow the person on whom the order has been served to apply for variation or discharge of the order. It is general practice for the bank to be informed beforehand as a matter of courtesy and sensible policing, not least because the bank can inconvenience the authorities by delaying the giving of information within the range—normally up to seven days—granted by the court, or because the bank has supplied the information informally already and the authorities have decided that it is sufficiently useful to justify applying for the Order. However, on occasions, the bank itself may be suspected of high-level involvement in money laundering, so unlike *R. v. Manchester Crown Court; Ex parte Taylor*,[17] no-one will be informed even orally in advance. Supplementary problems may be caused in relation to information about third parties overseas that is seized during a raid. In *R. v. Southwark Crown Court; Ex parte Customs & Excise* and *R. v. Southwark Crown Court; Ex parte Bank of Credit and Commerce International*,[18] the

17. [1988] 1 W.L.R. 705.
18. [1989] 3 W.L.R. 1054.

Divisional Court quashed an order of the circuit judge preventing *copies* of information about Panamanian General Noriega's accounts seized during a raid on the Bank of Credit and Commerce International from being communicated to the United States authorities.

Section 24 continues to cause great alarm in banking circles, even though it is a defence (subs. 4) to prove, inter alia, that one did not know or suspect that the arrangement related to *any* person's proceeds of drug trafficking. If the police have already revealed *their* suspicions about the customer, this defence might be hard to sustain. This generates problems in how to deal with the account of someone thus suspected. Often, for intelligence purposes, the account will be allowed to run. But at other times, the police may want the bank to act in a manner which may not protect the bank by law. An example occurred in December 1987, when a press leak allegedly emanating from the police brought to a head criticism of one major bank because even though the bank knew of his arrest on drugs charges, a man was allowed to withdraw from his account in an unsalubrious area of Liverpool £1,500: a fairly insubstantial sum, far from the image of the international narcotics trafficker used in Parliament as the justification for this legislation, but almost his entire liquid assets. This caused an enormous fuss, and bank officers were threatened with prosecution. The general policy of most banks has changed so that if the police confirm in writing that the Crown Prosecution Service is applying for a Restraint Order—which can be obtained only from the High Court in London, not from a High Court Judge elsewhere—the bank will release the information and risk a civil lawsuit from the client.

Sometimes—particularly in the laundering sphere and organised crime groups—the same people are involved in drug trafficking, fraud, and terrorism, but the legal framework for reporting requirements is *offence*-based, not *offender*-based. In practice, there has developed a certain fluidity in access to banking information in Britain, depending largely on whether the bank is one of the major ones or not, though even among large banks, there are substantial variations. Where the officers (police and customs) are trusted and have been shown to be reliable, information may be given for intelligence purposes on condition that it will not be used evidentially without its being obtained officially via a Production Order. Where this system breaks down, it is usually because the police seek to short-circuit their own hierarchies and the banking hierarchies—or are not aware what the proper procedures are—not appreciating the risks that the bankers are running from laws whose implications are uncertain or from their own superiors if they co-operate with the police without the plain legal protection of a court order.

Some police consider that the D.T.O. Act entitles them to require information from banks without any legal formality other than their own (reasonable or unreasonable, but genuine) suspicion of drug trafficking; a view of the law that is intriguing. (If it is correct, why would the Act have specified procedures through the Crown Court for granting Production Order access to the police?) It is possible, for instance, that a court might hold that criminal as well as civil liability for assisting in the disposal of the proceeds of drug trafficking arises where suspicion—which need not be reasonable—exists, and that such suspicion is established by virtue simply of receiving the suspicions of someone in authority. So, *provided that drug trafficking by the account holder or its disposal through her/him could be established*, it would be dangerous for the banker to refuse the request for information, and certainly for the banker to inform the account holder, to give her/him the opportunity to object to any Production Order, for this communication to the account holder might give rise to prosecution under s. 31 of the D.T.O. Act.

THE CRIMINAL JUSTICE ACT 1988

The third, relatively modest, legislative inroad into customer confidentiality was the *Criminal Justice Act* 1988. The obscurely drafted s. 98 does not impose an obligation to report suspicions, but rather exempts from liability for breach of contract a bank that decides to disclose "to a constable" a suspicion or belief (or "any matter on which a belief or suspicion is based", presumably such as documentation) that property is directly or indirectly the proceeds of a crime or is being used for a crime to which the Part of the Act applies. No analogue of s. 24 of the D.T.O. Act liability arises for other offences by virtue of the *Criminal Justice Act* 1988, except where the banker's actions would be tantamount to aiding and abetting an offence—such as fraud—itself, as distinct from aiding the disposal of the proceeds of the offence. Major international fraud not being as serious a crime as supplying cannabis to a group of friends, it was impolitic to *require* banks (or other bodies such as accountants) to report suspicions, but it was politically possible to enable them to do so without risking lawsuits for breach of contract and implied confidentiality. Ironically, excusal from punishment for noncompliance apart, such legislative "permissives" make banks feel more uncomfortable than do *requirements* to report, for they confront them actively with moral choice rather than making them passive instruments of the criminal law.

THE PREVENTION OF TERRORISM (TEMPORARY PROVISIONS) ACT 1989

The final area of *police* power to which I will refer here is in relation to terrorism. Many provisions of the *Prevention of Terrorism (Temporary Provisions) Act* 1989 are draconian. Not only are there powers similar to P.A.C.E. 1984 under Sched. 7 of the Act, but it is an offence (s. 18) for anyone who has information which he or she knows or believes might be of material assistance to preventing an act of terrorism "connected with" the affairs of Northern Ireland or in bringing terrorists or their aides to justice not to communicate it to the authorities as soon as reasonably practicable. "Terrorist funds" include (s. 11(3)(b)) "the proceeds of the commission of such acts of terrorism or of activities engaged in furtherance of or in connection with such acts" and (para. (c)) "the resources of a proscribed organisation". Section 11(1) of the *Prevention of Terrorism (Temporary Provisions) Act* 1989 states that:

A person is guilty of an offence if he enters into or is otherwise concerned in an arrangement whereby the retention or control by or on behalf of another person of terrorist funds is facilitated, whether by concealment, removal from the jurisdiction, transfer to nominees or otherwise.

Section 11(2) states:

In proceedings against a person for an offence under this section it is a defence to prove that he did not know and had no reasonable cause to suspect that the arrangement related to terrorist funds.

Section 12(2) provides that a person such as a banker does not commit an offence if, inter alia, he discloses his suspicions to a constable *and* if (para. (b)):

the disclosure is made after he enters into or otherwise becomes concerned in the transaction or agreement in question but is made on his own initiative and as soon as it is reasonable for him to make it.

(Provided that he does not go on to assist the suspected terrorist against the wishes of the officer.) Prosecutions can arise only with the consent of the Attorney-General, but the maximum penalty for assisting in the retention or control of terrorist funds—like that under the D.T.O. Act—is 14 years' imprisonment. It seems plain that s. 11—like "reverse onus" rules generally, as used in confiscation proceedings, which require the equivalent of civil disclosure provisions from the defence—has the advantage for prosecutors of increasing the pressure for defendants to give evidence in the witness box. However, the wording is different from that of the D.T.O. Act, inasmuch as the subjective "suspect" is replaced by the objective "had no reasonable cause to suspect", and even this quasi-objective issue is a matter for defence demonstration rather than proof by the prosecution. The risk for bankers here is that at the time they handled the funds, they might not have considered the transactions suspicious, whereas in retrospect, perhaps they should have thought more about them. Thus, to cope with the provision, banks may have to establish regular reviews of bank transactions, applying agreed criteria to decide whether or not there is "reasonable cause" to suspect the source of the moneys to be terrorism. It is very difficult to do this on a systematic basis, but although this is being done to some extent to comply with the provisions of the D.T.O. Act—from which identical wording was dropped following lobbying from the British Bankers' Association and the Law Society—it clearly places greater burdens on bank staff who can no longer plead the "thoughtless idiot" line of defence. There are also problems of who is liable under this section; is it just the front-line staff who handled the transactions, or is there some vicarious liability for supervisory staff who ought to have looked at the transactions, whether or not they actually did? Some banks have authorisation for voluntary reporting of suspect cases at the level of the Deputy General Manager: will he or she be the person to go into the dock?[19]

---

19. Hitherto, no senior British bankers have been indicted in relation to alleged money laundering, a fact that possibly increases deterrence, since there are no judge-directed or jury acquittals to ease the minds of bankers.

It seems plain that the objective is to put pressure on everyone by giving them fewer grounds on which they might hope that the courts— whether juries in England, Scotland, and Wales, or judges alone in Northern Ireland—might excuse them. It is moot whether the risks of prosecution and sentence will be effective in rendering bank officials proof against potential threats to their families from Republican or Loyalist groups against whom they inform (or even with whom they refuse to do business): though terrorist groups are given more to think about by this legislation, they know that most people would rather face jail than be kneecapped or murdered. Bank staff in Northern Ireland, particularly, are afraid that the provisions will jeopardise their safety, for the I.R.A. will lay the blame on bank managers if there should be any leak of the paper trail. (Though informants or police surveillance could equally be the source.) But the legislation may inhibit terrorist groups by making them less confident that their wishes will be obeyed by bankers.

THE POWERS OF THE DEPARTMENT OF TRADE AND INDUSTRY

That part of money laundering that relates to white collar crime funds is regulated—if that term is appropriate—by non-police agencies as well as by police. It may be a difficult line to draw when corporate misconduct or insider trading become "money laundering": this merely points up the all-embracing nature of the term, a quality it shares with "crime prevention". Nevertheless, on the view that when the criminally obtained funds are transferred, they are "laundered", we should note that the Department of Trade and Industry (D.T.I.), which has the task of investigating company misconduct, has a number of different sorts of powers. Although its inspectors under the *Companies Act* 1989 can require information from any past or present officer of the company, there is no general power to question officers of the company about matters not in the books, nor are bankers, employees, or "financial consultants" included within the category of people who are required to answer questions. The *Financial Services Act* 1986 extended the powers of the D.T.I. and of "competent authorities" (Sched. 13)—such as investigators from self-regulatory organisations—in relation to persons carrying on investment business. Apart from provisions applying to the managers and trustees of unit trusts or other collective investment schemes (s. 94), the major powers are granted under ss 105 and 177. Section 105 gives the Secretary of State or a competent authority the power to require a person whose affairs are to be investigated to answer questions or furnish information "with respect to any matter relevant to the investigation". Likewise, documents (including computer-held data) must be produced if requested and, subject to legal professional privilege, "the person producing them or any connected person" (extending as far as bankers, auditors, and solicitors) may be required to explain them. Evidence compulsorily obtained is admissible in subsequent criminal proceedings: failure to comply without reasonable excuse is a summary offence punishable by up to six months' imprisonment and/or a fine.[19a]

Section 177 of the *Financial Services Act* 1986 relates to insider dealing and is more extensive than the other investigation powers, perhaps reflecting the catch-22 difficulty of establishing without a full enquiry whether or not insider dealing has occurred. Subsection (3) creates a duty for any person whom the inspectors consider is or may be able to give information:

(a) to produce to them any documents in his possession or under his control relating to the company in relation to whose securities the contravention is suspected to have occurred or to its securities;

(b) to attend before them; and

(c) otherwise to give them all assistance in connection with the investigation which he is reasonably able to give.

As with ss 94 and 105 of the Act, statements obtained under compulsion are admissible in evidence and these informational requirements extend to bankers provided that the Secretary of State is satisfied—not necessarily "reasonably", for that word is not contained in the text—that the disclosure or production is necessary to the investigation and that the bank customer "is a person who the inspectors have reason to believe may be able to give information concerning a suspected contravention": see s. 177(8).

Under s. 178, if anyone refuses to co-operate, the inspectors may certify this in writing and a court may enquire into the case. If, after hearing any witness produced by the offender and any statement made by the defence, the court is satisfied that the person had no reasonable excuse to refuse to give the information requested, it may punish him as for contempt of court or direct that the Secretary of State may exercise powers to restrict or cancel the person's authorisation to undertake investment business, either generally or in specific areas. This may be done even though the offender is not within the jurisdiction of the court, if the court is satisfied that he or she was notified of the right to appear before it and of the powers available to the court. Section 178(6) expressly states that it is *not* a reasonable excuse for non-co-operation to claim

in a case where the contravention or suspected contravention being investigated relates to dealing by him on the instructions or for the account of another person, by reason that at the time of the refusal—

(a) he did not know the identity of that other person; or

(b) he was subject to the law of a country or territory outside the United Kingdom which prohibited him from disclosing information relating to the dealing without the consent of that other person, if he might have obtained that consent or obtained exemption from that law.

19a. For more discussion of D.T.I. powers, see further *R. v. Spens* [1991] 4 All E.R. 421 and *R. v. Seelig* [1991] 4 All E.R. 429.

The extensiveness of the requirement to disclose is indicated by the judgment of the House of Lords in the case of Jeremy Warner, the journalist who refused to disclose his source of leaked takeover information to the Department of Trade Inspectors. The court took the robust view that if the information is necessary for the prevention of crime—taken in the most general sense—there is no reasonable excuse for witholding it. Lord Griffiths observed that " 'necessary' has a meaning that lies somewhere between 'indispensable', on the one hand, and 'useful' or 'expedient' on the other . . . The nearest paraphrase I can suggest is 'really needed'."[20] In the less defensible (from a public interest viewpoint) case of X Ltd v. Morgan-Grampian (Publishers) Ltd,[21] the House of Lords similarly ruled that the potential damage to the plaintiff's business was very substantial and there was no counterbalancing public interest in publication. Journalists are less popular than bankers with the judiciary, but if the courts can over-ride so readily the normal presumption of journalistic privilege in s. 10 of the Contempt of Court Act 1981, bankers too may expect little tolerance.

One question that arises is what will happen to bankers with sought-after account holders' branches in strong secrecy nations, who could not "have obtained exemption from that law"? Nor is it yet certain how the phrase "if he might have obtained that consent" will be interpreted. Will it count as a reasonable excuse for the banker if the person under investigation refuses to give consent though consent might lawfully have been given? There is still ample scope for judicial interpretation and for argument by defence counsel.

THE SERIOUS FRAUD OFFICE

A special provision in s. 2(10) of the Criminal Justice Act 1987—inserted partly in response to pressure from the banks—requires the personal fiat of the Director (or a designate where it is impractical for the Director to act) to investigate any bank accounts: this places a layer of bureaucracy and time in the way of speedy information trawl. There are sanctions for non-co-operation, though they are much lower than the maxima for substantive fraud offences. As in s. 105 of the Financial Services Act 1986, s. 2(13) states that:

> Any person who without reasonable excuse fails to comply with a requirement imposed on him under this section shall be guilty of an offence and liable on summary conviction to imprisonment for a term not exceeding six months or to a fine not exceeding level five on the standard scale or to both.

An accountant has been imprisoned for five months for refusing to respond to an s. 2 order, of which 574 notices were issued in 1989-1990 and 765 in 1990-1991.[22]

20. Re an Inquiry under the Company Securities (Insider Dealing) Act 1985 [1988] 1 All E.R. 203.
21. [1990] 2 W.L.R. 1000.
22. Serious Fraud Office, Second Annual Report (1990); Third Annual Report (1991).

Except for revenue intelligence, which will be disclosed to others only for the purpose of a criminal prosecution by either the Serious Fraud Office or, in relation to an inland revenue offence, to the Crown Prosecution Service (see s. 3 of the Act) information obtained may be passed on not only to the police but to Department of Trade Inspectors, the Official Receiver, and, under s. 3(6):

(l) any body having supervisory, regulatory, or disciplinary functions in relation to any profession or area of commercial activity; and

(m) any person or body having, under the law of any country or territory outside Great Britain, functions corresponding to any of the functions of any person or body mentioned . . . above.

So the possibility of developing international intelligence and supervisory interchange is very considerable: s. 3(4) also permits the Director to enter into agreements to supply for an (unspecified) specified purpose information that is in his possession.

So much for the heavy "must disclose" powers. What about the "permissives", where the bank is relieved of its supposed contractual obligations of confidentiality but is not actually required to tell? In the United Kingdom, there is no general legal obligation on the part of a bank to satisfy itself as to the identity of its customers, and proof of identity was tightened only following the publication of guidelines in December 1990 by the Joint Money Laundering Committee. This is notwithstanding the fact that the D.T.O. Act and, a fortiori, the *Prevention of Terrorism (Temporary Provisions) Act* 1989, have led many banks and building societies to verify all customers' identities at least to the extent of checking electoral rolls, debt registers, etcetera, which many used to do only if there was some financial risk to the bank such as a request to borrow money. Simple deposit account holders were seldom checked up on: banks were pleased to have the custom. My 1989 experimental survey of several building societies reveals that all they required was some item of identification with my signature on it. Whether they would have checked further after opening the account remains open, but by then, I could have laundered my funds. Though very large syndicates would be unlikely to rely on building society accounts, this relative laxity may be why in recent completed narcotics trafficking cases, funds have been found in building societies rather than in bank accounts.

One of the major facts affecting the banks in England (and overseas) is in relation to narcotics. Wherever legislation creates penalties for failure to report or disclose, this opens up not only the "legal duty" but also possibly the "interests of the bank" grounds for relief from civil liability for breach of confidence.[23] Normally, the "interests of the bank" notion is applied to the bank's ability to drop confidentiality when it is a party to legal proceedings. But the notion could be widened. There is no hard evidence on the extent to which publicity for under-reporting per se—rather than fear of bank insolvency or intensified police/revenue interest in clientele—will lead basically legitimate clients to desert the bank. But since it presumably is not in the interests of the bank to have

23. See generally, *Tournier v. National Provincial Union of England* [1924] 1 K.B. 461.

its employees jailed and to receive bad publicity for assisting money laundering, this can open up considerably the opportunities for disclosure. However, even this is not self-evident, for in a competitive market for funds, ready disclosure of information may harm the interests of the bank also: even legitimate clients who suspect that account details may be passed on to the police or to a government department—and thence, who knows?—may choose to bank elsewhere. Furthermore, banks (or parts of banks) that knowingly launder money will not avail themselves of disclosure opportunities, except perhaps as part of a subtle strategy to legitimate themselves in the eyes of the authorities. However, as we have seen, recent legislation imposes serious consequences not only of imprisonment but also of asset confiscation for those bankers who know or suspect that the money is the proceeds of drug trafficking, or who know or have reasonable cause to suspect that the funds are terrorist moneys.

INTRA-ORGANISATIONAL COMMUNICATION

I now come to a rather different issue: the question of policy communication within banks and within the police. One of the public relations—and criminal liability—problems that confronts the banks is that outsiders such as the police, press, and courts have very little idea of the complexity of decision-making structures within banks, nor of the conflicts within institutions—such as between sales and security personnel—that may affect either official policy or deviations from official policy. Let us take as an example the question of reporting suspected fraud and/or money laundering. This logically entails an awareness that there is something odd and suspicious about a transaction or series of transactions. Does any obligation to disclose require proof of actual suspicion by those who handled the transactions, or does it apply some objective test of when a reasonable person ought to be suspicious (as in the *Prevention of Terrorism Act* 1989)? This is a critical issue, since the *subjective* test rewards the thoughtless idiot—or someone who can convince the jury that he or she is one—by granting immunity from punishment, while the *objective* test risks punishing those who make genuine mistakes in good faith in circumstances where suspiciousness was not self-evident, for example in relation to cash deposits and withdrawals by a well-established client for whom the sums are not plainly absurd.

Wilful blindness or even active conspiracy in money laundering sometimes occurs: such is alleged on the part of senior officials of the Bank of Credit and Commerce International who, as a result of Operation C-Chase, are currently facing criminal charges in the United States for money laundering and other drug offences.[24] But even assuming a genuine desire to comply, and complete integrity throughout the bank,

24. The Bank has been fined $14 million following a plea bargain, presumably to avoid the dangers of R.I.C.O.-generated asset confiscation. In 1990, one more junior officer of the B.C.C.I. was jailed in England under s. 24(1) of the *Drug Trafficking Offences Act* 1986. In July 1991, the bank was closed down altogether, following revelations of massive internal fraud.

it is hard to develop a realistic set of instructions that will guide the civic conscience of bank employees *at all levels from director to assistant cashier* without paralysing the banking activities or the handling capacity of the police. This is a different problem from that which we see in responding to requests for information from the police, for in the latter, except where the information is requested without a court order, no judgment of suspiciousness on the part of "the banker" is called for. (Though vicarious liability problems arise where the bank headquarters may not know what its branch staff are doing.) It is where we are asking bankers to use initiative that real organisational communication problems arise. This depends not only on the ethics but also on the nature of the normal banking activities of the branch: unlike mainland High Street branches, where bank staff generally know customers personally, offshore branches in the Channel Islands, for instance, will normally have scanty information about clients unless they wish to borrow money. Inter-bank international electronic payments transfers, perhaps involving currency swaps by the (presumed) corporate clients of third-party banks that are common as hedges, would not be expected to excite the sort of interest that would lead to a report to the National Drugs Intelligence Unit.

Another area of "bank secrecy" which is giving rise to problems is constructive trust. The bank was not a defendant in the action, but some relevant further discussion of mental states arose in *A.G.I.P. (Africa) Ltd v. Jackson*,[25] in which one chartered accountant and an employee working from the Isle of Man were found liable to account as constructive trustees for moneys transferred with employee complicity from A.G.I.P. in Tunisia to nominee accounts opened for the employee by the accountants at Lloyds Bank in London. It is questionable whether a similar constructive trust would be placed upon banks, unless they acted as financial advisers on A.G.I.P. lines. But the ruling does raise questions about when it is proper and legally safe for professionals *not* to look behind the rationale for the establishment of nominee companies, which often are used for facilitating crime as well as for lawful privacy. More generally, the conditions under which one has a "duty to the public", referred to by Bankes L.J. in *Tournier* as a circumstance under which banks may disclose, would generate irresolvable conflict among most philosophers. What we have is a conflict between two principles: the duty of an agent to his principal, and the duty of a citizen towards the state. If we extend the duty to the state to situations that further "the prevention of crime"—as in insider dealing enquiries[26]—almost anything can count as permitting or requiring disclosure, since there are few things that do not assist the commission of some crime or other. The courts traditionally have sought to use some imprecise notion that confidentiality should be preserved except where required by law or where there is danger to the state (as in wartime).[27] But statute law, and the greater willingness of judges to accept that even lawyer/client documentation that does not relate to the defence of a

---

25. [1989] 3 W.L.R. 1380.
26. See *Re an Inquiry under the Company Securities (Insider Dealing) Act 1985* [1988] 1 All E.R. 203.
27. *Weld-Blundell v. Stephens* [1920] A.C. 956, 965.

criminal trial can be revealed to the police, has changed the overall position of professionals generally, as well as bankers in particular.

INTERNATIONAL POLICE-BANK PROBLEMS

The English courts have tended to take a strong line against extraterritorial invasions of banking privacy.[28] However, there cases occurred largely before the inroads into banking confidentiality in England already discussed, and it may be possible to deduce an attitude shift in the direction of greater openness to foreign courts from the decision of the House of Lords in *Re State of Norway's Applications (Nos 1 and 2)*,[29] which took a generous approach to the Norwegian authorities' request to interview senior bankers from Lazards in relation to alleged tax liabilities from the estate of a Norwegian businessman. Lord Goff supported the approach of the lower courts to the Norwegian letter of request, observing[30] that this "was in substance a request for what, by English law, would be regarded as assistance in obtaining evidence". He went on to balance the public interest in preserving confidentiality of bankers' dealings with their clients against "the public interest in the English court assisting the Norwegian court in obtaining evidence in this country", upholding the lower court's decision to require the witnesses to give evidence in Norway but allowing them to withhold the identity of the settlor, unless at least one of them stated in evidence that the settlor was acting in relevant respects as the nominee or agent for the alleged tax avoider, who was deceased. In *R. v. Chief Metropolitan Stipendiary Magistrate; Ex parte Secretary of State for the Home Department*,[31] the Queen's Bench Division likewise supported the extraditability of a Norwegian for tax evasion.

If co-operation with the information requirements of foreign states occurs in cases with a strong fiscal element, one may expect still more accommodation in other areas of suspected misconduct, creating further inroads into banking confidentiality, except where statutory provisions or objections to extreme extraterritorial claims generate specific reasons to resist. Whether or not one agrees with their seriousness rankings, we may expect the English courts to take a less aggressive jurisdictional line in relation to offences of drug trafficking, terrorism, and insider dealing than in relation to anti-trust and other offences that they may deem to be "purely economic". Thus, in *R. v. Southwark Crown Court; Ex parte Customs and Excise*,[32] the Divisional Court took the view that information obtained as a consequence of a Production Order under the D.T.O. Act could be communicated to a foreign agency to:

> serve suitably the ordinary obligations of our law enforcement agencies to co-operate with their colleagues in achieving their common aims.

28. See *Westinghouse* [1978] A.C. 547; *X A.G. v. a Bank* [1983] 2 All E.R. 464.
29. [1989] 1 All E.R. 745.
30. Ibid. at 762.
31. [1989] 1 All E.R. 151.
32. [1989] 3 W.L.R. 1054.

The court even took the view that where an overseas country could not be trusted to respect the confidentiality of the material sent to it, that ought not to influence a court in the way it exercised its discretion to grant an order, though it might reasonably affect the willingness of the domestic agency to apply for a Production Order to assist that overseas agency. However, without further proceedings, the *originals* of the documents should not be sent overseas, even where secondary evidence (for example, photocopies) were inadmissible there in evidence. The court brusquely rejected as unimpressive the claims of the bank that information should not be sent to the United States lest this lead to reprisals, presumably at the behest of General Noriega's associates, against the bank's staff in Panama:

> The courts of this country are not to be deflected from making orders in aid of the international battle against drug trafficking for fear of reprisals no matter from where the threat of them emanates.

English courts have also exercised a self-denying ordinance to refuse orders that would seek to infringe the jurisdiction of foreign courts on behalf of parties in Britain.[33]

Sometimes, United States cases impinge upon English law. In the mid 1980s, a case in which the Internal Revenue Service wished to examine further payments of $900,000 to a Hong Kong corporation, Garpeg Ltd, by Gucci Shops Inc. and Aldo Gucci (later imprisoned), led to a tough response by the Hong Kong Court of Appeal, denying access to the accounts.[34] Nevertheless, the United States Tax Court upheld the summons against Chase Manhattan under what was then Restatement Ch. 40 of the Foreign Relations Law.[35] However, such displays of national independence do not always provide *financial* protection for the *bank*, which tends to be caught in the middle of these jurisdictional conflicts. For example, in June 1988, in *Securities & Exchange Commission v. Wang and Lee*,[36] an insider dealing case in which Lee was said to have made U.S. $19 million in illegal profits, the District Court of New York gave the Securities and Exchange Commission a temporary freezing order directing banks holding the defendants' assets anywhere to retain them. (Wang, a former financial analyst with Morgan Stanley, pleaded guilty to criminal charges of passing inside information to Lee, and entered into a financial settlement with S.E.C. Because the information Wang possessed was confidential and was able to be prohibited by an injunction from being communicated to others, the information had some "property-like" characteristics and could be treated by the United States courts as subject to a proprietary constructive trust, giving the power to trace assets through bank

33. *R. v. Grossman* (1981) 73 Cr. App. R. 302; *MacKinnon v. Donaldson Lufkin and Jenrette Securities Corp.* [1986] 1 All E.R. 653.
34. White, "Principles of confidentiality in cross-border banking", in Cranston (ed.), *Legal Issues of Cross-Border Banking* (1989), pp. 18-19.
35. See *United States v. Chase Manhattan Bank*, 84-1 C.C.H. 1984 Stand (S.D.N.Y., 27 March 1984).
36. Unreported. I am grateful to both parties who supplied me with this documentation.

accounts. The United States generally makes such public tracing rights easier: all drug money is legally the property of the federal government, giving the government the right to trace.)

In August and October 1988, the District Judge for the Southern District of New York—where many of the major white collar crime cases are heard—made orders which required the Standard Chartered Bank (S.C.B.), on pain of contempt, to pay into the registry of the United States District Court a sum equal to the aggregate balances in personal and corporate accounts maintained at the bank's Hong Kong branch that were alleged by the Commission to be controlled by Lee; and which directed that the sum be paid over to unidentified "defrauded investors" to reimburse their losses and to the United States Treasury, in payment of a civil penalty assessed against Lee, pursuant to the *Insider Trading Sanctions Act* 1984 (which provides for triple penalties). The low frustration tolerance of United States courts could hardly be in greater contrast to the principles of comity expressed in *R. v. Grossman*[37] and in *MacKinnon v. Donaldson Lufkin and Jenrette Securities Corp.*[38] Under protest, the S.C.B. paid U.S.$12.5 million into court in New York, while the defendant Lee (who remained outside the United States and did not defend the S.E.C. suit) and the corporations allegedly controlled by him—which had never been served with any papers related to the civil suit by the S.E.C.—sued it in Hong Kong for repayment of money deposited there. The Hong Kong courts decided that the United States court order had no extraterritorial effect on the accounts in Hong Kong, but permitted Standard Chartered to delay repaying its depositors. If it had been decided by the Hong Kong courts simply that the proper law of the contract between the Bank and Lee was Hong Kong, the bank risked having to pay U.S.$12.5 million to both parties, as well as incurring considerable legal costs.[39]

Standard Chartered appealed against the District Judge's order to the 2nd Circuit Court of Appeals, arguing, inter alia, that the forced transfer and deposit of Standard Chartered's funds confiscated the assets of an innocent third party—the S.C.B.—without doing anything to make those or any other funds safe from Lee, who had the right to obtain his money from the Hong Kong branch at which the proper law of the contract existed. Part of the S.C.B. argument was also that the S.E.C. failed to pursue discovery and constructive trust remedies in the Hong Kong courts which it ought properly to have done. It might additionally have questioned whether the Hong Kong courts would be able to enforce extraterritorially S.E.C. penalties which in effect may be penal law provisions. (International law looks at the substance, not just the form, of law, so some civil and administrative penalties are treated as penal ones and are not enforceable internationally.) To the extent that the S.E.C. penalties are *un*enforceable, the only remedies for Americans

37. [1981] 73 Cr. App. R. 302.
38. [1986] 1 All E.R. 653.
39. See *Libyan Arab Foreign Bank v. Bankers Trust Co.* [1988] 1 Lloyd's Rep. 259.

against Lee and his alleged companies would be the equitable claims of defrauded investors.[40]

In July 1989, the cases against all parties were settled out of court. Instead of the triple penalty he faced under the *Insider Trading Sanctions Act* 1984—and the $38 million actually proposed by the judge—Lee agreed to pay the Securities and Exchange Commission $25 million, including the $19 million profits from his trading (and including the $12.5 million that the S.C.B. had been ordered to pay into the United States court). To satisfy the proprieties of the bank's claim, the New York Court Registry issued a cheque to S.C.B. in New York for $12.5 million, minus Wang's specifically United States money; and the S.C.B. in New York then remitted money back to S.C.B. in Hong Kong who, after deducting costs of some $300,000 towards their legal expenses agreed by the New York Court, then credited the sum to the Hong Kong accounts. The S.C.B. in Hong Kong then followed instructions by their customer, Lee, to send to the receiver in the United States the sums agreed.

The advantage of this settlement for the S.E.C. was the avoidance of an appellate precedent in a case that seems to this author fairly weak, inasmuch as the S.E.C. clearly did not pursue all reasonable remedies according to comity with the Hong Kong courts or with the innocent bank which, before the making of the order to pay funds into New York, had fully complied with worldwide asset-freezing orders, had rejected— at risk to itself—demands by account holders for payment, and was vigorously defending in the Hong Kong courts actions by two account holders for repayment. It was not surprising that the "maximum bid" position of the S.E.C. led to the Standard Chartered Bank being supported on appeal by amicus curiae briefs from, inter alia, the United Kingdom government and the Federal Reserve Bank of New York, and supported also by the British Bankers' Association, the Committee of London and Scottish Bankers, the International Bankers' Association, the Institute of International Bankers, the Hong Kong Association of Banks, the Canadian Bankers' Association, and the New York Clearing House Association.

In its brief, the S.E.C. urged the Court of Appeals to create a "hot pursuit" principle in civil litigation, which forces repayment of sums that are transferred just *prior* to the making of freeze orders. Frustrating though such transfers are for the authorities and for victims, as the S.C.B.'s reply brief reasonably states:

> It cannot be the rule that a Commission telephone call saying that it intends to seek a freeze order the following week has the effect of an injunction. It is the function of the courts to determine whether an order that stops ordinary commercial process is appropriate and

40. Section 61 of the *Financial Services Act 1986* might provide civil remedies enforceable overseas, but has not yet been tried out even in the United Kingdom: though Browne-Wilkinson V.C., did open this up as a possibility in granting a Mareva injunction to the Securities and Investments Board in *Securities & Investment Board v. Pantell S.A.* [1989] 2 All E.R. 673. The current attitude of the United Kingdom government to civil action against insider dealing is negative, as may be deduced from the Secretary of State's evidence to the house of Commons Select Committee on Trade and Industry (1990): see *Company Investigations*, Third Report, H.C. 36.

until it does so, upon a legally sufficient showing, no freeze or injunction is in effect.

We cannot know what the court of Appeals would have held, but assuming that it was not "got at" by the State Department or influenced by other pending cases which required co-operation, the S.E.C.'s willingness to settle out of court indicates that it was far from confident of victory. This case may be compared with the controversy over the interpretation of the restraint provisions of the D.T.O. Act and allied legislation, discussed above, pp. 338-339.

THE FUTURE OF UNITED KINGDOM BANK SECRECY

The *Drug Trafficking Offences Act* 1986 and the *Prevention of Terrorism (Temporary Provisions) Act* 1989 have had some effect in getting British bank managers to enquire into the genuineness of the identities of their *new personal* customers and to keep a closer eye on the relationship between customers' actual and expected transactions (given the kind of work the customers claim to do). Terror works, though regular nagging from Head Office is required to keep branches alert, since individual branches are aware of relatively few cases of laundering and therefore find it hard to develop guidelines or to sustain a policy of laundering-spotting. During 1991, staff training videos developed by the British Bankers' Association have had a consciousness-raising effect.

But there is a fine line between wilful blindness and recklessness—that is, seeing that there is a risk and ignoring it—on the one hand, and sheer thoughtlessness on the other. The way that judges and juries may draw this line in practice[41] may depend on (i) the degree of opprobrium attached to the conduct itself—and judicial intolerance of white collar and narcotics crime has been increasing; and (ii) the perception of the villainousness of the people or institution involved—were there prior warnings or convictions? Whatever the risk of criminal convictions of bank staff, however, the banks are concerned also about the bad publicity that attaches to them if they are seen to be un-co-operative in investigations into serious crime: an image problem that has been skilfully and sometimes crudely exploited by the police when they are refused information they want. Some of these image problems for banks can arise when accounts are held for former "respectables" who are later treated as disreputable: particularly Third World politicians caught out by changes in government. This has been a problem for the Swiss, but it is also a problem for the United Kingdom banks when headlines appear such as "Marcos cash trial leads to Barclays",[42] even though there is no hard evidence that except where bank insolvency is feared, customer business is affected by such publicity. Despite prosecutions in the United

---

41. See further, Levi, *Regulating Fraud: White Collar Crime and the Criminal Process*, op. cit.; and Levi [1989] "Suite Justice: sentencing for fraud" (June 1989) Crim. L. Rev. 420-434.

42. *The Observer*, 25 June 1989.

States for money laundering, the Bank of Credit and Commerce International might well have survived had it not been for massive frauds upon it.

One critical question is whether or not bankers are going to freeze assets at the request of the police, pending such court authorisation. Except in the legally ambiguous areas of drug trafficking and terrorism, to do so would place them on very dangerous legal territory. This reliance upon *police* assurances might become more problematic still because of differences in the interpretation of the appropriate use of Restraint Orders on the part of police, on the one hand, and the Crown Prosecution Service and Serious Fraud Office, on the other. Currently, most prosecutors interpret the *Criminal Justice Act* 1988 narrowly as meaning that they are permitted to apply for a Restraint Order only when they are satisfied that a Compensation Order will not be made, for compensation has priority over confiscation, yet sentencers are required to take the confiscation order into account when awarding compensation! Since the Act requires sentencers to justify the *non*-imposition of compensation orders, these will normally be applied. Therefore, it is argued, confiscation orders are appropriate only for "victimless crimes", even though unless the victim has substantial assets (and knowledge of the identity of the principal suspect), *civil* Mareva action will be impossible, and there may be no assets remaining to be compensated or confiscated. The extraterritorial effect of order—s. 38(3) D.T.O. Act; s. 102(3) *Criminal Justice Act* 1988—is likewise going to generate some interesting conflicts with banks and branches overseas. In relation to the *Prevention of Terrorism (Temporary Provisions) Act* 1989, the possibility of some jurisdictions defining "terrorism" as a "political offence" may also affect the willingness of those jurisdictions to co-operate in the freezing of assets already overseas. It is also possible—despite the label of confiscation provisions as "non-penal", fortified by the presumption that they are not germane to the consideration of imprisonment—that countries overseas will refuse to enforce them on the well-established convention of public international law that countries will not enforce the penal provisions of other states.

After some initial problems in interpreting the D.T.O. Act—which generated a great deal of extra work in dealing with reports from branches, as well as uncertainty about (i) how much to tell branches to do and (ii) what "suspicion" meant in practice—the growing involvement of banks in police and customs narcotics investigation is now working much more harmoniously, and since it is often prima facie impossible to tell whether large cash transfers relate to drugs, to terrorism, or to fraud (including tax fraud), the information flow is beginning to develop quite strongly. Future proactive reports are likely to continue to exceed 3,000 cases per annum. Whether something that turns out to be fraud rather than drug trafficking or terrorism is passed on to those whose task it is to act against fraud is a grey area: the permeability of inter-agency Chinese Walls depends on personal relationships and institutional interest. One advantage enjoyed by Customs and Excise over the police is that they are centrally co-ordinated with a much smaller number of personnel authorised to deal with the banks—16 in Great Britain—compared with hundreds of police officers whose assignments are often not long term and many of whom never deal with the banks often enough to develop a rapport of mutual trust. Generally, interaction between "repeat players" generates far fewer problems than the involvment of "one shot" players who have no long term interest in stable relationships and have less understanding of the world that bankers inhabit.

One area of possible contention is who is going to pay for all this co-operation. Some controversy exists as to the justification for the high cost of self-regulation in financial services.[43] However, whatever the merits of the opposing views, regulation is plainly in the interest of market participants themselves. The same cannot be said for the costs imposed on banks for obedience to legislation on money laundering, which can be represented as a targeted tax rather than a donation by shareholders pro bon publico. Granted that the heavy compliance costs borne by banks in the United States and Australia do not arise in the United Kingdom (or other European countries), because we do not have currency transfer reporting requirements, there is nevertheless a cost which has to be borne by somebody. Currently, the customer whose account is investigated pays for bank costs only if he or she signs an authority for the police to inspect the account. For other information obtained by court order or under executive authority, the costs are borne by customers generically and shareholders. (Though some Restraint Order and Confiscation/Forfeiture Order costs are part-reimbursed by prosecution agencies.) Will policing and government agencies be required to make greater financial contributions to the policing of banking transactions? If so, this will have to be budgeted for and administered, with consequent potential rows over the fairness of charges.

On the international side, there will continue to be greater pressure to co-ordinate efforts against money laundering. In June 1980, the Committee of Ministers of the Council of Europe adopted Resolution R(80) 10, which concluded that "the banking system can play a highly effective preventative role while the co-operation of the banks also assists in the repression of such criminal acts by the judicial authorities and the police". The Basle Committee on Banking Regulations and Supervisory Practices has expressed the view in a statement of December 1988 that "banking supervisors have a general role to encourage ethical standards of professional conduct among banks and other financial institutions". In an accompanying Statement of Principles, the Committee asserts the following:

> With a view to ensuring that the financial system is not used as a channel for criminal funds, banks should make reasonable efforts to determine the true identity of all customers requesting the institution's services. Particular care should be taken to identify the ownership of all accounts and those using safe-custody facilities. All banks should institute effective procedures for obtaining identification from new customers. It should be an explicit policy

43. Seldon (ed.), *Financial Regulation—or Over-Regulation?* (1988).

that significant business transactions will not be conducted with customers who fail to provide evidence of their identity.

. . . As regards transactions executed on behalf of customers, it is accepted that banks may have no means of knowing whether the transaction stems from or forms part of criminal activity. Similarly, in an international context it may be difficult to ensure that cross-border transactions on behalf of customers are in compliance with the regulations of another country. Nevertheless, banks should not set out to offer services or provide active assistance in transactions which they have good reason to suppose are associated with money laundering activities.

Banks should co-operate fully with national law enforcement authorities to the extent permitted by specific local regulations relating to customer confidentiality. Care should be taken to avoid providing support or assistance to customers seeking to deceive law enforcement agencies through the provision of altered, incomplete, or misleading information. Where banks become aware of facts which lead to the reasonable presumption that money held on deposit derives from criminal activity or that transactions entered into are themselves criminal in purpose, appropriate measures, consistent with the law, should be taken, for example, to deny assistance, sever relations with the customer and close or freeze accounts.

The December 1988 Statement of Principles concludes:

All banks should formally adopt policies consistent with the principles set out in this Statement and should ensure that all members of their staff concerned, wherever located, are informed of the bank's policy in this regard. Attention should be given to staff training in matters covered by the Statement. To promote adherence to these principles, banks should implement specific procedures for customer identification and for retraining internal records of transactions. Arrangements for internal audit may need to be extended to establish an effective means of testing for general compliance with the Statement.

There are unresolved questions of how this will be implemented (particularly in relation to business customers and to checks on persons opening new accounts), and how overseas branches and subsidiaries outside the Group of Ten countries—who are merely exhorted to follow the principles—will react. It should not be forgotten that some of the concern on the part of Third World citizens about banking secrecy is about the ability of corrupt *governmental* personnel—who presumably would have passed the test of fitness and propriety to be bank customers—to hide funds overseas. But the Statement represents an official perspective on the appropriate role of the banks in assisting crime prevention and the police. This perspective is being reinforced— probably coincidentally, though they are responding to the same perceived public attitudes and needs—by the present willingness of the

English judiciary to embrace world-wide Mareva injunctions and other mechanisms for freezing assets within and outside the jurisdiction.[44]

THE EUROPEAN COMMUNITY'S DIRECTIVE ON MONEY LAUNDERING

Criminal law matters are normally an issue reserved to member governments individually, and are not a competence—in the legal technical rather than efficiency sense—of the Community as a whole. However, in the interests of developing a single European market in financial matters, the United Kingdom and other E.C. countries have agreed to treat attempts to combat money laundering as within the competence of the Community. The Explanatory Memorandum to the Directive Proposal of March 1990 seeks to justify its involvement by noting that

> the soundness and stability of the particular institutions involved as well as the prestige of the financial system as a whole could be jeopardised, thereby losing the confidence of the public. The Community, which is responsible for adopting the necessary measures to ensure the soundness and stability of the European financial system, cannot be indifferent to the involvement of credit and financial institutions in money laundering.

One might regard this with suspicion as the "thin end of the wedge" for Community interference in domestic criminal justice issues—by analogy with the unbounded value of "crime prevention" as a rationale for police powers, discussed earlier—inasmuch as much significant crime for gain involves the use of financial institutions at some stage. However, given the problems that arose for Banco Ambrosiano and for the Bank of Credit and Commerce International as a result of their involvement in money laundering internationally, there is a plausible case here in relation to capital adequacy (and the consequences of large fines for money-laundering), even if there is no evidence that the public is likely to be disturbed or directly harmed if the major banks *do* take deposits from international criminals. One should, in other words, distinguish between those laundering activities that imperil soundness and stability, for example, non-arms length loans to fraudsters, and those that are in some sense immoral but not unsound from a banking viewpoint. (Though no doubt some might view the imprisonment of bank directors as being unsound business!)

Potentially, the ambit of money laundering rules is very wide: Art. 1 of the draft *European Community (E.C.) Directive* of 24 October 1990 defines it—if "define" is the appropriate word—as:

> the conversion or transfer of property, in the knowledge that such property is derived from a serious crime, for the purpose of

---

44. These provisions are giving rise to immense complications, as the volume of cases indicates. For a more developed discussion, see Levi, *Customer Confidentiality, Money Laundering, and Police-Bank Relationships: English law and practice in a global environment* (1991).

concealing or disguising the illicit origin of the property or of assisting any person who is involved in committing such an offence or offences to evade the legal consequences of his action;

the concealment or disguise of the true nature, source, location, disposition, movement, rights with respect to, or ownership of property, in the knowledge that such property is derived from a serious crime or from an act of participation in such a crime;

the acquisition, possession, or use of property, in the knowledge, at the time of receipt, that such property was derived from a serious crime or from an act of participation in such a crime, and;

participation in, association or conspiracy to commit, attempts to commit and aiding, abetting, facilitating, and counselling the commission of any of the actions established in the preceding paragraphs of this indent.

Knowledge, intent or purpose required as an element of the abovementioned conduct may be inferred from objective factual circumstances.

Money laundering shall be regarded as such even where the conduct which generated the property to be laundered was perpetrated in the territory of another Member State or in that of a third country.

The delineation of what constitutes "serious crime" is a matter of major conflict, with some countries currently wishing to restrict it to drug trafficking and others to any other offences regarded as serious by the member states. The final version of the Directive restricts obligatory E.C. action to drug trafficking, though countries may extend it to other crimes.

Article 3 states:

1. Member States shall ensure that credit and financial institutions require identification of their customers by means of a supporting document when entering into business relations (particularly when opening an account or savings accounts or when offering safe custody facilities).

2. The identification requirement shall also apply for any transaction with occasional customers . . . involving a sum which, at the time of the transaction, amounts to E.C.U. 10,000 or more, whether the transaction is carried out in a single operation or in several operations which appear to be linked.

3. In the event of doubt as to whether the customers referred to in paragraphs 1 and 2 are acting on their own behalf, institutions shall take reasonable measures to obtain information on their real identity.

4. The institutions shall carry out such identification, even where the amount of the transaction is lower than the amount laid down, wherever there is suspicion of money laundering.

5. Credit and financial institutions shall not be obliged to carry out identification where the other party in the business relationship

or transaction referred to above is also a credit or financial institution covered by this Directive.

This elaborate formulation draws a distinction between regular customers—who are required to produce evidence of identity only when they establish business relations—and occasional customers who are required to produce identification if their transaction, whether in cash or otherwise, is above an agreed monetary threshold. The term "party" in subs. 5 may be ambivalent, since it normally refers to a principal, and thus a securities dealer acting as an agent might be free from the obligation to make checks on someone with whom he or she deals.

Article 3a requires customer identification materials to be kept for five years after the end of business relations with the customer; information such as ledger records likewise to be kept for five years; and supporting transaction documentation to be kept for "only" three years. These requirements have important evidentiary implications, for example, in relation to handwriting examination.

An earlier draft of Art. 4 of the Directive raised interesting issues by requiring financial institutions to "examine with special attention any unusual transaction not having an apparent economic or visible lawful purpose". How these requirements would have been applied in practice is mysterious, but the recent formulation requires special attention for "any transaction which they regard as particularly likely, by nature, to be related to money laundering".

COUNCIL OF EUROPE CONVENTION ON LAUNDERING, SEIZURE AND CONFISCATION OF THE PROCEEDS FROM CRIME

The Council of Europe also has produced a Convention (8 November 1990), signed by Belgium, Cyprus, Denmark, Germany, Iceland, Italy, Netherlands, Norway, Portugal, Spain, Sweden, and the United Kingdom in relation to laundering, seizure, and confiscation. Article 6 states:

1. Each party shall adopt such legislative and other measures as may be necessary to establish as offences under its domestic law, *when committed intentionally* [emphasis added]:

   a. the conversion or transfer of property, knowing that such property is proceeds, for the purpose of concealing or disguising the illicit origin of the property or of assisting any person who is involved in the commission of the predicate offence to evade the legal consequences of his actions;

   b. the concealment or disguise of the true nature, source, location, disposition, movement, rights with respect to, or ownership of, property, knowing that such property is proceeds;

   and, subject to its constitutional principles and the basic concepts of its legal system:

    c. the acquisition, possession or use of property, knowing, at the time of receipt, that such property was proceeds;

    d. participation in, association or conspiracy to commit, attempts to commit and aiding, abetting, facilitating and counselling the commission of any of the offences established in accordance with this Article.

Article 6(2)(c) provides that "knowledge, intent or purpose required as an element of an offence set forth in that paragraph may be inferred from objective, factual circumstances", though note that it is the permissive "may", not the obligatory "shall". Subsection 2(a) also commends consideration of criminalisation where the offender "ought to have assumed that the property was proceeds".

Much of the Convention is concerned with international co-operation, which is to be refused only under exceptional circumstances set out in Art. 18. One important part of that Article is subs. (7), which states:

> A party shall not invoke bank secrecy as a ground to refuse any co-operation under this chapter. Where its domestic law so requires, a Party may require that a request for co-operation which would involve the lifting of bank secrecy be authorised by either a judge or another judicial authority, including public prosecutors, any of these authorities acting in relation to criminal offences.

In relation to the freezing and seizure of assets, Art. 13(1) states:

> At the request of another party which has instituted criminal proceedings or proceedings for the purpose of confiscation, a party shall take the necessary provisional measures, such as freezing or seizing, to prevent any dealing in, transfer or disposal of property which, at a later stage, may be the subject of a request for confiscation or which might be such as to satisfy the request.

So international freezing cannot take place without some formal criminal justice procedure, an issue which currently arouses police complaints in the United Kingdom, since prosecutors, not themselves, have monopoly on freezing applications. Third party rights are protected by the provisions of Art. 22: subs. 2(a) states that recognition may be refused if third parties "did not have adequate opportunity to assert their rights". However, it is unstated whether the adequacy of the opportunity will be viewed substantively or formally.

In the light of complaints that some countries tend to dismiss mutual assistance requests for dubious reasons (including corruption),[45] it is interesting that Art. 12(2) states that:

> Before lifting any provisional measure taken pursuant to the Article, the requested Party shall, wherever possible, give the requesting Party an opportunity to present its reasons in favour of continuing the measure.

Likewise, Art. 30 requires requested parties to "give reasons for any decision to refuse, postpone, or make conditional any co-operation". Again, responding to 20th century communications and the necessity for

45. See Ziegler, *La Suisse Lave Plus Blanc* (1990).

speedy action, Art. 23(2) allows judicial authorities, including public prosecutors, to communicate directly instead of through a central authority in cases of urgency. Likewise, requests or communications may be made through Interpol: subs. 3. Requests for information that do not involve coercive action can be transmitted direct, eliminating potential inter-police communication obstacles: subs. 5.

In short, a substantial amount of legal movement is taking place in Europe and elsewhere in the field of international mutual assistance in relation to money laundering and the freezing and seizing of assets. The moral and political pressure is so great that it is hard for countries to resist agreement: how the formal rules work out in practice is another question—for example, what counts as prompt response?—but the requirement to explain does constrain previously laggard nations.

But what is all this extra policing of banking transactions likely to achieve? One cynical approach is to argue that in sensitising and reforming the many, all we do is to impose barriers to entry into the money laundering market which (via bank-unauthorised personal or bank-authorised institutional "counting fees") drives up the price of corruption for the remaining few. The sophisticated offenders generate business fronts that can be used to launder funds in a way that is unlikely to be caught by even the most conscientious proactive monitoring on the part of the banks. (Though targeted surveillance, from the inside or outside, can succeed against particular syndicates, and this may benefit greatly from bank co-operation.) In the meantime, there may be some overall diminution of criminal activity as the barriers to entry into the international or national laundering game prove too burdensome for some potential players, and there may be some national displacement of crime, as mobile criminals operate in areas they perceive as more lightly regulated. For to argue that deterrent effects are only partial is not to show that there is *no* deterrent effect at all.

Let us take drug trafficking as an example. Although most people are convinced that opiate addiction is a serious social evil, the likely net effect of internationalising money laundering rules on reducing total levels of drug supply, drug abuse, and drug-related property crime, or reducing terrorism, let alone on reducing fraud (including tax evasion), has to be viewed critically. As the 1988 and 1989 struggles against drug traffickers in Panama and Colombia demonstrate, the global political economy of the narcotics business is easier to condemn than to do something effective about. Both at a domestic and international level, to catch some offenders—even major ones—is not necessarily to reduce crime and vice: the crime-reducing effect of convictions and confiscation depends on the organisation of the criminal markets and upon the willingness and capacity of new or existing offenders to enter them. [46] It is always arguable that a criminal justice policy is failing because it is not being implemented with sufficient vigour, but supply-side controls have heave social and economic costs, [47] and more positive as well as

46. Reuter, *Disorganised Crime* (1983).
47. Wagstaff and Maynard, *Economic Aspects of the Illicit Drug Market and Drug Enforcement Policies in the United Kingdom* (Home Office Research Study No. 95, 1988).

repressive things could be done on the narcotics demand side. The end purpose of policing banking transactions is often forgotten in the thrill of the chase, which becomes an end in itself.

The Jack Committee[48] takes a very strong line in support of the principle of banker-customer confidentiality, arguing that the banks are far too ready to reveal details about customers without their express consent to other financial services groups, whether within-group or external credit reference agencies. The report is relatively silent on the subject of when bankers *may* disclose, except to recommend the abolition of the "duty to the public" criterion in *Tournier v. National Provincial Union of England*[49] in the following terms,[50] correctly suggesting that "necessary in the interests of justice or national security or the prevention of disorder or crime" involves too vague concepts to generate certainty for banks as to when they may or must breach confidentiality. As regards disclosure under compulsion by law, the Report contains an unsophisticated discussion which includes nothing on the operational, practical difficulties for bankers or policing agencies. However, the Committee did express its great unease at the legislative trend when it observed:[51]

> We do not question, that these statutory interventions in customer confidentiality are, in each individual case, justified by the public interest at stake. But it cannot be doubted that cumulatively, they amount to a formidable burden on bankers, not made easier to bear when there is some uncertainty as to the precise nature of the obligations imposed by law . . . [T]hey constitute a serious inroad into the whole principle of customer confidentiality as conceived at the time of *Tournier*.

It went on to recommend:[52]

> all existing statutory exemptions from the duty of confidentiality should be consolidated in the new legislation. The law should also. provide that any new statutory exemptions from the duty of confidentiality should be made by reference to this new provision, with the sanction that, if they did not do so, they would not over-ride the central duty.

This final suggestion is unspecific—though presumably the Committee would be unhappy if consolidation took the form of the *Prevention of Terrorism (Temporary Provisions) Act* 1989—and poses constitutional difficulties regarding parliamentary sovereignty in the absence of a Bill of Rights. Those who might seek to rationalise access powers across the board at a reduced level would have to confront not only a variety of political interests, but also the fact that the powers were created for different purposes. Moreover, though the demand to "trust the executive" can be dangerous for democracy, it is reasonable for Parliament, when deciding how much discretion to give each separate

48. Review Committee, *Banking Services*, Law and Practice Report (Cm 622).
49. [1924] 1 K.B. 461.
50. Review Committee, *Banking Services*, op. cit., p. 35.
51. Ibid., p. 30.
52. Ibid., p. 37.

agency, to take into account the quality of administrative (as opposed to judicial) control over the use of powers. However, the Jack Report does stand as a *critique* of the conceptually incoherent development of legislation, determined more by what the political market will bear than by intellectual or moral principle.

Recent legislation has meant that the United Kingdom police (or other agencies such as the Serious Fraud Office and Department of Trade and Industry Inspectors) can wield the iron fist to get information out of banks in relation to known clients.[53] This, in insider dealing and some other banking cases can involve the threat of de-authorisation from conducting investment business in the United Kingdom.[54] However, in the *proactive* cases where the state wants bankers to report suspicions of fraud or narcotics trafficking on their own initiative, it is inevitable that some bank employees do not and will not suspect cases which "actually" are money laundering, just as they may defensively report cases that "actually" are *not* money laundering (or are not *drug* or *terrorism* money laundering). Police and customs officers vary in their opinions on how much filtering they want the financial institutions to engage in: some realise that they could become overwhelmed by "aggressive compliance", particularly given tight personnel budgets which constrain the processing of the data. Likewise, banks vary in the extent to which they filter such suspicions before passing them on centrally to the police and customs. In the case of companies, there is a thin dividing line between normal financial transfers and "money laundering". The difference resides in the fact that the latter occurs other than for the normal *purpose* of lawful business conduct. Money is unlawfully siphoned out of the company, or the company itself is being used as a conduit or "front" for unlawful transactions or false invoices. But how is the *banker* to know? The way in which the banker might be likely to know would be if the company turnover suddenly increases, it

53. I have not dealt here fully with issues such as the absence of any privilege against self-incrimination in D.T.I. and S.F.O. investigations: see Levi, *Regulating Fraud: White Collar Crime and the Criminal Process*, op. cit. However, an indication that the courts are beginning to take these issues more seriously may be found in the judgment of the Court of Appeal in *M.J.O'C. (The Independent*, 23 November 1990), where it was held that although the appellants were required to disclose their assets in connection with a Restraint Order on their assets made under s. 77 of the *Criminal Justice Act* 1988, this should be accompanied with a condition along the lines of: "No disclosure made in compliance with this order shall be used as evidence in the prosecution of an offence alleged to have been committed by the person required to make that disclosure or by any spouse of that person."

54. Some powers have been stregthened in the *Companies Act* 1989 and in the *Criminal Justice (International Co-operation) Act* 1990. When the *Criminal Justice (International Co-Operation) Act* 1990 came into force, it enabled *Police and Criminal Evidence Act* production orders to be obtained on behalf of overseas jurisdictions even where there is no corresponding offence under United Kingdom law, provided that the Home Secretary is satisfied that an offence under the law of the requesting country or territory has been committed or that proceedings or investigations in respect of an offence that is reasonably suspected of having been committed are under way (s. 4). This should generate greater official reciprocity, which has improved greatly since the United Kingdom government agreed to take foreign, for example Swiss, examining magistrates' demands for interview as equivalent to "the institution of proceedings" which in turn can give rise to *Bankers' Books (Evidence) Act* 1879 applications.

trades in seemingly inappropriate areas, one partner abnormally takes out large sums in cash from the firm's accounts, and/or when its turnover rises to the extent of triggering extra "super-banking" financial management services, which the owners decline. But the assumption that currently, bankers routinely monitor thousands of accounts per branch is almost certainly a mistaken one.

This article has sought to present an overview of the developments in law and practice in relation to money laundering in the United Kingdom. From a socio-political perspective, many of these powerful trends in the globalisation of regulation result from concern about the impact of drug trafficking and terrorism rather than white collar crime and tax evasion. But the obscurity—to bankers and often to law enforcement officers—of the origins of funds means that these phenomena are difficult to compartmentalise: money is simply money! From a jurisprudential policy view, unless banks and the public agree to treat banking as a sphere of private activity—which has not been a human rights issue that has grabbed the public's imagination hitherto—policing demands on banks will increase, backed by the force of law. These are only partly counterbalanced by banks' need for police assistance, though banks are an increasingly attractive target for fraudsters. Although few civil libertarians regard banks as very deserving institutions, and many citizens may be cynical about the motivation of bankers who defend customer confidentiality, the moral and empirical justifications for their new (and, by bankers in respect of most crimes, largely unwanted) role as extensions of the modern State intelligence and regulatory apparatus repay close attention. I hope that this review of evolving law and practice in the United Kingdom will contribute to that academic and policy debate.

17

Money Laundering Legislation In The United States

A Perspective From The Banking Industry

JOHN J. BYRNE*

Bankers may not seem like soldiers, but in the United States that is what we have become: the front-line in the very real battle to rid our country of the terrible scourge of drugs. No matter how we perceive the government's efforts, the goal of the banker is clear: to eliminate financial institutions as places where illegal moneys can be moved to hide their origins. I will discuss the legislative and regulatory developments of money laundering deterrence in the past five years and how our industry has responded to this patchwork of laws that were, more often than not, passed without considering their utility and effect.

OVERVIEW OF THE BANK SECRECY ACT

To understand how United States bankers have dealt with their money laundering deterrence responsibilities, it is important to review the various laws and regulations that cover financial institutions. The major requirement emanates from a 1970 law commonly known as the *Bank Secrecy Act*.[1] This law was passed to assist the government with tracking moneys that were being hidden in tax evasion schemes.[2] Thus, the Act was not initially designed to prevent what we commonly know as drug money laundering. The Act is a record-keeping and reporting statute. The most frequently cited requirement under this law is that financial institutions must report all transactions in currency over $10,000 to the Internal Revenue Service.[3]

* Senior Federal Legislative Counsel, American Bankers Association, Washington, D.C. Paper delivered at R.M.S. Seminar, "Cash Transaction Reporting, Money Laundering, and Confiscation of Proceeds of Crime", Sydney, 21 August 1990; Melbourne, 24 August 1990.

1. *Currency and Foreign Transactions Reporting Act* (Pub. L. No. 91-508).
2. In fact, the original proposal that resulted in the *Bank Secrecy Act* was labelled the so-called "Swiss Bank" Bill and its purpose was to require:

    the maintenance of appropriate types of records by insured banks where such records may have a high degree of usefulness in criminal, tax, or regulatory investigations or proceedings. [See House Report 91-975.]
3. The regulations implementing the *Bank Secrecy Act* did not become effective until 1 July 1972. There have been many changes to the *Bank Secrecy Act* over the years, but the $10,000 threshold has remained the same.

In 1975, the United States banking industry filed 3418 cash reports or C.T.Rs (currency transaction reports) for the entire year. In 1989, our industry filed almost 7 million! While these numbers seem impressive, many are concerned that the volume of C.T.Rs makes it impossible to use the form to initiate investigations. In fact, according to I.R.S. estimates, it takes 45 days before a C.T.R. is placed on the federal database in Detroit, Michigan. No matter how committed we are as an industry to stemming the tide of money laundering, it is clear that there must be some policy adjustment or increased resource allocation or we will continue to inundate the government with paper.[4]

MONEY LAUNDERING LEGISLATION IN THE 1980s

Cash reports continued to be filed in the 1980s but the amounts were not significant. It took several major institutions being fined for failure to report cash transactions before there was a dramatic change in filings.[5] It is interesting to note that the General Accounting Office (G.A.O.) took the government to task for not enforcing the *Bank Secrecy Act* before the major fines were levied in 1985.[6] However, the fines in 1985 took the banking industry by storm. All the major newspapers and the electronic media jumped on the bandwagon and began to engage in bank-bashing. Most importantly, Congress decided to legislate.

In 1986, Congress enacted the *Money Laundering Control Act* (M.L.C. Act).[7] Ironically, it was not a crime until the passage of that Act to disguise the source of ownership of drug funds derived from illegal activity. While the American Bankers Association supported the creation

4. The Treasury Department is planning to promulgate a regulation on the electronic filing of C.T.Rs. This may add necessary efficiency to the filing process.
5. In a statement to the House Banking Committee in 1985, an I.R.S. official suggested that the increase in filings occurred after the sentencing of the Bank of Boston for *Bank Secrecy Act* violations.
   The following shows the increase in C.T.R. filings from 1984 to 1988:

Year	Filings	Dollar amount reported
1984	704,521	$ 39,695,822,146
1985	1,847,859	78,225,644,407
1986	3,563,986	136,999,133,842
1987	4,905,867	208,555,516,059
1988	5,743,942	249,071,682,196

6. The General Accounting Office stated that the Treasury Department:
   [G]ave relatively low priority to *Bank Secrecy Act* compliance when applying examination resources, being concerned primarily with other mission-related objectives; lacked detailed procedures, or applied existing procedures inconsistently; failed to adequately document the work performed, so that often neither we nor they could ascertain how well examiners were performing the compliance examinations, and failed to designate examiners with a wide range of experience and training to assure compliance with the Act, and could better communicate and co-ordinate with one another and thereby enhance the overall compliance.
   Senate Hearing 99-540, p. 90.
7. *Anti-Drug Abuse Act* 1986, Pub. L. No. 99-570, Title I, s. 1352(a), 100 Stat. 3207 (codified as amended at 18 U.S.C. 1956, 1957 (Supp. IV 1986)).

of this necessary statute,[8] our industry bore the brunt of excessive rhetoric the like of which was never seen. James Harmon, the Executive Director and Chief Counsel of the President's Commission on Organised Crime, stated in the *New York Times*, 3 March 1984:

> Part of the solution to this country's organised crime problem may be found in the boardrooms of the financial institutions which service this city and the world. All too often, banks condone money laundering because their balance sheets make no distinction between legal and illegal money.

It was this type of attack that pushed the industry to emphasise their aggressive stance towards the problem. The A.B.A. provided a witness every time the Congress held a hearing on money laundering. The A.B.A. began a series of educational efforts designed to assist all of our members in developing effective compliance programs. We became the leading source of information on money laundering prevention in the country.

Thus in 1986, the first money laundering statute was crafted with the A.B.A.'s support. The statute created several new laws. First, 18 U.S.C. 1956 establishes monetary penalties and jail fines for virtually any dealings with the profits of a wide range of "specified unlawful activities" when those dealings are aimed at furthering some "specified unlawful activity", or at concealing the source or ownership of the funds, or constitute violations of the *Bank Secrecy Act* under Title 31. The second provision, 18 U.S.C. 1957, makes it illegal to engage in transactions involving criminally derived property.[9] This second statute has been the cause of some confusion within and out of the government. In fact, the United States Attorneys' Manual instructs that cases brought under this statute must be approved by the Justice Department.[10]

The final new criminal offence created in the M.L.C. Act was the crime of structuring transactions or evading or assisting an individual in avoiding reporting. 31 U.S.C. 5324 provides for stiff criminal fines for

8. Boris F. Melnikoff, Group Vice President and Corporate Director of Special Services at First Atlanta told the House Judiciary Committee on 13 June 1985:
   > The A.B.A. supports making the laundering of money a crime, provided specific criminal elements such as intent and scienter are included in the definition. The crime of money laundering must be drafted with precision so as to exact the most effective, fair result. The thrust of any newly defined crime of "money laundering" should be on the individual who initiates or causes to be initiated a transaction involving a financial institution, with the intent to promote unlawful activity or with knowledge or reason to know that the transaction reports income directly or indirectly derived from unlawful activity. This definition would affect customers and employees of financial institutions alike.

9. This section is limited to criminally derived funds over $10,000 and the statute does not require that these funds are being used for any additional criminal purpose, only that the receiver knows that they are from an unlawful activity. The purchase of any personal chattel or real estate, knowing that the proceeds of such purchase were from a criminal activity, could constitute a violation under this statute.

10. The manual states:
    > Prosecutors are again directed to Section 9-111.000 of the United States Attorneys' Manual for guidance in exercising the discretion vested them by this section. Remember, however, that no prosecution may be brought under Section 1957 without first obtaining the concurrence of the Narcotic and Dangerous Drug Section.

    Justice Department *Handbook on Anti-Drug Abuse Act* 1986 (March 1987).

actions such as depositing $8,000 in three successive days if the prosecution can prove wilfulness or negligence. Congress felt the need to craft this proposal because the courts did not uniformly agree as to whether the reporting requirements fell only on the financial institution or on the individual.[11] In addition, the breaking down of transactions (commonly known as smurfing) under $10,000 to avoid reporting became the most common method of laundering.

While the creation of this statute may have been placed in the back seat to the money laundering crime, Congress does give us an example of what constitutes structuring:

> [A] person who converts $18,000 in currency to cashier's cheques by purchasing two $9,000 cashier's cheques at two different banks or on two different days with the specific intent that the participating bank or banks not be required to file [reports] for those transactions, would be subject to potential civil and criminal liability. A person conducting the same transactions for any other reasons or a person splitting up an amount of currency that would not be reportable if the full amount were involved in a single transaction (for example, splitting $2,000 in currency into four transactions of $500 each), would not be subject to liability under the proposed amendment.[12]

THE BANKING INDUSTRY RESPONDS

There was universal recognition within the banking industry that the government's new weapons were broad and should be understood immediately and promptly implemented in our compliance programs. Since another major component of the new laws created was the requirement that all financial institutions have compliance programs, all of the bank regulatory agencies were going to examine banks to determine the validity of their written policies.[13]

---

11. See *Hearing Before the Senate Committee on Banking, Housing and Urban Affairs*, 99th Cong., 2d Sess. 22, 30 (anti-smurfing law meant to cure inadequacies in current law in three federal circuits); at 48-49 (proposed anti-smurfing law corrects the problems revealed in case law); at 67 (anti-smurfing statute should close money laundering "loophole"; anti-smurfing statute "needed as prosecutions . . . continue to suffer from adverse case law"; anti-smurfing statute "should help clarify the state of the law and permit continued vigorous prosecution"); at 92 (anti-smurfing statute will cure confusion caused by case law and preclude unjustified dismissals); at 95 (anti-smurfing statute is designed to cure shortcomings in *Bank Secrecy Act*); at 134-136 (case law has created two major gaps in reporting law that anti-smurfing law should overcome); at 226 (anti-smurfing law is designed to overcome several recent court decisions); *Hearing before the House Comm. on Banking, Finance and Urban Affairs*, above at 792 (anti-smurfing statute is aimed at overcoming problems of structured transactions caused by recent cases); at 846 (describing recent case law as a severe blow to government efforts to use reporting requirements).
12. See Senate Report No. 433, 99th Cong., 2nd Sess., p. 22 (1986). Also, for an excellent analysis of this law, see Welling, above, Chapter 11.
13. For example, in a 26 February 1987 circular to insured State non-member banks, the Federal Deposit Insurance Corporation stated:
    The F.D.I.C. has adopted a rule which requires that all insured state non-member banks, including insured state branches of foreign banks, establish and maintain

Several educational programs were created in 1987 and the A.B.A. went to 27 sites and instructed thousands of bank employees on what were acceptable compliance programs. Fortunately, by 1987, most of the excessive rhetoric had subsided and government officials were willingly providing their time and expertise to the banking community.

One of the most frequent questions we received in the wake of the 1986 laws was the application of the crime of structuring to a banker's responsibility on reporting suspicious transactions. Prior to the law against structuring, financial institution employees were quick to assist customers with questions on the level of currency that triggered reporting. Now, that same activity is a felony![14] Bankers and especially the front-line tellers feel that they are now in the untenable position of refusing to respond to customer inquiries on legitimate questions concerning why reports were being filed.[15]

Not only was no clarity forthcoming, but bankers were told that reluctance on the part of an individual to proceed with a transaction after being informed about the filing of a C.T.R. is an indication that money laundering is taking place.[16] Therefore, in a United States bank, if you do not complete a transaction because a form may be filed, the bank will report you to the government.

THE 1988 OMNIBUS DRUG BILL

On 18 November 1988, the President signed the 1988 version of the omnibus drug Bill. Many saw it as another cynical attempt by Congress to prove to the American people that legislation alone could eliminate a serious problem. In reality, the *Omnibus Drug Initiative Act* 1988 (Pub. L. No. 100-690) mainly added additional record-keeping and reporting

13. *continued*

procedures to assure and monitor compliance with the *Bank Secrecy Act*. The rule requires each bank to develop and provide for the continued administration of a compliance program that, at a minimum, provides for:

(1) a system of internal controls to assure ongoing compliance;
(2) independent testing of compliance by bank personnel or by an outside party;
(3) a designated individual or individuals responsible for co-ordinating and monitoring day-to-day compliance, and;
(4) training for appropriate personnel.

The compliance program shall be reduced to writing, approved by the bank's board of directors and noted in the minutes.

The final rule became effective on 27 January 1987. Banks must have developed and implemented their compliance programs by 27 April 1987. The program and procedures will be reviewed during the course of regulatory examinations.

14. A wilful violation of 31 U.S.C. 5324 constitutes a criminal offence punishable by imprisonment of not more than five years or a fine of not more than $250,000 or both.

15. In fact, in a 1988 law review article by the former Director of Enforcement for the Department of the Treasury, the following act was considered "characteristic" of persons trying to evade reporting:

The person, after being informed that the institution intends to file a C.T.R. on the transaction, asks the officer or employee handling the transaction whether he should deposit less than $10,000.

See generally Rusch, "Hue and Cry in the Counting House: Some Observations on the Bank Secrecy Act" (1988) 37 Cath. L. Rev. 478.

16. See Office of the Comptroller of the Currency, *Policies and Procedures for Enforcement of the Bank Secrecy Act* (1990).

burdens on financial institutions. Financial institutions argued that those burdens would have little effect on the battle already being waged by the industry to aid law enforcement. The provisions, however, were passed overwhelmingly without the benefit of any real debate.

THE $3,000 RECORD-KEEPING REQUIREMENT

Despite considerable evidence to the contrary, Congress decided to require financial institutions to keep additional records on certain cash transactions under $10,000. 31 U.S.C. 5325 was added to the *Bank Secrecy Act* to provide new identification and record-keeping requirements for financial institutions that sell certain monetary instruments in excess of $3,000.[17]

The law provides that no financial institution can issue or sell a bank cheque, cashier's cheque, traveller's cheque, or money order to any individual in amounts in excess of $3,000 unless:

* the individual has a transaction account with such financial institution and the financial institution: (a) verifies that fact through a signature card or other information maintained by such institution in connection with the account of such individual; and (b) records the method of verification in accordance with regulations the Secretary of the Treasury shall prescribe; or

* the individual branch furnishes the financial institution with such forms of identification as the Secretary of Treasury may require in regulations that the Secretary shall prescribe, and the financial institution verifies and records such information in accordance with the regulations.

The regulations implementing this Act were finally completed in 1990 and made effective on 13 August. While the A.B.A. is working diligently to assist our members with compliance,[18] we remain sceptical that these records will deter drug traffickers since banks already report suspicious transactions in increments under $10,000.

TARGETING OF FINANCIAL INSTITUTIONS

The addition to the *Bank Secrecy Act* in 1988 of 31 U.S.C. 5326 was equally troubling to bankers. With little or no support from the Treasury Department, the House Banking Committee proposed that the Treasury be given the authority to isolate or "target" certain geographic regions or specific financial institutions, and require those institutions to report cash transactions under the current reporting threshold of $10,000.

17. The original proposal, contained in H.R. 5176, passed the House in 1986, but was rejected by the Senate. In 1988, even though there was now a law prohibiting transactions under $10,000 designed to avoid reporting, the House fought for the $3,000 law. The A.B.A. questioned the necessity of this new authority.
18. See generally American Bankers Association, *A Guide to the $3,000 Record-keeping and Reporting Rule* (1990).

The response from the industry was immediate. The facts showed that the financial industry had been, for several years, reporting transactions under $10,000 that were deemed "suspicious". These types of transactions (that is, structured transactions) were being reported on a regular basis to the Treasury or the other bank regulators because the banks had a reason to believe that a violation of law had occurred. There was absolutely no evidence that geographic targeting was a necessary requirement. In fact, members of the Criminal Investigative Division of the Internal Revenue Service (I.R.S.) had denounced the requirement as causing unnecessary paperwork, which would send the wrong message to the financial industry.

Opposition within the industry and the government agencies did not deter the House Banking Committee from passing this provision, and it became part of the final version of the drug bill. Under the new s. 5326 of Title 31, the Secretary of Treasury may order a specific financial institution or group of financial institutions in a particular geographic area to obtain information and maintain a record about transactions in which the bank is engaged and any person participating in the transaction.

The Treasury Department has issued regulations on the scope of the targeting authority and the A.B.A. has recommended to its members that any institution that is a target not disclose that order to anyone. In yet another legislative proposal on money laundering in 1990, [19] there is a provision clarifying the prohibition against disclosing a targeting order.

OTHER CHANGES TO THE 1988 LAW

One of the major concerns with the omnibus drug Bill of 1986 was the creation of the crime of engaging in a transaction derived from illegal proceeds (18 U.S.C. 1957). This statute, very broadly worded and ambiguously defined, has caused major concern within the industry.

In 1988, 18 U.S.C. 1957 was amended so that the term "monetary transaction" does not include any transaction necessary to preserve a person's right to representation as guaranteed by the Sixth Amendment to the Constitution. The criminal defence bar had long sought a change that would make it clear that bona fide attorneys' fees could be accepted without running afoul of the statute.

While it is now relatively clear that attorneys' fees can be accepted in order to defend a client under a charge of violating 18 U.S.C. 1957, the banking industry remains concerned that the statute could be used recklessly against industry officials. Therefore, the A.B.A. continues to push for a "safe harbour" for financial institutions under 18 U.S.C. 1957.

18 U.S.C. 1956 was amended by the 1988 Bill to provide that whoever conducts or attempts to conduct a financial transaction with the reckless intent involving property "represented by a law enforcement official to be the proceeds of specified unlawful activity" shall be fined or imprisoned for 20 years. The change indicates that any representation

19. Section 11 of H.R. 3848.

made by a law enforcement officer or any other person at the direction of, or with the approval of, a federal official authorised to investigate or prosecute violations of the section is now covered. Thus, individuals can be prosecuted for money laundering offences even if the moneys involved were not illegal but in fact were moneys used by the government in "sting" operations.

One of the major provisions in the 1988 Act was the creation of the Office of National Drug Control Strategy.[20] The Director of that office is commonly known as the "Drug Czar". In the first drug control strategy plan released in 1989, the office stated:

> Another critical area of concern is money laundering. The magnitude of their drug-generated wealth gives foreign traffickers the capability to penetrate—and potentially dominate—both legitimate and illegitimate commercial markets, to corrupt United States and foreign officials, and to destabilise foreign governments. Defeating this problem needs attention at the national level, and the rewards to be gained by success in this are potentially very large.

In 1989, the A.B.A. formalised its long-standing commitment to money laundering deterrence.

THE A.B.A. MONEY LAUNDERING TASK FORCE

In order to ensure that there was a formal mechanism for swift banker response to all of the proposals and attacks on the banking industry, the American Bankers Association created a money laundering task force.

One of the first major acts of this group was the submission to William Bennett of its recommendations in the drug war. In the document entitled *Toward a New National Drug Policy—The Banking Industry Strategy*, the task force made the following recommendations:

- Government-industry co-operation is essential for any successful national drug policy. Establishment of a formal financial industry advisory board will greatly enhance communications between these two critical groups.
- The government should establish a mechanism for prompt dissemination of money laundering activities and trends to the financial industry.
- There should be a thorough review of all record-keeping and reporting regulations designed to attack the drug money laundering problem. There is a need for a study addressing the law enforcement utility of the *Bank Secrecy Act*.
- Successful prosecutions resulting from active support from the banking industry should be publicised by the government whenever possible.
- The problems with tracking possible laundering schemes through the use of wire transfers and other complex transactions should be addressed.

20. Section 1005 of the *Anti-Drug Abuse Act* 1988 (21 U.S.C. 1504).

To the credit of the task force, all five of these recommendations have been addressed in one form or another in the past year. In addition, coming on the heels of the *Statement of Principles* issued by the Basle Committee on Banking Regulation and Supervisory Practices, the A.B.A. released the following statement:

> In December 1988, the Basle Committee on Banking Regulation and Supervisory Practices issued a Statement of Principles on money laundering. This Committee is well aware of the ground-breaking nature of such a statement, as is the international banking community. The American Bankers Association has agreed to endorse the principles embodied in that document and we have recommended the same course of action to our international counterparts. We believe that this endorsement is simply a formal acknowledgement of what we have all believed: that money laundering is a "borderless issue" and mandates total global commitment. This is a good first step, but the principles must be supported by binding laws and regulations to be effective. The A.B.A. supports the need for the international community to enact laws similar to United States money laundering laws so we can work together to make financial institutions universally dangerous places for launderers.[21]

A.B.A.'s MONEY LAUNDERING DETERRENCE AND BANK SECRECY ACT SURVEY

In May 1990, the A.B.A. released its survey on *Money Laundering Deterrence and Bank Secrecy Act Compliance*. While many readers focused on the survey's estimate of $129 million spent in 1989 on

---

21. The A.B.A. *Statement of Principles* was contained in testimony before the House and Senate Banking Committee and read in part:
    - United States financial institutions should continue to be at the forefront of efforts to combat the laundering of profits from illegal drug trafficking.
    - United States financial institutions should comply fully with all laws and regulations relating to money laundering. Employees of these financial institutions should be trained in the rules applicable to reporting of transactions and to identifying possible money laundering schemes. The management of all financial institutions should indicate strong support for employee efforts to combat money laundering.
    - The employees of financial institutions should report suspicious transactions or other activities to authorities when there is sufficient reason to believe that illegal activities may be taking place, consistent with basic principles of customer privacy.
    - Financial institutions and their employees should work actively with law enforcement authorities when those authorities request their assistance in investigations of money laundering.
    - Financial institutions should work with government institutions to develop new methods to effectively combat money laundering.
    - United States financial institutions should work through their trade associations to encourage international co-operation and agreement on cross-border efforts to combat money laundering.

compliance,[22] there were many other interesting results. According to the survey, only 7 per cent of responding banks are aware of any prosecution cases that resulted from their filing of C.T.Rs, or from their reporting of a suspicious currency transaction. This result amplifies the need for institutions to receive some feedback on what information is effective and utilised by the government.

In addition, the survey confirms banker commitment to compliance policies on "knowing your customer". This result emphasises a dedication to monitoring activity far beyond those required on reporting cash transactions. Treasury may issue "know your customer" regulations if the Senate money laundering bill is enacted. A.B.A. is committed to this policy concept and our task force will share its "know your customer" guidelines with the Treasury.

The survey respondents were asked: "In your experience, what is the most effective procedure to prevent money laundering?" Some of the prevalent answers included:

- know your customer;
- alert and trained tellers;
- deal only with known customers; and
- suspicious activity reporting.

A.B.A. is filling these needs through training and product development. In fact, our Association produced a nationwide teleconference in October 1990 that reached over 25 States and several thousand bank employees. In addition, the A.B.A. offered a major two-day seminar in 1990 held in conjunction with the American Bar Association as well as holding two more programs in 1991.

LEGISLATIVE AND REGULATORY PROPOSALS IN 1990-91

Since 1986, there have been two major laws and a series of regulations concerning money laundering as well as a myriad of legislative proposals that have been offered by members of Congress to prove their mettle during election years. 1990 was no exception. Congress and the Administration once again placed several new proposals on the table.

22. The House Banking Committee recognised the cost of compliance stating:
    The Congress must recognise that compliance by the financial community with the *Bank Secrecy Act* is difficult and costly. The submission of over six million forms requires significant commitment by depository institutions. Depository institution staff must be trained and supervised if C.T.Rs are to be properly competed and submitted every time a cash transaction exceeds the minimum amount for reporting purposes. It is the responsibility of the federal government to make sure that the system is properly maintained and utilised so as to justify the time, money and effort expended by the financial community. Whenever possible and practical, the federal government should take steps to reassure both the American taxpayers and the financial industry that their efforts do result in the apprehension and conviction of money launderers and others who have broken the law.
    House Report 101-446, p. 20.

On 25 April 1990, the House of Representatives passed H.R. 3848 by an overwhelming margin. The Bill, the "Depository Institution Money Laundering Amendments of 1990", was originally introduced in response to the plea bargain in the money laundering case of *United States v. Bank of Credit and Commerce International* (B.C.C.I.). As the House Banking Committee pointed out in its report on the Bill: "[c]learly, a majority of the members of the Banking Committee felt that additional sanctions were warranted in those cases where the financial institution itself is convicted of money laundering crimes."[23] In 1991, the House passed a similar Bill 406-0.

The original version of H.R. 3848 would have mandated the automatic revocation of the bank charter but the final Bill was a compromise that allows the appropriate federal regulator to appoint a conservator for any financial institution convicted of money laundering *only* after considering:

- the extent to which senior management was involved in the offence;
- whether the institution had policies and procedures to prevent money laundering;
- the degree to which the institution had co-operated with law enforcement procedures; *and*
- whether the institution had implemented new procedures to prevent the occurrence of similar money laundering crimes in the future.[24]

The final Bill would *require* the regulator to hold a hearing to consider revoking the charter of any financial institution when an institution *and* directors or officers are convicted of money laundering. The regulator must consider the same factors of revocation as for the conservatorship proceedings.

For State-chartered banks, the F.D.I.C. shall consider the revocation factors *and* must notify the appropriate State regulator ten days before deposit insurance is revoked.

H.R. 3848 also contains several other provisions unrelated to charter revocation including:

- Allowing the removal from the financial institution of persons who have been convicted of money laundering or of structuring transactions to evade the *Bank Secrecy Act* reporting requirements:

23. House Report 101-446, p. 18 (3 April 1990).
24. The American Bankers Association, in a joint letter to the Chairman of the House Banking Subcommittee on Financial Institutions, Supervision, Regulation and Insurance pointed out that:

> the most troubling aspect of this proposal is that the revocation is automatic and mandatory, with no provisions for regulatory discretion. Depository institutions' charters will be revoked, or federal deposit insurance withdrawn, even if senior management is totally innocent. Such a revocation would cause great hardship to customers and communities served by these depository institutions. For example, the citizens of a community, rural or urban, that is served by a single depository institution would be deprived of any banking services. This will occur even if the corporation were only found guilty under legal theory that "attributed" a low level employee's illegal conduct to innocent and well-meaning senior management.

31 U.S.C. 5324. The person will also be banned from affiliating with *all* financial institutions in the future.

- Section 10 of H.R. 3848 was the focus of much debate as to Congress' role in establishing record-keeping requirements on international funds transfers. After a vote on the House floor defeating an amendment that would have initiated record-keeping in certain areas, the House agreed on a provision giving Treasury the ability to complete its rulemaking on international funds transfers by 1 January 1991. It is important to note that Treasury must now consult with the Federal Reserve Board and consider the usefulness of such regulations and the effect such regulations will have on the cost and efficiency of the payment system. The Treasury may issue its notice of proposed rulemaking shortly.

- In what may be a major breakthrough for the financial industry, a provision creates a "safe harbour" from civil liability under the *Right to Financial Privacy Act* for good faith reporting of suspicious transactions to authorities *and* the subsequent refusal to do business by the institution with that person.

- Finally, H.R. 3848 contains a provision that is an important step for banks that are in States which feel the need to enact parallel cash reporting laws.[25] Under the House-passed bill, State financial institution regulators would gain access to C.T.Rs maintained by Treasury. This may negate the need for duplicate reporting.

In the Senate, a Bill (s. 2327), introduced by Senator Kerry (D-MA), and co-sponsored by several members of the Senate Banking Committee (including Chairman Don Riegle (D-MI)) also grants charter revocation authority to the regulators for money laundering convictions of the institution. The Bill differs from the House, however, in that the conviction has only to be on the institution and *not* officers and directors.[26] The conviction also can be for any criminal violation of the *Bank Secrecy Act* reporting statute. The Bill passed the full Senate but Congress adjourned before the House and Senate could complete action on the Bills. The Senate Bill was reintroduced in 1991. The co-sponsors of the original Bill have indicated that this legislation "will give law enforcement a new tool in the war on drugs, . . . [but] . . . [i]t will not punish a community which relies on the bank for its source of loans and contributions to the local economy. [Nor will it] . . . penalise a bank for the actions of low-level employees or officials acting beyond the scope of their employment. [And] [i]t will not place additional administrative burdens on banks."[27] (The 1991 Bill has a later effective date, which has also not been met as the 1991 Bill has also not yet been enacted.)

It is important to note that Senator Kerry (D-MA), Chairman of the Foreign Relations Subcommittee on International Terrorism and Narcotics, and Senator McConnell (R-KY), the ranking Republican,

25. There are six States that contain some cash reporting requirements with several others considering such proposals.
26. However, the extent of senior management involvement must be considered by the regulators.
27. Cong. Rec. S3109 (22 March 1990), Vol. 136, No. 32.

advocated charter revocation in a report,[28] but recommended that federal bank regulators "consider revocation" for a money laundering violation "to the extent that the operational integrity and viability of the institution is compromised."[29] Bankers were especially supportive of the provisions that protect persons who acquire or succeed to the interest of an institution which has violated the money laundering statutes or currency reporting laws as long as the acquisition was made in good faith and not for the purpose of evading the law.[30]

The other major Senate Bill on money laundering was Senator Alfonse D'Amato's *Money Laundering Enforcement Act* (s. 2651) that was incorporated into the Committee Bill that passed in July. This Bill contained many of the same provisions from an Administration Bill drafted by the White House Office of National Drug Control Policy. The Senator introduced another Bill in 1991 which closely follows s. 2651.

The major thrust of Sen. D'Amato's approach concerns the problem of illegal money transmitters. The Bill requires Treasury to issue regulations, by 1 July 1991, that banks, thrifts and credit unions identify their "non-bank" financial institution customers (money transmitters, cheque cashers, foreign exchange dealers, issues and redeemers of travellers' cheques and casinos). It would be a federal crime to operate a money transmitting business in violation of state law. The A.B.A. supports the concept of enforcing the reporting law against other businesses, but we remain concerned that the regulations not be unduly burdensome to banks.

Treasury would also receive the authority to issue compliance procedures "to guard against money laundering". This will give the agency the ability to issue "know your customer" regulations.

A.B.A.'s Money Laundering Task Force, and the industry in general, have recommended that financial institutions base their regulatory compliance on "know your customer". This means activities such as verifying the business of a new account holder and reporting activity in an account that is disproportionate to that customer's known business. Immediate reaction to unusual transaction activity should be the goal for all banking institutions. Identification procedures beyond the regulatory minimum should be considered to include situations such as verifying whether a document for identification that is seemingly altered is genuine. With these several concepts in play, individuals will find it increasingly difficult deliberately to utilise a financial institution for illegal purposes.

28. *Drug Money Laundering, Banks and Foreign Policy*: a report on anti-money laundering law enforcement and policy based on oversight hearings before the Senate Foreign Relations Committee and Hearings before the Senate Banking Committee, p. 79.
29. Ibid.
30. On 7 August 1989 the Fifth Circuit ruled in *Alamo Bank v. United States* 880 F. 2d 828 (1989) that Alamo was liable for the failure to file certain currency transaction reports (C.T.Rs) of a bank that they acquired almost three years after the alleged criminal conduct. On 21 February, the Supreme Court decided not to review the case. Since a charter revocation is the final act for a financial institution, this decision will have an even greater chilling effect on bank mergers, savings and loan mergers and those of credit unions. Therefore, the "successor liability" provision grants protection for good faith acquiring banks.

Financial institutions already have a well known "know your customer" standard that does ensure compliance with both the M.L.C. Act and the *Bank Secrecy Act*. While we may not always agree as to what constitutes "know your customer", it is important that this concept be advanced within the industry.

The Senate Bill also parallels H.R. 3848 in its treatment of wire transfers but adds the authority for Treasury to include record keeping requirements for international fund transfer orders made by money transmitters and cheque cashers.

THE NEED FOR A FINANCIAL INSTITUTION "SAFE HARBOUR" AND THE RIGHT TO FINANCIAL PRIVACY ACT

With a myriad of laws and regulations placed on the financial industry for money laundering deterrence, A.B.A. has argued that it is critical that there be protection for actions taken by institutions doing their part in the war on drugs.

One outstanding concern of the banking industry is the level of adequate protection from criminal and civil liability for reporting transactions that are deemed suspicious to the proper law enforcement activity. Of course any disclosure to government authorities must be accomplished only by clear procedures that protect the financial privacy of our customers.[31]

With the spate of legislative changes to the federal *Right to Financial Privacy Act* (R.F.P. Act)[32] in the past several years, there is a concern that institutions should have the ability to refuse business with individuals or corporations who may reasonably be suspected of engaging in illegal activity.

Banks now find themselves in a position of having to monitor all customer transactions, file currency transaction reports, report suspicious criminal activities,[33] avoid assisting in structured money laundering transactions or receiving the proceeds of criminal activities. Banks are in the difficult position of complying as "good corporate citizens" while being subjected to potential lawsuits for privacy violations, defamation, breach of contract and lender liability.

---

31. As the A.B.A. stated in 1972:
    [w]e believe that additional positive legislation is needed to assure the public that their bank records will not be available to government agencies except under proper safeguards, and [A.B.A.] suggested that could be accomplished by the addition of simple language requiring a subpoena or summons before such material could be examined. ("No Fishing", *American Banker*, 18 August 1972).
32. 12 U.S.C. 3401ff. The R.F.P. Act generally provides that, except in accordance with certain exceptions or requirements, no government authority can gain access to the financial institution. In addition, a financial institution may not provide the customer's financial records to a government authority except in accordance with the R.F.P. Act.
33. In addition to filing C.T.Rs, financial institutions must file "criminal referral forms" to the government if money laundering or other criminal violations are suspected.

There is now a distinct possibility that well-run financial institutions will face criminal and civil liability because of the lack of adequate protection under the law. Public policy plainly requires that financial institutions take aggressive attitudes towards potential money laundering, and the American Bankers Association completely supports this policy. However, we believe that now is the time for Congress to review possible avenues that may be expanded to give good corporate citizens the needed protections for the support they are giving law enforcement.

There is a history of "safe harbour" protections long supported by certain federal agencies. The policy is simple: as long as the regulated entity maintains a diligent and serious compliance effort and fully reports all legal violations, the entity should not face prosecution or civil liability.

The Securities and Exchange Commission (S.E.C.) adopted a safe harbour program for dealing with the misuse of corporate funds, such as illegal political contributions, kickbacks, and payments to individuals and officials overseas. The S.E.C. implemented a voluntary compliance program to the effect that, if a corporation conducted its own investigations and then remedied its problems, the S.E.C. would give credit to the corporation when it was deciding whether to pursue an enforcement action.[34] More recently, the S.E.C. advocated the use of a safe harbour in the context of the *Bank Secrecy Act*. In a comment letter to the Department of Treasury, the S.E.C. recommended a "safe harbour be provided in your [Treasury's] regulations for firms that have developed and effectively implemented procedures reasonably designed, in light of the size, sophistication and structure of the firm, to uncover multiple, same day transactions". The S.E.C. went on to point out that "this approach will encourage more effective surveillance of currency transactions by financial institutions while providing those firms protection against liability where they have implemented good faith procedures".[35]

In addition, the American Bar Association's House of Delegates has passed a resolution that the United States "adopt prosecution policies to encourage compliance with the *Bank Secrecy Act* and the M.L.C. Act by establishing guidelines and standards governing prosecution of financial institutions."

Finally, the recent publication of the G-7 Financial Action Task Force, *Report on Money Laundering*, confirms the need for a safe harbour on the international level. Recommendation 16 of the report states:

> If financial institutions suspect that funds stem from criminal activity, they should be permitted or required to report promptly their suspicions to the competent authorities. Accordingly, there should be legal provisions to protect financial institutions and their employees from criminal or civil liability for breach of any restriction on disclosure of information imposed by contract or by any legislative, regulatory or administrative provision, if they report in good faith, in disclosing suspected criminal activity to the

34. (1976) 31 Bus. Law. 1279 at 1281.
35. See, S.E.C. letter to Jonathan Rusch (20 March 1987).

competent authorities, even if they did not know precisely what the underlying criminal activity was, and regardless of whether illegal activity actually occurred.[36]

These are just some examples of the support for the "safe harbour" concept. The House and Senate have already passed a version of this policy. According to the House Banking Committee:

The Committee is concerned that financial institutions have been reluctant to report suspicious transactions to law enforcement authorities because of concern for potential civil liability resulting from the filing of the report. Financial institutions are also reluctant to cease doing business with customers whom they suspect are engaged in illegal activities out of concern for liability to those customers. In one case, a court held the bank civilly liable for terminating a business relationship with a customer, even though the bank had been told (erroneously) by federal law enforcement authorities that the customer was engaged in illegal activities.

In order to encourage financial institutions to report suspicious transactions and to encourage financial institutions to terminate relationships with customers who may be engaged in illegal transactions but who have not yet been charged with any offence, the Committee amends the R.F.P. Act to provide an exemption from civil liability for any institution which, in good faith, files a suspicious transaction report or who refuses to do business with a customer that the institution has in good faith reported.

The Committee emphasises that this exemption from liability applies only when the referral has been made in good faith. It does not apply to the filing of a referral simply as an attempt to evade liability for an otherwise impermissible purpose or motive.

The Committee intends "good faith" to mean that the report has been filed with an honesty of intention, observing the reasonable standards of fair dealing in filing the report.[37]

An amendment to the Senate Bill will require the Justice Department to study the safe harbour issue. We have recommended that the Justice Department adopt a prosecution policy that takes into consideration the level of management from which the money laundering violation occurred, the compliance program of the institution, as well as the extent of co-operation from within the institution.[38]

PUBLIC RELATIONS ISSUES

Not only is it critical continually to educate the Congress and the government on what banks are doing to counter the money laundering

36. See Financial Action Task Force "Synopsis of the Forty Recommendations of the Report" (1990).
37. House Report 101-446, pp. 33-34. The amendment was supported by the Treasury who cited *Ricci v. Key Bancshares of Maine* 768 F. 2d 456 (1st Cir. 1985) as reason for allowing a bank to "sever relations" with a customer because of activities underlying a suspicious transaction report.
38. One of the factors to be considered by regulators prior to charter revocation contains just such recommendations.

menace, it is imperative that we give the public information on our compliance and success stories.[39]

The A.B.A. developed radio and print public service announcements on the banker's role in the war on drugs. When bankers became frustrated over the amount of information we would be asked to receive from our customers, A.B.A. was approached to get the word out to the public as to why we would be asking for identification and recording information.

A.B.A. ran radio ads in 1500 markets and took out print ads in major news magazines telling the public that patience was needed to assist our government's efforts in slowing down drug trafficking. The ads were an instant success and A.B.A. has received commendation letters from various enforcement agencies who appreciated our support for the government.

THE CRITICAL DEBATE ON WIRE TRANSFERS

As mentioned earlier, the A.B.A.'s Money Laundering Task Force took the courageous step of predicting that many in Congress and in the government would look to the electronic wire transfer as the next area for regulation in money laundering. Unfortunately, many used our comments on the need to address the wire issue as an indication that the banking industry was seeking regulation. Thus, our comments were used by several individuals for political gains rather than constructive dialogue.

The A.B.A. wrote to the Treasury Department on 2 January 1990 that we were "committed to any workable policy that would hinder the flow of moneys derived from illicit activity". We pointed out that it was possible "to establish effective monitoring and controls on international wire transfers originated in the United States".

However, due to the enormity of the wire transfer issue, the A.B.A. added that "an international wire transfer policy may have the side effects of slowing the global payments system, hindering legitimate world trade, and penalising the international competitiveness of United States financial institutions".[40]

A.B.A. recommended that international wire transfers regulations must be measured against the industry's ability "to comply with minimal service disruption and costs while addressing the need to stop the flow of illegal moneys". More importantly, it was essential that Treasury consider that "by their very nature, international wire transfer systems are subject to a myriad of regulations and market practices, varying with the countries involved in each transfer".

39. As the Basle Committee cogently pointed out:
      Public confidence in banks, and hence their stability, can be undermined by adverse publicity as a result of inadvertent association by banks with criminals. In addition, banks may lay themselves open to direct losses from fraud, either through negligence in screening undesirable customers or where the integrity of their own officers has been undermined through association with criminals.
40. Letter to Amy Rudnick, Department of Treasury (2 January 1990).

This was but one example of the complexities of the problem. The A.B.A. was also the first banking group to voice our concern on potential wire transfer legislation. On 27 September 1989, before a Senate Foreign Relations Subcommittee, the A.B.A.'s Money Laundering Task Force Chairman, Earl Hadlow, told the Committee that the volume of wire transfers "makes it clear that the federal cash reporting requirements could not be applied to wire transfers." The A.B.A. also wrote to House Banking Committee Chairman, Henry Gonzalez (D-TX) on 22 March 1990 that:

> The Treasury Department is in the midst of a complex, detailed study relating to the over 400,000 wire transactions in the United States per day. To mandate specific reporting requirements and record retention legislatively will negate the tremendous amount of work already underway and will have unintended negative side effects. The A.B.A. recommends this regulatory approach be allowed to go forward.

The A.B.A. made it clear why Congress should wait for the Treasury to complete their rule-making. Unfortunately, the banker concerns about wire legislation were attacked. One member even went so far as to state:

> We heard about balancing. But what are we balancing? Yes, the banks will have to do some extra paper work. Maybe it will cut back on the paper work in our prisons; maybe it will cut back on the paper work in our drug treatment programs; maybe it will cut back on our paper work in the morgues where thousands of people die from drug overdoses. [41]

Fortunately, this posturing did not persuade the House and the amendment failed 283 to 127. The Treasury Department was still considering final regulations on wire transfers in late 1991.

CONCLUSION

Does each and every one of these new laws have an impact on slowing down the drug trafficking? No. Clearly, the creation of the money laundering laws as well as the heightened awareness by the government and the industry to their respective roles in the drug war has had a major effect. However, some of the increases in reporting or recording routine transactions will take bankers away from the more serious attempts to eliminate the movement of drug money. Deterrence works if risks are raised sufficiently. Fortunately, through the passage of several major laws, we believe that the risks involved in attempting to launder money through financial institutions are now great. The voluntary reporting of suspicious transactions is on the rise and this will add to overall effective deterrence.

It cannot be overemphasised that not all of the recent changes have been useful. Therefore, the A.B.A. continues to urge that Congress and the banking industry be kept apprised of the law enforcement utility of information submitted to the government. Even though there is general

41. Cong. Rec. H. 1730 (25 April 1990).

agreement within the industry on the need for extensive co-operation in the war on drugs, there is good faith scepticism on the utility of all of the required information submitted to the government. [42]

We must remember that the International Financial Action Task Force did not unanimously adopt a cash reporting structure as one of its recommendations and that the Drug Enforcement Agency (D.E.A.) has raised questions about the utility of reporting. While we are not adding our voices to the list of those who are completely opposed to the emphasis on routine reporting, it is clear that the system is not above review. The banking industry calls for an objective analysis of the proper role of cash reports and reports of suspicious transactions in the efforts to deter money laundering. Both the House and Senate are considering legislation to require a study on the C.T.R. and suspicious transaction reporting system. This is indeed welcome news.

It is important to re-emphasise that not only has the industry filed close to seven million cash reports (C.T.Rs) in 1989, but the industry's effort has been singled out for high praise from the government. [43]

In addition, the New York State legislature in a recent report stated:

> Bank compliance with money laundering laws and regulations is at an all time high, and represents the cornerstone of efforts to detect and stop criminal activity. [44]

The banking industry and the A.B.A. supported most of the legislative efforts aimed at deterring money laundering in 1986. It is therefore frustrating to hear attacks on bankers for not accepting each and every legislative proposal offered by Congress or the agencies. Knowing that our reporting makes a difference will go a long way toward easing that frustration.

---

42. Former Deputy Assistant Secretary for Law Enforcement at the Treasury Department, Gerald L. Hilsher told an audience in September 1988 that:
    In my opinion, the Treasury Department has done a poor public relations job in not telling the private sector what the Treasury Department is doing with this information and what kinds of cases the Treasury Department is making. The Treasury Department needs to keep better statistics because although Title 31 convictions are not the only measure of B.S.A. effectiveness, we have not brought forth statistics on other aspects of B.S.A. utility. The federal government has good examples of individual cases brought as a result of B.S.A. compliance, but the Treasury Department, for example, can't state the degree to which B.S.A. compliance has resulted in increased tax revenues. One of the recommendations that I will be making . . . is to do a better job of tracing Title 31 involvements in criminal and tax cases, so that next year, perhaps, we can bring these statistics to the financial community to show that we do have a program that makes sense.
43. In fact, Attorney-General Richard Thornburgh singled out the banking industry for its tremendous work in this area. The Attorney-General told an audience at the 26 October 1989 joint conference of the American Bankers Association-American Bar Association that the work of the Justice Department "has been immeasurably helped by your own increased attention to your obligations to report all financial transactions over $10,000 to Treasury. We are grateful for your diligence, which has aided us in catching these criminals. I recognise your sincere concern and commend your willingness to co-operate."
44. See, *Financial Institutions And the Problem of Money Laundering: A Guide to State and Federal Action*, A Report by Senator Hugh T. Farley, Chairman, New York State Senate Committee on Banks, New York State Senate Select Committee on Interstate Operation (April 1990), p. 9.

It is important that the banking industry emphasises to its regulators the need to stop the flow of paper, a situation that is reaching epidemic proportion. In our ongoing effort to prove that routine reports are less effective than specific reports, we will continue to point out all of the examples of suspicious transaction reporting by the industry that have resulted in investigations and/or indictments.

The creation of FINCEN, the Financial Crimes Enforcement Network that is to be a "government-wide, multi-source, intelligence and analytical network to support the investigation and prosecution of money laundering and other financial crimes", is an excellent step toward addressing the paper trail problem. The banking industry abhors money laundering and is working extremely hard to eliminate it from within our industry.

However, the co-operation we have been offering to the government and Congress must be met by reviewing all of the laws affecting banks. The A.B.A. will continue to co-operate, educate and push for reform.

18

The Practical Impact of United States Criminal Money Laundering Laws on Financial Institutions

WHITNEY ADAMS*

INTRODUCTION

After the February 1985 criminal conviction of the Bank of Boston, followed by a $2.25 million civil fine against the Crocker National Bank, and a $4.75 million civil fine against Bank of America, much public attention focused on banks' responsibilities to report cash transactions under the *Bank Secrecy Act* ("B.S.A.").[1] As a result of substantial amendments in 1986 to the B.S.A.,[2] and announced Congressional priority given to attacking money laundering,[3] the United States federal banking agencies directed all banks to establish effective programs for ensuring compliance with the B.S.A. reporting and record-keeping requirements.[4] Very little attention was given, however, to the sweeping *Criminal Money Laundering Control Act* 1986 (M.L.C. Act) until 1988. Although these statutes, 18 U.S.C. ss 1956 and 1957, expanded potential criminal liability to every function of financial institutions, the Treasury Department, bank regulatory agencies, and the

---

* Ms Adams, who practises with Rogers & Wells, is the Chairperson of the American Bar Association's Criminal Justice Section's White Collar Crime Committee.

1. Pub. L. No. 91-508, 12 U.S.C. s. 1829b; 12 U.S.C. ss 1951 ff; 31 U.S.C. ss 5311 ff. See 31 C.F.R. Pt 103. See generally, *California Bankers Assoc. v. Schultz* 416 U.S. 21 (1974).
2. Section 1359 of the *Anti-Drug Abuse Act* 1986, Pub. L. No. 99-570, amending 12 U.S.C. s. 1818, 12 U.S.C. s. 1464(d), 12 U.S.C. s. 1730, 12 U.S.C. s. 1786. See 31 U.S.C. s. 5324.
3. See e.g., S. Rep. 99-433, 99th Cong., 2d Sess. (3 September 1986).
4. See 52 Fed. Reg. 2858 (27 January 1987). E.g. 12 C.F.R. s. 21.21 (O.C.C.); 12 C.F.R. s. 563.17-7 (Office of Thrift Supervision). The 1986 B.S.A. legislation also authorised the federal bank regulatory agencies to issue civil fines and cease and desist orders against banks failing to establish procedures or correct problems in procedures after notice and opportunity to correct. Although the B.S.A. authorises the Treasury Secretary to impose compliance procedures on financial institutions, 31 U.S.C. s. 5318, Treasury has never issued regulations implementing this provision. Instead, it has delegated authority to the bank regulatory agencies and the S.E.C., to monitor compliance of banks and brokerage firms. See e.g. 31 C.F.R. s. 103.46.

374

Securities and Exchange Commission did almost nothing to alert financial institutions to these criminal statutes' dramatic implications.[5]

Indeed, for many banks, the first government "alert" on the M.L.C. Act came in late 1988 or early 1989 via news headlines of the indictments of Bank of Credit and Commerce International (B.C.C.I.) subsidiaries and Banco Occidente. Much of this media attention focused on the fact that the government's allegations did not charge the banks with illegal cash transactions but wire transfers. After these two cases were resolved through plea negotiations, a strong movement emerged in Congress to regulate wire transfers and impose a "death penalty" on banks convicted of money laundering. In the 1990 session of Congress both Houses passed modified "death penalty" bills requiring federal regulators to hold hearings to consider revoking any bank's federal charter and insurance whenever the bank and its officers or directors are convicted of a B.S.A. or money laundering offence.[6] Although this legislation was not finalised due to the press of the United States budget crisis and a parliamentary snafu, similar legislation is almost certain to pass in 1991.

Criminal exposure, apart from significant fines[7] and forfeiture provisions, has, of course, extremely serious implications for financial institutions because of various collateral consequences from indictment or conviction. Banks face potential termination or suspension of F.D.I.C. insurance,[8] revocation of federal or State banking charters,[9] and the imposition of cease and desist orders,[10] the violation of which under the new *Financial Institutions Reform, Recovery, and Enforcement Act* 1989 (FIRREA) can expose the bank to additional civil penalties of $1 million per day.[11] Adverse publicity associated with a pending

5. E.g. the Federal Reserve, while issuing various alerts regarding B.S.A. compliance, issued no similar alerts regarding the M.L.C. Act's implications until 8 December 1988. See S.R. 88-36 (E.I.S.) (8 December 1988). See also Federal Home Loan Bank Board Thrift Bulletin (18 October 1988) (alerting members to the 1986 M.L.C. Act).
6. This legislation would also have required the Treasury Department to impose regulations on international wire transfers by 1 January 1991.
7. See e.g. *United States v. Ponce Federal Bank FSB* 883 F.2d 1 (1st Cir. 1989) (affirming district court's imposition of $2.5 million fine for five B.S.A. violations to which the bank pleaded per agreement in which the government recommended fines of $1.5 million); *United States v. B.C.C.I.* (unreported, M.D. Fla, 1989, No. 88-330-Cr.-T-13(B)) (plea agreement providing for $15 million in forfeiture). See also *United States v. First Bank of Georgia* (unreported, N.D. Ga, 22 June 1990, Cr. 90-213) ($500,000 fine for conviction of one count of violating 18 U.S.C. s. 1956).
8. See 12 U.S.C. s. 1818(a).
9. See e.g. 12 U.S.C. s. 1818(c), (e), (g), (h), and (s).
10. See e.g. *Order Issued on Consent entered between B.C.C.I. and the Board of Governors of the Federal Reserve System* (9 May 1989) (order issued following indictment but before conviction and requiring bank to overhaul its customer procedures and prohibit suspicious activities).
11. FIRREA, Pub. L. No. 101-73, 103 Stat. 446 (12 U.S.C. s. 1818(i)(2)(C) and (D)). Presumably the government would argue that FIRREA civil penalties for violations of such cease and desist orders would not be prevented by *United States v. Halper* 109 S.Ct 1892 (1989), because the violation would occur after the conduct giving rise to the criminal offence.

criminal investigation, or the bank's indictment, can also provoke a massive flight of deposits.[12]

Criminal prosecution under United States law also can provoke unusually severe consequences for securities and commodity brokers. A criminal conviction can render a broker dealer (or any of its affiliates) ineligible to engage in the mutual fund business, and the mere fact of a criminal investigation may have to be regularly disclosed to mutual fund investors.[13] Broker dealers would also face suspension or licence revocation before the S.E.C. and in all 50 States.[14]

These drastic collateral consequences take on an alarming dimension in the financial institution context because of the generally broad scope of United States criminal corporate liability, the money laundering statutes' incorporation of the wilful blindness standard of knowledge,[15] and the relatively new, and yet to be fully tested, theory of collective knowledge.[16]

The government will rarely have difficulty in establishing respondeat superior criminal liability against a financial institution under United States law which provides that a corporation may be prosecuted for the criminal acts of its employees committed within the scope of their real or apparent authority and done with the intent to benefit the corporation.[17] The conduct of financial transactions is readily within the apparent authority of virtually any bank employee.[18] Moreover, the intent-to-benefit rule will not be much of a hurdle for the prosecutor,

12. Under the forfeiture statutes, the government can freeze substantial assets of the bank at the time of indictment. In *United States v. Banco De Occidente (Panama)* (unreported, N.D. Ga, 1989, No. 89 Cr. 86A) the government froze millions of dollars that would have resulted in the demise of the bank according to the bank's lawyers. The bank pleaded guilty to two conspiracy counts and agreed to a forfeiture of $5 million as part of a plea agreement in 1989.
13. See e.g. S.E.C. Form N-1A, item 9; Form N-2, Pt. I, item 10. See also 17 C.F.R. ss 4.21(a)(13)(i) and 4.31(a)(7).
14. See 15 U.S.C. s. 78o(b)(4); 15 U.S.C. s. 80(b)(3); s. 204(a), *Uniform Securities Act.* Criminal conviction also leads to automatic disqualification as an E.R.I.S.A. plan manager, 29 U.S.C. s. 1160(a), and from state registration exemptions.
15. See *United States v. Jewell* 532 F.2d 692 (9th Cir.), cert. denied, 426 U.S. 951 (1976).
16. *United States v. Bank of New England, N.A.* 821 F.2d 844 (1st Cir.), cert. denied, 484 U.S. 943 (1987).
17. See *New York Central and Hudson River Railroad Co. v. United States* 212 U.S. 481 (1909); *United States v. Automated Medical Laboratories Inc* 770 F.2d 399 (4th Cir. 1985); *United States v. Gold* 743 F.2d 800 (11th Cir. 1984), cert. denied, 469 U.S. 1217 (1985); *United States v. Cincotta* 689 F.2d 238 (1st Cir.), cert. denied, 459 U.S. 991 (1982); *United States v. Hilton Hotels Corp.* 467 F.2d 1000 (9th Cir. 1972), cert. denied, 409 U.S. 1125 (1973).
    Criminal liability under this standard may also be applicable to any successor corporation that acquires an institution whose employee committed criminal acts: *United States v. Alamo Bank* 880 F.2d 828 (5th Cir. 1989), affirming 705 F. Supp. 336 (S.D. Tex., 1988).
18. See generally, *United States v. Bi-Co Pavers Inc.* 741 F.2d 730 at 737 (5th Cir. 1989); *United States v. Hilton Hotels Corp.* 467 F.2d 1000 at 1007 (1972).
    Most brokerage employees probably have similar apparent authority but, because of S.E.C., C.F.T.C., and exchange registration requirements, brokerage firms might have slightly better arguments than banks for excluding some employees from the apparent authority to handle certain financial transactions.

even if the employee's conduct is contrary to corporate policy and actually detrimental to its interests, because financial institutions receive some pecuniary benefit from virtually any financial transaction their employees conduct.[19] In a recent money laundering prosecution of a bank, the court sustained the bank's conviction even though the employee whose conduct provided the basis for the convictions was acquitted.[20] The court held that acquittal of the individual could have resulted from jury lenity and did not require reversal of the finding of guilt as to the corporate entity.

The United States Senate report[21] on the M.L.C. Act legislation specifically explained that the wilful blindness standard, as described in *United States v. Jewell*,[22] is applicable to its scienter requirements. Under *Jewell*, the jury may essentially equate deliberate lack of knowledge with actual knowledge, if it finds that the defendant was aware of the high probability of a fact's existence and had a conscious purpose to avoid learning the truth—unless he or she actually believes that the fact does not exist.[23] The Senate Report makes clear that Congress did not intend to authorise money laundering prosecution of those who transact with persons they merely suspect of criminal involvement, in the absence of other evidence. In *United States v. Bank of New England*,[24] the wilful blindness instruction was interpreted in the corporate setting to mean "flagrant organisational indifference" to regulatory requirements, and this standard was applied to a specific intent ("wilfully") scienter requirement.

Bank of New England increased concerns in the white collar defence bar more because of its "collective knowledge" standard, which permits the jury to aggregate the knowledge of employees and impute this collective knowledge to the corporation. Thus, if one employee knows of the duty to report a certain type of transaction, another knows that such a transaction occurred, and a third knows that no report was filed, the knowledge of all three is collectively attributed to the bank. *Bank of New England's* roots are not on entirely solid ground[25] and later cases

---

19. See *United States v. Carter* 311 F.2d 934 (6th Cir.), cert. denied, 373 U.S. 915 (1963).
20. *United States v. L.B.S. Bank-New York Inc.* 1990 U.S. Dist. Lexis 9949 (E.D. Pa, 1990).
21. S. Rep. No. 99-433, 99th Cong. 2d Sess. 9-10 (3 Sept. 1986), citing 532 F.2d at 700.
22. 532 F.2n 692 (9th Cir.), cert. denied, 426 U.S. 951 (1976).
23. *United States v. Jewell* 532 F.2d 692 at 700. See also *United States v. Valle-Valdex* 554 F.2d 911 (9th Cir. 1977). The wilful blindness instruction should not be available unless the government has presented evidence that the defendant purposely contrived to avoid learning all of the facts: *United States v. Pacific Hide and Fur Depot Inc.* 768 F.2d 1096 at 1098 (9th Cir. 1985). But see *United States v. St Michael's Credit Union* 880 F.2d 579 at 584-86 (1st Cir. 1989) (sustaining wilful blindness instruction in prosecution of bookkeeper for C.T.R. violations where evidence showed she had been told of C.T.R. requirements by bank auditor and would have been aware of cash transactions by virtue of her position).
24. 821 F.2d 844 at 855 (1987).
25. See *United States v. Time-D.C. Inc.* 381 F.Supp. 730 (W.D. Va, 1974) (corporation not liable for one alleged violation where it had not been put on notice of all of the facts constituting the offence).

appear to limit it, [26] but nonetheless the collective knowledge standard presents serious risks in defending the corporate client today.

Because of the broad scope of potential corporate liability for the acts of corporate employees, counsel representing a financial institution in a United States money laundering case may be well advised to assume its probable liability if the alleged substantive offences can be sustained. Hence, what follows is a brief overview of the more important United States money laundering statutes and recent interpretative case law.

B.S.A. CURRENCY TRANSACTION REPORTING REQUIREMENTS

Reporting Requirements

The B.S.A.'s major requirement of financial institutions is to report any currency transactions of more than $10,000 by submitting to the I.R.S. a Form 4789 (Currency Transaction Report or C.T.R.) within 15 days following the transaction. [27] Multiple transactions on one day with a financial institution (including all branches) must be treated as one *if* the institution has knowledge that they are by or for the same person. [28] The Treasury Department has stated that financial institutions are not required to adopt systems to detect multiple same-day transactions, but

26. See *First Equity Corp. of Florida v. Standard and Poor's Corp.* 690 F.Supp. 256 (S.D.N.Y., 1988), affd, 869 F.2d 175 (2d Cir. 1989) (at least one single employee must have the culpable state of mind to find the corporation liable): Accord *United States v. L.B.S. Bank-New York Inc.* 1990 U.S. Dist. Lexis 9949 (E.D. Pa, 1990); see also *Kern Oil & Refining Co. v. Tenneco Oil Co.* 792 F.2d 1380 (9th Cir. 1986), cert. denied, 480 U.S. 906 (1987).

27. 31 U.S.C. s. 5313; 31 C.F.R. ss 103.22, 103.26(a). A revised C.T.R. form became effective 1 January 1990. The major changes to the C.T.R. are a requirement to report the date of birth and social security number of the person conducting the transaction and the person on whose behalf it is conducted (see Treasury B.S.A. Administrative Ruling 89-5). The new form also contains a check-off box to denote whether the transaction is "suspicious". This reporting requirement may apply to individuals who act as financial institutions by conducting financial transactions for others for a fee. See *United States v. Rigdon* 874 F.2d 774 (11th Cir. 1989); *United States v. Hawley* 855 F.2d 595 (8th Cir. 1988), cert. denied, 109 S. Ct. 1141 (1989). But see *United States v. Bucey* 876 F.2d 1297 (7th Cir. 1989).

28. 31 C.F.R. s. 103.22(a). See 51 Fed. Reg. 45108 (17 December 1986); 52 Fed. Reg. 11436 (8 April 1987); 55 Fed. Reg. 1021 (11 January 1990); *United States v. Besmajian* 910 F.2d 1153 at 1158 (3d Cir. 1990). Night or weekend deposits are treated as next business day deposits. Before April 1987, the only written instruction on multiple transactions was found on Form 4789 itself and I.R.S. Publication 1178 (Rev. 4-83). See e.g. *United States v. Tobon-Builes* 706 F.2d 1092 (11th Cir. 1983).

The C.T.R. must identify the person conducting the transaction and the person on whose behalf the transaction was made. See 31 C.F.R. 103.27, 54 Fed. Reg. 3023 (23 January 1989). This regulation was adopted to correct an ambiguity identified in *United States v. Murphy* 809 F.2d 1427 (9th Cir. 1987) and *United States v. Gimbel* 632 F. Supp. 713 (E.D. Wis., 1984). Accord *United States v. Bucey* 876 F.2d 1297 (7th Cir. 1989). But see *United States v. Palma* (unreported, S.D. Tex., 19 May 1989, Cr. No. H-88-201). See also *United States v. Bosch* 914 F.2d 1239 (9th Cir. 1990).

if existing systems aggregate data, they must be used to detect multiple deposits.[29]

The B.S.A. (31 U.S.C. s. 5322(a)) provides misdemeanour criminal penalties of up to one year's imprisonment and up to $1,000 in fines for anyone wilfully[30] violating the Act or regulations. Felony enhancement is provided in 31 U.S.C. s. 5322(b) for anyone wilfully violating the Act or regulations while violating another federal law[31] or as part of a pattern of illegal activity involving transactions of more than $100,000 in a 12-month period; the felony provision authorises up to a $500,000 fine and/or up to ten years' imprisonment.[32]

Recent Amendments

Amendments in 1988 expanded the statutory definition of financial institution under 31 U.S.C. s. 5312(a)(2) to include businesses involved in vehicle sales (auto, air, boat) and real estate closing or found by the Treasury Secretary to be engaging in similar or related activity or whose cash transactions have a high degree of usefulness in criminal, tax, or regulatory matters.[33]

The 1988 legislation also added a new identification/reporting requirement (31 U.S.C. s. 5325), implemented by Treasury Regulations

29. See 52 Fed. Reg. 11436 (8 April 1987). See *United States v. American Investors of Pittsburgh* 879 F.2d 1087 at 1099 (3d Cir. 1989); *United States v. St Michael's Credit Union* 880 F.2d 579 at 585 (1st Cir. 1989) (financial institutions are not required to aggregate into one reportable transaction separate currency transfers by the same person on the same day at the same branch); *United States v. Paris* 706 F. Supp. 184 at 187 (E.D. N.Y., 1988). Treasury's preface to the April 1987 rules states that "knowledge" means "knowledge on the part of a partner, director, officer or employee of a financial institution, or on the part of any existing system at the institution that permits it to aggregate transactions". Treasury also adopted the concept of knowledge by "wilful blindness" as discussed in *United States v. Jewell* 532 F.2d 692 at 700.
      In 1990, Treasury proposed a new rule that would require banks with deposits exceeding U.S.$100 million to maintain systems to aggregate currency transactions by or on behalf of the same customers during a business day. 55 Fed. Reg. 36663 (6 September 1990). This proposal is not expected to be finalised until 1992.
30. This scienter requirement has been interpreted to mean a "knowing failure to obey the law with specific intent to disobey the law": *United States v. Sans* 731 F.2d 1521 at 1530 (11th Cir. 1984), cert. denied, 105 S.Ct 791 (1985). See *United States v. Kington* 875 F.2d 1091 at 1105 (5th Cir. 1989) (re evidence sufficient to show knowledge of C.T.R requirements). Cf. *United States v. Alzate-Restrepo* 890 F.2d 1061 (9th Cir. 1989) (evidence that various postings at airport announcing C.M.I.R. reporting requirements sufficient to establish the defendant's knowledge of the reporting requirement).
31. See *United States v. Kington* 875 F.2d 1091 at 1106 (5th Cir. 1989) (C.T.R. non-filings in the course of bank fraud).
32. Individual B.S.A. violations may constitute separate felony counts if they form the requisite pattern of activity and occur in a 12-month period. E.g. *United States v. So* 755 F.2d 1350 at 1355 (9th Cir. 1985); *United States v. Valdes-Guerra* 758 F.2d 1411 (11th Cir. 1985); *United States v. Dickinson* 706 F.2d 88 at 96 (2nd Cir. 1983). To form a pattern, the transactions must be "repeated and related": *United States v. St Michael's Credit Union* 880 F.2d 579 at 586-87 (1st Cir. 1989), quoting *United States v. Bank of New England* 821 F.2d 844 at 853. Where the institution has never filed a C.T.R., the prosecution is not required to establish a linkage: *St Michael's Credit Union* at 587.
33. Treasury was given regulatory authority over these entities. 12 U.S.C. s. 1953(b).

103.29[34] providing that no financial institution may issue or sell a bank, traveller's or cashier's cheque or money order for $3,000 or more in cash except to an account holder or to a person providing identification as specified in the regulation. The other significant amendment was enactment of a "targeting" provision, 31 U.S.C. s. 5326, giving the Secretary authority to order financial institutions in a targeted geographic area to (i) obtain any information the Secretary demands concerning any transaction described in the order; (ii) maintain a record of such information for as long as the Secretary requires; and (iii) file a report of such information as required in the Secretary's order. Treasury adopted targeting rules in August 1989.[35]

"Structuring" Offence

Under the pre-1986 B.S.A. statute, many courts held that customers who "structured" or otherwise contrived transactions to evade the reporting requirements could not be held criminally responsible under the B.S.A.[36] Congress passed legislation in 1986 to over-rule these decisions[37] by prohibiting the "structuring" of currency transactions to evade the C.T.R. reporting requirements.[38]

The term "structures" is not defined in the statute, but the legislative history[39] indicates that Congress intended to cover the type of conduct discussed in existing case law in which persons broke down and separately made cash deposits or withdrawals in $10,000 or less amounts in one account on different days or in different accounts in order to evade the C.T.R. reporting requirements.[40]

34. See 55 Fed. Reg. 20139 (22 May 1990).
35. See 31 C.F.R. ss 103.26, 103.33(d), 54 Fed. Reg. 33679-80 (16 August 1989).
36. See e.g. *United States v. Mastronardo* 849 F.2d 799 (3d Cir. 1988); *United States v. Gimbel* 830 F.2d 621 at 625 (7th Cir. 1987); *United States v. Varbel* 780 F.2d 758 (9th Cir. 1986); *United States v. Denmark* 779 F.2d 1559 (11th Cir. 1986); *United States v. Larson* 796 F.2d 244 (8th Cir. 1986); *United States v. Anzalone* 766 F.2d 676 (1st Cir. 1985). But see *United States v. Besmajian* 910 F.2d 1153 (3d Cir. 1990).
    Recently, courts have tended to sustain structuring convictions under the old law if high level bank officials were involved in the structuring. See *United States v. Kington* 875 F.2d 1091 at 1105 (5th Cir. 1989); *United States v. Rigdon* 874 F.2d 774 (11th Cir. 1989); *United States v. Donahue* 885 F.2d 45 (3d Cir. 1989); *United States v. Polychron* 841 F.2d 833 (8th Cir.), cert. denied, 109 S. Ct 135 (1988); *United States v. Pilla* 861 F.2d 1078 (8th Cir. 1988). See *United States v. Paris* 706 F. Supp. 184 (E.D.N.Y. 1988) (attempting to synthesise cases).
37. See S. Rep. No. 99-433 99th Cong., 2d Sess. (3 September 1986) at 3; H. Rep. No. 99-746, 99th Cong., 2d Sess. 18-19 (1986); and *United States v. Herron* 825 F.2d 50 at 55-56 (5th Cir. 1987).
38. 31 U.S.C. s. 5324. The prosecution must prove that the defendant knew of the reporting requirements and set out to evade them. See e.g. *United States v. Puerto* 730 F.2d 627 (11th Cir.), cert. denied, 105 S. Ct 162 (1984).
39. S. Rep. 99-433, 99th Cong., 2d Sess. (3 September 1986); H. Rep. No. 99-746. See *United States v. Scanio* 705 F. Supp. 768 (W.D.N.Y., 1988).
40. See e.g. *United States v. Heyman* 794 F.2d 788 (2d Cir. 1986); *United States v. Tobon-Builes* 706 F.2d 1092 (11th Cir. 1983). See also *United States v. Gimbel* 830 F.2d 621 (7th Cir. 1987); *United States v. Thompson* 603 F.2d 1200 (5th Cir. 1979); *United States v. Tota* 672 F. Supp. 716 (S.D.N.Y., 1987). For another example of structuring, see *United States v. American Investors of Pittsburgh* 879 F.2d 1087 (3d Cir. 1989) (brokerage firm president and other officers regularly stored cash in a bank safe deposit box and dribbled in cash deposits).

The United States Treasury Department has adopted an extremely broad definition of "structuring" to include any currency transaction conducted "in any manner" if for the purpose of evading C.T.R. reporting.[41] Recently, the Second Circuit held that a structuring conviction requires only proof that the defendant knew of the reporting obligation and intended to avoid it.[42] The government thus may not be required to prove that the defendant knew that structuring is unlawful.[43] Treasury has also notified banks that they are required to file criminal referrals on persons who appear to have engaged in structuring,[44] but, other than providing some obvious examples of structuring,[45] Treasury has not given any more clear definition of the term. Courts have rejected, however, challenges that the statute is unconstitutionally vague.[46]

Thus banks and broker dealers are essentially left to identify such transactions on their own, possibly to be second-guessed later on. Unfortunately, the second-guessing could come in the context of a criminal prosecution. In *United States v. L.B.S. Bank—New York Inc.*[47] the government charged the bank with a s. 371 conspiracy for, among other things, failing to report a customer's attempted structuring as required by F.D.I.C. regulation 12 C.F.R. s. 353.1.[48] The bank moved to dismiss on vagueness, among other, grounds.[49] The bank was convicted

41. 31 C.F.R. s. 103.11(n), 54 Fed. Reg. 3023 (23 January 1989). Treasury also has recently adopted a regulation making it illegal to structure the transportation of monetary instruments to avoid C.M.I.R.S. 54 Fed. Reg. 28416 (6 July 1989). See 31 U.S. s. 5316.
42. *United States v. Scanio* 900 F.2d 485 (2d Cir. 1990).
43. The court rejected the defendant's argument that a Treasury proposed rule requiring banks to post notices of s. 5324 (53 Fed. Reg. 7948 (1988)) indicated the government's agreement with the proposition that it had to prove a defendant's knowledge of s. 5324. Treasury withdrew this proposed rule in 1989 (54 Fed. Reg. 20398).
44. Treasury Administrative Ruling 88-1, 53 Fed. Reg. 40063, 40064-66 (13 October 1988). Other regulations, imposed by the bank regulatory authorities, require criminal referrals on any suspected violations of federal laws. See below, n. 48.
45. 53 Fed. Reg. 40063 (13 October 1988) and 54 Fed. Reg. 3023, 3025-26 (23 January 1989).
46. *United States v. Camarena* 863 F.2d 880 (table, unpublished) (per cur.), cert. denied, 109 S. Ct 3158 (1989); *United States v. Maroun* 739 F. Supp. 684 (D. Mass. 1990); *United States v. Davenport* 740 F. Supp. 1371 (S.D. Ind., 1990); *United States v. Thakkar* 721 F. Supp. 1030 (S.D. Ind., 1989); *United States v. McKinney* 919 F.2d 146 (D. Or., 1989); *United States v. Scanio* 705 F. Supp. 768 (W.D.N.Y., 1988). In May 1989, Treasury withdrew a proposed regulation that would have required financial institutions to warn customers of the structuring prohibition.
47. 1990 U.S. Dist. Lexis (E.D. Pa, 1989).
48. The F.D.I.C. regulation requires a criminal referral when the financial institution has a known factual basis for a belief that a crime has been or may have been committed. The O.C.C. (12 C.F.R s. 21.11(h)(5)) and Office of Thrift Supervision (12 C.F.R. s. 563.18(d)(iv)) have the same type of regulation. The Federal Reserve Board has not adopted a regulation requiring criminal referrals but takes the position that such a requirement flows from the bank's obligation to maintain safe and sound banking practices. See S.R. 88-9 (F.I.S.) (18 March 1988); cf. S.R. 85-22 (F.I.S.) (16 August 1985). The bank regulatory agencies have adopted uniform forms for making criminal referrals. See Federal Reserve Form 2230.
49. The defence also challenged F.D.I.C.'s authority to issue 12 C.F.R. s. 353.1 and made Fourth and Fifth Amendment challenges to the C.T.R. and criminal referral regulations.

in 1989 after the court denied the motion to dismiss,[50] but the issue may resurface on appeal.

Reporting of Wire Transfers

In 1988, the government returned its first indictment of a bank under s. 1956 in a case based solely on non-currency transactions and principally involving alleged wire transfers.[51] Following that indictment, Treasury, through bank regulatory agencies, issued general guidelines in late October 1988 on wire transfers,[52] and in late October 1989 issued an advance notice of proposed rulemaking requesting comments on reporting and record-keeping requirements governing international funds transfers.[53] Treasury's notice appeared to envision requiring banks to secure the identification of any sender or recipient of an international wire transfer.

Banks and some brokerage firms opposed aspects of the proposal, principally any requirement affecting incoming transfers from foreign countries. Annually, dollar denominated wire transfers in the United States electronic payments system average approximately $325 trillion. Volume only on the Clearing House for Interbank Payments (C.H.I.P.S.) (95 per cent of which is international) averages about $700 billion *per day*. Despite the enormous burdens that any wire transfer reporting requirement would impose on the banking channels (and the lack of any proven cost-effectiveness of B.S.A. reporting), Treasury is proceeding with proposed wire transfer record-keeping rules because Congress is likely to pass legislation that will require Treasury to have final rules.

On 15 October 1990 Treasury proposed final wire transfer rules[54] requiring banks to maintain certain identifying information regarding the originators and beneficiaries of wire transfers. The originating bank must retain the name of the originator and person on whose behalf the funds transfer was originated, the amount and date of the funds transfer, the payment instruction, and the name of the beneficiary and identity of the beneficiary's bank. Beneficiary banks must maintain the name of the recipient and person on whose behalf the funds were received as well as the amount and date of the funds transfer, the payment instruction and the name and account number of the originator. Intermediary banks must retain whatever information they receive from the preceding bank in the funds transfer process. Comments on the proposed rules were

50. *United States v. L.B.S. Bank-New York Inc.* 1990 U.S. Dist. Lexis 9949 (E.D. Pa, 1989) (Memorandum and Order denying pre-trial motions of defendants).
51. *United States v. Awan* (unreported, M.D. Fla, 5 October 1989, Cr. No. 88-330-Cr-T-13B. According to the indictment, which grew out of a government undercover operation, government agents collected currency from alleged narcotics sales, deposited the currency in undercover accounts at local banks, wire transferred the proceeds to another undercover account at a Florida bank, and then wire transferred the funds again to certain of the defendant bank's foreign branches.
52. See O.C.C. Advisory Letter 88-5 (26 October 1988). Financial institutions were strongly recommended to report suspicious wire transfers or other transactions to their local I.R.S. criminal investigation division or local United States Customs Service.
53. 53 Fed. Reg. 45770-71 (31 October 1989).
54. 55 Fed. Reg. 41696 (15 October 1990). This rule is not expected to be finalised until 1992.

completed in January 1991, and some of the most severe criticisms were lodged by the Federal Reserve Board. As of the end of 1991, a revised unpublished draft rule was under consideration by the Treasury Department.

CRIMINAL MONEY LAUNDERING OFFENCES

More significant than the B.S.A. reporting requirements are the Title 18 M.L.C. Act criminal provisions outlawing a wide range of financial transactions beyond those involving merely the physical transfer of cash. In general, M.L.C. Act s. 1956 creates a criminal offence for knowingly engaging in domestic or international financial transactions involving criminally-derived funds with the intent to promote the unlawful activity or knowledge that the transaction is designed to conceal the ownership, source or control of the funds or to avoid reporting requirements. Section 1957 prohibits knowingly engaging in virtually any financial transaction exceeding $10,000 when the defendant knows that the property is criminally derived and the property is in fact derived from specified unlawful activity.[55] The *Anti-Drug Abuse Act* 1988 and the Omnibus Crime Bill 1990, which passed in late October 1990, significantly expanded these statutes. In addition, M.L.C. Act violations give rise to possible forfeiture of bank collateral under forfeiture laws which are discussed below, pp. 395-398.

Section 1956

Section 1956 imposes criminal penalties of up to 20 years' imprisonment and/or fines up to $500,000 or twice the value of the property involved, whichever is greater.[56] Section 1956(a)(1) applies to domestic transactions, and s. 1956(a)(2) applies to "transporting" instruments or funds out of or into the United States.

The 1988 M.L.C. Act amendments created a new government "sting" offence by adding to s. 1956(a) a subpara. (3) imposing the same penalties on anyone who after 18 November 1988, conducts or attempts to conduct a financial transaction involving property *represented by a law enforcement officer* to be the proceeds of specified unlawful activity, or property used to conduct or facilitate specified unlawful activity; to conceal property believed to be proceeds of specified unlawful activity, with the intent to promote specified unlawful activity; or to avoid a state or federal reporting requirement.[57] Although the statute is loosely

55. The M.L.C.A. also added civil and criminal forfeiture statutes, 18 U.S.C. ss 981 and 982, which were expanded in 1988. See below, p. 395.
56. Under the United States sentencing guidelines, a s. 1956 conviction carries a Base Offence level of 20 (or 23 if based on an intent to promote specified unlawful activity), if the value of the funds was less than $100,000. Offence levels increase up to 24 (or 27) if the value goes up to $1 million, etc. Under Sentencing Guidelines for Organisations, effective 1 November 1991, these offence levels translate into fines ranging up to four times the amount of funds laundered through the institution.
57. The term "represented" means any representation made by a law enforcement officer or by another person at the direction of, or with the approval of, a federal official authorised to investigate or prosecute violations of 18 U.S.C. s. 1956: 18 U.S.C. s. 1956(a)(3). Defence motions to dismiss sting indictments based on inadequate allegations of the "representation" element have thus far not been successful.

drafted, it probably requires proof that the defendant believed the property was proceeds of specified unlawful activity. Otherwise the "representation" element is subject to a strong constitutional challenge for vagueness. The 1990 Crime Bill extended this sting provision to s. 1956(a)(2).

In *United States v. Silberman*[58] the government brought one of the first s. 1956(a)(3) "sting" indictments[59] against a California businessman and others alleging a series of transactions in undercover funds represented to be proceeds of drug trafficking. The defence raised a number of significant legal challenges to the indictment that were rejected by the court. In the summer of 1990 the defendant was convicted on one count of the indictment.

Domestic Transactions[60]

Section 1956(a)(1) has essentially four elements. Penalties may be imposed on anyone who:

(i) conducts or attempts to conduct a financial transaction;

(ii) knowing that the property represents proceeds of some form of unlawful activity;

(iii) the transaction in fact involves proceeds of specified unlawful activity; and

(iv) (scienter)

(a) with intent to promote specified unlawful activity or engage in conduct violating I.R.S. Code Sections 7201, 7206[61]

(b) knows that the transaction is designed to conceal proceeds of specified unlawful activity or

(c) knows that transaction is designed to avoid a reporting requirement under State or federal law.

Important definitions

"A financial transaction"

Section 1956(c)(4), defining "financial transaction", was clarified in the 1990 Crime Bill to mean (i) the movement of funds by wire or other means or involving monetary instruments which affect interstate commerce; or (ii) any transaction "involving the use of a financial institution" (as defined in the B.S.A. and its regulations) engaged in, or

58. Unreported, S.D. Cal, second superseding indictment filed 2 March 1990, No. 89-0417-JCI-Crim.

59. See also *United States v. Brumlik* (unreported, M.D. Fla, 1989, Cr. No. 89-234-Cr; *United States v. L.B.S. Bank-New York Inc.* 1990 U.S. Dist. Lexis 9949 (E.D. Pa, 1989).

60. Extraterritorial jurisdiction (s. 1956(f)) is provided for conduct by a United States citizen or, if not by a United States citizen, if conduct occurs "in part" in the United States (s. 1956(f)(1)) and the transaction(s) involve funds/instruments of a value exceeding $10,000 (s. 1956(f)(2)). Anytime trades are executed in United States dollars, this standard could arguably be satisfied because all dollar transactions are booked in United States correspondent banks.

61. The 1988 Amendments added the income tax scienter element only to s. 1956(a)(i); evasion/fraud scienter is not included in the new sting provision (see text above, p. 383 or the other M.L.C. Act provisions, e.g. 18 U.S.C. ss 1956(a)(2) and 1957.

the activities of which, affect interstate commerce. The term is thus not limited to transactions involving financial institutions.[62]

In *United States v. Awan*[63] the government charged, as single counts under s. 1956(a)(1), a series of deposits, wire transfers and credit transactions, and the defence move to dismiss on the ground that they were duplicitous.[64] The court rejected this contention, concluding that the indictment plainly charged that each series of transactions involved the same "proceeds" and thus constituted a continuing course of conduct.

In *Awan*, the defence also argued that the counts charging a s. 846[65] conspiracy (to aid and abet narcotics distribution) and s. 371 conspiracy to violate s. 1956 were multiplicitous. The court rejected this argument but put the government on notice that it would grant a r. 29 motion to dismiss the s. 846 count if the government's only evidence at trial consisted of proof of money laundering. Significantly for banks, the court held that Congress, in enacting the M.L.C. Act indicated it did not intend "to permit money laundering (without additional narcotics activity) to be punished under both Title 21 conspiracy law" and the M.L.C. Act.[66]

"Proceeds"

Under s. 1956(a)(1), the property involved in the transactions must be "proceeds" of specified unlawful activity and the defendant must know that the property represents "proceeds" of some form of criminal activity. The statute does not define the term "proceeds", and some defence counsel have argued that the term necessarily is more limited than the phrase "criminally derived property" used in s. 1957. To date, however, courts have adopted an expansive view of the meaning of "proceeds" in s. 1956.[67] Recently, the Eighth Circuit adopted an extremely broad view in holding that the government is not required to trace the proceeds to a specific predicate offence: *United States v. Blackman*.[68] In *Blackman*, the court held that the government had satisfied its burden of proof that the proceeds were derived from a drug-trafficking offence by evidence that the defendant had been involved in drug trafficking, had no legitimate source of income, transferred money by Western Union[69] and used the funds for a downpayment on the purchase of an automobile.[70] In the court's view, this circumstantial

---

62. See also S. Rep. No. 99-433, 99th Cong., 2d Sess. (3 September 1986) at 13.
63. Unreported, M.D. Fla, 5 December 1989, Cr. No. 88-330-Cr.-T-13 (B).
64. See *United States v. Woods* 780 F.2d 955 (11th Cir.), cert. denied, 476 U.S. 1184 (1986).
65. 21 U.S.C. s. 846.
66. *United States v. Awan* (unreported, M.D. Fla, 5 December 1989, No. 88-330-Cr-T-13B, slip op. at 15).
67. See *United States v. Mainieri* 694 F. Supp. 1394 (S.D. Fla, 1988) (holding that the term "proceeds" is clear in context to mean "source of the money").
68. 897 F.2d 309 (8th Cir. 1990).
69. The government's expert witness testified that drug dealers commonly use wire services in furthering drug activities.
70. The government's expert witness testified that drug dealers prefer to drive automobiles that are encumbered by a lien to protect the car from government seizure under forfeiture laws.

evidence was sufficient to create the inference that the money used to purchase the automobile was proceeds from drug distribution.

In *United States v. Awan*[71] the defence argued that the term "proceeds" in s. 1956 did not encompass funds placed in several different government undercover bank accounts and commingled with other funds before being transferred to the defendant bank. The court held that the statute covers "proceeds" exchanged through a series of intervening transactions and changed in form, even if commingled with other funds under general banking principle. Moreover, passing the allegedly illicit funds through the hands of undercover agents, accounts, and/or banks did not transform them in to government funds because they were not transacted in "the normal course of Government business", slip op. at 20-21, citing *United States v. Ospina*.[72]

Knowledge that the property represents proceeds of "some form of unlawful activity"

As defined in s. 1956(c)(1), the defendant does not need to know exactly what crime generated the funds involved, but only that the funds are the proceeds of some felony under federal or State law.[73] The 1990 Crime Bill expanded this knowledge to include knowledge of foreign law violations. The purpose of this amendment was apparently to take account of the fact that the statute covers drug law offences against foreign nations.[74] Unfortunately the legislative history does not provide this explanation. Thus, the statute as broadened could be read to permit the prosecution of a person who believes her or his funds are merely derived from violations of foreign currency control laws or any other foreign law violations, provided, of course, that the other elements of the offence are established.

The "knowing" scienter requirement includes "wilful blindness"[75] and can be shown by evidence of out-of-the-ordinary dealing or commissions.[76] Congress rejected, however, a proposal to require a reckless or "reason to know" scienter standard.[77]

"Specified unlawful activity"

"Specified unlawful activity," as defined in s. 1956(c)(7), includes most United States federal white collar and drug offences: all R.I.C.O. predicate offences in 18 U.S.C. s. 1961(e) (except B.S.A. offences, which are included in the operative language of s. 1956); continuing criminal enterprise drug offences in 21 U.S.C. s. 848; drug offences under foreign law; and a variety of fraud offences, such as theft, embezzlement, and bank bribery. The 1988 legislation added certain federal customs,

71. Unreported, M.D. Fla, 5 December 1989, Cr. No. 88-330-Cr-T-13B (Order Denying Defendants' Joint Motions to Dismiss Second Superceding Indictment and denying Defendants' Joint Motion to Dismiss Counts One and Two).
72. 798 F.2d 1570 (11th Cir. 1986).
73. See also S. Rep. No. 99-433, 99th Cong., 2d Sess. (3 September 1986) at 8.
74. 18 U.S.C. s. 1956(c)(7)(B).
75. See S. Rep. No. 99-433, 99th Cong., 2d Sess. (3 September 1986) at 9-10.
76. See H. R. Rep No. 855, 99th Cong., 2d Sess. 13 (1986).
77. See S. Rep. No. 99-433, 99th Cong., 2d Sess. (3 September 1986) at 9.

copyright, and drug offences.[78] The 1990 Crime Bill added a number of environmental crimes and bank fraud crimes.[79] As of mid 1990, about 40 per cent of money laundering indictments in the United States were based on fraud and other non-drug related predicate offences.[80]

"With intent to promote specified unlawful activity"

The term "promote" was substituted in the final legislation for the term "facilitate", which would have been less burdensome on the prosecution.[81] Compare 18 U.S.C. s. 1952(a)(3) (proscribing use of any facility of interstate commerce to "promote" any unlawful activity): *United States v. Polizzi*.[82]

Knowledge that the transaction is designed to avoid a reporting requirement under State or federal law

Reporting requirements would include those under 26 U.S.C. s. 6050I and 31 U.S.C. s. 5311 et seq. States that currently have reporting requirements include California, Florida, Georgia, Hawaii, Maine, Maryland, North Carolina and Rhode Island.

An argument can be made that this knowledge element is unconstitutionally vague on the ground that it effectively transfers the intent of the customer to the bank employee.[83] Thus far courts have rejected this argument.[84]

Section 1956(a)(2): International Transportation

Subsection 1956(a)(2) imposes the same, 20 year, $500,000 fine, maximum penalties on anyone who transports funds or monetary instruments under prescribed circumstances. Section 1956(a)(2) imposes penalties on anyone who:

    (i) transports transmits or transfers a monetary instrument or funds;

    (ii) into or out of the U.S.;

    (iii) (scienter)

        (A) with the intent to promote specified unlawful activity or

        (B) knowing that the funds represent proceeds of some form of unlawful activity under State or federal law and either

78. Those added were 18 U.S.C. ss 542, 549, 2319, 1590, 830, and 857.
79. The 1990 Crime Bill added felony violations of the *Water Pollution Control Act* (33 U.S.C. s. 1251), *Ocean Dumping Act* (33 U.S.C. s. 1401), *Act to Prevent Pollution from Ships* (33 U.S.C. s. 1901), *Safe Drinking Act* (42 U.S.C. s. 300F), and *Resources Conservation Act* (42 U.S.C. s. 6901). The legislation gives the United States Environmental Protection Agency authority concurrent with the Department of Justice to investigate money laundering offences predicated on these offences.

    The new legislation also added the crimes of fraud by a bank officer or employee (18 U.S.C. ss 1005-06), fraud by any person on the Federal Deposit Insurance Corporation (18 U.S.C. s. 1007), and fraud in any loan application to a federally regulated depository institution (18 U.S.C. s. 1014).
80. Bureau of National Affairs, 4 *B.N.A. Criminal Practice Manual* 487 (17 October 1990).
81. See S. Rep. No. 99-433, 99th Cong., 2d Sess. (3 September 1986) at 10.
82. 500 F.2d 856 (9th Cir. 1974); cert. denied, 419 U.S. 1121 (1975).
83. See Strafer (1989) 27 Am. Crim. L. Rev. 149.
84. See *United States v. Ortiz* 738 F. Supp. 1394 (S.D. Fla, 1990).

—knowing that the transport is designed to conceal proceeds of specified unlawful activity or

—knowing that transport is designed to avoid reporting requirements under State or federal law.

Important Definitions

"Proceeds"

The 1990 Crime Bill amended s. 1956(a)(2)(B) to clarify that it does not necessarily require proof that the proceeds be of specified unlawful activity. The 1990 amendment provides that the prosecution may establish culpable knowledge under this statute by proving "that a law enforcement officer represented the matter specified in subpara. (B) as true, and the defendant's subsequent statements or actions indicate that the defendant believed such representations to be true." Thus government undercover funds arguably may be used as a basis for a s. 1956(a)(2) prosecution. At least two courts had taken this view even before the clarifying amendment: *United States v. Parramore*;[85] *United States v. Awan.*[86]

"Monetary instrument or funds"

The definition of "monetary instrument" in s. 1956(c)(5) was originally limited to include any United States coin or currency, cheque, and securities or negotiable instruments in bearer form or "otherwise in such form that title thereto passes upon delivery".[87] The 1990 Crime Bill expanded this definition to include foreign currency denominated instruments and to clarify that the "bearer form" limitation applies only to investment securities and negotiable instruments. Thus, the statute covers cheque and most banking instruments. The term "funds" is not defined.

"Transports"

Before 1988, s. 1956(a)(2) was limited to transportation of monetary instruments or funds. The Department of Justice took the position[88] that the term included wire transfers, apparently in part because of the inclusion of the term "funds". The 1986 legislative history, however, does not support this view. This provision grew out of a house Bill expanding the then existing requirement of reporting the international transportation of monetary instruments and there is no explanation in the 1986 legislative history suggesting any broader meaning. The 1988

85. 20 F. Supp. 799 at 802-804 (N.D. Cal., 1989), per Lynch J. In his analysis, Judge Lynch ruled in part on the legislative history of the 1988 "sting" amendment which reflected statements that s. 1956(a)(1) could not be used in undercover operations but made no reference to a similar interpretation of s. 1956(a)(2).
 Two courts have held that charging ss 1956(a)(1) and 1956(a)(2) (see above, p. 383) are not multiplicitous because s. 1956(a)(1) requires proof of "in fact" derivation of the proceeds from specified unlawful activity. See *United States v. Parramore* 720 F.Supp. 799 (N.D. Cal., 1989); *United States v. Awan* (unreported, M.D. Fla, 5 Dec. 1989, No. 88-330-Cr-T-13B).
86. Unreported, M.D. Fla, 5 December 1989, No. 88-330-Cr-T-13B.
87. See S. Rep. No. 99-433 at 13.
88. See Department of Justice, *Handbook on the Anti-Drug Abuse Act of 1986* (1987) p. 73, n. 59.

M.L.C. Act legislation amended the operative language to be "transports, *transmits, or transfers*," and an explanatory comment by Senator Biden[89] in 1988 indicated that the intent of this amendment was to "clarify" Congress's intent in 1986 to include wire transfers in s. 1956(a)(2).

In *United States v. Awan*, the defence moved to dismiss s. 1956(a)(2) counts on the ground that, as enacted in 1986, the statute did not cover wire transfers but only physical transportations. The court rejected this argument on the basis of Senator Biden's explanation that the 1988 amendment was intended only to clarify Congress' intent to include wire transfers in the 1986 Bill.

Section 1957

Section 1957 essentially requires proof only that the defendant knowingly engaged or attempted to engage in a monetary transaction involving funds with the knowledge that they were greater than $10,000 and were criminally derived, and that in fact were derived from specified unlawful activity. Section 1957 was designed in part to prosecute those who provide goods and services to criminal elements and knowingly accept criminally derived proceeds as payment.[90]

Section 1957 is arguably broader than s. 1956 because it does not require proof that the defendant intended to promote an illegal activity or knew that the transaction was designed to conceal the proceeds or to avoid reporting requirements. It does not, however, contain a "sting" provision like s. 1956(a)(1). Nor does it contain the tax fraud, scienter elements added to s. 1956(a)(1) in 1988.

Section 1957 imposes penalties of up to a ten year term of imprisonment and/or a fine of up to twice the amount of the criminally derived property involved in the transaction or $250,000[91] for any

---

89. 134 Cong. Rec. S 17367 (10 November 1988).
90. When enacted, s. 1957 gave the defence bar serious concerns because it would allow prosecution of a defence attorney who knowingly received and deposited more than $10,000 in criminally derived funds as legal fees. In response, D.O.J. adopted a formal "prosecution policy" regarding prosecutions of defence attorneys under s. 1957 for receipt of criminally derived funds as legal fees in a criminal case.

   Under this D.O.J. policy, prosecutions would be brought only with the approval of the Assistant Attorney-General of the Criminal Division and would not be brought in any case in which the defence attorney received the funds as bona fide fees for representation of the client/payer in a criminal matter unless (i) the defence attorney had *actual knowledge* of the criminal derivation of the property and (ii) the defence attorney acquired such actual knowledge from a source other than confidential attorney-client communications or her or his own efforts in provided effective representation for the client/payer in the criminal case. See *United States Attorney's Manual* (1991) s. 9.105-400.

   In 1988 Congress provided a very limited exemption for attorney fee transactions "necessary to preserve a person's right to representation as guaranteed by the Sixth Amendment." This amendment probably became meaningless upon the Supreme Court's decisions in *United States v. Monsanto* 109 S. Ct 2657 (1989) and *Caplin and Drysdale, Chartered v. United States* 109 S. Ct 2646 (1989). Compare *United States v. Kelly* 888 F.2d 732 (11th Cir. 29 September 1989) (reversing a s. 846 conviction of a defence attorney based solely on his conversations with his client-turned-informer).
91. See 18 U.S.C. s. 1957(b)(1) and 18 U.S.C. s. 3623. Under the Sentencing Guidelines, a s. 1957 conviction carries a Base Offence Level of 17, increased by 5 if the defendant knew the proceeds were derived from narcotics-related activity.

knowing receipt of criminally derived funds exceeding a value of $10,000 and involving a financial institution.

This offence has essentially seven elements. Penalties may be imposed on anyone who:

- engages or attempts to engage
- in a monetary transaction,
- in criminally derived property,
- of a value exceeding $10,000,
- knowing that the property is criminally derived and is of a value exceeding $10,000[92]
- property is in fact derived from specified unlawful activity and
- takes place in the United States or its territorial jurisdiction or takes place outside the United States but the defendant is a United States person.

Important Definitions

"Engages or attempts to engage"

The statute does not define "engage", nor does the legislative history shed any light on the question. Arguably the term is thus narrower than the term "conducts" in s. 1956.

"Monetary transaction"

This term is defined in s. 1957(f) as a deposit, withdrawal, transfer, or exchange in, or affecting, interstate or foreign commerce,[93] of funds or a monetary instrument as defined in 18 U.S.C. s. 1956(c)(5),[94] by, through, or to a financial institution as defined in 31 U.S.C. s. 5312.[95]

Knowledge that property is criminally derived

Criminally derived property is defined in s. 1957(f)(2) as any property constituting or derived from proceeds obtained from any criminal offence and thus may impose broader liability than its counterpart in s. 1956. The defendant need not know that the offence from which the property is derived was specified unlawful activity.[96]

"Property" is derived from specified unlawful activity

"Specified unlawful activity" has the meaning given in s. 1956. See *United States v. Baker*[97] (s. 1957 prosecution based on alleged financial transactions in proceeds of mail fraud, and interstate transportation of stolen securities).

92. See *United States v. Baker* (unreported, M.D. Fla, 28 July 1989, No. 89-83-Cr-T-15(B)) (government "must prove that the defendant knew the monetary transaction in which he engaged was in criminally derived property of a value greater than $10,000".)
93. See 18 U.S.C. s. 1952 and case law thereunder.
94. The original Act defined "monetary instrument" by reference to 31 U.S.C. s. 5312. The effect of the 1988 amendment was to expand the definition.
95. Unlike s. 1956, s. 1957 defines financial institution without reference to Treasury regulations but to the statute itself. As a consequence, while commodity brokers may not be financial institutions for purposes of s. 1956, they are for purposes of s. 1957. See 31 U.S.C. s. 5312(a)(2)(H).
96. See 18 U.S.C. s. 1957(c).
97. Unreported, M.D. Fla, 28 July 1989, No. 89-83-Cr.-T-15B.

COMPLIANCE IMPLICATIONS FOR FINANCIAL INSTITUTIONS

On 1 November 1991, the United States adopted "Guidelines for Sentencing of Organisations"[98] which significantly harshen criminal fines and other sanctions but offer substantial reductions in penalties if the institution has established programs in accord with the Guideline standards to reasonably ensure compliance and detection and reporting of possible violations. These standards provide a road map for financial institutions in attempting to reduce the risk of criminal prosecution or conviction in the United States.

Compliance Program: Commitment, Detection, and Muscle

Commitment

The institution must have a strong written policy forbidding any employee involvement in conduct constituting or having the appearance of facilitating B.S.A. or M.L.C. Act violations. When educating employees about money laundering, the bank must stress the importance of the corporate policy and tell them that violators will be disciplined, possibly reported to law enforcement agencies, and subject to criminal prosecution. The bank should obtain employees' signatures acknowledging that they have been notified of and understand this corporate policy.

The institution must also designate a high-level compliance officer who reports directly to the C.E.O. and who conveys an image of strength, intelligence, and a "cop" mentality. The bank needs to ensure genuine commitment at the highest level of management which understands the importance of quickly addressing compliance issues and recognises that lack of adequate compliance can become the institution's guillotine.

The bank must document its commitment by adopting a written compliance program that goes well beyond the minimum standards of the United States bank regulatory agencies' uniform regulations on B.S.A. compliance programs. These regulations require that a written compliance program be approved by the bank's board of directors, have a designated compliance officer, and provide for regular staff training, a system of internal control, and independent testing.[99] Beyond these generalities, the regulations are not helpful in guiding institutions toward effective compliance. Moreover, they are limited to B.S.A. compliance[100] and thus do not address most of the banking and brokerage functions affected by the M.L.C. Act and its related forfeiture laws.

---

98. See 56 Fed. Reg. 22787 (1991).
99. See 12 C.F.R. s. 21.21, (O.C.C.); 12 C.F.R. s. 563.17-7 (Office of Thrift Supervision); 12 C.F.R. Part 326 (Federal Deposit Insurance Corporation); 12 C.F.R. s. 208.14 (Federal Reserve System). The S.E.C. has not adopted similar regulations for broker-dealers.
100. See e.g. O.C.C. Handbook for Compliance, Examination Planning, Tier I and Tier II Procedures.

Detection

Any effective compliance program must have a nervous system for detecting possible violations of corporate policy and the muscle to carry out corporate policy. Having an effective nervous system means ensuring that corporate management is receiving the information that can be legally imputed to the corporation under the collective knowledge standard, regardless of whether it is actually conveyed. In the present climate, this will occur only if the bank extends coverage to all functions of the institution, not just the teller function. Compliance training must also be directed to the private banking officers, credit officers, the legal department, the wire transfer staff, and back-office personnel.

"Know your customer" policies and procedures

A diligent "know your customer" (K.Y.C.) policy is one of the most essential components of a money laundering compliance program. A K.Y.C. policy serves several purposes. Merely asking the questions will often deter undesirable customers from using the bank. Getting answers may call into question the legitimacy of the potential customer. And a good knowledge of the customer's business is essential for evaluating whether the customer's transactions are consistent with legitimate activity.

Starting point for developing a K.Y.C. policy

Many bank counsel and compliance officers find that the most difficult part of developing enhanced K.Y.C. policies and procedures is the beginning—convincing management to allocate resources and convincing operating units that they should shoulder yet another burden when banks and broker/dealers are already drowning from over-regulation. A first step is to convince the C.E.O. that the job must be done because of the substantial risks outlined in the beginning of this chapter. It should also be pointed out that eventually Treasury regulations are going to require an effective K.Y.C. policy and having one now facilitates compliance with rapidly evolving lending standards, United States wire transfer regulations and requirements being imposed by foreign jurisdictions. Banks operating internationally are already subject in some foreign jurisdictions, notably Switzerland, to know-your-customer requirements. Also, enhanced K.Y.C. procedures can promote good relations with, and expand banking services for, legitimate customers.

Secondly, it should not be assumed that the bank needs to retain outside consultants to do the job. Some of the best programs have been developed primarily in-house with occasional outside guidance from legal and compliance experts. In-house-developed programs have at least three advantages: (i) they ensure that the design of the project takes full advantage of the expertise of the staff familiar with the bank's operations and clientele; (ii) they promote more immediate acceptance of the procedures during implementation; and (iii) they cost a lot less.

A small or medium-sized institution may prefer to develop one, uniform account opening form and procedures. Larger institutions may find it more effective to permit variations among operating units or along functional lines (for example, retail branch operations, commercial lending, international department).

Identifying basic K.Y.C. principles: lessons from criminal prosecutions of financial institutions

The other difficult part of developing good K.Y.C. policies is determining what are the essential elements. This is particularly difficult because the United States government has not issued any K.Y.C. guidelines. One good starting point is to look at the facts of criminal cases in which banks have been in trouble. One of the most important cases to learn about is the prosecution of the Bank of Credit and Commerce International (B.C.C.I.). That case, which resulted in a sanction of approximately $15 million against the bank, teaches that what was standard K.Y.C. policy a few years ago will no longer suffice.

In the B.C.C.I. case, a United States undercover officer purporting to be a registered investment adviser opened a corporate account with B.C.C.I.'s Tampa, Florida branch in January 1987. Before opening the account, the bank obtained a photographic identification (Florida driver's licence) of the "adviser", the Florida articles of incorporation of his company, and a notarised corporate resolution giving the "adviser" authority to open and be a signatory on the account. The branch also obtained a written reference from a well-established Florida bank confirming the integrity of the "adviser." The Tampa account had little activity and no large transactions. Some six months later, after a Tampa branch officer had met with the "adviser" at his place of business, the "adviser" opened an individual and corporate account with B.C.C.I.'s Panama branch following an introduction from the Tampa branch. In the following year, he met with B.C.C.I. private banking officers in Miami and foreign branches and one of the B.C.C.I. private banking officers visited the "adviser's" registered brokerage firm in New York to confirm his business relationship with the brokerage firm and his reputation in New York financial circles. The "adviser" conducted 14 transactions averaging $1 million each, in which funds from other United States banks were wire transferred to foreign B.C.C.I. branches and used as collateral for loans to the "adviser's" other foreign accounts. B.C.C.I. received no cash and no out-of-the-ordinary commissions or fees. Its criminal liability was based solely on the undercover officer's alleged statements to six B.C.C.I. officers that his customers' funds were associated with cocaine sales.

At the time of the events charged in the indictment, B.C.C.I. had a world-wide policy, stated in a compliance manual and in separate written directives, that its employees were not to violate the laws of any country or deal with customers involved in contraband. It also had a policy of reviewing the activity in any new account for the first few months. No government agency had issued any warnings regarding the use of wire transfers in money laundering, and "cash" collateralised loans were a common occurrence in international banking. Shortly after the B.C.C.I. indictment, the United States Treasury issued a notice warning banks to look for suspicious wire transfers, and a year later the O.C.C. included "cash" collateralised loans in a list of warning signs bankers should look out for.

The B.C.C.I. case teaches at least the following lessons: (i) at the account opening stage, obtaining the standard identification and bank reference information may be insufficient, depending on the circumstances, to "know" the customer and protect the bank; (ii) a K.Y.C. policy must apply not only to deposit accounts but also loans and funds transfers; (iii) merely adopting policies against employee involvement in illegal activity gives the institution no protection; (iv) monitoring of accounts for unusual or suspicious transactions must be an ongoing process; (v) the bank is at substantial risk if it relies only on government pronouncements as to what types of transactions are suspicious; (vi) the bank's foreign branches and subsidiaries must be covered by policies and procedures designed to ensure compliance not only with their jurisdiction's requirements but also with United States money laundering laws.

Essential elements of a good K.Y.C. Policy and Procedure

Any effective K.Y.C. policy must accomplish the following objectives:

- establish the minimum documentation required to ensure identification of all customers and a basis for believing that the source of any customer's deposit or collateral is legitimate;
- identify categories of customers for whom additional documentation must be required before account opening;
- identify categories of customers for whom the account documentation must be updated periodically;
- provide for documenting the source and basis of verifying any information obtained;
- provide for enforcement of a rule that no account will be opened or maintained without the required documentation; if the follow-up documentation is not obtained, the account relationship should be terminated;
- identify categories of customers whose accounts should be reviewed on a monthly, quarterly etc. basis and establish procedures for monitoring account transactions for suspicious activity;
- develop written descriptions of staff responsibilities and internal controls that ensure adherence to K.Y.C. procedures; and
- provide for independent auditors to review random samples of new account openings for compliance with existing procedures.

At the time an account is opened, the degree of the bank's inquiry necessarily should depend on the type of account and the bank's prior knowledge about the customer. Warning signals at this stage include reluctance to give bank references, details concerning the customer's business or occupation, or copies of financial statements. In today's world, given the scope of corporate criminal liability in the United States, any financial institution that does not request new corporate customers' financial statements is at risk. And the bank needs seriously to consider requiring financials for any wealthy individuals whose accounts are expected to reflect high volume or turnover.

Other warning signs include reluctance to provide information on the intended use of the account, inquiries from the customer about getting on the bank's exempt list for C.T.R. reporting, and the absence of any apparent reason for the customer's selecting the bank (such as physical proximity of the bank to the customer's residence or business).

Due diligence in the credit process: protecting the collateral from forfeiture

The 1988 United States money laundering indictment of B.C.C.I. involved extensions of cash collateralised credit facilities, a routine form of credit, particularly in international banks doing business with customers from third world debt countries.[101] The case illustrates, however, the importance of training credit officers that credit review today means ascertaining not only the credit worthiness of the borrower, but also the borrower's *legitimacy*.

Credit is also critical because of the forfeiture provisions of United States laws, which authorise forfeiture of any proceeds or property traceable to, or used to facilitate, money laundering, drug and R.I.C.O. violations. The civil and criminal forfeiture provisions of the M.L.C. Act, 18 U.S.C. ss 981, 982, which were originally limited to gross receipts, were significantly expanded in 1988. The civil provision now reaches any property involved in a M.L.C. Act or B.S.A. violation and was expanded in 1990 to cover numerous additional fraud crimes. The Government may establish entitlement to forfeiture merely upon a showing of probable cause to believe the property derives from or was used to facilitate a money laundering violation.[102] United States courts have been liberal in permitting the government to use broad account and tracing techniques to reach other property.[103] The criminal M.L.C. Act forfeiture provision, expanded to cover B.S.A. as well as M.L.C. Act violations, requires at sentencing the forfeiture of any property involved in the offence "or any property traceable to such property".[104]

To appreciate fully the importance of enhanced due diligence in the credit function, bankers need only be told the story of *Calero-Toledo v. Pearson Yacht Leasing Co.*[105] In that case, the United States Supreme Court upheld the forfeiture of a yacht because one marijuana cigarette was found on board and the owner had not exercised due diligence to avoid allowing the property to be used illegally.

Since title to any forfeitable property vests in the government when the crime is committed, the bank's security interest may be subordinate to the government's interest in any property subject to forfeiture.[106] Under the M.L.C.A. and other forfeiture laws, banks may contest

---

101. Almost two years after the B.C.C.I. indictment, the United States Office of the Comptroller of the Currency issued an Advisory Letter (No. 90-5, 29 March 1990) warning banks to exercise "particular caution" in making loans fully collateralised by cash equivalents.
102. See *United States v. Southside Finance* 755 F. Supp. 791 (N.D.J. 11 1991); *United States v. All Moneys* (1477, 048.62), 754 F. Supp. 1467.
103. See *United States v. Banco Cafetero Panama* 797 F.2d 1154 (2d Cir. 1986).
104. 18 U.S.C. s. 982(a). Section 982(b) permits forfeiture of "substitute assets", except substitution cannot be required if the defendant "acted merely as an intermediary who handled but did not retain the property in the course of the money laundering offence." The 1990 Crime Bill rendered this exception inapplicable if the defendant conducted three or more transactions involving US $100,000 or more in any 12-month period. Thus, the substitute assets provision will now apply in many banking transactions.
105. 416 U.S. 663 (1974).
106. See *United States v. Stowell* 133 U.S. 1 at 16-17 (1890); 18 U.S.C. s. 1963(c); S. Smith, *Prosecution and Defence of Forfeiture Cases* ss 4.3, 4.35.

forfeiture of their interest in collateral by proving their innocent "ownership" status. Significantly, however, the bank or owner bears the burden to prove its absence of knowledge of, or consent to, the violation, and any knowledge of its employees may be imputed to the corporate entity: see *United States v. 141st Street Corporation*.[107] That case involved an apartment building used in part for narcotics trafficking. The building owner's innocent ownership claim was rejected due to substantial evidence that its agents, the building manager and building superintendent, had actual knowledge of the violation. The court held that the owner had not proved absence of its consent because it had failed to establish that it had done "all that reasonably could be expected to prevent the illegal activity once [the owner] learned of it".[108]

In another recent decision involving a mortgage lien holder, Republic National Bank,[109] the Federal District Court in Miami provided important guidance on proving lack of knowledge to establish innocent ownership status.[110] In that case, the court held that the bank mortgagee had not established an innocent owner status and therefore forfeited its $800,000 interest in a property due to the bank's "blind indifference" to suspicious circumstances of the mortgagee loan transaction. The decision is extremely significant in setting a new due diligence standard for financial institutions in the lending process.[111]

107. 911 F.2d 870 (2d Cir. 17 August 1990), cert. denied, 111 S. Ct. 1017 (1991).
108. The *141st Street* case was brought under 21 U.S.C. s. 881(a), the civil forfeiture provision of the *Comprehensive Drug Abuse Prevention Act*. That statute requires a claimant to establish innocent ownership by proving either lack of knowledge or lack of consent. Some courts have construed the showing to be conjunctive but the majority, including the Second Circuit in this case, construe the language in the disjunctive. The M.L.C.A. civil forfeiture provision requires only a showing of lack of knowledge. 18 U.S.C. s. 981(a)(2). Thus this case may not have value in interpreting innocent owner claims under the M.L.C.A. forfeiture. The Justice Department has, however, sought legislation that would amend all significant forfeiture laws to provide for the same standards. See below, n. 111.
109. *United States v. One Single Family Residence located at 6960 Miraflores Avenue, Coral Gables* 731 F. Supp. 1563 (S.D. Fla, 1990), appeal dismissed, 932 F.2d 1433 (11th Cir. 1991). This case was decided under the civil forfeiture provision of the *Comprehensive Drug Abuse Prevention and Control Act* 21 U.S.C. s. 881, which excludes forfeiture if the owner shows the violation was without its "knowledge or consent." The M.L.C. Act forfeiture provision recognises a similar defence only if lack of knowledge is proven. Since the court's decision focuses exclusively on the knowledge issue, it will have precedential value in cases under the M.L.C. Act civil forfeiture provision.
110. In addition to deciding important questions of innocent ownership proof, the court's decision addressed two other issues. First, following previous decisions, it adopted a fairly lenient standard for the government in establishing probable cause that the collateral is derived from illegal activity; the government must establish more than a suspicion but less than prima facie proof of a substantial connection. Secondly, the Court held that the relation back doctrine (whereby title vests in the government at the time of the violation) does not preclude a purchaser of property after the offence from raising the innocent owner defence.
111. In 1990, the Department of Justice sought legislation incorporating the wilful blindness standard of this case into all significant federal forfeiture laws. The D.O.J. proposed amendments would have provided that innocent ownership claims must be established by proving absence of knowledge, consent, and wilful blindness. This proposal was not enacted in the 1990 Crime Bill but will probably be considered in a future session of Congress.

The government's evidence showed the probability that a convicted narcotics trafficker, Inglesias, used narcotics proceeds to purchase land and build a house in Coral Gables with an appraised value of $1.2 million. Tipped off that the I.R.S. was on his trail, Inglesias put the house up for sale; obtained, through a Panamanian shell corporation, an $800,000 loan from Republic secured by a one-year balloon note mortgage; and had the loan proceeds transferred to a Swiss bank. In rejecting Republic's claim of innocent owner status, the Court found that the following circumstances, in combination, were so suspicious as to be evidence of the bank's actual knowledge:

- the corporate borrower and its stockholder, Munoz, were unknown to the bank and the second guarantor on the note, who *was* a long-standing bank customer, had no known connection with the borrower;

- the borrower was a Panamanian shell corporation (a "preferred" vehicle for trafficker laundering) that had no known source of repayment or assets other than the collateral;

- the bank did not inquire into the purpose of the loan, conduct a title search, or assess the corporate shareholder's financial standing;

- although the collateral was sufficient to cover the loan, the transaction was unusual in that it lent two thirds of the appraised value, was structured as a one-year balloon note, did not contain a repayment schedule or the borrower's undertaking to use the sale proceeds for repayment (the court said that "banks are [not] in the business of lending money with the intent to force sale of the property");

- the bank quickly approved the transaction outside normal channels, and its president was intimately involved in the process;

- the second guarantor used part of the loan proceeds to give a $3,000 honeymoon trip to the son of the bank's president; and

- most of the proceeds were transferred to the borrower's Swiss bank account.

In the court's view, these factors made Republic's claim far inferior to the successful claim made by a bank in a Louisiana case, which at the time was the only other reported decision considering the innocent owner defence for commercial lending institutions. In that case[112] the bank had a long relationship with the borrower, lacked awareness of the borrower's legal problems, and conducted a title search. However the bank did not review the borrower's financials because the loan was fully secured by the property—one of the factors the court in this case used against the bank.

Republic introduced expert witness testimony that the transaction was not commercially unusual in South Florida. The court rejected this testimony but said that such evidence, even if credited, is not determinative if the circumstances as a whole indicate that the bank officer deliberately closed his eyes to facts giving every reason to believe the collateral was criminally derived.

112. *United States v. A Fee Simple Parcel of Real Property* 650 F. Supp. 1534 (E.D. La, 1987).

The Republic Bank case teaches several lessons: (i) the lending process must involve more than a credit risk analysis. The process must include due diligence to establish a good faith belief in the legitimacy of the borrower and its funds, as well as the use of the collateral; (ii) the process must be documented; and (iii) the institution's officers and employees must be made aware of its strict policy against transactions in proceeds derived from illegal activity and trained to spot "red flags" of such transactions.

In addition, the bank should consider requiring warranties and representations from the borrower as to the legality of the customer's activity and the source of the funds, a representation that no criminal charges or forfeiture proceeding is pending, and the obligation to notify the bank of any proceeding that could give rise to a forfeiture.[113] Any line of credit agreement should allow the bank to terminate its obligation to make advances when the possibility of forfeiture arises.

Automation

Automation is critical to developing an effective detection system. Computer systems need to be devised to flag questionable transactions for further review, such as multiple currency transactions on the same or different days in the same or related accounts; patterns of deposits of bearer instruments; patterns of small deposits followed by high volume debits to the same payees; and aberrational wire transfers, or transactions that are unusually large or voluminous, given the nature or prior history of an account. The theories for such computer detection systems have long been used in other contexts, such as credit card use, and are not unduly complicated to install. These types of systems will not tell the bank what is suspicious activity, but they are enormously helpful in pinpointing activity that warrants review by knowledgeable staff. Defending against a criminal investigation can cost an institution several million dollars or more. Effective software packages or programs can be purchased or designed to detect unusual transactions for as little as U.S. $50,000 to U.S. $100,000, depending on the size of the institution and the sophistication of its existing computer system.

Employee awareness

While automation is essential to an effective compliance program, the human computer is the most vital component of the corporate nervous system. Employees at all levels must be sensitised to be on the look out for questionable activity and report it immediately to management and compliance officers. To achieve this level of sensitivity, banks must provide (and document) regular training programs on money laundering techniques, regulatory changes, etc.

Many financial institutions are attempting to develop enhanced money laundering awareness programs but have been hampered by the fact that neither the United States nor foreign governments are providing institutions with guidance on how to detect money laundering transactions. For example, one of the possible signs of a "smurfing" operation is recurring deposits of personal cheques from various banks

113. See office of the Comptroller of the Currency, Advisory Letter 90-5, 29 March 1990.

in small, even denominations such as $3,000, $5,000 and $7,000. To date, however, the United States government has not formally alerted banks to monitor personal cheque deposits. Moreover, it was not until October 1988 that United States banks were alerted to the need to monitor wire transfers, and the guidance issued was very general.[114] And, while government prosecutions have focused on narcotic-related money laundering, the statutes plainly cover an extremely broad range of "specified unlawful activity" ranging from wire and mail fraud to tax evasion and securities fraud. Yet no guidelines have been provided to financial institutions for detecting these activities.[115]

Detecting suspicious transactions

The recent history of criminal money laundering enforcement in the United States teaches that financial institutions cannot rely on government to alert them to the evolving methods and schemes devised to launder legitimate proceeds; they must themselves stay abreast of these developments by following press accounts and criminal indictments, staying in touch with local law enforcement and drawing on other resources, such as former law enforcement officers and prosecutors.

A study of criminal money laundering cases to date reveals that in most money laundering schemes, some or many of the following warning signs will probably appear.

- New customer fails to provide identification or provides evasive or obscure answers to questions regarding its nature of business or occupation, permanent address, or references.

- Customer appears to be acting as the agent for another but evades or is reluctant to provide information in response to questions about the principal.

- Legal entity provides only general, boiler plate articles of incorporation and cannot provide evidence of a legitimate business enterprise (such as names of suppliers or purchasers).

- Customer's bank references are not from well-known reputable institutions and customer cannot provide other credible references.

- Person who does not have an account relationship conducts large cash transactions with the institution on a regular basis (especially if the person deals in United States currency).

- In countries with cash reporting requirements, customer deposits several cash transactions at different times on the same day or on different days in amounts slightly under a reporting threshold.

114. See O.C.C. Advisory Letter 88-5 (26 October 1988).
115. Some useful guidelines or warning signs of money laundering are contained in a December 1989 O.C.C. publication *Money Laundering* and the F.D.I.C. Manual of Examination Policies for F.D.I.C. Examiners (*Bank Fraud and Insider Abuses*) (3-87) (*Money Laundering*, Appendix A, p. 16). These warning signs largely relate to cash transactions but they do flag other types of transactions, such as: a large volume of wire transfers for non-customers or to/from offshore banks; a large volume of cashier cheques or money order deposits; a large number of small deposits and a small number of large cheques with the balance of the account "remaining low"; and a large volume of deposits to different accounts which are then transferred to one account.

- Customer conducts frequent or large cash transactions and cannot satisfy the institution that the cash derives from a legitimate business that would be expected to generate cash.
- Person or legal entity opens a number of accounts under one or more names (or has several accounts with different institutions in the same locale), regularly makes inter-account transfers followed by wire transfers abroad of aggregated funds, and cannot satisfy the institution that the multiple accounts and transfers relate to a legitimate business or commercial purpose.
- Account experiences a high volume of wire transfer activity associated with places or amounts that do not appear commensurate with the owner's business or occupation.
- Account receives frequent deposits of bearer instruments (cashier or bank cheques, money orders, or personal cheques with blank payees) in amounts below reporting thresholds (for example, U.S.$10,000 or U.S.$3,000).
- Account shows a pattern of deposits and immediate debits of similar amounts ("in and out" pattern), often associated with bounced cheques or overdrafts.
- Account shows a pattern of outgoing wire transfers funded by cash debits from account funded by multiple deposits of monetary instruments.
- Customer requests unusual wire transfers in which transaction appears inconsistent with normal funds transfer practices (for example, advises that funds will be returned from different sources).
- Person or entity seeks a credit relationship whereby loan is collateralised by a deposit and there is no established connection between the borrower and depositor or there are other signs that the cash collateralised loan may be used solely as a device to disguise the transfer of funds.
- Customer pays down a problem loan suddenly.
- Account receives numerous deposits by wire or cheque and then customer orders the transfer of the funds to another city or country.
- New customer requires urgent transfer of large amount of funds.
- Customer makes or receives numerous wire transfers to or from numbered accounts.
- Account has high volume of deposits and withdrawals that do not appear consistent with customer's type of business or occupation.
- Customer is engaged in a type of business that has been associated with money laundering (for example, shipping, air transportation, cash intensive retail sales, export-import brokers, agriculture or ranching) and has a high volume of transactions.
- Account regularly receives deposits of third-party cheques or cheques in which the payee appears to have been written or added by someone other than the drawer.
- Customer frequently gives instructions to "pay upon proper identification" or to issue bank cheques for non-customers.

- Account receives regular payments from accounts in countries commonly associated with production, processing or marketing of narcotics.
- Account exhibits any transaction or pattern of transactions that appears aberrational given the customer's known business or occupation (for example, unexplained large increase in deposits and withdrawals).
- Customer implies or suggests that he or she does not wish her or his identity revealed to regulatory authorities or requests information regarding how to conceal transactions from government authorities.
- Customer suggests payments of a gratuity or gift to a staff member.
- Customer seeks credit but exhibits a lack of concern regarding cost of the funds or is evasive as to the purpose of the loan.
- Investments customer exhibits lack of concern regarding risks or commissions.
- Customer implies or gives indication that her or his business is wholly or partly involved in an activity related to narcotics distribution or controversial investment or sales efforts.

The foregoing list is merely illustrative and is not intended to suggest that the appearance of any one factor automatically suggests that the customer is engaged in illegal activity. Rather, the appearance of these or any other warning signs simply suggests that the prudent course is to inquire more fully into the circumstances.

Moreover, money laundering techniques are mercurial—as soon as the bank learns to watch for one type of transaction, the bad guys devise new ways to carry out their schemes. In the final analysis, employees must be trained to look for unusual patterns, but to determine what is unusual, the banker must have a thorough knowledge of the customer's business.

Internal controls (muscle)

Having the nervous system is not enough without muscle. When criminal subpoenas arrive, the bank's legal counsel should investigate immediately to ensure that none of the bank's employees have been involved in any illegal activity. The bank should be aware that a criminal grand jury subpoena is an invitation to make at least a discrete inquiry. When evidence of employee wrongdoing is uncovered, the bank must be prepared to terminate or otherwise discipline the employee, and, in appropriate circumstances, report the matter to government authorities.

Internal control and audit systems must form the core muscle function. The bank's auditors must be trained in money laundering detection, and audit criteria should be reviewed and expanded to test for compliance in every function, not just cash reporting testing.[116]

116. If an outside accounting firm is engaged for independent testing, bank management should ensure that meaningful criteria and procedures are used. Accounting firms have developed very good testing procedures for whether systems are in place reasonably to ensure currency transaction reporting. Few, if any, however, appear to have developed procedures for testing systems designed to identify the subjective and often non-quantitative phenomenon of money laundering or suspicious activities. Indeed, accounting firms are specialists in measuring and evaluating under highly objective criteria, and they thus may not be the best source for independent testing of most money laundering compliance functions.

Internal control functions should include periodic review of selected deposit and loan accounts for adequacy of documentation under the "know your customer" standard[117] and for questionable transactions. Deposit accounts having transactions exceeding selected parameters should be scrutinised by reviewing the credit and debit items to determine whether the activity is consistent with the customer's business as documented in the file. For example, the review should include analysis of whether there is any pattern in deposits (for example, even numbered personal cheques at or under $10,000, bearer instruments, same payors, different handwriting on the cheques, etc.) or debits (for example, wire transfers to bank secrecy havens, cashier cheques, large numbers of small incoming cheques with small numbers of large cheques to the same individual payors deposited in secrecy haven banks). In addition, the review should attempt to ascertain whether the payors and recipients of credits and debits have an apparent connection with the customer's legitimate business (for example, are the (customer) deposits in a retail electronic store's account largely cash and personal cheques in odd numbered amounts or are they huge volumes of currency, money orders, and $9,000 cashier cheques; are its large payments to recognised electronics wholesale distributors or are they wire transfers to individuals?) This is the type of review that some bank examiners conduct when they get wind that a bank may be involved in money laundering; a careful bank should be doing it to try to avoid the trouble in the first instance.

In addition, the bank should systematically review its deposit, cashier cheque issuance, and wire transfer functions for B.S.A. compliance and any unusual patterns of activity. For example, the bank to bank (correspondent) wire transfer function should be reviewed for suspicious patterns of large wire transfers (for example, a sudden large increase in transfers coming from a small southwest bank going to a bank in a bank secrecy haven country). Large increases in cashier cheque sales should be detected and checked for compliance with any Treasury "$3,000 rule" identification requirements, and overall cash intakes should be monitored for aberrational increases.

Due diligence in an acquisition

In this age of financial institutions' consolidations through mergers and acquisitions, any acquiring institution should include, in its pre-acquisition due diligence, a careful inquiry to determine whether the acquisition could likely expose it to criminal B.S.A. or M.L.C. Act liability. Successor liability for the criminal conduct of the predecessor corporation's employees is provided in most States' corporation statutes,[118] and a valiant effort to avoid such liability was recently rejected by the Fifth Circuit in *United States v. Alamo Bank of*

---

117. The review should consider not only whether the file contains sufficient information on the identity and business of the customer, but also whether that information has been reasonably verified.

118. See e.g. *United States v. Mobile Materials Inc.* 776 F.2d 1476 (10th Cir. 1985).

Texas. [119] While technically the successor can never protect itself from such liability, prosecutors are far less likely to prosecute an otherwise innocent successor if it can show that it was sensitive enough to the importance of B.S.A. and M.L.C. Act compliance to have made a thorough pre-acquisition scrutiny that revealed no indication of a problem. Such due diligence should include, at a minimum, review of the takeover candidate firms' written policies, compliance program, examination and auditors' reports, criminal referral program, as well as criminal subpoenas and related memoranda or reports of counsel.

A Track Record of Co-operation with the Government

To keep the government's sword in its scabbard, the bank needs a good track record in examination reports and a good relationship with its federal and State banking examiners, [120] who increasingly are a pipeline to United States Attorney's offices. [121] Federal prosecutors who investigate banks obtain recent audit reports from the bank regulatory agency. While prosecutors do not usually put much stock in these reports if they are positive, they give them a lot of weight if they are negative. Thus bank officials must strive to ensure that examination reports do not criticise the bank's money laundering deterrence efforts.

The bank also needs a good track record of compliance with grand jury subpoenas, which means timely and thorough productions to United States attorneys. And the bank needs a good track record of making criminal referrals to prosecutors. Under United States federal banking regulations, [122] all federally regulated banks are required to submit a criminal referral form to designated regulatory and law enforcement agencies and the relevant Office of United States Attorney whenever they have a known factual basis to believe any of certain crimes, including money laundering, has been or may have been committed. Brokerage firms are not currently required to make such reports but are encouraged to do so.

119. 880 F.2d 828 (5th Cir. 1989). In that case, the government indicted a national bank and its acquiring state bank for B.S.A. violations that occurred three years before the acquisition. The state bank argued that, upon the acquisition and the surrender to the Comptroller of the Currency of the national bank's charter it ceased to exist as an entity and by operation of federal law, its liabilities did not pass through to the successor bank.

120. The bank should also appreciate the importance of having its compliance staff engage in regular schmoozing with local I.R.S., F.B.I. and customs agents. Bankers who get to know their local federal law enforcement representative in customs, the F.B.I. or I.R.S. can get a lot of relevant information and build enormous credibility.

121. Treasury has issued guidelines to all bank regulatory agencies directing them to refer B.S.A. violations for civil or criminal penalties. See F.H.L.B.B. Regulatory Bulletin 400 RB 8 (13 December 1988). Also, the 1988 Drug Bill amended the *Right to Financial Privacy Act* ("R.F.P.A."), 12 U.S.C. s. 3412, to authorise federal bank regulatory agencies to disclose R.F.P.A.-protected records to D.O.J. upon supervisory certification that the records may be relevant to a federal criminal law violation and were obtained in the agency's exercise of its regulatory function. D.O.J. may use such records *only* for criminal investigative or prosecutive purposes.

122. See above, n. 48.

Criminal referrals were very controversial among United States banks a few years ago because of exposure to civil damages under the *Right to Financial Privacy Act* 1978 (R.F.P. Act) 12 U.S.C. s. 3401 ff., other privacy laws and common law defamation. That controversy largely subsided with adoption in 1986 of an amendment to the R.F.P. Act, 12 U.S.C. s. 3403(c), providing banks a limited safe harbour from civil liability—not criminal liability—for disclosure in a criminal referral to law enforcement of information relating to customer and account identification and a description of the suspicious activity. No other account information should be provided without a proper subpoena or court order. [123]

The more serious issue is whether criminal referrals expose the bank to possible criminal prosecution for the conduct reported if a bank employee turns out to have been involved. Obviously, a criminal referral should not be made without a thorough inquiry of the facts and, normally, advice of counsel. While O.C.C. and F.D.I.C. regulations and the Federal Reserve Criminal Referral Form require referrals in very short time frames (seven days), the time does not begin to run until the bank has sufficiently complete information, that is, a known, factual basis, to conclude that a crime has been or may have been committed. Making such a determination often requires an extremely careful evaluation of multiple facts. Making criminal referrals, based on hunches or rumour or incomplete information, is folly and could expose the bank to unwarranted investigation, possible criminal prosecution, or civil liability. But if the facts, fully developed, indicate possible criminal activity, the bank has no choice but to report it. If employee criminal involvement is indicated, the bank probably has only one choice: suspend the employee, report the conduct, co-operate with the government, and persuade the government not to draw its sword against the bank because it has been a good corporate citizen and has a model compliance program.

Having an effective compliance program with internal controls and a good record of responsiveness is going to be extremely persuasive to most prosecutors. The Department of Justice is becoming increasingly aware that if, as a policy matter, the government expects banks to be cops, it had better stop trying to put them in jail. [124] Nonetheless, under current procedures there is no criminal safe harbour policy and some

---

123. See S. Rep. No. 99-433, 99th Cong., 2d Sess. 15 (1986). Compare *Young v. United States* 882 F.2d 633 (2d Cir. 1989) (assuming R.F.P.A. exempts "tips" from customer privacy laws). Some states, including California and Florida, have similar statutory protections.

   Proposed legislation introduced by Senator Biden (S.1970) in a previous session of Congress would have further amended R.F.P.A. s. 3403(c) to provide banks with immunity from civil suit for refusing to do business with a customer after making a criminal referral on that customer. 135 Cong. Rec. S 16723 (21 November 1989). See *Ricci v. Key Bancshares of Maine Inc.* 662 F. Supp. 1132 (D. Me, 1987) (upholding $15 million punitive damage award against a bank for terminating the customer's line of credit based on an incorrect tip from the F.B.I.).

124. A recent apparent illustration of D.O.J.'s inclinations in this regard is the prosecution of employees of Security Pacific in which news reports indicated that the bank, which was not indicted, had co-operated in the investigation. This proposal was reintroduced in 1991 but was not enacted.

prosecutors unwisely ignore this compelling argument. To attempt to deal with this problem, the American Bar Association recently adopted a policy encouraging the United States Department of Justice to adopt prosecution policies reflecting safe harbour considerations.

When Co-operation Fails

If the bank is unsuccessful and there is an indictment, the institution's strategy obviously will depend on the particular facts and its compliance track record. A detailed description of practice pointers in preparing for a money laundering case is beyond the scope of this chapter. A few general observations, however, should be made.

First, motions to dismiss B.S.A. and money laundering indictments have not been very successful, despite defence counsel ingenuity. For example, constitutional challenges to the M.L.C. Act for vagueness and first amendment abridgement have been routinely rejected by the courts, which have found the statutes' scienter requirements to be sufficiently clear and narrow.[125] Similarly, courts have rejected defence claims of selective prosecution[126] and "outrageous government conduct" in targeting the defendant in an undercover operation.[127] Nonetheless, for tactical reasons, such motions should be seriously considered.

Pre-trial preparation for a money laundering prosecution against a bank usually involves review and analysis of government tape recordings of undercover officers' conversations with bank officials. Bank counsel should ensure that the prosecution provides good quality tapes (that is,

125. See *United States v. Restrepo* 884 F.2d 1381 (2d Cir. 1989); *United States v. Awan* (unreported, M.D. Fla, 1989, Cr. No. 88-330-Cr-T-13B); *United States v. Kimball* 711 F.Supp. 1031 (D.Nev., 1989); *United States v. Mainieri* 694 F.Supp. 1394 (S.D. Fla, 1988) (s. 1956); *United States v. Baker* (unreported, M.D. Fla, 28 July 1989) No. 8983-Cr-T-15(B) (s. 1957).
126. In *Yick Wo v. Hopkins* 118 U.S. 356 at 373-74 (1886), the United States Supreme Court recognised that the equal protection clause of the United States constitution forbids selective prosecution based on race, national origin or other invidious factors. Courts adhere to a presumption that prosecutors act in good faith and impose a heavy burden on a selective prosecution claimant to show that others similarly situated have not been prosecuted and that the government's selection of her or him for prosecution was based on an impermissible factor. See *United States v. Bassford* 812 F.2d 16 (1st Cir. 1987). Thus, although most United States money laundering indictments against banks have involved foreign owned banks (for example, B.C.C.I., L.B.S., Banco Occidente, National Mortgage Bank of Greece), few cases have raised a defence of selective prosecution. In a recent decision arising from the convictions of a Puerto Rican banker for Bank Secrecy violations, the Court of Appeals considered and rejected a claim of discriminatory prosecution, concluding that the government had presented sufficient nondiscriminatory reasons (surplus cash deposits in Puerto Rico banks) for selecting the defendant and other Puerto Ricans for prosecution: *United States v. Penagaricano-Soler* 911 F.2d 833 (1st Cir. 1990).
127. United States Courts recognise in principle that government undercover operations may involve conduct that is so "outrageous" as to violate due process such as when the government manufactures virtually the entire criminality. See *United States v. Russell* 411 U.S. 423 at 431 (1973); *United States v. Twigg* 588 F.2d 373 (3d Cir. 1978). Essentially, the claimant must show that he or she was not engaged in illegal conduct before the undercover operation and was victimised by government misconduct that "shocks the conscience". Such claims are almost invariably unsuccessful. See *United States v. Penagaricano-Soler* 911 F.2d 833 (1st Cir. 1990); *United States v. Silberman* (unreported, S.D. Cal. 1990, No. 89-0417-JCI-Crim.).

not high speed copies) and may find it advisable to retain an expert in recording devices and techniques if the tapes appear to have gaps or unusual sounds. Defence counsel should also consider retaining a linguisitic expert to assist in evaluating the actual communication revealed on the tapes; linguistic analysis can be especially helpful when the conversation is key to the issue of intent and knowledge, which is often the case. Experts in banking procedures and money laundering techniques should be consulted to explore whether the banking transactions at issue are typical or aberrational.

In the final analysis, the only good defence a bank can have before a jury is a strong showing that it had adopted an effective compliance program. Under the standards of collective knowledge and "flagrant" indifference adopted in the *Bank of New England* case, the bank was convicted. But when a similar instruction was given in a criminal case against Shearson Lehman Brothers in Philadelphia, the jury acquitted the corporation, apparently in large part due to evidence of a strong B.S.A. compliance program. One of the most determinative factors in the jury's acquittal was probably the testimony of the chief compliance officer who conveyed a "tough cop" image.

Another tactic that the bank should consider in defending a money laundering prosecution is to attack the government for not providing guidance and never questioning similar transactions during bank examinations. Defence counsel's strategy should emphasise that the government's own examiners who reviewed the bank year after year never found anything wrong; thus, the bank should not be found to have been "flagrantly indifferent".

The best policy now, for any financial institution, is to adopt effective compliance measures, and establish good relationships with the local United States Attorney's Office and other authorities, such as the I.R.S., F.B.I., Customs, and the federal and State bank regulatory agencies, so that they will trust the bank's management and not be inclined to draw the criminal sword against the bank.

19

Minimising Exposure to Liability under the New Legislation

Developing Effective Corporate Compliance Systems

BRENT FISSE*

INTRODUCTION: THE NEED FOR EFFECTIVE COMPLIANCE CONTROLS

Australia now has an extensive web of legislation on money laundering, cash transaction reporting, and confiscation of proceeds of crime. At the federal level, the *Proceeds of Crime Act* 1987 (P.O.C. Act) and the *Cash Transaction Reports Act* 1988 (C.T.R. Act) impose far-reaching controls and severe penalties.[1] There are also hard-hitting provisions for monetary penalties and civil forfeiture under the *Customs Act* 1901.[2] At the State and Territorial level, almost all jurisdictions have legislation specifically on confiscation of proceeds of crime.[3]

These legislative initiatives are driven by several powerful factors. First, governments are determined to combat drug trafficking and tax fraud, and there is much political support for the strategy of attacking the

*   Professor of Law, University of Sydney. Paper presented at R.M.S. Seminar, "Cash Transactions Reporting, Money Laundering, and Confiscation of Proceeds of Crime", Sydney, 21 August 1990; Melbourne, 24 August 1990.
1. See further Dabb, "Cash Transactions Reporting and Proceeds of Crime Legislation: The New Generation of Commonwealth Law Enforcement". Paper presented at R.M.S. Seminar, "Cash Transactions Reporting, Money Laundering, and Confiscation of Proceeds of Crime", Sydney, 21 August 1990; Melbourne, 24 August 1990.
2. For useful reviews see Scott, "The Customs Act/The Proceeds of Crime Act 1987" in *Confiscation of Assets* (1988) College of Law, Continuing Legal Education; Thornton, above, Chapter 2. The *Customs Act* provisions may affect the position of financial institutions but the *Cash Transaction Reports Act* 1988 (Cth) (C.T.R. Act) and *Proceeds of Crime Act* 1987 (Cth) (P.O.C. Act) are of more immediate relevance and provide the focus of discussion in this paper.
3. E.g. *Confiscation of Proceeds of Crime Act* 1989 (N.S.W.); *Drug Trafficking (Civil Proceedings) Act* 1990 (N.S.W.). See also *Crimes (Confiscation of Profits) Act* 1986 (S.A.); *Crimes (Confiscation of Profits) Act* 1986 (Vic.); *Crimes (Confiscation of Profits) Act* 1989 (Qld); *Crimes (Confiscation of Profits) Act* 1988 (W.A.); *Crimes (Forfeiture of Proceeds) Act* 1988 (N.T.).

money trail in crime.[4] Secondly, Australia plays a leading role internationally in developing measures against money laundering[5] and is closely allied to the United States, where very high priority is given to the strategy of controlling crime by bombarding the money trail.[6] Thirdly, confiscation of proceeds of crime may produce significant additional revenue for the state (consider, for example, the estimate that U.S.$220 million daily is generated by United States drug sales).[7]

Financial institutions need to take account of the legislative assault on the money trail in crime and devise compliance systems accordingly.[8] The more significant forms of reducible or avoidable loss are these:

- fines or monetary penalties;[9]
- injunctions;[10]
- adverse publicity;[11]
- damages payable to clients for breach of confidence or defamation;[12]
- disruption and loss of morale as a result of involvement in litigation or a publicity crisis;[13]
- personal liability of corporate officers;[14]
- legal costs in defending claims or prosecutions.

Compliance measures help to keep these risks to a minimum and reduce the demand for crisis management. Moreover, even if legal liability is incurred, compliance efforts can mitigate the extent of loss.[15] A solid preventive system may also help to preserve the company's credibility and its ability to negotiate when dealing with plaintiffs,

4. Many leading politicians, including Lionel Bowen, Michael Tate, Nick Greiner and Michael Pickering, have favoured hitting the money trail as a general strategy of crime control. See e.g. "Spoils of War", *Sunday Telegraph*, 18 March 1990, p. 139 (Pickering); "More Criminals May Lose Assets", *Sydney Morning Herald*, 1 June 1990, p. 5 (Greiner).

5. As is evident from Australia's signature to the United Nations *Convention against Illicit Traffic in Narcotic Drugs and Psychotropic Substances* in 1988 (the Vienna Convention) and the active role it has played as one of 15 members of the international Financial Action Task Force on Money Laundering.

6. See generally the monthly newsletter, *Money Laundering Alert*.

7. See further Pinner, above, Chapter 3. Cf. Fraser, above, Chapter 4.

8. Many legal issues arise; see further O'Sullivan and Mitchell, above, Chapter 8.

9. See e.g. P.O.C. Act, s. 81 (fine of $600,000 for corporation convicted of money laundering).

10. E.g. C.T.R. Act, s. 32.

11. See generally Fisse and Braithwaite, *The Impact of Publicity on Corporate Offenders* (1983).

12. On protection of privacy see further O'Connor, above, Chapter 9.

13. Consider e.g. the immense time and resources incurred by E. F. Hutton in fielding the Hutton banking fraud case; see United States House of Representatives, Committee on the Judiciary, Subcommittee on Crime, *E. F. Hutton Mail and Wire Fraud Case*, Report, 99th Cong., 2nd Sess., 1986; Carpenter, *The Fall of the House of Hutton* (1989).

14. Corporations Law, s. 232(4).

15. This has been the experience under the *Trade Practices Act* 1974 (Cth): see e.g. *Trade Practices Commission v. General Corporation Japan (Australia) Pty Ltd* (1989) A.T.P.R. 40-922. See further Freiberg, "Monetary Penalties under the Trade Practices Act" (1983) 11 Aust. Bus. L. Rev. 4.

investigators, prosecutors, judges, shareholders, journalists and politicians. It has also been claimed that a compliance programme "helps to create a healthy environment in which to work, improves morale among employees and gives them confidence, and builds a corporate reputation for good citizenship".[16]

Neglecting compliance and letting things take their course is hardly a commendable option:

- flying blind, or proceeding on the basis of "creeping incrementalism",[17] is inconsistent with sound managerial theory, in particular the postulate of strategic decision making;[18]

- doing nothing may result in situations where the company is taken by surprise and hence placed at a disadvantage in litigation or dealings with enforcement agencies or news media;

- studious non-commitment to compliance is a lightning rod for civil or criminal liability.

The impact of money laundering legislation upon the United States banking industry is sobering.[19] One watershed was the Bank of Boston case in 1985 where the bank pleaded guilty to criminal charges involving the failure to file hundreds of reports of international currency transactions over $10,000. The bank was fined $500,000 and subjected to a storm of adverse publicity. Later in 1985 a civil penalty of $2.25 million was imposed on the Crocker National Bank for failure to report currency transactions totalling $3.9 billion. In 1986, the Bank of America was fined $4.75 million for 17,000 violations. In 1986 the Bank of New England was fined $1.24 million for *Bank Secrecy Act* violations. More recently, in 1989, the Ponce Federal Bank was fined $2.5 million, and the United Orient Bank $2 million. These are some of the more superficial effects. Behind the scenes, much work has gone into compliance initiatives and participation in a flurry of legislative development.

The purpose of this chapter is to suggest a framework for consideration where a money laundering control system is being devised. I stress the word "suggest" because, as far as I have been able to discover, we now lack any empirical study of the comparative experience of Australian financial institutions in complying with the

16. Bruns, "Corporate Preventive Law Programs" (1985) 4 *Preventive Law Reporter* 30 at 31.
17. See further Goodin, *Political Theory and Public Policy* (1982), Ch. 2.
18. See further Ansoff, *Corporate Strategy* (1965), Ch. 6. Thus Ansoff argues that project decisions are likely to be of poorer quality than in firms with strategy (p. 102):
    Without focus for its efforts, the staff will lack the depth of knowledge in any particular area needed for competent analysis. Without strategy criteria, it will lack tools for recognising outstanding opportunities. As a result managers acting on such advice will be forced into extreme forms of behaviour. Conservatives will refuse to take what under better information might be reasonable risks; entrepreneurs will plunge without appreciation of potential costs and dangers.
19. See Byrne, above, Chapter 17. On the criminal fines imposed see (1990) 1 (10) *Money Laundering Alert* 8.

money trail legislation.[20] Most of what I have to say is based on general principles extracted from a wide cross-section of corporate regulation and applied to this particular context.

THE RECENT LEGISLATIVE CONTROLS

The central features of the main Commonwealth money trail legislation are set out below.

Cash Transaction Reports Act 1988 (Cth)[21]

A "cash dealer" has several obligations under the *Cash Transaction Reports Act* 1988 (Cth) (C.T.R. Act):

- When opening new accounts or facilities or adding new signatories to existing accounts, cash dealers must verify the identification of the person opening the account or facility.[22]

- A cash dealer must report to the Cash Transaction Reports Agency details of a currency transaction involving $10,000 or more unless the transaction is exempt.[23]

- A cash dealer must report to the Agency suspect transactions (cash or otherwise)[24] where there are reasonable grounds to suspect that the information about the transaction may be relevant to the investigation of an evasion or attempted evasion of a taxation law, may be relevant to the investigation or prosecution of an offence against a law of the Commonwealth or a Territory, or may be of assistance in the enforcement of the *Proceeds of Crime Act*.[25]

A "cash dealer" includes:[26]

- banks, building societies and credit unions;

- insurance companies and insurance intermediaries;

- securities dealers and futures brokers;

20. Compare the detailed survey and analysis of costs in American Bankers Association, *Money Laundering Deterrence and Bank Secrecy Act Survey* (1990) (see Byrne, above, Chapter 17). On the projected costs of compliance with the C.T.R. Act and related questions see Australia, Attorney-General's Department, *Cash Transaction Reports Legislation and Materials* (1988), especially Ch. 4 of the Report by the Senate Standing Committee on Legal and Constitutional Affairs. See further Cullen, "Money Laundering Legislation: Perspectives from the Australian Banking Industry". Paper presented at R.M.S. Seminar, "Cash Transactions Reporting, Money Laundering, and Confiscation of Proceeds of Crime", Sydney, 21 August 1990; Melbourne, 24 August 1990.
21. See generally Hewett and Kalyk, *Understanding the Cash Transaction Reports Act* (1990).
22. C.T.R. Act, ss 18-23.
23. C.T.R. Act, s. 7.
24. The requirement to report a suspect transaction under the C.T.R. Act is not confined to transactions involving cash (i.e. notes and coin). The requirement to report suspect transactions applies to all transactions and is not affected by any of the limits applying to significant cash transaction reports.
25. C.T.R. Act, s. 16.
26. C.T.R. Act, s. 3(1).

- managers and trustees of unit trusts;
- firms dealing in travellers' cheques;
- currency and bullion dealers;
- casinos and gambling houses;
- TABs and bookmakers;
- a person (other than a bank, building society or credit union) who carries on a business of:
  - collecting currency, and holding currency collect, on behalf of other persons;
  - preparing pay-rolls on behalf of other persons in whole or in part from currency collected; and
  - delivering currency (including pay-rolls).

"Currency" means coin and paper money of Australia or of a foreign country.[27]

"Transaction" is not defined under the C.T.R. Act. The view of the Agency is that a "transaction" includes negotiations or discussions preliminary to actual dealings to which the cash dealer is a party.[28] Negotiation involves a degree of positive activity on the part of the negotiating party; it would not be enough that a cash dealer merely answers enquiries. The basis of this position is partly as follows:

> The inclusion of negotiation is consistent with the objectives of s. 16 which is to compel the reporting of suspect transactions; those objectives would be partially frustrated if the statutory notion of a "transaction" required the existence of a dealing; in those circumstances, a cash dealer could withhold from entry into a dealing because of relevant suspicion, leaving the subject matter of suspicion unreported, to the obvious detriment of the public interest. The evident purpose of the legislation is to involve citizens or associations of citizens, who have status of cash dealers, in active obligations in promotion of the public interest concerning matters of grave concern.

Obligations are also imposed on persons generally:

- adequate identification documents must be produced when opening a new account with a financial institution or other cash dealer;[29]
- no one may open a bank account or similar account in a false name;[30]
- everyone is obliged to report to the Agency or to Customs currency transfers to and from Australia for an amount of $5,000 or more that the person proposes to make (certain exceptions apply, for example, to banks and airlines);[31]

27. C.T.R. Act, s. 3(1).
28. C.T.R. Agency, Guideline No. 1, *Suspect Transactions Reporting*.
29. C.T.R. Act, s. 18.
30. C.T.R. Act, s. 24.
31. C.T.R. Act, s. 15.

- no one may structure transactions so as to avoid the reporting requirements. [32]

Breach of the obligations imposed by the C.T.R. Act is subject to severe penalties. Thus, failure to report suspicious transactions is subject to a jail term of up to two years and a fine of $5,000, or both, and corporations are subject to a fine of up to $25,000. [33] Vicarious liability is imposed. [34]

Proceeds of Crime Act 1987 (Cth)

The *Proceeds of Crime Act* 1987 (Cth) (P.O.C. Act) provides for discretionary forfeiture and/or pecuniary penalties where D has been convicted of an indictable offence. [35] Provision is also made in some circumstances for automatic forfeiture of property subject to a restraining order. [36]

"Tainted property" is subject to forfeiture where a forfeiture order is made after D has been convicted of a relevant offence. "Tainted property" is defined in s. 4(1) as property used in, or in connection with, the commission of the offence, or proceeds directly or indirectly derived from the offence. [37] "Property" is defined as real or personal property of every description, whether tangible or intangible (thus, bank accounts are covered), and wherever situated, and any interest in relation to such property. A court has discretion as to whether a forfeiture order should be made, and in exercising that discretion may take into account such factors as hardship, [38] the use to which the property is ordinarily put or is intended, [39] and the gravity of the relevant offence. [40]

Pecuniary penalties may be imposed where D has been convicted of an indictable offence. [41] D may be ordered to pay a penalty equal to the value of the benefit to D resulting from the commission of the offence. Penalties are assessed according to s. 27 which details a number of guides for making assessments. [42] In the case of "serious offences" all of D's property at the time the application for a pecuniary penalty order is made, and all property since the earliest relevant offence (or within the previous five years if the earliest offence occurred more than five years previously), are presumed to be proceeds of crime. [43]

Where D has been convicted of a "serious offence", and a restraining order remains in force in relation to D's property six months after that

32. C.T.R. Act, s. 31.
33. C.T.R. Act, s. 28.
34. C.T.R. Act, s. 34.
35. P.O.C. Act, ss 19, 26.
36. P.O.C. Act, s. 30.
37. The nexus between offence and property forfeited is a perennial issue in forfeiture legislation; see e.g. *R. v. Hadad* (1989) 16 N.S.W.L.R. 476; *R. v. Ward* [1989] 1 Qd R. 194.
38. P.O.C. Act, s. 19(3).
39. P.O.C. Act, s. 19(3).
40. P.O.C. Act, s. 19(4).
41. P.O.C. Act, s. 26.
42. Cf. *Customs Act* 1901 (Cth), s. 243c.
43. P.O.C. Act, s. 27(6).

conviction, the property is automatically forfeited.[44] "Serious offence" means a "serious narcotics offence" as defined (that is, an offence involving a traffickable quantity of drugs), organised fraud, or money laundering in relation to the proceeds of a serious narcotics offence or organised fraud.[45]

Restraining orders may be made in relation to the property of D where D has been convicted of an indictable offence, or has been or is about to be convicted of such an offence.[46] Detailed provision is made for ancillary orders, variation and revocation.[47]

Several major offences have been created, namely money laundering,[48] receiving or possessing money or property reasonably suspected to be the proceeds of crime,[49] and organised fraud.[50] All of these offences carry severe maximum punishments (for example, for money laundering, human offenders face $200,000 and/or 20 years' jail). They also impose vicarious liability on individual as well as corporate persons for the conduct of their agents and employees.[51]

The P.O.C. Act covers a wide range of other matters, including mutual assistance in enforcement,[52] and search and seizure.[53]

CORPORATE OFFICERS AND REASONABLE CARE AND DILIGENCE IN COMPLIANCE

Corporate officers are well advised to heed the implications of the new money trail legislation. Consider in particular the impact of s. 232(4) of the Corporations Law,[54] which requires corporate officers to use reasonable care and diligence in the exercise of their powers and in the discharge of their duties. Failure to comply with s. 232(4) is an offence, and attracts a variety of civil remedies.[55]

Assume that the board of directors of a merchant bank delegates all tasks of money laundering prevention to a compliance manager and then exercises no supervisory role over his or her compliance activities. Assume further that the compliance manager takes an unduly optimistic

44. P.O.C. Act, s. 30.
45. P.O.C. Act, s. 7.
46. P.O.C. Act, s. 43.
47. P.O.C. Act, Pt III, Div. 2.
48. P.O.C. Act, s. 81.
49. P.O.C. Act, s. 82.
50. P.O.C. Act, s. 83.
51. P.O.C. Act, s. 85.
52. P.O.C. Act, ss 23, 23A. See further United Nations, *Convention against Illicit Traffic in Narcotic Drugs and Psychotropic Substances* (1988), Art. 7; McClean, "Mutual Assistance in Criminal Matters: The Commonwealth Initiative" (1988) 37 Internat. & Comp. L. Q. 177.
53. P.O.C. Act, Pt III, Div. 1.
54. Corporations Law 1989 (Cth), s. 232.
55. The maximum penalty is a fine of $5,000. The remedies available include injunctions and damages under s. 1324. It may also be noted that, unlike the tort of negligence or statutory offences of failing to exercise due diligence to prevent a contravention, liability under s. 232(4) is not conditional upon the causing of damage or the failure to try to prevent a contravention which has actually occurred.

or casual view of the compliance function delegated and that the company's financial health is badly affected by a number of middle managers who have engaged in money laundering. In supposing that the compliance officer would prepare adequate compliance procedures, and in refraining from demanding any assurances of adequacy, have the members of the board violated s. 232(4) by failing to use reasonable care and diligence in monitoring the company's compliance efforts? Should they have insisted on at least quarterly reports by the compliance officer as to the nature and extent of the company's compliance system?

It may be argued that, in the absence of any reason to suspect that the compliance officer would not properly discharge the function delegated, there is no liability. Certainly there is some support in the case law for this position.[56] However, prevention of liability for money laundering and protection of assets from confiscation is a matter of such significance for a merchant bank that failure to monitor such compliance by requiring periodic reports and assurances may well be considered to amount to a lack of reasonable care by the directors in exercising their power to manage the business of the company.[57] Losses associated with non-compliance in this area may be much more significant than some of the traditional items of financial business on the agenda of board meetings,[58] and hence it would be unwise to assume that the duty under s. 232(4) is confined only to the traditional areas of fiscal command expected of directors in the past. It should also be remembered that much is known today about how organisations can malfunction and, since many of the likely causes of malfunction are relatively easy to remedy, it is foolhardy for corporate officers to ignore them. Another pertinent factor is the current hardening of social attitudes against corporate malfeasance, and the growing antipathy toward corporate directors who do not direct.

A FRAMEWORK FOR COMPLIANCE

The following framework is suggested by reported experience and empirical studies of corporate compliance in a variety of regulatory contexts:[59]

56. *Re City and Equitable Fire Insurance Co. Ltd* [1925] Ch. 407 at 429, per Romer J.; *Graham v. Allis Chalmers* 188 A. 2d 125 (1963). See further Corkery, *Directors' Powers and Duties* (1987), pp. 137-139; Warnick, "The Liabilities of the Inattentive Company Officer" (1988) 18 U.W.A. L. Rev. 91. Reasonable care in delegation requires more than blind faith; consider Perkins, "Avoiding Directors' Liability" [1986] Harvard Bus. Rev. 8 at 12.
57. Compare *Gould v. Mount Oxide Mines Ltd* (1916) 22 C.L.R. 490 at 530; Perkins, "Avoiding Directors' Liability" [1986] Harvard Bus. Rev. 8 at 12.
58. E.g. review of leases of premises, the financial ramifications of which may pale into insignificance when compared with a major scandal involving money laundering.
59. See further American Bankers Asssociation, *Currency Transaction Reporting* (1988); Bank of Boston Corporation, *Bank Secrecy Act: Overview* (1987); Braithwaite, *To Punish or Persuade: Enforcement of Coal Mine Safety* (1985); Braithwaite, "Taking Responsibility Seriously: Corporate Compliance Systems" in Fisse and French (eds), *Corrigible Corporations and Unruly Law* (1985), Ch. 3; Fisse and Braithwaite, op. cit.; Adams, "The Practical Impact of Criminal Money Laundering Laws on Financial Institutions" American Bar Association (1990) *White Collar Crime National Institute* 599.

- clearly-stated compliance policies which are backed and reinforced by top management;[60]
- systematic identification and management of risks created by the company's operations;[61]
- clear allocation of responsibility for compliance functions to specified personnel;[62]
- readable compliance manuals setting out relevant standards (legal, corporate, and industry-self-regulating) and enforcement agency guidelines,[63] together with operating procedures for particular units in the organisation;[64]
- routine controls for monitoring and enforcing compliance together with safeguards for ensuring command of compliance problems by senior management;[65]
- review of loan and other contractual documentation in order to optimise the degree of self-protection;[66]
- control of documentation, including standard contractual terms for protection where secured assets are subject to confiscation, and procedures for avoiding the creation or retention of unnecessarily damaging or incriminating documentation;[67]

60. See e.g. Bruns, "Corporate Preventive Law Programs" (1985) 4 *Preventive Law Reporter* 30 at 31; Arkin, *Business Crime* (1985), para. 6A-7; Dinnie, "Corporate Crime: Prevention is Better than Cure" in *Policing Corporate Crime* (1987) 74 *Proceedings of the Institute of Criminology, University of Sydney* 46 at 48.
61. Dinnie, op. cit. This task includes watching pressures for non-compliance, as discussed in Braithwaite and Fisse, "Preventive Law and Managerial Auditing" (1988) 3 (1) *Managerial Auditing Journal* 17.
62. Braithwaite, op. cit., pp. 32-34, 65-66; Kent, "Risk of 'Smoking Gun' Papers is Outweighed by the Benefits" (1987) 6 (3) *Preventive Law Reporter* 12 at 15-16.
63. E.g. C.T.R. Agency Guideline No. 1.
64. Note Haarer, "Avalanche of Compliance Problems Means More 'Hats' for House· Counsel" (1987) 6 (3) *Preventive Law Reporter* 3 at 6:
    Procedures are "policies explained". They should be intended as informative "road maps of the workplace" which detail the importance of the policies in a practical sense, the consequences of violating those policies and each employee's obligation in connection with policy adherence. Employee handbooks and innovative procedure manuals illustrating policy application in a catechetical setting are examples of this critical education tool.
65. See further Shearing and Stenning (eds), *Private Policing* (1987); Campbell, Fleming and Grote, "Discipline without Punishment—At Last" [1985] Harvard Bus. Rev. 162.
66. Consider e.g. the possible merit of using reservation of title clauses or leases so as to avoid transfer of title to a potential offender whose assets may be subject to forfeiture or restraint. Cf. *Drug Trafficking (Civil Proceedings) Act* 1990 (N.S.W.), s. 59 (re arrangements to defeat operation of statute).
67. See further Fedders and Guttenplan, "Document Retention and Destruction: Practical, Legal and Ethical Considerations" (1980) 56 Notre Dame L. Rev. 5; Curtis, "Establishing and Implementing a Document Retention Program" in A.B.A., *Organising Corporate Compliance Efforts* (1983), Ch. 11; Trower, "Records Retention: An Important Subject Often Gets a Low Priority" (1987) 6 (3) *Preventive Law Reporter* 28; "Legal Ethics and the Destruction of Evidence" (1979) 88 Yale L. J. 1665; Walter and Richard, "Corporate Counsel's Role in Risk Minimisation: Lessons from Bhopal" (1986) 4 *Preventive Law Reporter* 139 at 143-44; Kent, "Risk of 'Smoking Gun' Papers is Outweighed by the Benefits" (1987) 6 (3) *Preventive Law Reporter* 12.

- investigative and reporting procedures structured so as to maximise the protection possible from legal professional privilege;[68]
- action plans in the event of discovery of illegality and for resolution of complaints received from employees, clients, members of the public, or enforcement agencies;[69]
- education and training of personnel;[70]
- regular interaction with the enforcement agencies responsible for administering the relevant statutes;[71]
- liaison with insurers and promotion of favourable insurance track record.[72]

The exact mix and emphasis depends on various factors, most notably organisational structure,[73] nature of financial operations, quality and number of personnel, ability of top management to instil a culture of compliance without laying down detailed rules, and the extent to which achieving compliance and liability control is seen as a line rather than a staff function.[74]

The framework above reflects a liability control, or risk management, perspective. The old-fashioned view of compliance systems revolved around the provision of legal services, whether by way of advice on particular transactions, education of personnel as to legal requirements, or periodic review of contractual and other documentation. A different approach has emerged over the last decade.[75] According to this approach, the basis on which compliance programmes should be built is not only provision of legal services but management of risk of exposure to liability and related losses. This approach transcends legal advice and legal auditing:[76]

68. See discussion and references below, pp. 432-436.
69. See e.g. Dinnie, op. cit. at 51.
70. The C.T.R. Agency has available a good training video on cash transactions reporting. See generally Holtz, "Company Education Programs must Motivate Employees to Listen" (1987) 6 (3) *Preventive Law Reporter* 26.
71. See generally Sigler and Murphy, *Interactive Corporate Compliance: An Alternative to Regulatory Compulsion* (1988).
72. Most of the risks from money trail legislation are not presently insurable but some insurance companies may be prepared to provide insurance for companies that have appropriate controls in place.
73. See further Braithwaite and Fisse, "Varieties of Responsibility and Organisational Crime" (1985) 7 *Law and Policy* 315.
74. For a review of the factors in favour of an integrated approach see Fisse, "Risk Minimisation Through Preventive Law" (1987) 25 (7) L. Soc. J. 54.
75. Especially the experience of Allied Chemical (now Allied Signal): Kent, "Risk of 'Smoking Gun' Papers is Outweighed by the Benefits" (1987) 6 (3) *Preventive Law Reporter* 12; Fisse and Braithwaite, op. cit., Ch. 6. See Further Sigler and Murphy, op. cit.; Beckenstein and Gabel, "Antitrust Compliance: Results of a Survey of Legal Opinion" (1982) 51 Antitrust L. J. 459.
76. Note Kent, "Risk of 'Smoking Gun' Papers is Outweighed by the Benefits" (1987) 6 (3) *Preventive Law Reporter* 12 at 13:
    It may come as a mild shock to the lawyer reader of this article, but the real secret to compliance in this area is not the lawyer—he or she is merely one cog in the compliance wheel. Rather, the secret lies in the active involvement by a sufficient number of competent multidisciplined environmental professionals. These folks should be primarily at the plant level, but with a sufficient number of staff to develop, implement and monitor the various environmental programs.

- liability control systems justify their existence not on the quality or intensity of legal or other input by staff experts but on the contribution made to the company's profitability and reputation;[77]
- management attitudes tend to carry more weight than the views of discrete compliance staff or outside professional advisers;[78]
- compliance depends greatly on the day-to-day accountability of line managers and supervisors for operations under their span of command;[79]
- legal auditing requires that compliance be monitored and the monitoring function is best undertaken as a line as well as a staff responsibility;[80]
- suspected non-compliance is more likely to be reported upwards in an organisation through managers and supervisors than via specialised legal staff;[81]
- self-protective documentation programmes require not only legal auditing but also procedures which are ingrained down the line;[82]
- responding to complaints from consumers, employees, or enforcement agencies is not only a defensive legal function but a feedback mechanism for managerial learning;[83]
- education and training are more obviously achievable through routine operational procedures than by reliance merely on periodic lectures and seminars conducted by compliance staff or solicitors from law firms.[84]

None of this is to deny the importance of the role of legal advisers.[85] The point is that legal services fall within the broader and more fundamental framework of liability control.

CORPORATE POLICY

A cornerstone of a compliance system is a statement of corporate policy resolved by the board of directors and signed by the managing director.

77. Many companies (e.g. Exxon and Allied) stress the financial costs of non-compliance.
78. E.g. the lawyers at General Electric were ineffectual in controlling price fixing in the heavy electrical equipment conspiracies.
79. See further Braithwaite, "Taking Responsibility Seriously: Corporate Compliance Systems" in Fisse and French (eds), *Corrigible Corporations and Unruly Law* (1985), Ch. 3.
80. See further Fisse and Braithwaite, op. cit., Chs 15, 17.
81. The classic example is the information blockage at General Electric which led to its implication in the heavy electrical price-fixing conspiracies of the late 1950s and early 1960s.
82. See e.g. Walter and Richard, "Corporate Counsel's Role in Risk Minimisation: Lessons from Bhopal" (1986) 4 *Preventive Law Reporter* 139; Kent, "Risk of 'Smoking Gun' Papers is Outweighed by the Benefits" (1987) 6 (3) *Preventive Law Reporter* 12.
83. See e.g. Witherell, *How to Avoid Products Liability Lawsuits and Damages* (1985), pp. 255-259.
84. Thus, the thrust of safety education and training at Allied is the pervasive learning process achieved by having standard operating procedures designed to manage risk as a matter of everyday routine.
85. See Witherell, op. cit., p. 246.

The policy statement provides a platform for action within the organisation.

Consider the advice offered by Robert Powis in relation to the United States money laundering legislation:[86]

> A policy statement that clearly spells out senior management's commitment to full compliance . . . should be formulated and distributed to all employees. This statement should make it clear to all employees that the bank policy is to avoid handling the proceeds of drug traffickers and other criminals and to avoid doing business with individuals who are drug traffickers or who are money launderers for drug traffickers. Banks may consider adopting a policy instructing their employees to do business only with individuals, businesses, and other entities whose reputations are sound. The employee who establishes the customer relationship could be charged with the responsibility to determine that customer's character and reputation. One bank's policy directs employees to notify an appropriate senior official whenever it appears that the bank's reputation and that of the customer are not compatible for any reason. The statement should also make it clear that the bank does not want to be "used" for money laundering schemes.
>
> The policy statement should encourage officers and employees to promptly report to the I.R.S. all criminal violations of the *Bank Secrecy Act* and all transactions wherein there is a suspicion of criminal violations to a central location within the bank. The statement should spell out a policy of co-operation with federal enforcement agencies consistent with the provisions of the *Right to Financial Privacy Act*. Consideration should be given to a policy of restricting certain kinds of transactions (wire transfers, purchasers of monetary instruments) to "customers only".

From this may be distilled the following points of focus for a statement of corporate policy:

- the commitment of top management to compliance and the direct relevance of compliance to the company's profitability and reputation;
- the need to avoid doing business with money launderers;[87]
- the importance of timely reporting where required by the legislation;
- the desirability of notifying senior management about questionable customers;

86. Powis, *Bank Secrecy Act Compliance* (2nd ed., 1988), pp. 67-68.
87. Consider ibid., pp. 1-2:
> *Failure to comply with the provisions of the Bank Secrecy Act can cause embarrassment, bad publicity, and loss of business to your financial institution.* Consider the Bank of Boston case: "Bank Officials Linked With Mob." "Bank Looks the Other Way While Drug Dealers Launder Cash." These were the headlines; these were the stories. They make juicy reading, even if they are not true. They can cost an otherwise respected financial institution its good name, which was built up over many years of honest dealing. They can also cost money in terms of lost business. [Emphasis added.]

- the value attached to protection of customer privacy and confidentiality of sensitive information;
- the need to comply with all internal procedures and the internal disciplinary consequences of non-compliance.

Compliance policies are unlikely to be taken seriously unless reinforced by senior management. Empirical research has confirmed the importance of the attitude of top management toward compliance efforts.[88] Much depends on top management commitment (i) to back up the judgment of compliance staff against line managers, (ii) to clearly define line manager accountability for compliance, (iii) to take a personal interest in monitoring compliance performance, (iv) to insist on compliance training programmes, and (v) to foster communication about compliance problems to senior management.[89]

Managerial reinforcement can be achieved in many ways, including these:

- Acting as a top-level "trouble-shooter" who may be approached by employees about a money laundering problem;
- Participating as a keynote speaker in compliance training sessions with managers and supervisors;
- Performing as a narrator or interviewee in video training films;
- Writing notes and comments about money laundering in company newsletters and posters.

RISK IDENTIFICATION AND CONTROL

Two critical elements of liability control are the identification of relevant risks and the adoption of a system for managing them. If required to do so in discovery proceedings or in investigations by enforcement agencies, is it possible to point to a document that summarises the risks faced by the organisation and what has been done to control them?

It is natural for banks and financial institutions to focus on their reporting obligations under the C.T.R. Act, and on such related matters as transactions structured to avoid reporting.[90] However, as explained below, the money trail legislation contains several less obvious traps for the unwary.

The *Proceeds of Crime Act* 1987 (Cth) creates serious yet sweepingly defined offences of money laundering. Under s. 81 money laundering is an offence punishable by a fine of $200,000 and/or 20 years' jail (in the case of a corporation the maximum fine is $600,000). Receiving or

---

88. See Clinard, *Corporate Ethics and Crime: The Role of Middle Management* (1983).
89. Braithwaite, "Taking Responsibility Seriously: Corporate Compliance Systems" in Fisse and French (eds), op. cit., Ch. 3.
90. On structured transactions see s. 31; Hewett and Kalyk, op. cit., pp. 131-133; Fisse and Fraser, above, Chapter 10; Welling, above, Chapter 11. Difficulties arise in determining what banks and finance corporations are supposed to do to avoid being placed in a situation where it would be reasonable to conclude that two or more transactions are illicitly structured. Is it necessary to modify computer programs where existing programs are unable to fast-track multiple deposits at multiple branches?

possessing money or property reasonably suspected to be proceeds of crime is an offence under s. 82. The guilty mind required for liability under s. 81 or s. 82 is broadly defined. The mental element required for liability under s. 81 or s. 82 of the P.O.C. Act is not confined to intention, knowledge or recklessness (compare *Confiscation of Proceeds of Crime Act* (N.S.W.), s. 73, where the offence of money laundering requires knowledge). Under s. 81, liability extends to an unreasonable failure to know that the money or other property is derived or realised, directly or indirectly, from some form of unlawful activity. Under s. 82, D is subject to liability unless he or she can prove on the balance of probabilities that he or she had no reasonable grounds for suspecting that the property referred to in the charge was derived or realised, directly or indirectly, from some form of unlawful activity.

These objective tests of liability are inconsistent with the emphasis traditionally attached to subjective tests of liability for serious offences;[91] subjective blameworthy states of mind have been insisted upon in a long line of High Court decisions, from *R. v. Parker*,[92] to *R. v. Crabbe*,[93] to *He Kaw Teh v. The Queen*[94] and *R. v. Giorgianni*.[95] It is also remarkable that the mental element of money laundering is so radically different from the mental element of receiving, the offence that is a forebear of the offence of money laundering. The mental element required for receiving is knowledge, or at least belief, that the goods received are stolen.[96] The courts have repeatedly refused to equate negligence or even wilful blindness with knowledge.[97] By contrast, an unreasonable failure to know that one is dealing with the proceeds of crime is sufficient under s. 81. Gullibility, carelessness, or excessive optimism is enough to snare a person for money laundering yet not for receiving. It should be noted that money laundering under s. 81 is hardly a minor offence; the maximum punishment is double that typically provided for receiving.

Another potential trap is the adverse possible impact of the provisions for confiscation on banks or other financial institutions who have lent money on the security of an offender's property. Extensive provision is made for the protection of third party interests but lenders may nonetheless find themselves out in the cold.

The P.O.C. Act provides important safeguards for protecting the property interests of innocent third parties. Discretionary forfeiture

91. It should also be realised that ss 81 and 82 do not adhere to the model provided by the money laundering offences enacted under the United States *Money Laundering Control Act* in 1986; under the corresponding United States provisions knowledge is required: 18 U.S.C. s. 1956(a)(b). See further Plombeck, "Confidentiality and Disclosure: The Money Laundering Control Act of 1986 and Banking Secrecy" (1988) 22 *International Lawyer* 69.
92. (1963) 111 C.L.R. 610.
93. (1985) 156 C.L.R. 464.
94. (1985) 157 C.L.R. 523.
95. (1985) 156 C.L.R. 473.
96. *R. v. Raad* [1983] 3 N.S.W.L.R. 344; *R. v. Crooks* [1981] 2 N.Z.L.R. 53.
97. *R. v. Raad* [1983] 3 N.S.W.L.R. 344; *Anderson v. Lynch* (1982) 17 N.T.R. 21; *R. v. Fallon* (1981) 28 S.A.S.R. 394; *R. v. Crooks* [1981] 2 N.Z.L.R. 53. See further Spencer, "Handling, Theft and the Mala Fide Purchaser" [1985] Crim. L. Rev. 92.

orders require that an offender be convicted of an offence;[98] by contrast, there is no such requirement under the forfeiture provisions of the *Customs Act* 1901 (Cth).[99] Where third parties have an interest in property subject to a forfeiture order they may apply to a court to have their interest restored;[100] to succeed they must satisfy the court that they were not involved in the commission of an offence in respect of which the forfeiture order was made or, where the interest was acquired at the time of or after the commission of such an offence, that the interest was acquired for sufficient consideration and without their knowing or being placed on reasonable suspicion that the property was tainted. The automatic forfeiture provisions are also conviction-based, but there must be a conviction for a "serious offence".[101] Forfeiture takes place not by court order but spontaneously where property subject to a restraining order remains in force six months after the conviction. As in the case of discretionary forfeiture, innocent third parties may apply to a court to have their interest restored.[102] Restraining orders are circumscribed by a variety of protections for third parties, including notice of application for an order, notice of an order, and rights of exemption from and revocation of an order.[103]

The worst hazard is the automatic forfeiture process under s. 30 of the P.O.C. Act.[104] Where a third party's property is subject to a restraining order it can be forfeited upon effluxion of six months from the time when another person has been convicted of a relevant serious offence. Although provision is made for innocent parties to protect interests in the property subject to potential forfeiture, the onus is on them to come forward and make application to a court. Passive neglect or casual inaction may thus lead to loss. Worse, even care and attention may not be enough. It is difficult for lenders to keep track of criminal proceedings against borrowers; for instance, it may be impossible to make a quick computer-based check of all the proceedings that might conceivably affect the interest of the lender.

Lenders also face peril in the context of discretionary forfeiture orders where they are given no notice of the forfeiture proceedings. Where a security over property is registered the interest of the lender may come to the attention of the court which in turn may see to it that the lender is notified. However, in the common situation where the security is unregistered there is much less chance of the lender being alerted. There is also the danger that, if the lender is put on notice, it will be too late. Under s. 21(7) of the P.O.C. Act a third party has six months from the date of forfeiture order in which to apply for relief, a period that may be extended under s. 21(8) but only if the applicant can satisfy the court that there has been no neglect in failing to apply within the six month period.

98. As under *Proceeds of Crime Act* (Cth), s. 19.
99. See *Customs Act* 1901 (Cth), ss 229A, 243B, 243C.
100. P.O.C. Act, s. 21.
101. P.O.C. Act, s. 30.
102. P.O.C. Act, s. 31.
103. P.O.C. Act, ss 45, 47, 48, 56.
104. There is no equivalent under the *Confiscation of Proceeds of Crime Act* 1989 (N.S.W.).

The new legislation makes extensive provision for vicarious liability, as under s. 85 of the P.O.C. Act[105] and s. 34 of the C.T.R. Act. The effect of s. 85 of the P.O.C. Act is to impose vicarious and hence strict liability on individual and corporate defendants for the offences prescribed by s. 81 (money laundering), s. 82 (receiving or possessing money or property reasonably suspected to be the proceeds of crime), and s. 83 (organised fraud). The general principle at common law is that liability is personal, not vicarious,[106] and although there are numerous statutory exceptions to that principle it is rare to find vicarious liability in the context of offences carrying jail terms.[107]

Assume that a junior teller in a bank innocently receives a deposit of $5,000 from a customer but in circumstances where there is reason to know that the money is tainted property. The teller has committed the offence of money laundering under s. 81 of the P.O.C. Act and, by virtue of s. 85, the bank is vicariously and hence strictly liable for the same offence; in the case of the bank the maximum penalty is $600,000.

Another potential trap under the legislation is the extent of civil and criminal liability for agents. The vicarious liability provisions under s. 85 of the P.O.C. Act and s. 34 of the C.T.R. Act (parallel provisions exist under other statutes) extend liability to the mental state and conduct of agents as well as servants, subject to the limitation that the agent or servant be acting within the scope of his or her actual or apparent authority. The extension of liability to agents means that an organisation needs to view the potential scope of liability through a wide-angle lens. The potential scope of liability is much broader than some suppose.

Assume that a car dealer receives a deposit of $100,000 for a new B.M.W. 7 Series car, with a balance of $100,000 financed by Credit Limited, a finance corporation, under loan documentation completed by the dealer on behalf of Credit Limited. The car dealer fails to report her or his reasonable grounds for suspecting the transaction. By reason of s. 34 of the C.T.R. Act, Credit Limited is liable for the conduct and mental state of the car dealer if that dealer is its agent, and, as a cash dealer, it thereby becomes liable for the offence of failing to report a suspicious transaction. If the dealer had reason to know that the $100,000 cash deposit was tainted property (as is likely), then, by virtue of s. 85 of the P.O.C. Act, Credit Limited is also liable for the offence of money laundering under s. 81. The conventional assumption in such a case appears to be that what the car dealer gets up to is her or his own affair, but that assumption does not necessarily reflect the position in law. The critical question is whether the dealer is acting as the agent of the cash dealer. This is a complex question, which depends on how the relevant relationships and transactions between the various parties are structured.

To recognise the potential traps outlined above is to point toward responsive action. The following pointers emerge:

105. See also *Confiscation of Proceeds of Crime Act* 1989 (N.S.W.), s. 76.
106. *Tesco Supermarkets Ltd v. Nattrass* [1972] A.C. 153.
107. Section 85 echoes s. 84 of the *Trade Practices Act* (Cth) as amended in 1986 but it should be noticed that, unlike the offences under the P.O.C. Act, the offences and violations under the *Trade Practices Act* do not expose defendants to jail sentences.

- honesty is not enough to avoid liability for money laundering offences: reasonable care must be taken to ensure that one is not dealing with tainted property;
- financial institutions need to be on the alert against forfeiture of assets over which they hold security; there is no easy method of tracking whether assets are subject to forfeiture but some system is needed (for example, watching court lists in the newspaper for proceedings against customers);
- compliance procedures need to reflect the possibility of vicarious liability for low as well as for high level employees: control procedures are required for all employees involved in transactions with customers;
- agents may engage in conduct for which a bank or other financial institution is vicariously liable: contractual arrangements and compliance procedures need to be structured and targeted accordingly.

One commendable precaution against being taken by surprise is to have a procedure specifically requiring employees to voice their concerns about potential money laundering problems to senior management.[108]

ACCOUNTABILITY

Effective compliance requires clear allocation of authority within the organisation.[109]

There are various reasons for pin-pointing accountability by specifying the responsibilities of individuals and sub-units within an organisation. These reasons are perhaps self-evident but bear repetition:

- blurred lines of authority can lead to oversight;
- unambiguous lines of responsibility help to ensure that each task is carried out without undue delay;
- areas where "fail-safe" systems are necessary can be identified more readily;
- personnel are given less opportunity to find excuses for not taking action, or to pass the buck to others;
- control over cost can be enhanced by allocating the costs of non-compliance to the budgets of the operating units concerned;
- internal disciplinary action against non-compliance is promoted where the rules and responsibilities are clearly stated in advance;
- detailed job descriptions facilitate training.

108. See below, "Monitoring and Early Warning", pp. 427-429.
109. As evident from Braithwaite, op. cit., a study of coal-mining safety practices. At all five coal mining safety leaders in the United States, the line manager, not the safety staff, was accountable for the safety of his workforce. A universal feature was also clear definition of the level of the hierarchy responsible for different types of safety breakdowns; personnel knew where the "buck" stopped for different kinds of failures.

The task of working out and administering a scheme of accountability for compliance is now a matter for companies themselves to resolve. One key person is the officer responsible for sending C.T.R.A. forms to the Cash Transaction Reports Agency, and for liaising with the Agency. In defining the responsibilities of the C.T.R.A. contact officer, it may be helpful to take account of the advice given in the American Bankers Association handbook, *Currency Transaction Reporting* (1988).

The A.B.A. handbook recommends the appointment of an administrator whose role depends on the size of the bank. In small banks, the administrator would be an operations specialist combining currency reporting duties with other responsibilities. In medium and large banks a full-time administrator is contemplated. The responsibilities of the administrator are taken to include:

- reviewing completed reporting forms for accuracy, errors, and omissions before filing them with the appropriate government agency;
- reviewing the bank's monitoring system daily to determine compliance with reporting requirements;
- maintaining the bank's central exemption list and serving as the point of approval for additions to and deletions from that list;
- helping to determine an exemption amount for individual customers;
- corresponding directly with the Internal Revenue Service regarding requests for special exemptions from the reporting requirements;
- retaining copies of completed report forms, exemption lists, and other evidence of compliance for at least five years;
- reporting to senior management, at least quarterly, the results of the bank's compliance program (including violations, potential loss exposure, and changes to the regulations);
- reading, researching, interpreting, and generally staying abreast of relevant legislative requirements (including communicating with the bank's legal counsel when necessary);
- co-ordinating the development, implementation, and revision of bankwide operating procedures to ensure compliance;
- helping to develop a formal training program for customer contact personnel;
- disseminating information regarding new or amended compliance requirements to the appropriate administrative departments or customer contact personnel;
- helping to develop a compliance checklist to be used by the bank's internal auditors.

The A.B.A. handbook also proposes the use of currency reporting liaison officers in each branch or department. The ideal choice is said to be the branch or department manager, assistant, or operations supervisor. The responsibilities of such a liaison officer include:

- serving as the principal liaison person between the branch or banking office or department and the central currency reporting administrator;
- verifying the completeness of reporting forms before routing them to the currency reporting administrator;
- spot-checking teller documentation to determine whether currency reporting forms are completed when necessary, and reporting the results of such reviews to the administrator;
- initiating requests for additions to the bank's exemption list;
- co-ordinating the implementation of changes required by new or amended currency reporting requirements;
- co-ordinating the training of personnel in currency reporting requirements as revised;
- making quarterly reports to the currency reporting administrator about compliance activities and the state of currency reporting compliance for the branch, banking office, or department.

COMPLIANCE MANUALS, ACTION SHEETS, AND COMPUTERISATION

The main purposes of compliance manuals are as follows:
- to set out a company's compliance policy and to instil that policy throughout the organisation;
- to specify the legal, corporate, and industry standards to be followed, together with relevant enforcement agency guidelines;
- to lay out the operating procedures for achieving compliance with those standards or guidelines;
- to delineate accountability for compliance;
- to demonstrate that the company has taken due precautions.

The content of compliance manuals varies from company to company, and from operating unit to operating unit within an organisation. There are no immutable rules as to coverage but a comprehensive compliance manual for senior management might well include the following:
- a statement of company policy regarding compliance;
- a supporting statement of the reasons why the policy is important to the company, together with an outline of the ways in which implementation of that policy is to be reinforced by management;
- a summary of the relevant legal, corporate, and industry standards;
- a summary of the company's operating procedures that are most relevant to achieving compliance with the relevant standards;
- a flowchart indicating lines of accountability for money laundering control functions;
- a detailed specification of those compliance procedures that are relevant to the functions of senior management or that apply across

all operating divisions (for example, procedures relating to compliance monitoring);

• cross-references to area-specific manuals for particular operating units within the firm;

• cross-references to legal opinions and advice on central issues;

• action plans prepared by management.

Manuals are appropriate for senior management and branch or department managers. For customer contact staff compliance procedures need to be reduced to plain step-by-step instructions. This can be done by preparing action sheets which take contact staff step by step through what they need to do in relation to a significant cash transaction, a suspect transaction, or use of a false name. Even for branch or departmental managers an action sheet may be a useful way of crystallising what they need to do. Suitably designed action sheets can also provide a convenient record of compliance.

The format of compliance manuals varies widely. One modern trend is to provide computerised manuals with "hypertext" links to related information.[110] This approach enables instant access to pertinent material. It also provides a convenient medium for rapid updating.

Beyond manuals, there is the use of computerisation to automate the process of compliance itself. The C.T.R. Agency and the Australian banking industry have led the world in developing computerised processes for direct reporting of significant transactions. It is estimated that over 90 per cent of significant cash transactions reports in the banking industry will be made directly from tapes supplied by the banks. One important consequence of this approach is to reduce the need for exemptions, a cumbersome and costly feature of currency transaction reporting in the United States. Another is to avoid the paper mountain that significant cash transaction reporting would otherwise generate (in the United States 7 million currency transaction report forms were filed in 1989). Unfortunately, other compliance obligations, most notably suspect transaction reporting, cannot be automated to anywhere near the same extent.

A perennial concern about compliance manuals is that gaps in their coverage, or failure to attain self-set standards, will provide fertile evidence against the company or its officers in the event of legal action. For this reason, a disclaimer clause should be included. An example:

This compliance manual does not and does not purport to provide an exhaustive statement of the goals, policies, procedures, practices, or routines that govern the money laundering control function of this organisation. The ethos and culture of the company transcend any attempt to codify our way of corporate life and could never be captured in a document. It should also be stressed that the standards or obligations endorsed as a matter of company policy may well exceed the standards or obligations imposed by law. The law imposes generalised minimum standards. This manual goes beyond those minimum legal standards. It projects particular models and

110. See further Hawkridge, Newton and Hall, *Computers in Company Training* (1988).

expectations to which we aspire as working ideals. To treat those working ideals as standards legally binding upon the company in its dealings with outsiders would be as absurd as treating biblical commandments as a criminal code.

MONITORING AND EARLY WARNING

Compliance policies and procedures need to be monitored to help ensure compliance.[111] In the context of the *Trade Practices Act* 1974 (Cth) the point has repeatedly been made that the duty to take reasonable care requires not only the adoption of sound policies and procedures but also the supervision and enforcement of them.[112] Thus, in *Trade Practices Commission v. General Corporation Japan (Australia) Pty Ltd*,[113] General was penalised $130,000 for resale price maintenance largely as a reflection of the "totally inadequate" steps taken to impress upon employees and senior management the need to adhere to a compliance policy established by the board of directors. In *Trade Practices Commission v. Commodore Business Machines (Australia) Pty Ltd*,[114] the penalty of $195,000 marked the court's dissatisfaction with Commodore's incomplete efforts to implement legal advice it had received on resale price maintenance. A similar approach is to be expected in the context of money trail legislation.

United States banks are required to have not only a system of currency reporting procedures but also an auditing programme to help ensure that

111. See further Haarer, "Avalanche of Compliance Problems Means More 'Hats' for House Counsel" (1987) 6 (3) *Preventive Law Reporter* 3 at 6:

>Sad but true is the fact that many companies believe that publishing a policy provides absolution from future lawsuits or criminal convictions. Dissuading management from the illusion that policies can be "winked at" after they are published is a key responsibility of house counsel.
>
>Similarly, counsel must educate management that merely promulgating a written policy to the employee population will not excuse civil or possible criminal consequences if an employee fails to adhere to the policy.
>
>Management must understand that the power of its authority requires a corresponding duty to control employee activity and that delegation by management to subordinates will rarely excuse the corporation or its top management from liability if continuing efforts at legal compliance are not consciously and consistently administered.

112. As in *Universal Telecasters Qld Ltd v. Guthrie* (1977) 18 A.L.R. 531; *Videon v. Beneficial Finance Corporation* (1981) A.T.P.R. 40-246; *T.P.C. v. Queensland Aggregates Pty Ltd* (1982) A.T.P.R. 40-317. See also *Re Holland Furnace Co.* 341 F.2d 548 (1965). How frequent and how extensive the checks and reviews should be varies from context to context. If a bank has encountered a string of money laundering episodes, weekly or even daily reviews of control procedures by an executive director may be warranted. If the bank has a clean record, it may be sufficient for the board to act on the basis of an annual compliance report prepared by the personnel in charge of compliance. In the event of a major catastrophe, it may be necessary for the board itself to take an active role in resolving what should be done to revise existing compliance procedures. A task force approach has been adopted in response to some major corporate episodes of non-compliance, with board representation on the task force; see Fisse and Braithwaite, op. cit., Chs 5, 6.

113. (1989) A.T.P.R. 40-922. See also *T.P.C. v. B.P. Australia Ltd* (1986) A.T.P.R. 40-652.

114. (1990) A.T.P.R. 41-019.

the procedures are followed.[115] The programme can be carried out by a bank's internal auditors, or by an accounting or consulting firm. There is no requirement of compliance auditing under the C.T.R. Act but what is required by law in the United States may influence prudential practice in Australia.

An auditing programme is intended to ensure that:[116]

- internal compliance controls and procedures are adequate, effective, and efficient;
- officers and employees are properly trained in the procedures for compliance;
- reporting requirements are being complied with;
- compliance policies and procedures are in fact being followed;
- senior managers receive a proper evaluation of the state of compliance.

The A.B.A. handbook makes the following recommendations:

- the audit programme should be conducted annually but more frequent audits may be required in relation to any trouble spots within the organisation;
- an auditing checklist should be developed, with a testing section (sampling and selection guidelines) and a review section (explaining what to look for once the sampling and selection process is completed);
- the audit should include at least five to ten days of transactions at each branch office being audited;
- the test days should include a high-volume day, such as a payday or a holiday eve (that is, a time likely to be used by money launderers).

An excellent example of an auditor's checklist for currency transaction reporting is contained in the I.B.M. P.C. compliance tutorial program prepared by the A.B.A. The Auditing Checklist provides bank auditors with an automated means of evaluating a bank's compliance and the adequacy of internal controls to assure ongoing compliance. A "no" answer to any of the questions indicates a violation of law or an internal control weakness (there are over 50 questions). Once an audit is completed using the program, the auditor is able to print a summary of the findings along with recommendations for improvement.

In addition to the monitoring controls mentioned above, it is advisable to make provision for early signs of danger to be reported to senior management as and when they occur. Preventive intelligence and effective channels of communications within an organisation are essential to the task of avoiding violations or minimising the loss flowing from them.[117]

115. See American Bankers Association, *Currency Transaction Reporting* (1988), p. 48.
116. Ibid., p. 56.
117. See e.g. Coffee, "Beyond the Shut-Eyed Sentry" (1977) 63 Virginia L. Rev. 1099.

Cases have often arisen where even widespread illegality at the level of middle management has passed unnoticed by top management.[118] A notorious example is General Electric's experience during the heavy electrical equipment conspiracies of the late 1950s and early 1960s. Systematic price-fixing by sales executives took place for years without being detected by top management. General Electric was fined $437,500 for its part in the conspiracies and many middle managers were convicted. The company had a firmly-worded compliance policy on antitrust but its reporting and monitoring procedures had failed. Although much effort had been expended on advice and compliance auditing by the legal staff, the outbreak of price-fixing had passed undetected. In light of this and other similar episodes, numerous companies have revised their reporting systems so as to "bubble up" news of suspected illegality to senior management.

The solution adopted by many American companies (for example, General Electric, Allied-Signal, Dow Chemical) has been to supplement traditional one-over-one reporting relationships with extra reporting channels through which the concerns of personnel about possible areas of non-compliance can readily be communicated to top management. Expanding upon this practice, John Braithwaite has made these suggestions:[119]

- make sure that routine formal reporting relationships are designed well enough, and appropriately enough to the unique environment of the company, to ensure that most recurrent problems of non-compliance are reported to those with the power to correct them;

- make sure there is a free route to the top, bypassing line reporting relationships, to reduce the likely success of conspiratorial blocking of bad news;

- create a corporate culture with a climate of concern for compliance problems which are not an employee's own responsibility, an organisation "full of antennas" in which there is a commitment to being alert to noticing and reporting how others, as well as oneself, can solve compliance problems.

DOCUMENTATION CONTROL

A documentation control programme serves various purposes:

- compliance with statutory or self-regulatory record-keeping requirements;

- improving self protection by reviewing standard term contracts in order to guard against newly discovered forms of risk;

- generation of useful evidence for defence against lawsuits;

---

118. See e.g. *T.P.C. v. Dunlop Australia Ltd* (1980) A.T.P.R. 40-167; *T.P.C. v. General Corporation Japan (Australia) Pty Ltd* (1989) A.T.P.R. 40-922. Consider also Exxon in relation to allegations of the payment of bribes by its Italian subsidiary in the mid 1970s.

119. Braithwaite, "Taking Responsibility Seriously: Corporate Compliance Systems", in Fisse and French (eds), op. cit., pp. 46-47.

- neutralisation, within legal and ethical limits, of otherwise misleading or harmful documents;
- protection against disclosure of confidential documents;
- insulation from liability by clearly marking and isolating responsibilities to be borne by subsidiaries, independent contractors, consumers, successor companies, and other parties;
- assistance in monitoring compliance efforts.

The money trail legislation affects record keeping in three major ways. First, s. 23 of the C.T.R. Act requires cash dealers to keep certain information about accounts for seven years after the day when an account is closed. However, there is no provision in the Act requiring a record to be kept of any report made under the Act. Nor does it seem that the record keeping requirements under the P.O.C. Act[120] apply to reports made under the C.T.R. Act.[121] The main consideration for cash dealers is protection against litigation from customers. Suspect transaction reporting is the prime area of concern here, and it is advisable to retain a copy of the report filed, together with action sheets and notes; a seven-year retention period seems advisable to allow for statutory limitation periods.[122] Secondly, the P.O.C. Act imposes a regime of required record-keeping.[123] Financial transaction documents must be retained for a specified period related to the category of document involved. Thus, documents relating to the telegraphic or electronic transfer of funds must be kept for seven years from the day of the transaction.[124] Third, the sensitive nature of suspect transaction reporting places a premium upon confidential and accurate record keeping practices. Although suspect transaction reports are most unlikely to be made available under the *Freedom of Information Act* 1982 (Cth), subsequent law enforcement action may lead a customer to suspect that a suspect transaction report has been made and in turn to take action for defamation or breach of confidence. Sound documentation control is essential to successful defence against legal action by any such aggrieved customer.

Another aspect of documentation control is reviewing standard contractual documentation in light of the risks posed by confiscation of proceeds of crime legislation. Two Wall Street lawyers, Danforth Newcomb and Cathleen Shine, have recommended that banks take care to revise their loan documentation in light of the risk of crime-related forfeiture.[125] One precaution is to obtain a representation from the client that no confiscation of the assets secured is threatened or pending. The main point of such a precaution is to strengthen the bank's case if it is later placed in the position of having to establish that its security interest arose in circumstances where it had no reason to suspect that the

120. See P.O.C. Act, ss 76-78.
121. An issue canvassed in Pinner, above, Chapter 3.
122. E.g. the six year limitation period under the *Limitation Act* 1969 (N.S.W.), s. 14(1).
123. See P.O.C. Act, ss 76-78.
124. P.O.C. Act, ss 76, 77.
125. Newcomb and Shine, "Asset Forfeiture: A Primer for Bankers" in A.B.A., *Money Laundering Enforcement: Legal and Practical Developments* (1989) 395.

secured assets were the proceeds of crime.[126] A second precaution is to impose a specific obligation upon a borrower to notify the bank of any proceeding that could lead to confiscation of a secured asset. Another precaution again is to have a specific default provision that allows the bank to terminate the loan once the risk of confiscation arises.

Care also needs to be taken in documentation when handling further inquiries from the C.T.R. Agency or other law enforcement agencies in relation to suspect transaction reports. Under s. 16(5) action pursuant to s. 16 is immunised against liability. This immunity may be critical in cases where aggrieved customers sue for breach of confidence of defamation. Information volunteered to the C.T.R. Agency or to any other law enforcement agency will not be protected under s. 16(5). The immunity applies only to action pursuant to s. 16, and there must be a request for information under s. 16(4) before the giving of information is pursuant to the section. The request under s. 16(4) should therefore be filed. It is also advisable to make it crystal clear in any communication with the C.T.R. Agency or other law enforcement agency that the information provided is at the request of the C.T.R. Agency under s. 16, and is given solely for the purpose of complying with s. 16. Any communication should be put in writing and headed in such a way as to indicate that it is confidential and conveyed pursuant to s. 16

A final issue of documentation control worth mentioning is the inevitable "hot file"[127] which, if left in the company's records, may easily turn out to be the incriminating "smoking gun" in later litigation. For instance, there may be complaints on record from employees that a branch manager is suspected of arranging unreported currency transactions for drug traffickers or tax evaders. Shredding the record in such a case is dangerous, for a number of reasons:

- if their complaints are ignored, the complaining employees may go straight to the C.T.R. Agency or the police;

- if litigation is underway or expected, destroying relevant evidence creates a real risk of criminal liability (for example, for contempt of court or for attempting to pervert the course of justice)[128] as well as civil liability for fraud;

- if files relevant to a contested issue are inexplicably missing, an adverse inference can readily be drawn and this may be critical to the outcome of the case;

- unsuccessful attempts to cover up a problem may easily spark a public relations disaster;[129]

126. See above, p. 421.
127. The file need not be red hot to be damaging; see Witherell, *How to Avoid Products Liability Lawsuits and Damages*, p. 240: "it is not so much *what* is said but *how it appears in court*, with the court having benefit of 20/20 hindsight, that really matters."
128. See generally Fedders and Guttenplan, "Document Retention and Destruction: Practical, Legal and Ethical Considerations" (1980) *Notre Dame Law Review* 5; Note, "Legal Ethics and the Destruction of Evidence" (1979) 88 Yale L. J. 1665.
129. See e.g. Fisse and Braithwaite, *The Impact of Publicity on Corporate Offenders*, Ch. 18 (Air New Zealand and Mt. Erebus Disaster).

- hot files have a habit of being copied by employees, and subsequently falling into the hands of the media.[130]

It is thus advisable to neutralise the potentially damaging file rather than to shred it. Neutralisation is possible using the "loop-closing" procedure developed by General Motors in the context of product liability.[131] When a question is raised about the safety of a product, the loop thereby opened is required to be closed by a written answer either resolving the problem or denying that a problem exists. Loop-closing does not involve falsification of the record[132] but getting the position straight in order to avoid "a welter of unjustified litigation". In the example above there is no realistic alternative but to investigate the complaints, and to close the loop by documenting the outcome. The danger of unfolding highly prejudicial information that might be used against the bank (for example, in a prosecution for money laundering or for failing to report suspect transactions) can be managed by using a legal adviser to conduct the inquiry and to shield the results by means of legal professional privilege, an avenue discussed in the next section.

LEGAL PROFESSIONAL PRIVILEGE

An organisation sensing that it has a problem of non-compliance with the law faces a dilemma. The first horn of the dilemma is pressure to find out what has occurred. Apart from the possible risk of liability for negligence, it is good business practice to avert governmental investigation or adverse publicity by nipping it in the bud.[133]

---

130. Note Witherell, *How to Avoid Products Liability Lawsuits and Damages*, pp. 239-40 re the "save your hide" syndrome that often leads to hot files:

> While it is easy to criticise those engaging in this practice, it is probably unfair to do so. Most often the practice stems from inept management that creates a climate of distrust of one's superiors, of the company's management, and of possibly everyone else in the operation. It is deplorable when professionals feel so frustrated in their failure to communicate with management that they must resort to this approach. It is a warning signal that management, if alert to the problem as it should be, should heed, as it is a symptom of an unhealthy organisation.

131. See Fisse and Braithwaite, *The Impact of Publicity on Corporate Offenders*, pp. 36-37.
132. Cf. Epstein, "Polluted Data" [1978] *The Sciences* (July-August) 16.
133. See further Mathews, "Internal Corporate Investigations" (1984) 45 Ohio State L. J. 655 at 671-672:

> an internal self-investigation is less painful than a government investigation. I have articulated over the years a set of fourteen "Rules of Thumb in Defending S.E.C. Investigations".
>
> Rule Two: Take control of the investigation—get the S.E.C. out as quickly as possible.
>
> > a. Obviously, neither defence counsel nor his clients should engage in sharp tactics that smack of obstruction of justice, but within acceptable legal and ethical bounds, counsel should influence as much as possible the speed and scope of the investigation.
> >
> > b. If necessary, have the client offer to investigate itself, or to have an independent special counsel conduct the investigation. The goal is to have a nonprosecutorial person, rather than a government enforcement agency, conduct whatever investigation is required.

Accordingly, companies often find themselves obliged to make thorough internal investigations.[134] The other horn of the dilemma is the danger that effective internal investigations will dramatically increase the risk of exposure to liability.[135] Taking statements from employees and preparing a detailed investigative report creates a high risk of providing ready-made evidence for enforcement agencies and plaintiffs.

As explained below, legal professional privilege can be used to help resolve the dilemma.[136] It should be remembered, however, that legal professional privilege provides only a partial shield against liability. Facts cannot be concealed merely by communicating them to a lawyer; enforcement agencies and plaintiffs are still free to get evidence by other means, including questions put to the company requiring it to disclose the facts as known to its employees.[137]

Nonetheless, the importance of shielding internal interview notes is plain. The information contained in such notes may be far more incriminating than briefer responses sufficient to satisfy civil discovery, or what is necessary to satisfy a demand for information under a statutory power of investigation:

> Pleading . . . resembles nothing so much as naval warfare before the advent of radar, when each side made blind forays into the sea area of the other, while giving away as little as possible about the disposition of his own forces.[138]

Moreover, enforcement agencies and private litigants often begin their inquiries months or even years after the event, by which time recollections tend to fade without leaving scarlet trace.[139]

133. *continued*
> I do concede, however, that the self-investigation may, in the short run, be more costly to the corporation in terms of legal fees than allowing the government to expend its resources in the investigation. . . . major investigations by outside counsel and independent accounting firms are expensive. Consequently, in some cases in which I have represented smaller, financially insecure companies, I have advised them not to conduct an internal investigation and instead to let the S.E.C. expend its budget in developing the facts.
134. See further Mathews, "Internal Corporate Investigations" (1984) 45 Ohio State L. J. 655; Morvillo, "Voluntary Corporate In-House Investigations—Benefits and Pitfalls" (1981) 36 *Business Lawyer* 1871.
135. See Block and Barton, "Internal Corporate Investigations: Maintaining the Confidentiality of a Corporate Client's Communications with Investigative Counsel" (1979) 35 *Business Lawyer* 5 at 6.
136. Arkin, *Business Crime* (1985), paras 6.02, 6-3.
137. See Bray, *The Principles and Practice of Discovery* (1985), pp. 138-142, 364-365. For a useful assessment of the advantages and limitations of legal professional privilege as a tool of risk management see Sigler and Murphy, op. cit., pp. 74-76. Statutory investigative powers (e.g. C.T.R. Act, s. 16(4); P.O.C. Act, s. 36) do not over-ride legal professional privilege unless they provide so expressly or by clear implication: *Baker v. Campbell* (1983) 153 C.L.R. 674; *Commissioner of Taxation v. Citibank Limited* (1989) 20 F.C.R. 403; *Bond Corporation Holdings Ltd v. Australian Broadcasting Tribunal* (1988) 3 B.R. 121; 84 A.L.R. 669. But see *Corporate Affairs Commission v. Yuill* (1991) 65 A.L.J.R. 500.
138. Justice, *Going to Law: A Critique of English Civil Procedure* (1974), p. 13.
139. See generally Nath, "Upjohn: A New Prescription for the Attorney-Client Privilege and Work Product Defences in Administrative Investigations" (1981) 30 Buffalo L. J. 11.

It may also be pointed out that exploiting legal professional privilege can give personnel the misleading impression that the object is to evade the law rather than to comply with it. This is a real risk where a compliance programme is dedicated to documentation control and other defensive or obstructionist devices. However, there is little danger if legal professional privilege is exploited as part of a comprehensive liability control system where the value of compliance is stressed and reinforced by senior management and where the need to avoid potentially damaging incidents is emphasised. Seen in that light, legal professional privilege is not inimical to compliance; rather, it is a means of damage control where primary compliance efforts have failed.

One major stumbling block is the requirement that the communication be for the sole purpose[140] of obtaining legal advice or for assisting litigation. Organisations have often fallen into the trap of conducting multi-purpose inquiries into episodes of suspected non-compliance rather than dividing up the task and channelling the most legally sensitive matters through the company's legal advisers. This trap has defeated claims of legal professional privilege in several reported decisions,[141] including *Grant v. Downs*,[142] a decision of the High Court of Australia.[143]

The sole purpose test under *Grant v. Downs* can be satisfied provided that corporate communications are carefully structured in advance. The basic strategy required is to divide sensitive inquiries into two or more

---

140. *Grant v. Downs* (1976) 135 C.L.R. 674. Contrast the dominant purpose rule under New Zealand and English law: *Waugh v. British Railways Board* [1980] A.C. 521; *Stuart v. Guardian Royal Exchange of New Zealand Ltd* [1985] 1 N.Z.L.R. 597.
141. A rare exception is *Waterford v. Commonwealth* (1987) 61 A.L.J.R. 350.
142. (1976) 135 C.L.R. 674. Cf. *Waugh v. British Railways Board* [1980] A.C. 521.
143. In *Grant v. Downs* (1976) 135 C.L.R. 674, an action was brought for negligence in the care and supervision of the deceased who had died from exposure after escaping from a psychiatric centre. Discovery was sought of certain official reports into the death but this was resisted on the basis that the documents were protected by legal professional privilege. The claim of privilege rested mainly on an affidavit of a senior officer of the New South Wales Health Commission. The affidavit set out the administrative reasons for making routine official reports in the event of death or injury to mental patients. The reports had three basic purposes: to promote internal disciplinary action, to facilitate revision of security and preventive procedures, and to equip the Department of Health's legal representatives with a contemporaneous detailed report on which they could found their advice to the Department or represent it in legal proceedings. The High Court of Australia held that the reports in question were not covered by legal professional privilege. In the opinion of the majority (Stephen, Mason, and Murphy JJ.), legal professional privilege did not cover documents prepared for legal advisers unless the sole purpose is submission for legal advice or use in legal proceedings. This test plainly had not been satisfied because the reports were for administrative as well as legal purposes (at 690):

> [T]he documents have about them a flavour of routine reports such as would be made by any institution or corporation relating to an occurrence of the kind that took place so as to inform itself of the circumstances in which the death of the patient occurred and with a view to disciplinary action and the reform of any procedures that might be found to be defective.

clearly separated channels.[144] Directed through the first channel is a preliminary routine inquiry to advise management briefly of the circumstances surrounding the problem.[145] A second channel is then used for a fuller confidential investigation conducted by the company's legal representatives for the sole purpose of providing the company with legal advice or of assisting it in litigation.[146]

Several steps are probably necessary to guard against the risk of a court treating second-channel reports as routine reports which the corporation would have been expected to create for the purpose of informing itself adequately for administrative purposes.[147] The non-routine nature of the investigative inquiry should be spelt out in the instructions to the legal adviser, and reference made to the need for legal advice and for recourse to professional skills not possessed by management. In particular, mention should be made of the legal issues about which management is apprehensive and the need for a full inquiry to be made by a lawyer in order to ascertain exactly what the risks of liability are and to provide advice as to legal solutions which might be adopted.[148] It is also advisable to include an instruction to the effect that the purpose of seeking legal advice is to enable management to handle questions of liability for past conduct and that any question of administrative changes will be left to separate inquiry.[149]

Another possible obstacle is the rule requiring existing or anticipated litigation before communications between lawyer or client and third parties can be privileged.[150] It has been held in several cases that communications with a third party are not privileged unless made for the purpose of conducting or aiding the conduct of existing or anticipated

144. Compare *Re Grand Jury Subpoena (Doe)* 599 F.2d 504 (1979); Kent, "Risk of 'Smoking Gun' Papers is Outweighed by the Benefits" (1987) 6 (3) *Preventive Law Reporter* 12 at 15. The strategy discussed in the text relies on two channels of inquiry. In some contexts a third channel of inquiry may be necessary, as for the purpose of insurance. Consider the implications of *National Employers' Mutual General Insurance Association Ltd v. Waind* (1979) 141 C.L.R. 648; *Leader Westernport Printing Pty Ltd v. I.P.D. Instant & Duplicating Pty Ltd* (1988) 5 A.N.Z. Ins. Cas. 60-856. On the downside is the need to use a lawyer to conduct sensitive inquiries among personnel who may remain silent if confronted by a lawyer rather than by a managerial colleague. However, this downside might well be eliminated where the lawyer is also an active member of the managerial team and respected as such. Satisfying the sole purpose test under *Grant v. Downs* does not require that the lawyer conducting the inquiry be perceived solely as a lawyer by the personnel interviewed: it is sufficient that the inquiry be conducted for the sole purpose of giving or obtaining legal advice.
145. See Block and Barton, "Internal Corporate Investigations" (1979) 35 *Business Lawyer* 5 at 9.
146. It is immaterial that the resulting document, if prepared for the sole purpose of legal advice or use in litigation, contains some material which relates to matters of policy or administration: *Waterford v. Commonwealth* (1987) 61 A.L.J.R. 350.
147. See *Grant v. Downs* (1976) 135 C.L.R. 674 at 688 per Stephen, Murphy, and Mason JJ.: a document is not protected by the privilege if it "would have been brought into existence . . . in any event" for some purpose other than legal advice or for use in litigation.
148. See Block and Barton, op. cit. at 9, 11.
149. Reflecting *Waugh v. British Railways Board* [1980] A.C. 521 at 537 per Lord Simon.
150. As applied in *Re Australian Bank Employees' Union; Ex parte A.B.N. Australia Ltd* (1987) 61 A.L.J.R. 277.

litigation.[151] The status of this rule is unclear, but even if it were upheld it would have little bearing on sensitive inquiries conducted before litigation is anticipated. There is solid authority for the proposition that the rule does not apply to communications with third parties who are employees of the client.[152] The road is thus open for a corporate client to use legal professional privilege to help protect internal interviews with employees even if at that stage there is no reasonable anticipation of litigation.

COMPLAINTS MANAGEMENT

The functions of complaints management are basically these:

- receipt of complaints from consumers, employees, enforcement agencies or the general public;
- investigation of complaints where warranted, whether or not any legal claim has yet been filed;
- resolution of complaints, either by management or by referral to a legal adviser;[153]
- formulation of action plans for coping with conceivable crises, including use of a task force to deal quickly with any major problem;
- providing feedback about money laundering problems or solutions discovered as a result of complaints;
- documenting action taken in response to complaints.

Some complaints can be avoided simply by putting customers in the picture about the impact of the new legislation. The major banks and the Australian Bankers Association have prepared customer information leaflets that go some distance toward allaying the concerns that customers may legitimately have about protection of their privacy. However, not all of these leaflets focus on the interest that banks have in protecting customer privacy. It would seem appropriate to include a message about the importance of protecting customer privacy and the fact that steps are taken to protect the confidentiality of client histories and other information.

Where civil claims are made by customers, timely and tactful action can defuse the issue and, through settlement, avoid potentially damaging litigation.[154] Such an approach can also facilitate the early discovery of information about a problem and thereby help to avoid future claims. Similar considerations apply to possible allegations that the company has

151. *Wheeler v. Le Marchant* (1881) 17 Ch. D. 675; *Nickmar Pty Ltd v. Preservatrice Skandia Insurance Ltd* (1985) 3 N.S.W.L.R. 44; *Macedonia Pty Ltd v. Federal Commissioner of Taxation* (1987) A.T.C. 4565; Eagles, "Legal Professional Privilege and the Corporate Client" (1987) 12 N.Z. Universities L. Rev. 297. But see *Weir v. Greening* [1957] V.R. 296 at 300-301 per Sholl J.
152. *Nickmar Pty Ltd v. Preservatrice Skandia Insurance Ltd* (1985) 3 N.S.W.L.R. 44.
153. See generally Witherell, op. cit., pp. 255-260. On handling adverse publicity see Irvine, *When You are the Headline: Managing a Major News Story* (1987); Fisse and Braithwaite, op. cit., pp. 228-229; Collins and Przybylski, "Reacting to Unfavourable Television Publicity" (1986) 2 Trade Prac. Advertising and Marketing L. B. 37.
154. See Witherell, op. cit., pp. 255-259.

committed an offence. Prompt commitment by the company to finding out the cause of the problem and to taking corrective action removes much of the incentive enforcement agencies otherwise have to launch or maintain a prosecution. A complaint response capacity can also be useful in dealing quickly with threatened adverse publicity.

Effective complaint response requires co-ordination with legal advisers. Decisions made at this point can shape and determine the course of events in any litigation, and reliance on legal professional privilege and other avenues of legal self-protection may be critical to success or failure in defence.

Speed is of the essence in effectively responding to claims or warnings. The history of organisational behaviour is littered with instances where compliance systems have not been used by management as planned, and where control of a crisis has been lost as a result. An infamous example is the handling of the news media by N.A.S.A. in the wake of the Challenger disaster.[155]

N.A.S.A. had a public affairs contingency plan for shuttle accidents since 1983.[156] That plan was in part as follows:

> Status of the crew will be the prime public consideration under any emergency situation. Consequently the facts, once confirmed, should be announced as quickly as possible. No longer than 20 minutes should elapse before an announcement is made.

However, that plan was not implemented after the explosion of the Challenger. It took five hours before a statement was released by an official spokesperson and that statement provided very little information. Only after the Rogers Commission began its inquiry did N.A.S.A. release information sufficient to reassure the public that all aspects of the accident were being investigated and would be disclosed. In the opinion of one critic, this failure of internal compliance devastated N.A.S.A.'s credibility:

> It only took a few hours, but N.A.S.A.'s management myopia and subsequent siege mentality regarding the news media seriously damaged a highly effective press relations program that had been developed and refined over a quarter century of space flight. It also turned the media against N.A.S.A. in an attack that would continue unA.B.A.ted for six months. In the process the image of an organisation that represented the best of American know-how and technology would come to be perceived as a bureaucracy whose inept management decisions had cost the lives of the seven astronauts.[157]

EDUCATION AND TRAINING

Education and training are critical to the success of compliance. The traditional methods include compliance manuals, lectures, seminars, and

155. Irvine, op. cit., pp. 13-14.
156. Ibid.
157. Ibid., p. 14.

video-tape programmes.[158] As with educative methods generally, the efficacy of such techniques is variable and uncertain:

> Education is widely accepted as a compliance measure, but it is rarely subjected to much analysis. How much reliance can be placed on education? How effective are the various educational techniques? If a dramatic presentation is made once a year, how much of its impact will be retained eleven months later? Is it more effective to focus on potential criminal penalties or to attempt to explain the application of the law? Or is it best to focus on the social objectives represented by the particular legislation? Is a multi-media presentation more effective? Is there an actual correlation between educational programs and the conduct of the attendees? For the most part these questions are not only not answered, they are rarely, if ever, asked.[159]

These questions underscore the point that the prime method of education and training is day-to-day practice in the workplace. The most effective form of compliance instruction in an organisation is a well-designed standard operating procedure that manages the task of compliance as everyday routine. Thus, in the context of suspect transaction reporting, there is merit in providing counter staff with a step-by-step action sheet that tells them what to do and what to consider when filling in the relevant items on C.T.R.A. Form 16. Given the common sense of integrating training and day-to-day work, it seems regrettable that the focus of the national training levy scheme appears to be on forms of training discrete from routine procedures.

Training sessions have a useful supplementary role. A section on money laundering and cash transaction reporting can readily be included in induction sessions and periodic refresher courses, as is typically the practice in the banking and finance industry. Action sheets and compliance manuals provide a useful launching pad for this purpose. Some banks, including the Bank of Boston, have gone further by developing detailed training packages for instructors; these include testing routines as well as key points for discussion and form completion exercises. Robert Powis has gone even further in suggesting training for directors, the Chief Executive Officer and senior officers of the bank:[160]

> Senior officers and directors should participate in an executive forum with experts in the *Bank Secrecy Act*. The objective of this forum would be to increase knowledge and sensitivity regarding the responsibilities and risks of non-compliance with the Act. It would also provide them with an understanding of the Act's requirements, the points of vulnerability and risks for the bank, and a discussion of effective compliance policies and procedures. Perhaps most important, there should be a discussion of costs and resources needed to run an effective compliance program as required by regulations, and to maintain the bank's reputation versus the costs

158. See further Holtz, "Company Education Programs must Motivate Employees to Get Involved" (1987) 6 (3) *Preventive Law Reporter* 26.
159. Sigler and Murphy, op. cit., p. 84.
160. Powis, op. cit., p. 72.

associated with the negative publicity arising from serious non-compliance. There would also be a discussion of indirect costs that may arise from future legislative proposals.

Computer-based training[161] may also be relevant, partly because it offers an efficient, standardised means of instruction:

In training, increased standardisation is often equated with increased effectiveness. Conventional "stand-up" or instructor-led training is notoriously unstandardised, varying with the trainer and training centre. Computer-based training, commonly known as "C.B.T.", appears to offer standardisation. Eastman Kodak, for example, decided to use microcomputers to standardise its training of field service engineers. The trainees were widely scattered, worldwide, yet the training had to be done quickly and in standardised form. Texaco Tankerships' trainees are even more widely scattered, on board ships moving across the oceans. Yet tanker crews need standardised and frequent training in safety and emergency procedures. C.B.T. is providing this.

C.B.T. cannot guarantee standardisation of performance, as opposed to standardisation of training, because ultimately, of course, on-the-job performance depends on the individual as well as the training. But it can increase the chances of performance being up to a particular standard. Kearsley suggests that some companies want increased control over training. With printed manuals, branch offices use the existing material differently or neglect it altogether, with very uneven results. Unstandardised training can be expensive in company systems that demand uniformity (such as banks and insurance companies). Standardised training can be introduced through C.B.T. because the software can be developed to include frequent testing and recording of progress and scores.[162]

INTERACTION WITH ENFORCEMENT AGENCIES

Many subscribe to the view that avoiding enforcement action depends not so much on knowing oneself as on knowing one's regulators. In extreme form this is the "capture theory" of business regulation. More realistically, the point is simply that enforcers are more likely to adopt a "softly, softly" approach to violations if one has previously shown an interest in compliance by liaising with the relevant enforcement agencies. It is significant that the C.T.R. Agency has been one of the main Australian enforcement agencies to foster such an approach. The stance of other agencies with responsibilities in this area (for example, the N.C.A.) is much less clear.

There is a growing literature on the merits of interaction between government and corporations. A recent leading contribution is Sigler and Murphy's book, *Interactive Compliance*.[163] Government and business,

---

161. See further Hawkridge, Newton and Hall, op. cit.
162. Ibid., p. 12.
163. Op. cit. An earlier important work on the significance of compliance-based enforcement efforts is Hawkins, *Environment and Enforcement* (1984).

it is claimed, have become trapped in an accelerating contest of tit-for-tat. The way out of this mindless contest, it is suggested, is a system of mutual support and co-operation. The interactive system envisaged would involve an increased commitment to internal compliance controls by corporations and fuller recognition by government agencies of corporate compliance initiatives. There would also be a sharing of expertise, as by government compliance specialists working within corporations and corporate specialists within government. Such an approach is largely consistent with the direction that has been taken by the C.T.R. Agency. It remains to be seen whether the Agency will follow the Trade Practices Commission by providing detailed assistance with the development of compliance systems on a user pays basis.[164]

CONCLUSION: THE FABLE OF MANUEL DE COLUMBIA'S GOOD, CLEAN DRUG CASH

Money laundering legislation represents a sea change in social control and, from the standpoint of financial institutions, may be seen as having created a flood of obligations and hazards. The task of this chapter has been to address the problem by suggesting a framework for a system of control gates.

It is of course possible to look at the subject of compliance from many other angles. Consider the thesis of Manuel de Columbia, spokesman for the Drug Launderers of America, that society needs money launderers to turn bad money into good money:[165]

> Perhaps the proceeds did come from selling dope, but before the bankers got through with it, they were financing condominiums in the Everglades. I know most of these money launderers personally, and I would trust them with my sister.

For better or worse, however, the law has yet to recognise either economics or humour as a good excuse.

---

164. It might be maintained that, in the context of loosely defined obligations (e.g. the suspect transaction reporting obligation), it is the function of government to develop model compliance procedures and thereby to show that the task of compliance is both manageable and not unduly costly.
165. Art Buchwald, "Good, Clean Drug Cash", *International Herald-Tribune*, 25 January 1990.

Index

Accomplice, 192
  attempting to cause failure to report
      (U.S.), 213-214
  bank customers, 234

"Account", 156-157

Account verification, 170

Accountability, 423-425

Acquisitions
  inquiry, 402-403

"Affairs", 247

Agents, 159
  liability, 422

Aggregation, 378-379
  issue addressed by U.S. regulation,
      209-212
  under original U.S. reporting statute,
      206-209

American Bankers Association
  advertising campaign, 369-370
  Money Laundering Task Force, 361-362
  recommendations on administration and
      liaison, 424-425
  survey on money laundering, 362-363

Anti-Drug Abuse Act (U.S.), 383

Anton Piller orders, 287

Assets
  disclosure of, 318-319
  freezing, 286-287
  overseas, 321
  tracing, 285-286

Attainder, 50-51, 76, 103, 108, 144

Attempt (offence), 188

Auditing programme, 427-428

Australian Securities Commission, 286,
      292
  powers, 291

Bank account, 412
  false name, 265

Banking (Foreign Exchange) Regulations
      1946, 275

Bank Secrecy Act (U.S.), 32, 35, 203,
      354-355, 374—see also Currency
      and Foreign Transaction
      Reporting Act (U.S.)
  "financial institution", 379
  identification of customers, 379-380
  informants, 282-283
  reporting requirements, 378-379
  "structuring" offence, 381-382
  "targeting" provisions, 380
  wire transfers, 382-383

Banks—see also Compliance systems;
      Suspect transactions
  accountability, 423-425
  American Bankers Association Money
      Laundering Task Force, 361-362
  branches
    transactions combined in U.S.,
        209-210
  collateral, 420
  compliance programme (U.S.), 391-406
  computing systems, 398
  constructive trust, 337
  convicted of money laundering (U.S.),
      364-365
  corporate officers' liability, 413-414
  costs
    complying with legislation, 68-69
    policing transactions, 344
  currency transfers, 272
  customers' liability, 205-206, 234
  defences to prosecution, 406
  disclosure requirements, 314-315
    insider trading, 333-334
  employee awareness, 398-399
  employee criminal involvement, 404
  future of bank secrecy (U.K.), 342-346
  immunity clause, 289
  insurance, 416
  "interests of the bank", 335-336
  international transfer of information,
      338-342
  internal controls, 401-402
  "know your customer" policy, 392-394
  need to co-operate with government,
      403-406
  policy decisions about disclosure,
      336-338

Banks—*Continued*
  preparing for money laundering case,
      405-406
  preventing money laundering, 363
  protecting collateral from forfeiture,
      395-398
  reporting requirements, 315
    background (U.K.), 323-325
    Department of Trade and Industry's
        powers (U.K.), 332-334
    drug trafficking, 328-330
    exemption from liability for breach of
        contract (U.K.), 330
    fraud (U.K.), 334-336
    production orders, 325-328
    protection for good faith reporting
        (U.S.), 365
    search warrants, 325
    terrorism, 330-332
  response to U.S. legislation, 354-373
  revocation of charter when convicted,
      375
  risk management strategy, 416
  role in detecting money laundering, 293
  security interest, 430-431
  sharing information (U.K.), 335
  staff training, 437-439
  tellers, 162-165
  vicarious liability, 422; *see also*
      Vicarious liability

Basle Committee on Banking Regulations
    and Supervisory Practices,
    344-345, 362

"Benefit", 81-82

Bona fide purchaser for value without
    notice, 245; *see also* Third
    parties
  Drug Trafficking (Civil Proceedings) Act
      (N.S.W.), 250

Bookmakers, 411

Bribery, 62

Brinks-Mat robbery, 323-324

Broker dealers, 376, 381, 403

Building societies, 335, 410; *see also*
    Banks

Burden of proof
  amount of benefit, 309-313
  structured transaction provisions, 182

Capone, Al, 259

"Cash dealer", 32, 157-159, 410

Cash Transaction Reports Act (Cth),
    31-32, 410-412
  "account", 156-157
  Agency, 156
  agents, 159
  "cash dealers", 32, 157-159, 410
  "currency", 411
  currency reporting, 275
  currency transfers, 160-161
  exemptions from reporting, 159-160
  immunity clause, 289
  legislation
    success, 47
  obligations, 411
    cash dealers, 155-156
    public, 156
  relationship with Privacy Act, 167-172
  reporting provisions, 281-282
  sharing information, 156
  structured transaction provisions,
      173-198
  "structuring", 32
  "suspect transaction", 32
  suspect transaction reporting, 161-166
    accountants, 161-162
    bank tellers, 162-165
    "cash dealers", 161-162
    guidelines (Agency), 165-166
    lawyers, 161-162
  "transaction", 411
  vicarious liability, 412, 422

Cash Transaction Reports Agency, 33, 156
  co-ordinating role, 41
  Director's liability, 165-166
  guidelines, 165-166
  resources, 45

Casinos, 266-267, 411

Charging order (U.K.), 317

Charter revocation, 364-365

Chinese underground banking system,
    279-280

Chop (Chinese negotiable instrument),
    279

Civil actions
  against organised crime, 65
  recovery of overseas assets, 321-322

Collateral
  forfeiture of, 395-398

Collective knowledge, 376-378, 392

Companies Code
  investigations, 286

Compensation of victims (U.K.), 319-320

Complaints management, 436-437

Compliance systems, 391-406, 407-440
    accountability, 423-425
        currency-reporting administrators,
            424
        liaison officers, 424-425
    action sheet, 426, 438
    auditing programme, 427-428
    complaints management, 436-437
    computerisation, 426
    corporate policy statement, 417-419
    defence to prosecution, 406
    documentation control, 429-432
    legal professional privilege, 432-436
    liaison with enforcement agencies,
        439-440
    manuals, 425-427
    monitoring procedures, 427-429
    risk identification and control, 419-423
    suggested framework, 414-417
    training, 437-439
    U.S. programme, 391-406

Complicity, 186-187, 192

Computers
    compliance system, 426
    use in detection, 398
    use in training, 439

Confidentiality
    exemptions
        criticism of public interest criterion,
            351
        "safe harbour" protections for banks,
            365, 367-369

Confiscation of proceeds of crime
    background, 14-15
    basis, 22-23
    compensation of victims, and, 319-320
    Customs Act (Cth)
        proof, 22-23
    England, 305-322; see also Criminal
        Justice Act (U.K.) and Drug
        Trafficking Offences Act (U.K.)
        confiscation orders, 306-309
    legal fees, 24-27
    legislation
        Confiscation of Proceeds of Crime
            Act (N.S.W.), 78-79
        conviction-based approach, 92-95
        Customs Act (Cth), 16-17
        history, 15-16
        incapacitating offenders, 90-92
        objectives, 79-80
        Proceeds of Crime Act (Cth), 17-19,
            76-78
        proportionality of confiscation orders
            and pecuniary penalties, 85-90
        rationale, 29-30
        suggested reforms, 104-105
    rationale, 13-14
    restraining orders, 23-24

Confiscation of Proceeds of Crime Act
        (N.S.W.), 78-79
    conviction-based approach, 92-95
    legal fees, 96
    safeguards for third parties, 101-102
    "serious offence", 78-79
    "tainted property", 78
    vicarious punishment of third parties,
        102-103

Confiscation orders, 306-309

Conservatorship proceedings
    bank convicted of money laundering,
        364

Conspiracy, 187-188, 191-192
    double jeopardy, 240-242

Constitutionality, 87-89, 164, 405
    U.S. anti-smurfing statute
        due process, 229-230
        Fourth Amendment, 227-228
        privilege against self-incrimination,
            228-229

Constructive trust, 337
    proceeds of crime
        identity of beneficiary, 153-154
        unconscionability and unjust
            enrichment, 153-154
        unlawful killing, 151-153

Conversion, 22

Copyright offences, 387

Corporate liability, 192-194, 376-378

Corporate officers
    duty to use reasonable care and
        diligence, 413

Costigan Royal Commission, 14

Costs
    policing banking transactions, 344

Council of Europe Convention, 348-350

Court orders—see also Production orders,
        Search warrants
    monitoring orders, 29
    production orders, 28
    search warrants, 29

Credit unions, 410

Criminal Justice Act (U.K.), 330
    charging order, 317
    compensation of victim, 319-320
    disclosure, 314
    identification of proceeds, 313-315
    police powers, 315
    restraint orders, 316
    scope of confiscation orders, 306-308
        "pecuniary advantage", 308

Criminal Money Laundering Control Act, (U.S.), 374-375
transactions involving criminally-derived funds with intent (s. 1956)
domestic transactions, 384-387
elements of offence, 384, 387-388
"financial transactions", 384-385
international funds transfer, 387-388
knowledge, 386, 387
"monetary instrument", 388
penalties, 383, 387
"proceeds", 385-386, 388
"specified unlawful activity", 386-387
"sting" provisions, 383-384
"transports", 388-389
"with intent to promote unspecified unlawful activity", 387
transactions over $10,000 knowing criminally derived (s. 1957)
elements of offence, 390
"engages or attempts to engage", 390
knowledge, 390
"monetary transaction", 390
penalties, 389-390
"specified unlawful activity", 390

Cruel and unusual punishment, 87-88

"Currency", 411

Currency and Foreign Transaction Reporting Act (U.S.), 354; see also Bank Secrecy Act (U.S.)
introduction of statute, 203-205
problems with original statute
aggregation, 206-209
customers' liability, 205-206
revision of original legislation
aggregation, 209-212
branch transactions combined, 209-210
structuring as a crime, 212-213
sanctions, 212-213

Currency dealers, 411

Currency import and export reporting
Cash Transaction Reports Act (Cth), 275

Currency transfers, 160-161, 272

Customs Act (Cth)
discretionary forfeiture orders, 421
forfeiture legislation, 16-17
pecuniary penalties, 19-20
proof, 22-23
restraining orders, 23
third party property rights, 27

Defamation 165, 166

Defence
bona fide purchaser for value without notice, 245
Drug Trafficking (Civil Proceedings) Act 1990 (N.S.W.)
legal professional privilege, 255
no notice/no reason to expect restraining order, 255
privilege against self-incrimination
ignorance of law of structuring transactions, 219-227, 243
no knowledge or suspicion that proceeds of drug trafficking, 329
no knowledge that arrangement related to terrorist funds, 331

Deodand, 50-51, 105, 108, 121, 142

Department of Trade and Industry (U.K.)
powers, 332-334

Detention of suspects (U.K.), 315

Deterrence, 90, 134, 324

Detinue, 22

Directors
liability, 413-414

Disclosure
assets, of, 318-319
England, 314-315

Double jeopardy
U.S. anti-smurfing statute
bank reporting statute, 234-236
conspiracy, 240-242
s. 1001 (concealing material fact, etc), 236-240

Double Tax Treaties, 300-301

"Drug-derived property", 246, 250-251

"Drug-related activity", 245

Drug Trafficking (Civil Proceedings) Act (N.S.W.)
"affairs", 247
assets forfeiture orders
legal expenses, 250
privilege, 248
relief against hardship, 249-250
requirements, 248
"drug-derived property", 246, 250-251
"drug-related activity", 245
examination
ambit, 247
privilege against self-incrimination, 246-247
relevance of criminal proceedings, 246
use of evidence in other proceedings, 247

Drug Trafficking (Civil Proceedings) Act
    (N.S.W.)—*Continued*
  exclusion orders
    bona fide purchaser for value without
        notice, 250
    burden of proof, 251
    defined, 250
    evidence, 251
    negative onus, 252
    "hardship", 249
    "illegally acquired", 250
    "interest", 246
  legal expenses, 253-255
  offences, 255-256; *see also under*
        individual offences
  proceeds assessment orders
    assessment, 251-252
    definition, 252
    "proceeds", 253
    sale of property, 253
  purpose, 244-245
  restraining orders, 245-246

Drug Trafficking Offences Act (U.K.),
    328-330
  assumptions concerning amount of
        assets, 309-313
  identification of proceeds, 313-315
  "proceeds", 310
  scope of confiscation orders, 308-309
  "drug trafficking", 308

Due process, 229-230

Duplicity, 385

Electronic data, 34-35

"Engages or attempts to engage", 390

Environmental crimes, 387

Equity—*see* Constructive trust

European Community Directives
  identification of customers, 347-348
  "money laundering", 346-347
  "serious crime", 347

European Convention on Human Rights,
    311-313

Evidence
  assets, as to, 319
  rules
    relevance to Drug Trafficking (Civil
        Proceedings) Act (N.S.W.), 245

Exchange controls, 276-278

Exclusion orders, 250-252; *see also under*
    Drug Trafficking (Civil
    Proceedings) Act (N.S.W.)

"Expenses", 82, 83, 253

False name accounts, 42

Family—*see* Third parties

Financial Crimes Enforcement Network,
    373

"Financial corporation", 157-158

"Financial institution", (U.S.), 379

Financial Institutions Reform, Recovery
    and Enforcement Act (U.S.), 375

"Financial transaction"
  Money Laundering Control Act (U.S.),
    384-385

Fitzgerald report, 46

Forfeiture
  automatic, 110, 113-119, 412-413, 421
    effect on sentence, 115-118
    history, 113-115
  Customs Act (Cth), 16-17
  discretionary, 112
  discretionary on conviction—criminal
        process, 111, 119-125
    adjusting components of sentencing,
        122-125
    forfeiture as part of sentencing,
        119-122
  discretionary under civil process, 111,
        132
  discretionary under proceeds of crime
        legislation, 111, 125-132
    forms of legislation, 125-127
    relationship between confiscation
        orders and sentence, 125-132
  forms, 109-112
  history, 50-51, 106-107
  in personam, 141-143
  in rem, 141-143
  mortgage property, 395-396
  Proceeds of Crime Act (Cth), 17-19
  purposes
    deterrence, 134
    incapacitation, 133-134
    protection and prevention, 134-136
    rehabilitation, 137
    restoration, 136-137
  rationale, 52
  success, 44-45, 73
  suggested reform
    abolition or restriction of non-judicial
        forfeitures, 143
    judicial forfeiture as part of "sanction
        package", 148
    judicial forfeiture limited by "least
        restrictive alternative" principle,
        147-148
    judicial forfeiture limited by
        proportionality, 144-147
    seizure to be separated from
        forfeiture, 144
  third parties, 69-70, 100-104, 420-421

446

INDEX

Forfeiture orders
Drug Trafficking (Civil Proceedings) Act
(N.S.W.), 248-250

Fourth Amendment rights, 227-228

Fraud, 78, 334-336, 413
offences, 386-387

Freezing assets, 286-287

Freezing orders, 64—see also Mareva
injunctions
common law (U.K.), 316
Council of Europe Convention, 349
request of police rather than court, 343

Futures brokers, 158, 410

Gambling, 266-268

Gold, 279, 411

Handwriting examination, 348

Hardship, 87, 249-250, 317

"Hawala" system, 280

Hodgson Committee (U.K.), 82-83, 84,
137

Identification of customers
Bank Secrecy Act (U.S.), 379-380
Cash Transaction Reports Act (Cth),
410, 411
priority for banks, 344
proof (U.K.), 335
U.S. legislation, 359
wire transfers (U.S.), 382-383

"Illegally acquired", 250

Immunity clause, 289

"In connection with", 19

Informants, 282-283

Information
access to, 171-172
sharing—see Sharing information

Information Privacy Principles, 167-168

In personam forfeiture, 141-143

In rem forfeiture, 141-143

In rem proceedings, 143

Insider trading, 333-334, 340, 341

Insurance companies, 410

"Integration", 37

"Interest", 246

International transfers
currency
duty to report, 411
funds—see Wire transfers
information, 338-342

Interpol, 291-292, 350

Investigation powers
Department of Trade and Industry
(U.K.), 332-334

Jack Committee, 351

"Know your customer" policy, 392-394

Knowledge—see also Collective
knowledge, Wilful blindness
assisting in retention of benefit of drug
trafficking (U.K.), 314
corporate liability, 376-378, 396
Council of Europe Convention, 349
European Community Directives, 347
loan cases, 395-398
Money Laundering Control Act (U.S.)
proceeds of unlawful activity, 386
property criminally derived, 390
transaction designed to avoid
reporting, 387
structuring transactions (U.S.), 218-227,
243, 381

"Layering", 37

Legal fees, 24-27, 63-64, 95-100, 250, 360
drug offenders, 99
Drug Trafficking (Civil Proceedings) Act
(N.S.W.), 253-255
money laundering, 99-100

Legal professional privilege, 255, 299,
325-326, 328, 416, 432-436
copies of documents (U.K.), 326
exemptions (U.K.), 326

Limitations period, 430

Loans
need for diligence of bank, 395-398

Mareva injunctions, 286, 320-322
  definition, 321
  world-wide, 346

Mens rea—*see also* Knowledge
  money laundering, 93-94, 95, 287-288,
      420
    compared to receiving (offence), 420
    Proceeds of Crime Act (Cth), 420
    structured transaction provisions
        (C.T.R. Act (Cth))
      common law presumptions, 175-180
    structuring transactions (U.S.), 216

Mental element—*see* Mens rea

"Monetary transaction", 390

Money laundering
  banks' role in detection, 293
  calculating size of problem, 260-261
  Confiscation of Proceeds of Crime Act
      (N.S.W.), 79
  conviction of bank, 375
  definition, 36, 66, 201, 257-258,
      346-347
  detection, 280-282, 399-401
  estimating income, 285
  European initiatives, 346-353
  freezing assets, 286-287
  havens, 278-279
  informants, 282-283
  Internal Revenue Code (U.S.), 269
  international co-operation
    Interpol, 291-292
    mutual assistance treaties, 289-291
  investigation and analysis, 284-285
  legislation
    effectiveness, 68
  mens rea, 93-94, 95, 287-288, 420
  morality of, 261-263
  offences, 287; *see also* Offences
  offshore
    agitation of funds (laundering cycles),
        273-274
    repatriation of funds, 274-275
    smuggling funds offshore, 272-273
  origin of term, 258
  penalty, 78
  prosecution, 287-289
  purpose, 259-260
  revocation of bank charter for
      conviction, 375
  seizing assets, 286-287
  stages, 37
  statistics, 66-67
  tracing assets, 285-286
  undercover operations, 283-284
  underground banking systems, 279-280
  U.S. legislation, 354-373
    American Bankers Association Money
        Laundering Task Force, 361-362

Bank Secrecy Act, 354-355, 374,
    378-383; *see also* Bank Secrecy
    Act (U.S.)
Criminal Money Laundering Control
    Act, 374-375, 383-390; *see also*
    Criminal Money Laundering
    Control Act (U.S.)
Financial Institutions Reform,
    Recovery and Enforcement Act,
    375
legal fees, 360
Money Laundering Control Act,
    355-357
Money Laundering Enforcement Act,
    366
Office of National Drug Control
    Strategy, 361
Omnibus Drug Initiative Act, 358-359
revocation of charter where bank
    convicted, 364-365
suggestions for prevention, 363
targeting specific institutions, 359-360
warning signs, 399-401
wire transfers, 275-276
within jurisdiction
  bogus mortgages, 270
  financial institutions, 264-266; *see
      also* Refining money
  gambling, 266-268
  lawyers' trust accounts, 270
  purchasing legitimate businesses,
      268-269
  real estate investment, 270
  secret purchases of assets and shares,
      269-270
  "smurfing", 271

Money Laundering Control Act (U.S.),
    355-357; *see also* Criminal Money
    Laundering Control Act (U.S.)

Money trail
  definition, 257
  origin of term, 259

Monitoring orders, 29
  Proceeds of Crime Act (Cth), 285

Mortgagee's rights to restrained property,
    28

Multinational Convention on Mutual
    Administrative Assistance in Tax
    Matters, 303

Mutual assistance
  international, 350
  Proceeds of Crime Act (Cth), 413
  requests
    Council of Europe Convention, 349
  treaties, 289-291, 294, 302

Mutual Assistance in Criminal Matters Act
    (Cth), 290, 294, 302

Narcotics—*see also* Customs Act (Cth),
        Proceeds of Crime Act (Cth)
  "in connection with", 19
  pecuniary penalties, 19-22

Negligent misstatement, 166

Negotiations, 411

New South Wales Crime Commission, 244

Notice
  illegality of, 223-224

Offences—*see also* Double jeopardy
  assisting in retention of benefit of drug
        trafficking (U.K.), 314
  assisting to avoid reporting (U.S.), 356
  causing failure to report (U.S.), 213-214
  causing filing of report containing
        omission or misstatement (U.S.),
        214-215
  Drug Trafficking (Civil Proceedings) Act
        (N.S.W.)
    breaching or disclosing court order to
        monitor transactions, 256
    dealing with restrained property, 255
    failure to comply with production
        orders, 255-256
    obstructing execution of search
        warrants, 256
  failure to comply without reasonable
        excuse (U.K.), 332-333
  failure to respond to order to
        investigate bank accounts (U.K.),
        334
  money laundering, 287
  Money Laundering Control Act (U.S.)
    s. 1956, 383-389
    s. 1957, 389-390
  structuring transactions (U.S.), 215-218,
        356-357

Office of National Drug Control Strategy,
        361

Omnibus Crime Bill (U.S.), 383

Omnibus Drug Initiative Act (U.S.),
        358-359

Onus of proof
  conversion or detinue, 22
  Drug Trafficking (Civil Proceedings) Act
        (N.S.W.), 245

Orders—*see* Anton Piller orders, Court
        orders, Exclusion orders,
        Forfeiture orders, Freezing
        orders, Proceeds assessment
        orders, Production orders,
        Restraint orders, Search warrants

Organised crime
  Australian approach, 56
  economic analysis, 56-71
    "insurance" schemes, 62-64
    "pattern" of activity, 53-54
  scope, 72-73
  size of economy, 42-44
  U.S. approach, 52-55

Organised fraud
  offence, 78

Pay-rolls, 411

Penalties
  Bank Secrecy Act (U.S.), 379
  Cash Transaction Reports Act (Cth), 412
  money laundering, 413
  Money Laundering Control Act (U.S.)
    s. 1956, 383, 387
    s. 1957, 389-390
  pecuniary, 19-22
    Customs Act (Cth), 19-20
    Proceeds of Crime Act (Cth), 20
    quantifying benefits, 20-21
  Proceeds of Crime Act (Cth), 412

"Placement", 37

Police and Criminal Evidence Act (U.K.),
        325-328

Police powers (U.K.), 315

Prevention of Terrorism (Temporary
        Provisions) Act (U.K.)
  defence, 331
  offence, 331
  retribution against banks, 332

Privacy
  balanced against threat to society, 218

Privacy Act (Cth)
  background, 167-168
  relationship with Cash Transaction
        Reports Act, 167-172

Privilege against self incrimination,
        228-229, 318, 352
  Drug Trafficking (Civil Proceedings) Act
        (N.S.W.), 246, 255-256

"Proceeds", 253, 310
  Money Laundering Control Act (U.S.),
        385-386, 388

Proceeds assessment orders, 252-253; *see
        also under* Drug Trafficking
        (Civil Proceedings) Act (N.S.W.)

Proceeds of crime
  assessment models, 81-84
  definition, 1-2, 287

Proceeds of Crime Act (Cth), 77-78,
    125-127, 412-413
  analogy to tax enforcement, 294-304
  conviction-based approach, 92-95
  forfeiture legislation, 17-19
  "in connection with", 19
  legal fees, 96
  investigative powers, 28-29
  mens rea, 287-288, 420
  money laundering offences, 287
  mutual assistance, 413
  penalties, 20, 413
  "proceeds of crime", 287
  "property", 77, 412
  purpose, 44
  restraining orders, 23-24
  safeguards for third parties, 101-102
  "serious narcotics offence", 413
  "serious offences", 18, 78, 413
  success, 45
  "suspicious transaction", 288
  "tainted property", 77, 412
  third party property rights, 27-28
  tracing assets, 285
  "unlawful activity", 287
  vicarious liability, 78, 413, 422
  vicarious punishment of third parties,
    102-103

Production of documents, 297-299

Production orders, 28
  Drug Trafficking (Civil Proceedings) Act
    (N.S.W.), 255
  Drug Trafficking Offences Act (U.K.),
    314, 328
  insider trading, 333-334
  Police and Criminal Evidence Act
    (U.K.), 325-328
  Proceeds of Crime Act (Cth), 285, 296

"Property", 77 412

Proportionality, 135, 137

Public Trustee, 245, 253

Punishment
  purposes
    deterrence, 134
    incapacitation, 133-134
    protection and prevention, 134-136
    rehabilitation, 137
    restoration, 136-137

Racketeer Influenced and Corrupt
    Organisation statute (R.I.C.O.),
    52-56
  offences, 386

Real estate agents, 158

"Reasonable expenses", 96-97

"Reasonable to conclude" test
  aggregation of deposits, 185-186
  attempt (offence), 188
  burden of proof, 182
  complicity, 186-187
  conspiracy, 187-188
  indicia specified, 181-182
  purpose, 180-181
  retrospectivity, 182-185

"Reasonable grounds to suspect", 163

Recklessness, 386

Refining money
  Cash Transaction Reports Act (Cth), 265
  casinos, 266
  definition, 264
  motives, 265

Rehabilitation, 137

Relation-back provision, 64-65

Reporting legislation
  Internal Revenue Code (U.S.), 269
  United States, 32-36

Reporting scheme (U.S.), 232-233

Restraint orders, 23-24, 43, 316
  Drug Trafficking (Civil Proceedings) Act
    (N.S.W.), 245-246
  Mareva injunctions and, 321

Right to Financial Privacy Act (U.S.), 404

"Safe harbour" provisions (U.S.), 365,
    367-369
  civil, 404
  criminal, 404-405

Sanctions
  structuring transactions (U.S.), 212-213

Search powers
  Cash Transaction Reports Act (Cth), 285
  Commissioner of Taxation, 296
  Proceeds of Crime Act (Cth), 285

Search warrants, 29, 325
  Commissioner of Taxation, 296
  Drug Trafficking (Civil Proceedings) Act
    (N.S.W.), 256
  Proceeds of Crime Act (Cth), 297

Securities dealers, 158, 410

Seizure
  assets, 286
  Council of Europe Convention, 349
  currency
    Cash Transaction Reports Act (Cth),
      285-286

Self-regulation, 344

Sentencing
  relevance of confiscation orders, 307,
      312, 343

Serious Fraud Office, 334-336

"Serious offence", 18, 78, 413
  Confiscation of Proceeds of Crime Act
      (N.S.W.), 78-79

"Serious narcotics offence", 413

Shares
  purchase of, for money laundering,
      270, 271

Sharing information, 33, 41, 45 46, 156,
      335

Smurfing—see also Structuring
      transactions to avoid reporting
  definition, 173, 199, 271

Solicitors
  "cash dealers", 158, 161-162

"Specified unlawful activity", 386, 390

Standard of proof, 128, 132
  conversion or detinue, 22
  drug confiscation proceedings (U.K.),
      308

Stewart Royal Commission, 14

"Sting" offence, 383-384

Structuring transactions to avoid
      reporting, 32, 47, 412
  Bank Secrecy Act (U.S.), 380-382
  definition, 32
    U.S. Treasury Department, 381
  description (U.S.), 380
  example, 357
  offences, 173-174
    mental element, 174-180
    parties, 189-194
    "reasonable to conclude" test,
        180-189; see also "Reasonable to
        conclude" test
  protection for cash dealers, 194-196
  suggested reforms, 197-198
  U.S. federal criminal law, 199-243; see
        also Currency and Foreign
        Transactions Reporting Act (U.S.)
    analogy to tax law, 217-218
    causing failure to report, 213-214
    causing filing of report containing
        omission or misstatement,
        214-215
    constitutionality, 227-230
    crime, 212-213, 215-218
    original reporting statute, 203-205

elements and theory of offence,
    215-218
investigation, 232
knowledge of illegality, 218-227
prosecution, 232
relationship to other federal crimes,
    232-242
"structure", 216-217
unit of prosecution, 230-231

Successor liability, 402-403

Suspect transaction
  Australian experience, 41-42
  definition, 32, 38, 288
  duty to report, 38-39
  reports, 37-39
  U.S. experience, 39-41

TABs, 411

"tainted property", 77, 412
  Confiscation of Proceeds of Crime Act
      (N.S.W.), 78

Takeovers
  inquiry, 402-403

Tape recordings, 405-406

Targeting provisions (U.S.), 380

Tax enforcement
  Carribean Basin Initiative, 301-302
  Commissioner's powers, 296
  Double Tax Treaties, 300-301
  information exchange agreements with
      tax havens, 301-302
  investigation powers, 296-297
  investigative techniques, 299
  Multinational Convention, 303
  mutual assistance treaties, 302
  production of documents by third
      parties, 298-299
  production of documents held offshore,
      297-298

Tax evasion, 42, 164, 257-258, 262, 354
  purpose of money laundering, 201, 202

Tax havens, 278, 294, 295—see also
      under Money laundering and
      Tax enforcement

Tax law
  analogy to structuring transactions,
      217-218

Terrorism, 314, 343
  reporting relevant information, 330-332;
      see also Prevention of Terrorism
      (Temporary Provisions) Act (U.K.)

Third parties, 121, 143
    confiscation orders, and, 317-318
    forfeiture, 69-70, 100-104
    innocent "ownership" status, 396-397
    production of documents by, 298-299
    protection of property interests,
        420-421
    property rights, 27-28
    Council of Europe Convention, 349

Tracing proceeds of crime
    internationally
        analogy to tax enforcement, 294-304

Tracing rights, 339-340

"Transaction", 163, 411

Travel agents, 158

Travellers' cheques, 411

Truth in sentencing, 138

Two-transaction rule, 189-190

Undercover operations, 283-284

Underground banking systems
    Interpol investigations, 292

Unit trust scheme, 158-159, 161-162, 411

Unjust enrichment, 80, 81-84

Unjust terms of acquisition, 88-89

"Unlawful activity", 287

Vicarious liability, 80, 94, 191-194,
        376-378; see also Collective
        knowledge
Cash Transaction Reports Act (Cth),
        412, 422
Confiscation of Proceeds of Crime Act
        (N.S.W.), 79
Proceeds of Crime Act (Cth), 78, 413,
        422

Whistleblower laws, 283

White collar crime, 72; see also Money
        laundering, Organised crime

Wilful blindness, 336, 342, 376, 377, 386,
        420

Williams Royal Commission, 14, 42-43

Wire transfers, 275-276, 281, 384, 385,
        388-389, 400
    potential regulation (U.S.), 370-371
    reporting requirements (U.S.), 382-383
    suspicious patterns, 402

"With intent to promote specified
        unlawful activity"
    Money Laundering Control Act (U.S.),
        387

Woodward Royal Commission, 43, 267